GLOBAL ISSUES

2013 EDITION

GLOBAL ISSUES

SELECTIONS FROM CQ RESEARCHER

2013 EDITION

Los Angeles | London | New Delhi
Singapore | Washington DC

Los Angeles | London | New Delhi
Singapore | Washington DC

FOR INFORMATION:

CQ Press

An Imprint of SAGE Publications, Inc.

2455 Teller Road

Thousand Oaks, California 91320

E-mail: order@sagepub.com

SAGE Publications Ltd.

1 Oliver's Yard

55 City Road

London EC1Y 1SP

United Kingdom

SAGE Publications India Pvt. Ltd.

B 1/I 1 Mohan Cooperative Industrial Area

Mathura Road, New Delhi 110 044

India

SAGE Publications Asia-Pacific Pte. Ltd.

3 Church Street

#10-04 Samsung Hub

Singapore 049483

Printed in the United States of America

Library of Congress Control Number: 2013936045

ISBN: 978-1-4522-4153-1

This book is printed on acid-free paper.

Acquisitions Editor: Charisse Kiino

Associate Editor: Nancy Loh

Editorial Assistant: Davia Grant

Production Editor: Stephanie Palermini

Copy Editor: Brenda White

Typesetter: C&M Digitals (P) Ltd.

Cover Designer: Candice Harman

Marketing Manager: Erica DeLuca

Permissions Editor: Jennifer Barron

Certified Chain of Custody
Promoting Sustainable Forestry
www.sfiprogram.org
SFI-01268

SFI label applies to text stock

13 14 15 16 17 10 9 8 7 6 5 4 3 2 1

Contents

Annotated Contents

CONFLICT, SECURITY, AND TERRORISM

Assessing the United Nations

As the government of Bashar Assad slaughters thousands of civilian protesters in Syria, the United Nations stands impotent — blocked from intervening by Russian and Chinese vetoes in the U.N. Security Council. The inaction contrasts dramatically with the U.N.'s success in stopping similar atrocities during an anti-government resistance movement in Libya that led to the overthrow of longtime dictator Moammar Gadhafi. The stark difference between U.N. action and inaction in the two venues helps explain the wide range of opinions about the effectiveness of the global organization, created in 1945 to preserve peace after World War II. Some critics say the U.N. is too heavily influenced by countries run by dictators, while others say it is dominated by industrial democracies. Several countries are conducting studies to determine which U.N. agencies are most cost-effective, and some in the United States want to make all U.N. contributions voluntary. Meanwhile, many U.N. agencies quietly continue to feed the hungry, aid needy children and enable mail, telecommunications and aircraft to move smoothly across borders.

Islamic Sectarianism

Sectarian rifts are almost as old as Islam itself. They surfaced in 632, shortly after the death of the Prophet Muhammad, when Muslims disagreed over who should succeed him. Although the original sectarian split was violent, Islam's two major branches — Shiism and

Sunnism — have co-existed peacefully more often than not over the centuries. But recently, sectarian tensions once again have erupted into full-scale violence in the wake of the U.S. invasion of Iraq and 2011's Arab Spring democracy movement. The volatile situation is not just about theology. Competition for power and privilege intensifies the hostility and distrust. In postwar Iraq, sectarian attacks killed 325 people in July 2011, the highest monthly toll since August 2010. Currently, the epicenter of the sectarian crisis is Syria, where the Sunni opposition is battling the Shiite Alawite regime of Bashar Assad. Experts fear the violence could engulf significant parts of the Middle East. Meanwhile, other countries have lined up on either side of the fight, with Iran, Russia and China supporting the Syrian regime and Saudi Arabia, Turkey, the Gulf States and the West supporting the rebels.

Small Arms Trade

From brutal civil wars in Africa to vicious drug-cartel rivalries in Mexico, violence around the world has one thing in common: vast quantities of hand-held weapons such as Kalashnikov assault rifles, mortars and rocket-propelled grenades. Nearly a billion small arms are scattered across the globe, about three-quarters of them in civilian hands. Many have been recycled from recent conflicts, such as last year's Libyan civil war; some have come from former Soviet Union stockpiles. While most are used for hunting, sport shooting and personal protection, millions end up in the hands of rebel groups, gangs and criminals. Some experts argue that the growing proliferation of small weapons can exacerbate a potentially violent situation, but others insist the mere presence of weapons does not necessarily promote violence. In the summer of 2012, the U.N. tried to negotiate a treaty governing the global trade in all weapons. Some negotiators wanted small arms included, but gun-rights groups opposed overly restrictive regulations on the small arms trade.

Unrest in the Arab World

The wave of popular uprisings that toppled dictators in Tunisia, Egypt and Libya is still roiling the Arab world, but other governments have held on by cracking down on protests or instituting modest reforms. Meanwhile, Syria is engulfed in a bloody civil war that many experts predict will force President Bashar Assad from office but leave the country devastated and politically unstable. Some experts say the events have transformed political attitudes in Arab nations. Others stress that a majority of those countries still have authoritarian regimes. The political dramas are playing out against the backdrop of pressing economic problems, including high unemployment among Arab youths. In addition, the growing power of Islamist parties and groups is raising concerns among advocates of secular government and creating risks of sectarian disputes among different Muslim sects.

U.S. – Europe Relations

Following World War II, the U.S. alliance with Western Europe stood as the cornerstone of American foreign policy in the face of Cold War threats from what was then the Soviet Union. Forged in the North Atlantic Treaty Organization (NATO) — the alliance's enduring defense pact — the partnership is rooted in the shared values of democracy, rule of law and free-market principles. But with the emergence of China and India as global economic powers, the Arab Spring revolutions and Iran's uncertain nuclear ambitions, the United States has shifted its political and security priorities to the Asia-Pacific region, leaving Europe worried that its historic ties with the United States are fraying. In May 2012, President Obama hosted two meetings of European leaders that could help define the trans-Atlantic alliance for years to come: a NATO summit in Chicago and a summit of the Group of 8 industrialized nations at Camp David, the presidential retreat.

Russia in Turmoil

In 2012 as Russians went to the polls to choose a president, there was little doubt about the outcome. Vladimir Putin, who had been president or prime minister since 1999, beat four challengers, winning more than 63 percent of the vote. Yet despite years of rapid economic growth fueled by rising oil and gas exports, Putin's efforts to extend his authoritarian rule faced a new and destabilizing challenge. Tens of thousands of people took to the streets during the campaign and immediately afterwards to protest pervasive corruption and a rigged campaign. Putin has dealt firmly with political opponents — many of whom have been exiled, imprisoned on dubious charges, or died in mysterious circumstances. Now many are wondering if Russia's 2012 winter of protests may have planted the seeds for a future popular revolution inspired by the "Arab Spring" movement that toppled dictators across the Middle East in 2011 and 2012. The upheaval has strained relations with the West — as has Russia's recent support for the repressive Syrian regime — leading to questions about what lies ahead for Russia, a nuclear power and the world's second-largest oil producer.

Future of the EU

Europe's debt crisis has cast doubt over the future of the European integration project, launched out of the ashes of World War II. At the center of an unfolding drama are Germany and Greece, two countries that epitomize a culture clash taking place between austerity-prone northern Europeans and their more spendthrift Mediterranean counterparts. Greece is on its knees, weighed down by a vast sovereign debt burden and a viciously contracting economy. Its desperate plight has raised wider concerns about the future of the euro – the common currency used by Greece and 16 other countries in the 27-member EU. In response, Europe's leaders, determined to save the euro, have forged ahead with ever closer economic union with fiscally strong Germany firmly in the driving seat. By contrast, the United Kingdom's confidence in the EU has been severely shaken, and Britain is even considering exiting the club. Subsumed by these internal shocks, EU nations have had little time to think about admitting more members, although Croatia is set to join in July, 2013.

Rising Tension over Iran

Successive U.S. presidents have insisted that a nuclear-armed Iran is "unacceptable." Iran's Islamic leadership protests that its nuclear program is for peaceful purposes only, but the body of evidence from U.N. inspections raised nagging questions that the Iranians have failed to answer, such as why facilities for a peaceful program would be buried hundreds of feet underground. A nuclear Iran would alter the strategic balance in the tense Middle East and, some say, possibly trigger a regional atomic arms race. Although the United States and Europe have imposed tough economic sanctions on Iran, the Iranians have not stopped enriching uranium or begun operating their nuclear program with more

transparency. Israel has long considered a pre-emptive strike on nuclear facilities in Iran — which has vowed to destroy the Jewish state — an option, but the Obama administration has insisted that sanctions be given time to work — or fail.

INTERNATIONAL POLITICAL ECONOMY
Millennium Development Goals

World leaders from 189 countries gathered at the United Nations in 2000 to approve an ambitious plan to change the world. By 2015, they vowed, countries would meet broad, measurable objectives — which would become the eight Millennium Development Goals (MDGs) — designed to, among other things, eliminate extreme poverty and hunger, promote gender equality, achieve universal primary education and fight HIV-AIDS, malaria and other diseases. With the 2015 deadline approaching, some MDG targets appear out of reach. Others — such as halving the percentage of people living in extreme poverty and lacking access to safe drinking water — were met in 2010. But some critics say the MDGs have been inherently unfair because regions such as sub-Saharan Africa were far behind other regions at the outset, so they had much farther to go to meet the targets. As the international community prepares to draft new goals, it seeks lessons from the first round of MDGs on what works, what doesn't and whether goal-setting is the best way to solve global problems.

Booming Africa

Once considered hopeless, much of sub-Saharan Africa is booming. Seven of the world's 10 fastest-growing economies currently are in Africa. High prices for the continent's oil and mineral exports have brought a surge of government revenue and investment, but the growth is occurring in commodity-poor countries as well. Better governance, less war and the rapid spread of cell phones and other communication technologies are fostering growth even in nations with few natural resources. Debt forgiveness and the rise of China, India and other emerging markets as trading partners and sources of investment also have spurred economies forward. Demographers say that with the continent's working-age population projected to expand by a third by 2020, Africa could benefit from a "demographic dividend" that would fuel sustained economic growth, even as populations in developed countries and Asia are growing older. Yet, the population boom also poses challenges: Africa's economies must provide enough jobs for the growing number of workers with expectations of a better life.

Euro Crisis

Amid Europe's continuing economic troubles, in September 2012, riots erupted in several nations, notably Spain and Greece, as citizens protested radical government efforts to cut spending and raise taxes. Rising debt has damaged the euro currency and pushed many nations into deep recession, high unemployment and widespread poverty. Some experts say Europe's economic woes are holding back economic recovery in the United States by undermining consumer confidence, exports and investments and that the U.S. government should do more to help Europe fix its problems. Otherwise, they warn, a new global economic crisis on the scale of the 2008 crash could hit Europe, the United States and the rest of the world. Other experts argue, however, that it is not in the United States' interest to help rescue the European economy.

China in Latin America

China's global expansion has reached Latin America and the Caribbean, where the Asian giant has been pursuing an aggressive trade policy for a decade. Besides investing heavily in the region's abundant natural resources and shipping huge quantities of cheap industrial goods into the area, China is also interested in buying Latin America's food commodities — especially soybeans. While trade with China has provided a historic bonanza for Latin producers, a growing trade imbalance — favoring China — has soured the initial euphoria. In exchange for Latin America's raw materials, China exports manufactured goods that are clobbering Latin competitors, threatening to return the region to its 1970s-era over-dependence on commodity exports. China also has emerged as a major investor — and financier — for the region, helping it to weather the 2008–09 global recession. China's sudden emergence as a significant player in the hemisphere also has sparked concern that China might eventually undermine U.S. influence and interest in the vast region — a fear that Beijing carefully tries to assuage.

State Capitalism

Since the 2008 financial crisis China, Russia and Saudi Arabia have been among the best-performing economies in the world. All three countries practice so-called state capitalism, in which the government plays a dominant role in the economy and owns a large share of the nation's companies. As economic growth in the United States and Japan remains tepid, and parts of the European Union are mired in a double-dip recession, many developing world governments are questioning whether Western market capitalism is the best path for growth. Many also blame the excesses of unfettered Western-style capitalism for the recent global financial crisis and the ensuing worldwide recession. China, on the other hand, has lifted 600 million people out of poverty in three decades, and Russia's economy has doubled in size since Vladimir Putin began rolling back post-Soviet free-market reforms. Some economists see trouble ahead, however, because when governments manipulate markets for political purposes it can lead to inefficiencies, corruption and political tensions over time.

INTERNATIONAL ISSUES
Women's Rights

The women's rights movement has made enormous strides globally in the last 15 years, with most countries signing treaties to end gender discrimination. But with conservative Muslim parties gaining power in some post-Arab Spring governments, feminists fear women's rights in the Middle East — already lagging by world standards — may be further threatened. Although women were at the forefront in 2011's protests, female candidates have been scarce in recent elections. One solution being considered: electoral gender quotas, already used in about 100 countries. In developed nations, women comprise the majority of recent university graduates, but females receive smaller paychecks than their male counterparts and rarely reach top management positions. Some experts attribute this to women's tendency to work part-time or take time off for parenting. Nordic countries are encouraging fathers to share parenting duties, while some countries are boosting the number of female business leaders through mandatory gender quotas for corporate boards.

Human Trafficking and Slavery

Long hidden and often denied, the global epidemic of human trafficking and slavery is finally being exposed on the world stage. A five-year-old chained to a rug loom in India, a domestic servant enslaved and beaten in the Middle East and sex slaves trafficked within the United States are among the 21 million men, women and children held in some form of bonded labor, slavery or forced prostitution around the world today. With millions of vulnerable victims being trafficked across international borders, this inhuman crime racks up more than $32 billion in profits each year. As nations seek effective ways to combat what President Barack Obama recently called "a debasement of our common humanity," some experts say legalizing prostitution and some forms of child labor might remove financial incentives for the illicit trade. While some nations have cracked down on traffickers, resulting in increased prosecutions and convictions, many more need to join the fight, according to activists, who say the biggest obstacle to halting the trade in human beings is the lack of political will.

Vanishing Biodiversity

Earth's biodiversity — the profusion of plants and animals that work together to support life — continues to shrink. Species are going extinct at a rate most scientists find alarming — possibly as many as 150 a day — while the populations of many surviving species are declining rapidly. Endangered species range from plants and large animals such as tigers and rhinoceroses to smaller creatures such as insects and honeybees. All play key roles in sustaining healthy ecosystems, which provide a variety of costly environmental services for free, such as filtering water and scrubbing carbon from the air. Some researchers believe the Earth could be approaching a so-called tipping point, in which biodiversity loss causes global ecosystems to change rapidly and dramatically, but other scientists doubt the theory. Meanwhile, there is widespread concern about humanity's ability to sustain itself in a world of diminishing biodiversity if the global population reaches 9.5 billion by 2050, as is projected. While many more areas are being protected today than in the past — including the bio-rich Amazon rainforest — conservation efforts are not keeping up with the loss of biodiversity.

Preface

In this pivotal era of international policymaking, scholars, students, practitioners and journalists seek answers to such critical questions as: Will the Arab Spring lead to more changes? Can state-run economies sustain their success? Is species loss approaching a "tipping point?" Students must first understand the facts and contexts of these and other global issues if they are to analyze and articulate well-reasoned positions.

The 2013 edition of *Global Issues* provides comprehensive and unbiased coverage of today's most pressing global problems. This edition is a compilation of 16 recent reports from *CQ Researcher,* a weekly policy brief that unpacks difficult concepts and provides balanced coverage of competing perspectives. Each article analyzes past, present and possible political maneuvering, is designed to promote in-depth discussion and further research and helps readers formulate their own positions on crucial international issues.

This collection is organized into three subject areas that span a range of important international policy concerns: conflict, security, and terrorism; international political economy; and international issues. Fourteen of these reports are new to this edition.

Global Issues is a valuable supplement for courses on world affairs in political science, geography, economics and sociology. Citizens, journalists and business and government leaders also turn to it to become better informed on key issues, actors and policy positions.

CQ RESEARCHER

CQ Researcher was founded in 1923 as *Editorial Research Reports* and was sold primarily to newspapers as a research tool. The magazine was renamed and redesigned in 1991 as *CQ Researcher*. Today, students are its primary audience. While still used by hundreds of journalists and newspapers, many of which reprint portions of the reports, *Researcher*'s main subscribers are now high school, college and public libraries. In 2002, *Researcher* won the American Bar Association's coveted Silver Gavel Award for magazine excellence for a series of nine reports on civil liberties and other legal issues.

Researcher staff writers — all highly experienced journalists — sometimes compare the experience of writing a *Researcher* report to drafting a college term paper. Indeed, there are many similarities. Each report is as long as many term papers — about 11,000 words — and is written by one person without any significant outside help. One of the key differences is that the writers interview leading experts, scholars and government officials for each issue.

Like students, staff writers begin the creative process by choosing a topic. Working with *Researcher*'s editors, the writer identifies a controversial subject that has important public policy implications. After a topic is selected, the writer embarks on one to two weeks of intense research. Newspaper and magazine articles are clipped or downloaded, books are ordered and information is gathered from a wide variety of sources, including interest groups, universities and the government. Once the writers are well informed, they develop a detailed outline and begin the interview process. Each report requires a minimum of ten to fifteen interviews with academics, officials, lobbyists and people working in the field. Only after all interviews are completed does the writing begin.

CHAPTER FORMAT

Each issue of *CQ Researcher*, and therefore each selection in this book, is structured in the same way. A selection begins with an introductory overview, which is briefly explored in greater detail in the rest of the report.

The second section chronicles the most important and current debates in the field. It is structured around a number of key issues questions, such as "Is the euro crisis slowing the U.S. recovery?" and "Is the U.N. worth the money the world spends on it?" This section is the core of each selection. The questions raised are often highly controversial and usually the object of much argument among scholars and practitioners. Hence, the answers provided are never conclusive, but rather detail the range of opinion within the field.

Following those issue questions is the "Background" section, which provides a history of the issue being examined. This retrospective includes important legislative and executive actions and court decisions to inform readers on how current policy evolved.

Next, the "Current Situation" section examines important contemporary policy issues, legislation under consideration and action being taken. Each selection ends with an "Outlook" section that gives a sense of what new regulations, court rulings and possible policy initiatives might be put into place in the next five to ten years.

Each report contains features that augment the main text: sidebars that examine issues related to the topic, a pro/con debate by two outside experts, a chronology of key dates and events and an annotated bibliography that details the major sources used by the writer.

CUSTOM OPTIONS

Interested in building your ideal CQ Press Issues book, customized to your personal teaching needs and interests? Browse by course or date, or search for specific topics or issues from our online catalog of *CQ Researcher* issues at http://custom.cqpress.com.

ACKNOWLEDGMENTS

We wish to thank many people for helping to make this collection a reality. Thomas J. Billitteri, managing editor of *CQ Researcher*, gave us his enthusiastic support and cooperation as we developed this edition. He and his talented staff of editors and writers have amassed a first-class collection of *Researcher* articles, and we are fortunate to have access to this rich cache. We also thankfully acknowledge the advice and feedback from current readers and are gratified by their satisfaction with the book.

Some readers may be learning about *CQ Researcher* for the first time. We expect that many readers will want regular access to this excellent weekly research tool. For subscription information or a no-obligation free trial of *Researcher,* please contact CQ Press at www.cqpress.com or toll-free at 1-866-4CQ-PRESS (1-866-427-7737).

We hope that you will be pleased by the 2013 edition of *Global Issues.* We welcome your feedback and suggestions for future editions. Please direct comments to Charisse Kiino, Publisher, College Publishing Group, CQ Press, 2300 N Street, NW, Suite 800, Washington, DC 20037; or send e-mail to *ckiino@ cqpress.com.*

— *The Editors of CQ Press*

Contributors

Brian Beary, a freelance Irish journalist based in Washington, specializes in European Union (EU) affairs and is the U.S. correspondent for the daily newspaper, *Europolitics.* Originally from Dublin, he worked in the European Parliament for Irish MEP Pat "The Cope" Gallagher in 2000 and at the EU Commission's Eurobarometer unit on public opinion analysis. Beary also writes for the Brussels-based *Parliament Magazine* and *The Globalist.* His most recent report for *CQ Global Researcher* was "Emerging Central Asia." He also authored the recent CQ Press book, *Separatist Movements, A Global Reference.*

John Felton is a freelance journalist who has written about international affairs and U.S. foreign policy for nearly 30 years. He covered foreign affairs for the Congressional Quarterly Weekly Report during the 1980s, was deputy foreign editor for National Public Radio in the early 1990s and has been a freelance writer specializing in international topics for the past 15 years. His most recent book, published by CQ Press, is The *Contemporary Middle East: A Documentary History.* He lives in western Massachusetts.

Roland Flamini is a Washington-based correspondent who specializes in foreign affairs. Fluent in six languages, he was *Time* bureau chief in Rome, Bonn, Beirut, Jerusalem and the European Common Market and later served as international editor at United Press International. While covering the 1979 Iranian Revolution for *Time*, Flamini wrote the magazine's cover story — in which Ayatollah Ruhollah Khomeini was named Man of the Year — and was promptly expelled because authorities didn't like what they read. His books include a study of Vatican politics in the 1960s, *Pope, Premier, President*. His most recent report for *CQ Global Researcher* was "Rising Tension Over Iran."

Sarah Glazer, a London-based freelancer, is a regular contributor to *CQ Global Researcher*. Her articles on health, education and social-policy issues also have appeared in *The New York Times* and *The Washington Post*. Her recent *CQ Global Researcher* reports include "Future of the Euro" and "Sharia Controversy." She graduated from the University of Chicago with a B.A. in American history.

Christopher Hack is a London-based freelance writer and economic analyst working for *The Economist* Intelligence Unit and *The Observer* and *Guardian* newspapers, among others. He writes on contemporary events in Britain and Europe and is a former foreign correspondent in Beirut, Lebanon, for the BBC and *Time*. He earned a Joint Honors degree in politics and economics in 1993 at the University of London.

Leda Hartman is a nationally award-winning print and public radio journalist who specializes in global affairs. Her articles have appeared in *The New York Times* and *The Christian Science Monitor*, and her radio stories have aired on programs such as "Morning Edition," "All Things Considered," "Marketplace" and "The World." She also was an editor for two public radio global affairs programs, "Latitudes" and the "World Vision Report."

Associate Editor **Kenneth Jost** graduated from Harvard College and Georgetown University Law Center. He is the author of the *Supreme Court Yearbook* and *The Supreme Court from A to Z* (both CQ Press). He was a member of the *CQ Researcher* team that won the American Bar Association's 2002 Silver Gavel Award. His previous reports include "Understanding Islam" (2006) and a series of regional reports on democratization, including "Democracy and the Arab World" (2004). He also writes the blog *Jost on Justice* (http://jostonjustice.blogspot.com).

Reed Karaim, a freelance writer in Tucson, Arizona, has written for *The Washington Post, U.S. News &World*

Report, Smithsonian, American Scholar, USA Weekend and other publications. He is the author of the novel, *If Men Were Angels*, which was selected for the Barnes & Noble Discover Great New Writers series. He is also the winner of the Robin Goldstein Award for Outstanding Regional Reporting and other journalism honors. Karaim is a graduate of North Dakota State University in Fargo.

Robert Kiener is an award-winning writer whose work has appeared in the *London Sunday Times, The Christian Science Monitor, The Washington Post, Reader's Digest*, Time Life Books, *Asia Inc.* and other publications. For more than two decades he lived and worked as an editor and correspondent in Guam, Hong Kong, Canada and England and is now based in the United States. He frequently travels to Asia and Europe to report on international issues. He holds an M.A. in Asian Studies from Hong Kong University and an M.Phil. in International Relations from Cambridge University.

Danielle Kurtzleben reports on business and economics for *U.S. News & World Report* and previously worked at the Pew Research Center's Project for Excellence in Journalism. Originally from rural northern Iowa, Danielle holds a B.A. in English from Carleton College (Northfield, Minn.) and an M.A. in Global Communication from George Washington University's Elliott School for International Affairs. She has appeared on C-SPAN and the Washington, D.C., public radio affiliate, WAMU, and she is also a regular contributor to the career website Brazen Life.

Jason McLure is a New Hampshire-based freelance writer. Previously he was a campaign correspondent for Reuters and an Africa correspondent for Bloomberg News and *Newsweek* and worked for *Legal Times* in Washington, D.C. His writing has appeared in publications such as *The Economist, The New York Times* and *BusinessWeek*. His last *CQ Global Researcher* was "Booming Africa." His work has been honored by the Washington, D.C., chapter of the Society for Professional Journalists, the Maryland-Delaware-District of Columbia Press Association and the Overseas Press Club of America Foundation. He is also coordinator of the Committee to Free Eskinder Nega, a jailed Ethiopian journalist.

Tom Price, a contributing writer for CQ Researcher, wrote "Globalizing Science" for the February 1, 2011, *CQ Global Researcher*. Currently a Washington-based freelance journalist, he previously was a correspondent in the Cox Newspapers Washington Bureau and chief politics writer for the *Dayton Daily News* and *The Journal Herald* in Dayton. He is author or coauthor of five books, including *Changing The Face of Hunger* and, most recently, *Washington, DC, Free & Dirt Cheap* with his wife Susan Crites Price. His work has appeared in *The New York Times, Time, Rolling Stone* and other periodicals. He earned a bachelor of science in journalism at Ohio University.

Kenneth J. Stier is a freelance writer who has worked for various wire services, newspapers and news organizations on several continents, including *TIME, Newsweek, Fortune* and CNBC. He has lived in several countries in Asia, including Vietnam where he opened a news bureau in Hanoi for dpa, Germany's main news agency, as part of the first group of Western reporters allowed to reside in the reunified country after the Vietnam War. He has also spent extended periods of time in Latin America and the Caucasus, where he was in Tbilisi for Georgia's Rose Revolution. He lives in Brooklyn, New York.

1

Assessing the United Nations

Tom Price

A U.N. peacekeeper from Brazil patrols Pettion Ville, Haiti, in 2010. The U.N. mission in Haiti — established in 2004 — was beefed up after the January 2010 earthquake destroyed much of the capital, Port-au-Prince. The U.N. spends about $7 billion a year on peacekeeping missions — less than Wall Street pays out in yearly bonuses.

From *The CQ Researcher*, March 20, 2012.

As shells fired by the Syrian army fell on Homs in late February 2012, resident Omar Shaker described his city's plight: "They bombed all the water tanks on the roofs of buildings. There's no water. Some people have gone without bread for days. If they don't die in the shelling, they will die of hunger.

"People don't care if it's the devil intervening to save us," Shaker said. "We need the world's help."[1]

But help was not on the way. Despite pleas from the Arab League and Gulf Cooperation Council for United Nations action, Russia and China kept the U.N. on the sidelines by vetoing Security Council resolutions condemning the attacks on civilians and calling for Syrian President Bashar Assad to leave office. It was just one more frustrating example of the 193-member organization's too-frequent inability to stop bloodshed, Secretary-General Ban Ki-moon lamented.[2]

The victors of World War II created the U.N. in 1945 "to save succeeding generations from the scourge of war."[3] Since then, however, more than 22 million people have died in more than 300 wars.[4] Today, the initially hopeful "Arab Spring" protests — which overthrew despotic governments in Tunisia, Egypt, Libya and Yemen — have cost thousands of lives, including more than 8,000 slaughtered in Syria by the Bashar Assad regime, according to the United Nations.[5] Despite the U.N.'s many successes, the recent failures to keep the peace have handed ammunition to critics who question the organization's value — a question that has been asked periodically throughout the U.N.'s existence.

Without the United Nations, there likely would have been more wars, and they probably would have lasted longer and claimed

1

U.N. Peacekeepers Span the Globe

The United Nations maintains 16 peacekeeping operations on four continents, including a "special political mission" in Afghanistan, established in 2002 to help bring sustainable peace and development to the country. The oldest peacekeeping mission is in the Middle East, where military observers have been authorized since 1948 to monitor tensions between Arabs and Israelis. Peacekeeping, which costs $7 billion this fiscal year, involves 98,653 uniformed personnel from 115 countries; the 19,000-strong contingent monitoring the post-war peace in the Democratic Republic of Congo is the largest.

Current U.N. Peacekeeping Operations

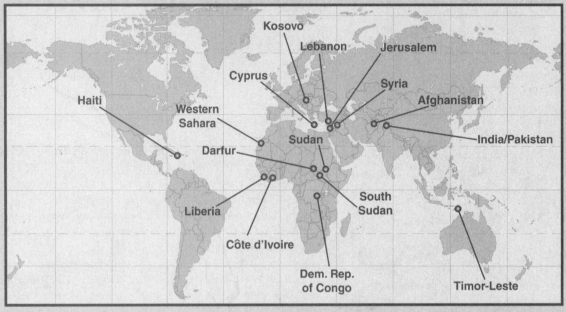

Source: "United Nations Peacekeeping," www.un.org/en/peacekeeping/operations/current.shtml

more casualties, says Swadesh Rana, former chief of the U.N.'s Conventional Arms Branch. Moreover, no nuclear, biological or radiological weapon has been used since the U.N.'s creation, says Rana, now a World Policy Institute senior fellow. And few, if any, U.N. member nations are engaged in cross-border armed conflict today, although there are tense standoffs in various parts of the world, she points out. As many as 36 countries were engaged in such conflicts about 20 years ago, as the Cold War was winding down, she says.

The United Nations also has worked to fulfill — with greater or lesser success — the other promises of its charter, such as "to reaffirm faith in fundamental human rights" and "to promote social progress and better

standards of life."[6] Various U.N. agencies fight hunger and poverty, promote economic development, defend human rights, provide relief during and after wars and natural disasters, support education, nurture culture and carry out other humanitarian activities.

And even though the United Nations has many critics, few contend the world would be better off without it. The arguments involve whether the global body's strengths outweigh its weaknesses and by how much. Newt Gingrich, former speaker of the U.S. House and a candidate for the 2012 Republican presidential nomination known for his fiery rhetoric, called the U.N. "amazingly bureaucratic" and "very corrupt." While campaigning in January he said he would "cut out a substantial amount of American money going to the U.N."

Nevertheless, he added, "I am not for withdrawing from the U.N."[7] In fact, with former Senate Democratic Leader George Mitchell in 2005, Gingrich co-chaired a study of the U.N. that concluded "an effective United Nations is in the interests of the United States."[8]

The U.N. is "sometimes frustrating to deal with," says Philippe Bolopion, a former French journalist who heads Human Rights Watch's activities at U.N. headquarters in New York City. "Yet it's an irreplaceable forum to advance human rights issues."

That's a common assessment: even pro-U.N. activists find the organization imperfect but necessary.

"It's bloated," says Tony Hall, former U.S. ambassador to the U.N. food and agriculture agencies in Rome. "There are tremendous bureaucracies. Some programs have had leadership issues." But the World Food Programme and other relief agencies work effectively, he says, and "they can go into areas that [the United States] cannot — into countries that we don't have relations with." In places like North Korea and Sudan, he adds, "as bad as those governments are, they have innocent people who need help."

American Will Davis, director of the U.N. Development Programme's Washington Office, says the organization exists "not because the U.N. is some perfect machinery that's going to lead us to some utopian future, but because there's really no alternative. It exists to attack problems that no individual country can tackle or has the political will to tackle on its own."

Canadian Anne Bayefsky, a senior fellow at the conservative Hudson Institute think tank who favors abolishing the

World Favors Greater UN Power

An overwhelming majority of people surveyed around the world wants the United Nations to have more power, such as to investigate human rights violations or authorize military force to prevent genocide or defend countries that have been attacked.

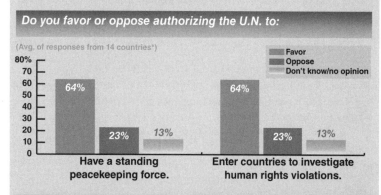

Do you favor or oppose authorizing the U.N. to:

(Avg. of responses from 14 countries*)

- Favor
- Oppose
- Don't know/no opinion

Have a standing peacekeeping force. — 64% Favor, 23% Oppose, 13% Don't know/no opinion

Enter countries to investigate human rights violations. — 64% Favor, 23% Oppose, 13% Don't know/no opinion

Should the U.N. Security Council be able to authorize military force to:

(Avg. of responses from 10-12 countries**)

- Should
- Should not
- Don't know/no opinion

Defend an attacked country? — 74% Should, 17% Should not, 9% Don't know/no opinion

Prevent severe human rights violations such as genocide? — 73% Should, 19% Should not, 8% Don't know/no opinion

Stop a country from supporting terrorist groups? — 69% Should, 24% Should not, 7% Don't know/no opinion

Prevent a country from acquiring nuclear weapons? — 52% Should, 37% Should not, 11% Don't know/no opinion

Forcefully restore an overthrown democratic government? — 48% Should, 40% Should not, 12% Don't know/no opinion

* Argentina, Armenia, China, France, India, Israel, Peru, Philippines, Poland, Russia, South Korea, Thailand, Ukraine and the United States.

** China, France, India, Israel, Mexico, Palestinian territories, Poland, Russia, South Korea, Thailand, Ukraine and the United States.

Source: "World Publics Favor New Powers for the UN," WorldPublic Opinion. org, May 2007, www.worldpublicopinion.org/pipa/articles/btunitednationsra/355.php?nid= &id=&pnt=355&lb=btun

U.N., calls attempts to reform it "almost a perennial joke." She and other critics complain that undemocratic countries wield too much power and subvert U.N. ideals. "Most of what we expected from the U.N. — mainly protecting

U.N. Actions Stir Outrage and Ridicule

Some top jobs go to anti-female, anti-Semitic governments and individuals.

The next time a liberal asks why conservatives don't respect the United Nations, *National Review* advised its conservative readers last year, "you could tell them this: North Korea is chairing the Conference on Disarmament. If that's not good enough, you could add this: Iran is a member of the Commission on the Status of Women. That should answer their question."[1]

The U.N. certainly provides plenty of fodder for its critics to condemn or ridicule.

As Australia's nationwide newspaper, *The Australian*, asked in a headline: "Is the UN Stark Raving Mad?" The paper condemned North Korea's chairmanship of the disarmament conference as "a case of lunatics taking over the asylum. The wacky regime that constantly violates the U.N.'s nuclear controls, is the target of U.N. sanctions, and is the leading proliferator of nuclear technology to Iran and Syria is now putatively in charge of the organization responsible for negotiating multilateral arms control agreements."[2]

Under the headline "The depraved United Nations," *Jerusalem Post* columnist Isi Leibler complained of Iran's election as a General Assembly vice president and charged that the U.N. had been captured by "dictatorships and tyrannies" and "transformed into a platform for promoting genocide."[3]

Human rights activists also expressed disbelief in 2010, when Iran was elected to the 45-member U.N. Commission on the Status of Women and Saudi Arabia to another agency — U.N. Women — charged with promoting women's rights. Shirin Ebadi, the Iranian woman who won the 2003 Nobel Peace Prize for her campaigns for women's rights, said it was "a joke" for countries that oppress women to be placed on such panels. Iranian laws discriminate against women in divorce cases and require testimony from two women to equal testimony of one man in court, she said, and the women's rights situation in Saudi Arabia "is even worse."[4]

Saudi Arabia forbids women to drive, restricts their use of public facilities when men are present and requires them to get permission from male relatives to participate in many activities. The monarchy recently announced that women would be allowed to vote in 2015. According to Human Rights Watch, Iran restricts what women can study in college and requires a male guardian's permission to marry.[5]

Equally jaw-dropping: Syria was appointed to two human-rights-related committees of the United Nations Educational, Scientific and Cultural Organization (UNESCO) even as the Syrian government was killing protesters in its own country. Astonishingly, UNESCO's Arab members selected Syria for the posts in November, shortly before the country was suspended from the Arab League because of its violent attacks on demonstrators. Other countries quickly launched a campaign to expel Syria from the panels.[6]

Rep. Ileana Ros-Lehtinen, R-Fla., chair of the U.S. House Foreign Affairs Committee, called Syria's appointments a "stunning display" of "irresponsible and dangerous behavior" and "an affront to those suffering at the hand of tyrants all around the world."[7]

Possibly the greatest outrage and ridicule have been generated by the activities of Princeton Law Professor Richard Falk, the U.N.'s special rapporteur for human rights in the Palestinian territories. Falk is accused of anti-Semitism and has suggested that the Bush administration may have been complicit in the 2001 terrorist attacks on the World Trade

peace and security and human rights — can be done better by a redesigned multilateral institution run by and for democracies in the interests of democracy," she says.

But others argue that the U.N.'s universal membership — which includes repressive as well as democratic governments — is essential for its actions to have global credibility. "Working to find agreement with countries that have disparate worldviews has always been a difficult endeavor," former U.N. Secretary-General Kofi Annan said. "Nevertheless, it is important and worthwhile."[9]

Hall, a longtime human-rights activist and former member of Congress, views universal U.N. membership the same way he views bilateral diplomacy. "Should we have an embassy in North Korea?" he asks rhetorically. "I believe we should. If we're able to discuss at the table, we should always sit at the table."

As the U.N. stumbles in trying to address ongoing violence in the Middle East, here are some questions diplomats and others are asking about the institution's value to the world:

Center and the Pentagon. He wrote the foreword to *The New Pearl Harbor*, by David Ray Griffin, a retired American professor of the philosophy of religion and theology who suggests that the World Trade Center towers were destroyed by "controlled demolition" rather than by hijacked airplanes.[8] Falk himself has written about a "large and growing grassroots constituency" that believes the truth about 9/11 "is not yet known, or . . . is known but being actively suppressed."[9]

And last year Falk caused controversy when he posted a cartoon on his blog depicting a dog — wearing a sweater labeled "USA" and a yarmulke with a Star of David — chewing a bloody skeleton and urinating on Lady Justice.[10]

While acknowledging that many of these appointments are outrageous, U.N. supporters downplay their significance. Some positions rotate, so North Korea — for instance — simply got its turn to chair the disarmament conference for a brief time. Iran and Saudi Arabia can be outvoted on the women's panels, supporters note, and other U.N. bodies are more important.

More significant, they point out, the United States, U.K. and France hold three of the five permanent seats on the organization's most powerful body — the Security Council — where any one of them can block a Security Council action with a veto.

— *Tom Price*

Iranian human rights advocate Shirin Ebadi, who won the 2003 Nobel Peace Prize for her campaigns for women's rights, said it was "a joke" for countries that oppress women to be placed on key U.N. human rights panels.

AFP/Getty Images/John Thys

[1]"The Week," *National Review*, Aug. 15, 2011.

[2]"Is the UN Stark Raving Mad?" *The Australian*, July 4, 2011, p. 15, www.theaustralian.com.au/news/opinion/is-the-un-stark-raving-mad/story-e6frg71x-1226086716084.

[3]Isi Leibler, "Candidly Speaking: The depraved United Nations," *The Jerusalem Post*, Sept. 8, 2011, www.jpost.com/Opinion/Columnists/Article.aspx?id=237091.

[4]Bill Varner, "Iran, Saudi Arabia Seats on UN Women's Board Would Be a 'Joke,' Ebadi Says," Bloomberg, Nov. 9, 2010, www.bloomberg.com/news/2010-11-09/iran-saudi-arabia-seats-on-un-women-s-board-would-be-a-joke-ebadi-says.html.

[5]"World Report 2012: Iran," Human Rights Watch, www.hrw.org/world-report-2012/world-report-2012-iran; Alexia Bedat, "Women's Rights in China, Saudi Arabia and Iran," Testimony to the UN Human Rights Council, UN Watch, Sept. 15, 2011; Varner, *op. cit.*

[6]Kareem Fahim and Steven Erlanger, "Aid official and priest are killed in Syria," *The International Herald Tribune*, Jan. 27, 2012, p. 4.

[7]"Ros-Lehtinen Says Selection of Syria for UNESCO Human Rights Panel Affront to Victims Around the World," U.S. House Foreign Affairs Committee, Nov. 22, 2011, http://foreignaffairs.house.gov/press_display.asp?id=2099.

[8]David Ray Griffin, "Was America Attacked by Muslims on 9/11?" www.davidraygriffin.com/articles/was-america-attacked-by-muslims-on-911.

[9]Richard A. Falk, "9/11: More than meets the eye," *The Edinburgh* (Scotland) *Journal*, Nov. 9, 2008, www.journal-online.co.uk/article/5056-911-more-than-meets-the-eye.

[10]Gil Shefler, "US, Jewish groups demand Falk resign over blog entry," *The Jerusalem Post*, July 10, 2011, www.jpost.com/International/Article.aspx?id=228618.

Is the U.N. worth the money the world spends on it?

During his brief campaign for the Republican presidential nomination, Texas Gov. Rick Perry suggested that "it's time for us to have a serious discussion about defunding the United Nations."[10]

U.S. House Foreign Affairs Committee Chair Ileana Ros-Lehtinen, R-Fla., calls the U.N. "big, bloated" and "dysfunctional."

But former U.N. executive Rana calls the organization's budget a bargain. The U.N. spends about $7 billion a year on 16 peacekeeping missions scattered around the globe, she notes — or about $1 for each of the world's 7 billion inhabitants. The rest of the U.N.'s activities — from hunger relief to facilitating international air travel — costs about $8 billion, or another $1.15 per person.

Other advocates point out that the U.N.'s peacekeeping expenses make up less than half of 1 percent of global military spending.[11] It costs more to run the New York City School system.[12] Wall Street pays out more in yearly bonuses.[13]

AFP/Getty Images/Mahmud Turkia

Libyans dance in the streets of Tripoli on Oct. 20, 2011, following the capture of longtime dictator Moammar Gadhafi by opposition forces. After Gadhafi launched a brutal crackdown on dissenters last spring, the U.N. Security Council authorized "all necessary measures" to protect Libyan civilians. With protection from NATO aircraft, the opposition forces overthrew the regime and killed Gadhafi.

However, critics don't focus solely on how much the organization costs. They also question whether the money is well spent. "There's very little scrutiny paid to whether [U.N.] activities are living up to expectations," says Brett Schaefer, a fellow at the Margaret Thatcher Center for Freedom at the conservative Heritage Foundation think tank in Washington.

The U.N. tends to add new activities — or "mandates," in U.N. parlance — without assessing whether older mandates continue to be needed, Schaefer says.

For example, he points out, "The Economic Commission for Europe was designed to transition Europe from World War II. The commission continues to exist, with over 100 employees and a budget of over $50 million, even though no one can demonstrably say what contribution it makes to a mission that has been overtaken by events." The commission says its "major aim" is to "promote pan-European economic integration." Yet most of Europe already belongs to the European Union, a wealthy economic and political confederation with 27 members.

The U.N.'s first two peacekeeping missions — in the Middle East (1948) and on the India-Pakistan border (1949) — still have boots on the ground after being deployed more than 60 years ago, Schaefer notes, because the conflicts they were commissioned to resolve are still simmering: the Palestinian-Israeli conflict and

the India-Pakistan dispute over Jammu and Kashmir. "The presence of the operations for six decades argues that they are not contributing to the resolution of those problems," he adds.

Moreover, he says, because U.N. dues are assessed according to a nation's wealth — resulting in most of the dues being paid by a handful of developed countries — most members aren't motivated to police U.N. spending.

The world's 10 wealthiest countries pay 72 percent of the U.N.'s core budget and an even larger share of peacekeeping expenditures. The United States funds 22 percent ($569 million) of the core budget and 27 percent of peacekeeping costs. The 39 countries with the lowest assessments altogether cover less than one-tenth of 1 percent of the core budget — or $23,631 each.[14]

Schaefer does not oppose all U.N. spending. "Some peacekeeping activities are worthwhile," he says, pointing to the current operation that oversees South Sudan's secession from Sudan and the creation of a new nation there. "It addresses a present crisis, and it greatly contributed to the transition to independence."[15]

The U.N. also has "noncontroversial, useful" agencies that facilitate the global economy and fight disease, he adds.

Similarly, some of the U.N.'s strongest supporters acknowledge its flaws while arguing that it makes profound contributions to peace, relief and development. The U.N. delivers "mixed results," says Martin Rendón, vice president for public policy and advocacy at the United States Fund for UNICEF, a support organization that raises money for the U.N. children's program. "It's not on target to meet all the goals that have been set. But fewer people are hungry today, and fewer people are poor today because of the U.N.

"In the 1980s, we used to say that 40,000 children were dying every day from preventable causes," he continues. "Now we say it's 21,000." That's still too high, he says, but moving in the right direction.

UNICEF offers "very good value for the money," according to a U.K. study of multilateral aid programs released in November. Several other U.N. agencies — including the U.N. Development Programme, U.N. High Commissioner for Refugees (UNHCR), U.N. Peacebuilding Fund and the World Food Programme — were rated as providing "good" value.[16] The study prompted the United Kingdom to stop providing funding for four U.N. agencies and warned four others that they also will lose funding if they don't improve.

Overall, the U.N. is worth what the U.K. spends on it because it is "able to work in many more countries than the U.K. can reach on its own — and at a scale beyond any single country — on a broad range of activities the U.K. could not tackle by itself," says Alan Duncan, the U.K.'s minister for international development. "Some agencies are worth every penny, and others need to be helped to improve or they will see their funds reduced or cut" entirely.

Do undemocratic countries wield too much power in the United Nations?

At its birth near the end of World War II, the United Nations was dominated by the industrial democracies and their allies. Four of the five permanent, veto-wielding members of the Security Council — the United States, the United Kingdom, France and the anticommunist nationalist government of China (which now controls only Taiwan) — were democracies or allies.

Today, free countries hold a minority — 45 percent — of the seats in the U.N. General Assembly, according to Freedom House, a human rights group. About a third are "partly free" and a quarter are "not free."[17]

That helps to explain why undemocratic countries — including some of the most repressive — seem to exercise so much power, according to Bayefsky, of the Hudson Institute. "The current U.N. bears little resemblance to the original drafters' vision," she says. "Democracies don't control what happens in the General Assembly. They play a largely defensive role in the Security Council."

That's because of the U.N.'s one-country-one-vote policy, which means the tiny Caribbean Island of Saint Lucia (which has a population 170,000 and pays $23,631 a year in U.N. dues) has the same General Assembly vote as the United States, according to Kim

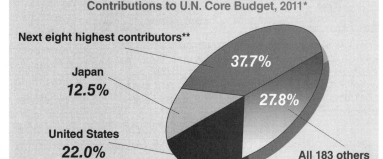

U.S. Contributes Most to UN

The United States contributed 22 percent of the U.N.'s core budget in 2011 — or $582 million — more than any other nation and nearly as much as the amount given by 183 other members combined. Japan ranked second with a contribution of about 13 percent. Dues are assessed according to a nation's wealth, but every country — regardless of how much it contributes — has a single vote in the General Assembly.

Contributions to U.N. Core Budget, 2011*

Next eight highest contributors** — 37.7%

Japan — 12.5%

27.8%

United States — 22.0%

All 183 others

Does not include peacekeeping expenses or independently funded agencies like UNICEF.

** Germany, U.K., France, Italy, Canada, China, Spain and Mexico

Total U.N. Budget, 2011
$2.6 billion

Source: "Assessment of Member States' Contributions to the United Nations Regular Budget for the Year 2011," United Nations Secretariat, December 2010, pp. 2-7, www.un.org/zh/members/contribution_2011.pdf

Holmes, a Heritage Foundation scholar who was assistant secretary of state for international organization affairs in the George W. Bush administration.[18]

Because there are few criteria for U.N. membership, Holmes said, totalitarian and authoritarian regimes have the same voting power as free nations. As a result, "the all-too-frequent clash of worldviews between liberty and authoritarian socialism" often has stymied effective action, she said.

According to Bayefsky, "Islamic states and their cronies form an automatic General Assembly majority" that enables them to pass resolutions condemning Israel while blocking or delaying actions against despotic regimes.[19]

U.N. supporters acknowledge the unwelcome actions of authoritarian states but argue that the real power resides in the wealthy industrial democracies and in the Security Council, where any one of the five permanent members — the United States, U.K., France, Russia and China — can veto any action.

Protesters march in the Jan. 6, 2012, funeral procession of a man killed outside his home in the besieged Syrian city of Homs. He was among more than 8,000 people killed during a crackdown on anti-government dissenters in the past year. The efforts by Russia and China to block Security Council action on the crisis have sparked international outrage.

"Every time [Iranian President Mahmoud] Ahmadinejad speaks at the U.N. General Assembly, my blood boils, too," says Peter Yeo, executive director of the Better World Campaign, which advocates for the United Nations in the United States. "But we have to look at the totality of the activities being undertaken by the U.N. and see that, on the whole, it serves American interests."

Davis, at the U.N. Development Programme's Washington office, suggests "paying close attention to what it is they're dominating." Authoritarian countries don't control what's important, he adds.

Many democratic governments agree. When controversy erupted over North Korea's becoming chair of the U.N. Disarmament Conference, for instance, the United States reacted with a shrug. "It's a consensus-based organization, so nothing can be decided just because the chair is a country that we have issues with," State Department spokeswoman Victoria Nuland said. The U.S. government chose "not to make a big deal out of this, because it's a relatively low-level, inconsequential event."[20]

Similarly, South Korean officials noted that the chairmanship rotates and "have not considered any action with regard to it."[21]

Sounding like Americans who insist the Founding Fathers intended Congress to be inefficient, Adam Chapnick, deputy director of education at the Canadian Forces College, said the United Nations is "working exactly the way its founders intended. They anticipated

that some parts of the U.N. would be dysfunctional, but, curiously, they believed that dysfunction could serve a useful purpose in the long run."

The Security Council was to hold the real power, according to Chapnick, author of *The Middle Power Project: Canada and the Founding of the United Nations.* As the U.N. was being organized, Chapnick said, U.K. Foreign Secretary Anthony Eden said the General Assembly would "enable representatives of the smaller powers to blow off steam."[22]

Around the world, the United States is widely seen as the U.N.'s powerhouse. "The U.S. basically controls the U.N. and can almost always make the U.N. do what the U.S. wants," said a majority of people polled in six predominantly Muslim states — Egypt, Turkey, Jordan, Iran, Indonesia and Azerbaijan — plus the Palestinian Territories and Nigeria, where half the population is Muslim. Agreement ranged from 68 percent in Egypt to 53 percent in Turkey and a plurality of 43 percent in Indonesia. Only in Azerbaijan, a former Soviet republic, did a plurality (49 percent) agree with the alternative: "Through its veto the U.S. can stop the U.N. from doing things, but the U.S. cannot make the U.N. do things the U.S. wants."[23]

Should democracies leave the U.N. Human Rights Council?

Last year, about three months before Libya launched a brutal attempt to suppress Arab Spring demonstrations, Libyan officials sat for their Universal Periodic Review by the U.N. Human Rights Council in Geneva. During the hearing, any U.N. member could comment on Libya's record. Many lined up to do so, including some of the world's worst human rights violators.

According to the council's report on the hearing, Syria "commended [Libya] for its democratic regime," and North Korea praised Libya "for its achievements in the protection of human rights." Saudi Arabia commended Libya for "the importance that the country attached to human rights."[24]

Four days earlier, the council had examined the United States, and North Korea had complained of "persistent reports of human rights violations committed by the United States at home and abroad." Iran, Nicaragua, Cuba and other less-than-free states weighed in with similar critiques.[25]

The comments illustrate how the review process has been, in the words of Heritage Foundation scholar Schaefer, "hijacked by countries seeking to shield themselves from criticism . . . laughably affirming their commitment to fundamental human rights and freedoms."[26]

In testimony before the House Foreign Affairs Committee, Hillel Neuer, executive director of U.N. Watch, an independent monitor of the U.N., quoted Human Rights Watch executive director Kenneth Roth, who likened the predecessor Human Rights Commission to "a jury that includes murderers and rapists, or a police force run in large part by suspected murderers and rapists determined to stymie investigation of their crimes."[27]

Only 20 of the council's current 47 members (42.5 percent) are rated "free" by Freedom House. Fifteen (32 percent) are rated as "partly free" and 12 members (25.5 percent) as "not free." The human rights group includes four council members on its 20-country list of the "worst of the worst" — China, Cuba, Saudi Arabia and Libya, which won a council seat when Gadhafi was in power.[28]

Calling the council "fundamentally illegitimate," House Foreign Affairs Committee Chairwoman Ros-Lehtinen says democracies should be "pushing for a massive structural overhaul or create an alternative body with real standards for membership. The council has continually undermined its own credibility by ignoring human rights abuses in Cuba, China, Russia, Saudi Arabia, Venezuela and many other countries," she charges, while it "focuses disproportionately on the democratic, Jewish state of Israel."

Since its creation in 2006, the council has seen about half of its country-specific resolutions aimed at Israel, Schaefer said. He joined Ros-Lehtinen in calling for democracies to "begin exploring the option of creating an alternative, effective human rights body outside of the U.N. system."[29]

Not all human rights activists agree. Some say the council performs better than the Human Rights Commission that it replaced, and they see improvement since the United States joined the panel in 2009. They cite recent actions, such as the council's condemnation of Syria's crackdown on demonstrators; its move to investigate human rights violations in Iran, Libya and Côte d'Ivoire; and its program to assess freedom of assembly around the world.[30]

Perhaps most dramatic, the council passed a resolution last June to end discrimination based on sexual orientation and gender identity. It commissioned a report by the U.N. High Commissioner for Human Rights, which, when it was issued in December, catalogued anti-gay laws and practices around the world and called for their repeal.[31]

The council's stand will help activists respond to governments that say "we have poverty and people starving, so we cannot focus on LGBT [lesbian-gay-bisexual-transgender] rights," says Grace Poore, a Malaysian who coordinates the Asia and Pacific islands work of the International Gay and Lesbian Human Rights Commission. "We'll see if it actually trickles down and translates into something on the ground."

Hossein Alizadeh, an Iranian who is Poore's counterpart for the Middle East and North Africa, says the council's actions "send a signal to countries that often state that LGBT rights are not compatible with their culture or religious beliefs, and therefore it's irrelevant to their human rights framework. It affirms the universality of humans' rights, regardless of their sexual orientation or sexual identity."

Looking at the broader picture, Philippe Dam, a Frenchman who advocates for Human Rights Watch at the council's headquarters in Geneva, sees "positive trends," which he attributes in part to U.S. involvement. The "most repressive [council members] have been more isolated in recent votes," Dam says. Democracies in Latin America, Africa and Asia have become more active, he adds.

Democracies must stick with the council, said former U.N. Secretary-General Annan, or "we leave the field free to tyrants to call the shots."[32]

BACKGROUND

Dreams of Peace

Hope ran high after World War II, as the victorious gave birth to the United Nations. They had beaten back world conquest by the most brutal regimes in modern history, and they now had created an organization designed to guarantee that such a conquest could never threaten again.

In 1944, even as fighting continued to rage worldwide, diplomats from the United States, the United Kingdom, the Union of Soviet Socialist Republics (U.S.S.R.) and Nationalist China met to plan a peaceful future for the planet. In the Dumbarton Oaks mansion, atop a hill in Washington's historic Georgetown neighborhood, they hammered out plans for the U.N.[33]

CHRONOLOGY

1940s *As World War II ends, U.N. is founded to preserve peace.*

1944 Diplomats from United States, U.K., U.S.S.R. and Nationalist China meet to plan new body to end wars.

1945 U.N. Charter is signed; Food and Agriculture Organization begins to address U.N.'s humanitarian goals.

1946 U.N. Children's Emergency Fund is created to serve children suffering effects of World War II.

1948 Israel declares statehood; Jordan, Iraq, Lebanon, Egypt and Syria attack Israel; fighting stops after U.N.-brokered truce a month later, but resumes and ends again; U.N. deploys its first military observer group to monitor the truce.

1950 U.N. mediator Ralph Bunche wins Nobel Peace Prize for negotiating 1949 Arab-Israeli armistices; U.N. observers monitor India-Pakistan truce in dispute over Kashmir.

1950s-1970s *Cold War proceeds; free and communist countries support allies in proxy wars.*

1950 U.N. sends troops to defend South Korea after invasion from Communist North Korea.

1953 Armistice ends Korean War.

1956 Egypt nationalizes Suez Canal; U.K., France and Israel capture canal; invaders agree to U.N. withdrawal demands; U.N. peacekeepers oversee pullout.

1961 World Food Programme is established to provide emergency food relief and fight chronic hunger.

1962 Cuban missile crisis sparks fear of nuclear war; U.N. serves as stage for debate while U.S. and U.S.S.R. resolve confrontation.

1963 Security Council endorses arms embargo against South Africa in effort to end white minority rule.

1966 U.N. Development Programme is created to promote economic development in poor countries. U.N. imposes economic sanctions against white-ruled Rhodesia (now Zimbabwe) in Southern Africa.

1967 Egypt blockades Israeli oil supply route, sparking "Six-Day War;" Israel seizes Golan Heights, Sinai, Gaza, East Jerusalem and West Bank. . . . Security Council says peace will require Israeli withdrawal from occupied land and Arab recognition of Israel's right to exist. Neither occurs.

1969 U.N. Population Fund created to provide reproductive health services to the poor and victims of conflict and disaster.

1973 After surprise attack by Egypt and Syria, Israel pushes Arab troops back across 1967 cease-fire lines. United States and U.S.S.R. broker truce without U.N. help.

1990s *Cold War ends. U.N. focuses on smaller conflicts, atrocities.*

1990 Iraq invades Kuwait; U.N. authorizes liberation of Kuwait.

1991 U.S.-led coalition liberates Kuwait.

2000s-Present *Terrorism, civil wars replace nation-vs.-nation warfare.*

2001 Al Qaeda terrorist attacks in the United States prompt U.N. to authorize military action against Afghanistan, which harbors the terrorists.

2005 U.N. condemns terrorism; says it has responsibility to protect citizens from "genocide, war crimes, ethnic cleansing and crimes against humanity" if their own governments fail to protect them.

2011 "Arab Spring" erupts across North Africa and the Middle East. . . . Security Council authorizes NATO bombing to protect civilians after Libyan dictator Moammar Gadhafi cracks down on anti-government demonstrators; Gadhafi is overthrown and killed.

2012 Arab League calls for U.N. action against Bashar Assad regime in Syria after it kills thousands of protesters. Russia and China veto Security Council resolution. . . . Iran is suspected of defying U.N. strictures against nuclear weapons, raising specter of military attack by Israel or United States.

The following April — as the Allies conquered Italy and Germany and pressed toward victory over Japan — an expanded cast of 50 nations convened in San Francisco to write the U.N. charter, which was approved on June 25.

The next day, speaking at the charter's signing, U.S. President Harry S Truman defined the new organization's task as keeping the world "free from the fear of war." A month later, as the U.S. Senate ratified the charter by a vote of 89-2, Democratic Sen. Theodore Bilbo of Mississippi proclaimed it "a great document which we believe will usher in the millennial dawn."[34]

The charter created two very different bodies to govern the new organization.

The General Assembly, where each nation cast one vote, would pass budgets, conduct debates and vote on nonbinding resolutions. The 11-member Security Council, with five permanent members who each could exercise a veto, was charged with maintaining peace and could authorize sanctions and the use of force. As U.N. membership grew, the council was enlarged to 15 in 1965.

The vetoes belonged to the four nations that met at Dumbarton Oaks, plus France. But the real point of the veto was to require the United States and the Soviet Union to agree on major U.N. actions. The world was dividing into two camps — the industrial democracies and their allies against the Soviet Union and its communist satellites. The United States and its allies dominated the 51-member organization. (Poland was added at the last moment.) But it would be impossible for the organization to act effectively if the two leaders were split on U.N. decisions.

To show that it was more than a military alliance, the U.N. established the Food and Agriculture Organization to increase farm productivity, improve the nutrition and lives of rural populations and contribute to world economic growth. In 1946, the U.N. created the United Nations International Children's Emergency Fund, its initial task to provide urgent relief to children suffering from the effects of the war. Funded voluntarily, UNICEF received its first substantial government contributions from the United States and Canada in 1947 and saw its first national fundraising organization established — the U.S. Fund for UNICEF.

Peacekeeping Begins

The Middle East conflict between Arabs and Jews became the new organization's first major military crisis — a conflict that persists today. The United Kingdom controlled Palestine under a League of Nations mandate, and Jews wanted a homeland there for the hundreds of thousands who had survived the Nazi Holocaust but been driven from their homes.

In November 1947, the General Assembly approved partitioning Palestine into separate Jewish and Arab states. Confusion ensued later, when the United States reversed its position and called for creation of a U.N. trusteeship in the region.

Britain removed its troops on May 14, 1948, and the Provisional State Council in Tel Aviv immediately proclaimed the establishment of the State of Israel. Despite its earlier second thoughts, the United States quickly became the first country to recognize the new nation. Almost as quickly, Jordan, Iraq, Lebanon, Egypt and Syria launched the first Arab-Israeli war.

A U.N. representative negotiated a truce in June, and the international organization deployed its first military observer group to the region. U.N. mediator Ralph Bunche managed to negotiate armistices between Israel and its Arab foes in 1949, for which he won the 1950 Nobel Peace Prize — the first of 10 awarded to the U.N. and its staff. The agreements left Israel in control of 20 percent more land than it received in the partition, while some 700,000 Arabs fled the territory.[35] On May 11, Israel joined the U.N.

By then, the U.N. had deployed military observers to the India-Pakistan border to monitor the uneasy peace between the two newly independent nations, who had clashed over control of the disputed territory of Jammu and Kashmir.

In 1950, with Mao Zedong's Communist Party in control of mainland China and the Nationalist government relocated in Taiwan, the Soviets attempted and failed to transfer the Nationalists' Security Council seat to the communists. (That didn't occur until 1971.) Soviet U.N. Ambassador Jacob Malik boycotted council meetings in protest.

The boycott proved bad strategy for the communists, however. When communist North Korea invaded South Korea on June 25, Malik was not present to veto the Security Council resolution that approved the U.N.'s defense of the south. Sixteen countries sent troops into the war under U.S. command.

Three years of fighting resulted in the deaths of more than 450,000 U.N. troops, mostly South Koreans, and 500,000-1.5 million soldiers from North Korea and Communist China, which entered the war as U.N. troops

Unsung Agencies Help Prevent Chaos

From the mail to outer space, U.N. programs grease the global gears.

The United Nations usually commands public attention during times of conflict, controversy or tragedy — when its peacekeepers stand between enemies on a cease-fire line, when its relief workers rush to the aid of disaster victims or when nations debate how U.N. power should be deployed.

But much of the 67-year-old organization's work is done quietly and without controversy, by agencies supplying what Will Davis, director of the U.N. Development Programme's Washington Office, calls "the grease between the gears in an ever globalizing world."

"Every time we board an aircraft for a trip abroad, we entrust our safety to the International Civil Aviation Organization," said S. Jayakumar, Singapore's former senior minister. "Any time we call a friend or family in another country, we rely on the International Telecommunications Union."[1]

Some U.N. agencies — such as the Universal Postal Union and the International Telecommunications Union — were established in the 19th century and were incorporated into the U.N.'s portfolio after its founding. Other bodies — such as the Office for Outer Space Affairs — were created to deal with new challenges.

U.N. agencies that deal with peacekeeping, hunger and disease are well known. Here are some of the important, but lesser known, U.N. agencies:

Office for Outer Space Affairs — If Newt Gingrich were elected U.S. president and established a colony on the Moon, as he has vowed to do, this office, created in 1958 to advise the U.N.'s new Committee on the Peaceful Uses of Outer Space, likely would address questions of ownership and appropriate lunar activity. International treaties say no nation can claim ownership of a celestial body and all space activity must be peaceful.

The office, which adopted its current name in 1992, also monitors space debris, which poses a growing threat to space vehicles, and maintains a register of objects launched into outer space.[2] In 2009, at the request of countries worried about space debris, it prepared "Space Debris Mitigation Guidelines," which urge space agencies to remove spacecraft from orbit once their missions end.

The office also staffs a round-the-clock hotline to act on requests for satellite imagery during disasters and prepares reports on international space law.[3]

Universal Postal Union — Negotiated by representatives of 22 nations in 1874, the Treaty of Bern established the General Postal Union to replace a series of bilateral postal agreements with a single system for moving mail from country to country. The name was changed to the Universal Postal Union four years later. It became part of the United Nations system in 1948 and continues to serve

advanced on the Chinese border. An armistice, signed July 27, 1953, left the North-South border near the 38th parallel, where it had been at the war's beginning. U.N. forces, mostly South Koreans and Americans, have been stationed at the tense demilitarized zone (DMZ) between the two countries ever since.

The U.N. deployed peacekeepers again after the Suez Canal crisis of 1956. Egypt had nationalized the canal in July. In October, British, French and Israeli troops invaded — the Europeans to overturn the nationalization, the Israelis to attack anti-Israeli terrorist bases.

Britain and France vetoed Security Council resolutions — proposed by the United States and the U.S.S.R. — calling for an end to the invasion. But a precedent had been established earlier for General Assembly action when vetoes

stymied the Security Council. Although General Assembly resolutions carried no enforcement power, the U.N. at that time was highly respected in Europe, and the U.K., France and Israel agreed to a ceasefire.

U.N. peacekeepers entered Egypt in November to oversee the withdrawal of the invasion forces. They remained as a buffer between Israel and Egypt until the Arab-Israeli war of 1967.

Cuban Missile Crisis

In 1962, the Security Council served as a stage upon which the Cuban missile crisis unfolded, although U.N. action did not end the U.S.-U.S.S.R. standoff.

On Oct. 22, President John F. Kennedy announced in a somber televised address that the Soviet Union as the primary forum for cooperation among postal systems, setting rules for international mail exchange, mediating disputes, providing advice and offering technical assistance.[4]

International Telecommunication Union — Founded in 1865 as the International Telegraph Union (ITU), this is the U.N.'s oldest agency and possibly the one that has had to cope with the most change. In the early years after the telegraph's 1844 invention, telegraph lines did not connect between nations, so messages had to be transcribed, translated if necessary and retransmitted at each international border.

As they did with international mail, countries at first developed bilateral and regional agreements to standardize equipment and connect lines. The International Telegraph Convention, signed in Paris on May 17, 1865, established the union to address technological issues and establish international tariff and accounting rules.

As new technologies developed, the union had to establish international standards for telephones, wireless telegraphy, radio, television, space communication, mobile communication, digital communication and, now, media convergence. Reflecting its expanding responsibilities, the ITU became the International Telecommunication Union in 1932 and became a U.N. agency in 1949. In 1989, it accepted responsibility for helping developing countries establish modern telecommunication systems.[5]

International Civil Aviation Organization — While the postal and telecommunication unions ensure that communications flow across borders, the International Civil Aviation Organization (ICAO) makes sure pilots and air traffic controllers around the world can understand each other and that aircraft and airports are safe.

Created in 1944 at a conference in Chicago and becoming fully operational in 1947, the ICAO promulgates uniform global standards and regulations for training and licensing of air and ground personnel, communication, air traffic control, aircraft airworthiness and navigation. The organization also serves as a forum for discussion of international aviation issues.[6]

— *Tom Price*

[1]"United Nations: Exaggerated hopes, exaggerated fears," *The* (Singapore) *Straits Times*, Oct. 1, 2003.

[2]For background, see Konstantin Kakaes, "Weapons in Space," *CQ Global Researcher*, Aug. 16, 2011, pp. 395-420.

[3]"United Nations Office for Outer Space Affairs," www.oosa.unvienna.org/oosa/en/OOSA/index.html; David Adam, "Property rights on the moon," *The* (London) *Guardian*, Oct. 24, 2005, p. 25; Neil MacFarquhar, "U.N. Weighs How to Answer a Knock on Earth's Door," *The New York Times*, Oct. 8, 2010, www.nytimes.com/2010/10/09/world/09nations.html; Heidi Blake, "Satellites threatened by orbiting rubbish dump," *The* (London) *Daily Telegraph*, May 27, 2010, p. 23.

[4]"Universal Postal Union," www.upu.int/en/the-upu.html.

[5]"ITU's History," International Telecommunication Union, www.itu.int/en/history/overview/Pages/history.aspx.

[6]"About ICAO," www.icao.int/Pages/icao-in-brief.aspx.

was erecting missile sites in Cuba, a communist island just 90 miles from Florida. He announced he had imposed a blockade of military shipments to Cuba, demanded that the Soviet Union remove the missiles and warned that "further action" would be taken if the missiles remained. He also declared that a missile attack in the Western Hemisphere would trigger "a full retaliatory strike upon the Soviet Union" and requested an emergency Security Council meeting.

The meeting began the next day and was watched by a television audience that feared the outbreak of nuclear war. Adlai Stevenson Jr., the U.S. ambassador to the U.N., introduced a resolution condemning the missile placement. Soviet Ambassador Valerian Zorin called for a U.N. denunciation of the blockade.

Two days later, the meeting reached its highest drama. After repeatedly challenging Zorin to deny the missile placement, while Zorin declined to respond, Stevenson declared: "I am prepared to wait for my answer until hell freezes over, if that is your decision. And I am also prepared to present the evidence in this room." He then unveiled photos of the missile sites, taken from a U-2 spy plane.

Private communications between Kennedy and Soviet Premier Nikita Khrushchev ended the crisis, with Khrushchev agreeing to withdraw the missiles and Kennedy agreeing to remove U.S. missiles from Turkey, although he would not link the two actions in public, so as not to be seen as giving in to Khruschev.

The 1960s saw the U.N. pushing against the remaining minority-white governments in Africa. In 1963 the Security

AFP/Getty Images/Jens Schlueter

A Somali refugee and her child live in a squatter's hut outside the U.N.'s giant Dadaab refugee settlement near the Kenyan border with Somalia. Aiding refugees is one of the most important humanitarian activities undertaken by the United Nations. Some say the U.N. High Commissioner for Refugees is one of several humanitarian agencies that functions effectively, because — unlike the U.N.'s regular budget — its funding is voluntary, so donor countries can stop giving money if the agency is seen as ineffective.

Council endorsed a voluntary arms embargo against South Africa. In 1966 the General Assembly stripped South Africa of its mandate to govern South-West Africa, which later became Namibia. The same year, the Security Council imposed sanctions on minority-run Rhodesia, now known as Zimbabwe.

During the '60s, the U.N. also stepped up its humanitarian and development work. The World Food Programme was established in 1961, the U.N. Development Programme in 1966 and the U.N. Population Fund in 1967.

The U.N. failed to prevent or halt the war in Vietnam, however. Nor did it prevent the slaughter of more than a million Cambodians on that nation's "killing fields" by the brutal Pol Pot government. And its relevance was challenged in 1967, when Egypt (at the time called the United Arab Republic) demanded the U.N. remove its international military observers.

U.N. Secretary-General U Thant agreed. Egypt then blockaded the Strait of Tiran, cutting off Israel's main oil shipping route. The blockade, considered an act of war under international law, spurred an Israeli preemptive air strike on June 5 that destroyed most of the military aircraft in Egypt, Jordan, Iraq and Syria. The U.N. brokered a cease-fire after

Israel had rapidly won what became known as the Six-Day War, in which it seized control of the Golan Heights from Syria, the Sinai and Gaza from Egypt and East Jerusalem and the West Bank from Jordan. In November, the Security Council passed Resolution 242, which declared that peace in the Middle East required Israeli withdrawal from territory it captured in the Six-Day War and Arab recognition of Israel's right to exist, neither of which has occurred.

Arabs and Israelis fought again in 1973, and once again the U.N. sent peacekeepers to supervise the ceasefire. The truce was arranged by U.S. and Soviet diplomats, however, an indication that the U.N. had little influence in the region, according to journalist/historian Stanley Meisler in his *United Nations: A History.*[36]

The United Nations sent another peacekeeping force to the Middle East following a 1978 Israeli invasion of Lebanon, which was aimed at weakening the Palestine Liberation Organization, a Palestinian nationalist organization, elements of which had engaged in terrorist acts against Israel. Four years later, U.N. troops could not prevent Israel from entering Lebanon again after hostilities flared once more.

Amid the peacekeeping failures, the U.N. at least was able to claim success in its humanitarian efforts, when in 1980 the World Health Organization declared smallpox to have been eradicated from Earth, three years after the last case had been reported.

From 1988 to 1993, the U.N. initiated 14 peacekeeping missions, more than it had deployed in the previous four decades. But peacekeeping was not always successful, largely because the troops' "monitoring" mandate often forbids them from intervening in conflicts. In 1994, for example, peacekeepers in Rwanda did not prevent the ethnic slaughter of more than 800,000 people, mostly Tutsi, by the Hutu majority. And in 1995, Dutch peacekeepers could not protect Bosnian Muslims, some 8,000 of whom were massacred by Bosnian Serbs in Srebrenica.

The Security Council did act after Iraq invaded Kuwait in August 1990, although the U.N. did not lead the military response. The Security Council authorized "all necessary means" to liberate Kuwait after U.S. President George H. W. Bush — at the invitation of the Saudi government — sent troops to Saudi Arabia to counter any further Iraqi aggression. But the war was fought by a U.S.-led coalition, not under the U.N. flag. After Iraq's quick defeat, the United States, U.K. and France did not seek U.N. permission to establish no-fly zones to protect Kurds in northern Iraq and Shiite Muslims in the South.

To avoid a potential Russian veto in the Security Council, NATO skipped seeking U.N. authority in 1999, when it intervened to stop the Serbs from slaughtering Albanians in Kosovo. NATO bombing drove Serbs to negotiations. After an accord was signed, NATO and Russian peacekeepers maintained the ceasefire while U.N. administrators helped establish a government.

After the Sept. 11 attacks against the United States by Al Qaeda in 2001, the U.N. authorized military action against the Taliban government in Afghanistan, which had harbored the Al Qaeda terrorist organization that carried out the attacks. But President George W. Bush failed to win Security Council authorization to invade Iraq again in 2003 on the later-discredited grounds that Iraq possessed weapons of mass destruction. The United States invaded anyway, with the support of countries in what Bush called the "Coalition of the Willing."

'Oil for Food' Scandal

The aftermath of the second Iraq war uncovered one of the U.N.'s worst scandals — in the so-called "oil-for-food" program.

After the first Persian Gulf War, the U.N. had imposed severe sanctions on Saddam Hussein's government. Beginning in 1996, to provide relief for its citizens, Iraq was allowed to sell oil and use the proceeds to buy food, medicine and other necessities and pay reparations to Kuwait. But after the second war, Saddam's government was discovered to have diverted funds from the sale, with the help of corrupt U.N. employees.

Marking the millennium, the U.N. and other international organizations agreed in 2000 to set what became known as the Millennium Development Goals to be achieved by 2015. They called for ending extreme poverty and hunger, providing universal primary education, promoting gender equality, reducing child mortality, improving maternal health, pursuing environmentally sustainable development, reversing the spread of major diseases such as HIV/AIDS and malaria and creating a global partnership for development.[37]

At a U.N.-sponsored summit in 2005, world leaders for the first time unanimously condemned terrorism "in all its forms and manifestations, committed by whomever, wherever and for whatever purposes."

They also agreed to a new doctrine, which would be used for the first time during the "Arab Spring." Dubbed the "responsibility to protect" and abbreviated "R2P," it declared that a nation has the responsibility to protect its population from "genocide, war crimes, ethnic cleansing and crimes against humanity." If a nation failed to do so, the U.N. had the responsibility to intervene.[38]

In late 2010 and early 2011, as anti-government demonstrations sprang up across the Arab world, Libyan dictator Moammar Gadhafi launched an especially brutal crackdown on protesters. Distressed by the bloodshed and the threat of more, the Arab League asked the U.N. to impose a no-fly zone to restrict Libyan troop movements.

On March 17, the Security Council authorized "all necessary measures" to protect Libyan civilians. Two days later, U.S. war planes destroyed Libya's air defenses and attacked Libyan troops and tanks. NATO then took over the operations, continuing to hamper Gadhafi's forces. Protected by NATO aircraft and joined by defecting Libyan soldiers, opposition forces overthrew the Gadhafi regime and killed the long-time dictator.

Libya "changed the dynamic of the Security Council," German U.N. Ambassador Peter Wittig says. "Quite a number of Security Council members adhere to orthodox political doctrine: The Security Council should not get involved in affairs of U.N. member states." But Gadhafi's "ruthless brutality" forced even them to act.

While much of the world rejoiced at Gadhafi's downfall, the reaction of Russia's former ambassador to Libya helps to explain why Russia and China often oppose actions against oppressive governments. Vladimir Chamov complained that Russian businesses were harmed because Russia did not veto the Security Council resolution.

"Russian companies had agreed to very lucrative long-term contracts . . . which they could lose and have already lost — which in a sense can be considered the betrayal of Russia's interests," he said.[39]

CURRENT SITUATION

Responsibility to Protect?

Reflecting on U.N. actions in Libya and other places last year, Secretary-General Ban Ki-moon declared in early 2012 that "history took a turn for the better" in 2011. U.N. members seriously accepted the "responsibility-to-protect"

Should all UN payments be voluntary?

YES
Rep. Ileana Ros-Lehtinen, R-Fla.
Chair, House Foreign Affairs Committee

Written for *CQ Global Researcher,* March 2012

The U.N.'s many problems stem from deep flaws in its very foundations. The Obama administration's tactical efforts for U.N. reform — while paying our U.N. dues in full without conditions — has failed to solve the organization's systemic problems. We need sweeping reforms. My bill, the United Nations Transparency, Accountability and Reform Act, conditions our U.N. contributions on shifting funding from an assessed to a voluntary basis.

At the U.N. we pay too much and get too little in return, because those who call the shots don't pay the bills. The U.N.'s regular budget is funded through assessments based on a complicated formula that factors in "gross national income." The United States pays for 22 percent of the U.N.'s regular budget but only has one vote, while two-thirds of the other member countries combined pay for only 1 percent. Those countries vote together to pass budgets and set priorities, but the cost is passed on to the United States. As long as we continue paying our dues in full with no strings attached, we surrender our strongest leverage to stop wrongdoing, advance our interests and support our allies.

Voluntary funding will enable the American people to determine, through their representatives in Congress, how much of their hard-earned money goes to the United Nations and how it is spent. Voluntary funding already works well at several U.N. bodies, including UNICEF and the World Food Programme (WFP). Catherine Bertini, a former WFP director, has said: "Voluntary funding creates an entirely different atmosphere at WFP than at the U.N. At WFP, every staff member knows that we have to be as efficient, accountable, transparent and results-oriented as possible [or] donor governments can take their funding elsewhere."

With no consequences for abuse, the U.N. has taken our funding for granted. In the past decade, its budget has more than doubled. The Human Rights Council is dominated by rogue regimes like Cuba, China, Russia and Saudi Arabia and spends its time bashing Israel instead of addressing real human rights abuses. The Conference on Disarmament was chaired in 2011 by North Korea; Iran serves on the Commission on the Status of Women; and the Syrian regime serves on the executive board and human rights committee for the U.N. Educational, Scientific and Cultural Organization (UNESCO).

Voluntary funding creates the incentive structure necessary to reform the U.N. and make it transparent, accountable, objective and effective.

NO
Rep. Howard Berman, D-Calif.
Ranking Democrat, House Foreign Affairs Committee

Written for *CQ Global Researcher,* March 2012

Despite its many flaws, failures and shortcomings, the United Nations often plays an essential role in supporting American foreign policy and national security interests. U.N. peacekeepers separate warring parties and create conditions for reconciliation at a fraction of the cost of deploying the U.S. military. U.N. Security Council resolutions have provided the legal basis for assembling an international coalition of countries determined to prevent Iran from developing nuclear weapons. All of these important U.N. activities are funded by assessed dues.

In the name of U.N. "reform," some have argued that our government should move to a system of voluntary contributions, in which we would selectively pay for U.N. programs that we deem vital to our national interests. Such headline-grabbing proposals are totally unrealistic and run counter to the principles that governed the U.N.'s establishment. Transitioning to a system of voluntary financial support, as opposed to paying our assessed dues, would require a U.N. Charter revision and renegotiation of the treaty establishing the organization.

The U.N. Charter has been amended only four times in its 66-year history, most recently in 1973 when the body approved an enlargement of the Economic and Social Council to better reflect the growth in U.N. member states. For one member state to force through an amendment unraveling the financial stability of the organization would be greeted with near unanimous opposition. And aside from the political infeasibility, if the United States were to unilaterally abandon its treaty obligations over payment of assessments, it would undercut the financial underpinnings of the entire U.N. regular budget.

Other nations would respond in kind by adopting their own selective approach to financing the organization. U.N. programs vital to U.S. national security interests undoubtedly would face funding reductions. For example, the U.N. special political missions in Iraq and Afghanistan — which are funded through the U.N. regular budget, largely at the insistence of the United States — would almost certainly see severely diminished financial support from other U.N. member states and thus reduced legitimacy. Other U.S. priorities at the United Nations, such as the advancement of women's rights, the protection of human rights and counterterrorism cooperation would likely face reduced funding under a voluntary funding scheme.

A course of picking and choosing what one likes and doesn't like is best left for a food buffet, not for selectively funding U.N. programs and maintaining our standing within the international community.

doctrine, he said. "The results were uneven but, at the end of the day, tens of thousands of lives were saved."

However, he continued, the world already faces "the next test of our common humanity" — in Syria. And, so far, the world is failing.

"Stop the violence, I told President Assad," Ban said. "The path of repression is a dead-end. . . . Change now, act bold and make decisive reforms before it is too late, before more innocents die."[40]

Yet Assad refuses, and his forces have killed more than 8,000 dissidents and civilians since March 2011. The atrocities now have risen to the level of war crimes, according to Navi Pillay, the U.N.'s High Commissioner for Human Rights. But, unlike in last year's Libyan crisis, Russia and China have blocked U.N. action in Syria.[41] Even as Syrian forces were firing on civilians in the city of Homs on Feb. 4, the two permanent Security Council members vetoed a resolution to support an Arab League plan that called for Assad to leave office. The other 13 council members voted yes. Russia and China also had vetoed an October resolution that condemned Assad's crackdown. And Syrian officials cannot be brought before the International Criminal Court in the Hague without the Security Council's approval.[42]

Earlier, the six Gulf Cooperation Council states — Bahrain, Kuwait, Oman, Qatar, Saudi Arabia and United Arab Emirates — called on the U.N. to take "all needed measures" to stop the violence in Syria.[43]

The vetoes created "a sad day for this council, a sad day for Syrians and a sad day for all friends of democracy," French U.N. Ambassador Gerard Araud said after the vote. Russia and China "made themselves complicit in a policy of repression carried out by the Assad regime."[44]

Unlike when addressing the Libya problem, the Security Council "failed to live up to its responsibility," Germany's Wittig lamented. "The people in Syria have been let down again."[45]

The stalemate exposed the U.N.'s "chief failing," Ban said, which is "the reluctance to act in the face of serious threats. The result, too often, has been a loss of lives and credibility that haunt us ever after."[46]

It's also put the "responsibility to protect" doctrine "in major crisis," said Stewart Patrick, director of international institutions and global governance at the Council on Foreign Relations.[47]

And although Syria may pose the U.N.'s most urgent crisis, the organization's agenda is crowded with other challenges as well. U.N. investigators are probing Iran's nuclear program and its human rights record. The Palestinian Authority is pressing for admission as a sovereign state. Some members of the U.S. Congress are pushing to make U.N. payments voluntary. Several countries are conducting systematic assessments of U.N. effectiveness. And, all the while, the U.N. carries out its ongoing peacekeeping, development and relief efforts.

Policing Iran

Early this year, a team from the International Atomic Energy Agency (IAEA) traveled to Tehran to probe Iran's suspected nuclear weapons program.[48] In late February, the team said it could not complete its investigation because Iran had blocked access to important records and sites.[49] An IAEA report last November had triggered international alarm bells after agency officials released satellite images, letters and other documents they said showed Iran has carried out activities "relevant to the development of a nuclear explosive device."[50]

While Iran contends it is working only on a peaceful energy program, some of its activities are specific to weapons development, the IAEA said. These include high-explosives testing, development of a detonator to trigger a nuclear charge, computer modeling of a nuclear warhead core, preparatory work for a nuclear weapons test and development of a nuclear payload for Iran's *Shahab 3* intermediate range missile, which can reach Israel.[51]

The Security Council, with the support of Russia and China, has authorized sanctions on Iran, although neither country has imposed sanctions themselves.[52] The United States and Europe have ratcheted up sanctions on Iran's oil output and banking, however.[53]

Iran's supreme leader, Ayatollah Ali Khamenei, has acknowledged that the sanctions are "painful and crippling." But Iran has not agreed to scrap its nuclear program. Instead, Khamenei and President Mahmoud Ahmadinejad have threatened military reprisals and a blockade of the Strait of Hormuz, a major oil-shipping route. World leaders also worry that Israel might launch a military strike against Iran's nuclear facilities, at least one of which is in the process of being buried deep inside a mountain — out of the reach of Israeli missiles.[54]

Unlike the nuclear inspectors, the U.N.'s new special rapporteur on human rights in Iran, Ahmed Shaheed, has not been granted entry into Iran. But, from outside the country, he said, "I am able to gather a substantial amount of information which points to widespread abuse of human rights."[55]

A report by Shaheed last October described horrific repression. The General Assembly in November denounced Iran for, among other things, torture, cruel and degrading treatment of prisoners, pervasive violence against women, restrictions on freedom of assembly and "severe limitations and restrictions on the right to freedom of thought, conscience, religion or belief."[56]

In his own report last March, Ban said he was "deeply troubled" by reports of "increased executions, amputations, arbitrary arrest and detention, unfair trials and possible torture," as well as mistreatment of lawyers, journalists and human rights and opposition activists.[57] The judiciary also continues to sentence men and women to execution by stoning, he said.

New Controversies

Controversy has erupted inside the U.N. over the Palestinian Authority's campaign for membership. The authority's admission to the U.N. Educational, Scientific and Cultural Organization last year triggered an automatic cutoff of U.S. funding under U.S. law and gave impetus to a congressional campaign to make all U.N. payments voluntary.

U.S. House Foreign Affairs Committee Chair Ros-Lehtinen, who has introduced voluntary-payments legislation, argues that "U.N. bodies funded on a voluntary basis — such as UNICEF, the World Food Programme and the U.N. High Commissioner for Refugees — function better and are more deserving of funding because they recognize that, if they fall short, donor countries can and will stop giving them money."

The Heritage Foundation's Schaefer agrees that voluntarily funded programs tend to be "extremely useful activities" that are "more responsive to the member states" and their concerns. However, he adds, organizational expenses — such as maintaining headquarters, facilitating meetings and providing translations — are essentials that should be financed by all members.

Yeo of the Better World Campaign warns that Americans might be unpleasantly surprised by the impact of voluntary funding. Mandated dues "support U.N. missions that nobody else would fund," he says. "Which countries are going to line up for the U.N. to work in Iraq and Afghanistan?"

Duncan, Britain's minister for international development, says every country should contribute toward costs, just as taxpayers help pay for a country's defense and justice departments. But, the money must be spent "in a transparent manner and highly focused on results."

Britain, Australia and Norway are among nations that tie their voluntary contributions to the results of systematic evaluations of U.N. agencies. After their first round of reviews last year, for instance, Australian evaluators recommended maintaining or reducing funding of some agencies while doubling contributions to UNICEF and substantially increasing support for the World Food Programme and the U.N. High Commissioner for Refugees.[58]

Other evaluations are being conducted by the 16-country Multilateral Organization Performance Assessment Network and the evaluation network of the Paris-based Organisation for Economic Co-operation and Development.

While those evaluations proceed, 16 U.N. peacekeeping operations continue on four continents, and humanitarian and development missions are being conducted by such U.N. agencies as UNICEF, the High Commissioner for Refugees, the U.N. Development Programme and the World Food Programme.[59]

OUTLOOK
Thwarting Violence

Secretary-General Ban has declared 2012 "the Year of Prevention." Instead of trying to end conflicts or atrocities after they begin, he wants the United Nations to mark his second term, which began in January, by thwarting violence before it happens in the first place.

That requires "strengthening our capacities for mediation, fact-finding and peaceful settlement," he said, as well as building strong civil societies around the world. "Genocide, war crimes, ethnic cleansing and other crimes against humanity . . . occur far less often in places where civil society is robust, where tolerance is practiced, and where diversity is celebrated."[60]

Ban promised that the U.N. would increase its efforts to promote human rights and democratic values and practices and asked the Security Council to take better advantage of its power to investigate potential threats before they become crises.

Several public opinion polls indicate there is global support for strengthening the U.N. and expanding its authority. A poll in predominantly Muslim regions, for example, found that nearly two-thirds of respondents supported making the U.N. "significantly more powerful in world affairs," and majorities backed using U.N. military force to stop a country from supporting terrorist groups, prevent nuclear proliferation and restore a democratic government that had been overthrown.[61]

Another survey, in countries that contain 56 percent of the world's population, found majority support for empowering the U.N. to regulate international arms trade.[62] And, in a poll of 23,518 people in 23 countries, majorities in all but two countries supported increasing the U.N.'s power.[63]

Dam, the Human Rights Watch advocate, wants the U.N. to require members to cooperate with efforts to promote human rights and to single out those that don't. States must be made to "pay a political cost for their lack of cooperation," Dam says.

Rick Leach, president and CEO of World Food Program USA, predicts that his and other U.N. agencies will engage more with the private sector. For instance, "UPS is helping us look at logistics operations," Leach says, referring to the United Parcel Service. And the World Food Programme is purchasing more food from subsistence farmers and teaching farmers to become more productive, using funds and business expertise from the Bill and Melinda Gates and Howard Buffett foundations. The goal is to turn aid recipients into farmers who can support their families by selling their products in the private marketplace.

Others want to see the U.N. develop better management practices. Former Ambassador Hall says U.N. agencies need to hire external organizations to evaluate their operations, just as external auditors examine corporate books. "Institutions that do that and then follow through on the (recommendations) are your best."

Schaefer, of the Heritage Foundation, wants the U.N. to finish a systematic evaluation of all its programs, a process that began in 2005. And the Better World Campaign's Yeo wants U.N. executives to "more aggressively adopt best practices for the management of large institutions."

However, Rana, the former U.N. executive, urges caution in applying corporate theory to the global public institution. "Reforms based on the corporate world do not necessarily apply well to the U.N. Secretariat," she says.

NOTES

1. "Red Cross urges daily 2-hour halt in Syria clashes," The Associated Press, *USA Today*, Feb. 21, 2012, www.usatoday.com/news/world/story/2012-02-21/syria-clashes/53186210/1?csp=34news.

2. Ban Ki-moon, "Address to the Stanley Foundation Conference on the Responsibility to Protect," Jan. 18, 2012, www.un.org/apps/news/infocus/sgspeeches/statments_full.asp?statID=1433.

3. "Preamble to the United Nations Charter," United Nations, www.un.org/en/documents/charter/preamble.shtml.

4. Kim R. Holmes, "Smart Multilateralism," in Brett D. Schaefer, ed., *ConUNdrum: The Limits of the United Nations and the Search for Alternatives* (2009), p. 25.

5. Oliver Holmes and Erika Solomon, "*Violence across Syria; soldiers killed in ambushes,*" Reuters, March 13, 2012, www.reuters.com/article/2012/03/13/us-syria-idUSBRE8280G820120313.

6. "Preamble to the United Nations Charter," *op. cit.*

7. "Former Rep. Newt Gingrich, R-Ga., Presidential Candidate, Holds a Town Hall Meeting In Meredith, NH," Political Transcript Wire, Jan. 6, 2012.

8. Newt Gingrich and George Mitchell, "Foreword," in "American Interests and U.N. Reform," Task Force on the United Nations, United States Institute of Peace, www.usip.org/files/file/usip_un_report.pdf, June 2005.

9. Kofi Annan, "Despite flaws, U.N. Human Rights Council can bring progress," *The Christian Science Monitor*, Dec. 8, 2011.

10. Brian Montopoli, "Rick Perry: Time to consider defunding United Nations," CBS News, Oct. 18, 2011, www.cbsnews.com/8301-503544_162-20122309-503544.html.

11. "Financing Peacekeeping," United Nations, www.un.org/en/peacekeeping/operations/financing.shtml.

12. "About Us," New York City Department of Education, http://schools.nyc.gov/AboutUs/default.htm; "Is the United Nations Good Value for the Money?" United Nations, www.un.org/geninfo/ir/index.asp?id=150.

13. "Wall Street Bonuses," *The Economist*, Feb. 24, 2011, www.economist.com/node/18231330; "Is the United Nations Good Value for the Money?" *op. cit.*

14. "Assessment of Member States' contributions to the United Nations regular budget for 2012," U.N. Secretariat, December 2011, www.un.org/ga/search/view_doc.asp?symbol=ST/ADM/SER.B/853.

15. For background, see Jason McLure, "Sub-Saharan Democracy," *CQ Global Researcher*, Feb. 15, 2011, pp. 79-106.

16. "The Multilateral Aid Review," UK International Development Department, March 2011, www.dfid.gov.uk/What-we-do/How-UK-aid-is-spent/a-new-direction-for-uk-aid/Multilateral-Aid-Review. For background, see Jina Moore, "Peacebuilding," *CQ Global Researcher*, June 21, 2011, pp. 291-314.

17. "Freedom in the World 2012," Freedom House, http://freedomhouse.org/sites/default/files/inline_images/Table%20of%20Independent%20Countries%2C%20FIW%202012%20draft.pdf.

18. "Assessment of Member States' contributions to the United Nations regular budget for 2012," *op. cit.*; "Background Note: Saint Lucia," U.S. State Department, Dec. 16, 2011, www.state.gov/r/pa/ei/bgn/2344.htm; "U.S. POPClock Projection," U.S. Census Bureau, January 2012, www.census.gov/population/www/popclockus.html; Holmes, *op. cit.*

19. Anne Bayefsky, "Palestinian 'Head of State' at the U.N.," FoxNews.com, Aug. 3, 2011, www.foxnews.com/opinion/2011/08/03/palestinian-head-state-at-un-get-ready-for-statehood-steamroller.

20. "US unfazed by NK's presidency of U.N. disarmament body," *Korea Times*, July 12, 2011, www.koreatimes.co.kr/www/news/nation/2012/02/113_90697.html.

21. *Ibid.*

22. Adam Chapnick, "The U.N. May Be Dysfunctional, But It's the Kind of Dysfunction That Its Founders Intended," George Mason University, History News Network, July 5, 2011, http://historynewsservice.org/2011/07/the-u-n-may-be-dysfunctional-but-its-the-kind-of-dysfunction-that-its-founders-intended.

23. "People in Muslim Nations Conflicted About UN," University of Maryland Program on International Policy Attitudes, Dec. 2, 2008 (Polling conducted from late 2006 to September 2008), www.worldpublicopinion.org/pipa/articles/btunitednationsra/575.php?lb=&pnt=575&nid=&id=.

24. "The Review of the Libyan Arab Jamahiriya," U.N. Human Rights Council Working Group on the Universal Periodic Review, Jan. 4, 2011, www2.ohchr.org/english/bodies/hrcouncil/docs/16session/A-HRC-16-15.pdf.

25. "Report of the Working Group on the Universal Periodic Review, United States of America," U.N. Human Rights Council, Jan. 4, 2011, www2.ohchr.org/english/bodies/hrcouncil/docs/16session/A-HRC-16-11.pdf.

26. Brett Schaefer, "Treatment of Libya Illustrates the Fatuousness of the Human Rights Council," Heritage Foundation, March 1, 2011, http://blog.heritage.org/2011/03/01/treatment-of-libya-illustrates-the-fatuousness-of-the-human-rights-council.

27. Hillel Neuer, "The State of Human Rights at the U.N.," Testimony before the U.S. House Foreign Affairs Committee, U.N. Watch, Jan. 25, 2011, www.unwatch.org/site/apps/nlnet/content2.aspx?c=bdKKISNqEmG&b=1316871&ct=9085407.

28. "Membership of the Human Rights Council 20 June 2011-31 December 2012," U.N. Human Rights Council, www2.ohchr.org/english/bodies/hrcouncil/membership.htm; "Freedom in the World 2012," Freedom House, http://freedomhouse.org/sites/default/files/inline_images/Table%20of%20Independent%20Countries%2C%20FIW%202012%20draft.pdf.

29. Brett Schaefer, "The U.S. Should Pursue an Alternative to the U.N. Human Rights Council," Heritage Foundation, June 23, 2011, www.heritage.org/research/reports/2011/06/the-us-should-pursue-an-alternative-to-the-un-human-rights-council.

30. Ted Piccone, "Why the U.S. Must Stay on The U.N. Human Rights Council," Brookings Institution, April 01, 2011, www.brookings.edu/opinions/2011/0401_human_rights_piccone.aspx; "Stop

human rights violations in Syria," U.N. Human Rights Council, May 5, 2011, www.ohchr.org/EN/NewsEvents/Pages/HRCStophumanrights violationsinSyria.aspx.

31. For background, see Reed Karaim, "Gay Rights," *CQ Global Researcher*, March 1, 2011, pp. 107-132.

32. Annan, *op. cit.*

33. Unless otherwise noted, information for this historical chapter was drawn from: Stanley Meisler, *United Nations: A History* (2011); Schaefer, *op. cit.*; *Time-Life Books History of the Second World War* (1989); David Masci, "The United Nations and Global Security," *CQ Researcher*, Feb. 27, 2004; Lee Michael Katz, "World Peacekeeping," *CQ Global Researcher*, April 1, 2007; "Internet Modern History Sourcebook," Fordham University, www.fordham.edu/halsall/mod/modsbook.asp; "United Nations Peacekeeping," United Nations, www.un.org/en/peacekeeping; "History of the United Nations," United Nations, www.un.org/en/aboutun/history/1951-1960.shtml.

34. Meisler, *op. cit.*, p. 19.

35. "Timeline of the Arab-Israeli Conflict and Peace Process," Institute for Curriculum Services, www.icsresources.org/content/factsheets/ArabIsraeliTimeline.pdf.

36. Meisler, *op. cit.*, p. 184.

37. "Millennium Development Goals," United Nations, www.un.org/millenniumgoals.

38. "Fact Sheet: 2005 World Summit High-Level Plenary Meeting," United Nations, Sept. 14-16, 2005, www.un.org/summit2005/presskit/fact_sheet.pdf.

39. "Germany, Russia learn high cost of abstaining," *The Australian*, March 25, 2011, p. 10.

40. Ban Ki-moon, *op. cit.*

41. "Wounded British journalist smuggled safely out of beseiged city of Homs," *op. cit.*; John Size, "Russia, China veto UN draft resolution on Syria," CTVNews.ca, http://ottawa.ctv.ca/servlet/an/plocal/CTVNews/20120204/un-security-council-syria-resolution-voting-day-120204/20120204/?hub=OttawaHome.

42. Richard Spencer and Adrian Blomfield, "UN inquiry says Assad should be charged over war crimes," *The* (London) *Daily Telegraph*, Feb. 24, 2012, p. 20, www.canada.com/news/inquiry+says+Assad+should+charged+over+crimes/6196914/story.html.

43. Liz Sly, "Arab states seek U.N. help as Syria steps up violence," *The Washington Post*, Jan. 24, 2012, www.washingtonpost.com/world/middle_east/arab-states-seek-un-help-as-syria-violence-escalates/2012/01/24/gIQAL1f8NQ_story.html?hpid=z5. For background, see Jennifer Koons, "Future of the Gulf States," *CQ Global Researcher*, Nov. 1, 2011, pp. 525-548.

44. Size, *op. cit.*

45. *Ibid.*

46. Ban Ki-moon, *op. cit.*

47. "R2P in Crisis Following U.N. Syria Vote," Council on Foreign Relations, www.cfr.org/syria/r2p-crisis-following-un-syria-vote/p27303.

48. Ali Akbar Dareini, "UN nuclear team arrives in Iran," The Associated Press, Jan. 28, 2012, www.tribtoday.com/page/content.detail/id/567202.html.

49. Joby Warrick and Thomas Erdbrink, "IAEA mission to Iran ends in failure," *The Washington Post*, Feb. 22, 2012, www.washingtonpost.com/world/national-security/iaea-mission-to-iran-ends-in-failure/2012/02/21/gIQANEcLSR_story.html.

50. For background, see Roland Flamini, "Rising Tension Over Iran," *CQ Global Researcher*, Feb. 7, 2012, pp. 57-80.

51. "Revealed: Proof of Iran's N-bomb plan," *The* (Singapore) *Straits Times*, Nov. 13, 2011.

52. "U.N. Security Council Passes Iran Sanctions," Jewish Telegraphic Agency, June 9, 2010, www.thejewishweek.com/news/breaking_news/un_security_council_passes_iran_sanctions.

53. Mark Landler and Clifford Krauss, "Gulf Nations Aid U.S. Push To Choke Off Iran Oil Sales," *The New York Times*, Jan. 13, 2012, p. 4, www.nytimes.com/2012/01/13/world/asia/asia-buyers-of-iran-crude-get-assurances-of-alternate-supply.html?pagewanted=all.

54. Robert F. Worth and David E. Sanger, "U.N. Nuclear Inspectors' Visit to Iran Is a Failure, West Says," *The New York Times*, Feb. 4, 2012, p. 4. Also see Simon Mann Washington, "New Iranian missile 'could strike US,' " *The* (Melbourne) *Age*, Feb. 4, 2012, p. 9.

55. "UN envoy slams Iran for human rights violations," ABC Radio (Australia), Oct. 21, 2011, www.abc.net.au/pm/content/2011/s3345574.htm.

56. "General Assembly Condemns Iranian Regime's Abuses," Voice of America, Dec. 26, 2011, www.voanews.com/policy/editorials/middle-east/General-Assembly--136166128.html.

57. "A Special Rapporteur Needed for Iran," Voice of America, March 16, 2011, www.voanews.com/policy/editorials/A-Special-Rapporteur-Needed-For-Iran-118173714.html.

58. "Independent Review of Aid Effectiveness," Australian Government, April 2011, www.aidreview.gov.au/publications/aidreview.pdf.

59. "Current peacekeeping operations," United Nations, www.un.org/en/peacekeeping/operations/current.shtml.

60. Ban, *op. cit.*

61. "People in Muslim Nations Conflicted About UN," *op. cit.*

62. The countries surveyed were China, India, the United States, Russia, France, Thailand, Ukraine, Poland, Iran, Mexico, South Korea, the Philippines, Australia, Argentina, Peru, Armenia, Israel and the Palestinian territories.

63. "Nation Poll Finds Strong Support for Dramatic Changes at U.N.," BBC, March 21, 2005 (Polling conducted Nov. 15, 2004 to Jan. 3, 2005 by GlobeScan and University of Maryland Program on International Policy Attitudes), www.worldpublicopinion.org/pipa/articles/btunitednationsra/72.php?lb=&pnt=72&nid=&id=.

BIBLIOGRAPHY

Selected Sources

Books

Boutros-Ghali, Boutros, *Unvanquished: A US-UN Saga*, Random House, 1999.
In counterpoint to U.S. complaints about the United Nations, a former secretary-general blames American attempts to dominate the organization for damaging the U.N. during his term.

Gold, Dore, *Tower of Babble: How the United Nations Has Fueled Global Chaos*, Three Rivers Press, 2005.
A former Israeli ambassador to the U.N. chronicles the many ways he feels the institution has failed since shortly after its inception and says it cannot work in its current incarnation. He proposes that democracies take a two-track approach to repelling immediate threats: working both outside and inside the U.N. to fix its "crippling flaws" over the long term.

Meisler, Stanley, *United Nations: A History*, Grove Press, 2011.
A longtime *Los Angeles Times* foreign correspondent, whose assignments included the U.N., traces the organization's history from the first four-power planning conference in 1944 to U.N.-authorized attacks on Libyan dictator Moammar Gadhafi after the 2011 Arab Spring uprisings.

Schaefer, Brett D., ed., *ConUNdrum: The Limits of the United Nations and the Search for Alternatives*, Rowman & Littlefield Publishers, 2009.
An international affairs fellow at the conservative Heritage Foundation in Washington has compiled essays about the U.N. from 16 conservative scholars. Topics addressed include multilateralism, international law, international interventions, environmental policy, human rights, economic development, trade, arms control and health.

Articles

Anstee, Margaret Joan, "What Price Security?" *Global Governance*, Jan. 1, 2011, p. 1.
The U.N's first female undersecretary applies her unique perspective to argue that security requires human development as well as military power. The U.K. native first became a U.N. field worker in the Philippines in 1952 and served in postings throughout the world.

Hancock, Herbie, "Without the U.S., a diminished UNESCO," *The Washington Post*, Dec. 3, 2011, www.washingtonpost.com/todays_paper/A%20Section/2011-12-04/A/29/32.1.3339981937_epaper.html.
A famed American jazz musician contends that culture plays a critical role in fostering international understanding

and that UNESCO plays a critical role in exposing the world's occupants to each other's culture.

Kabendera, Erick, "Anna Tibaijuka: 'Not easy for African women in the UN system,' " *New African*, August-September 2011, p. 68.
In an interview, Tanzanian Anna Tibaijuka, who became U.N. deputy secretary-general, describes the obstacles African women say they face when they try to advance through the U.N. bureaucracy.

Lynch, Colum, "Mideast conflict has shaped U.N.'s history, mission," *The Washington Post*, Sept. 18, 2011, p. 7.
Arab-Israeli conflicts have demanded U.N. attention and created controversy since shortly after the organization's birth.

Reports and Studies

"Keeping the Momentum: One Year in the Life of the UN Human Rights Council," Human Rights Watch, Sept. 22, 2011, www.hrw.org/sites/default/files/reports/hrc0911ForWeb.pdf.
The global human rights advocacy group finds "some notable progress" in the operations of the U.N.'s highest-ranking — and highly controversial — human rights body.

"Multilateral Aid Review: Ensuring maximum value for money for UK aid through multilateral organizations,"
U.K. Department for International Development, March 2011, www.dfid.gov.uk/Documents/publications1/mar/multilateral_aid_review.pdf.
A British government evaluation of 43 multilateral organizations, including prominent U.N. humanitarian and development agencies, concludes that nine offer very good value for the money spent by U.K. taxpayers, 16 offer good value, nine adequate value and nine poor value.

"People in Muslim Nations Conflicted About UN," University of Maryland Program on International Policy Attitudes, Dec. 2, 2008, www.worldpublicopinion.org/pipa/articles/btunitednationsra/575.php?lb=&pnt=575&nid=&id=.
Polling in Egypt, Turkey, Jordan, Iran, Indonesia, the Palestinian Territories, Azerbaijan and Nigeria finds support for a strengthened United Nations and a belief that the United States dominates the organization.

Blanchfield, Luisa, "United Nations Reform: U.S. Policy and International Perspectives," U.S. Congressional Research Service, Dec. 21, 2011, www.fas.org/sgp/crs/row/RL33848.pdf.
Congress' nonpartisan research arm examines various attempts at reforming the United Nations over the years, congressional actions aimed at U.N. reform and potential U.S. policy considerations for dealing with the organization.

For More Information

Better World Campaign, 1800 Massachusetts Ave., N.W., 4th Floor, Washington, DC 20036; 202-462-4900; www .betterworldcampaign.org. Founded in 1999 with funding from Ted Turner's $1-billion contribution to benefit the United Nations; advocates for increased U.S. support for the U.N.

Human Rights Watch, 350 Fifth Ave., 34th Floor, New York, NY 10118; 212-290-4700; www.hrw.org. Keeps tabs on U.N. activities and publishes more than 100 reports annually on human rights conditions around the world.

Multilateral Organization Performance Assessment Network, www.mopanonline.org. A 16-nation consortium founded in 2002 to evaluate multilateral organizations, including U.N. agencies. Organization's management is rotated among members and currently is housed in the German Federal Ministry for Economic Cooperation and Development.

United Kingdom Department for International Development, 1 Palace St., London SW1E 5HE; +44 1355 84 3132; www.dfid.gov.uk. Runs Great Britain's foreign aid program. Publishes many reports on development and evaluates multilateral aid organizations, including U.N. agencies.

United Nations, First Avenue and 46th St., New York, NY; www.un.org. Website is portal to all U.N. activities. List of UN information centers in various countries is at unic. un.org/aroundworld/unics/en/whereWeWork/index.asp.

U.N. Watch, Case Postale 191, 1211 Geneva 20, Switzerland; +41 22 734-1472; www.unwatch.org. A nonprofit advocacy organization (and an affiliate of the American Jewish Committee); keeps a critical eye on U.N. activities.

Voices From Abroad:

KANAT SAUDABAYEV

Minister of Foreign Affairs, Kazakhstan

A storied contribution

"Over the past 65 years, the United Nations has made an enormous contribution to peace and security on our planet and to the solution of many social, economic, humanitarian and other problems. It is in our common interests that the United Nations continues to demonstrate leadership in promoting peace and cooperation and sustainable progress on Earth."

Speech before 65th session of U.N. General Assembly, September 2010

SYED YUSUF RAZA GILANI

Prime Minister, Pakistan

Using its power

"The U.N. must use its offices to achieve a fresh consensus on broad contours of this anti-terror policy. The U.N. must also spell out a strategy to address the rightful grievances of people."

Associated Press of Pakistan, July 2011

BAN KI-MOON

Secretary-General, United Nations

Peacekeeping must evolve

"We may be entering a new phase, with diverse and multifaceted situations where peacekeeping may play a role. Peacekeeping will need to evolve to meet specific demands in a variety of environments and to flexibly and nimbly bring together multiple capabilities in a coherent and effective manner."

India Blooms News Service, August 2011

UN   UN IN WESTERN EYES

Cagle Cartoons/Mike Keefe

ED LUCK

Special Adviser, United Nations

Strong principles

"Today, the principle of human protection and responsibility to protect are so strong that even governments traditionally worried about sovereignty did not want to stand in the way of forceful council action."

The Nation (Thailand), March 2011

SIMON ADAMS

Former pro-vice chancellor Monash University, Australia

The U.N.'s failures

"From the killing fields of Cambodia to East Timor, Rwanda, Bosnia and Kosovo, mass-atrocity crimes were generally met with international diplomatic passivity. The United Nations proved incompetent or impotent in the face of monstrous human rights challenges."

Canberra (Australia) Times, April 2011

HANY BESADA

Senior Researcher, North-South Institute, Canada

Response necessary

"The [Libyan] violence has created a massive humanitarian crisis, displacing hundreds of thousands of foreign workers and Libyans alike. Failure to develop an effective response to halt these events would render the R2P [Responsibility to Protect] doctrine ineffective and undermine the credibility of the United Nations."

Korea Times (South Korea), May 2011

INGA-BRITT AHLENIUS

Under-Secretary-General Internal Oversight Services United Nations

Lacking accountability

"There is no transparency; there is a lack of accountability. Rather than supporting the internal oversight, which is the sign of strong leadership and good governance, you have strived to control it, which is to undermine its position. I do not see any signs of reform in the [U.N.] organization."

Financial Post (Canada), August 2010

BABACAR GAYE

Military adviser, U.N. Mission in Sudan

Protect the Sudanese

"We could have and should have had more visibility to deter any violence against [Sudanese] civilians."

The Guardian (England),
June 2011

VLADIMIR PUTIN

Prime Minister, Russia

Learn from the past

"I very much hope that the USA and other countries will take dismal experience into account and not try to use the force scenario in Syria. . . . Having learnt from bitter experience, we oppose the adoption of UN Security Council resolutions that could be interpreted as a signal to military intervention in internal Syrian processes. . . . Russia together with China prevented in early February the adoption of [such a] resolution."

Moskovskiye Novosti, February 2012

2

Islamic Sectarianism

Leda Hartman

Waving photos of dead relatives and friends, Pakistani Shiites in Quetta protest the rise in sectarian violence in the majority-Sunni country. Sunni extremists, who view Shiites as heretics, have carried out scores of bombings and shootings against minority Shiites in recent years.

On July 18, in Damascus, the unthinkable happened: A bomb exploded at a meeting of the Syrian regime's innermost circle, killing four top officials in charge of putting down the country's 16-month-long rebellion.

But the nation's leader, President Bashar Assad, reportedly was not there. According to opposition forces and an American diplomat, Assad had retreated to the coastal town of Latakia, the stronghold of his own Alawite people.[1] In recent months as the insurgency has escalated, thousands of civilians have been killed by loyalist troops, and the fragile mosaic of Syrian society appears to have been shattered.

The rebels — mostly from the nation's majority Sunni Muslims — are rising up against nearly 100 years of rule by the minority Shiite Alawites, who have been aligned with Syria's Christians and Druze.* (See box, p. 32.)

"When countries are well-managed and citizens feel they have a say in political and economic developments, sectarian identities and tensions decrease and eventually disappear," wrote Rami Khouri, a columnist for the *Beirut Star*, Lebanon's English-language daily. "But when authoritarian gangs and oligarchic ruling families plunder their countries and treat their citizens like idiots without rights or feelings, sectarianism sprouts like the natural self-defense mechanism that it is."[2]

The dynamic that Khouri described is in full force in Syria and plays a role in other Muslim countries with sizable populations

From *The CQ Researcher*, August 7, 2012.

*Shiites are often called Shia.

Sunnis Rule Most of Muslim World

The overwhelming majority of the world's 1.6 billion Muslims — 85 percent — are Sunnis. Shiites predominate in only three Middle Eastern countries — Iran, Iraq and Bahrain. Except for Iran, Sunnis have traditionally ruled over Shiites, even in places where Shiites held the majority. Currently, Syria is the only country in which Shiites rule over a Sunni majority. Experts fear that an upsurge in sectarian strife in Syria could trigger a proxy war that could spread throughout the region and eventually draw in Western nations.

Muslim Sectarian Hot Spots

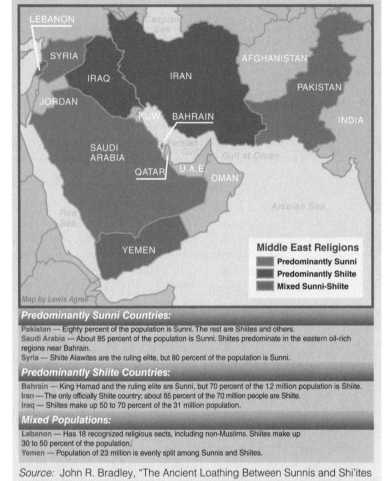

Predominantly Sunni Countries:

Pakistan — Eighty percent of the population is Sunni. The rest are Shiites and others.
Saudi Arabia — About 85 percent of the population is Sunni. Shiites predominate in the eastern oil-rich regions near Bahrain.
Syria — Shiite Alawites are the ruling elite, but 80 percent of the population is Sunni.

Predominantly Shiite Countries:

Bahrain — King Hamad and the ruling elite are Sunni, but 70 percent of the 1.2 million population is Shiite.
Iran — The only officially Shiite country; about 85 percent of the 70 million people are Shiite.
Iraq — Shiites make up 50 to 70 percent of the 31 million population.

Mixed Populations:

Lebanon — Has 18 recognized religious sects, including non-Muslims. Shiites make up 30 to 50 percent of the population.
Yemen — Population of 23 million is evenly split among Sunnis and Shiites.

Source: John R. Bradley, "The Ancient Loathing Between Sunnis and Shi'ites Is Threatening to Tear Apart the Muslim World," Daily Mail, March 2011, www.dailymail.co.uk/debate/article-1367435/ Middle-East-unrest-Sunni-Shiite-conflict-threatens-tear-Muslim-world-apart.html

"In many ways, sectarianism is the new politics of the Muslim world," observes Toby Jones, an associate professor of Middle East history at Rutgers University.

About 85 percent of the world's 1.6 billion Muslims — or 1.3 billion — are Sunnis, and the rest are Shiites. Four countries — Iran, Iraq, Bahrain and Azerbaijan — have Shiite majorities, but they are in power only in Iran and Iraq. Traditionally (except in Iran), Sunnis have ruled over Shiites, even when the Sunnis were in the minority. Syria is the only country in which a Shiite minority rules over Sunnis.

Sectarian conflict is not unique to Islam, of course. Experts cite bloody periods in Christian history such as the Reformation and the long conflict between Protestants and Catholics in Northern Ireland. In fact, Sunnis and Shiites have co-existed for centuries throughout the Muslim world.

But in the political vacuums that developed after the Iraq War and the Arab Spring, sectarian divisions have intensified, as previously disenfranchised groups from Islam's two branches have struggled for power.[3] "The problem is not in co-existing, but in who has the upper hand in terms of government control and oil money, things like that," explains Columbia University history professor Richard Bulliet.

Experts fear those struggles could spill over into neighboring countries, triggering a proxy war that could spread throughout the region and eventually draw in Western nations. The growing Sunni-Shiite conflict is damaging Islam's reputation as a religion of peace, according to nearly two-thirds of the Arabs surveyed in 2008 by Doha Debates, a Qatar-based free-speech forum. At least 77 percent of respondents blamed the United States for instigating

of both Sunnis and Shiites: Iraq, Lebanon, Bahrain, Pakistan and Yemen. (*See map.*)

sectarian tensions by invading Iraq and toppling the Sunni-led government of Saddam Hussein.[4] (*See graph.*)

Most mainstream Muslims want less division between the branches. "Moderate Muslims in Islam think that anybody who says there is only one God and Muhammad is his prophet is Muslim," says Gawdat Bahgat, a political science professor at National Defense University in Washington. "So moderate Muslims on both sides believe you should respect this and not question their beliefs."

In many places, however, Sunni-Shiite relations have deteriorated even further since the Doha poll. Sectarian violence — mainly Sunni attacks on Shiites — is on the upswing in Iraq, reflecting the political tug-of-war between the Shiite-controlled government and the Sunni opposition.[5] In Afghanistan, where sectarian attacks are rare, two Shiite shrines were bombed in December.[6] In March, the violence bled into Europe, when Belgium's biggest Shiite mosque was the target; the suspect was a member of the ultra-orthodox, hardline Sunni Salafist sect.[7] And since the Arab Spring began in 2011, many Shiite pro-democracy activists in Bahrain have been imprisoned and tortured by the minority Sunni monarchy.

In Syria, where the authoritarian Assad regime is Alawite — an offshoot of Shiism — most of its civilian victims have been Sunnis. In May, June and July, government forces and the Alawite militia, called the "shabiha," massacred hundreds of people in the Sunni villages of Houla, Qubair and Tremseh, and by mid-July the regime was bombing Syria's largest city, Aleppo.[8] The U.N.'s High Commissioner for Human Rights said both the shabiha and Syrian government could be prosecuted for crimes against humanity.[9]

While the sectarian strife in individual countries might be, as Bulliet says, a fight over who gains power or controls a country's natural resources, it's also part of a broader struggle over which group will dominate the Middle East. The struggles are, in a sense, proxy battles

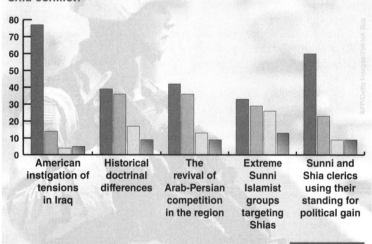

Muslims Say U.S. Worsened Sunni-Shiite Divide

More than three-quarters of Muslims surveyed in the Middle East blamed the 2003 U.S. invasion of Iraq for exacerbating Sunni-Shiite tensions in Iraq and the rest of the Middle East. Another factor was the age-old rivalry between Saudi Arabia, a Sunni Arab nation, and Iran, a country of Shiite Persians.

To what extent do you blame each of the factors for the Sunni-Shia conflict?

Source: "This House Believes That the Sunni-Shia Conflict Is Damaging Islam's Reputation As a Religion of Peace," Doha Debates, April 2008, clients.squareeye.net/uploads/doha/polling/shia_sunni.pdf; a total of 993 people from throughout the region responded to the survey.

Extent factor is to blame
- A lot
- A little
- Not at all
- Don't know

in the age-old religious and ethnic rivalry between the region's two centers of power: Iran, a Shiite Persian theocracy since its 1979 revolution, and Saudi Arabia, an Arab Sunni monarchy where the state religion is Wahhabism — an ultra-conservative form of Sunnism.

For instance, Iran supports the Shiite Alawite government in Syria, while Saudi Arabia supports the mostly Sunni opposition. Likewise, militant Islamic groups in the Middle East are divided along sectarian lines: Lebanon's Hezbollah and Iraq's Mahdi army are both Shiite, while Al Qaeda's terrorist network is made up of Sunnis from the hardline orthodox Wahhabi, Salafist and Deobandi sects.

Why is sectarianism on the upswing? For starters, says Bahgat, Muslims tend to identify themselves by their religion more than by their nationality. "In the United States and most of the Western world, we

How to Tell a Sunni From a Shiite

Names and prayer styles often vary.

As with any religion, it's usually not considered polite to ask outright what branch of Islam someone belongs to. For most Muslims, it's a non-issue, because they live in countries that are predominantly Sunni.

But in countries such as Iraq and Lebanon, with mixed Sunni-Shiite populations, Muslims tend to look for subtle clues that indicate whether another Muslim is Sunni or Shiite.

A major indicator is geography. The overwhelming majority — about 85 percent — of the world's 1.6 billion Muslims are Sunni. But Shiites make up the majority in Iran, Azerbaijan, Bahrain and southern Iraq. There are also Shiite majorities in southern Lebanon, northern Yemen and the oil-producing region of eastern Saudi Arabia. And significant numbers live in Kuwait, Afghanistan, Pakistan and Syria.[1]

Names are another indicator. Ali and Hussein are popular among both Sunnis and Shiites, but have a special resonance for Shiites. Ali was the name of Muhammad's son-in-law, the man Shiites believe should have been his immediate successor. Hussein was the name of Ali's son, who was killed by the army of the caliph Yazid and is an important symbol of Shiite martyrdom.

Zulfikar — the name of Ali's sword — is a Shiite name. Zulfikar Ali Bhutto was prime minister of Pakistan from 1973-77. Although he was a secular, modernist Muslim, "Zulfikar" paired with the name "Ali" indicates a Shiite family background.

Other names are favored only by Sunnis. "There are certain names" — such as Abu Bakr, Omar, Osman or Yazid — "that a Shiite would never have," says Jonathan Brown, an assistant professor of Islamic Studies at Georgetown University's School of Foreign Service and a Muslim.

That's because those names refer to the three Muslim leaders who immediately succeeded Muhammad, bypassing Ali. In fact, the most powerful political state in Muslim history, the Sunni Ottoman Empire, derives from the name Osman.

In matters of worship, all Muslims believe in the five tenets of Islam: the declaration of faith, prayer, charity, fasting and pilgrimage to Mecca. All Muslims pray five times a day. But some Shiites allow some prayers to be combined, so they may pray only three times a day.[2]

"The style of praying also differs between the two branches. Shiites pray with their arms at their sides," says Brown, although a Sunni school of thought predominant throughout northern Africa prays that way, too. But if you are in Turkey, and people are praying with their arms by their sides, he says, they are probably Shiite. By contrast, most Sunnis pray by laying their right hand on top of the left, on their diaphragm, between the chest and the navel.

Also, Shiites pray by putting their foreheads on a little stone of compacted dirt or mud, which represents the earth of Karbala, the Iraqi city where Ali's son Hussein died. Unlike the Sunnis, Shiites commemorate Ashura, the day Hussein died, with ritual mourning processions that can include self-flagellation.

— Leda Hartman

---

[1]Vali Nasr, *The Shia Revival* (2006), pp. 12-13.

[2]"Sunni and Shi'a," BBC, Aug. 19, 2009, www.bbc.co.uk/religion/religions/islam/subdivisions/sunnishia_1.shtml.

define ourselves by our national identity," he explains. "We are Americans first. Christians and Jews, white and black, are second or third." In most Middle Eastern countries religious identity is more important. "They have not completely understood or accepted the concept of national identity," he added. "They are Shia or Sunni, Christian or Muslim. This is very clear in countries like Iraq and Lebanon."

The Middle East also lacks democratic institutions that could encourage people of different persuasions to live together peacefully. "The region is known for the mosaic structure of society," says Abdeslam Maghraoui, an associate professor of political science at Duke University. "The problem comes when you don't have procedures to say, 'Hey look, this is how we define our rights, this is how we can have a balance where you can fulfill your potential to be who you are without infringing on the rights of others.'"

Pluralism hasn't had a chance to develop in the Middle East because the region historically has been dominated by authoritarian powers that force people to jostle for position, says Jones, especially in oil-producing states where petroleum revenue is distributed as patronage. "The preference is not for reconciliation," he explains. "The preference is to protect access to a system of privilege."

But the most important factor, analysts say, may be the lack of trust. People from one sect don't trust that the other side would be fair if they were in power, and vice versa. In Iraq, for instance, the U.S. invasion deposed the Sunni Baath Party and opened the way for a Shiite-controlled government, leaving the Sunnis marginalized.

Such factors help explain why the situations in Egypt, Libya and Tunisia — where autocratic leaders were ousted during last year's Arab Spring — differ from what's happening in Syria and Bahrain. The North African countries are overwhelmingly Sunni, and sectarian divisions aren't much of an issue. But in Syria and Bahrain, where minority regimes rule over a majority of the opposite sect, the situation is more complex and much more volatile.

Meanwhile, unlike in Libya, Western powers are reluctant to step in with direct military action in Syria because they fear that a Syrian civil war could spill over into other countries where sectarian tensions simmer. However, on August 1, Reuters reported that President Obama had secretly authorized covert U.S. support for the rebels and that agencies such as the CIA are operating from a secret base in Turkey.[10]

Those fears appear to be well-founded. Sunnis from Iraq and Lebanon have gone to Syria to join the insurgents fighting the Alawite government.[11] There also have been fatal skirmishes in northern Lebanon between Sunnis who support the Syrian uprising and Alawites who back Assad.[12]

As the standoff in Syria continues, some fear that Islamic sectarianism in the Middle East could re-ignite Cold War-era animosities, as the United States and the other NATO powers call for Assad's ouster while Russia and China remain his ally.

Meanwhile, the human cost continues to rise unabated, and its after-effects may be felt for some time. Khalid Ali al-Sardi, a Sunni student at the University of Bahrain, told *New York Times* reporter Souad Mekhennet that he used to have Shiite friends who would come to his home to share a meal. Then, last year, he was badly beaten up by a group of Shiite protesters.

"Why did this happen to all of us here in Bahrain?" al-Sardi asks. "We thought Shiites and Sunnis had lived as brothers and sisters together. We all are losing. Why does no one see that?"[13]

As sectarian tensions escalate in the Middle East, here are some of the questions being debated by academics, Middle East experts and Muslims themselves:

Is the Sunni-Shiite split primarily about theology?

All Muslims believe in the five tenets of Islam: the declaration of faith, prayer, charity, fasting and making a pilgrimage to Mecca. But sectarian divisions emerged early in Islam, over who should succeed the Prophet Muhammad after his death.

A larger group of Muslims, who later became known as the Sunnis, chose one of Muhammad's companions, Abu Bakr. A smaller group, later known as the Shiites, supported Muhammad's son-in-law, Ali. The larger group won out, and throughout history, the Sunnis have maintained control of most of the Muslim world — even in places where Shiites comprise the majority — except in Iran and postwar Iraq.

Joshua Landis, director of the Center for Middle East Studies at the University of Oklahoma, sees religious differences as a major underpinning of today's sectarian conflict.

"It has a lot to do with theology," Landis maintains. "If you want to look at it ideologically, the easiest thing to do would be to compare it to a pre-Enlightened Europe. In a sense, the Middle East is in the midst of a pre-Enlightenment era. Theology and God still are the main sources of truth for most Middle Easterners. People take their religion seriously. It's driven by politics, but also by a world view where God is talking truth with a big 'T.'"

Although moderates from both branches accept one another without questioning each other's beliefs, in today's heated climate some Muslims, particularly Sunnis, disavow the others. "Many Sunnis believe Shia are Muslims," says Bahgat, at the National Defense University, but some extremist Sunnis believe the Shia "are not Muslims."

Theologically based violence is especially visible in Pakistan, where Shiite Iran and Sunni Saudi Arabia have vied for influence for decades and where most of the recent violence has been fomented by Sunnis targeting Shiites. Many Sunni extremists belong to the Deobandi

Islam's Two Branches Have Many Offshoots

Eighty-five percent of the world's Muslims are Sunni, while the rest are Shiite. The split developed in the 7th century over who should succeed the Prophet Muhammad. Sunnis believed the best-qualified leader should succeed him, while Shiites believed Muhammad's blood descendants were his rightful successors. Since then, several small sects have broken off from mainstream Sunnism and Shiism. Some sects are more prevalent in certain countries.

Major Sunni Groups

Mainstream Sunnism includes four broad schools of thought, mainly divided along geographical lines. The Hanafi are prevalent in much of the Arab world and South Asia; the Hanbali in Saudi Arabia; the Maliki in North, Central and West Africa; and the Shafii, mainly in East Africa and Southeast Asia.

Salafists/Wahhabis — Practitioners of these ultra-conservative branches follow the practices of the early Muslims and distrust modernist interpretations of the Quran, Islam's holy book. Wahhabism — Saudi Arabia's state religion — began with an 18th-century Arabian scholar named Muhammad Ibn Abd al-Wahhab. Among other things, it provides the rationale for the global jihad against infidels espoused by today's terrorists and is known for its strict limits on women's rights. The terrorist group Al Qaeda is generally made up of Salafists and Wahhabis.

Deobandis — Based primarily in Pakistan and named after a city in northern India where it was founded, this ultra-conservative branch developed in the late 19th century in part as a response to British colonialism. The Deobandis believe Islamic societies have become too Westernized. Like Salafists, Deobandis restrict women's rights and regard Shiites as heretics. The extremist Taliban group, based in Pakistan and Afhganistan, is primarily Deobandi.

Major Shiite Sects

Twelvers — Centered in Iran, Shiism's largest mainstream sect recognizes 12 imams and believes the last imam — a messianic figure — will appear at the end of time to usher in peace and justice.

Ismailis — This geographically and ethnically diverse group of 15 million recognizes seven imams.

Zaidis — Mostly based in Yemen, this group recognizes only five imams. In belief and practice, the Zaidis are the Shiite group most similar to the Sunnis.

Alawites — This Shiite offshoot of 3 million followers is most prevalent in Syria. Their rituals incorporate elements of Christianity and other religions. Some mainstream Sunnis and Shiites don't consider them Muslims.

Alevis — Similar to the Alawites but based mostly in Turkey, the Alevis downplay formal rituals and stress gender equality.

Druze — Prevalent in Syria, Lebanon, Israel and Jordan, this group's secretive belief system includes elements of Christianity, Gnosticism and Zoroastrianism. Many mainstream Muslims view the Druze as non-Muslims.

Source: "The Sword and the Word," The Economist, May 2012, p. 67, www.economist.com/node/21554513; "Deobandi Islam," GlobalSecurity.org, www.globalsecurity.org/military/intro/islam-deobandi.htm

"The Shia of Pakistan have not yet been officially declared a non-Muslim minority, but they have clearly lost their bid for power," wrote Vali Nasr, dean of The Johns Hopkins University's Paul H. Nitze School of Advanced International Studies (SAIS). "The extremist face of Sunnism has proven itself capable of reacting to the Shiite challenge, using violence but also theology and religious ideology to roll back Shiite gains."[15]

According to some experts, the power struggle is more important than theology in the sectarian conflict. In fact, the Sunni-Shiite schism after Muhammad's death was "purely political," wrote Islamic history scholars Bernard Lewis, professor emeritus of Near Eastern Studies at Princeton University, and Buntzie Ellis Churchill, the former president of the World Affairs Council of Philadelphia. It was "a dispute over the succession to the prophet Mohammed as the head of the Muslim state and community which he had founded."[16]

Geopolitics continues to be at the root of the conflict today, says Leena El-Ali, vice president of strategic development at Search for Common Ground, a Washington-based nongovernmental organization focusing on conflict resolution. "Very often we forget that what we describe in sectarian terms is actually a conflict about worldly political power, period," she says. "There are fault lines in certain countries whereby the political power is officially or de facto distributed along sectarian lines. So there you see people lining up behind different sorts of sectarian groupings because of the implications for political power."

El-Ali should know. She lived through the Lebanese civil war of 1975-90, when Christians, Sunnis and Shiites were all fighting each other. "It sounded to the

sect, which inspired the Taliban, or have been educated in madrassas (Islamic religious schools) built and financed by the hardline Saudi Wahhabis.[14]

outside world that people were fighting over religion — 'mine is better than yours, you're a heretic' — and that was never, ever the issue," she says. "The issue was quite simply political power. And we run the risk now, when it comes to the Sunni-Shiite thing, to give the same wrong impression in some cases."

Sectarian divisions also have been exacerbated by economics, says Bahgat. "The minority in most countries are Shia who have been deprived of jobs and economic opportunities," he says. "So in many countries the Shia minority also happen to be the poor."

Are concerns about sectarian conflict overblown?

Although Muslim sectarian violence dominates today's headlines, some experts say it's important not to lose sight of the bigger picture, both numerically and historically.

"I think the norm in Islamic history is a relatively peaceful co-existence," says Charles Kurzman, professor of sociology at the University of North Carolina at Chapel Hill. "These communities have lived next to each other and even intermingled for centuries. They have intermarried in many communities, and we rarely see trouble rising to the level of communal violence."

Kurzman says nothing in the Sunni-Shiite split makes for inherent conflict, and for the overwhelming majority of Muslims, co-existence remains the norm. Even in the "handful of countries and cases" where violence does exist, he adds, the conflict has been triggered by external factors such as the U.S. invasion of Iraq or the Arab Spring movements in North Africa, which inspired similar movements in Bahrain and Syria.

Sheikh Mahmood Shaltoot, the grand imam of Al Azhar University in Cairo, Egypt, wrote in a 1959 *fatwa*, or Islamic legal opinion, that Shiism "is a school of thought that is religiously correct to follow in worship as are other Sunni schools of thought."[17]

Further, he continued, "Muslims must know this, and ought to refrain from unjust prejudice to any particular school of thought, since the religion of Allah and His Divine Law (Shari'ah) was never restricted to a particular school of thought."[18]

It's also important to compare Islamic sectarianism to religious conflicts in other times and places. Even the rivalry between the Sunni Ottoman Empire and Persia's Shiite Safavid dynasty during the 16th-18th centuries "never reached the level of the bitter and bloody wars of

Residents survey the damage caused by a truck bomb that killed 44 people in a market in Diwaniya, 95 miles south of Baghdad, on July 3, 2012. One of the latest in a series of sectarian attacks in Iraq, the bombing was near a Shiite mosque where pilgrims gather on their way to Karbala to celebrate the birthday of al-Mahdi, one of their most important imams. Sunni extremists were thought to have detonated the bomb.

religion that followed the Reformation in Europe," according to Lewis and Churchill.[19]

In his book *The Missing Martyrs*, Kurzman compares terrorist incidents around the world to other forms of violence and finds that terrorism represents only a tiny portion of the world's bloodshed. Thus, worries about Muslim sectarian tensions leading to violence and terrorism are exaggerated, he says.

"Both of these grand narratives are flawed," he says. "We would be better served to look at particular cases and also put these things in perspective. Not to ignore them — these are very real problems and have very real victims — but at the same time to recognize it's not nearly so bad as many of us feared it would be, and is not nearly the global tsunami that it may have appeared to be."

Others, however, note a sea change in the intensity and volatility of sectarian tension, especially when it's viewed in context with other issues.

"Is sectarianism — the fact that there's a Sunni-Shiite split — an inherently destabilizing fact in world politics? No, it's not," says Jonathan Brown, an assistant professor of Islamic studies at Georgetown University and a Muslim. "But, considering that sectarianism is fuel for a fire originally caused by political concerns, economic

CHRONOLOGY

1453-1924 *Sunni Ottoman Empire, headquartered in Istanbul, rules much of the Muslim world, stretching from Eastern Europe to the Arabian Peninsula and parts of North Africa.*

1501-1722 Safavids break away from Ottoman Empire and establish Shiite theocracy in Persia (modern Iran). They suppress Sunnism and other religions.

1783 Sunni Al Khalifa family expels Shiite Persians from Bahrain; establishes monarchy that rules over majority Arab Shiites.

1923 French take power in Syria and Lebanon and put Alawites — an unorthodox branch of Shiism — in charge of Syria and Maronite Christians in charge of Lebanon.

1932 Abdul-Aziz bin Saud establishes monarchy in Saudi Arabia, with ultra-orthodox Sunnism (Wahhabism) as the state religion. Minority Sunnis take power in Iraq.

1941 Lebanon declares its independence from France. . . . French mandate formally ends in 1943 but French power structure is retained.

1946 Syria becomes a sovereign state, but keeps French power structure.

1958 Iraq becomes a republic after military coup. Minority Sunnis take power.

1970s-1980s *The seeds of today's sectarian conflicts are planted in Syria, Pakistan, Iraq and Lebanon; Iranian Revolution creates a Shiite theocracy.*

1970 Alawite Hafez Assad seizes power in Syria. The Shiite Alawites rule majority Sunni population for more than 40 years, with support from Christian and Druze minorities.

1977 President Zulfikar Ali Bhutto, a secular Shiite, is ousted in a military coup in Pakistan.

1979 Shah of Iran abdicates; Ayatollah Ruhollah Khomeini establishes a Shiite theocracy. In Iraq, Sunni Baath leader Saddam Hussein seizes power. Gen. Zia ul-Haq, a fundamentalist Sunni, becomes president of Pakistan.

1981 Sunni monarchy in Bahrain puts down Shiite insurgency.

1982 Syria's Assad crushes uprising in Hama, a Sunni Muslim Brotherhood stronghold; thousands of civilians are killed. A militant Shiite group, Hezbollah, forms in Lebanon.

1980-1988 Iraq's Sunni leader Saddam Hussein invades Iran. Iraq's Shiites fight on the Iraqi side against Iran's Shiites. War ends in stalemate, with hundreds of thousands of deaths on each side.

1989 Ayatollah Khomeini dies.

1990s-2000s *Hardline Muslim extremist groups emerge; Sunni extremist group, Al Qaeda, attacks the United States, which then invades Afghanistan and Iraq.*

1990 North and South Yemen unite; Ali Abdullah Saleh becomes president of an autocratic regime.

1991 Saddam brutally suppresses Shiite uprising in southern Iraq, killing thousands. . . . United States establishes Fifth Fleet at a naval base in Bahrain.

1996 Sunni monarchy crushes second Shiite uprising in Bahrain.

2001 Al Qaeda hijacks four airliners and attacks targets in New York and Washington, killing 3,000 people. The United States retaliates by invading Al Qaeda safe-haven, Afghanistan. For the next 11 years U.S. battles Al Qaeda and the Sunni fundamentalist regime known as the Taliban.

2003 United States invades Iraq, claiming Saddam has weapons of mass destruction. Sunni Baath party is deposed and Shiite leader Nuri al-Maliki comes to power. Sunni Baathists and Al Qaeda launch anti-U.S. insurgency.

2006-2007 Sunni-Shiite violence in Iraq escalates.

2010 Bahrain arrests Shiite opposition leaders, claiming they are plotting to overthrow the Sunni monarchy.

Feb. 17, 2011 Arab Spring movement, which began in December in Tunisia, migrates from Sunni-dominated North Africa to Bahrain, where it takes on a sectarian flavor. Majority Shiites demand equal rights from Bahrain's Sunni monarchy, which cracks down hard on the protesters.

March 15 Sunni-led protests erupt against Syria's minority Alawite regime.

Nov. 23 Independent inquiry finds Iran was not involved in the Bahraini uprising, but that the government tortured and used excessive force against protesters.

Dec. 7 Sunnis bomb two Shiite mosques in Afghanistan.

Dec. 18 U.S. withdraws from Iraq.

Dec. 19 Shiite-controlled Iraqi government issues arrest warrant for Sunni vice president, Tariq al Hashemi, claiming he oversaw death squads. Hashemi denies the charges; flees Iraq.

April 20, 2012 Thousands of protesters, mostly Shiites, rally against Bahrain's Sunni monarchy. Riot police use tear gas and stun grenades.

May 13 Five people are killed in Tripoli, signaling an escalation of sectarian clashes in Lebannon.

May 21 A suicide bombing at a military rehearsal for Yemen's National Day parade kills nearly 100; extremist Sunnis claim responsibility.

May 26 Syrian military begin the first of three major assaults on Sunni villages, killing hundreds.

June 1 U.N. High Commissioner for Human Rights Navi Pillay says Syrian regime could face charges of crimes against humanity.

June 13 At least 70 Iraqis are killed in a wave of attacks targeting Shiite pilgrims. A militant Sunni group claims responsibility.

June 15 Russians ship defensive missile systems to Syria.

June 16 Car bombs target a Shiite pilgrimage in Baghdad, Iraq, killing 32.

June 18 Suicide bomber in Baquba, Iraq, targets a Shiite funeral, killing at least 15 and wounding 40. At least 130 Shiites are killed in sectarian attacks in June.

June 22 Some 25 members of Syria's Alawite militia are killed in Aleppo. Western intelligence officials warn that Sunni extremists have joined the rebel forces. Syria shoots down a Turkish fighter jet that inadvertently flew into Syrian air space.

June 24 Two high-level Syrian military officers join dozens of others who have defected to Turkey.

July 18 Rebel bombing in Damascus kills four top security officials, including the Defense minister.

July 24 Assad regime uses warplanes to bomb Aleppo, Syria's largest city, after rebel incursions there. . . . Death toll from sectarian attacks in Iraq reaches two-year monthly high of 325.

Aug. 1 Reuters says President Obama has secretly authorized covert U.S. support for the Syrian rebels.

---

concerns and strategic concerns — right now that is a very dangerous mixture of fire and fuel, which has been burning very fiercely for the last couple of years and will continue to do so."

That dynamic could not only cause increased armed conflict but also endanger the goals of the Arab Spring movement, he says. It could make "the anxieties of the regimes and the majority controlling groups supersede much nobler aspirations," he says, such as the protest movements "trying to better the lives of people and increase their ability to participate in government and demand accountability."

As an example, he cites the situation in Bahrain, where the ruling Sunni monarchy has defined the opposition as a Shiite uprising led by Iran. "The fact that

these people had legitimate grievances was forgotten," says Brown.

The sectarian label in Bahrain, among other places, has led to the torture and deaths of many people, adds Rutgers University's Jones. What's more, it has aggravated a religious divide that wasn't as bitter when the pro-democracy movement began. Jones says nonviolent activists could eventually turn to violence in desperation, or sectarian tension could become permanent or long-lasting in parts of the Middle East.

"What's more likely is that you'll have a generational, structural reality in which people identify along sectarian lines, and that will paralyze politics," Jones says. "That means the kinds of unrest we see in places like Syria, even in Iraq and in parts of the Gulf, will

Why Are the Sufis Under Attack?

Extremists see the tolerant mystics as heretics.

In early July, in northern Mali's fabled Timbuktu, members of the radical Islamist group Ansar Dine used picks and shovels to destroy the ancient mausoleums of several saints revered by the local Sufis.[1]

Technically, it wasn't a sectarian assault, since Ansar Dine is Sunni, as are Mali's Sufis, who practice a mystical form of Islam. But the two groups are as far apart as you can get in their approach to Islam.

Ansar Dine, along with its allies Al Qaeda and the Taliban, espouses an ultra-conservative, puritanical strain of Islam that is associated with the Wahhabi, Salafist and Deobandi sects of Sunnism. (*See chart, p. 32.*) The movement began with the 18th-century Arabian scholar Muhammad Ibn Abd al-Wahhab.

"Wahhabi theology saw the world in white and black categories," wrote John Esposito, professor of religion and international affairs at Georgetown University, "Muslim and non-Muslim, belief and unbelief. They regarded all Muslims who did not agree with them as unbelievers to be subdued (that is, fought and killed) in the name of Islam." Thus, Wahhabism has provided the rationale for the global jihad against infidels espoused by today's terrorists.

Al-Wahhab formed an alliance with a tribal leader named Muhammad ibn Saud, who established the dynasty that still rules Saudi Arabia today. The Wahhabi interpretation of Islam is the country's official religion.[2]

Closely related to the Wahhabis are the Salafists, whose name comes from the Arabic phrase "those who have gone before," connoting a return to the purity of early Islam. The Salafist movement first developed in late 19th-century Egypt in reaction to the modernization and reform associated with foreign influence and has since spread to many parts of the Muslim world.[3]

At around the same time, the Deobandi movement emerged in northern India — partly in response to British colonialism — and spread to other South Asian countries, notably Pakistan and Afghanistan.[4]

At the other kinder, gentler end of the spectrum is Sufism. Grounded in traditional Muslim law and scholarship, it also incorporates a variety of mental and physical disciplines to achieve a direct and personal experience of God. Sufism's focus is on the esoteric, inner connection with the divine, perhaps most familiarly captured in the image of the dancing mystics known as the whirling dervishes, who are said to be "revolving in harmony with all things in nature."[5]

Sufis can be either Sunni or Shiite. They're inclusive in their outlook, even embracing local traditions and practices that may be somewhat outside the bounds of Islam.

The phrase that epitomizes Sufism is *sulk e kul*, or "peace with all," says Akbar Ahmed, an Islamic studies professor at American University and Pakistan's former ambassador to the United Kingdom. "Sufis believe we are all creatures of God, that there are many paths to God," Ahmed says. "You may be a Buddhist, a Christian, a Hindu. If you're striving to understand God, that's fine, and good luck to you."

Ahmed says it helps to view Muslims not in terms of Sunni and Shiite, but in terms of three groups: the literalists (the conservatives); the modernists (those who may speak English, wear Western dress and engage internationally while still maintaining their faith); and the mystics (the Sufis).

He illustrates these distinctions through the example of a traditional Sufi practice — chanting the name of God over and over. "Now, imagine there are 500 people chanting this, it's late at night, you've said your prayers, you're thinking of God," Ahmed says. "It's highly spiritual. But it almost smacks of something that's off the beaten path of orthodoxy. A literalist

more or less be a perennial problem, just waiting for the match to be ignited."

Is Sunni-Shiite reconciliation possible in the near future?

Jones, of Rutgers, doesn't see reconciliation on the near horizon, and he blames the Middle East's power structures.

Regional governments "have basically had to buy their way or co-opt their way or oppress their way into remaining in power," he says. And none of them has "the political will to stand above the fray and mediate.

"People want to talk to each other. They want to have relationships. But they don't have the space to create that," Jones observes.

... would say, 'What the hell is going on? This is not an Islamic ritual!' A modernist . . . would say, 'This is mumbo jumbo!' The Sufis would say in response, 'Well, we bless both of them. May their eyes be opened to the reality.'"

Such tolerance makes Sufis the target of extremists, especially the militant Salafists who comprise the majority of today's global terrorist groups. "Salafists and others who believe in a more orthodox brand of Islam harbor a particular animosity toward Sufism, whose mystical interpretation of the divine affords a more heterodox faith, steeped sometimes in local pre-Islamic traditions and a reverence for saints and wise men," wrote *Time* columnist Ishaan Tharoor.[6]

To Sunni extremists, Sufis — like Shiites — are infidels. And for the last generation, extremists in Pakistan have attacked Sufis almost as much as they have Shiites.

Sunni extremists — who recently declared northern Mali an independent nation called Azawad — have set their sights on the region's Sufis and in doing so have destroyed more than the ancient shrines.[7]

"The attack on Timbuktu's cultural heritage," says UNESCO's director general, Irina Bokova, "is an attack against this history and the values it carries — values of tolerance, exchange and living together, which lie at the heart of Islam. It is an attack against the physical evidence that peace and dialogue is possible."[8]

Still, Sufism continues to resonate with Muslims worldwide — both Sunnis and Shiites, literalists and modernists. Many see it as a potential bridge builder and a counterweight to extremism. In fact, in 2009, Tahroor reported, "the Algerian government announced it would promote the nation's Sufi heritage on radio and television in a bid to check the powerful influence of Salafism."[9]

When he's asked if the Muslim world can co-exist peacefully in the near future, Ahmed considers for a moment. Then he laughs gently. "Yes," he says, "if we listen to the mystics."

— Leda Hartman

Islamist militants destroy an ancient Sufi shrine in Timbuktu, Mali, on July 1, 2012. Although the country's Sufis are Sunnis, extremist Sunni rebels in northern Mali consider the shrines idolatrous and have wrecked seven tombs — designated by UNESCO as world heritage sites.

[1]Rukmini Callimachi, "Islamists Continue Destroying Timbuktu Heritage," The Associated Press, July 2, 2012, http://hosted2.ap.org/APDEFAULT/cae69a7523db45408eeb2b3a98c0c9c5/Article_2012-07-02-AF-Mali-Timbuktu/id-995898803faf4d0da5de0b946e6fa2cb.

[2]John L. Esposito, *What Everyone Needs to Know about Islam* (2011), p. 54.

[3]Bernard Lewis and Buntzie Ellis Churchill, *Islam: the Religion and the People* (2009), pp. 158-159.

[4]Vali Nasr, *The Shia Revival* (2006), pp. 100-101.

[5]Esposito, *op. cit.*, p. 61. Also see "Sufism and Dervishes," www.whirling dervishes.org.

[6]Ishaan Tharoor, "Timbuktu's Destruction: Why Islamists Are Wrecking Mali's Cultural Heritage," *Time*, July 2, 2012, http://world.time.com/2012/07/02/timbuktus-destruction-why-islamists-are-wrecking-malis-cultural-heritage/.

[7]For background, see John Felton, "Small Arms Trade," *CQ Global Researcher*, June 19, 2012, pp. 281-304.

[8]Ishaan Tharoor, "Can Sufism Defuse Terrorism and Radical Islam?" *Time*, July 22, 2009, www.time.com/time/world/article/0,8599,1912091,00.html.

[9]*Ibid.*

People also don't trust that they will be treated fairly by the other side if power switches hands because one side tends to have the power and wealth, and the other does not, he says.

"Iraq is your model for that," he says. The U.S. invasion led to the overthrow of Saddam Hussein's Sunni regime and resulted in establishment of a Shiite government, he says, which has become increasingly authoritarian. "We didn't have a change in the system. We had a change in sides for who controlled the system. That's exactly the dynamic that's feared across the region."

The University of Oklahoma's Landis is even more pessimistic. "In that core of the Middle East, we don't have a good example" of egalitarian co-existence. Even Lebanon, often touted as an egalitarian, multicultural society, has a dysfunctional government plagued by political paralysis and factional distrust, he says.

"People don't trust each other because they don't see where it works," says Landis. "The religious groups fight each other in a zero-sum game into complete submission, and it goes on for a decade or two, and hundreds or thousands of people are killed, and it makes misery." In comparison, a dictatorship might look preferable, he says.

El-Ali at Search for Common Ground agrees that issues of sectarianism get tangled up with concerns about access, privilege and power. Her goal is to untangle the web — to clarify exactly what needs to be fixed and in doing so, lower the temperature. "I am quite hopeful," she says.

Even in violence-wracked Syria, she says, "The issues are not Alawite versus Sunni. The issues are about living a life of dignity and freedom — free from fear — and where the law protects you and guarantees your rights."

To achieve that, all groups must work toward reform together, or the same inequality that existed before will just happen in reverse, she says. When she broaches this idea, she's often met with cynicism. But when she persists, she says, people begin to listen.

She's also encouraged by last year's Arab Spring. "For the first time in a very long time, the Arab seems to have shed his sense of victimhood," she says. "This has kind of shaken up things. The cynicism was always accompanied by a doomed response — 'The powers that be make all the decisions; you are kidding yourself' — and always blaming someone else and portraying oneself as a victim and powerless." But the members of the young generation that ushered in the awakening "don't want to be victims."

Other peacemakers turn to religion as a way to unite people, rather than divide them. "Even if you're devout, war can make you forget the positive, healing aspects of faith," says Qamar-ul Huda, a scholar of Islam and a senior program officer at the U.S. Institute for Peace, in Washington.

Huda works with religious leaders from different branches of Islam in several Muslim countries. He asks them how they developed their opinions of each other. Often, he finds that biases originate not from theology but from one's family, community, the political structure or a person's economic standing. Huda then stresses the common points in Islam that would resonate with any Muslim: the oneness of God; a sense of responsibility to the local and the global communities; the sacredness of each life; forgiveness and practicing reconciliation. And he then asks clerics — many of whom are afraid to call for reconciliation — what they're doing to alleviate the suffering around them.

"When you ask religious leaders, 'What are you doing?' either it's guilt, or they say, 'Yeah, right, we're not doing anything.' And they just jump up and say, 'Yeah, we need to do something. What can we do?'"

Huda has had some successes. In Pakistan, with its history of intense sectarian violence, people who wouldn't sit down with each other before now work together to head off conflict before it starts. He also has helped to develop a peace education curriculum for some of Pakistan's madrassas, which in some cases have been seen as incubators for terrorism.

"It's not a banana split every day," Huda says, "but there are wonderful things happening."

BACKGROUND

Roots of the Division

The division between Sunnis and Shiites stems from a dispute that erupted shortly after Muhammad's death in 632 over who would succeed him and lead the roughly 100,000 Muslims in the Arabian Peninsula.

The largest group — who would become known as Sunnis — favored Abu Bakr, one of Muhammad's close companions. A smaller group — who eventually would become the Shiites — favored Muhammad's cousin and son-in-law, Ali. The Sunnis wanted to choose the most-qualified person, while the Shiites wanted succession based on Muhammad's male descendants.[20]

Abu Bakr was selected as Islam's first caliph, or leader, probably because Ali, still in his early 30s, "lacked seniority within the Arabian tribal system," wrote researcher Febe Armanios.[21] Eventually, Ali became the Muslims' fourth leader after the second and third caliphs, Omar and Othman, were murdered. But tensions flared when the governor of Damascus took up arms against Ali for failing to prosecute Othman's killers. The two sides eventually agreed to a truce, but some of Ali's followers opposed it and murdered him while he was at prayer.[22]

The conflict continued into the next generation, when the governor's son, Yazid, became caliph, and Ali's son, Hussein, was asked to overthrow Yazid in 680. The two forces met near Karbala, in what is now Iraq. Hussein, who was vastly outnumbered, fought to the death and became a powerful symbol of martyrdom.

The Battle of Karbala remains a watershed event in Shiite history and is commemorated each year in a day of mourning called Ashura, when Shiites participate in public processions and perform symbolic acts of self-flagellation.[23]

Karbala not only led to the division of Islam into two branches but also shaped each branch's very different world views.

"Shiite rhetoric is couched in the rhetoric of a fight against injustice and tyranny, so at its root is the idea that the world is unjust and must be challenged," says Akbar Ahmed, an Islamic studies professor at American University in Washington, D.C., and Pakistan's former ambassador to the United Kingdom. Sunnism, on the other hand, "is the opposite. Sunni Islam is establishment Islam," he explains," and holds that "the world is what it is, and you must not disrupt it; you must not create chaos. So you see, straightaway you have a different attitude to how the world is seen."

The name Sunni refers to "one who follows the Sunnah," or the sayings, customs and judgments of Muhammad. The Sunnis are non-hierarchical, and their caliphs tended to be political rather than religious leaders. Shiite means simply "partisans of Ali." The Shiites venerate a series of imams, or spiritual leaders, who they believe are descendants of Muhammad, and their leaders can be both religious and political.[24]

Over time, divisions developed within each branch. The Sunni have four main schools of thought: the Hanafi, Maliki, Shafii and Hanbali, generally associated with different geographic areas. (*See chart, p. 32.*)

The Shiites have three main groups, generally distinguished by how many imams each reveres. Twelvers — the largest Shiite group, comprising a majority in Iran, Iraq and Azerbaijan and substantial populations in Bahrain and Lebanon — venerate 12 imams. The Ismailis, a geographically and culturally diverse group, venerate seven; and the Zaydis, based mainly in Yemen, five.

There also are two distinct offshoots of mainstream Shiism: the Alawites and the Druze, whose beliefs incorporate elements of Christianity, Gnosticism and Zoroastrianism.[25] Some Sunnis and Shiites don't consider the Alawites to be Muslims, and even less so the Druze.[26]

Throughout Muslim history, empires and dynasties have defined themselves in religious and/or political terms. The most powerful was the Sunni Ottoman Empire, based in Turkey, which ruled a vast swath of the Mediterranean world from the 15th century to the end of World War I. At its height, it stretched from Eastern Europe to the Arabian Peninsula and parts of North Africa. The Shiite Safavid dynasty — centered in Persia (modern Iran) — ruled from the 16th-18th centuries.

The Safavids derived from a Sufi order that originated in Azerbaijan. When they took control of Persia in 1501, it was the first time that Persia had native rulers since the Arab Muslims conquered the country in 644. The Safavids established the Twelver branch of Shiism as the state religion and demanded that inhabitants either convert or leave.

Sunni-Shiite violence erupted twice during the Ottoman era. First, the Ottomans and the Safavids fought a long war for control of Iraq in the 17th century.[27] Then, in the 18th century the Wahhabis — ultra-orthodox Sunnis who had risen to power in the Arabian Peninsula — declared the Shiites heretics and mounted bloody attacks on them in the Iraqi cities of Najaf and Karbala.

"If you want to have a war with other Muslims," says Georgetown's Brown, "you'd better figure out a way to make them [heretics]; otherwise you can't have a holy war."

With that defeat the Sunnis have almost always ruled over the Shiites, except in Iran and for three centuries in North Africa and the Levant. "The really significant differences between the two arose from their different experience — the one of dominance, the other of subordination and all the social and psychological consequences of this difference," wrote Lewis.[28]

That dynamic has had a profound impact on sectarian relations throughout Islamic history.

Enter the Europeans

The presence of European powers in the Muslim world after World War I not only created animosity toward the West but also exacerbated sectarian divisions, largely because of how the Europeans granted power and privilege among the Arabs.

With the postwar fall of the Ottoman Empire — which the Arabs helped bring about — European powers established a "quasi-colonial network" in the Persian Gulf and the Levant, says Rutgers University's Jones. The exceptions were Turkey, which became an independent secular republic in 1923, and Saudi Arabia, which established itself as an independent kingdom in 1932.

The rest of the Arab lands were subjugated by Britain and France, which devastated Arab leaders who had been promised independence in exchange for helping to overthrow the Ottomans.[29] With the League of Nations' approval, Britain and France took control of what is now Iraq, Syria, Lebanon, Jordan, Israel and the Palestinian territories.[30]

The Europeans created a new power structure that favored minorities and disregarded the centuries-old Islamic social order, says Jones. "Over the course of the early to middle part of the 20th century, [the Europeans] used this as a colonial strategy — to empower the minority, bind them to the imperial power and make them dependent at the expense of the majority. It was divide and rule, absolutely," says Jones.

For example:

• In Iraq, the British put the minority Sunnis in power over the majority Shiites, a dynamic that persisted until the U.S.-backed coalition overthrew Saddam Hussein in 2003.

• In Syria, the French removed the ruling Sunni elites from power by brutally suppressing rebellion and replaced them with a coalition of minorities — including the Shiite Alawites, the religion of the current ruling family, the Assads.

• In Lebanon, the French distributed power along religious lines, largely favoring the Maronite Christians (Catholics based in the Middle East who trace their heritage back to a 4th-century monk).

The legacy of these arrangements is still at play in all three countries today, says Landis, of the University of Oklahoma. "We have seen bloody conflict in every one of these states, as the majority that was suppressed by the minority claws its way back to the top," he says.

Sectarian tensions eased somewhat in the 1950s and '60s, the heyday of the secular, anti-Western, pan-Arab nationalist movement. "A lot of Muslim activists who were trying to rally Muslims against Western colonialism and imperialism understood very clearly that you have to heal the Sunni-Shiite divide," observes Georgetown's Brown. "You can't resist the West if you are divided."

During the nationalist period, religious identity became weaker, and many Sunnis and Shiites intermarried, says the National Defense University's Bahgat. But nationalism declined after Israel defeated Egypt and its allies during the 1967 Six Day War. Traditional tribal attachments revived, political leaders turned back to their own countries' affairs and sectarian identities revived.

"Now with this failure of Arab nationalism," says Bahgat, "political Islam is on the rise."*

"In my opinion, there is nothing wrong with this," Bahgat continues. "People choose whatever they like. But with political Islam on the rise, people started thinking, 'I'm Shiite, Sunni or other sects.' This is how reconciliation is under attack now."

Modern Sectarianism

Three game-changing events shaped recent Muslim history before the Arab Spring occurred in 2011: the 1979 Iranian Revolution, the Iran-Iraq War (1980-88) and the U.S. invasion of Iraq in 2003.

"The Iranian Revolution was the genesis of modern sectarianism," says Rutgers' Jones. Spearheaded by the Shiite cleric Ayatollah Ruhollah Khomeini, the uprising ousted the iron-fisted, pro-Western Shah Mohammad Reza Pahlavi and created the modern world's first Islamic theocracy.[31]

"In one sweep," wrote historian J. E. Peterson, "the movement deposed an authoritarian monarch, reversed the process of secularization, trumpeted justice for the working classes and enforced the observance of a conservative view of Islam. It also initially espoused the spread of 'Islamic Revolution' to the rest of the region."[32]

At first, the rest of the Muslim world applauded the new Shiite state for standing up to the West. "Even if you are a Sunni and an Arab," says Georgetown's Brown, "it still resonates in some parts of your heart." But Khomeini's call for "relieving the oppressed people of the Earth" and his penchant for putting himself forward as the leader of the Muslim World threatened Sunni rulers, especially in Iraq and Saudi Arabia.[33]

In 1980, Saddam Hussein, whose secular Sunni regime ruled over a Shiite majority in Iraq, felt threatened by the new Shiite theocracy next door. He invaded Iran, with

---

*Political Islam is the movement to mix religion with politics, often involving a strict interpretation of Islamic law, known as Sharia.

financial help from Sunni monarchies in the Gulf States.[34] Hundreds of thousands died on both sides before the blood-bath ended in a stalemate in 1988. During the war, Iraqi Shiites had fought alongside their Sunni Iraqi compatriots against Iran's Shiites. But after the war, the Iraqi Shiites tried to overthrow Saddam but were viciously suppressed. Ironically, Iran was the only country that supported them.[35]

The Shiite majority eventually came to power in Iraq after the United States deposed Saddam in 2003, creating the world's only Arab country with a Shiite-dominated government and reviving Gulf State fears that their own restive Shiite populations might try to overthrow their Sunni rulers. The threat of sectarian civil war in Iraq seemed especially high in 2006 and 2007, as Sunnis bombed a Shiite shrine and a mobile phone video of Saddam's hanging showed him trading insults with his Shiite guards.[36]

Simmering Tensions

Sectarian conflict re-emerged during the late 20th century in other Muslim countries with mixed populations, especially where majority populations were oppressed by their minority rulers.

In Syria, Hafez Assad, an Alawite, became president after a military coup in 1970. In 1982 he brutally crushed a Muslim Brotherhood revolt in the predominantly Sunni stronghold of Hama, presaging today's civil war in Syria. Often described as one of the single deadliest acts by any modern Arab government against its own people, Assad (the father of today's president Bashar Assad) turned the full brunt of the military on Hama, killing from 10,000 to 40,000.[37]

In Bahrain, the disenfranchised Shiite majority twice tried unsuccessfully to overthrow the Sunni monarchy, in 1981 and 1996. And in 1975 civil war erupted in Lebanon — a multicultural mix of Christians, Sunnis, Shiites and Druze — and raged till 1990.

Muslims, who had become the majority in Lebanon, wanted more representation, but the French-installed Maronite Christians didn't want to relinquish power. Meanwhile, the militant Shiite group Hezbollah, allied with Iran, emerged in southern Lebanon in reaction to incursions by Israel and to the arrival of large numbers of Sunni Palestinian refugees from Israel.[38] At one point, all three groups were fighting each other. Today, an uneasy peace reigns in Lebanon.

Around the same time, sectarian conflict developed in northern Yemen. Historically, Sunnis and Shiites there

Reuters/Stringer

A Sunni Muslim gunman fires during clashes that erupted in the Bab al-Tebbaneh neighborhood in Tripoli, Lebanon, on May 13, 2012, that killed three people, The fighting between members of Lebanon's Alawite minority, which supports Syrian President Bashar Assad, and members of Lebanon's Sunni majority, which supports the Syrian rebels, stoked fears that Syria's civil war could bleed into neighboring Lebanon.

had lived in harmony, intermarrying and praying at each other's mosques. But that began to change in the 1980s, when ultra-orthodox Salafist Sunnis from Saudi Arabia settled along Yemen's northwestern border where the Zaidis, a Shiite sect, lived. At the time, the government was trying to reduce the influence of religion in Yemen. In response, some Zaidis formed a militant group called the Houthis, which opposed both the Salafists and the government. Occasionally, the tension turned violent.

"The leadership of the Zaidi community felt they were in danger of being eradicated," says Gregory Johnsen, a Yemen scholar at Princeton University. "So they fell back into a corner and lashed out."

Pakistan probably has experienced the worst deterioration of sectarian tranquility in the late 20th century. Like Yemen, Pakistan had a tradition of various religious communities living in harmony. But since the 1980s, thousands of people have been killed in sectarian violence, often perpetrated by ultra-conservative Sunnis against Shiites and Sufis.[39]

In the late 1970s, three events changed Pakistan's climate: a military coup in 1977 by Gen. Zia ul Haq; the 1979 Iranian Revolution and the Soviet invasion of Afghanistan in 1979.

Zia, a fundamentalist Sunni, deposed the secular, leftist Shiite president, Zulfikar Ali Bhutto, and used conservative

Islam to legitimize his military regime. "He claimed that the state had been established in the name of Islam and that Islamization was the only way the state could attain its national identity," says Samina Ahmed, South Asia project director for the International Crisis Group, a nonprofit that advocates conflict resolution. Under Zia's regime, new laws encouraged discrimination against minority groups, including the Shiites, creating what Ahmed calls a "monster of extremism and intolerance."

Meanwhile, the revolution in neighboring Shiite Iran sparked a proxy war in Pakistan between Iran and Sunni Saudi Arabia. Both countries encouraged their own forms of sectarianism, says Naveed Ahmad, a Pakistani investigative journalist and academic. "The Saudi influence definitely filtered in, broadening all the rhetoric of Wahhabism, and claims that the Shia were infidels," he says. "The Iranian reaction was very open and very crude. They were talking the same way."

Another factor encouraged the violence. When the Soviets invaded Afghanistan, both Sunnis and Shiites sent fighters to vanquish their common enemy. But when they came home, they brought their weapons. "I was a very young student, going to school," Ahmad recalls, "and I knew that people . . . could get a good Kalashnikov anywhere in central or western Pakistan without much problem."

The violence began when the Sunnis attacked the Shiites, who set up their own militant groups in response. The conflict continued, and some would say worsened, under President Pervez Musharraf, who like Zia, took power in a military coup.

Now Musharraf has been replaced, and the militants are part of Pakistan's landscape, says Samina Ahmed. "If the state hadn't discriminated against the minority sects during the Zia years, would we have seen the violent conflict we see today between Sunni and Shiite?" she asks. "I don't think so."

CURRENT SITUATION

Syrian Powder Keg

Of all the countries in the Middle East, Syria has the most potential to set off a regional conflagration.

Syria's crisis pits the majority Sunnis against the ruling Shiite Alawites and their supporters, who have traditionally included Christians and Druze. The current leader, Bashar Assad — the younger son of Hafez Assad — had been trained as an ophthalmologist in London but returned to Syria to be groomed for succession after his older brother, Basil, died in a car accident in 1994. Bashar took power in 2000 after Hafez's death.

The current troubles began in March 2011 as an Arab Spring pro-democracy-style uprising against the 42-year-long Assad dynasty. Since then it has disintegrated into lethal sectarian conflict with a heavy civilian death toll. Pluralism and power-sharing seem impossible.

"So many Syrians — when you catch them in an off moment — will say, 'We're not prepared for democracy,'" says Landis, of the University of Oklahoma. "They'll say, 'Arabs are bloody-minded. They are little autocrats, and they need a strong leader. Otherwise they'll just kill themselves.'"

Indeed, more than 19,000 people have died since the uprising began, according to the Syrian Observatory for Human Rights; the United Nations said in May that 10,000 had died and 120,000 refugees had fled into Jordan, Iraq, Lebanon and Turkey.[40] Both sides have committed human-rights abuses.[41]

Even if the Assad regime falls, it's anyone's guess when and in what form stability will return to Syria, mainly because the opposition is not united. It consists of radical Islamists — who want to establish a theocratic Muslim caliphate across the Arab world — secularists, nonviolent protesters, armed rebels, expatriates and local residents.[42] Other minorities who are protected by the Alawites, including Christians and Druze, are afraid of being marginalized if a Sunni government takes power.[43] Even the Alawites are divided, with some condemning the regime's brutal crackdown.[44]

The conflict has spilled beyond Syria's borders. Starting in February, fatal skirmishes have erupted in northern Lebanon between Shiites and Sunnis. The rivalry between Iran and Saudi Arabia also plays a role: Iran counts Syria as its only Arab ally, while Saudi Arabia, Qatar and Turkey are helping fund the opposition's Free Syrian Army.[45] And recent intelligence confirms that members of Al Qaeda and other jihadists have joined the Sunni rebels.[46]

Meanwhile, CIA officers are in Turkey — Syria's weapons pipeline — trying to keep sophisticated weapons out of extremist hands.[47] Others worry who might gain access to the regime's chemical weapons if Assad falls. A

Is sectarian reconciliation among Muslims likely anytime soon?

YES
Leena El-Ali
Vice President, Strategic Development
Search for Common Ground

Written for *CQ Global Researcher*, August 2012

Until the Iraq War exploded onto our screens in 2003, I never heard talk of a Sunni-Shia divide, even during the 15-year civil war in my home country of Lebanon. The difference between Sunni and Shia was essentially a 7th-century disagreement about who should have succeeded Islam's prophet, Muhammad, as leader of the nascent Muslim community in Arabia.

Since the Iraq War, other factors have helped establish this consciousness of Sunni and Shia difference. One factor is the rise of Sunni extremist groups, such as Al Qaeda, which habitually pronounce on who is a real believer and who is not — a development that has directly harmed far more Muslims in numerous countries than it has Westerners.

Another factor was the 2005 assassination of former Lebanese Prime Minister Rafiq Hariri, a prominent and hugely influential Sunni leader, and the tense standoff that has developed between the Shia Hezbollah Party and the Sunni community over the investigation.

Finally, the Arab Spring has broadly pitted a ruling Sunni regime against a predominantly Shia population in Bahrain, and a ruling Shia regime (Alawite) against a majority Sunni population in Syria.

Grim as all this sounds, there is cause for optimism. First, the concept of a human being judging the quality or validity of another's belief is so antithetical to Islam that it would pretty much require the erasure of 13 centuries' worth of Muslim custom and tradition.

Secondly, all vying for political power — or for participation in it — is ultimately just that, even if it pits one sect against another along the way. This can happen even within the same religion. Witness Lebanon today, where after a 15-year Christian-Muslim civil war, we now have a Christian community that is split right down the middle, with half of it supporting the (Muslim) Sunni-led coalition and the other half the (Muslim) Shia-led one.

We can help bring about reconciliation sooner if we name the objectives of various groups rather than calling members of those groups names — even if religious ones. Calling one another names only delays the return to normal relations between the two sects of Islam, as practical considerations get mixed up with issues of identity. Moreover, it inflates the problem, given that nearly 90 percent of the world's Muslims are Sunni.

NO
Abbas Barzegar
Assistant Professor, Georgia State University;
Affiliate, Middle East Institute

Written for *CQ Global Researcher*, August 2012

During the 20th century, sectarian affiliation was generally secondary to nationalist or pan-Islamic ideologies in the Middle East. Recently, however, the rapid rise of vitriolic sectarian rhetoric and violent outbursts have shocked most Middle East political analysts. Unfortunately, with escalating turmoil in the Muslim world, this is the most inopportune moment in modern history for Sunni-Shiite reconciliation.

Much of today's Islamic sectarian discord can be attributed to the consolidation of Shiite clerical rule in post-revolutionary Iran. Fearing Ayatollah Khomeini's plan to "export the revolution," most Arab states — especially the Gulf monarchies — instituted broad public-education campaigns to curb the revolution's appeal to the "Arab street."

The campaigns equated Sunni Islam with Arab national identities to the point that even pan-Islamist activism was trumped by sectarian parochialism. Anti-Shiite rhetoric took on the force of law. For example, even in Malaysia, typically cited as an example of Muslim pluralism, Shiism is illegal. In May 2012, Egyptian authorities shuttered a Shiite religious center in Cairo when fear of Shiite proselytism angered orthodox Sunni clerics.

But religious institutional rivalry pales in comparison to ideologies that sanction violence in the name of sectarian truth. Militant jihadists' treatises have revived medieval discourses of alleged humiliation and defeat, leading to terrible acts of violence in the name of self-defense. Similar allegations of Shiite sexual licentiousness, heresy and covert Iranian plots now abound in the Sunni opposition's rhetoric in Syria. Likewise, officials in Bahrain have skillfully framed the pro-democracy movement there as a cover for Iranian domination. Iran's geopolitical ambitions and well-financed Shiite evangelical campaign only add verisimilitude to such narratives.

Perhaps the acclaimed Lebanese director Nadine Labaki's latest film, "Where do we go now?" best demonstrates my pessimistic outlook on sectarian reconciliation. It is set in a fictitious Lebanese village inhabited by Christians and Muslims who get along well. Then, sectarian tension elsewhere leads to violence among the men, compelling the women to devise creative solutions to halt the hostility. The film illustrates how quickly dormant discourses of community identity can re-emerge to rearrange the social order.

I believe the sectarian tension in today's Middle East eschews anything but pragmatic cooperation between the Sunnis and Shiites.

top Syrian official recently said that such weapons are only meant to be used against foreign "aggressors."[48]

The international community, meanwhile, seems paralyzed, with Russia and China continuing to stand behind the regime and the West and Gulf States calling for its ouster. Events on the ground seem to have simply outrun diplomacy. On Aug. 2, former U.N. Secretary-General Kofi Annan said he would resign as special Arab League envoy to Syria, complaining that international disunity is exacerbating the conflict.

"Eventually it's going to be okay, but it's going to be a hell of a struggle," says Landis. "And if you add in 10 years of civil war and instability — which all their neighboring countries faced when they went through the same effort to get rid of a minority and put the majority on top — it's miserable."

The single bright spot, ironically, seems to be within Syria itself, in the form of a multi-faith underground support and rescue network whose volunteers risk their lives to bring food, clothing and medical supplies to areas destroyed by the regime. "They [the regime] want to get rid of the idea that people can help each other," a participant told *The New York Times*. "They don't want there to be solidarity among the Syrian people."[49]

Regional Tensions

Sectarian fault lines have deepened elsewhere in the Middle East as well. In Iraq, for instance, suicide bombings against Shiites are on the rise, allegedly by Sunni militants linked to Al Qaeda. More than 325 people died just in July.[50]

Meanwhile, the government's unity is fragile. In December, the Shiite prime minister, Nuri al-Maliki, charged the Sunni vice president, Tariq al-Hashemi, with orchestrating anti-Shiite death squads. Hashemi denied the charges, calling them politically motivated, and fled to Turkey, which has refused to extradite him. Nevertheless, he is being tried in absentia in Baghdad. Maliki, meanwhile, is facing no-confidence calls in Parliament from critics who say he is concentrating too much power in his own hands.

A major Shiite-Sunni flashpoint in Iraq is the question of who will rebuild a shrine in Samarra — revered by both sects — which was destroyed in a 2006 bombing. In June a suicide car bombing targeted a Shiite religious office hoping to oversee the project, and a homemade bomb found in the offices of its Sunni counterpart was detonated by authorities.

"That the shrine is still a focus for Iraq's sectarian divisions illustrates how far Iraq is from salving its psychic wounds," wrote Tim Arango and Yasir Ghazi in *The New York Times.*[51]

Meanwhile, in tiny Bahrain, the restive Shiite majority says it has habitually been discriminated against by the country's minority Sunni monarchy. When a pro-democracy movement broke out in the early days of the Arab Spring, both Shiites and Sunnis were involved. But the monarchy lost no time in portraying the movement as an Iranian-backed Shiite uprising.

"The initial response was to claim that the Shiites . . . wanted to create an Islamic theocracy modeled on Iran's Islamic Republic," says Rutgers' Jones. "Of course, nothing could be further from the truth. But that kind of language justified a brutal crackdown [and] paralyzed American diplomacy and foreign policy in the region."

A November 2011 report by the Bahrain Independent Commission of Inquiry, an international panel commissioned by Bahrain's King Hamad bin Isa al Khalifa, found no evidence of Iranian involvement in the protests. But the report found that the government had used excessive force and torture against protesters. Moreover, on Aug. 1, the Cambridge, Mass.-based group Physicians for Human Rights claimed the Bahraini government has killed at least 30 civilians by "weaponizing" tear gas; the government denied the charges.[52] The United States has registered concern about those findings.[53] But, with a key U.S. naval base in Bahrain and a desire to maintain friendly access to the region's oil, the United States may be reluctant to upset the balance of power in the Gulf.[54]

"Imagining a political system that may not allow oil to flow as we want it to is too much of a risk," Jones maintains. "So the U.S. isn't going to let a little thing like human rights get in the way of that."

The commission's report created momentum to end the conflict, but that push now seems to have stalled, says Mariwan Hama-Saeed, a researcher at New York-based Human Rights Watch. He says the Bahraini government can't fairly negotiate with the opposition because many of its leaders are in jail — for demanding more political rights. "It's very tense," he says. "Nobody talks to anyone. Like friends from the other sect — even when they want to talk, they don't want to talk politics, or they're just silent. Everybody's scared."

Landis predicts the Shiites in Bahrain "will just have to suck their lemons." But others, such as Jones, worry about a turn towards radicalization, even terrorism. If that happens, Bahrain might agree to be annexed by its large, powerful, Sunni neighbor, Saudi Arabia.

That's exactly the plan a young Bahraini prince described to Columbia University's Bulliet a dozen years ago. "I said, 'You know, in the long run, your family is either going to have to share power, or turn the country over to Saudi Arabia, because you just can't stand up permanently to a substantial majority population,'" Bulliet says. "He said, 'Yes, that's what we're going to do. We're going to give up sovereignty and become part of Saudi Arabia.'"

Then, the prince began describing Shiites in the most racist terms possible, Bulliet adds. "And I thought, 'Wow, if that is the view [he has] grown up with — that the only way we can stand up to the vermin who inhabit our island is to give up sovereignty and become part of Saudi Arabia — then the Shiites can't win against them."

In poverty-stricken Yemen, there isn't much of a central government to rebel against — but factions on both sides of the sectarian divide are trying. In the south, the government is battling Al Qaeda. In the north, it's confronting the Houthi — militant Zaidis who oppose the government's alliance with the United States. The Houthi also are fighting the ultra-orthodox Sunni Salafists who have moved into their territory from Saudi Arabia.[55]

"It's a very complicated, murky picture," says Princeton's Yemen scholar Johnsen.

Such developments have weakened the traditional harmony that existed between the mainstream Sunnis and Shiites who make up the majority of Yemenis. Plus, the Persian-Arabian rivalry plays a role here as it does in other Middle Eastern hotspots.

"You have a kind of spectrum," says Laurent Bonnefoy, a political science researcher at the French Institute for the Near East in Jerusalem. "At one end of the spectrum you would have the Zaidi revivalists; at the extreme other end you would have the Salafists. They stigmatize each other as being led by Iran or Saudi Arabia." Still, Bonnefoy remains optimistic that the political process Yemen has adopted since the fall of its autocratic president, Ali Abdullah Saleh, in February will lead to stability.

Johnsen is less sanguine. "At this point, I'm not sure it's helpful to even talk about one Yemen anymore," he says. "There are several Yemens, and the country is slowly drifting apart."

In Pakistan, Sunni extremists continue to target Shiites, but "having spent decades turning a blind eye to . . . groups with a clear agenda based on hatred and intolerance, Pakistan's government appears helpless" to stop it, wrote blogger Mustafa Qadri in Britain's *Guardian*.[56]

Still, there are signs of hope, says the International Crisis Group's Ahmed. The two moderate parties that dominate the country's politics understand the need to reduce sectarian violence, she says. "If we see that process sustained," she adds, "then the political culture in Pakistan can go back to where it was — where the vast majority of moderate Pakistanis will not allow the extremists to hijack them."

OUTLOOK

Historical Process

Examples of harmony and reconciliation among Muslims of different branches abound.

Each year more than 2 million Muslims of every persuasion peacefully make the pilgrimage to Mecca, Muhammad's birthplace.[57] Muslim peacemaking clerics and conflict resolution experts work to build bridges between the branches. Muslims co-exist harmoniously in countries such as India, Azerbaijan and Oman.[58]

But the risk of continued violence in the heart of the Muslim world remains high. Looking ahead, much will depend on the course of the crises in Syria and Bahrain, the likelihood of maintaining stability in Iraq and Lebanon and the frequency of Sunni attacks on Shiites in Pakistan.

Jones of Rutgers University predicts that where disenfranchised groups — such as the Sunnis in Syria and the Shiites in Bahrain — have been met with violence by the ruling regime sectarian divisions will become permanent. "Part of what's so devastating and so dangerous about this is that the outcome is to make sectarianism more pronounced," he says. "This is toxic and it's structural, at this point." But it didn't have to be this way, he says. At the beginning of the Arab Spring people from different faiths and backgrounds united to push for equal rights.

El-Ali, at Search for Common Ground, hopes the Arab Spring will offer a different vision of the future. "The question is going to be, 'Is this young energy going to learn from the mistakes of previous generations that took to the streets in different parts of the region and tried to do things by force, and descended into mayhem and chaos?" she asks. That's why it's so important to offer a vision of the future in these countries, she adds, "to try to be builders and not destroyers."

Promoting education and economic development would help, says Bahgat of the National Defense University. He suggests that Islamic societies expose more people to different ways of life, without necessarily aping the Western model. This would help people of different persuasions accept each other, he says.

In the end, he says, Muslims may have little choice but to try to do just that. Western powers will come and go, but the people living in the Middle East will stay. "No sect will disappear," Bahgat says. "They will always live together — Sunni and Shia, Muslim and Jews. That is why they have to figure out how to have a peaceful relationship with each other."

With the heart of the Islamic world in flux, it's unclear what the future holds for the region. But most experts agree that for the foreseeable future the transition will be neither smooth nor nonviolent.

It took democratic nations centuries to get to the point where diverse populations live together in relative equality, points out Duke University's Maghraoui. "It was a struggle," he says, "bloody, convoluted. It went forward. It went backward. It was a process, a historical process. And in the Middle East, we have not seen this process. It has been dominated by authoritarian regimes, until the Arab Spring emerged."

NOTES

1. Damien McElroy, "Syria: Bashar al-Assad 'flees to Latakia,'" *The Telegraph*, July 19, 2012, www.telegraph.co.uk/news/worldnews/middleeast/syria/9412126/Syria-Bashar-al-Assad-flees-to-Latakia.html.

2. Rami Khouri, "Sectarianism starts at home," *The Globe and Mail*, July 26, 2011, www.nowlebanon.com/NewsArchiveDetails.aspx?ID=294678#ixzz21SuYGJtb.

3. For background on the Arab Spring, see Roland Flamini, "Turmoil in the Arab World," *CQ Global Researcher*, May 3, 2011, pp. 209-236.

4. "This House Believes the Sunni-Shia Conflict is Damaging Islam's Reputation as a Religion of Peace," The Doha Debates, April 29, 2008, http://thedohadebates.com/debates/item/?d=2&s=4&mode=opinions.

5. Kareem Raheem, "Iraq Attacks Kill at Least 53, Pilgrims Targeted," Reuters, June 13, 2012, www.reuters.com/article/2012/06/13/us-iraq-violence-idUSBRE85C05920120613.

6. "Shias Targeted in Afghan Shrine Blasts," *Al Jazeera*, Dec. 7, 2011, www.aljazeera.com/news/asia/2011/12/201112674650869183.html.

7. "The Sword and the Word," *The Economist*, May 12, 2012, www.economist.com/node/21554513.

8. "Houla: How a Massacre Unfolded," BBC, June 8, 2012, www.bbc.co.uk/news/world-middle-east-18233934.

9. Stephanie Nebehay, "Syrian Forces Face Prosecution for Houla — UN," Reuters, June 1, 2012, www.trust.org/alertnet/news/syrian-forces-face-prosecution-for-houla-un.

10. Khaled Yacoub Oweis, "Rifts Widen in Syrian Opposition," Reuters, May 21, 2012, www.reuters.com/article/2012/05/21/us-syria-opposition-idUSBRE84K1A220120521. Also see Mark Hosenball, "Obama Authorizes Secret U.S. Support for Syrian Rebels," Reuters, Aug. 1, 2012.

11. "Syria Boosts Fears of Sunni Shia War," UPI, April 19, 2012, www.upi.com/Top_News/Special/2012/04/19/Syria-boosts-fears-of-Sunni-Shiite-war/UPI-50411334854300/.

12. "North Lebanon Fighting Kills 1; Ninth in Five Days," Reuters, May 17, 2012, www.reuters.com/article/2012/05/17/us-lebanon-clashes-idUSBRE84G09N20120517.

13. Souad Mekhennet, "Bahrain's Shiite-Sunni Animosities Linger on Campus a Year After Clashes," *The New York Times*, March 28, 2012, www.nytimes.com/2012/03/29/world/middleeast/bahrains-shiite-sunni-animosities-linger-on-campus-a-year-after-clashes.html?pagewanted=all.

14. "Deobandi Islam," Global Security, www.global security.org/military/intro/islam-deobandi.htm.

15. Vali Nasr, *The Shia Revival* (2006), p. 168.

16. Bernard Lewis and Buntzie Ellis Churchill, *Islam: The Religion and the People* (2009), p. 61.

17. "Al-Azhar Verdict on the Shia," Al-Shia.org.

18. *Ibid.* For background, see Sarah Glazer, "Sharia Controversy," *CQ Global Researcher*, Jan. 3, 2012, pp. 1-28.

19. Lewis and Churchill, *op. cit.*, p. 65.

20. John L. Esposito, *What Everyone Needs to Know about Islam* (2011), p. 43. For background, see Kenneth Jost, "Understanding Islam," *CQ Researcher*, Nov. 3, 2006, pp. 913-936.

21. Febe Armanios, "Islam: Sunnis and Shiites," Congressional Research Service, Library of Congress, Feb. 23, 2004.

22. *Ibid.*

23. *Ibid.*

24. Lewis and Churchill, *op. cit.*, p. 62.

25. Armanios, *op. cit.* Also see Robert Mackey, "Syria's Ruling Alawite Sect," *The New York Times*, June 14, 2011, http://thelede.blogs.nytimes.com/2011/06/14/syrias-ruling-alawite-sect/.

26. "The Sword and the Word," *op. cit.*

27. "Safavid and Ottoman Eras," "History of the Middle East Database," www.nmhtthornton.com/mehistory database/safavid_and_ottoman_eras.php.

28. Lewis and Churchill, *op. cit.*

29. J. E. Peterson, "Introduction to the Middle East," *Political Handbook of the World* (2007), http://library.cqpress.com/phw/document.php?id=phw2008-1000-43952-2033610&type=query&num=J.E.+Peterson&.

30. "Syria's Role in the Middle East," "PBS Newshour," Sept. 14, 2006, www.pbs.org/newshour/indepth_coverage/middle_east/syria/history.html.

31. For background, see D. Teter, "Iran Between East and West," *Editorial Research Reports*, Jan. 26, 1979, available at *CQ Researcher Plus Archive.*

32. Peterson, *op. cit.*

33. Mike Shuster, "The Partisans of Ali," NPR, Feb. 14, 2007.

34. Peterson, *op. cit.*

35. Shuster, *op. cit.*

36. Michael Scott Moore, "Was Saddam's Execution a Message to Shiites?" *Der Spiegel International*, Jan. 3, 2007, www.spiegel.de/international/the-world-from-berlin-was-saddam-s-execution-a-message-to-shiites-a-457559.html.

37. "1982: Syria's President Hafez al-Assad crushes rebellion in Hama," "From the Archive blog," *The Guardian*, www.guardian.co.uk/theguardian/from-the-archive-blog/2011/aug/01/hama-syria-massacre-1982-archive.

38. *Ibid.*

39. Alistair Lawson, "Pakistan's Evolving Sectarian Schism," BBC, Oct. 4, 2011.

40. "Syria troops hit back at rebels in Damascus and Aleppo," BBC, July 23, 2012, www.bbc.co.uk/news/world-middle-east-18943316. Also see Stephanie Nebehay and Tom Miles, "Tens of thousands flee Syria as fighting surges," Reuters, July 20, 2012.

41. Stephanie Nebehay and Mariam Karouny, "Both Sides in Syria Abuse Human Rights," Reuters, May 25, 2012, www.reuters.com/article/2012/05/24/us-syria-idUSBRE84N0ZJ20120524.

42. Khaled Yacoub Oweis, "Rifts Widen in Syrian Opposition," Reuters, May 21, 2012, www.reuters.com/article/2012/05/21/us-syria-opposition-idUSBRE84K1A220120521.

43. Jack Healy, "Syrian Kurds Flee into Iraqi Refugee Limbo," *The New York Times*, March 8, 2012, www.nytimes.com/2012/03/09/world/middleeast/syrian-kurds-flee-into-iraqi-refugee-limbo.html?pagewanted=all.

44. Neil MacFarquhar, "Syrian Alawites Divided by Assad's Response to Unrest," *The New York Times*, June 9, 2012, www.nytimes.com/2012/06/10/world/middleeast/syrian-alawites-divided-by-assads-response-to-unrest.html?pagewanted=all.

45. Eric Schmitt, "C.I.A. Said to Aid in Steering Arms to Syrian Opposition," *The New York Times*, June 21, 2012, www.nytimes.com/2012/06/21/world/middleeast/cia-said-to-aid-in-steering-arms-to-syrian-rebels.html?pagewanted=all. Also see Mark Landler and Neil MacFarquhar, "Heavier Weapons Push Syrian Crisis Toward Civil War," *The New York*

Times, June 12, 2012, www.nytimes.com/2012/06/13/world/middleeast/violence-in-syria-continues-as-protesters-killed.html?pagewanted=all.

46. Mark Hosenball, "As Militants Join Syria Revolt, Fears Grow over Arms Flow," Reuters, June 22, 2012, www.reuters.com/article/2012/06/22/us-syria-armsrace-idUSBRE85L0MS20120622.

47. Schmitt, *op. cit.*

48. "Syria threatens to use chemical weapons against foreign powers — video," *The Guardian*, July 24, 2012, www.guardian.co.uk/world/video/2012/jul/24/syria-chemical-weapons-video?newsfeed=true.

49. "Syrians Defy Leaders to Aid Those in Need," *The New York Times*, May 14, 2012, www.nytimes.com/2012/05/15/world/middleeast/syria-aid-movement-defies-assad-government.html?pagewanted=all.

50. "Iraq sees deadliest month in two years," BBC News, Aug. 1, 2012, www.bbc.co.uk/news/world-middle-east-19076257.

51. Tim Arango and Yasir Ghazi, "Violence Spreads in the Struggle for Baghdad Shrine," *The New York Times*, June 4, 2012, www.nytimes.com/2012/06/05/world/middleeast/bombing-in-baghdad-linked-to-dispute-over-samarra-shrine.html.

52. "Report of the Bahrain Independent Commission of Inquiry," Bahrain Independent Commission of Inquiry, Nov. 23, 2011, www.bici.org.bh/BICIreportEN.pdf. See also "Bahraini authorities 'weaponising' tear gas," BBC, Aug. 1, 2012, www.bbc.co.uk/news/world-middle-east-19078659.

53. "U.S. Statement at the Universal Periodic Review of Bahrain," U.S. Mission to the U.N. (Geneva), May 21, 2012, http://geneva.usmission.gov/2012/05/21/bahrain/.

54. For background, see Jennifer Koons, "Future of the Gulf States," *CQ Global Researcher*, Nov. 1, 2011, pp. 525-548.

55. Chiara Onassis, "Yemen: The Sunni-Shia Divide, Sectarian Violence on the Rise," Bikyamasr.com, Feb. 27, 2012, http://bikyamasr.com/58961/yemen-the-sunni-shia-divide-sectarian-violence-on-the-rise/.

56. Mustafa Qadri, "Pakistan Is in Denial over Spreading Sectarian Violence," *Guardian*, April 19, 2012, www.guardian.co.uk/commentisfree/2012/apr/19/pakistan-sectarian-violence.

57. Esposito, *op. cit.*, p. 22.

58. "The Sword and the Word," *op. cit.*

BIBLIOGRAPHY

Selected Sources

Books

Commins, David, *The Wahhabi Mission and Saudi Arabia,* **Library of Modern Middle East Studies, 2009.**
A professor of history at Dickinson College examines the rise of Wahhabism, a controversial hardline Sunni sect prevalent in Saudi Arabia, Afghanistan, Pakistan and other parts of the Muslim world. Commins also evaluates the challenge that radical militants in Saudi Arabia present to the Middle East.

Gonzalez, Nathan, *The Sunni-Shia Conflict: Understanding Sectarian Violence in the Middle East,* **Nortia Press, 2009.**
A lecturer in Middle East studies and international politics at California State University says Muslim sectarian rivalries are based on geopolitics rather than theology and contends that power vacuums allow regional leaders to use sectarianism for their own ends.

Haddad, Fanar, *Sectarianism in Iraq: Antagonistic Visions of Unity,* **Hurst/Columbia University Press, 2011.**
A Middle East scholar and analyst examines the relationship between Iraq's Shiites and Sunnis as it evolves from coexistence to conflict. He focuses on the Shiite uprising in 1991 and the fall of Saddam Hussein's Baath Party in 2003.

Hazleton, Lesley, *After the Prophet: The Epic Story of the Shia-Sunni Split in Islam,* **Doubleday, 2009.**
A veteran journalist describes the epic origins of the sectarian split that began while the Prophet Muhammad lay dying.

Johnsen, Gregory, *The Last Refuge: Yemen, al-Qaeda and America's War in Arabia,* **W. W. Norton, 2012.**
A Yemen scholar at Princeton University charts the rise, fall and resurrection of Al Qaeda in Yemen over the last 30 years. Johnsen brings readers inside the Sunni terrorist group's training camps and safe houses and examines successes and failures in fighting a new type of war in one of the most turbulent countries in the world.

Nasr, Sayyed Hossein, *The Heart of Islam: Enduring Values for Humanity,* **Harper One, 2004.**
A professor of Islamic Studies at The George Washington University and one of Islam's most respected intellectuals writes about the religion's core values.

Weiss, Max, *In the Shadow of Sectarianism: Law, Shi'ism, and the Making of Modern Lebanon,* **Harvard University Press, 2010.**
An assistant professor of history and Near East studies at Princeton University examines the complicated roots of Shiite sectarianism in Lebanon, going back to the French mandate after World War I.

Articles

Blanford, Nicholas, "In Lebanon, a Worrying Sectarian Spillover from Syria," *The Christian Science Monitor,* **June 3, 2012, www.csmonitor.com/World/Middle-East/2012/0603/In-Lebanon-a-worrying-sectarian-spillover-from-Syria.**
Analysts worry that sectarian violence in Syria could reignite civil war in Lebanon.

Diehl, Jackson, "Lines in the Sand: Assad Plays the Sectarian Card," *Foreign Affairs,* **May/June 2012, www.worldaffairsjournal.org/article/lines-sand-assad-plays-sectarian-card.**
A *Washington Post* foreign affairs specialist offers an explanation of how Syria has become the focal point of sectarian and regional conflict.

Feldman, Noah, "Choosing a Sect," *The New York Times Magazine,* **March 4, 2007, www.cfr.org/religion-and-politics/choosing-sect/p12772.**
A Harvard law professor at the Council on Foreign Relations explores the debate about whether the United States should side with one Islamic sect.

Reports and Studies

Blanchard, Christopher, "Islam: Sunnis and Shiites," *Congressional Research Service,* **Jan. 28, 2009, www.fas.org/sgp/crs/misc/RS21745.pdf.**
This study presents a history of the original split and a description of the differences and similarities between both branches, and the relationship to sectarian violence.

Jha, Saurav, "Saudi-Iranian Tensions Widening into Sunni-Shiite Cold War," *World Politics Review,* **April 29, 2011.**
The crisis in Bahrain has deepened the Saudi-Iranian Cold War, exacerbating regional tensions.

Kuwait Study Group: "Identity, Citizenship and Sectarianism in the GCC," Chatham House, February 2012, www.chathamhouse.org/sites/default/files/public/Research/Middle%20East/0212kuwaitsummary_identity.pdf.
This workshop summary examines the evolving identity of the Gulf States, particularly the authoritarian, male-dominated ruling regimes, juxtaposed with traditions of inclusiveness and multiculturalism.

Shuster, Mike, "The Partisans of Ali," NPR, www.npr.org/series/7346199/the-partisans-of-ali.
This five-part radio documentary traces the religious and historical differences between Sunnis and Shiites, and the impact of sectarian conflict.

For More Information

Center for Arab Unity Studies, P.O. Box 113-6001, Hamra, Beirut, Lebanon; +961 1 750084; www.caus.org. Researches Arab society and Arab unity without any partisan or government ties.

Center for Islamic Pluralism, 202-232-1750; www.islamicpluralism.org. A think tank that opposes the radicalization of Islam in America.

Center for Religious Freedom, 1319 18th St., N.W., Washington, DC 20036; 202-296-5101; www.freedomhouse.org/religion. Defends against religious persecution of all groups throughout the world.

Center for the Study of Islam and Democracy, 1050 Connecticut Ave., N.W., Suite 1000, Washington, DC 20036; 202-772-2022; www.islam-democracy.org. Merges Islamic and democratic political thought into modern Islamic discourse.

Conflicts Forum, Beirut, Lebanon; +961 3 803028; www.conflictsforum.org. Aims to shift Western opinion towards a deeper understanding of Islam and the Middle East.

Doha Debates, Qatar Foundation, P.O. Box 5825, Doha, Qatar; www.thedohadebates.com; Fax: +974 4454 1759. An independent public forum that conducts televised debates on controversial topics, with participants from all over the Arab world.

Institute for Social Policy and Understanding, 1225 I St., N.W., Suite 307, Washington, DC 20005; 202-481-8215; www.ispu.org. Provides analysis, insight and context on critical issues, especially those related to Muslims.

School of Sufi Teaching, London, England and centers worldwide; +44 20 8556-7713; www.schoolofsufiteaching.org. Offers instruction in teachings of Sufism.

Search for Common Ground, 1601 Connecticut Ave., Suite 200, Washington, DC 20009; 202-265-4300; www.sfcg.org. Nonprofit that advocates conflict resolution.

Voices From Abroad:

RAMI KHOURI

Director, Issam Fares Institute for Public Policy Lebanon

The root causes

"When countries are well managed and citizens feel they have a say in political and economic developments, sectarian identities and tensions decrease and eventually disappear. But when authoritarian gangs and oligarchic ruling families plunder their countries and treat their citizens like idiots without rights or feelings, sectarianism sprouts like the natural self-defence mechanism that it is."

Globe and Mail (Canada), July 2011

India/*The National Herald/Paresh Nath*

SHEIKH YUSUF AL-QARADAWI

Islamic theologian, Egypt

Simply unacceptable

"Unfortunately, we have seen that in a big country, such as Iraq, another language, . . . the language of political sectarianism, is being used. This is a divisive sectarianism. The ummah, which was once united, is meant to be divided. . . . This is what Al-Maliki, those who are behind him, and his allies want to do. . . . This sectarianism is unacceptable."

Al Jazeera (Qatar), December 2011

MICHEL SULAYMAN

President, Lebanon

Liberating the youth

"It is critical in a diverse country such as Lebanon to draft laws that could liberate the youth from sectarianism, primarily the election law that is based on proportional representation and preserves the major characteristic of Lebanon's covenant of coexistence between the Lebanese."

The Daily Star (Lebanon), July 2011

SHEIKH KHALID BIN ALI AL KHALIFAH

Minister of Justice and Islamic Affairs, Bahrain

Things to consider

"There are societies that have turned political differences into issues of existence, and our priorities now are to implement consensus of the National Dialogue and make constitutional amendments in line with people's demands. . . . We can't stop preachers, because people will see it as targeting the whole congregation, and at the moment we are working with international organizations to train clergymen on the principles of giving speeches. There are some serious violations, and I agree with parliament that they have to be dealt with, but several factors have to be taken into consideration first."

Gulf Daily News (Bahrain), March 2012

ALHAJI MUHAMMAD SA'AD ABUBAKAR

Sultan of Sokoto state Nigeria

Stop blaming sects

"Most of the crises are not caused by the Boko Haram sect, so we have to ask ourselves, why is there violence in the northeast [of Nigeria]. Who are those behind them? The government must fish them out and tell us those responsible for the crises. This thing did not start today, stop blaming every violence on Boko Haram."

Daily Trust (Nigeria), July 2011

SHEIKH ANAS SUWAYD

Islamic cleric, Syria

Discrimination against Sunnis

"In Hims [Syria], there is sectarianism par excellence because the regime is discriminating against the Sunnis . . . in an unimaginable manner. Imagine that electricity is cut off for eight hours a day in all Sunni neighbourhoods in Hims, and the Sunni neighbourhoods are deprived of bread for days if people staged demonstrations, [but] bread would be passed secretly to them from other neighbourhoods."

Al Jazeera (Qatar), January 2012

WOLE SOYINKA

Author, Nigeria

Picking up the gauntlet

"The gauntlet of religious sectarianism has been thrown down. African leaders must pick it up, and lend succor to those who are plagued with this constriction of citizen choice."

The New Times (Rwanda), July 2012

WADAH KHANFAR

Former Director General Al Jazeera Network, Qatar

Preserving national character

"The Syrian popular consciousness has been able to protect the revolution from the virus of sectarianism and ethnicity by preserving its national character. . . . The Syrian street knows that the language of sectarianism will only serve the interests of the regime, and it will divert the revolution from the path of democracy."

The Guardian (England), February 2012

3

Small Arms Trade

John Felton

A youth carries an AK-47 assault rifle in Côte d'Ivoire, where civil conflict broke out following a disputed presidential election in late 2010. The proliferation of small, light, portable arms — such as the ubiquitous AK-47 — make it easier for paramilitary units, insurgents and government military units to recruit children, often forcibly, into service as soldiers. Imitations of the AK-47 — initially manufactured in the Soviet Union — now are produced in several dozen countries. No one knows exactly how many exist, but experts estimate at least 100 million.

From *The CQ Researcher*, June 19, 2012.

AFP/Getty Images/Georges Gobet

Since its independence in 1960, Mali has easily crushed periodic insurgencies by the semi-nomadic Tuaregs — known as the "blue men of the Sahara" for their brilliant blue robes — who want a separate state in their vast corner of Africa's western Sahara.

Then, in late March, armed with Kalashnikov assault rifles and other small weapons, several hundred Tuaregs easily overwhelmed lightly armed Malian security forces and seized control of several major towns — including the storied ancient city of Timbuktu. Within days the Tuaregs had declared an independent nation — Azawad — in a Texas-size portion of the country.[1]

Ironically, the most important factor in the Tuaregs' sudden success is linked to last year's civil war in Libya, where — in one of the most dramatic episodes of the so-called Arab Spring — rebels ousted and killed the mercurial dictator, Moammar Gadhafi.[2]

Gadhafi had recruited hundreds of Tuareg fighters from Mali — equipping them with Kalashnikovs, mortars, rocket-propelled grenades (RPGs) and other hand-held weapons. After the war ended in October 2011, the Tuaregs returned to northern Mali, many still armed to the teeth.

"The Libyan crisis shook up the order of things," a rebel spokesman told *The New York Times*. "A lot of our brothers have come back with weapons."[3]

Whether the rebels can hold onto Azawad remains an open question. But the spread of weapons from the upheaval in Libya has reverberated broadly across Africa and the Middle East. Looted Libyan arms reportedly have surfaced in Algeria, Egypt, Niger, Nigeria and Somalia. An Israeli military official said in April that

U.S. Is Top Small Arms Trader

Governments and private companies in a handful of countries — led by the United States — dominated the legal trade in small arms between 2001 and 2008, according to the most recent survey of authorized weapons trades. China, along with other developing countries, has begun manufacturing small arms, but it does not release information about its exports. Often arms are imported into one country and then shipped illegally to other destinations, where they end up fueling civil conflicts or arming terrorists, drug cartels and other violent groups.

Exporters of Small Arms, 2001-2008
(estimated annual average value of exports)

Category		Value ($US million)	Countries
Top Exporters	Tier 1	$500+	United States
	Tier 2	$100-$499	Austria, Belgium, Brazil, China, Germany, Italy, Russia
Major Exporters	Tier 3	$50-$99	Canada, Czech Republic, Finland, France, Israel, Japan, Norway, South Korea, Spain, Sweden, Switzerland, Turkey, United Kingdom
	Tier 4	$10-$49	Bulgaria, Croatia, India, Iran, Mexico, Netherlands, North Korea, Pakistan, Poland, Portugal, Romania, Saudi Arabia, Serbia, Singapore, Slovakia, South Africa, Taiwan, Ukraine

Importers of Small Arms, 2001-2008
(estimated annual average value of imports)

Category		Value ($US million)	Countries
Top Importers	Tier 1	$500+	United States
	Tier 2	$100-$499	Canada, France, Germany, Saudi Arabia, U.K.
Major Importers	Tier 3	$50-$99	Afghanistan, Australia, Belgium, Cyprus, Italy, Japan, Netherlands, Norway, South Korea, Spain
	Tier 4	$10-$49	Austria, Azerbaijan, Colombia, Denmark, Egypt, Finland, Greece, India, Iraq, Israel, Libya, Mexico, Pakistan, Poland, Portugal, Russia, Sweden, Switzerland, Thailand, Turkey, United Arab Emirates, Venezuela

Sources: "Small Arms Transfers: Importing States," Small Arms Survey, November 2011, p. 1, www. smallarmssurvey.org/fileadmin/docs/H-Research_Notes/SAS-Research-Note-12.pdf; "Small Arms Transfers: Exporting States," Small Arms Survey, October 2011, p. 1, www.smallarmssurvey.org/fileadmin/docs/H-Research_Notes/SAS-Research-Note-11.pdf

2011 book *The Shadow World: Inside the Global Arms Trade.* "In some cases it elevates small tussles into fully fledged wars, and it is no coincidence that some of the most egregious acts of violence have been preceded by massive inflows of weaponry.[5]

"The arms trade in Africa has militarized social conflict," he continued, "and, when that happens, mass deaths, poverty, widespread displacement and human rights violations are sure to follow."

Former U.N. Secretary General Kofi Annan in 1996 described small arms as "weapons of mass destruction" because "the death toll from small arms dwarfs that of all other weapons systems."[6]

Outside sources are providing small but powerful weapons, mostly the famed Kalashnikov assault rifle and its numerous imitators, to combatants in dozens of countries. Small arms are "the weapon of choice in much of the world" today because they are "relatively easy to get hold of, are cheap and relatively easy to use and are not controlled as well as they should be," says Roy Isbister, a small arms expert at Saferworld, a London-based arms control advocacy group.

They're also highly portable. In fact, their chief characteristic is that most can be carried and used by one person.

The very portability of small arms contributed to their role in the dozens of armed conflicts that broke out around the world in the decades after

two rockets fired into Israel from the Sinai Peninsula in Egypt had been smuggled from Libya.[4]

"The easy supply of weapons makes these conflicts exponentially more violent and deadly," wrote South African journalist Andrew Feinstein, author of the World War II. Some conflicts, notably in Africa and Southeast Asia, were direct consequences of the Cold War between the United States and the Soviet Union — and both superpowers supplied vast arsenals of assault rifles and other small arms to their favored governments or guerrilla groups. After the collapse of communism in the early 1990s, a new upsurge of conflicts over ethnic, tribal and national claims erupted in Eastern Europe and sub-Saharan African. Many of these conflicts were fought primarily with Kalashnikovs and other weapons from former Soviet arsenals.

The Small Arms Survey, an independent research group in Geneva, Switzerland, estimates that there are nearly 900 million pistols, rifles, mortars, grenades and other small arms and light weapons available throughout the world today. (*See definitions, p. 58.*) Undoubtedly, there are more weapons in the world than ever before, but the lack of comprehensive record-keeping in the past makes accurate historical comparisons impossible.

"The demand for weapons in the world remains very high," says Paul Holtom, a senior researcher at the Stockholm International Peace Research Institute. "There clearly is a sense of insecurity in the world, and insecure people tend to want to be armed."

Civilians, which can include rebel groups, gangs and criminal enterprises, own about three-fourths of the world's small arms; the rest are held by armies, police and security forces. Nearly 300 million of the privately owned weapons are in the United States, the world's largest producer, exporter and importer of armaments of all kinds.[7]

Most small arms trade is legal — such as sales of sporting arms to hunters — and does not concern law enforcement officials or human rights groups, say Nicholas Marsh, a researcher at the Norwegian Initiative on Small Arms Transfers, and others. But millions of small arms and a large but unknown percentage of the world's military-style firearms and weapons end up in the hands of terrorists, drug smugglers and leaders of guerrilla groups of all kinds.

"It's just a few steps from an arms transfer being legal to becoming illegal, and thus a source of concern," notes Eric Berman, managing director of the Small Arms Survey.

Gun Ownership vs. Violence: Is There a Link?

Except for Iraq, countries with the world's highest gun-ownership rates generally do not have the highest rates of violent death. Of the 15 countries with the highest rates of violent deaths, seven are in Latin America and the Caribbean and six are in Africa. The United States, with the world's highest gun-ownership rate, is not among the world's 50 most violent countries.

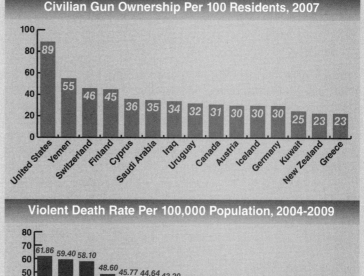

Civilian Gun Ownership Per 100 Residents, 2007

United States	89
Yemen	55
Switzerland	46
Finland	45
Cyprus	36
Saudi Arabia	35
Iraq	34
Uruguay	32
Canada	31
Austria	30
Iceland	30
Germany	30
Kuwait	25
New Zealand	23
Greece	23

Violent Death Rate Per 100,000 Population, 2004-2009

El Salvador	61.86
Iraq	59.40
Jamaica	58.10
Honduras	48.60
Colombia	45.77
Venezuela	44.64
Guatemala	43.20
South Africa	38.39
Sri Lanka	37.09
Lesotho	33.67
Central African Republic	32.95
Sudan	32.30
Belize	31.34
Dem. Republic of the Congo	31.29
Swaziland	26.47

Sources: "Armed Violence: Spotlight on Lethal Effects," Small Arms Survey, May 2012, p. 2, www.smallarmssurvey.org/fileadmin/docs/H-Research_Notes /SAS-Research-Note-17.pdf; "Small Arms Survey 2011," Small Arms Survey, 2011, p. 2, www.smallarmssurvey.org/fileadmin/docs/ H-Research_Notes/SAS-Research-Note-9.pdf

'Lords of War' Days Are Over for Arms Dealers

Dictators now are turning to China, other sources for weapons.

Most arms merchants operate legally, experts say. And then there are unscrupulous dealers, such as the notorious Russian gun-runner Viktor Bout.

In the late 1990s U.S. and other government officials began watching the young businessman, who seemed able to transfer gigantic quantities of weapons into the hands of rebel forces and governments in remote places, especially in Africa. Using front companies around the world and a large fleet of old cargo planes, Bout delivered weapons from former Soviet stockpiles to conflict zones in central and West Africa.

Many went to the warring parties in eastern Democratic Republic of the Congo (DRC)[1] or to any government that would pay well, including the Taliban in Afghanistan and the infamous regime of former Liberian leader Charles Taylor — recently convicted as a war criminal.[2]

Although the Clinton administration in 2000 placed Bout on its international "most wanted" list, just three years later the U.S. Department of Defense was chartering his airplanes to transport weapons and other supplies into Iraq after the U.S. invasion.[3]

Bout is now serving 25 years in a U.S. federal prison after being convicted in November 2011 for conspiring to kill American citizens, officers and employees, growing out of his agreement to sell antiaircraft missiles and other weapons to individuals he thought were members of the Revolutionary Armed Forces of Colombia, a guerrilla army known as FARC. The men were actually U.S. government informants.[4]

While Bout ranks among the most successful and prolific illegal arms dealers in recent decades, he also may have been one of the last to make repeated deliveries of large quantities of weapons, several experts say. "The image of the 'Lord of War' is a bit out of date now," says Nicholas Marsh, a researcher at the Norwegian Initiative on Small Arms Transfers. "If you are an African dictator, you are probably getting your arms from Beijing, not from some arms dealer."

Matthew Schroeder, a small-arms expert at the Federation of American Scientists, in Washington, D.C., agrees. Arms trafficking and diversion will always occur, he says, but "the Wild West days are over, hopefully."

Experts say several developments are curtailing shady arms merchants' ability to operate under the radar, including tougher U.N. monitoring of arms embargoes and increased international regulation of arms brokering.

"A lot of the Eastern European countries that used to be major sources of illicit weapons have cleaned up their acts," Marsh says. That's because when those countries apply to join the European Union (EU), they must start regulating their arms trade. "Places like Bulgaria and Romania were told, 'If you are going to join the European Union, you have to set up export controls.' " Moreover, he continues, "the benefits of joining the EU were enormously larger than what they were earning from selling Kalashnikovs and rocket-propelled grenades under the table."

Russia also is better controlling its arsenals, Marsh adds. "It's no longer true that you can drive up to a Russian military base, bribe the commander and drive off with a load of weapons."

"We have international laws regulating the sale of iPods and bananas, but no treaty regulating the transfer of weapons being used to kill people the world over," argues Bishop Elias Taban, the president of the Sudan Evangelical Alliance. "As a result, states are left to self-regulate, creating a patchwork of laws and loopholes that can be exploited by arms smugglers. (*See "At Issue," p. 69.*)

In fact, since 1996 more than a dozen international agreements to regulate weapons trading have been adopted by the U.N. and regional and multilateral organizations. But none of them is universal, legally binding and comprehensive. (*See box, p. 64.*)

Experts say having a large number of guns in a country does not necessarily make it an especially violent place, nor does a lack of guns guarantee tranquility. For instance, the United States, Switzerland and Finland are among the world's top gun-owning nations (89 guns per 100 people in the United States, 46 in Switzerland

Nevertheless, illegal private arms deliveries continue to surface. In December 2009 Thai authorities intercepted a 35-ton shipment of weapons, including RPGs and surface-to-air-missiles, from North Korea reportedly headed for Iran. Listed as "oilfield equipment," the shipment was being handled by a New Zealand shell company, SP Trading. The plane carrying the weapons reportedly was flown by a crew working for Alexander Zykov, a weapons dealer in Kazakhstan.[5]

Today, arms experts are more concerned about the proliferation of arms manufacturing, including by developing countries.

"The number of suppliers was much more limited in the past, but now there is a desire by a number of states to produce military equipment and even civilian firearms and ammunition themselves," says Paul Holtom, a senior researcher at the Stockholm International Peace Research Institute.

"Some of those states will not have the types of export controls you might want them to have," he adds, "so there could be problems in the future."

— John Felton

Russian arms dealer Viktor Bout, shown here in Bangkok in 2010, is serving 25 years in a U.S. federal prison after being convicted in November 2011 for conspiring to kill U.S. citizens, officers and employees. Bout had agreed to sell antiaircraft missiles and other weapons to U.S. government informants posing as Columbian rebels.

[1] For background, see Josh Kron," Conflict in Congo," *CQ Global Researcher*, April 5, 2011, pp. 157-182.

[2] Douglas Farah and Stephen Braun, *Merchant of Death* (2007), pp. 8-10.

[3] *Ibid.*, p. 225.

[4] Noah Rosenberg, "Russian Weapons Trafficker Avoids Getting Life in Prison," *The New York Times*, April 5, 2012, www.nytimes.com/2012/04/06/nyregion/russian-arms-dealer-is-sentenced-to-25-years.html?_r=1&ref=viktorbout.

[5] "Govt acts on arms smuggling controversy," *The National Business Review*, New Zealand, Jan. 8, 2010, www.nbr.co.nz/article/govt-acts-arms-smuggling-controversy-117048. Also see "Inside the shell: drugs, arms and tax scams," *The Sydney Morning Herald*, May 15, 2011, www.smh.com.au/national/inside-the-shell-drugs-arms-and-tax-scams-20110514-1enkz.html; and Simon Shuster, "Shadowy arms deal tracked to Kazakhstan," The Associated Press, Jan. 20, 2010, www.utsandiego.com/news/2010/jan/20/ap-impact-shadowy-arms-deal-traced-to-kazakhstan/.

and 45 in Finland).[8] But all three countries have lower homicide rates than Haiti, where there is only one gun per 100 residents.[9]

Peter Danssaert, an arms researcher at the International Peace Information Service in Antwerp, Belgium, says "socio-economic inequality, socio-psychological circumstances and the presence of a culture of violence" are more important than the number of guns in determining the level of violence in a country.

According to the international peace advocacy agency known as the Geneva Declaration, more than 526,000 people each year are killed by guns or other weapons, but only about 10 percent are the result of warfare or civil conflict. The rest occur in personal disputes, during the commission of crimes or as the result of actions by law enforcement or state security agencies.[10]

In the past, a handful of developed countries — the United States, Russia, Italy, Germany and a few other

What Are 'Small Arms'?

There is no single, universally accepted definition of the term "small arms." The United Nations, Western nations and many nongovernmental organizations often use the term "small arms and light weapons" to describe a broader category that includes military-style weapons such as automatic rifles, rocket-propelled grenades and portable antiaircraft missiles.

The so-called International Tracing Instrument, a U.N. agreement adopted in 2005, defines small arms as weapons designed for individual use, including:

- revolvers and self-loading pistols
- rifles and carbines
- submachine guns
- assault rifles and
- light machine guns.

Light weapons are defined as those designed for use by two or three persons, although some may be carried and used by a single person. They include:

- heavy machine guns
- hand-held and mounted grenade launchers
- portable antiaircraft guns
- portable anti-tank guns
- recoilless rifles
- portable anti-tank missile and rocket launchers
- portable antiaircraft missile launchers and
- small mortars (with a caliber of less than 100 millimeters).

Source: "International Instrument to Enable States to Identify and Trace, in a Timely and Reliable Manner, Illicit Small Arms and Light Weapons," "Section II: Definitions," www.poa-iss.org/InternationalTracing/ITI_English.pdf

European nations — consistently produced and sold the vast majority of the world's small arms. (*See chart, p. 54.*) But that has been changing recently, according to some observers, as China has become a major weapons manufacturer and exporter. And just as Washington and Moscow used arms sales to achieve political or commercial goals, especially during the Cold War, Beijing often sells weapons as part of broader deals to secure oil, minerals and other resources, experts say.

"The Chinese are making large deals for resource extraction in the developing world, and arms are definitely a component of that," says Marsh. In some cases, China is charging below-market rates or "even giving weapons

away" as a sweetener for long-term commercial contracts in Africa, Asia and Latin America, Marsh says.

Moreover, some developing countries are producing their own weapons and ammunition. Notably, Venezuela is scheduled to begin manufacturing a recent generation (AK-103) of the Kalashnikov under an official license from Russia.[11]

Much of the small arms trade has been covert. During the Cold War, for example, U.S. and Soviet intelligence agencies quietly shipped tons of weapons to favored countries or insurgent groups. And private dealers thrived on the secrecy, often playing a major role in supplying weapons — sometimes even selling to both sides of a conflict. These dealers create multiple commercial entities to disguise their activities, violating national and international laws, including U.N. arms embargoes.

The devastating impact of the easy availability of weapons in civil conflicts after the Soviet Union collapsed in 1991 — coupled with the murkiness of the arms trade — have led to numerous international efforts to reduce the global flow of weapons, or at least make the trade more transparent. In 2001 the United Nations adopted a voluntary agreement — called the Program of Action — to combat illicit small arms sales. Groups of African and Latin American countries have taken similar steps, with limited results.

Two major U.N. conferences this summer will focus on the global weapons trade. In July, member nations will try to negotiate an Arms Trade Treaty, which could impose legally binding standards on trade in all types of non-nuclear weapons — from small arms to tanks and aircraft. (*See "At Issue," p. 69.*) And in August, a U.N. conference will review progress under the Program of Action.

Some developing countries want to strengthen the Program of Action, but that's not likely, says Isbister. "There is no appetite for that, and nobody is placing it on the agenda," he said, in part because diplomats are focusing more attention on the trade treaty.

As the United Nations, government officials and nongovernmental organizations grapple with the growth in the small arms trade, here are some of the questions being asked:

Can the U.N. curb the illicit trade in small arms?

Since 1990, the U.N. Security Council — which can ban the sale of weapons to a specific country or group or impose legally binding standards on the global arms trade — has imposed 21 mandatory arms embargoes, of varying complexity, against governments or groups.[12]

About half of those embargoes remain in effect, according to the Stockholm International Peace Research Institute. The longest-running embargo, in effect since 1992, prohibits arms exports to Somalia.

The U.N. General Assembly also has adopted three major agreements intended to control specific aspects of the weapons trade, including small arms. Two were adopted in 2001: the Program of Action called on governments to voluntarily curb illegal arms sales, and the Firearms Protocol asked countries to criminalize the illicit manufacture and trade of weapons, including small arms. In 2005 the General Assembly approved the International Tracing Instrument, which encourages countries to adopt universal standards for marking small arms and light weapons and to keep accurate records of arms transfers.

It is still unclear how these measures would be affected if the proposed Arms Trade Treaty is adopted in July. Major details of the treaty have not been ironed out, and a handful of countries could block adoption of any treaty or force major amendments, depending on what types of weapons are included and what voting procedures are adopted.

Regardless of what happens in New York, the U.N.'s experience in trying to enforce Security Council arms embargoes demonstrates the difficulty of imposing

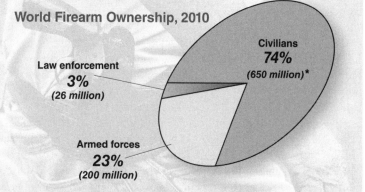

Civilians Own Most Firearms

Of the nearly 900 million firearms — handguns, rifles, shotguns and machine guns — worldwide in 2010, about three-quarters were owned by civilians.*

World Firearm Ownership, 2010

Civilians
74%
(650 million)*

Law enforcement
3%
(26 million)

Armed forces
23%
(200 million)

* Civilians can include private-security employees and members of gangs or "non-state armed groups," such as rebels or insurgents.

Source: "Small Arms Survey 2011," Small Arms Survey, 2011, p. 1, www.smallarmssurvey.org/ fileadmin/docs/H-Research_Notes/SAS-Research-Note-9.pdf

global standards, even in cases of egregious human rights violations, says Holtom at the Stockholm Institute. "None of the embargoes has been anywhere near 100 percent effective," he says. "The best you can say is that most of them put obstacles in the paths of the embargoed actors."

For example, Holtom cites a 2007 study by his colleague Pieter D. Wezeman, which examined the impact of two arms embargoes intended to reduce violence in Sudan's Darfur region.[13] The U.N. embargoes "appear to have had no measurable effect on the actual flow of weapons to the region," Wezeman concluded.[14]

Another major conflict in Africa highlighted the Security Council's slowness in even addressing the obvious problem of massive arms shipments into a volatile region. Starting in 1998, Rwanda, Uganda and other countries in the Great Lakes region of Africa invaded the Democratic Republic of the Congo (DRC), in part to protect or attack various ethnic groups in the eastern part of the country but also to loot Congo's vast natural resources.[15] Despite the international dimensions of the conflict and the resulting deaths of up to 5 million people, the Security Council failed to impose arms embargoes against the participants until 2003 — after the worst of the fighting was over and key actors had signed a peace agreement. In late 2002 and early 2003, for example, Rwanda imported 400 tons of ammunition from Albania, according to a report by the Stockholm Institute. "Vast deliveries of this kind have coincided with Rwandan military support to the Congolese rebel groups," the report said.[16]

The U.N.'s first embargo in the region, adopted in July 2003, prohibited arms shipments to insurgents and militias in eastern Congo, but not to any of the neighboring countries that were arming them.[17] And just before the embargo took effect, outside powers sent "a noticeable upsurge" of supplies to armed groups in Congo, according to a subsequent U.N. investigation.[18]

The Security Council tightened the embargo in April 2005, expanding sanctions to "any recipient" in Congolese territory — but, again, Rwanda, Uganda and other regional governments were exempted. "As a result, their forces are able to buy arms on the international market without limitation — using [profits from] minerals extracted in the DRC. The arms can then be easily smuggled back into the DRC, where effective policing is non-existent," South African author Feinstein wrote.[19]

The Security Council also has never imposed arms embargoes against narco-traffickers or criminal gangs — the chief sources of armed violence in many countries, particularly in Latin America. Because most of that violence is considered a domestic matter, it is outside the reach of the Security Council, even though drug violence spills across international borders.

The success of the three broad U.N. arms agreements is mixed, according to several experts. On one hand, the act of adopting the agreements, especially the Program of Action on illicit arms transfers, demonstrated international concern about the impact of international arms sales. In addition, dozens of countries have since written new laws and regulations designed to prevent illicit exports or imports of weapons.

"If you look at the Program of Action, it is legitimate to ask how effective it has been after a decade," says Berman, of the Small Arms Survey. "Has it stopped the illicit trade in small arms and light weapons? Absolutely not. But it has encouraged countries to do a better job of controlling arms sales, so I think it's fair to say the world is a better place because we have it."

Edward J. Laurance, a former U.N. consultant who helped to develop the Program of Action and now teaches international studies at the Monterey Institute of International Studies in California, says it was "watered down" so much during the 2001 negotiations that governments can claim they are abiding by it even though they are doing nothing.

"The language as it stands has not resulted in much progress," he says. "The problem is that nobody knows much about what governments have done."

Does the presence of small arms cause conflicts?

Most experts who study the small arms issue argue that the easy availability and growing proliferation of Kalashnikovs and similar military-style weapons can exacerbate a potentially violent situation.

"Having access to these types of weapons enhances the likelihood of a conflict escalating," says arms analyst Danssaert of the International Peace Information Service.

However, gun-rights supporters insist that the presence of guns neither guarantees nor promotes violence. In fact, many gun-rights advocates say weapons reduce violence by intimidating potential attackers.

Tom Mason, executive secretary of the Rome-based World Forum on the Future of Sport Shooting Activities, contends it is more important to consider the types of weapons present in a potentially violent situation than the mere presence of weapons.

"The problem that needs to be addressed vis-à-vis small arms is the hundreds of thousands of military arms dumped on some African country, and it is always fully automatic arms, usually the ubiquitous AK-47. That is the problem the U.N. should be focusing on, not civilian firearms."

Marsh, of the Norwegian Initiative on Small Arms Transfers, agrees that "there is no direct relationship between small arms and light weapons and their use in conflict." Fighters need weapons to sustain a conflict, and the types of weapons they use might determine how violent the conflict will be and who will prevail. But simply having weapons does not itself guarantee that individuals or groups will engage in violence or conflict, he says.

James Bevan, a British expert who has monitored arms embargoes for the United Nations and has witnessed first-hand several of the worst civil conflicts in Africa, says the key question is whether the government is willing or able to provide proper security for its people.

"If you look at the individual conflicts, very often the state in question is not an effective security provider or could itself be the source of insecurity," he says. "So, if you are a community under threat from an organization or a state with a violent agenda, you are going to look for weapons to protect yourself. The weapons are not the source of the insecurity in these cases, they are a symptom of it."

He also cautions that taking guns away from people — for example, as part of the disarmament programs often included in peace agreements — does not always guarantee peace.[20] For example, he says, the Ugandan government's forced disarmament of the Karimojong people in northern Uganda during the 1970s led to increased violence in the area.

"If you have ineffective police or security forces, [and] the government says, 'We are going to disarm you,' people are going to resist," he says. "From their perspective, they would be better off armed, otherwise they fear they will be overrun. So, you can't just go into the middle of a conflict and take weapons piecemeal out of the equation, because there will be consequences."[21]

Another problem occurs when wars end without appropriate arrangements for employing the combatants in civil society, says Aaron Karp, a former researcher at the Small Arms Survey who now teaches at Old Dominion University in Virginia. "In many cases, the worst thing that can happen in a country is that the war ends, because the killing goes up, not down," he says. "And that's because you have all these guys who have done nothing, often for years, other than carry a gun around.

"There are strategies to deal with that," he continues, "but if you don't do it right, the results can be pretty awful. That is the whole experience we have seen in Central Africa and Central America in recent years."

Does China arm dictators and other unsavory regimes?

Some experts say China has become one of the world's most important exporters of small arms to the developing world — including to despots who use them to hold onto power. However, China publishes very little information about its arms production and exports — particularly if the shipments are going to controversial

recipients and conflict zones — making it difficult to prove the allegation.

The Chinese government has repeatedly denied exporting arms to conflict zones. In a statement to the United Nations in July 2011, China said that it "has always adopted a prudent and responsible attitude in its arms export and exercises stringent control over arms exports in accordance with national laws and regulations, United Nations Security Council resolutions and relevant international obligations."[22]

Moreover, the statement continued, China's arms export policy strictly observes the following three principles:

- Arms exports should be conducive to the legitimate self-defense capability of the recipient country;
- Exports should not undermine the peace, security and stability of the region concerned and the world as a whole; and
- They should not be used as a means of interfering in the internal affairs of the recipient country.

Analyst Richard Grimmett at the Congressional Research Service estimates that China annually sold more than $1.9 billion worth of arms to developing countries between 2007 and 2010. Although the shipments included small arms as well as major weapons systems, such as missiles and airplanes, Grimmett concluded, "China's likely client base will be states in Asia and Africa seeking quantities of small arms and light weapons, rather than major combat systems."[23]

A U.N. expert panel monitoring a Security Council embargo against arms shipments to Sudan's conflict-ravaged Darfur region said in a 2011 report that China had sent numerous ammunition shipments to Sudan in recent years, despite the embargo. The Chinese government insisted that it had obtained assurances from Khartoum that the ammunition would not be used in Darfur. In carefully worded diplomatic language, however, the U.N. panel said it considered "reliance on Government of the Sudan statements as problematic in the light of past and present findings suggesting violations of end-user undertakings by the Government of the Sudan."[24]

The International Criminal Court in 2009 indicted Sudanese President Omar Hassan al-Bashir for war crimes and crimes against humanity in connection with

CHRONOLOGY

1940s–1980s *During decolonization after World War II, most former European colonies in Africa and Southeast Asia gain independence, but a handful engage in wars of independence, primarily with small arms. During the Cold War, the United States and Soviet Union provide small arms for various civil conflicts in developing countries.*

1947 Soviet military develops a new automatic rifle, the Avtomat Kalashnikova, the AK-47, named after the army sergeant credited with designing it. After entering production in 1949, the AK-47 becomes the world's most popular assault rifle.

1989 Rebel group led by Charles Taylor attacks Liberia, sparking 14 years of civil war that trigger related conflicts in neighboring Côte d'Ivoire and Sierra Leone.

1990s *Collapse of the Soviet Union leads to conflicts in the former Yugoslavia. . . . International community takes tentative steps to regulate arms trade.*

1990 U.N. Security Council imposes its first arms embargo, against Iraq, because of its invasion of Kuwait.

1992 Security Council imposes arms embargoes on Liberia and Somalia.

1996 U.N. adopts Wassenaar Arrangement, designed to strengthen international controls on weapons exports ranging from warships to small arms. Eventually 41 countries adopt the voluntary, nonbinding agreement.

1997 Rebels backed by Rwanda and Uganda invade Zaire and topple the government of dictator Mobuto Sese Seko, setting off a massive regional conflict. . . . Nobel laureates propose International Code of Conduct on Arms Transfers. . . . Organization of American States calls for stronger export controls on arms, ammunition and explosives; Canada, the United States and three other countries refuse to ratify the treaty.

1999 U.N.'s Group of Governmental Experts on Small Arms calls on countries to control international small arms trade.

2000s–Present *Civil conflicts continue in some parts of the world (notably Africa) but gradually diminish in others. . . . The U.N. develops several agreements intended to curtail illicit trafficking in small arms and light weapons.*

2001 U.N. adopts nonbinding Program of Action, designed to eradicate illicit trade in small arms.

2003 Amnesty International and Oxfam form the Control Arms Campaign to press for U.N. adoption of a legally binding treaty to regulate international trade in small and large arms.

2005 U.N. adopts the International Tracing Instrument calling on countries to require markings that can be used to track small arms as they are traded.

2006 General Assembly votes to begin crafting a legally binding arms trade treaty.

2008 U.N. Group of Experts calls for legally binding treaty governing the arms trade.

2009 General Assembly adopts resolution calling for negotiation in 2012 of a legally binding Arms Trade Treaty that would establish "common international standards for the transfer of conventional arms."

2011 U.S. federal court convicts notorious Russian arms dealer Viktor Bout of conspiring to kill American citizens by agreeing to sell antiaircraft missiles and other weapons to U.S. government informants he thought were members of the Revolutionary Armed Forces of Colombia, a guerrilla army known as FARC. He is later sentenced to 25 years in prison.

2012 International tribunal convicts former Liberian President Taylor of 11 war crimes related to his support of Sierra Leone rebels, including supplying them with weapons. . . . U.N. diplomats on July 2 will begin crafting proposed Arms Trade Treaty, a major binding treaty imposing new standards for international arms sales — possibly covering small arms.

rampages that have occurred in Darfur since 2003, in which hundreds of thousands of people have been killed and more than 2 million forced to flee their homes.[25]

China's arms sales to Sudan have fueled suggestions that Beijing uses the arms trade to help it gain access to minerals, oil and other natural resources needed for its

Progress in Regulating Arms Trade Is Slow

Enforcement is not a high priority for border agents.

When the U.N. General Assembly adopted the Program of Action in 2001 to combat the illicit arms trade, it included provisions encouraging wealthier countries to provide training, technology and equipment to countries needing assistance controlling the arms trade.

For example, the United States donated machinery to several African countries that enables them to mark — and thus trace — all firearms. And several dozen countries have adopted regulations governing small arms trading, says Sarah Parker, a senior researcher at the Small Arms Survey, a Geneva-based research group that monitors the arms trade.

However, she says, "It's difficult to know the extent to which these laws and procedures are actually being enforced."

Paul Holtom, a senoir researcher at the Stockholm International Peace Research Institute, says enforcement is lagging because border patrol agents in most countries "are more likely to be focused on trafficking in drugs or people or weapons of mass destruction. You will hear them say, 'We'll find weapons when we are looking for drugs or other things.'"

Plus, Parker says, all program participants are supposed to report biennially to the U.N. on their progress implementing the regulations, but about 40 countries have never filed a report. Many others have filed only a few or didn't provide enough detailed information.[1]

To improve compliance, the U.N. has developed International Small Arms Control Standards, which will be introduced at a U.N. conference in August on the status of the Program of Action. The standards, along with an easy-to-use software program, could transform the Program of Action "from being words on paper to a real set of international standards" that will help governments track their own progress and donors "see where their money is going," says Edward J. Laurance, a professor at California's Monterey Institute of International Studies.

Moreover, said representatives from more than two dozen countries at a March meeting at the U.N., the governments need equipment and training in such things as reporting and legislative drafting, intelligence gathering and prosecutorial and investigative techniques. For their part, officials from developed countries expressed frustration that the aid requests often are vague or duplicative.

"At times, when states have made numerous requests to multiple donor states for a wide range of needs, it has been difficult to prioritize those proposed projects and to ascertain whether they are already being addressed or considered by other donors," says Steven R. Costner, deputy director of the Office of Weapons Removal and Abatement at the U.S. State Department.

— John Felton

---

[1]Sarah Parker, "The PoA: Review of National Reports," Small Arms Survey, March 2012, www.smallarmssurvey.org/fileadmin/docs/H-Research_Notes/SAS-Research-Note-10.pdf.

---

rapid economic development. China is by far the biggest customer for Sudan's oil, followed by India and Malaysia. Khartoum must now share its oil wealth with the newly independent nation of South Sudan because the oilfields are located along the border between the two countries.[26]

"Since 2003, roughly 70 percent of all small arms purchased by Sudan have been supplied by the Chinese, in addition to the less glamorous vehicles of war such as 212 military trucks purchased in 2005," arms expert Feinstein wrote.[27] The advocacy group Human Rights First says most of northern Sudan's oil exports have been used to purchase arms.[28]

Analyst Marsh is convinced that China often discounts its weapons, or even provides them for free, as incentives for broader economic deals. "It's impossible to get accurate numbers, but one can assume they [the Chinese] often just give the guns away because they are not worth a huge amount. And if they have a huge resource extraction deal with Sudan, it's like the marketing department giving away T-shirts. They are worth a tiny proportion of the overall deal."

A report by the Stockholm Institute said some of China's arms sales to countries such as Sudan "may be better explained by a desire to strengthen or maintain long-standing military ties than by access to resources."[29]

International Agreements Regulate Some Small Arms

None are both comprehensive and legally binding.

Since 1996, more than a dozen U.N., regional and multilateral agreements have been adopted in an effort to curtail illicit trafficking in small arms and light weapons. But most are voluntary or apply only to certain regions or aspects of the trade. The international Arms Trade Treaty, being negotiated this summer at the United Nations, is proposed as a universal, comprehensive and legally binding treating covering all countries and, potentially, covering all weapons.

United Nations Agreements and Treaties

- **Wassenaar Arrangement on Export Controls for Conventional Arms and Dual-Use Goods and Technologies** —This 1996 voluntary agreement was designed to strengthen international controls on the exports of all conventional weapons, from warships to small arms. The 41 countries that participate in the program pledge to ensure their arms exports do not "undermine international and regional security and stability and are not diverted to support such capabilities."

- **Program of Action to Prevent, Combat, and Eradicate the Illicit Trade in Small Arms and Light Weapons in All its Aspects** — Adopted in July 2001, this nonbinding agreement — known as the Program of Action — asked U.N. member nations to take all necessary (but unspecified) steps to prevent, combat and eradicate the illegal small arms trade. Participants agreed to submit regular, voluntary reports on progress under the agreement, but dozens have failed to do so. A conference to review implementation is scheduled for August.

- **Protocol Against the Illicit Manufacturing of and Trafficking in Firearms, Their Parts and Components and Ammunition, Supplementing the United Nations Convention against Transnational Organized Crime** — Known as the Firearms Protocol, this 2001 agreement calls on member states to criminalize the illicit manufacture and trade of weapons, including handguns, submachine guns and light missiles. Although it took effect in July 2005, only 90 countries, not including the United States, have signed it and 52 have ratified it.[1]

- **International Instrument to Enable States to Identify and Trace, in a Timely and Reliable Manner, Illicit Small Arms and Light Weapons (International Tracing Instrument)** — Adopted in December 2005, this companion agreement to the U.N. Program of Action encourages — but does not require — countries to adopt universal standards for recording arms transfers and marking small arms during the manufacturing process. It does not apply to ammunition.

Regional Agreements

- **Protocol on the Control of Firearms, Ammunition and Other Related Materials in the Southern African Development Community (SADC) Region** — By signing this binding treaty in August 2001 (effective in 2004), the 15 members of the Southern African Development Community agreed to adopt laws regulating arms brokering. So far, however, most have yet to introduce such laws.

The British advocacy group Saferworld says its own study of China's dealings with conflict-affected countries indicates that "there is no overarching Chinese policy" to trade arms for resources. China has many centers of political and commercial power, the group said, each of which may have its own agenda.[30]

The report noted that China joined Russia in vetoing a proposed 2008 U.N. arms embargo against Zimbabwe, a country with which Beijing has close and long-established relations. South Africa in 2008 blocked a Chinese shipment of 3 million rounds of small arms ammunition plus rocket-propelled grenades and mortars

- **The Nairobi Protocol for the Prevention, Control and Reduction of Small Arms and Light Weapons in the Great Lakes Region and the Horn of Africa** — Signed in April 2004, this legally binding agreement, effective in 2006, requires 12 countries in the Great Lake and Horn of Africa regions to control the "illicit" trade in small arms and light weapons as well as the trade in weapons owned by governments or civilians.

- **Convention on Small Arms and Light Weapons, Their Ammunition and Other Related Materials** —This binding treaty signed in June 2006 by eight members of the Economic Community of West African States (effective in 2009) bans the transfer of small arms and light weapons (and related materials) across the borders of member states, except with specific exemptions.

- **Central African Convention for the Control of Small Arms and Light Weapons, Their Ammunition and All Parts and Components That Can Be Used for Their Manufacture, Repair and Assembly** — Adopted in 2010 by the 11 members of the U.N. Standing Advisory Committee on Security Questions in Central Africa, this binding treaty has yet to be ratified by any of the members. It would establish requirements for cross-border transfers of small arms and light weapons; bar possession of light weapons by individuals and require permits for the possession of small arms.

- **Inter-American Convention Against the Illicit Manufacturing of and Trafficking in Firearms, Ammunition, Explosives and Other Related Materials** — Signed in 1997, this was the first binding international treaty governing commercial trading in small arms and light weapons. The convention would establish basic controls over the manufacture and trade in firearms, ammunition and explosives, but it does not apply to government sales or exports. However, of the 34 Organization of American States members that signed it, only 29 have ratified it.

Holdouts are Canada, Jamaica, St. Vincent and the Grenadines and the United States.

- **European Union Common Position Defining Common Rules Governing Control of Exports of Military Technology and Equipment** — Adopted by the European Council in December 2008, the legally binding "Common Position" replaced an earlier voluntary Code of Conduct on Arms Exports, which had suggested criteria for governments to use in considering applications for weapons export licenses, including for small arms. It established eight specific criteria for EU countries to consider when approving weapons exports, such as arms embargoes, respect for human rights and the behavior of the country buying the weapons. Some EU countries — including the three largest European arms exporters: Germany, France and the U.K. — have failed to submit some of the required annual reports.

- **European Union Common Position on the Control of Arms Brokering** —This 2003 law requires EU member countries to regulate arms brokering.

- **Joint Action on Small Arms** — Adopted in 1998 and amended in 2002, this law requires European Union members to regulate the export of small arms and ammunition.

Multilateral Voluntary Agreements

- **Geneva Declaration** — Issued in 2006 and signed by more than 100 countries — not including China, Russia or the United States — the voluntary declaration states that the participants will "deal effectively both with the supply of, and the demand for, small arms and light weapons." Among other things, signatories agreed to fully implement the U.N. Program of Action to combat the small arms trade.

---

[1]"Status," http://treaties.un.org/Pages/ViewDetails.aspx?src=TREATY&mtdsg_no=XVIII-12-c&chapter=18&lang=en.

being sent to land-locked Zimbabwe through South Africa. The shipment is thought to have eventually been delivered to Zimbabwe via Angola instead.[31]

According to the Stockholm Institute, China has been a major weapons supplier elsewhere in sub-Saharan Africa, including Nigeria, which obtained some 40,000 assault rifles from Beijing in 2007. Beijing has become "the friendly arms supplier who won't ask any questions," says Marsh, citing China's arms sales to Zimbabwe's autocratic President Robert Mugabe. "The Chinese have kind of stepped into that role, and they are now responsible for a lot of the questionable transfers" that once came from Ukraine and other countries that inherited vast arms arsenals from the Soviet Union.

BACKGROUND

Rise of Conflicts

After the Cold War ended, civil conflicts erupted around the world during the 1990s and early 2000s, leading to the deaths or displacement of millions of people and destabilizing entire regions, particularly the Balkans, West Africa and Africa's Great Lakes region.

With few exceptions the weapons of choice were small, portable arms — assault rifles, mortars and RPGs — because they can be used in remote places by one person. The Kalashnikov (AK-47) assault rifle has become the iconic small weapon of the contemporary era. AK-47s were first manufactured in 1949 at a single factory in the Soviet Union, but imitations are now produced in several dozen countries around the world. No one knows exactly how many exist, but experts estimate at least 100 million.

Many Kalashnikovs and other weapons used in recent war zones came from the former Soviet Union's arsenals, especially those in former Soviet states, such as Belarus and Ukraine, which loosely controlled their left-over arms depots or sold the arms for quick cash. Unscrupulous arms dealers exploited the situation, buying huge quantities of arms at fire-sale prices and shipping them into war zones.

Perhaps no conflict came to symbolize the role of small arms more than the related civil wars in Liberia, Côte d'Ivoire (the Ivory Coast) and Sierra Leone — West African neighbors that were relatively peaceful until warlords spread death and destruction in the 1990s.

Liberian rebel leader Charles Taylor muscled his way into power in 1997, then supported Sierra Leone's Revolutionary United Front (RUF), a rebel group notorious for kidnapping children and forcing them to become child soldiers and for hacking off the hands and feet of civilians as a terror tactic.[32] On April 26, following a six-year trial, Taylor was convicted by an international tribunal for Sierra Leone of 11 counts of aiding and abetting the rebels who committed war crimes.[33] The court cited numerous cases when Taylor directly, and through intermediaries, provided "indispensable" arms and ammunition to the RUF forces in Sierra Leone. Taylor often paid for the weapons with illegally mined diamonds,

the court said.[34] The presiding judge on May 30 sentenced Taylor to 50 years in prison.[35]

But wars and civil conflicts are not the only places where small arms are used. Drug cartels and criminal gangs worldwide — especially in Latin America — rely on assault rifles and other weapons to guard supply routes and intimidate local authorities.

Several Central American countries that fought bloody civil wars in the 1970s and '80s now have some of the world's highest homicide rates, largely because of the activities of violent drug gangs, who use their illicit profits to buy weapons and political influence.[36]

By the mid-1990s, the upsurge in local conflicts had spawned campaigns, particularly in Europe, to restrict the small arms trade, which earlier international arms-control agreements had largely ignored. In May 1997 former Costa Rican president Oscar Arias and other Nobel Peace Prize recipients published an International Code of Conduct on Arms Transfers, which called on governments not to supply weapons, including small arms, to countries and other parties that violate basic human rights.[37] The code has never been adopted into law, but it did help spur later action at the United Nations.

In 2001 the U.N. General Assembly adopted two international agreements intended to reduce the illegal trade in small arms. Both have unwieldy titles: the Protocol Against the Illicit Manufacturing of and Trafficking in Firearms, Their Parts and Components and Ammunition, supplementing the United Nations Convention Against Transnational Organized Crime (known as the Firearms Protocol), and the Program of Action to Prevent, Combat and Eradicate the Illicit Trade in Small Arms and Light Weapons in All Its Aspects (known as the Program of Action). In addition, regional groups of Latin American and African countries have adopted similar agreements pledging to control the arms trade, although none is fully functioning yet.

Despite such diplomatic efforts, the global trade in small arms has not diminished and probably is growing, according to experts in the field. Precise figures on the global trade are not available, because some major arms exporters — such as China, Iran and North Korea — provide little or no information about how many weapons they sell and where they sell them.

Several other big producers — including Russia — do not publish information about exports of military weapons, whether large or small, says Holtom at the Stockholm Institute. The United States, the world's largest producer and trader of weapons — both big and small — does publish detailed figures for all its private and government arms exports, except for secret arms transfers by government agencies such as the CIA, the Pentagon and others.[38]

The Small Arms Survey in Geneva estimates that global sales of small arms and light weapons totaled about $7 billion in 2008, the most recent year for which it has published figures.[39] New estimates, to be released later this summer, likely will show slightly higher annual averages for later years, several experts said.

To put that in perspective, analyst Marsh in Norway says the annual worldwide trade in all armaments, including major weapons systems such as tanks and aircraft, averages about $26 billion, while small arms represent around $7 billion —"about the same as the annual trade in knitted and crocheted fabrics."

"Economically, the small arms business isn't all that important," he says. "That's not to say it can't be important in some cases. If a weapons plant is the major industry in a particular town, then it is very important there."

Small arms are commodities that "outlast their users and their previous owners' intentions," wrote *New York Times* war correspondent C. J. Chivers last year in a blog posting. "People sell them. Then market forces and social forces combine and take over, typically putting large portions of these weapons into the hands of those whom reasonable people would rather not see well-armed."[40]

Chivers should know. He has covered numerous conflicts and written a definitive book (*The Gun*) about the Kalashnikov, which he calls "the most abundant firearms on Earth" and the weapon of choice for insurgents, narcotics traffickers, gangs and even some of the world's militaries.[41]

He wrote that blog after discovering weapons looted from Libya's vast, unsecured arsenals before and after the ouster of Gadhafi. The U.N., the United States and several European countries are now spending millions of dollars trying to secure as many of those weapons as possible and clear Libyan towns and farms of thousands of land mines and other unexploded ordnance that litter the countryside.[42] Despite that work, experts say, Libyan weapons like those used by the Tuaregs in Mali are bound to show up elsewhere.

Aside from being diverted, such weapons stockpiles can explode, causing massive damage and loss of life. The Small Arms Survey counted 355 "unplanned explosions at munitions sites" worldwide between 1998 and earlier this year.[43]

A particularly deadly explosion in March killed some 223 people and wounded 2,500 at an arms dump near Brazzaville, the capital of the Republic of Congo.[44]

Government Exporters

Books, TV shows and movies often feature the activities of unscrupulous arms dealers. The notorious Iran-contra scandal in the 1980s, for instance, exposed the roles of such shady arms merchants as Adnan Khashoggi of Saudi Arabia and Manucher Ghorbanifar of Iran. They helped the Reagan administration secretly sell weapons to the Islamist government of Iran (in violation of official U.S. policy) and use the proceeds to buy weapons for Nicaragua's right-wing "contra" rebels, who were fighting the leftist Sandinista government.[45]

However, the vast majority of the world's arms sales are made, or at least approved, by governments.

"The majority of weapons, including those for warring parties, are transferred with full knowledge of governments," says arms researcher Danssaert in Belgium. "Diversion of weapons is also done with knowledge of governments. The logistics of arms transfers entails some sort of government involvement, whether on the sending side, the receiving end or both."

The U.N.'s Bevan, who has tracked hundreds of major weapons sales in Africa, says "99 percent of them started off as legally traded." They began as government-to-government sales or, if sold by a private firm, were officially approved. "The weak point is what happens after they are sold to the governments." Some governments, particularly in Africa, have little or no control over their arsenals or even their borders, so weapons can "leak" out through corruption or incompetence, he says.

Governments sell weapons and ammunition from their own stockpiles to raise cash, make room for new equipment or to provide military support for friendly governments or insurgents seeking to oust unfriendly regimes. He cites the 2010-11 flare-up of fighting in Côte d'Ivoire (the Ivory Coast), when neighboring West African countries provided arms either to the government or to rebel forces.

When a government sells weapons, Bevan says, the one abiding factor is always: "You don't give them your best stuff. You give them your old, surplus stuff and go out and buy new stuff for yourself."

For decades, the United States has been the world's top arms exporter, whether measured in value or quantity, and the largest weapons importer, especially sporting and hunting firearms. (*See chart, p. 54.*) In dollar value, the vast bulk of U.S. government sales involve major weapons systems. In 2010, for example, the United States delivered $8.6 billion worth of major weapons to the developing world, according to the Congressional Research Service.[46]

By contrast, U.S. global sales of small arms and light weapons to the developing world amounted to only $700 million in 2008 (the last year for which figures were available).[47]

In a few cases, Washington exports arms secretly or with minimal public notice, such as when it armed Somalia's Transitional Federal Government — which controls only a tiny portion of the country — when that government faced collapse in May 2009. The United States gave it about 40 tons of weapons and ammunition, both directly and indirectly through the Ugandan military, which is part of an African Union force helping the Somali government fight al-Shabaab, an Al Qaeda-linked Islamist insurgency.[48] The weapons were just the first of an unknown number of shipments that could be continuing.[49]

Critics, reportedly including some Obama administration officials, questioned the wisdom of providing weapons to a barely functioning government. Within months, the U.S.-supplied weapons reportedly were being sold on the streets of Mogadishu, apparently because the transitional government's forces could not use all of them.[50] In October 2010 the Stockholm Institute cited several "risks" associated with arming Somali's transitional government, such as the potential loss of weapons and "repeated and credible reports" that soldiers had used the weapons for "disproportionate and indiscriminate attacks resulting in civilian casualties."[51]

Bevan, the former U.N. arms monitor, says the Somalia situation is an example of how even governments with "generally responsible" arms transfer policies — such as the United States — can sometimes solve immediate problems but create bigger problems later.

"You could raise some serious questions about both the immediate and long-term consequences of inserting even more weapons into a situation like Somalia," he says. "For example, what is the government's capacity to manage those weapons and to restrict them from falling into the hands of allied clans? And what is the strength of the government, period? It's not clear these questions were asked at the appropriate time."

Elsewhere, the United States is just one of several outside powers providing weapons to parties involved in conflict. For instance, Belgian arms researcher Danssaert cites the rearming of both northern Sudan and South Sudan after a peace agreement was signed in 2005. The agreement had prohibited either side from rearming unilaterally.

"Both sides rearmed without asking for approval," Danssaert says. The United States provided $200 million to the private security firm Dyncorp to train the new South Sudan army and apparently "was aware of or even complicit in" the sale of firearms and other military equipment from Ukraine to South Sudan, he says. Meanwhile, China and Russia continued to supply weapons to the Sudanese government in Khartoum.

Sudan and South Sudan resumed a low-level war in March and April over disputed oilfields along the border, prompting international efforts to keep the fighting from exploding into another major war.[52]

CURRENT SITUATION

Arming Syrian Rebels?

The international community is watching in horror as the government of Bashar Assad continues its brutal crackdown on armed opposition forces in Syria. By early June, according to the United Nations, more than 10,000 insurgents and civilians had died and tens of thousands had been displaced.[53] A peace mission led by former U.N. Secretary General Annan has unsuccessfully tried to negotiate a cease-fire. The continuing violence has led to a debate about the wisdom of outsiders providing weapons to insurgents.

Some leading Republicans in the United States — including presumptive presidential nominee Mitt Romney — have called for arming the opposition.[54]

Should the Arms Trade Treaty cover small arms?

YES Bishop Elias Taban
President, Sudan Evangelical Alliance;
Former Soldier and Child Soldier

NO David Penn
Member, Executive Committee, The World
Forum on the Future of Sports Shooting
Activities, Rome

Written for *CQ Global Researcher*, June 2012

Written for *CQ Global Researcher*, June 2012

We all know the massive damage that a tank or fighter jet can do. When people visualize the devastation of violent conflict, their minds go to the big guns and bombs.

But I have spent more than 40 years at war. I became a child soldier at age 12, and I know firsthand that the weapons that can do the most harm — small arms such as AK-47s and handguns — are often considered the least. That is why I strongly believe that the Arms Trade Treaty being negotiated by the United Nations must include small arms if it is to have any hope of stemming the threat of violence in regions across the globe, including my home country of South Sudan.

Sudan has become a dumping ground for small arms. Much of the tragic loss of life we witness isn't caused just by large military weapons but by arms that any man, woman or child can carry.

The Arms Trade Treaty would slow the flow of these weapons onto black and grey markets and help keep them out of the hands of warlords, terrorists, drug dealers and thugs. We need to regulate tanks and jets, but it is not enough.

Entire genocides have been carried out with just machetes, so no treaty can end all violence. But an Arms Trade Treaty that doesn't include small arms is like a gun without a bullet; it won't accomplish very much.

Right now, we have international laws regulating the sale of iPods and bananas but no treaty regulating the transfer of weapons being used to kill people the world over. As a result, states are left to self-regulate, creating a patchwork of laws and loopholes that can be exploited by arms smugglers.

The Arms Trade Treaty would do nothing to inhibit the sale of weapons, including small arms, between legitimate state actors. But it would help keep those weapons out of the hands of those bent on doing evil. It would save lives.

My country needs to be beating our swords into ploughshares. We need to be burying our guns and building schools, hospitals and homes on the graves of guns instead.

But we cannot do this alone. We need the international community to help stop the flow of weapons into our country. The Arms Trade Treaty is an answer to my prayers, and the prayers of my people.

According to the Small Arms Survey, about 75 percent of firearms are in civilian possession. Generally, these are in the hands of law-abiding individuals who use them for hunting, species management, target shooting or as heritage items. These activities are benign, provide ecological, economic and social benefits and are supported by a legitimate trade.

The Arms Trade Treaty (ATT) is intended to regulate the international movement and "end use" of major military weapons systems such as tanks and missiles, which, unlike firearms, are rarely found in private ownership. The recipient government usually remains accountable for the entire consignment and its eventual disposal.

Use of small arms in low-intensity conflict has fueled a demand for their inclusion in any ATT. Commonly encountered "conflict" small arms are fully automatic rifles, such as the AK-47 and M16. Treaty control of fully automatic military small arms would generate little if any resistance from shooters.

But if the ATT defines "small arms" as encompassing shotguns, hunting and target rifles, pistols and antiques — with no exceptions — it would engender strong opposition, delay progress on a treaty and potentially weaken it if key nations refuse to ratify it. There is a declared majority against an ATT in the U.S. Senate (which has the power to ratify) unless civilian arms possession is protected.

The potential for misuse of civilian firearms should be viewed as a crime issue, not a conflict one. The U.N. has already addressed this via the Vienna Firearms Protocol, which requires that member nations establish effective export, import and transit licensing systems. This is reasonable and practicable. For instance, it exempts antiques and allows simplified procedures for temporary export and import of small numbers of firearms for "verifiable lawful purposes."

ATT-approval criteria designed to regulate military weapons contracts will be exhaustive and may be based upon, among other things, consideration of international humanitarian law and human rights law, the relevance of which to a small batch of target rifles is at best tenuous. The expense in obtaining approval for an international sale of a major weapons system would be nominal when compared to the overall cost. But it would be prohibitive, disproportionate and potentially punitive in relation to a small shipment of civilian firearms. An ATT should not encompass civilian firearms.

AFP/Getty Images/Junior D. Kannah

Residents of eastern Democratic Republic of the Congo (DRC) flee their homes on May 8, 2012, to avoid clashes between deserters and Congolese soldiers. Although peace agreements have formally ended civil war in the DRC, roving militias and rogue soldiers still terrorize villages in the east. They carry small arms often purchased on the black market with profits from the sale of so-called conflict minerals extracted in the area. A 2003 U.N. arms embargo has failed to halt the proliferation of small arms in the DRC.

"We don't think more arms into Syria is the answer," a State Department spokesman responded in February. That was still the U.S. position in early June.[55]

Nevertheless, Washington reportedly has tacitly endorsed Saudi Arabia and other Persian Gulf states providing weapons to the Syrian rebels.[56]

It is still unclear just how much weaponry has reached the Syrian opposition. Until recently, news reports suggested the rebels had received only limited amounts of arms and ammunition. But *The New York Times* reported in mid-June that the rebels were better-equipped and now had anti-tank missiles and other heavy arms.[57]

Meanwhile, the Syrian government continues "to import arms and ammunition freely," according to a report by the U.K. human rights group, Oxfam, because a U.N. Security Council move to embargo arms shipments to Syria has been blocked by Russia and China.[58]

Outside observers say the question of arming the opposition poses serious ethical, legal and practical questions. Barbara Frey, a University of Minnesota professor and former U.N. special rapporteur on human rights and small arms, says "the case of Syria is a difficult one. Nobody, at least nobody outside Russia, wants arms to

go to the Syrian government. But there is a legitimate debate over what level to arm the opposition."

Ideally, she says, "the international community needs to focus on what it can do to ratchet down arms transfers rather than ratcheting them up." However, international law could be seen as allowing arms aid for the rebels under the current situation, she says. "We have different legal regimes for peacetime and wartime, and now there is a war against the civilian population," she says.

Matthew Schroeder, a small arms expert at the Federation of American Scientists, says there should be limits to the types of weapons sent into Syria. "God help us if we send MANPADS," the shoulder-fired, portable antiaircraft missiles, he says. "If we do that, and if . . . they lose control of those weapons, then we've got a big problem."

The Syrian government already has "thousands" of portable antiaircraft missiles, Schroeder says. With such weapons in the hands of rebels, he says, "you would have the added complication of Syria being where it is, its proximity to Israel and Lebanon and Iraq. The world doesn't need any more MANPADS in Syria."

Treaty Negotiations

Starting on July 2, U.N. diplomats will spend four weeks trying to negotiate a major, binding treaty imposing new standards for international arms sales — which may or may not include small arms and light weapons.

Long a dream of human-rights and gun-control advocates, the proposed Arms Trade Treaty is strongly opposed by gun-rights advocates.[59] And several major arms exporters — notably China, Russia and the United States — reportedly have serious concerns about some of its potential provisions.

A "chairman's draft" — created during a series of meetings since 2009 and which will serve as the basis for the negotiations this summer — would apply to international sales of all types of weapons, from warplanes to handguns.[60]

Treaty advocate Karp at Old Dominion University says the treaty is "much bigger" than the U.N.'s 2001 Program of Action because it would establish "universal standards regarding all arms sales." The earlier agreement was not legally binding and addressed only "illicit" sales of small arms and light weapons. The proposed treaty also would define which sales are illicit, something the Program of Action left up to individual countries.

Unlike its predecessor, the Obama administration has supported the idea of a treaty and has been active in negotiations leading up to the July meeting. In an April 16 speech outlining the U.S. position, senior State Department official Thomas Countryman said, "We want any treaty to make it more difficult and expensive to conduct illicit, illegal and destabilizing transfers of arms [but not] make legitimate international arms trade more cumbersome."[61]

Treaty critic Mason, of the sport shooting group, says the conference must decide whether the treaty should cover civilian weapons, such as shotguns and ammunition. The United States likely will take a "strong" position that it should "stay away" from these issues, he says.

Countryman has said the United States would oppose any treaty that "would in any way infringe on" U.S. gun ownership rights. He also said the treaty should cover global trade in "everything from pistols to aircraft carriers." However, he argued that governing international trade in ammunition would be "financially onerous" to the U.S. arms industry and should not be included in the treaty, a position held by the industry.[62]

Saferworld's Isbister says nothing in the proposed Arms Trade Treaty would affect Americans' rights to own guns. He also calls the U.S. opposition to establishing export standards for ammunition "very puzzling" because "nobody is calling for the United States to do anything more than it already does. We are calling for other states to do more than they are doing."

Another question concerns the treaty's language on human rights. The chair's draft from last July states that parties to the treaty "shall not authorize a transfer of conventional arms if there is a substantial risk that those conventional arms would be used to commit or facilitate serious violations of international human rights law."

Frey, the former U.N. special rapporteur, says the language represents "a pretty vague standard" that is subject to interpretation. "But in all practicality," she says, "states will be held accountable only if the level of seriousness of abuse rises to the point where it leads to international condemnation."

Aside from the details of the document, the conference must decide how it will vote on the treaty. Past negotiations have proceeded on the basis of "consensus," which would allow any single country to block action. Treaty advocates, led by Mexico and several European

governments, want a looser definition of consensus so the treaty can be adopted even if a handful of countries disapprove. As a result, this may be one of the most contentious issues in the negotiations.

OUTLOOK
More Manufacturers

Experts on international security matters say it's impossible to know what the future holds for the small arms trade — except for the obvious conclusion that people will continue to fight and will use whatever weapons are available to do so.

"I don't think anyone is naive enough to believe we are going to do away with weapons, no matter what types of treaties or agreements countries might adopt," says Isbister of Saferworld. "The question is whether we can put enough procedures in place to reduce the number of weapons in the hands of irresponsible actors and thus make future conflicts somewhat less likely."

Advocates on all sides of the issue acknowledge that this year's battle over the Arms Trade Treaty likely will be just the first of many. "You need to look at this as a long-term process," Old Dominion's Karp says. "Even a weak treaty will have a long-term effect, because countries will feel compelled to change their attitudes and actions. And over time, the treaty may become stronger."

However, Isbister disagrees that an effective Arms Trade Treaty can be built through a step-by-step approach. "Treaties are not easy to improve as time goes on," he says. Plus, a weak treaty might establish arms trade standards that are "less robust" than existing regional agreements in Africa and the Americas, he says. "If states agree on a low standard, that would be a backward step," he says.

Whatever happens at the U.N. negotiations this summer, national governments will not give up their prerogatives to sell weapons and arm themselves as they see fit, the sport-shooting group's Mason says.

"All of these treaties have exemptions for 'national security' needs, which means a government can decide what is in its national security interest and what is not," he says. "This treaty will probably not affect the power of states, the military power, of any state one iota."

Laurance at the Monterey Institute says Mason's point simply reflects how international law has developed. "In the end, states have to think it's in their interest to do something like controlling arms exports. They can sign an agreement, but who is going to force them to carry it out?"

Complicating the future, experts say, is the growing number of countries beginning to produce weapons on their own. The implications of that trend are unclear, but having more weapons available in even more places will make controlling the arms trade all the more difficult, says Holtom, of the Stockholm Institute.

While in the past only a handful of countries could be considered serious weapons producers, he says, "Now, a number of states want to produce military equipment themselves. They are seeking their own indigenous ability to produce both ammunition and firearms."

NOTES

1. "MALI: A timeline of northern conflict," IRIN News, April 5, 2012, www.irinnews.org/Report/95252/MALI-A-timeline-of-northern-conflict.

2. For background, see Roland Flamini, "Turmoil in the Arab World," *CQ Global Researcher*, May 3, 2011, pp. 209-236.

3. Adam Nossiter, "Qaddafi's Weapons, Taken by Old Allies, Reinvigorate an Insurgent Army in Mali," *The New York Times*, Feb. 5, 2012, www.nytimes.com/2012/02/06/world/africa/tuaregs-use-qaddafis-arms-for-rebellion-in-mali.html?_r=1.

4. The Associated Press, "Official: Rockets fired at Israel came from Libya," *The Guardian*, April 20, 2012, www.guardian.co.uk/world/feedarticle/10204551.

5. Andrew Feinstein, *The Shadow World: Inside the Global Arms Trade* (2011), p. 436.

6. "Small arms, as deadly as WMD," Small Arms Review Conference 2006, Backgrounder, United Nations, www.un.org/events/smallarms2006/pdf/backgrounder.pdf.

7. "Estimating Civilian Owned Firearms," Small Arms Survey, p. 1, September 2011, www.smallarmssurvey.org/fileadmin/docs/H-Research_Notes/SAS-Research-Note-9.pdf.

8. *Ibid.*, p. 2.

9. "Homicide level for 2010, or latest available year," United Nations Office on Drugs and Crime, www.unodc.org/unodc/en/data-and-analysis/homicide.html.

10. "Global Burden of Armed Violence 2011," Geneva Declaration, p. 2, October 2011, www.cambridge.org/aus/catalogue/catalogue.asp?isbn=9781107023079.

11. "Venezuela to produce Kalashnikov assault rifles in 2012," *El Universal*, Sept. 16, 2011, www.eluniversal.com/2011/09/16/venezuela-to-produce-kalashnikov-assault-rifles-in-2012.shtml.

12. "Arms Embargo Database," Stockholm International Peace Research Institute, www.sipri.org/research/armaments/transfers/controlling/research/armaments/transfers/databases/embargoes.

13. For background, see Karen Foerstel, "Crisis in Darfur," *CQ Global Researcher*, Sept. 1, 2008, pp. 243-270.

14. Peter D. Wezeman, "United Nations Arms Embargoes, Their Impact on Arms Flows and Target Behavior: Case study: Darfur, Sudan, 2004-2006," Stockholm International Peace Research Institute, 2007, p. 9, http://books.sipri.org/files/misc/UNAE/SIPRI07UNAESud.pdf.

15. For background, see Josh Kron, "Conflict in Congo," *CQ Global Researcher*, April 5, 2011, pp. 157-182.

16. Damien Fruchart, "United Nations Arms Embargoes, Their Impact on Arms Flows and Target Behavior: Case study: Democratic Republic of the Congo, 2003-2006," Stockholm International Peace Research Institute, 2007, p. 5, http://books.sipri.org/files/misc/UNAE/SIPRI07UNAEDRC.pdf.

17. *Ibid.*

18. U.N. Security Council letter incorporating findings of a U.N. Panel of Experts, July 14, 2004, U.N. Document S/2004/551, www.un.org/Docs/journal/asp/ws.asp?m=S/2004/551.

19. Feinstein, *op. cit.*, p. 453.

20. For background, see Jina Moore, "Peacebuilding," *CQ Global Researcher*, June 21, 2011, pp. 291-314.

21. For details, see James Bevan, "Crisis in Karamoja: Armed Violence and the Failure of Disarmament in Uganda's Most Deprived Region," Occasional Paper 21, Small Arms Survey, June 2008, www.smallarmssurvey.org/fileadmin/docs/B-Occasional-papers/SAS-OP21-Karamoja.pdf.

22. "The Arms Trade Treaty: Report of the Secretary General," U.N. General Assembly, July 20, 2011, p. 11, www.un.org/ga/search/view_doc.asp?symbol=A/66/166&Lang=E.

23. Richard Grimmett, "Conventional Arms Transfers to Developing Nations, 2003-2010," Congressional Research Service, Sept. 22, 2011, p. 10, http://fpc.state.gov/documents/organization/174196.pdf.

24. "Report by the Panel of Experts on the Sudan established pursuant to resolution 1591 (2005)," United Nations, March 2011, p. 25, www.un.org/ga/search/view_doc.asp?symbol=S/2011/111.

25. Foerstel, *op. cit.*

26. Palash R. Ghosh, "Sudan: Future Oil Exporting Powerhouse?" *International Business Times*, March 16, 2012, www.ibtimes.com/articles/315327/20120316/sudan-south-oil-exports-civil-wars-china.htm.

27. Feinstein, *op. cit.*, p. 481.

28. "Investing in Tragedy," Human Rights First, March 2008, p. i, www.humanrightsfirst.org/wp-content/uploads/pdf/080311-cah-investing-in-tragedy-report.pdf.

29. Pieter D. Wezeman, Siemon T. Wezeman and Lucie Beraud-Sudreau, "Arms Flows to Sub-Saharan Africa," Stockholm International Peace Research Institute, December 2011, p. 14, http://books.sipri.org/product_info?c_product_id=435.

30. "China and conflict-affected states: Between principle and pragmatism," Saferworld, January 2012, p. 7, www.saferworld.org.uk/downloads/pubdocs/China%20and%20conflict-affected%20states.pdf.

31. Wezeman, *et al.*, *op. cit.*, pp. 46-47.

32. For background see John Felton, "Child Soldiers," *CQ Global Researcher*, July 1, 2008, pp. 183-211.

33. Marlise Simons, "Ex-President of Liberia Aided War Crimes, Court Rules," *The New York Times*, April 26, 2012, www.nytimes.com/2012/04/27/world/africa/charles-taylor-liberia-sierra-leone-war-crimes-court-verdict.html?hp&pagewanted=all.

34. Judgment Summary, *Prosecutor v. Charles Ghankay Taylor*, Special Court for Sierra Leone, Trial Chamber II, April 26, 2012, pp. 22-23, www.sc-sl.org/LinkClick.aspx?fileticket=86r0nQUtK08%3d&tabid=53.

35. Marlise Simons and J. David Goodman, "Judge Gives Taylor 50 years for 'Heinous' Crimes in War," *The New York Times*, May 20, 2012, www.nytimes.com/2012/05/31/world/africa/charles-taylor-sentenced-to-50-years-for-war-crimes.html?ref=world.

36. Michael Shifter, "Countering Criminal Violence in Central America," Special Report No. 64, Council on Foreign Relations, April 2012, www.cfr.org/central-america/countering-criminal-violence-central-america/p27740.

37. "Nobel Peace Laureates' International Code of Conduct on Arms Transfers," Nuclear Age Peace Foundation, May 1997, www.wagingpeace.org/articles/1997/05/00_nobel-code-conduct.htm.

38. "Small Arms Survey 2011, Annexes to Chapter 1," www.smallarmssurvey.org/fileadmin/docs/A-Yearbook/2011/en/Small-Arms-Survey-2011-Chapter-01-Annexes-1.1-1.2-EN.pdf.

39. *Ibid.*

40. C. J. Chivers, "The Perils of Libya's Loose Arms," *The New York Times*, March 4, 2011, http://atwar.blogs.nytimes.com/2011/03/04/the-perils-of-libyas-loose-arms/.

41. C. J. Chivers, *The Gun* (2010), p. 12.

42. For background, see Robert Kiener, "Dangerous War Debris," *CQ Global Researcher*, March 1, 2010, pp. 51-78.

43. "Unplanned Explosions at Munitions Sites," Small Arms Survey, March 15, 2012, www.smallarmssurvey.org/weapons-and-markets/stockpiles/unplanned-explosions-at-munitions-sites.html.

44. "Congo: Thousands still homeless after munitions blast," IRIN News, March 23, 2012, www.irinnews.org/Report/95143/CONGO-Thousands-still-homeless-after-munitions-blast.

45. *The Iran-Contra Puzzle* (1987), pp. B-4, B-5.

46. Grimmett, "Summary," *op. cit.*

47. "Small Arms Transfers: Exporting States," Research Note, Small Arms Survey, October 2011, www.smallarmssurvey.org/fileadmin/docs/H-Research_Notes/SAS-Research-Note-11.pdf.

48. "Background Briefing on U.S. Assistance to the Somalia Transitional Federal Government," State Department, June 26, 2009, www.state.gov/r/pa/prs/ps/2009/06a/125448.htm.

49. For background, see Jason McLure, "The Troubled Horn of Africa," *CQ Global Researcher*, June 1, 2009, pp. 149–176.

50. Elizabeth Dickinson, "Arming Somalia," *Foreign Policy*, Sept. 10, 2009, www.foreignpolicy.com/articles/2009/09/10/arming_somalia?page=full.

51. Pieter D. Wezeman, "Arms Flows and the Conflict in Somalia," SIPRI Background Paper, October 2010, http://books.sipri.org/files/misc/SIPRIBP1010b.pdf.

52. James Copnall, "Is war between the Sudans inevitable?" BBC News, April 20, 2012, www.bbc.co.uk/news/world-africa-17783636.

53. "After earlier obstructions, UN observers reach reported site of massacre in Syria," U.N. News Centre, June 8, 2012, www.un.org/apps/news/story.asp?NewsID=42185&Cr=syria&Cr1=.

54. Mark Landler, "Romney Calls for Action on Syria, but His Party is Divided," *The New York Times*, May 29, 2012, www.nytimes.com/2012/05/30/world/middleeast/romney-condemns-obamas-syria-policy.html?ref=middleeast.

55. "Lawmakers suggest US consider arming Syrian rebels, as graphic videos emerge," Fox News, Feb. 7, 2012, www.foxnews.com/politics/2012/02/07/lawmakers-suggest-us-consider-arming-syrian-rebels-as-videos-purport-to-show/.

56. Steven Lee Myers, "U.S. Joins Effort to Equip and Pay Rebels in Syria," *The New York Times*, April 1, 2012, www.nytimes.com/2012/04/02/world/middleeast/us-and-other-countries-move-to-increase-assistance-to-syrian-rebels.html?pagewanted=all.

57. Mark Landler and Neil MacFarquhar, "New Weapons Push Syrian Crisis Toward Civil War," *The New York Times*, June 13, 2012, www.nytimes.com/2012/06/14/world/middleeast/new-weapons-push-syrian-crisis-toward-civil-war.html?pagewanted=all.

58. "The Devil Is in the Detail," Oxfam, May 2012, p. 3, www.oxfam.org/sites/www.oxfam.org/files/bp-devil-detail-arms-trade-treaty-030512-en.pdf.

59. "NRA Delivers Remarks at United Nations Concerning Proposed Arms Trade Treaty," Institute for Legislative Action, National Rifle Association, July 14, 2011, http://nraila.org/legislation/federal-legislation/2011/7/nra-delivers-remarks-at-united-nations.aspx?s=NRA+Delivers+Remarks+at+United+Nations+Concerning+Proposed+Arms+Trade+Treaty&st=&ps=.

60. "Report of the Preparatory Committee for the United Nations Conference on the Arms Trade Treaty," March 8, 2012, p. 9, www.un.org/disarmament/convarms/ATTPrepCom/Documents/PrepCom4%20Documents/PrepCom%20Report_E_20120307.pdf.

61. "Positions for the United States in the Upcoming Arms Trade Treaty Conference," Remarks by Thomas Countryman, assistant secretary of state for International Security and Nonproliferation, U.S. Department of State, April 16, 2012, www.state.gov/t/isn/rls/rm/188002.htm.

62. "Controlling Proliferation: An Interview with Assistant Secretary of State Thomas Countryman," *Arms Control Today*, May 2012, www.armscontrol.org/act/2012_05/Controlling_Proliferation_An_Interview_With_Assistant_Secretary_of_State_Thomas_Countryman%20.

BIBLIOGRAPHY

Selected Sources
Books

Chivers, C. J., *The Gun*, Simon and Shuster, 2011.
An award-winning *New York Times* war correspondent provides a comprehensive history of the Kalashnikov assault rifle.

Farah, Douglas and Stephen Braun, *Merchant of Death: Money, Guns, Planes, and the Man Who Makes War Possible*, John Wiley & Sons, 2007.
Veteran journalists tell how Viktor Bout made a fortune supplying weapons to dictators and rebels around the world.

Feinstein, Andrew, *The Shadow World: Inside the Global Arms Trade*, Farrar, Straus and Giroux, 2011.
A former South African politician describes how money and political power fuel the global arms trade.

Greene, Owen and Nicholas Marsh, eds., *Small Arms, Crime and Conflict: Global governance and the threat of armed violence*, Routledge, 2012.
An academic survey of the small arms trade examines the role of weapons in civil conflict and criminal violence.

Stohl, Rachel, Matt Schroeder and Dan Smith, *The Small Arms Trade*, One World, 2007.
Three experts examine the global small arms trade.

Articles

"Mali: Rebels and their cause," *IRIN*, April 23, 2012, www.irinnews.org/Report/95339/MALI-Rebels-and-their-cause.
The U.N.'s news service interviews a former guerrilla leader on rebels' use of Libyan weapons to take over Azawad in Mali.

Lawson, Guy, "The Stoner Arms Dealers," Rolling Stone, March 31, 2011.
This highly readable account shows how two young Americans made millions of dollars selling faulty weapons to the Pentagon for use by Afghan security forces.

Magnier, Mark, "Gun culture spreads in India," Los Angeles Times, Feb. 20, 2012, http://articles.latimes.com/2012/feb/20/world/la-fg-india-guns-20120221.
Increasingly prosperous Indians, many fearing crime, now possess some 40 million guns, second only to the United States.

Pachico, Elyssa, "How Much Is Guatemala Arming the Zetas?" Offnews, April 13, 2011, www.offnews.info/verArticulo.php?contenidoID=29800.
A reporter describes the relationship between Guatemala's military (and the country's black market in weapons) and Mexican drug gangs, including the biggest, the Zetas.

Schmitt, Eric, and Robert W. Worth, "With Arms for Yemen Rebels, Iran Seeks Wider Mideast Role," *The New York Times*, March 15, 2012.
The continuing violence and political instability in Yemen could be just as dangerous as the rebellion in Syria, as this report on Iran's arming of Yemeni rebels illustrates.

Simons, Marlise, "Ex-President of Liberia Aided War Crimes, Court Rules," *The New York Times*, April 26, 2012.
An international criminal court in Sierra Leone held Charles Taylor accountable for aiding rebel groups that committed widespread war crimes during that country's civil conflict.

Reports and Studies

"The Devil Is in the Detail," *Oxfam*, May 2012, www.oxfam.org/sites/www.oxfam.org/files/bp-devil-detail-arms-trade-treaty-030512-en.pdf.
A major relief agency advocates for a strong and enforceable Arms Control Treaty.

"Global Burden of Armed Violence 2011," Geneva Declaration, www.genevadeclaration.org/measurability/global-burden-of-armed-violence/global-burden-of-armed-violence-2011.html.
The diplomatic initiative surveys trends in armed violence.

"The Small Arms Survey 2011: States of Security," Small Arms Survey, www.smallarmssurvey.org/publications/by-type/yearbook/small-arms-survey-2011.html.
The Geneva-based institute tracks major issues concerning small arms and light ammunition.

"Sudan: No End to Violence in Darfur: Arms Supplies Continue Despite Ongoing Human Rights Violations," Amnesty International, 2012, www.amnestyusa.org/research/reports/sudan-no-end-to-violence-in-darfur.
The human-rights group argues that the government of Sudan relies on outside help for its repressive actions.

Bevan, James, "Crisis in Karamoja: Armed Violence and the Failure of Disarmament in Uganda's Most Deprived Region," Small Arms Survey, June 2008.
A former U.N. arms monitor analyzes weapons proliferation in a remote region of Uganda.

Grimmett, Richard, "Conventional Arms Transfers to Developing Nations, 2003-2010," Congressional Research Service, Sept. 22, 2011.
A nonpartisan research agency that supplies policy analysis to Congress provides an annual survey of arms sales to developing countries.

For More Information

Conflict Awareness Project, 51 Francisco St., San Francisco, CA 94133; www.conflictawareness.org. Founded by former U.N. arms monitor Kathi Lynn Austin; focuses on "investigating, documenting and bringing to justice major arms traffickers, war profiteers and transnational criminal networks that fuel conflict around the globe."

Control Arms Campaign, P.O. Box 3795, New York, NY 10163; 212-682-3086; www.controlarms.org. Founded in 2003 by Amnesty International, Oxfam and other nongovernmental organizations to lobby governments on behalf of a strong Arms Trade Treaty.

Federation of American Scientists Arms Sales Monitoring Project, 1725 Desales St., N.W., 6th floor, Washington, DC 20036; 202-546-3300, ext. 193; www.fas.org/programs/ssp/asmp/index.html. Compiles detailed records on global arms transfers and policies.

International Action Network on Small Arms, Leonard Street, London EC2A 4LT, United Kingdom; 44-20-7065-0870; www.iansa.org. Coalition of nongovernmental organizations formed to advocate for policies opposed to armed violence and in favor of international gun-control measures.

International Peace Information Service, Italiëlei 98a, 2000 Antwerpen, Belgium; +32 3 225-0022; www.ipsiresearch.be. Think tank that concentrates on the international arms trade, environment and corporate social responsibility in sub-Saharan Africa.

Norwegian Initiative on Small Arms Transfers, Peace Research Institute Oslo, Hausmans Gate 7, 0186 Oslo, Norway; +47 22 05-4166; www.nisat.org. Maintains a comprehensive database of global small arms transfers and publishes studies of timely topics in the field.

Small Arms Survey, Graduate Institute of International and Development Studies, 47 Avenue Blanc, 1202 Geneva, Switzerland; +41 22 908-5777; www.smallarmssurvey.org. Conducts research projects on all aspects of the small arms trade and publishes an annual yearbook reporting on key issues.

Stockholm International Peace Research Institute, Signalistgatan 9, SE-169 70 Solna, Sweden; +46 8 655-9700; www.sipri.org. Think tank focusing on conflicts and arms control issues. Its numerous reports are detailed and meticulously researched.

United Nations Institute for Disarmament Research, Palais des Nations, 1211 Geneva10, Switzerland; +41 22 917-3186; www.unidir.org/html/en/home.html. U.N. think tank for weapons-related issues; publishes numerous reports from a range of perspectives. For small arms issues, click on "small arms" at the bottom of the website.

World Forum on the Future of Sport Shooting Activities, WFSA c/o ANPAM Viale dell'Astronomia, 30 I-00144 Roma, Italy; +39 06 590-3510; www.wfsa.net. Advocates for national and international policies that promote hunting.

Voices From Abroad:

RICHARD MUGISHA

Executive Secretary, East Africa Action Network on Small Arms, Uganda

A treaty for all
"The new [East African] Arms Trade Treaty must be robust enough to have a genuine impact on the lives of tens of thousands of innocent civilians suffering from armed violence every single day."

New Vision (Uganda), May 2012

La Vanguardia, Spain/Kap

AMBASSADOR JOY OGWU

Permanent U.N. Representative, Nigeria

Changing with reality
"One prime example [of a global problem] was the trade of illicit small arms and light weapons. As the world was extremely unequal, those threats were compounded by poverty, social cohesion and governance. The complex challenges underlined the urgent need for vision and leadership from the United Nations and member states. To that end, the [U.N. Security] Council should reposition itself to deal with that reality."

Leadership (Nigeria), November 2012

DAVID KIMAIYO

Director, Kenya National Focal Point On Small Arms and Light Weapons Kenya

A grassroots problem
"It is these arms which find their way into wrong hands causing insecurity in the country, and that is why we are taking the matter seriously so that it is tackled right from the grassroot level."

Nairobi (Kenya) Star, August 2011

PETER WEIDERUD

General Secretary International Parliamentary Forum On Small Arms and Light Weapons Sweden

Mismanagement is to blame
"You get three, four explosions like the one in Cyprus every year. Around 95 per cent come from mismanagement. Ammunition storage is dangerous if you don't deal with it effectively."

Cyprus Mail, July 2011

GOODLUCK JONATHAN

President, Nigeria

Fighting the challenge
"I have consistently warned about the spread of small arms across Africa and, especially the West African region, by foreign merchants of death who are ingenious and desperate to sell their wares at our expense.... This act has added weight to the ongoing violence in some parts of our country. The Nigerian Customs Service must continue to play its part as we fight these security challenges. You have, indeed, recorded some remarkable breakthroughs by seizing arms that are being clandestinely brought into this country."

Daily Champion (Nigeria), December 2011

FRANCIS SANG

Executive Secretary Regional Centre on Small Arms, Kenya

Suffering serious consequences

"Africa is often the dumping ground for such weapons from manufacturing countries and in addition plays host to the great number of armed conflicts. Without a doubt, the continent suffers serious consequences of the easy availability of small arms and light weapons."

The Namibian, March 2011

MODESTE MWAUZI

Coordinator for Small Arms and Light Weapons East African Community, Tanzania

Estimates only

"Unfortunately, it is very difficult to establish the exact number of illegal weapons in circulation anywhere, not even the U.N. or other research bodies venture into quoting any figures due to the difficulty of establishing these numbers."

Arusha (Tanzania) Times, April 2011

OLA IBRAHIM

Navy Chief of Staff, Nigeria

New challenges arise

"Littoral states rely on the global maritime environment for trade and commerce. However, in recent times, the Gulf of Guinea maritime environment is increasingly threatened by a myriad of security challenges such as piracy, smuggling, oil theft and trafficking in humans and small arms and drugs."

This Day (Nigeria), February 2012

4

Unrest in the Arab World

Kenneth Jost

Holding a copy of the Koran, a supporter of Egyptian President Mohammed Morsi rallies with members of the Islamist Muslim Brotherhood in Cairo on Dec. 14, 2012, in support of the country's draft constitution. The controversial document, which was approved later in December, guarantees freedom of worship to Jews, Christians and Muslims — but not to others — and reaffirms Islam as the state religion.

Getty Images/Daniel Berehulak

From *The CQ Researcher*, February 1, 2013.

With a brutal civil war raging, Syrian President Bashar Assad emerged into public view for the first time in several months on Jan. 6 to deliver a defiant speech blaming the conflict on criminals, terrorists and foreign influences. Assad, whose strongman father ruled Syria for 30 years before the son's succession in 2000, outlined a plan for a negotiated political solution but rejected any notion of stepping aside.

"This is a fight between the country and its enemies, between the people and the criminals," Assad said in a 50-minute oration before a cheering audience assembled in the Opera House in Damascus, Syria's capital city. "I would like to reassure everyone we will not stop the fight against terrorism as long as there is one single terrorist left in the land of Syria," he added.[1]

Assad spoke only four days after a United Nations-commissioned study said nearly 60,000 people had been killed in the conflict, which began with peaceful protests against the Assad regime in March 2011 as the so-called Arab Spring movement was hitting its stride elsewhere in the Arab World.[2] Three days earlier, Lakhdar Brahimi, the Algerian diplomat designated as a mediator by the U.N. and the 22-member League of Arab States, had warned that the conflict could claim another 100,000 lives over the next year. Without a peace agreement, Brahimi said at the league's headquarters in Cairo, Syria could be "transformed into hell."[3] (*See "Syria Timeline," p. 82; "Syria: Mounting Casualties," p. 88.*)

The grim news from Syria contrasts sharply with the ebullient reaction to the Arab Spring, a succession of anti-government protests and demonstrations in North Africa and the Middle East that

Freedom Continues to Elude Arab World

Revolutions and popular unrest across much of the Arab world have yet to lead to full democracy and individual rights in any of the region's countries. No country is rated as "free," and only six are rated "partly free," by the international human-rights group Freedom House. Furthermore, only Bahrain, Qatar and the United Arab Emirates have achieved even a middling score on political corruption by Transparency International, a Berlin-based anti-corruption advocacy group.

Arab Countries With Recent Pro-Democracy Protests

Country Type; head of government	Population	GDP per capita	Freedom House freedom rating, 2013	Transparency International corruption score, 2012 (0 to 100, with 0 being the most corrupt)
Algeria	37.4 million	$7,300	Not free	34
Republic; independent from France since 1962. Prime Minister Abdelmalek Sellal in power since September 2012.				
Bahrain	1.2 million	$27,700	Not free	51
Constitutional monarchy; independent from U.K. since 1971. King Hamad bin Isa Al Khalifa in power since 1999.				
Egypt	83.7 million	$6,500	Partly free	32
Republic; British protectorate until 1922. Mohammed Morsi elected president in June 2012, more than a year after former President Hosni Mubarak was deposed in a revolution.				
Iraq	31.1 million	$4,200	Not free	18
Parliamentary democracy; independent from British administration since 1932 as part of a League of Nations mandate. Prime Minister: Nouri al-Maliki, elected in 2006.				
Jordan	6.5 million	$5,900	Not free	48
Constitutional monarchy; independent from British mandate since 1946. King Abdullah II in power since 1999.				

began in Tunisia in December 2010. Within a two-month span, the "Arab street" — the oft-used metaphor for disaffected Arabs shut out of the political process — forced Tunisia's longtime president Zine El Abidine Ben Ali to flee the country and Egyptian leader Hosni Mubarak to step down after 30 years as president. By August 2011, a popular uprising in Libya, aided by military support from the United States and some NATO allies, had toppled the longtime dictator Moammar Gadhafi.

Country Type; head of government	Population	GDP per capita	Freedom House freedom rating, 2013	Transparency International corruption score, 2012 (0 to 100, with 0 being the most corrupt)
Kuwait	2.6 million	$41,700	Partly free	44
Constitutional emirate; independent from U.K. since 1961. The emir, Sheik Sabah Al Ahmed Al Sabah, has been in power since 2006.				
Lebanon	4.1 million	$15,500	Partly free	30
Republic; independent from French administration since 1943 as part of a League of Nations mandate. President Michel Suleiman, in power since 2008.				
Libya	5.6 million	$6,000	Partly free	21
Operates under a transitional government following the deposition and death of ruler Moammar Gadhafi. Prime Minister Ali Zaidan took office in October 2012.				
Morocco	32.3 million	$5,100	Partly free	37
Constitutional monarchy; independent from France since 1956. King Mohammed VI in power since 1999.				
Oman	3.1 million	$27,600	Not free	47
Monarchy; independent since mid-1700s following Portuguese and Persian rule. Sultan Qaboos bin Said al-Said in power since 1970.				
Qatar	2 million	$98,900	Not free	68
Emirate; independent from U.K. since 1971. Sheik Hamad bin Khalifa al Thani in power since 1995.				
Saudi Arabia	26.5 million	$24,400	Not free	44
Monarchy; founded in 1932 after several attempts to unify the Arabian Peninsula. King Abdullah bin Abdul Aziz Al-Saud in power since 2005.				
Syria	22.5 million	$5,100	Not free	26
Authoritarian regime; French mandate until 1946. President Bashar Assad's family has been in power for 42 years.				
Tunisia	10.7 million	$9,400	Partly free	41
Republic; independent from France since 1956. Moncef Marzouki elected in December 2001 as president of interim government, which will remain in power until a new constitution is drafted.				
United Arab Emirates	5.3 million	$47,700	Not free	68
Federation with some powers reserved for member emirates; independent from U.K. since 1971. President: Sheik Khalifa bin Zayed Al Nahyan, in power since 2004.				
Yemen	24.8 million	$2,300	Not free	23
Republic; independent from Ottoman Empire since 1918. South Yemen unified with North Yemen in 1990. President Abed Rabbo Mansour Hadi took power on Feb. 27, 2012 after Ali Abdullah Saleh stepped down after 22 years as president.				

Sources: "Corruption Perceptions Index 2012," Transparency International, 2012, cpi.transparency.org/cpi2012/results; "Freedom in the World 2013," Freedom House, January 2013, pp. 14-18, www.freedomhouse.org/sites/default/files/ FIW% 202013%20 Booklet.pdf; The World Factbook, Central Intelligence Agency, January 2013, https://www.cia.gov/library/publications/the-world-factbook.

The protests spread to other countries, from monarchical Morocco in the west to the Gulf state monarchies and emirates in the east. Two years later, the political atmosphere has shifted in much of the Arab world, but the pace of change has slowed. "Things aren't as exciting as they were two years ago, but there are changes that are taking place," says James Gelvin, a professor of history at UCLA and author of a compact overview, *The Arab Uprisings.*[4]

Paul Salem, director of the Carnegie Middle East Center in Beirut, Lebanon, part of the Carnegie Endowment for International Peace, acknowledges the country-by-country variations in the degree of political

Timeline: The Syrian Civil War

2011

March 15-16	Demonstrators demand release of political prisoners; at least 20 protesters die as demonstrations widen in following weeks.
April 21	President Bashar Assad lifts state of emergency, releases political prisoners; security forces kill 72 protesters.
July 29	Some security forces refuse to fire on protesters; defectors form Free Syrian Army.
Aug. 3	Syrian tanks move into Hama, killing at least 45 protesters.
Aug. 23	U.N. Human Rights Council condemns Syrian government's response to protests; opposition forms National Council of Syria, demands Assad's removal from office.
Nov. 12	Arab League suspends Syria's membership.
Dec. 19-20	Security forces execute 110 protesters in Jabal al-Zawiya region; two suicide bombings in Damascus kill 44 people.

2012

February-March	Syrian forces begin shelling of Homs; hundreds killed.
March 21	Peace plan presented to U.N. Security Council by Arab League is championed by special envoy Kofi Annan and accepted by Russia, China; Assad accepts plan, then reneges.
April	U.N. observers enter Syria to monitor progress of Annan plan; U.N. suspends monitoring after deaths of women, children.
May 10	Two car bombs kill 55 people outside military intelligence building in Damascus; ceasefire nullified as government continues shelling cities; death toll reaches 9,000.
June 22	Syrian forces shoot down Turkish fighter jet; fighting later crosses Turkish border.
Aug. 2	Annan resigns as special envoy amid escalating violence.
Oct. 2	U.N. reports that 300,000 refugees have fled Syria.
Nov. 29	Syrian government shuts down Internet, telephone service; launches major offensive surrounding Damascus; U.S. delivers 2,000 communication kits to rebel forces.
Dec. 11	Obama says U.S. will recognize Syrian rebels as legitimate government; U.S. designates Jabhat al-Nusra, an Islamist militia backing Syrian rebels, as terrorist organization.
Dec. 22	Syrian military forces begin using Scud missiles against rebels.

2013

Jan. 1	U.N. puts death toll at 60,000; says it could reach 100,000 in coming year.
Jan. 6	Assad, in Damascus, vows to remain in office, continue fight against "criminals," "terrorists" and "foreign influences."
Jan. 17	Homs massacre kills 106 people; U.K.-based Syrian Observatory for Human Rights blames pro-Assad forces.
Jan. 21	Syrian National Coalition (SNC) fails to agree on transitional government; new plan promised for governing rebel-held areas.

Source: Compiled by Ethan McLeod from various news sources

reform. "It's spring in many places, winter in many places," he says. Even so, he says events will have a lasting impact on the political climate throughout the Arab world.*

"What has happened is a transformation of public consciousness and public political values," says Salem, a Harvard-educated dual citizen of Lebanon and the United States. Arabs throughout the region are now disavowing dictatorships and committing to political accountability and competitive elections, Salem says. "This paradigm shift is throughout the region," he adds, "and will be with us for the next generation."

Other experts are less convinced that the Arab world, long resistant to democratization and human rights, is now firmly on a different path. "We have seen a little bit of movement in a few countries," says Seth Jones, associate director for the RAND Corp.'s International Security and Defense Policy Center in Washington. "But for the most part we are not seeing the broad democratization that most people had hoped for."

For now, none of the 16 Arab countries stretching from Morocco to Iraq are rated as free, according to the annual survey "Freedom in the World 2013" by the international human rights group Freedom House. The report, released on Jan. 16, raises Egypt's and Libya's rating to "partly free," bringing

---

* This report does not detail events and conditions in Iraq, which will be covered in a forthcoming report in March. It also does not encompass these six members of the League of Arab States: Comoros, Djibouti, Mauritania, Palestinian National Authority, Somalia and Sudan.

the total in that category to six along with Kuwait, Lebanon, Morocco and Tunisia. The 10 other countries are all listed as "not free." In seven countries, according to the survey, the status of political rights or civil liberties worsened over the past year.[5] (*See map, p. 80.*)

The uprisings caught most analysts by surprise, U.S. scholars Mark Haas and David Lesch write in *The Arab Spring*, published in November. The waves of democratization that swept across Latin America, Eastern Europe and Central Asia during the late 20th century were unfelt in the Arab world except for a short-lived and largely abortive "Arab spring" of 2005.[6] Yet Haas, a political scientist at Duquesne University in Pittsburgh, and Lesch, a historian at Trinity University in San Antonio, say conditions were ripe for revolutionary uprisings in the Middle East. They note in particular the anger and frustration felt by the Arab world's disproportionately young populations as the global economic crisis of 2008 raised prices and drove up unemployment in much of the region.[7]

The 2010-2011 uprisings have resulted in "some grudging but nonetheless impressive gains," according to the Freedom House report, despite widespread predictions that the push for political reform would fall victim to what it calls the region's "perennial antidemocratic currents." The report sees "generally positive" gains in Libya and Tunisia, but it voiced concern about events in Egypt.

The Freedom House report lightly faults the "flawed but competitive" presidential campaign that resulted in the election of Mohammed Morsi, a leader of the once-banned Muslim Brotherhood, the Islamist group behind the now-dominant Freedom and Justice Party. It then criticizes a number of Morsi's actions in office, including what it calls the hasty process to draft a new constitution and hold a referendum that resulted in its approval with 64 percent of the low-turnout vote in December. (*See sidebar, p. 92.*)

Freedom House says political rights had diminished in several other Arab countries, including Lebanon, Jordan and four Gulf states: Bahrain, Kuwait, Oman and the United Arab Emirates. Saudi Arabia retained its status in the survey as one of the "worst of the worst" countries in terms of political and civil rights. But Syria is singled out as having suffered "by far" the worst of the repercussions from the Arab Spring.

Assad responded to the popular uprisings in 2011, the report says, "by waging war against his own people." Over the next year, "amid inaction by the international community," the conflict developed what the report calls "starker sectarian overtones" as it drew in fighters affiliated with al Qaeda and other terrorist groups. Today, many experts foresee only more bloodshed in Syria's future. "By every measure, it's getting worse," says Andrew Tabler, a senior fellow with the Washington Institute for Near East Policy.

The Freedom House report stresses the importance of the stance that Islamist groups such as the Muslim Brotherhood take as they gain power or influence. Fears of the Islamists' influence led Christian and liberal secularists to boycott the drafting of Egypt's new constitution. In other countries, political reforms are complicated by sectarian conflicts within Islam's two major branches: Sunnis, the worldwide majority, and Shiites, who comprise about one-third of the Muslim population in the Middle East. Syria's ostensibly secularist regime is tightly linked to the country's Alawites, a small minority branch of Islam viewed as heretical by both Sunnis and Shiites.[8]

The U.S. role in the events has been limited. "I don't think these events have been driven by the United States," says Jeremy Pressman, an associate professor of political science at the University of Connecticut in Storrs. "I don't think the way they turn out will be primarily driven by what the United States does."

President Obama called for Mubarak to step aside in Egypt but only after the longtime U.S. ally's fate had been sealed by weeks of demonstrations in Cairo's Tahrir Square and the military's decision to side with the revolt. In Libya, the United States helped doom Gadhafi's rule, but only after Britain and France took the lead in establishing a no-fly zone to help protect the popular uprising. And in Syria, despite calls for stronger action, the administration has limited the U.S. role to economic sanctions, covert assistance, humanitarian aid and public calls for Assad to step down. (*See "At Issue," p. 97.*)

With the unrest now in its third year, many experts caution that the situation will not be resolved quickly. "We're at the beginning of a long process," says UCLA's Gelvin.

Gawdat Bahgat, an Egyptian-born professor of political science at the National Defense University in Washington, agrees. "The process of moving away from authoritarianism to democracy is very unsettled," he says. As the events play out, here are some of the questions being debated:

Has the Arab Spring stalled?

New York Times op-ed columnist Nicholas Kristof was in Bahrain in February 2011 as government troops fired for several days on unarmed protesters, killing seven and wounding at least 200 others. Two years and at least 50 deaths later, Bahrain's Sunni monarchy still holds tight power over the country's Shiite majority, thanks in part to military help from its Sunni-ruled neighbor Saudi Arabia. And when Kristof tried to return late in 2012, he found that he had been blacklisted and was not allowed back in to report on the continuing repression in the Gulf state, home to the U.S. Navy's 5th Fleet.[9]

Despite U.S. ties, Bahraini authorities have spurned the Obama administration's urgings to negotiate a political solution with the simmering opposition. And in January Bahrain's highest courts upheld prison terms ranging from five years to life for 20 leaders of the revolt, following their convictions by a military tribunal. "The uprising was basically snuffed out," says the Carnegie Endowment's Salem.[10]

Bahrain provides the most dramatic example of what the Freedom House report labels the "intransigence" exhibited by many Arab nations toward popular uprisings. The report tags neighboring Oman and the United Arab Emirates with downward arrows based on increased arrests of activists calling for political reform and a crackdown on online activism. In other countries, including Jordan and Kuwait, governments have successfully tamped down discontent with modest political reforms that have left the underlying power structures unchanged. And in Egypt, the report cites continuing controversies over Morsi's actions, including his dismissal of the lower house of parliament in June and his claim of broad executive powers in November, to warn that the fate of democracy in the Arab world's most populous nation "remains very much an open question."

The moves to repress or stifle popular movements lead some experts to predict little democratization for the foreseeable future. "That's likely to be the case for the next couple of years," says Jones, the RAND expert. Jones' colleagues, writing in a book-length study, say the

government security apparatuses in the region pose formidable obstacles to popular political movements. In addition, oil-endowed countries have used their economic wealth to buy off potential opposition with what Jones calls "staggering benefits" in the form of government jobs and subsidies for food and other necessities.[11]

In Egypt, Jones says, the early signs pointed to a model of democratization, but Morsi's power-grabs now temper the early optimism. "There's serious reason to be concerned about the use of his position to establish broad executive, legislative and, to some degree, judicial power," Jones says.

Other experts, however, say it is too early to write off the Arab Spring as spent. "There have been continuous protests and uprisings" since the initial months in 2010 and 2011, according to Gelvin, the UCLA professor. "We see them taking place all the time. They just don't get covered."

Bahgat, at the National Defense University, agrees that the first few months of the uprisings resulted in unrealistic expectations about the future pace of change. "It makes sense that there will be ups and downs," says Bahgat. "It is not one straight line. The setbacks make sense. People should expect them."

As for his native Egypt, Bahgat finds the controversial moves by Morsi and the Muslim Brotherhood unsurprising and less than alarming. "It makes sense to me that they are trying to grab as much power as they can," Bahgat says. "That reflects the balance of power that is in Egypt now. But maybe in 10 years or so, it may be different."

"I don't think things have stalled," says the University of Connecticut's Pressman. "We should not come to these summary judgments after two years." Still, Pressman cautions that further democratization is not assured. "I'm in no way saying things are guaranteed."

Economics, more than politics, may determine the future course of events, according to many of the experts. "The Middle East is not doing well," says Gelvin. "That's the elephant in the room that no one's talking about." The initial wave of uprisings, he notes, "was not only social-networking youth. It was also workers."

The uprisings have hurt tourism in Egypt and elsewhere and slowed foreign investment, according to Joshua Landis, director of the Center for Middle

Syria at a Glance

Government

President Bashar Assad — Leader of Syria and regional secretary of the Arab Socialist Ba'ath Party. Elected in 2000 in unopposed referendum and initially seen as a potential reformer. Heavily criticized for human-rights violations and political corruption.

Minister of Defense General Fahd Jassem al-Freij — Appointed in July 2012 after assassination of predecessor; Assad has divided al-Freij's power among various commanders.

Syrian army — Estimated 280,000-member land force, responsible for suppressing rebels. Suffered up to 60,000 defections to the opposition in the past year.

Opposition

Free Syrian Army (FSA) — Formed in July 2011 by Syrian Army defectors. Estimated force of 100,000 soldiers with basic military training; has grown from a select group of defectors along the Turkish border to a broader group of insurgent civilians and military groups. Many rebels have adopted the FSA name.

Colonel Riad al-Asaad — Former commander of the FSA. Established the FSA in late July 2011 after defecting from the Syrian army earlier that month.

Brigadier General Salim Idris — Syrian Army defector appointed to replace Riad al-Asaad as chief of staff of the FSA in December 2012.

National Coalition for Syrian Revolutionary and Opposition Forces (Syrian National Coalition) — Formed in November 2012 as an inclusive leadership council of 63 (now 70) members. Aims to replace Assad's regime and become the international representative for Syria, but internal divisions have presented problems in forming a government. Supports the FSA. Recognized by more than 140 countries as representative of Syrian people.

Coalition President Moaz al-Khatib — Former Sunni imam of the Ummayad Mosque in Damascus; imprisoned several times for speaking out against Assad and forced to flee Syria in July 2012.

Syrian National Council (SNC) — Coalition of several opposition groups dominated by Sunni Muslim majority. Military bureau coordinates activity for the Damascus Declaration for Democratic Change, the Muslim Brotherhood, Syrian Revolution General Commission and Kurdish and tribal factions.

President George Sabra — Elected chairman of the left-wing Syrian Democratic People's Party, banned by the country's government, in November 2012.

National Coordination Committee for Democratic Change — Comprises 13 leftist and three additional Kurdish political parties, plus an assortment of independent and youth activists. Calls for a withdrawal of military from streets, an end to military attacks against nonviolent protests and the release of all political prisoners. Favors economic sanctions on Assad as a means of applying international pressure. Rejects foreign military intervention.

Jabhat al-Nusra — Salafi Jihadist rebel group with links to al Qaeda; has gained popular support in recent months. Worked with FSA factions to carry out attacks and large-scale bombings in the past year. The United States designated it a terrorist organization in December.

Ahrar al-Sham battalion — Rebel group composed of conservative Salafist and Islamist groups; has close ties to Jabhat al-Nusra. Has drawn attention from other, more radical rebel groups in Syrian rebel front.

Sources: "Guide to the Syrian opposition," BBC, Nov. 12, 2012, www.bbc.co.uk/news/world-middle-east-15798218; "Structure of SNC," Syrian National Council, www.syriancouncil.org/en/structure/structure.html; Elizabeth O'Bagy, "Middle East Security Report 6: Jihad in Syria," Institute for the Study of War, September 2012, www.understandingwar.org/report/jihad-syria; Khaled Yacoub Oweis, "Syria's army weakened by growing desertions," Reuters, Jan. 13, 2012, www.reuters.com/article/2012/01/13/us-syria-defections-idUSTRE80C2IV20120113; Samia Nakhoul and Khaled Yacoub Oweis, "World Powers Recognise Syrian Opposition Coalition," Reuters, December 2012, www.reuters.com/article/2012/12/12/us-syria-crisis-draft-idUSBRE8BB0DC2012 1212; Yelena Suponina, "Free Syrian Army's Riad al-Asaad: Political resolution of the crisis in Syria is impossible," Voice of Russia, Aug. 9, 2012, english.ruvr.ru/2012_08_09/Political-resolution-on-the-crisis-in-Syria-is-impossible/.

— Compiled by Ethan McLeod and Darrell Dela Rosa

East Studies at the University of Oklahoma in Norman. "We're caught in this race of whether the new governments can see their countries through these very dangerous and difficult times," says Landis.

The RAND researchers say economic failures do not necessarily doom efforts at democratization, but they warn that transitions in the Arab world may be "especially fragile" and "more vulnerable to economic strains than many past cases."[12]

Do Islamic groups pose a threat to political reform in the Arab world?

Egyptians were getting ready to vote on a new constitution that promises freedom of religion when an Egyptian court on Dec. 12 sentenced Alber Saber, an avowed atheist, to three years in prison for blasphemy.

Saber, 27, born into a Christian family, had been arrested in September based on never-confirmed reports that he had posted the controversial anti-Islam film "The Innocence of Muslims" on his blog. Authorities found enough evidence, however, to charge him with blasphemy for insulting both Islam and Christianity. "Egypt is a religious state," Saber said after appealing the sentence. "If you disobey the norms, you get judged and sentenced."[13]

The new constitution, approved in two rounds of balloting on Dec. 15 and Dec. 22, guarantees freedom of worship to believers in the three "monotheist" religions — Judaism, Christianity and Islam — but not to others. It also carries over a provision from the 1971 constitution designating Islam as the state religion and Islamic law, known as Sharia, as the source of legislation.

Under Mubarak, the government had banned the Muslim Brotherhood but protected the country's Christians, who comprise only 1 percent of the population. With the Muslim Brotherhood's Freedom and Justice Party dominating the new government, Christians and non-believers worry about possible repression. "Expect to see many more blasphemy prosecutions in the future," says Heba Morayef, a Cairo-based researcher with Human Rights Watch, the New York City-headquartered advocacy and monitoring organization.[14]

Whatever happens in Egypt, experts agree that Islamic parties will play an increasingly important role in Arab countries. Political Islam "is the one ideology that has roots with the people," says University of Oklahoma professor Landis. "Secularists are a distinct

minority. We're going to see Islamic governments from one end of the Middle East to another."

For much of the 20th century, Islamist organizations such as the Muslim Brotherhood — which was founded in Egypt in 1928 and later spawned branches in other countries — advocated violence as a political tactic, leading to bans and crackdowns from established regimes. UCLA's Gelvin now sees "a paradigm shift" as the groups, well organized despite a history of government repression, see opportunities in the new political openings. "It doesn't mean that Islamist organizations are going to be completely pro-democracy and human rights," Gelvin says. "But opportunities have opened for them to participate in democratic government."

With their superior political organization, Islamist parties are bound to be "the most powerful actors in the new regimes, at least in the short run," scholars Lesch and Haas write in their overview.[15]

Bahgat, the National Defense University professor, agrees. "It makes sense that they are winning many elections," he says, citing the voting in Tunisia and his native Egypt as examples. "They are winning because they are better organized than all other political groups."

Salem, the Carnegie expert in Beirut, acknowledges the disagreements in Egypt and Tunisia between Islamists and what he calls "non-Islamists" and "old regime forces." But he professes to be unconcerned. "Issues are being contested," he says, "but the good thing is they're being contested through political processes."

The sectarian division within Islam between Sunnis and Shiites is also an important factor in the ongoing political developments, according to Toby Jones, an associate professor of history at Rutgers University in New Brunswick, N.J. "Religious and ethnic differences have crept into politics in ways that we haven't seen before," says Jones, who specializes in the modern Middle East. "It's relatively new. It's very dangerous."

Sunni rulers in the Gulf states as well as Assad in Syria depict the popular protests as sectarian-motivated as a stratagem to stay in power, Jones says. "They all have an interest in claiming that sectarianism is the force that is at work," Jones explains. "It gives them legitimacy."

The Freedom House report gives Tunisia good marks on political reforms so far but takes a wait-and-see attitude toward Egypt. "The moderate Islamists in Tunisia who constitute the government have said mostly the

CHRONOLOGY

2010-2011 *Arab Spring begins; autocrats ousted in Tunisia, Egypt, Libya; Syria in civil war.*

December 2010 Tunisian fruit vendor Mohamed Bouazizi sets fire to himself to protest treatment by police (Dec. 17); incident sparks nationwide riots; President Zine El Abidine Ben Ali vows to punish protesters; Bouazizi dies on Jan. 4.

January 2011 Protests break out in Algeria, Egypt, Jordan, Yemen. . . . Ben Ali flees Tunisia (Jan. 14). . . . Demonstrations in Cairo's Tahrir Square call for Egyptian President Hosni Mubarak to resign (Jan. 25).

February 2011 Mubarak resigns; military council forms interim government (Feb. 11). . . . Libyans protest arrest of activist in Benghazi (Feb. 15); protests spread; leader Moammar Gadhafi vows to stay in office. . . . Protests erupt in Bahrain (Feb. 14), Morocco (Feb. 20).

March 2011 Protests banned nationwide in Saudi Arabia (March 5). . . . U.N. Security Council authorizes no-fly zone over Libya (March 17); rebels begin to capture territory, form transitional government. . . . Syrian security forces kill several people in provincial city of Daraa protesting arrest of political prisoners (March 18); protests spread to Damascus, other cities; tanks used to quell protests. . . . President Bashar Assad orders release of political prisoners (March 25-26).

April-June 2011 Protests in Egypt demand quick transfer of power by military. . . . Assad lifts state of emergency in Syria (April 21); security forces continue crackdowns. . . . Death toll in Egypt uprising: at least 846, according to judicial panel (April 19). . . . Four protesters sentenced to death in Bahrain (April 28). . . . Death toll in Tunisia uprising: at least 300, according to U.N. investigator (May 21). . . . Yemeni President Ali Abdullah Saleh injured in rocket attack, flown to Saudi Arabia (June 4).

July-September 2011 Free Syrian Army formed by defectors (July 29). . . . Battle of Tripoli: rebels capture city; Gadhafi overthrown (Aug. 20-28). . . . Saudi King Abdullah grants women right to vote, run in municipal elections (Sept. 25).

October-December 2011 Gadhafi captured, killed (Oct. 20). . . . Moderate Islamist party Ennhada leads in elections for Tunisian parliament (Oct. 23). . . . Sunni groups form National Salvation Council in Syria; Islamist groups refuse to join (November). . . . Saleh agrees to yield power in Yemen (Nov. 23). . . . Parliamentary elections begin in Egypt (Nov. 28); Muslim Brotherhood's Freedom and Justice Party leads after balloting concludes (Jan. 3).

2012-Present *Protests ebb; new governments take shape; Syrian civil war continues.*

January-March 2012 Syrian conflict intensifies; Russia, China block U.N. Security Council action (Feb. 4). . . . Abed Rabo Mansour Hadi elected Yemeni president in single-candidate vote (Feb. 21). . . . Egyptian parliament creates Islamist-dominated Constituent Assembly to draft new constitution; liberal lawmakers protest (March 24).

April-June 2012 Egyptian Constituent Assembly dissolved by court order (April 10). . . . Mubarak receives life sentence for role in killings of protesters (June 2); wins retrial (Jan. 13, 2013). . . . New Constituent Assembly created; critics still dissatisfied (June 12). . . . Ben Ali convicted in absentia for role in killings of protesters in Tunisia; sentenced to life (June 19). . . . Muslim Brotherhood's Mohammed Morsi elected president in Egypt (June 24).

July-September 2012 Liberal National Front Alliance leads in Libyan parliamentary elections; Islamists distant second (July 7). . . . U.S. ambassador, three others killed in attack on consulate in Benghazi (Sept. 11).

October-December 2012 Egyptian court skirts challenge to Constituent Assembly (Oct. 23). . . . Bahrain bans all protests (Oct. 30). . . . Morsi curbs judiciary's powers (Nov. 22); withdraws move under pressure (Dec. 8). . . . Draft constitution approved by Constituent Assembly (Nov. 29-30); approved by voters (Dec. 15, 22).

January 2013 Death toll in Syria put at 60,000 (Jan. 2); Assad vows to remain in office (Jan. 6). . . . Libyan government sharply reduces death toll estimate in civil war: 4,700 rebels killed, 2,100 missing; government losses thought comparable (Jan. 8). . . . Women named to Saudi advisory council for first time (Jan. 11). . . . New violence in Egypt marks second anniversary of revolution; military chief fears "collapse" of state (Jan. 25-29).

Syrian Civil War Has Region's Highest Death Toll

More than 60,000 are dead and millions homeless.

Students at Aleppo University in Syria were busy with exams on Jan. 15 when at least two massive bomb blasts shattered the campus. Dozens were killed and scores were wounded in carnage remarkable even for a country devastated by nearly two years of civil war.

"The most painful scene was a chopped hand with a pen and notebook right next to it," one student told *The New York Times* over Skype. "I saw blood [and] flesh littered all around."[1]

Tens of thousands of Syrians have witnessed similar scenes as strongman Bashar Assad tries to retain his presidency in the face of potent resistance by a confederation of rebel groups, some controlled by Western-oriented reformers and others by Islamist extremists.

Syria's civil war has killed more than 60,000, according to a United Nations-commissioned estimate released Jan. 2. The conflict has also laid waste to vast portions of the country stretching along the western border from Aleppo to Damascus. At the same time, the war has led to a humanitarian crisis, with more than 2 million refugees displaced inside Syria and possibly 1 million requiring humanitarian aid within the next six months in Jordan, Lebanon, Turkey and elsewhere.[2]

Without a quick resolution to the conflict — a scenario widely viewed by international observers as unlikely — "thousands more will die or suffer terrible injuries as a result of those who harbor the obstinate belief that something can be achieved by more bloodshed, more torture and more mindless destruction," according to Navi Pillay, the U.N. High Commissioner for Human Rights.[3]

The Syrian conflict is by far the deadliest of a string of uprisings that have rocked the Arab world in the past two years, but the death count is in the thousands in at least two other countries. Libya's new government released new, sharply reduced estimates on Jan. 8 that the civil war there claimed at least 4,700 lives on the rebels' side, with 2,100 missing; government losses were thought to be similar. The Yemeni government estimated in March 2012 that more than 2,000 had died in the political unrest there.

The death toll was in the hundreds in two other countries: Egypt and Tunisia. A judicial panel in Egypt in April 2011 said 846 people died in the revolution there. An investigative panel in Tunisia reported in May 2011 that 300 people had died in the Tunisian uprising. In Bahrain, a reform group counts 91 deaths, but news organizations put the death toll less exactly at more than 50.[4]

The International Rescue Committee's Commission on Syrian Refugees has been responsible for supplying medical aid and humanitarian assistance to women affected by sexual violence and to refugees displaced by the conflict. The IRC commission says sexual violence and child kidnappings by Syrian army troops have been primary causes for many families' decisions to flee the country.

rights things and have done mostly things that advance democracy," says Arch Puddington, vice president for research and editor of the annual volume. But he calls Egypt "another case." Morsi's tendency "is to address his message to his fellow brothers," Puddington says, referring to Muslim Brotherhood members, "and to the entire population second."

Other experts are also cautious about prospects in Egypt. "We're going to have to see how it plays out," says Landis. But Bahgat expects the Muslim Brotherhood to face more serious political competition as time goes on.

"The Islamists will not be able to solve the economic problems," Bahgat explains. "In the next round of elections, other groups, most likely liberals, will get better organized, and the people will have less confidence in the Islamists."

Can a stable political solution be found in Syria?

The capture of a key Syrian military air base by rebels on Jan. 11 further weakens the Assad regime's hold on the country, but the victory is a mixed blessing for the United States and others hoping for democratic change

Aleppo, Syria's largest city with more than 2 million people, bristles with military checkpoints. Vast tracts of homes and businesses have been damaged or destroyed. Pedestrians risk being shot in crossfires on bombed-out streets.[5]

Aleppo became a prime target in late July 2012 as Syrian army forces began shelling the city in a thus-far unsuccessful attempt to drive out the rebels. The attack on the public university, the country's flagship educational institution, was unprecedented.

The responsibility for the Aleppo University bomb blasts is disputed. Pro-rebel factions contend that Assad directed the Syrian air force to bomb the university; Syria's state-run news service said an unnamed terrorist organization was responsible. The Syrian Observatory for Human Rights said the explosions could have resulted from government airstrikes or from car bombs, which have been used by rebel groups.

What students saw, however, remains undeniable and clear: "Two big holes, caused by two missiles," in what had been the campus square, student Abu Tayem said. "I could not see it any more, it's vanished."[6]

— *Ethan McLeod*

Bombs devastated Aleppo University on Jan. 15, 2013, killing at least 87 people. More than 60,000 people have died in Syria's civil war, and some experts say the toll could reach 100,000 or more.

AFP/Getty Images/STR

[1]Hwaida Saad and Rick Gladstone, "Dozens Killed as Explosions Hit Syrian University," *The New York Times*, Jan. 15, 2013, www.nytimes.com/2013/01/16/world/middleeast/syria-violence.html?pagewanted=2&_r=0.

[2]See "Syria: A Regional Crisis: The IRC Commission on Syrian Refugees," International Rescue Committee, January 2013, www.rescue.org/sites/default/files/resource-file/IRCReportMidEast20130114.pdf. For coverage, see Ashish Kumar Sen, "Refugees flood Syria's neighbors," *The Washington Times*, Jan. 17, 2013, www.washingtontimes.com/news/2013/jan/17/syrian-war-creating-historic-refugee-crisis/.

[3]"Data Suggests Syria Death Toll Could be More than 60,000, Says UN Human Rights Office," United Nations News Centre, Jan. 2, 2013, www.un.org/apps/news/story.asp?NewsID=43866.

[4]Information drawn from, Ian Black, "Libyan revolution casualties lower than expected, says new government," *The Guardian*, Jan. 8, 2013, www.guardian.co.uk/world/2013/jan/08/libyan-revolution-casualties-lower-expected-government; Ahmed al-Haj, "Yemen Death Toll: Over 2,000 Killed In Uprising," The Associated Press, March 18, 2012, www.huffingtonpost.com/2012/03/19/yemen-death-toll_n_1361840.html; Almasry Ahmed, "At least 846 killed in Egypt's revolution," *Egypt Independent*, April 19, 2011, www.egyptindependent.com/news/least-846-killed-egypt%E2%80%99s-revolution; "Tunisia: High death toll challenges claims of smooth transition," *Los Angeles Times*, May 22, 2011, latimesblogs.latimes.com/babylonbeyond/2011/05/tunisia-uprising-violence-repression-human-rights-torture-.html; "91 Killed Since 14th February 2011," Bahrain Justice and Development Movement, www.bahrainjdm.org/78-killed-since-14th-february-2011/.

[5]See C. J. Chivers, "Rubble and Despair Redefine Syria Jewel," *The New York Times*, Dec. 18, 2012, www.nytimes.com/2012/12/19/world/middleeast/aleppo-residents-battered-by-war-struggle-to-survive.html?pagewanted=all.

[6]Saad and Gladstone, *op. cit.*

in post-Assad Syria. The rebels who seized the Taftanaz military base in the northwestern province of Idlib were primarily from Jabhat al-Nusra, a jihadist group designated by the United States as a terrorist organization and thought to have ties to al Qaeda in Iraq. By gaining weapons and credit from the victory, analysts said, the jihadists strengthened their position and stoked fears among Syria's minority Alawite community of a sectarian bloodbath if Assad falls.[16]

At the outset, the uprising in Syria caught outside observers, not to mention the Assad regime itself, totally by surprise.[17] Assad, a Western-educated ophthalmologist, had been viewed as a reformer when elected president at age 37 in 2000 after his father's death. He remained well-liked in Syria despite the regime's crackdown on protests before 2011, according to Lesch, the Trinity University professor who came to know Assad well while writing a biography.[18] The regime seemed to satisfy the country's Sunni majority while also protecting the interests of the Shia minority and the Alawite community that was the elder Assad's home and the regime's political base. In addition, the initial protests in Damascus and elsewhere in early 2011 drew small numbers and were easily put down.

The unrest became more serious and the crackdown turned deadly when security forces killed at least five people in the southern provincial town of Daraa on March 18, 2011, as they were protesting the arrest of schoolchildren for anti-government graffiti. In the nearly two years since, the unrest has turned into a bloody civil war. Rebel forces now control parts of the country, but the government counters with lethal force, including missile attacks in civilian neighborhoods.

Tabler is one of many experts who believes Assad must either step aside or resign himself eventually to being deposed. RAND expert Jones agrees. "The prognosis for the Assad regime is bleak," Jones says. "It's likely to fall, but it's hard to put a time frame on that." Some Syria-watchers think Assad could fall from power any day, but many others expect him to hold on for a while.

"Syria is looking forward to a long, hard-fought struggle that's going to devastate the country," says University of Oklahoma professor Landis, who hosts an up-to-date blog, *Syria Comment.*[19]

The experts are equally bleak in their predictions for a post-Assad Syria. The Syrian opposition is loosely organized — "fragmented," as University of Connecticut professor Pressman puts it. "There is no clear leadership," says Bahgat, at the National Defense University. Gelvin at UCLA says Muslim Brotherhood groups "claim to be for democracy and human rights," but "we don't know much about them." The jihadist groups, he says, are better known. "They are very sectarian," Gelvin says. "For the most part, they are not interested in ruling Syria. They want to use Syria as a jumping-off point for a larger uprising in the Islamic world."

The opposition's support among the Syrian people is difficult to gauge but at the least subject to doubt. The nationalist Free Syrian Army, formed in summer 2011 by defectors from Assad's security forces, is said to be losing support as individual commanders turn into local warlords. Jihadist groups are gaining good will, in part because they are helping to provide food and supplies to beleaguered towns such as Aleppo in the northwest. Peter Harling, an analyst with the International Crisis Group, says the opposition has failed to woo Alawites within the regime or to reach out to other disaffected communities.[20]

Many Alawites fear a bloodbath if the rebels force Assad from power. "If I were Alawi, I would fight to the end," says Bahgat. "If Assad falls, the Alawi will pay a price."

Salem, with the Carnegie Endowment, agrees. "There's a lot of people who want to take revenge," he says.

The government is responding to its weakened position with "a scorched-earth policy," according to Salem. "Rather than cede power to another party, it prefers to destroy what is left and leave nothing standing to whoever comes after," he says. The remnants of Assad's government can continue the fight by retiring to the Alawite community's northwest coastal home, he notes.

"I see no signs that this conflict will do anything but worsen," Tabler concludes.

Landis is just as pessimistic about the political dynamic. Syria "is not going to be a democracy for a long time," he says.

BACKGROUND

Strangers to Democracy

The Arab world knew little of freedom or democracy before or during most of the 20th century. The defeat of the Ottoman Empire in World War I left Arab lands from Morocco to Iraq under European rule as colonies or protectorates. As Arab nations gained independence after World War II, they emerged not as democracies but as autocracies ruled by long-serving monarchs or by strongmen from the ranks of the military. The leaders used nationalist and pan-Arabist rhetoric to hold popular support even as social and economic problems festered.[21]

An Arab empire once stretched from Spain in the west to the Asian subcontinent in the east, but the Ottoman Empire displaced it by conquest in the 15th century. European colonial powers gained footholds in North Africa in the 1800s. Britain and France took over parts of the Ottoman Empire in the Middle East after their victory in World War I. Britain controlled Palestine, Transjordan and Iraq and exercised strong influence over Egypt after unilaterally granting it nominal independence in 1922. France got the territory that became Syria and Lebanon and maintained colonial rule over Morocco, Algeria and Tunisia. Italy controlled what was to become Libya. The Ottoman Empire had been decentralized and religiously tolerant but with no tradition of political rights. Britain and France were granted mandates by the League of Nations in order to guide the Arab nations to self-governance, but they instituted only limited reforms and installed compliant rulers who protected the Europeans' interests even as nationalism was emerging as a force. Meanwhile, Saudi Arabia was formed in 1932 as an Islamic kingdom on the Arabian peninsula, an area viewed as worthless desert until the discovery of oil later in the decade. The end of World War II brought independence for Jordan and Syria and, in 1948, the creation of the Jewish state of Israel — with unsettling consequences for the politics of the region.

The defeat of the then-seven member Arab League in the first Arab-Israeli War (1948-49) stoked nationalist and pan-Arabist sentiment in many of the now-independent Arab nations. In Egypt, a military coup ousted the pro-British monarchy in 1952 and created a republic that was transformed over the next four years into a one-party state led by Gamal Abdel Nasser. Nasser translated his pan-Arabist views into an agreement with Syria in 1958 to form the United Arab Republic, but the union lasted only until 1961 as Syria chafed under the domination of its larger partner. Nasser ruled Egypt until his death in 1970; his successor, Anwar Sadat, reinstituted a multiparty system and moved away from Nasser's Arab socialism during 11 years in office until his 1981 assassination by opponents of Sadat's landmark 1979 peace agreement with Israel.

Syria, meanwhile, experienced two decades of extreme political instability after gaining independence from the French after World War II. Politics came to be dominated by the Arab Ba'ath Party (translation: "resurrection" or "renaissance"), founded by pan-Arabist Syrians in 1947. Power lay, however, not with political institutions but with the military and security establishment. Baathists divided in the 1960s into civilian- and military-oriented wings, with Air Force officer Hafez Assad — the father of Bashar — emerging as a major figure in successive coups in 1963 and 1966. As minister of defense after 1966, Assad maneuvered against the de facto leader, Salah Jadid, and then gained unchallenged power after mounting successive military coups in 1969 and 1970.

Strongman rulers came to the fore in several other countries, generally stifling any significant moves toward democracy. In Tunisia, the anti-colonialist leader Habib

AFP/Getty Images/STR

Refugees fleeing Syria's civil war face harsh conditions, including supply shortages, freezing temperatures and snow, in a camp in Turkey on Jan. 9, 2013. The war has created what Human Rights Watch calls "a dire humanitarian situation." More than 2 million Syrians have been displaced internally, and possibly 1 million more may require humanitarian aid within the next six months in Jordan, Lebanon, Turkey and elsewhere.

Bourguiba became president in 1957 of what would become a single-party state; he held office until 1987 when Ben Ali engineered his removal on grounds of mental incompetency. In neighboring Libya, Gadhafi led a bloodless military coup in 1969, ousting a corruption-tainted monarchy while espousing reformist and nationalist views; he wielded power, often ruthlessly, until his death in the Libyan Revolution of 2011. In Iraq, Saddam Hussein rose through the ranks of the Ba'ath Party to become president in 1979, the beginning of a sometimes brutal, 24-year rule that ended with his ouster in the U.S.-led invasion in 2003. In Yemen, Ali Abdullah Saleh began a 33-year tenure as president in 1978 — first as president of North Yemen and after 1990 as president of the Yemeni Arab Republic following the unification with formerly Marxist South Yemen.

Saudi Arabia gained influence in the region through its oil wealth, but political power remained consolidated in the royal family through a succession of long-serving successors to the kingdom's founder, Ibn Saud (1932-1953).

Among the Gulf states, the island sheikhdom of Bahrain took a stab at parliamentary democracy after declaring independence from Britain in 1971, but Sheikh Isa bin Salman Al Khalifa clamped down on dissent after

Egypt's New Constitution Gets Mixed Reviews

Some say the document creates "prospects of a religious state."

Egypt's new constitution includes a host of provisions that appear to strengthen protections for individual rights. But human rights advocates in Egypt and in the United States say it is deeply flawed because it vests too much power in the president, creates significant exceptions for some rights and opens the door to instituting Islamic law at the potential expense of religious freedom.

"From a liberal democratic perspective, there is much to like in the document," writes Nathan Brown, a professor of political science and international affairs at George Washington University in Washington, D.C. But, Brown adds, "the document includes just as much that causes concern."[1]

Egyptian voters approved the new, 234-article constitution with about 64 percent of the vote in a low-turnout, two-stage referendum on Dec. 15 and 22 that drew only one-third of the electorate to the polls. Opponents complained the referendum was hastily called after a drafting process by the Islamist-dominated Constituent Assembly that was itself too rushed and too contentious. President Mohammed Morsi made a nationally televised address on Dec. 26, the day after the results were announced, to acknowledge unspecified "mistakes" in the process while promising "to respect the law and constitution."[2]

The new constitution, replacing one that was adopted in 1971, shortens the president's term from six years to four and imposes a two-term limit instead of allowing unlimited terms. But Brown says the constitution "is more presidential than might have been expected." And Hafez Abu Saeda, head of the Egyptian Organization for Human Rights, complained in advance of the referendum about provisions allowing the president to appoint the prime minister, dissolve parliament and name members of the Supreme Constitutional Court.[3]

In another analysis before the referendum, the U.S.-headquartered Human Rights Watch praised the charter for its "strong protection" against arbitrary detention, torture and inhumane treatment and for freedom of movement, privacy of communication and freedom of assembly and association. But it noted that other provisions imposed significant qualifications on those rights — such as provisions against "insulting" individuals or "the prophets." The group noted that criminal prosecutions for insulting the president or the judiciary have increased since Morsi took office.[4]

The new constitution carries over a provision from the 1971 charter — Article 2 in both documents — that declares Islam to be the state religion and Islamic law, or Sharia, the principal source of legislation. The new constitution adds a new provision, Article 219, that defines Sharia broadly to include what is translated into English as "general evidence and foundations, rules and jurisprudence as well as sources accepted by doctrines of Sunni Islam and the majority of Muslim scholars." In a separate provision, the constitution specifies that scholars at the Islamic Al-Azhar University shall be consulted on all matters of Sharia law.

Magdi Khalil, an Egyptian who serves as executive director of the Belin-based Mideast Freedom Forum, calls the provisions "catastrophic" because they "create prospects of a religious state."[5] But Brown and coauthor Clark Lombardi, an associate professor at the University of Washington School of Law in Seattle, say the meaning of the new provisions remains to be seen. "There will continue to be fierce argument," they write, "about what types of law are permissible in a self-styled Islamic state and, of course, about which are wise."[6]

— Kenneth Jost

---

[1]Nathan J. Brown, "Egypt's Constitution Conundrum," *Foreign Affairs*, Dec. 9, 2012, www.foreignaffairs.com/articles/138495/nathan-j-brown/egypts-constitution-conundrum.

[2]See David D. Kirkpatrick, "Despite 'Mistakes,' Morsi Says Constitution Fight Was Democracy in Action," *The New York Times*, Dec. 27, 2012, p. A8. See also Sarah el Deeb, "Egypt's Morsi: constitution dawn of new republic," The Associated Press, Dec. 26, 2012. A video of the speech, delivered in Arabic, is posted on an Egyptian news site: http://nilesports.com/news/2012/12/26/video-president-mohamed-morsi-speech-december-26-2012/. For other background, see Ingy Hassieb and Abigal Hauslohner, "Egyptian voters adopt faith-based constitution," *The Washington Post*, Dec. 24, 2012, p. A8; David D. Kirkpatrick and Mayy el Sheikh, "As Constitution Nears Approval, Egypt's Factions Face New Fights," *The New York Times*, Dec. 23, 2012, p. A1.

[3]"Egyptian Human Rights Experts Analyze Draft Constitution," Washington Institute for Near East Policy, Nov. 15, 2012, www.washingtoninstitute.org/policy-analysis/view/egyptian-human-rights-experts-analyze-the-draft-constitution.

[4]"Egypt: New Constitution Mixed on Support of Rights," Human Rights Watch, www.hrw.org/news/2012/11/29/egypt-new-constitution-mixed-support-rights.

[5]See "Egyptian Human Rights Experts," *op. cit.*

[6]Clark Lombardi and Nathan J. Brown, "Islam in Egypt's New Constitution," *Foreign Policy*, Dec. 13, 2012, http://mideast.foreignpolicy.com/posts/2012/12/13/islam_in_egypts_new_constitution.

leftists and Shiites won nearly half the seats in parliamentary elections in 1973. Elsewhere, constitutional monarchs — Jordan's King Hussein (1953-1999) and Morocco's King Hassan II (1961-1999) — dominated the political scene while instituting reforms: modest in Morocco, more extensive in Jordan.

Overall, Freedom House's survey of the 16 Arab lands from Morocco to Iraq in 1979 rated none of them as free, nine as partly free and seven as not free.[22]

'Freedom Deficit'

Arab and Muslim countries remained impervious to the advances for political rights and civil liberties in much of the world as the 20th century ended. Repression was the order of the day in many countries — with Egypt and Syria among the worst. In Egypt, an emergency decree ordered by Mubarak after Sadat's 1981 assassination by Muslim fundamentalists remained in effect until Mubarak was forced out of office in February 2011. In Syria, Assad put down Sunni opposition to his regime with a ruthlessness best exemplified by the 1982 massacre in the city of Hama that claimed at least 10,000 lives. By 2001, Mali in West Africa was alone among the 47 majority-Muslim countries to be rated by Freedom House as free.[23]

Mubarak rose from Air Force ranks to become Sadat's vice president and then to succeed to the presidency unopposed in a referendum held a week after the slaying. He won three additional six-year terms in successive referendums, also unopposed. Mubarak called the assassination part of a plot to overthrow the government.

The emergency decree adopted after Sadat's slaying sharply limited political activity and allowed detention and imprisonment of political dissidents. As many as 30,000 people may have been held as political prisoners during the period. Parliamentary elections were held under rules favoring Mubarak's governing National Democratic Party. The Muslim Brotherhood, the largest opposition group, remained under a ban imposed in 1954. Throughout the period, Mubarak remained an important U.S. ally, even as political conditions failed to improve and evidence of personal and government-wide corruption grew.

Assad ruled Syria through a combination of guile and ruthlessness for nearly 30 years until his death in June 2000. His secularist policies — including equal rights for women — drew opposition from the Muslim Brotherhood beginning in the mid-1970s. Assad responded to the Brotherhood's attempt to take control of the west central city of Hama in February 1982 by ordering the city shelled and having its civilian population pay the price in lives lost.

Assad's military-security apparatus crushed any incipient opposition with similar ruthlessness, including torture. But Assad also won loyalty through financial ties with Syria's business community, patronage in a bloated state sector and tough anti-Israeli rhetoric. The United States designated Syria a state sponsor of terrorism from 1979 on but also worked to win Assad's support for, or at least acquiescence in, Arab-Israeli peace negotiations.

Hussein in Iraq and Gadhafi in Libya earned reputations as the region's other two worst dictators and biggest problems for U.S. policy. Both countries were designated as state sponsors of terrorism, though Iraq was removed from the list during the 1980s when the United States supported Baghdad in its war with Iran. Both men ruled through a combination of cult-of-personality adulation and coldblooded repression of political dissent. Hussein survived Iraq's defeat by a U.S.-led coalition in the Gulf War in 1991, his stature within Iraq seemingly enhanced; he won show elections in 1995 and 2002 with 99.9 percent and 100 percent, respectively, of the vote. Gadhafi survived a retaliatory U.S. air strike on his home in April 1986 and, like Hussein later, appeared only to gain political stature at home from his successful defiance of Washington.

The rise of Islamist parties unsettled politics in several countries, resulting in repressive crackdowns — most notably, in Algeria. The Algerian government's decision to cancel parliamentary elections in 1991 to thwart a potential victory by the newly formed Islamic Salvation Front touched off a decade-long civil war that may have claimed as many as 200,000 lives. In neighboring Tunisia, Ben Ali followed suit by cracking down on Islamist groups, abandoning the political liberalization of his first years in office. In Bahrain, the Shiite majority, chafing under Sunni rule and adverse economic conditions, clamored for restoration of the post-independence constitution, but the government responded by jailing dissidents. Meanwhile, Yemeni president Saleh held on to power despite secessionist sentiment in the south that continued after the north's victory in a brief civil war in 1994.

Freedom House contrasted political developments in the Muslim world with changes in other regions in its 2001 annual report. Despite "significant gains for democracy and freedom" in Latin America, Africa, Eastern and Central Europe and South and East Asia, the report stated, the Muslim world "experienced a significant increase in repression."[24]

A year later, a group of Arab intellectuals convened by a United Nations agency cited what they called the Arab world's "freedom deficit" as a major factor in the region's lagging social and economic indicators.[25] The 180-page report, sponsored by the U.N. Development Programme's regional bureau for Arab states, concluded that despite supposed acceptance of democracy and human rights in constitutions and legal codes, representative democracy was "not always genuine and sometimes absent."

Freedoms of expression and association were "frequently curtailed," the report continued, and political participation was "less advanced" than in other developing regions. The report tied political conditions to "deep and complex economic and social problems," including "high illiteracy rates," "rampant poverty" and "mounting unemployment rates." But it closed on the hopeful note that the problems could be eased with political reforms.

Warming Trends?

The Arab world felt stirrings of political change during the early years of the 21st century, but only in 2011 did popular discontent succeed in toppling regimes. Political developments unfolded against the backdrop of increased global attention on the Muslim world as the United States waged war first against the anti-American Islamist terrorist group al Qaeda in Afghanistan and then against Saddam Hussein in Iraq. Sectarian politics complicated democratization in Iraq and figured in unfolding events elsewhere, including Syria. The ouster of leaders in Tunisia, Egypt and Libya in 2011 encouraged democratization advocates, but Syria's civil war defied resolution, and only limited reforms were instituted elsewhere.

Midway through the century's first decade, Freedom House in 2006 reported a "positive regional trajectory" for political and civil rights in the Middle East and North Africa. Among the gains cited was Lebanon's popular "Cedar Revolution," which set the stage for free elections after forcing the withdrawal of Syria's occupying troops.

The report also noted competitive elections in Egypt, Iraq and Palestine. The gains were easy to exaggerate, however. In Egypt, Mubarak won his first competitive presidential election in September 2005 with 89 percent of the vote, and the ruling National Democratic Party still commanded a two-thirds majority in parliament after December balloting despite 87 seats won by Muslim Brotherhood candidates running as independents. Parliamentary elections in Iraq the same month resulted in a fragile coalition government still riven by sectarian disputes. And in balloting a month later, the hard-line organization Hamas won a majority in the Palestinian parliament.

Five years later, the Arab street wrought more significant changes, starting in Tunisia.[26] The uprising — dubbed the Jasmine Revolution in the West but not in Tunisia itself — began with the Dec. 17, 2010, self-immolation of unlicensed street vendor Mohamed Bouazizi to protest his alleged mistreatment by police. Protests driven by unemployment and inflation as well as political repression spread through the country quickly and picked up more steam after Bouazizi's death on Jan. 4. With a nationwide strike called and the military backing the revolution, Ben Ali fled on Jan. 14 for exile in Saudi Arabia. After false starts, a transitional government with no holdovers from Ben Ali's regime scheduled elections in October. The once-banned Islamist party Ennahda won a 41 percent plurality of the vote, but the party's leader, the once exiled Rachid Gannouchi, pledged to support democracy and human rights. Meanwhile, Ben Ali was convicted in absentia in June of embezzlement and sentenced along with his wife to 35 years' imprisonment; the next summer, a military court convicted him, again in absentia, of his role in the deaths of protesters and sentenced him to life in prison. Saudi Arabia has refused to extradite him.

Events in Egypt proceeded even more rapidly than in Tunisia, especially after "Day of Revolt" protests in Cairo and several other cities on Jan. 25, 2011. Six days later, hundreds of thousands massed in Cairo's Tahrir Square — al Jazeera estimated the crowd at 2 million — to protest Mubarak's continued rule. Mubarak tried to quiet the unrest the next day by promising reforms and pledging not to seek re-election in September, but the protests continued with military leaders significantly pledging neutrality.

Mubarak tried again on Feb. 10 by delegating powers to his vice president, but the next day — prodded by a phone call from U.S. President Obama — Mubarak formally resigned. In parliamentary elections held between November 2011 and January 2012, the Muslim Brotherhood's Freedom and Justice Party won 47 percent of the seats; Morsi's election as president in June made him the first Islamist elected leader of an Arab state. Meanwhile, Mubarak had been convicted in June of failing to stop the killing of protesters and sentenced to life imprisonment.

The ouster of Gadhafi in the Libyan civil war took longer and required outside military assistance. Gadhafi's intelligence chief responded to information about a planned anti-government demonstration in February 2011 by arresting one of the leaders, Fathi Tarbel. Despite Tarbel's release shortly afterwards, the Feb. 15 arrest ignited protests that spread from the eastern city of Benghazi through much of the country. Gadhafi responded with brute force, calling in foreign mercenaries to aid his own troops and air force. In March, the U.N. Security Council authorized a no-fly zone to protect civilians; NATO set up the protective zone with U.S. help. Gadhafi's fate was sealed when rebels took over the capital city of Tripoli in late August; the fallen dictator was found on Oct. 20 hiding in a culvert west of the central coastal city of Sirte and killed on the spot. The liberal National Front Alliance won 48 percent of the seats in parliamentary elections in July 2012, with the Islamic Justice and Construction Party a distant second with 10 percent of the seats.

The uprising in Syria grew from protests over the March 2011 arrest of graffiti-writing school boys in Daraa into full-fledged civil war. Assad responded on March 30 with promises of political reform and some economic concessions, but then with force as the unrest continued. By summer, the death toll had exceeded 1,000. Military defectors formed the Syrian Free Army in July; the next month, opponents established the National Council of Syria, which demands Assad's resignation and democratic elections. The fighting continued even as former U.N. Secretary-General Kofi Annan attempted mediation; he abandoned the effort by August 2012 in the face of mounting casualties and a flood of refugees. With high-level defections from the regime, more and more observers concluded that Assad's days were numbered, but he defied opponents by pledging on Jan. 6 to stay in office.

Protests in the two lesser conflict zones —Yemen and Bahrain — achieved no substantial change. In Yemen,

On the Hot Seat

Egyptian President Mohammed Morsi (top) has been criticized by Freedom House for his dismissal of the lower house of parliament in June and his claim of broad executive powers in November. The democracy advocacy group warns that the survival of democracy in the Arab world's most populous nation "remains very much an open question." President Bashar Assad of Syria (bottom) blames the country's ongoing civil war on criminals, terrorists and foreign influences. Assad, whose strongman father ruled Syria for nearly 30 years before his succession in June 2000, responded to the popular uprisings in 2011 "by waging war against his own people," says Freedom House.

Saleh replied to protests beginning in January 2011 with a pledge not to seek re-election in 2013. With the protests continuing, Saleh was injured in a rocket attack in June and flown to Saudi Arabia for treatment. He returned in September and two months later handed over power to his deputy, Abed Rabbo Mansour Hadi, who won an uncontested presidential election in February 2012. In Bahrain, the government responded quickly to protests that began in the capital city of Manama in February 2011 by calling in help from Saudi troops the next month. The government clamped down by destroying the Pearl Monument, the focal point of the demonstrations; banning political parties; and arresting and prosecuting leading dissidents. New protests in October 2012 prompted an indefinite ban on all political gatherings.

CURRENT SITUATION

Transition Troubles

Egypt's Muslim Brotherhood-dominated government is working to consolidate power while grappling with economic difficulties and continuing opposition from liberal and secularist groups, many of whom protested in Cairo and elsewhere on Jan. 25 to mark the second anniversary of the beginning of the Egyptian revolution.[27]

Tens of thousands joined the opposition-organized protests in Cairo's Tahrir Square, Alexandria and Suez on Jan. 25, two years to the day after the first of the 2011 protests that culminated in Mubarak's resignation. Protesters complain that the new government, led by Morsi and dominated by the Muslim Brotherhood-founded Freedom and Justice Party, has betrayed the revolution's democratic aspirations and failed to reverse an economic slide blamed largely on declining foreign investment and tourism.

To avoid confrontations with the opposition, Islamist parties — which have prevailed so far in six elections for president, parliament and a new constitution — marked the anniversary in public gatherings elsewhere. Protesters clashed with police, however, resulting in more than 200 injuries to demonstrators or security forces. More than 40 deaths were reported in Suez.[28]

The disorder widened over the weekend of Jan. 26-27 after a court in Port Said sentenced 21 local soccer fans to death for their role in a brawl at a match between Port Said and Cairo teams on Feb. 1, 2012, that resulted in 74 deaths. Protests over the verdicts in several cities led Morsi to impose martial law. By Jan. 28, more than 50

people had been killed in demonstrations that fused anger over the verdicts with disapproval of Morsi's leadership.

"The government is trying to assure everybody that we are on the right track," says Bahgat, the Egyptian-born professor at National Defense University in Washington. "On the other side, the opposition and a good number of people are not happy."

Despite the protests, the Islamist parties have the advantages of better organization and greater unity than the opposition groups in the run-up to elections in April for the lower house of parliament. The opposition groups reportedly are divided over previously announced plans to run as a single ticket in April.[29]

The governing Freedom and Justice Party has officially designated itself as a "civil" party to counteract Christian and secularist fears that it intends to establish a theocracy. But the constitution that Morsi pushed toward voter approval in December reaffirms Islam as the state religion. Other Islamist parties now form the Islamist Alliance, which differs with the Freedom and Justice Party in taking a stricter approach on some issues of Islamic law and a harder line toward Israel.

Opposition groups formed the umbrella National Salvation Front in December in an unsuccessful effort to reject the proposed constitution. The groups range from the Wafd Party, successor to an elite-dominated party banned by Nasser in the 1950s, to the April 6 Youth Movement, the social media-based grouping that figured prominently in the January 25 Revolution.

Apart from election-related maneuverings, Morsi is working to put his stamp on the machinery of government even as his government faces two high-profile challenges: negotiations with the International Monetary Fund (IMF) over a $4.8 billion loan and the court-ordered retrial of Mubarak for failing to prevent bloodshed during the 2011 uprising.

The IMF loan is needed to offset the loss of foreign currency from investment and tourism and the resulting sharp decline in the value of the Egyptian pound. To approve the loan, the IMF is likely to require politically difficult reductions in subsidies for food and fuel. Bahgat expects an eventual agreement. "The IMF recognizes that Egypt is too big to fail," he says.

Meanwhile, Mubarak, 84 and in ill health, remains in a military hospital after his arrest and his conviction and life sentence in June 2012 for failing to stop the killings of protesters. An Egyptian appeals court reversed the conviction

Should the U.S. and its allies intervene militarily in Syria?

YES Andrew Tabler
Senior Fellow, Program on Arab Politics, Washington Institute for Near East Policy; Author, In the Lion's Den: An Eyewitness Account of Washington's Battle with Syria

Written for *CQ Global Researcher*, February 2013

"You break it, you buy it" may have proven true for the United States in Iraq, but great powers are often forced to help clean up conflicts they did not cause but that threaten their interests. If Washington continues its "light footprint" policy of non-intervention in Syria, the American people will likely have to foot the bill for a more expensive cleanup of the spillover of the Syria conflict into neighboring states and the overall battle against international terrorism.

Every indicator of the conflict between the Alawite-dominated Assad regime and the largely Sunni opposition has taken a dramatic turn for the worse, with upwards of 65,000 killed, 30,000 missing and up to 3 million Syrians internally displaced during one of the worst Syrian winters in two decades. The Assad regime shows no sign of ending the slaughter anytime soon, increasingly deploying artillery, combat aircraft and most recently surface-to-surface missiles against the opposition. Reports quoting high-ranking U.S. government officials say the Assad regime has already loaded chemical weapons into bombs near or on regime airfields for possible deployment.

Signs are growing of a sectarian proxy war as well, with the Islamic Republic of Iran and Lebanese Hezbollah backing their fellow Shia at the Assad regime's core and Qatar, Saudi Arabia and Turkey backing their Sunni brethren in the opposition. Al Qaeda affiliates, as well as jihadists, are now among the opposition's best-armed factions.

The Obama administration has refrained from directly intervening or supporting Syria's increasingly armed opposition, based on an argument that neither would make the situation better. But allowing the conflict to continue and simply offering humanitarian and project assistance treats merely the symptoms while failing to shape a political settlement that would help cure the disease: a brutal Assad regime that was unable to reform trying to shoot one of the youngest populations in the Middle East into submission.

The Obama administration spent its first two years encouraging a treaty between the Assad regime and Israel that would take Damascus out of Iran's orbit and isolate its ally Hezbollah. While the method proved wrong, the strategic goals of containing Iranian influence in the region and keeping it from obtaining a nuclear weapon remain as valid as ever. Helping the Syrian opposition push Assad and his regime aside more quickly would help the United States and its allies achieve those objectives.

NO Brian Fishman
Counterterrorism Research Fellow, New America Foundation

Written for *CQ Global Researcher*, February 2013

If we learn nothing else from more than a decade of war in Iraq and Afghanistan, it must be that high hopes and good intentions help begin wars but do not help end them. Limited war in Syria is a recipe for mission creep and another long-term U.S. commitment to war in the Middle East.

That is why proposals for increased American military intervention in Syria are unconvincing. Broad-based American military action could tip the scales against the dictatorial Syrian regime but would not resolve the deep political conflicts in Syria. And more constrained proposals for military intervention would be unlikely to resolve the conflict.

The United States has many laudable goals in Syria that could plausibly justify military force: undermining an Iranian ally, eliminating a dictator, safeguarding civilians. Indeed, the United States should never hesitate to use military force when it is necessary to protect U.S. interests, but it must use military force only when the killing and dying that it implies are likely to achieve American political goals. That is not the case in Syria.

Public discussions about Syria were hyper-optimistic after the outbreak of peaceful protests against Bashar al-Assad in early 2011. Bolstered by the successes of the Arab Spring, many hoped the protests would not turn violent; they did. Observers ignored the presence of jihadis in the insurgency for months after it became clear that groups linked to al Qaeda were a major force driving the fighting. Still, today the clear split between Arab and Kurdish elements of the rebel coalition is poorly reported in the American press. And many observers have underestimated the cohesion of the Syrian regime, even as the country collapsed around it.

The situation in Syria is undoubtedly terrible. Assad's regime limps on with backing from Iran, and al Qaeda has emerged as one of the most powerful militant networks in the country. But the idea that limited military action — a no-fly zone coupled with increased military aid to rebels — will resolve these challenges is more hyper-optimism from well-intentioned people. One example: The threat will increase that Syria's chemical weapons will be used or proliferate as the regime's hold on power weakens.

Limited military force will redefine but not end the civil war in Syria and it will commit the United States to "solving" Syria politically. During the 1990s in Iraq, no-fly zones failed to destroy Saddam Hussein's regime, and military action to depose him in 2003 heralded chaos that empowered al Qaeda and Iran. Advocates of force in Syria have not offered a plausible argument for why we would do better this time.

AFP/Getty Images/Mohammed al-Shaikh

Shiite Muslims in Malikiya, Bahrain, demonstrate against the government and in support of political prisoners on Dec. 4, 2012. Government action against protesters in Bahrain has led to an estimated 50-100 deaths. Besides Syria, Bahrain provides the most dramatic example of what Freedom House labels the "intransigence" exhibited by many Arab nations toward popular uprisings.

and sentence on Jan. 13, sending the case back to a lower court for a new trial and possibly further investigation. Mubarak and his security chief, Habib el-Adly, whose conviction also was reversed, were the only security officials found guilty in trials stemming from the more than 800 deaths in the uprisings.

Post-revolutionary transitions in neighboring countries to Egypt's west are proceeding on significantly different paths, with generally successful democratization in Tunisia but violence- and abuse-riddled chaos in Libya.

Tunisia conducted "relatively free and fair elections" for the National Constituent Assembly in October 2011, according to Human Rights Watch, resulting in an interim coalition headed by the moderate Islamist party Ennahda in partnership with two secularist parties.[30] The government has now scheduled voting for parliament and direct election of president for June 23, with a runoff for the presidency if needed on July 7. A draft constitution, as revised by the Constituent Assembly in December, includes some favorable rights-protecting provisions but needs additional measures to safeguard the judiciary's independence, according to Human Rights Watch.

The country, accustomed to relative internal peace before the revolution, is experiencing sporadic violence

attributed to radical religious groups viewed as aligned with the government. The groups are trying to "impose their political and ideological model on society through a variety of means," Slahhedine Jourchi, an analyst of Islamist movements in Tunisia, told The Associated Press.[31]

Libya also held a relatively successful parliamentary election in July 2012, eight months after the end of the civil war, according to Freedom House's report, but violence by regional militias, Islamist groups and others delayed the balloting and remains a major problem. The leading party in the voting was the National Forces Alliance, a coalition headed by the relatively liberal politician Mahmoud Jibril, with 39 seats, followed by the Muslim Brotherhood's Justice and Construction Party with 17 seats. Plans and timeline for drafting a new constitution were uncertain as 2012 ended.[32]

In the most serious episode of violence, an armed assault on the U.S. consulate in Benghazi killed U.S. Ambassador Christopher Stevens and three other Americans. The attack became a major political issue in the United States as Republicans criticized the Obama administration for initially terming as spontaneous an attack that later intelligence indicated was planned by a branch of al Qaeda.

Meanwhile, Jordanians voted in higher-than-expected numbers in parliamentary elections on Jan. 23, despite calls for a boycott by a protest group that views the parliament as weak, unrepresentative and corrupt. Loyalists to King Abdullah II appear to dominate the new, 150-member body, but leftists and Islamists increased the number of seats won. Under reforms announced by Abdullah, the new parliament is to choose the prime minister, but the king still has the power to dismiss governments and dissolve parliament.[33]

Battle Fatigue

Syrians are continuing to suffer under a brutal civil war as rebels consolidate territorial gains, the government steps up attacks in civilian areas and neither side nears a decisive victory.

Human-rights groups say the Assad regime is countering rebel forces' gains on the ground by increasing what they call indiscriminate aerial assaults in civilian areas, including deliberate targeting of bakeries and bread lines and, in at least one instance, a hospital. Government forces also frequently detain humanitarian workers and human-rights monitors, according to Lama Fakih, a researcher with the U.S.-based Human Rights Watch who regularly crosses into Syria from her native Lebanon.[34]

Rebel forces have also been linked to such abuses as kidnapping, torture and extrajudicial executions as well as use of child soldiers and destruction of Christian and Shiite religious sites, Fakih says.[35] The government also has used "numerous torture techniques" on prisoners, she says. With its superior firepower and more extensive security apparatus, the government's abuses are far greater than those of the rebels, Fakih adds.

The civil war, now near the end of its second year, has created what Human Rights Watch calls "a dire humanitarian situation." More than 2 million Syrians have been displaced internally, and another 600,000 have registered as refugees in neighboring countries — chiefly Turkey and Jordan.

In conflict zones, "Syria does not resemble anything like normalcy," Fakih says. In opposition-controlled territory, entire villages may be emptied as residents seek safe havens. There is less disruption elsewhere, including in Damascus, according to Fakih. But throughout the country the mood is "one of fatigue," she says.

Neither side shows any interest, however, in the recurrent calls for a ceasefire, such as the most recent appeal by the Arab League's general secretary, Nabil El-Araby, at the league's Jan. 21 meeting in Riyadh, Saudi Arabia. Militarily, Fakih agrees with the many experts who say that neither side can achieve a decisive victory over the other for the foreseeable future.

Assad, out of public sight since his Jan. 6 speech in Damascus, is widely reported to be determined not to step aside. "I can win the war even if Damascus is destroyed," Assad is reported to have told U.N. and Arab League envoy Brahimi when they met in December.[36]

The anti-government forces remain far from unified, however. Meeting in Istanbul, Turkey, the Syrian National Coalition failed on Jan. 21 in its second attempt to agree on a transitional government. The 70-member coalition had been formed in Qatar in November with Gulf and Western backing. The coalition said in a statement that a five-person committee would try again to come forward with a proposal within 10 days, according to Reuters' account.[37]

The disunity among seemingly mainstream Sunni Muslims in the anti-government camp appears to be benefiting Jabhat al-Nusra, the avowedly jihadist group designated by the United States as a terrorist offshoot of al Qaeda. Some Free Syrian Army commanders have been criticized for warlordism, according to news accounts, while al-Nusra forces have built up good will by helping to deliver food and supplies to opposition-controlled areas cut off by government forces.[38]

Among other countries in the region to confront popular pro-democracy unrest in the past two years, Bahrain appears to be taking the toughest line. After declaring martial law early in 2012, the Sunni-led government clamped down further on the Shiite opposition movement Oct. 30 by banning all protest gatherings.[39] In Washington, a State Department spokesman condemned the action. Two people were killed in bomb blasts in the capital of Manama the next week (Nov. 5). Protests have continued in the tiny Gulf kingdom. Security forces used tear gas and stun grenades in Manama on Jan. 18 to disperse protesters who numbered in the hundreds.

Other Gulf countries are also resisting political change. In Kuwait, police used tear gas and stun grenades on Jan. 6 to disperse a crowd estimated at 1,000 or more who had defied a ban on public demonstrations and continued protesting changes in voting laws. The United Arab Emirates has drawn fire from Egypt's Muslim Brotherhood-dominated government by arresting 11 Egyptian nationals accused of trying to form a Brotherhood cell despite the emirate's ban on political parties.

All of the Gulf countries have moved to limit political dissent, including on social media.[40] Human Rights Watch blasted a Qatari court for its decision on Dec. 4 to sentence poet Muhammad Ibn al-Dheeb al-Ajami to life imprisonment, apparently for poems criticizing the ruling family and one in January 2011 praising the Tunisian revolution. In July 2012 the group had urged Oman to drop cases against online activists for postings the government viewed as critical of the sultan.[41]

Meanwhile, al Qaeda continues to pose a threat to security in some countries in the region. The assassination of a deputy police chief in a city near the Yemeni capital of Sanaa on Jan. 16 marked the third slaying of a security official in Yemen since October. The killing was apparently in retaliation for the government's moves against al Qaeda. And in Algeria, the West Africa branch of al Qaeda seized a natural gas plant on Jan. 16 in retaliation for France's decision, with Algeria's support, to send troops to Mali to combat Islamists there. At least 29 militants were killed when Algerian troops retook the plant after a four-day siege; at least 38 of the plant's personnel were killed, including three Americans.

OUTLOOK

Unfinished Spring

"I t's not easy being Arab these days," the Lebanese journalist and historian Samir Kassir wrote in an evocative dissection of the Arab peoples and their political and cultural plight in 2004. He found "a deep sense of malaise" throughout the Arab world that he said would persist unless Arabs freed themselves from "a sense of powerlessness" in order to create an Arab "renaissance."[42]

Kassir lived long enough to see Syria end its occupation of his country during the earlier Arab Spring of 2005 but not long enough to enjoy his country's freedom from Syrian suzerainty. He was killed by a car bomb on June 2, 2005, a still unsolved assassination that was surely carried out by Syrian agents or Lebanese surrogates.

Some five-and-a-half years later, a Tunisian fruit peddler frustrated by the petty arbitrariness of a local police woman threw off his sense of powerlessness in a fashion so dramatic — he set himself on fire — as to inspire fellow Arabs throughout North Africa and the Middle East. This time, the Arab Spring toppled three dictators, helped ease a fourth out of office, shook strongman rulers in other countries and helped prompt modest reforms even in countries with only minimal agitation in the Arab street. In Saudi Arabia, King Abdullah granted women the right to vote and run in municipal elections in September 2011; he followed up on Jan. 11 by naming 30 women to serve on the advisory Shura Council for the first time in the kingdom's history.[43]

After two years, however, the Arab Spring must be seen as unfinished business, as Robert Malley, regional director for North Africa and the Middle East for the conflict-mediating International Crisis Group, put it in a presentation midway through the unrest's second year. Even in countries with changes of government — Tunisia, Egypt, Libya and Yemen — Malley saw "the same fights, the same unfinished, unconcluded fights, between military and civilian, between Islamist and secular, among Islamists, among tribes, between regions." Elsewhere, Malley saw

"uprisings that have not begun" and the likelihood of an "ever descending" civil war in Syria.[44]

Today, as the Arab unrest continues, experts agree that the course of future events remains uncertain. "We still don't know what the final political outcome of the Arab Spring will be," says Toby Jones, the Rutgers professor. Gelvin, at UCLA, agrees. "We shouldn't make predictions," he says. "Nobody foresaw any of this happening, and nobody saw the paths that these rebellions were going to take."

The United States has multiple and sometimes conflicting interests in the events, including continuing counterterrorism initiatives and maintaining oil supplies. "It's mixed for the United States," says Pressman, the University of Connecticut professor. Moves toward democracy undermine what he calls the "narrative" of U.S. adversaries, such as Iran and al Qaeda, but changes in leadership can be "unsettling" for relations. RAND expert Seth Jones notes that the United States inevitably has to work with both democratic and nondemocratic countries in the region.

Egypt looms as the most important test of the political openings in the Arab world, but two years after Mubarak's fall, many Egyptians are disappointed. "The expectations were very high," says the National Defense University's Bahgat. "Progress, if any, is very slow. This is why there is frustration."

Bahgat sees frustration in the West as well. The new constitution "falls short of what we in the West would like to see," he says.

Syria's civil war is widely expected to lead eventually to the fall of a fifth Arab dictator, Assad, but the path for a post-Assad Syria is hard to predict. "It's like looking into a crystal ball," says Tabler, the Washington Institute expert, "but it's increasingly cloudy." No one predicts an easy transition for a country riven by conflict with no experience in self-rule.

The chance of successful democratization in Syria is "very slight," says the University of Oklahoma's Landis.

For many experts, the Arab glass is not even close to half full. The Arab Spring has produced only "a slight increase" in democratization — "far short of a fourth wave," says Seth Jones, the RAND expert. "The vast majority of countries remain authoritarian."

From his Beirut watching post, however, Salem, the Carnegie expert, sees more reason for democracy advocates to cheer. "If you look at the arc of history," Salem says, "in 24 months we've seen an amazing leap forward in the Arab world in the direction of democratization."

NOTES

1. For coverage, see Anne Barnard, "Syria President's Defiant Words Are Another Roadblock to Peace," *The New York Times*, Jan.7, 2013, p. A1; Liz Sly, "In Syria, a Defiant Speech by Assad," *The Washington Post*, Jan. 7, 2013, p. A1. For the full text, see "President al-Assad: Out of Womb of Pain, Hope Should Be Begotten, From Suffering Important Solutions Rise," SANA (Syrian Arab News Agency), Jan. 6, 2013, http://sana-syria.com/eng/21/2013/01/06/460536.htm. Assad had not spoken in public since June 3, 2012. See Neil MacFarquhar, "Assad Denies Government Role in Massacre, Blaming Terrorism," *The New York Times*, June 4, 2012, p. A4.

2. For background, see Roland Flamini, "Turmoil in the Arab World," *CQ Global Researcher*, May 3, 2011, pp. 209-236.

3. See Megan Price, Jeff Klingner, and Patrick Ball, "Preliminary Statistical Analysis of Documentation of Killings in the Syrian Arab Republic," 2 January 2013, www.un.org/apps/news/story.asp?NewsID=43866. The analysis was commissioned by the United Nations Office of the High Commissioner for Human Rights. For coverage, see Ben Hubbard and Frank Jordans, "UN says more than 60,000 dead in Syrian civil war," The Associated Press, Jan. 2, 2013, http://bigstory.ap.org/article/syrian-rebels-attack-air-base-north. Brahimi spoke in a news conference at the headquarters of the Arab League in Cairo, Egypt. For coverage, see Kareem Fahim and Hwaida Saad, "Envoy to Syria Warns of Slide to Hellish Fiefs With Huge Toll," *The New York Times*, Dec. 31, 2012, p. A9, www.aina.org/news/20121231004313.htm; Carol Morello, "Surge in Syrian death toll predicted," *The Washington Post*, Dec. 31, 2012, p. A7.

4. James L. Gelvin, *The Arab Uprisings: What Everyone Needs to Know* (2012).

5. "Freedom in the World 2013: Democratic Breakthroughs in the Balance," Freedom House, Jan. 16, 2013, www.freedomhouse.org/sites/default/files/FIW%202013%20Booklet.pdf.

6. For background, see these *CQ Global Researcher* reports: Brian Beary, "The Troubled Balkans," Aug. 21, 2012, pp. 377-400; Brian Beary, "Emerging Central Asia," Jan. 17, 2012, pp. 29-56; and Roland Flamini, "The New Latin America," March 2008, pp. 57-84, 29-56. See also these *CQ Researcher* reports by Kenneth Jost: "Russia and the Former Soviet Republics," June 17, 2005, pp. 541-564; "Democracy in Latin America," Nov. 3, 2000, pp. 881-904; "Democracy in Eastern Europe," Oct. 8, 1999; pp. 865-888; and "Democracy in Asia," July 24, 1998, pp. 625-648.

7. See Mark L. Haas and David W. Lesch (eds.), *The Arab Spring: Change and Resistance in the Middle East* (2012), pp. 3-4. For previous coverage, see Flamini, "Turmoil," *op. cit.*, pp. 209-236; Kenneth Jost and Benton Ives-Halperin, "Democracy in the Arab World," *CQ Researcher*, Jan. 30, 2004, pp. 73-100.

8. For background, see Leda Hartman, "Islamic Sectarianism," *CQ Global Researcher*, Aug. 7, 2012, pp. 353-376.

9. See Nicholas D. Kristof, "When Bahrain Said: Get Lost," *The New York Times*, Dec. 23, 2012, p. A11, www.nytimes.com/2012/12/23/opinion/sunday/kristof-when-bahrain-said-get-lost.html.

10. Reem Khalifa, "Bahrain court upholds life sentences on opposition," The Associated Press, Jan. 7, 2013, http://bigstory.ap.org/article/bahrain-court-upholds-life-sentences-opposition; Kareen Fahim, "Court in Bahrain Confirms Jail Terms for 13 Dissidents," Jan. 8, 2013, p. A4. Seven of the dissidents were tried in absentia.

11. See Laurel E. Miller, *et al.*, *Democratization in the Arab World: Prospects and Lessons From Around the Globe* (2012), pp. 35-53, www.rand.org/content/dam/rand/pubs/monographs/2012/RAND_MG1192.pdf.

12. *Ibid.*, p. 325.

13. Quoted in Maggie Fick, "AP interview: Egypt atheist blasts Islamist regime," The Associated Press, Dec. 19, 2012, http://news.yahoo.com/ap-interview-egypt-atheist-blasts-islamist-regime-173344116.html. Other background drawn from article.

14. Quoted in David D. Kirkpatrick, "Cairo Court Sentences Man to 3 Years for Insulting Religion," *The New York Times on the Web*, Dec. 12, 2012, www.nytimes.com/2012/12/13/world/middleeast/cairo-court-orders-3-year-term-for-insulting-religion.html.

15. Lesch and Haas, *op. cit.*, pp. 5-6.

16. See Babak Dehghanpisheh, "Syrian rebels, led by Islamists, capture key military air base," *The Washington Post*, Jan. 12, 2013, p. A7, http://articles.washingtonpost.com/2013-01-11/world/36272269_1_base-in-idlib-province-air-base-taftanaz-airport; Anne Barnard, "Syrian Rebels Say They Seized Helicopter Base in North," *The New York Times*, p. A5, www.nytimes.com/2012/11/26/world/middleeast/syrian-rebels-said-to-have-seized-military-airport.html?gwh=2F79954EB2025D2A5374630DBD41370E.

17. See David W. Lesch, "The Uprising That Wasn't Supposed to Happen: Syria and the Arab Spring," in Haas and Lesch (eds.), *op. cit.*, pp. 79-96; Gelvin, *op. cit.*, pp. 100-118.

18. David W. Lesch, *The New Lion of Damascus: Bashar al-Assad and the Modern Syria* (2005).

19. Syria Comment, http://joshualandis.com. In an unscientific poll on the blog, 39 percent of respondents predict Assad will have lost Damascus by June 1, 61 percent disagree.

20. Harling quoted in Anne Barnard, "Rebels Find Hearts and Minds Elusive," *The New York Times*, Jan. 16, 2013, p. A4. See also David Ignatius, "Anarchy in Syria," *The Washington Post*, Jan. 13, 2013, p. A21.

21. Background on the six nations most affected by the recent unrest in the Arab world (Bahrain, Egypt, Libya, Syria, Tunisia and Yemen) drawn in part from individual chapters in Lin Noueihed and Alex Warren, *The Battle for the Arab Spring: Revolution, Counter-Revolution and the Making of a New Era* (2012). See also Gelvin, *op. cit.*; Haas and Lesch (eds.), *op. cit.*

22. Raymond D. Gastil, *Freedom in the World 1980: Political Rights and Civil Liberties* (1980), p. 26, http://books.google.com/books?id=LIvHFydpgBgC&printsec=frontcover&source=gbs_ge_summary_r&cad=0#v=onepage&q&f=false.

23. Adrian Karatnycky (ed.), *Freedom in the World 2000-2001*, www.freedomhouse.org/article/new-study-details-islamic-worlds-democracy-deficit. For coverage, see Verena Dobnik, "Annual study shows freedom gap between Islamic countries and rest of world," The Associated Press, Dec. 18, 2001.

24. Quoted in Dobnik, *op. cit.*

25. "Arab Human Development Report 2002: Creating Opportunities for Future Generations," United Nations Development Programme/Arab Fund for Social and Economic Development, www.arab-hdr.org/publications/other/ahdr/ahdr2002e.pdf. For coverage, see Barbara Crossette, "Study Warns of Stagnation in Arab Societies," *The New York Times*, July 2, 2002, p. A11; Karen DeYoung, "Arab Report Cites Development Obstacles," *The Washington Post*, July 2, 2002, p. A10.

26. For timelines in the following summaries, see www.washingtonpost.com/wp-srv/special/world/egypt-protest-timeline/index.html. See also individual chapters in Noueihed and Warren, *op. cit.*

27. For a well-organized, updated guide to events and issues in Egypt, see Carnegie Endowment for International Peace, "Guide to Egypt's Transition, http://egyptelections.carnegieendowment.org/. Background on political parties drawn from this source.

28. See David D. Kirkpatrick, "Deadly Riots Erupt on Anniversary of Egypt Revolt," *The New York Times*, Jan. 26, 2013, p. A1, www.nytimes.com/2013/01/26/world/middleeast/tens-of-thousands-fill-tahrir-square-on-anniversary-of-egyptian-revolt.html.

29. See Abigail Hauslohner, "Egypt's anti-Islamists lack cohesion," *The Washington Post*, Jan. 22, 2013, p. A4, http://articles.washingtonpost.com/2013-01-21/world/36472981_1_islamists-parliamentary-elections-liberal-al-wafd-party.

30. "Human Rights Watch: Tunisia," www.hrw.org/middle-eastn-africa/tunisia (visited Jan. 25, 2013). See also Tarek Amara, "Tunisia's ruling coalition agrees to hold elections next June," Reuters, Oct. 14, 2012, www.itv.com/news/update/2012-10-14/tunisias-ruling-coalition-agrees-to-hold-elections-next-june/.

31. Bouazza Ben Bouazza and Paul Schemm, "Violence plagues Tunisia's politics 2 years later," The Associated Press, Jan. 14, 2013, http://bigstory.ap.org/article/violence-plagues-tunisias-politics-2-years-later.

32. "Libya," www.freedomhouse.org/report/freedom-world/2013/libya. See also "Human Rights in Libya," Human Rights Watch, www.hrw.org/middle-eastn-africa/libya.

33. See two articles by Kareem Fahim in *The New York Times*: "Loyalist to Dominate Jordan's New Parliament," Jan. 25, 2013, p. A11; "Despite Boycott, More Than Half of Voters Are Said to Turn Out in Jordan Election," Jan. 24, 2013, p. A6; and Taylor Luck, "Jordanian officials claim vote turnout as a victory," *The Washington Post*, Jan. 24, 2013, p. A6.

34. For ongoing coverage, see these sites: Human Rights Watch, www.hrw.org/middle-eastn-africa/syria; Syrian Observatory for Human Rights, http://syriahr.com/en/.

35. For background, see John Felton, "Child Soldiers," *CQ Global Researcher*, July 2008, pp. 183-211.

36. "Assad will stay in power 'even if Damascus is destroyed,'" *Middle East Monitor*, Jan. 23, 2013, www.middleeastmonitor.com/news/middle-east/5060-assad-says-he-will-stay-in-power-qeven-if-damascus-is-destroyedq.

37. See "Syrian opposition fails to form transitional government," Reuters, Jan. 21, 2013, www.reuters.com/article/2013/01/21/us-syria-crisis-opposition-idUSBRE90J0EW20130121.

38. See, e.g., Kelly McEvers, "Jihadi Fighters Win Hearts and Mind by Easing Bread Crisis," NPR, Jan. 16, 2013, www.npr.org/blogs/thesalt/2013/01/18/169516308/as-syrian-rebels-reopen-bakeries-bread-crisis-starts-to-ease.

39. See Reem Khalifa, "Bahrain bans all protest gatherings amid violence," The Associated Press, Oct. 30, 2012, http://bigstory.ap.org/article/bahrain-bans-all-protest-gatherings-amid-violence; and subsequent AP dispatches.

40. See Brian Murphy, "Gulf rulers take sharper aim at Web dissent," The Associated Press, Jan. 9, 2013, http://bigstory.ap.org/article/gulf-rulers-take-sharper-aim-web-dissent. For background, see

Jennifer Koons, "Future of the Gulf States," *CQ Global Researcher*, Nov. 1, 2011, pp. 525-548.

41. www.hrw.org/news/2012/12/04/qatar-poet-s-conviction-violates-free-expression; www.hrw.org/news/2012/07/21/oman-drop-cases-against-online-activists.

42. Samir Kassir, *Being Arab* (English translation, 2004), published same year in French as *Considerations sur le malheur arabe*. The opening sentence, quoted in text, uses the French word facile (easy); the translator substituted the English word "pleasant."

43. See Rashid Abul-Samh, "Saudi women on Shura Council," *Al-Ahram Weekly*, Jan. 16, 2013; Neil MacFarquhar, "Saudi Monarch Grants Women Right to Vote," *The New York Times*, Sept. 26, 2011, p. A1. For background, see Sarah Glazer, "Women's Rights," *CQ Global Researcher*, April 3, 2012, pp. 153-180.

44. "The Arab Spring: Unfinished Business," Carnegie Council on International Ethics, June 27, 2012, www.carnegiecouncil.org/studio/multimedia/20120627/index.html.

BIBLIOGRAPHY

Selected Sources
Books

Ajami, Fouad, *The Syrian Rebellion*, **Hoover Institution Press, 2012.**
A senior fellow at the Hoover Institution traces Syria's history from the rise of the Assad family through the current civil war. Includes source notes.

Cook, Steven A., *The Struggle for Egypt: From Nasser to Tahrir Square*, *Council on Foreign* **Relations/ Oxford University Press, 2011.**
A senior fellow at the Council on Foreign Relations chronicles modern Egypt's major historical episodes, from the decline of British rule and Nasser's rise as a pan-Arab leader to the Sadat and Mubarak eras and the demonstrations at Tahrir Square that overthrew an entrenched regime. Includes detailed notes, 40-page bibliography.

Gelvin, James L., *The Arab Uprising:* **What Everyone Needs to Know, Oxford University Press, 2012.**

A professor of Middle East history uses a convenient question-and-answer format to explain the origins of and prospects for the current uprisings in Arab countries. Includes source notes, further readings, websites. Gelvin is also author of *The Modern Middle East: A History* (3d. ed., Oxford University Press, 2011).

Haas, Mark L., and David W. Lesch (eds.), *The Arab Spring: Change and Resistance in the Middle East*, Westview Press, 2012.
A collection of 12 essays explores the course of events in major countries affected or unaffected by the Arab uprisings and the regional and international implications of the events. Haas is an associate professor of political science at Duquesne University, Lesch a professor of Middle East history at Trinity University in Texas.

Lesch, David W., *Syria: The Fall of the House of Assad*, Yale University Press, 2012.
A professor of Middle East history at Trinity University in Texas details the gradual shift in the popular view of President Bashar Assad from hopeful reformer at the start of his tenure to repressive tyrant. Includes detailed notes.

Miller, Laurel E., *et al.*, *Democratization in the Arab World: Prospects and Lessons from Around the Globe*, RAND Corp., 2012.
Researchers from RAND Corp., a global policy think tank, compare the most recent uprisings in the Arab world with past revolutions in Europe and the Americas. Includes notes, detailed list of references.

Noueihed, Lin, and Alex Warren, *The Battle for the Arab Spring: Revolution, Counter-Revolution and the Making of a New Era*, Yale University Press, 2012.
The book explores the origins of the current Arab uprisings; the course of events in Tunisia, Egypt, Libya, Bahrain, Yemen and Syria; and the likely nature of future Arab politics. Includes detailed notes, brief bibliography and source list. Noueihed is a Reuters editor

based in London; Warren is a director of Frontier, a Middle East and North Africa consultancy, also based in London.

Osman, Tarek, *Egypt on the Brink: From Nasser to Mubarak*, Yale University Press, 2011.
An analysis of the past five decades of Egyptian politics explains the growth of Arab nationalism in the country amid deep religious and economic divisions in the Egyptian population. Osman, whose work has appeared in numerous international news outlets, attended American University in Cairo and Bocconi University in Italy.

Articles

Berman, Sheri, "The Promise of the Arab Spring," *Foreign Affairs*, 2013, www.foreignaffairs.com/print/135730.
An associate professor of political science at Columbia University's Barnard College compares Western countries' past responses to transitioning from autocracy to democracy to the current problems faced by Arab countries with authoritarian regimes.

Jones, Seth, "The Mirage of the Arab Spring," *Foreign Affairs*, 2013, www.foreignaffairs.com/print/135731.
A senior political scientist at the RAND Corp. warns that it remains difficult for Arab countries overthrowing unpopular governments to establish political stability and therefore should not be burdened by Western pressure to form democracies.

Reports and Studies

"Freedom in the World 2013," Freedom House, Jan. 16, 2013, www.freedomhouse.org/event/upcoming-event-freedom-world-2013-launch.
This annual report by a non-government organization that advocates for democracy, political freedom and human rights ranks the status of political freedom in countries in the Middle East and North Africa.

For More Information

Carnegie Endowment for International Peace, 1779 Massachusetts Ave., N.W., Washington, DC 20036; 202-483-7600; www.ceip.org. Foreign-policy think tank promoting active international engagement by the United States and increased cooperation among nations.

Council on Foreign Relations, 58 E. 68th St., New York, NY 10065; 212-434-9400; www.cfr.org. Nonprofit think tank specializing in U.S. foreign policy and international affairs.

Freedom House, 1301 Connecticut Ave., N.W., Suite 400, Washington, DC 20036; 202-296-5101; www.freedom house.org. Publishes annual report on the status of freedom, political rights and civil liberties worldwide.

Human Rights Watch, 350 Fifth Ave., 34th Floor, New York, NY 10118; 212-290-4700; www.hrw.org. Conducts research and advocates for human rights in the Middle East and other regions.

International Crisis Group, 149 Avenue Louise, Level 24, B-1050 Brussels, Belgium; +32-2-502-90-38; www.crisis group.org. Non-governmental organization committed to preventing and resolving conflict worldwide.

Middle East Institute, 1761 N St., N.W., Washington, DC 20036; 202-785-1141; www.mei.edu. Promotes a greater understanding of Middle East issues among the American public.

Project on Middle East Democracy, 1611 Connecticut Ave., N.W., Suite 300, Washington, DC 20009; 202-828-9660; www.pomed.org. Examines how democracies can develop in the Middle East and how the United States can best support the democratic process.

Washington Institute for Near East Policy, 1828 L St., N.W., Suite 1050, Washington, DC 20036; 202-452-0650; www.washingtoninstitute.org. Promotes policies that advance American interests in the Middle East.

5

U.S.-Europe Relations

Roland Flamini

German troops in the NATO-led International Security Assistance Force hand over security in Afghanistan's Badakhshan Province to Afghan forces during a ceremony on Jan. 24, 2012. Tensions over Afghanistan will be on the agenda when President Obama and European leaders meet in May in Chicago for the first NATO summit in the United States in 13 years. Some 130,000 NATO forces are engaged in combat, military training and peace-building missions in Afghanistan.

From *The CQ Researcher*, March 23, 2012.

When British Prime Minister David Cameron visited Washington on March 14, President Barack Obama directed a few light-hearted zingers his way, ribbing him over Britain's burning of the White House during the War of 1812. "It's now been 200 years since the British came here . . .," Obama joked. "They made quite an impression. They really lit up the place."

Joshing back, Cameron replied: "I can see you've got the place a little better defended today. . . .You're clearly not taking any risks with the Brits this time."

The kidding around reflected the growing friendship between Obama, 50, and Cameron, 45. Indeed, the night before, Obama took the conservative British leader to an NCAA basketball playoff game in Dayton, Ohio, during the March Madness tournament. (By coincidence, Ohio just happens to be a key state in the president's upcoming re-election bid.)

But Cameron's visit was far from all fun and games.

He and the president talked about a range of weighty and shared problems — the war in Afghanistan, unrest in the Middle East and global economic woes. "We stand together and we work together and we bleed together and we build together," Obama said of America's historical alliance with Britain.[1]

In some respects, Obama's comments could apply to America's ties with much of Europe. Despite India and China's rising economic and political power, U.S. trade and financial ties with Europe remain strong. But in other ways, the link between the two continents is increasingly strained and uncertain. Not only do Europe's fiscal problems threaten the U.S. economy, but the

How the U.S. and EU Compare

The United States is more than twice the size of the 27-nation European Union but has about 200 million fewer people. The EU's gross domestic product (GDP) of $16.4 trillion is about $2 trillion more than that of the United States. Productivity is higher in the United States, however, with per capita GDP of $46,437, about 40 percent more than in the EU.

GDP and Population, EU and United States

KEY METRICS	EU	U.S.
GDP (2009)	$16.4 trillion	$14.3 trillion
Percent of global GDP	28.19%	24.52%
Population (2010)	501 million	309 million
Percent of global population	7.31%	4.51%
Per capita GDP (2009)	$32,842	$46,437
Total area (sq. miles)	1,634,757	3,536,310

Source: "The European Union and the United States: A Long-Standing Partnership,"EU Focus, European Union, December 2010, p. 4, www.eurunion.org/eu/images/stories/eufocus-eu-usrels-dec-2010.pdf

vaunted, 63-year-old military alliance binding the U.S. and Europe — the North Atlantic Treaty Organization (NATO) — must seek a new direction, analysts say.

These and other issues will confront President Obama and European leaders when they meet in May — in Chicago for the first NATO summit in the United States in 13 years and at the Camp David presidential retreat in Maryland two days earlier for a summit of the Group of 8 (G8) industrialized nations.* Dominating the agenda will be Europe's debt crises, the war in Afghanistan and the global response to Iranian nuclear ambitions.

And overshadowing both summits will be the question of whether the NATO alliance can survive in its current form as the focal point of geopolitics shifts to the emerging Asia-Pacific region, particularly China. "This is a time of change in the U.S.-European relationship," says Frances Burwell, director of trans-Atlantic

---

*The G8 is composed of the United States, Canada, France, Germany, Italy, Japan, Russia and the United Kingdom.

relations and studies at the Atlantic Council think tank in Washington. "I think we're really at a crucial point, but it may be a turning point."

Defining NATO's 2014 Afghan exit strategy will weigh on the Chicago summit, centered on the question of how many of the 130,000 Alliance forces will remain in the country to continue fighting the Taliban insurgents, training Afghan security forces and building its institutions.

Tensions with the Afghan government and people increased this winter, first when copies of the Quran were inadvertently burned at Bagram Airfield, and six U.S. military personnel were killed in the wave of protests.[2]

Then, on March 11, a U.S. Army staff sergeant allegedly murdered 16 Afghan villagers, mostly women and children, in their homes.[3] The incidents add urgency to the effort to define NATO's 2014 Afghan exit strategy.

Since its formation in April 1949 in the aftermath of World War II and the start of the Cold War, the NATO alliance has been in the diplomatic and foreign policy DNA of the United States and its Western European allies. Charles Kupchan, a senior fellow at the Council on Foreign Relations think tank in Washington and professor of international affairs at the School of Foreign Service at Georgetown University, calls NATO "an institution vital to preserving the coherence and effectiveness of the West as a potential community."

But the end of the Cold War and the global shift in attention toward the Asia-Pacific region have profoundly changed the nature of U.S.-European relations. The question is how the strategic partnership can be strengthened and made more relevant to geopolitical and economic realities.

Some critics argue that the United States has let its commitment to the alliance slip as it has focused more on China. Others contend that Europe has been so preoccupied with managing the European Union (EU) that it hasn't paid sufficient attention to the alliance either.

For all the speculation about the trans-Atlantic alliance, however, the United States and Europe still seem united on fundamental issues of war and peace. The best example is Iran, which has sparked global tensions over what many believe are plans to build nuclear weapons. Since 2010, the European Union has imposed progressively tougher sanctions on Iran, culminating in January in a ban on Iranian oil imports to Europe — measures that brought U.S. and European sanctions policies against Iran into broad alignment.

It's hard to find anyone on either side of the Atlantic, especially in Europe, who favors abolishing NATO. Instead, the discussion tends to focus on the search for relevance. "NATO's institutional setup may be the offspring of another age," says Riccardo Alcaro, a specialist in trans-Atlantic affairs at the Institute of International Affairs think tank in Rome. "But the core interest that its member states have in it — being party to a permanent military alliance between Europe and North America — has not diminished an inch."

The NATO summit will bring together the heads of state of the alliance's 28 member countries, plus Russia and Japan. Two days earlier, on May 18-19, Obama will host the G8 summit. The major challenge facing that group is how to resolve Europe's debt crisis, now in its third year.

The crisis has put the economies of Greece, Portugal, Ireland, Spain and Italy in jeopardy and threatened the viability of the euro — the EU's common currency. European leaders have introduced austerity measures but resisted U.S. pressure to increase stimulus spending. Many economists say that by not pumping more money into the European economy, European nations are making the continent's economic woes worse and undermining the United States' recovery from its own financial crisis.

The European debt crisis is all the more serious because trans-Atlantic trade and investment are the backbone of the global economy. Combined EU and U.S. economic output, or gross domestic product (GDP), amounts to about 53 percent of the world total. U.S. investments in

U.S.-European Trade on the Decline

European Union exports to the United States accounted for 19 percent of the EU's total exported goods — or about 206 billion euros — in 2009, down from 28 percent in 2000. EU imports from the United States fell from 21 percent of total European imports in 2000 to 13 percent in 2009.

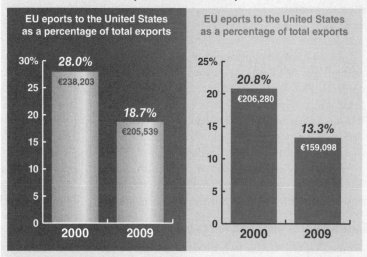

EU Trade in Goods with the United States, 2000 and 2009
(in millions of euros)

Source: "EU27 Surplus in Trade in Goods With the USA Almost Doubled in the First Six Months of 2010," Eurostat, European Union, November 2010, www.eurunion.org/eu/EU-US-Relations/EU-US-Facts-Figures.html

Europe easily top those in Asia. Together, the EU and United States command more than 40 percent of world trade, and their bilateral economic relationship was worth $898 billion in trade of goods and services in 2010 just short of $3 billion per day.[4]

The rise of China and other Asia-Pacific nations on the global economic and geopolitical scene has spurred concerns that the United States is losing interest in Europe. Obama himself, visiting Australia in November, assured Asian allies that America would stand by them in a crisis. "Let there be no doubt: In the Asia-Pacific of the 21st century, the United States is all in," he said.[5] Almost at the same moment, Washington announced it will station 2,500 U.S. Marines in Darwin, Australia, possibly open a base in the Philippines and will withdraw two U.S. Army brigades (5,000-6,000 men each) from Europe by the end of 2014 as a cost-cutting measure.[6]

"The Pacific focus inescapably means fewer resources for the traditional Atlantic partnership, symbolized by NATO," wrote *Washington Post* foreign policy columnist David Ignatius. "Given its recent economic jitters, Europe may feel abandoned."[7]

Secretary of State Hillary Rodham Clinton and Defense Secretary Leon Panetta in February both attended the annual Munich Security Conference, a gathering of defense ministers and foreign policy experts, where they reaffirmed America's commitment to the alliance with Europe. "Europe is and remains America's partner of first resort," Clinton declared.

Even so, "there's no question that the [Obama administration] sees Asia Pacific as the most challenging area," says Xenia Dormandy, a specialist on America's international role at Chatham House, a London think tank. "There's a real sense that America doesn't see Europe as a problem but as part of the solution. But the Europeans are still very much watching" developments.

As U.S. and European leaders weigh the future of the NATO alliance and the economic ties between the two continents, here are some of the questions being asked:

Should the U.S. pull all its forces out of Europe?

"Europe's GDP is greater than that of the United States, and its population is greater than the United States, so the notion that we need to continue to defend a continent that is eminently capable of defending itself is absurd," declares Christopher Preble, vice president for defense and foreign policy studies at the Cato Institute, a libertarian think tank in Washington.

The American military is not likely to be leaving Europe anytime soon. But questions are now being asked about how many of the 80,000 troops currently in Europe will still be there after 2014. The expected withdrawal of the two infantry brigades, beginning in late 2012, from Germany as part of Pentagon budget cuts has sparked speculation in Europe that a long but final drawdown of the U.S. presence may be beginning. And stirring such speculation, some observers say, may be part of an American plan.

Recent defense cuts combined with plans for leaner, more flexible, hi-tech American forces are factors behind the pullout. But the subtext may reflect growing impatience with Europe's habitual reliance on the U.S. military to do the heavy lifting when it comes to defense — combined with the hope that the Europeans might be goaded or scared into fending for themselves to a greater degree than they have in the past under the American security umbrella.

Every NATO country is required to spend at least 2 percent of GDP on defense. In reality, only four members besides the United States currently meet that obligation — the United Kingdom, France, Albania and — oddly — financially ailing Greece.

By contrast, the United States spends 5 percent. (*See chart, p. 112.*) In 2010, combined European spending on defense dropped to $275 billion, from $314 billion in 2008.

The euro crisis is partly to blame for the decline. But the other reason, argued Stephen Hadley, national security adviser in the George W. Bush administration, is that Europe has become a "free rider."

Hadley said the Europeans have been taking the United States for granted in providing defense and filling military-capability gaps. "Europe has become so enamored with soft power" — persuasion and diplomacy — "that it has stopped investing in hard power" — military action, he said. "In terms of hard security, it makes Europe a free rider."[8]

Dana Allin, senior fellow for trans-Atlantic affairs at London's International Institute of Strategic Studies, told the British House of Lords, "The history of U.S. relations with Europe ever since [World War II] has been trying to develop a semi-autonomous organization and alliance that can balance whatever the threat is. . . . Going back to the 1950s there was always a view that this should be possible. Europeans were becoming rich democracies and had a martial tradition."[9]

Today, says Charles Heyman, a defense analyst and former editor of *Jane's World Armies*, "The European Union as a whole is 10 percent richer than the United States based on GDP, and that is making a lot of American planners scratch their heads and say, 'What are we doing?'"

The U.S. presence in Europe is being questioned more widely than just by military planners. "Since the Cold War ended 20 years ago, the 80,000 troops still in Europe can be reduced to 20,000," wrote Laurence Korb, a defense analyst at the Center for American Progress, a liberal Washington think tank.[10]

"We now have a military alliance where many of the members do not want to engage in military operations . . .," wrote Robert Guttman, director of the Center on Politics and Foreign Relations at the Johns Hopkins University School of Advanced International Studies.

"Maybe we should call NATO a huge success, pat everyone on the back and dissolve the military organization and move on," he said.[11]

But the U.S. military could be staying on the continent simply because hot spots in the Middle East, Africa and Western Asia are much more easily reached from bases in Europe than in the United States. Indeed, the U.S. European Command (EUCOM) covers 93 countries in all and includes North Africa and parts of the Middle East. It also provides backup for the U.S. Africa Command. On the fringes of Europe are some explosive areas, including Georgia's border with Russia, Kosovo's border with Serbia, and Turkey and its Arab neighbors, Iraq and Syria, to say nothing of other areas of the Middle East.

There's also the influence factor. Alcaro of the Institute of International Affairs points out that it's a lot easier for the United States "to exert influence on European affairs and to keep European countries on its side on a number of issues, regional as well as global," if the American flag is flying in Europe.

Has Asia become the new focus of U.S. foreign policy?

Early in January, President Obama visited the Pentagon to introduce a new U.S. defense strategy employing advanced military technology to complement what, in the words of *The New York Times*, he described as "a smaller, more agile force across Asia, the Pacific and the Middle East." Obama's presence was highly unusual — presidents don't often visit the Pentagon — but it had a broader significance: It signaled the end of a decade of global politics shaped by the aftermath of the Sept. 11, 2001, terrorist attacks on New York City and the Pentagon.[12]

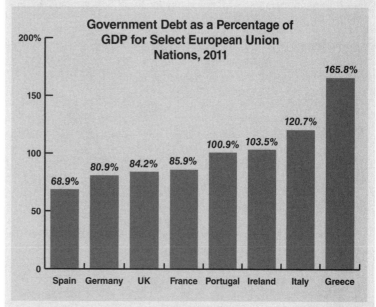

Debt Plagues European Nations

Debt held by the governments of Greece, Italy, Ireland and Portugal exceeds the countries' gross domestic product, threatening their economic stability.

Government Debt as a Percentage of GDP for Select European Union Nations, 2011

- Spain: 68.9%
- Germany: 80.9%
- UK: 84.2%
- France: 85.9%
- Portugal: 100.9%
- Ireland: 103.5%
- Italy: 120.7%
- Greece: 165.8%

Source: "General Government Gross Debt (Maastrict Debt) in % of GDP — Annual Data," Eurostat, European Union, March 2012,epp.eurostat.ec.europa.eu/tgm/table.do?tab=table&init=1&language=en&pcode=tipsgo10&plugin=0

Obama called it "turning the page on a decade of war . . . the end of long-term nation-building with large military footprints."[13] That approach had dominated strategic thinking in the George W. Bush administration. Under Obama, two major conflicts (Iraq and Afghanistan) were being declared over, and a decade of global military expansion was coming to an end.

Driving the new defense strategy was a fiscal crisis requiring a deep 8 percent cut in the Pentagon budget ($487 billion over 10 years) and a geographic reorientation toward Asia and the Pacific. "Mostly there is agreement that a more focused response . . . is needed to counter China's fast-growing military capabilities and address the concerns of allies in the region about how the emerging superpower will behave," noted *The Economist*. In short, China's emergence and the economic significance of Asia as a whole have made the region America's security priority.

Few NATO Members Meet Defense Obligations

The North Atlantic Treaty Organization (NATO) requires members to spend at least 2 percent of their gross domestic product (GDP) on defense. The United States spends the most, at 5.4 percent. Only four European members — Greece, the United Kingdom, Albania and France — meet the benchmark.

Defense Expenditures as a Percentage of GDP for NATO Members, 2010 estimates			
United States*	5.4%	Czech Republic	1.4%
Greece	2.9	Denmark	1.4
United Kingdom*	2.7	Germany	1.4
Albania	2.0	Italy	1.4
France	2.0	Netherlands	1.4
Poland	1.9	Romania	1.3
Turkey	1.9	Slovakia	1.3
Estonia	1.8	Belgium	1.1
Bulgaria	1.7	Hungary	1.1
Portugal	1.6	Spain	1.1
Slovenia	1.6	Latvia	1.0
Canada	1.5	Lithuania	0.9
Croatia	1.5	Luxembourg	0.5
Norway	1.5		

Figures include military pensions.
Iceland is not listed because it has no armed forces.

Source: *"Financial and Economic Data Relating to NATO Defence,"* North Atlantic Treaty Organization, March 2011, p. 6, www.nato.int/nato_ tatic/assets/ pdf/pdf_2011_03/20110309_PR_CP_2011_027.pdf

"We will be strengthening our presence in the Asia Pacific, and budget reductions will not come at the expense of that critical region," the president declared.[14]

But the budget cuts had to come from somewhere. And though Obama added the assurance that the United States intended "to continue investing in our critical partnerships and alliances, including NATO," analysts were speculating that the U.S. presence in Europe would shrink further.

The president left further explaining to senior Pentagon officials, including Gen. Martin E. Dempsey, chairman of the Joint Chiefs. "All of the trends, demographic trends, geopolitical trends, economic trends and military trends are shifting toward the Pacific," Dempsey said. "So our strategic challenges will largely emanate out of the Pacific region, but also the littorals of the Indian Ocean."[15]

Dempsey sees how China's submarines and missile platforms, soon to be backed up by an aircraft carrier taskforce, are projecting naval power into regions where the U.S. has dominated since 1945," commented *The Guardian* in Britain. "In short, he can read the writing on the Chinese wall." The general can foresee the United States having to stare down China the way it once did the Soviet Union, the paper said.

Panetta drove the point home. The Asia-Pacific region "is growing in importance to the future of the U.S. economy and our national security," he said. "This means, for instance, improving capabilities that maintain our military's technological edge and freedom of action."[16]

Nobody actually mentioned China, but Beijing noticed. "As promised, China would unwaveringly stick to its path of peaceful development," commented the Chinese government news agency Xinhua. It quoted Chinese Vice President Xi Jinping as saying that "a sound and stable China-U.S. relationship is not only vital to both sides but also crucial to peace, stability and prosperity of the Asia-Pacific region and that of the world as well."

And the *Global Times*, an English language offshoot of the Communist Party's *People's Daily*, swiftly made it clear China would be ready to match the United States step for step, wherever that uncharted path might lead. "Of course we want to prevent a new Cold War with the United States, but at the same time, we must avoid giving up China's security presence in the neighboring region," it said in an editorial.

A strong argument why the United States should focus on Asia-Pacific came in the form of a warning from Australian Foreign Minister Kevin Rudd, a

Mandarin-speaking sinologist. Rudd pointed out at the Feb. 1 Munich Security Conference that within the next decade China's economy is likely to be bigger than America's and that "there is analysis around that China's military expenditure may pass that of the United States by 2025." It will be, he said, "the first time in 200 years that the world has a non-democracy as the world's largest economy."

That will have a profound effect because the Chinese do not necessarily share "the longstanding liberal, international values which underpin the architecture of the post [World War II] global order," Rudd said. For the past 50 years, he said, the American military presence has ensured "Pax Pacifica" — the Asian-Pacific security balance — and it will remain the indispensable balancer throughout the region.[17]

Is a U.S. drift away from Europe reversible?

When the Soviet Union collapsed in 1989, there were 213,000 U.S. troops deployed in Western Europe, mainly in Germany, but also in the United Kingdom, Italy and Turkey. By 2011, U.S. troop levels in Europe had been pared to around 80,000.

When the planned pullout of the two Army brigades begins later this year, more American troops will still be deployed in Europe than anywhere else in the world — even though hardly a shot has been fired in anger in Western Europe since the end of World War II in 1945.

The military presence in Europe has symbolized America's enduring commitment to the trans-Atlantic alliance of shared values and — U.S. critics will say — allowed Europeans to develop complacent, "leave-it-to-the- Americans" attitudes toward security. Defense Secretary Panetta's predecessor, Robert Gates, called it "the demilitarization of Europe, where large swaths of the general public and political class are averse to military force and the risks that go with it."[18]

In Eastern Europe and the Baltic states, however, the American presence "provides the ultimate guarantee of protection from a resurgent Russia," according to Alcaro of the Institute of International Affairs — and the 2008 Russian incursion into Georgia, which is outside the NATO shield, underlined its importance. Alcaro argues that had Georgia been a NATO country, the Russians would not have risked a confrontation with the West by attacking.

The European Union's fledgling Common Security and Defense Policy envisions a standing multilateral force but is now on hold because of the continent's

AFP/Getty Images/Louisa Gouliamaki

Greek pensioners protest in Athens on Sept. 28, 2011, against further government austerity measures, including pension cuts and reduced health benefits. Greece, recently rescued from the brink of bankruptcy, is at the heart of the European debt crisis. The crisis has exposed huge government debts and threatened the eurozone economies of Spain, Portugal, Italy and Ireland as well as Greece.

economic problems. The policy doesn't inspire the same confidence as the Atlantic alliance, in part because NATO has tended to perceive it as an inferior rival.

The U.S. view is that there has been no drift away from the American commitment in Europe. The new defense strategy unveiled by President Obama in January stresses that view. The United States, the strategy document explains, is turning economic necessity to its advantage "to rebalance the U.S. military investment in Europe." That way it can structure "future capabilities" to create a lean, mean military suitable for a "resource-constrained era" (that is, one with budget pressures) and capable of meeting new military challenges wherever and whatever they may be, such as cyber warfare.[19]

The geopolitical center of gravity has been shifting toward the Asia-Pacific region for some time. "Many observers see the shift . . . as a natural, if long overdue, transition for the United States as it draws down in Iraq and Afghanistan," wrote Jonathan Masters an associate staff writer at the Council on Foreign Relations.[20]

But as German journalist Christoph von Marschall explained in the *German Times*, "in this subdued atmosphere of pervasive European self-doubt, a speech by President Obama convinced people a tectonic shift was under way in international politics."[21]

The U.S. troop drain from Europe is likely to continue even after 2014 because of Pentagon plans to reduce the military significantly and use the U.S. Air Force and Navy more forcefully than in past operations. The success of the Libyan operation, with NATO planes bombing Libyan forces, supported by a maritime blockade but no ground forces, is cited by American strategists as a model for future operations. Still, Dormandy of Chatham House says the Atlantic alliance will continue to exist foremost because "it gives more legitimacy (for countries) to come together under the banner of NATO."

Besides, as a report on the trans-Atlantic alliance by the Chicago Council on Global Affairs recently put it, a United States with economic problems and with its power "diluted by other centers of influence around the world . . . will be hard pressed to . . . preserve the openness and influence of the U.S.-led international order" and is going to need more, not less, support from its allies.[22]

The days of the unilateral U.S. force that can fight two major ground wars simultaneously are over, to be replaced by what the new strategy calls "fight and deter," meaning fight one war and prevent another. "The future is going to look at more collaborations of larger diverse groups of [NATO] member states with the will, the assets and the interest to take action," says Dormandy.

BACKGROUND

North Atlantic Treaty

By the end of World War II in Europe on May 8, 1945, more than three million Americans had fought in the conflict against Nazi Germany.[23] G.I.'s had been welcomed as liberators in Paris, Rome and elsewhere. But when the celebrations stopped and the Americans began to embark for home, Europeans realized they faced a new threat from the East.

The Soviet Union had at least 700,000 troops under arms and capable of overrunning war-weary Western Europe. Another fear was a ghost from the past: a possibly resurgent Germany.

To nail down a protective U.S. presence in Europe, the Western allies formed NATO — the North Atlantic Treaty Organization — in 1949.* NATO's first secretary

---

*The 12 original NATO members were the United States, Great Britain, France, Italy, the Netherlands, Belgium, Luxembourg, Norway, Denmark, Portugal, Iceland and Canada.

general, Britain's Lord Ismay, is purported to have said the purpose of the alliance was "to keep the Russians out, the Americans in, and the Germans down."[24]

At the heart of the treaty is Article 5, which ensures that "an armed attack against one or more of [the parties to the treaty] in Europe or North America shall be considered an attack against them all." In the face of such a threat, the article goes on, NATO will take "such action as it deems necessary, including the use of armed force, to restore and maintain the security of the North Atlantic area."[25]

Marshall Plan

NATO was actually the second U.S. postwar intervention in Europe. The alliance's participating European countries needed first to be rescued from the war's wreckage to their economies. So in 1947, the United States offered the Marshall Plan, named after Secretary of State George Marshall, who first proposed it in a commencement speech at Harvard University.[26]

Representatives from 17 European countries — including the Soviet Union — met in Paris and formulated a $22 billion plan (in 1947 dollars) for consideration by the United States. The plan focused on help to rebuild industry and agriculture and included requests for basic foods, such as sugar. Congress pared the request to $13 billion in grants and loans, and Marshall Plan aid began flowing to Europe in 1948. Stalin rejected it for Russia and its satellite countries, so 17 European countries received aid.[27]

Marshall Plan aid, an analyst wrote, was "the decisive kick that pushed Western Europe beyond the threshold of sustained recovery."[28] Britain was the top recipient with $2.7 billion; West Germany came second with $1.7 billion.

Marshall aid ended in 1951, but the North Atlantic Alliance is still in business six decades later.

With Russia "out" and Germany no longer regarded as a threat to European peace, many felt that NATO's role had come to an end and the alliance would be dissolved. Instead, NATO has expanded across Central and Eastern Europe, doubling in size. During the Cold War, NATO's anti-Soviet line of defense had extended from the Turkish border with the USSR in the south to Norway in the north, but the alliance never fired a shot against the potential enemy.

Since the 1990s, "NATO is not just about Europe and in Europe, but is increasingly seen as the hub of a global network of security," Ivo Daalder, U.S. permanent representative to NATO, said recently.[29] Since the end of the Cold War, the alliance has "focused on operations," Daalder said, in the Balkans (1992) and more recently in its first out-of-area missions in Afghanistan and Libya.

At times across the years, the NATO alliance has looked more like a misalliance. Its history is full of spirited — but eventually resolved — disputes. For example, in the 1960s it took NATO nearly a decade of internal debate to adopt and develop the so-called U.S. strategy of flexible response to an enemy attack: conventional forces first; if that failed, tactical nuclear weapons (short-range missiles for battlefield use); and if the enemy still wasn't pushed back from NATO territory, a strategic nuclear response would entail intercontinental rockets, which would bring the United States into direct conflict with the Soviets. Skeptical Europeans wondered whether the United States would ultimately be prepared to go to war for Europe.[30]

In 1966, French President Charles de Gaulle pulled France out of NATO's military command structure because he felt the United States was too dominant in the decision-making. At de Gaulle's insistence, NATO's headquarters moved from Paris to Brussels. Only intense damage control by the other allies prevented NATO's possible collapse.

In the end, no other country followed France's lead. Indeed, according to a recent analysis, the French departure was "a catalyst for action that actually strengthened the alliance in the long run."[31]

Missile Crisis

I n the late 1970s Washington pressed its European allies to deploy 108 U.S.-supplied Pershing II medium-range missiles and 462 ground-launched cruise missiles in response to Soviet deployment of the medium-range SS-20 missile, capable of carrying nuclear warheads to cities in Europe. Violent public opposition to the missiles erupted in Germany, Italy and elsewhere, and the issue became a critical test of the alliance's political resolve.[32]

Moscow worked hard to open a rift between the United States and its European allies. Ailing Soviet leader Leonid Brezhnev flew to Bonn, the West German capital, in an attempt to persuade Chancellor Helmut Schmidt to reject the U.S. missiles. The Germans gave Brezhnev a new Mercedes to add to his car collection but stood firm on the missiles, as did other NATO countries.

Following the collapse of the Soviet empire, NATO began expanding its membership to include former Soviet satellite countries, starting with Poland, the Czech Republic and Hungary in 1999. Moscow's one-time dominions, still nervous about their old master, welcomed NATO's (that is, America's) protective shield.

NATO troops saw action for the first time in the Balkans in the 1990s. In 1995, the alliance launched its first peacekeeping operation: the Implementation Force (IFOR) in Bosnia. Approximately 60,000 troops from the 16 NATO members and 17 non-NATO countries, including Russia, were tasked with making sure that the conditions of the Bosnia peace agreement, brokered by the United States and including a cease-fire, were observed. The main challenge was to keep Serb and Bosnian factions from renewing hostilities. Another was to create safe and secure conditions for repatriation of refugees and other humanitarian efforts.

Then in 1999, NATO planes began bombing targets in the former Republic of Yugoslavia (Serbia and Montenegro), and NATO forces were deployed in Kosovo to halt a Serbian ethnic-cleansing (genocide) campaign against Albanian Muslims. President Bill Clinton called the air strikes "a moral imperative."[33] Inevitably, the two offensives — and especially the air strikes — brought out the problems of waging war by consensus, since the 17 member states often disagreed on strategy.

"These problems included making war without admitting that it was war, and a clash of confused notions of how to use force effectively," according to an article in *Foreign Affairs* based on a published account of the war by U.S. Army Gen. Wesley Clark, the NATO commander at the time. Clark even had to take into account what NATO's legal advisers had to say on tactical options, according to the magazine.[34]

At one phase of the bombing, said *Foreign Affairs*, "Germany wanted to stop bombing Serbia's cities, Americans worried about bombing within Kosovo, and France wanted to stop the bombing in northern Serbia."[35] The Europeans were afraid continued attacks would derail peace negotiations.[36]

After almost four months of bombing, Serbian President Slobodan Milosevic ordered his troops to withdraw, but only because he believed that a NATO ground attack was imminent. In fact, *Foreign Affairs* said, such an attack wasn't even in the planning stage.[37]

CHRONOLOGY

1940s *U.S. establishes postwar connection with Western Europe through North Atlantic Treaty Organization (NATO) and Marshall Plan.*

1947 U.S. Secretary of State George C. Marshall announces extensive aid program for European recovery.

1949 NATO treaty signed in Washington by United States, Great Britain, France, Italy, the Netherlands, Belgium, Luxembourg, Norway, Denmark, Portugal, Iceland and Canada.

1950s-1960s *Cold War Europe divided by "Iron Curtain", with NATO forces in West and opposing Warsaw Pact nations in the East.*

1955 West Germany joins NATO; Soviet Union and seven Eastern European nations form Warsaw Pact.

1956 Israel, Britain and France invade Egypt after Egyptian leader Gamal Abdul Nasser nationalizes the Franco-British-owned Suez Canal. President Dwight D. Eisenhower pressures allies to pull out.

1957 Belgium, France, West Germany, Italy, Luxemburg and the Netherlands sign Treaty of Rome, founding document of European Union.

1961 East Germany begins Berlin Wall.

1966 France leaves NATO military structure; alliance moves to Brussels.

1970s-1980s *U.S. plan to deploy intermediate-range missiles sparks protests in Europe, tension with America's allies.*

1973 Denmark, United Kingdom and Ireland join European Community.

1987 United States and Russia sign Intermediate-Range Nuclear Forces Treaty (INF), removing U.S. and Russian missiles from Europe after less than a decade of deployment.

1989 Berlin Wall falls, allowing free travel between East and West Germany and leading to the formal reunification of Germany.

1990s-2000s *Europe, in further steps toward unification, establishes European Union, a unified currency (the euro) and a European single market.*

1990 Trans-Atlantic Declaration formalizes common goals of the United States and European Community.

1994 NATO planes enforce no-fly zone to protect Bosnian civilians from the Serbs. NATO eventually sends ground troops as well. Bosnia is NATO's first combat operation.

1999 Euro currency officially launched.

Sept. 12, 2001 Following the 9/11 terrorist attacks, NATO — for the first time in its history — invokes Article 5 of the treaty, holding that an armed attack against one state will be considered an armed attack against all. . . . Rift opens between Bush administration and France and Germany over Iraq War, but Britain, Spain and Eastern Europe support the conflict against Saddam Hussein.

2007 U.S.-EU Trans-Atlantic Economic Council formed to coordinate bi-lateral economic decision-making.

2009 Faced with a global debt crisis, G20 summit agrees to increase International Monetary Fund aid for European economies.

2010-Present *Economic crisis, wars, political upheavals cause global tension.*

2010 NATO summit in Lisbon agrees on establishing a missile defense shield for Europe acceptable to Russia. NATO also endorses 2014 as date for withdrawal of NATO forces from Afghanistan.

2011 NATO leads aerial offensive to protect civilians in Libya following uprising against the regime of Libyan leader Moammar Gadhafi.

2012 Discovery of charred copies of the Quran inadvertently burned at Bagram air base in Afghanistan sparks anti-NATO demonstrations in which 30 Afghans and six U.S. soldiers die. . . . EU sovereign debt crisis eases somewhat after Greece successfully negotiates 50 percent reduction of its debt to private creditors and receives $130 billion EU bailout.

Afghanistan and Iraq

Following the Al Qaeda terrorist attacks on New York and the Pentagon, NATO for the first time in its history invoked Article 5. Initially, the Bush administration rejected NATO's help in Afghanistan, preferring to work "with a more flexible international coalition" that was "unencumbered by the institutional constraints of alliance decision-making," wrote a British analyst, "while the U.S. was able to pick and choose only what it wanted — and needed — from NATO assets and member states."[38]

Subsequently, however, ISAF (International Security Assistance Force), a multinational coalition in Afghanistan deployed in December 2001, morphed into the NATO force deployed in Afghanistan, with U.S. forces as a separate command called Operation Enduring Freedom.

Two years later, France and Germany, although engaged in Afghanistan, refused to support the Bush administration's war in Iraq, and the United States put together what President Bush called the "coalition of the willing," which still included several NATO members.

"Passionate differences over the invasion of Iraq pushed trans-Atlantic and inter-European relations to an historic low point in 2003-2004," stated a recent study of U.S.-European relations prepared for members of Congress by the Congressional Research Service (CRS). "Iraq was the unforgettable defining element in their perceptions of President George W. Bush — too unilateral, too reliant on military force, too dismissive of international treaties and norms." But, CRS said, Iraq became shorthand for other areas of dispute between the United States and various European governments, such as U.S. rejection of the Kyoto climate treaty and the International Criminal Court, which pursues war crimes worldwide.[39]

The Iraq debate also revealed a deep division within Europe "between states that seek European identity through confrontation with America and those, led by Britain and Spain, that seek in it an instrument of cooperation," former U.S. Secretary of State Henry Kissinger wrote. He blamed the split on a resurgence of Gaullism — a reference to de Gaulle's nationalist philosophy — that, he wrote, "insisted on a Europe with an identity defined in distinction from the United States."[40]

But in 2005, Christian Democrat Angela Merkel replaced Socialist Gerhard Schröeder as chancellor of Germany, and relations with the Bush White House improved. Then in 2007, the pro-American Nicolas Sarkozy was elected president of France. Two years later, Sarkozy reintegrated France

NATO Photo

Delegates to the North Atlantic Treaty Organization meet in Washington, D.C., for the organization's first meeting on Sept. 17, 1949. Today every NATO country is required to spend at least 2 percent of GDP on defense, but only four members besides the United States currently meet that obligation – the United Kingdom, France, Albania and Greece. The heart of the treaty is Article 5, which ensures that "an armed attack against one or more [members] in Europe or North America shall be considered an attack against them all."

into all structures of the NATO alliance, 43 years after de Gaulle had broken away from military affairs.[41]

NATO'S presence in Afghanistan was not without friction because some countries, including Germany, tried to limit combat risks by imposing so-called caveats: Its troops were permitted to fire only in self-defense. "There's no question that there [were] exasperations with Germany in Afghanistan due to caveats and limitations," Allin of the International Institute of Strategic Studies told the House of Lords.[42]

On balance, however, NATO's deployment in Afghanistan was "a success for the cohesion of the alliance," argued Karl-Heinz Kamp, director of research at the NATO Defense College in Rome. When NATO took over in Afghanistan in 1973, "hardly anyone had assumed that the alliance would be able to remain fully engaged in the region for more than eight years (and still committed to stay until an acceptable level of stability is achieved)" and would have "successfully maintained unity of all members in Afghanistan."[43]

European Union

Meanwhile, the U.S. and Europe have other significant ties besides the North Atlantic alliance. Chief among them is U.S. support for the European process of integration culminating in the emergence of the European Union (EU), a political and economic confederation of nations established

EU Tribunals Trump National Courts on Key Issues

Critics worry that they wield too much clout.

British pub owner Karen Murphy wanted to keep her soccer-crazy customers happy — but she also wanted to cut down on expenses. So with a major soccer championship coming, she opted to bypass Sky Television, the big European media company that had an exclusive contract with the British soccer organization to broadcast its games in the U.K., and use a cheaper Greek satellite broadcaster to show the game.

The soccer organization filed and won a copyright infringement case against her, claiming exclusive rights to the game. But Murphy won on appeal to the European Union Court of Justice, which said the soccer authority's exclusive deal was "contrary to EU law."[1]

The Court of Justice and two lower EU courts — the General Court and the EU Civil Service Tribunal — form an increasingly potent legal force in European affairs. They hear hundreds of cases annually involving EU citizens, corporations and national courts seeking guidance on EU issues. Among the General Court's cases this year is a request from Microsoft Corp. for a reduction in an 899 million euro ($1.3 billion) fine imposed by the court in a 2008 antitrust case.

The Court of Justice, based in Luxembourg, is the highest in the European Union on issues covered by EU law, outranking national supreme courts. EU court decisions are binding on all 27 member countries.

In March, Spanish courts asked the Court of Justice to clarify an important addition to an EU online privacy-protection law. Called "the right to be forgotten," the new rule enlarges people's right to request the removal of personal data from Google and other search engines. Though the inquiry came from Madrid, the EU court's reply will be applicable throughout the European Union.[2]

"If today there exists something called [European] law, with its own particular features, characteristics, and issues, all this is due to the [European] Court's work," wrote Oreste Pollicino, a lecturer in public law at Bocconi University in Milan.[3]

And as far back as 1993, an American law professor and an Oxford University scholar called the European Court of Justice "an unsung hero" of European unification. Anne-Marie Burley, a University of Chicago law professor, and Walter Mattli, a professor of political economy at Oxford, wrote that "thirteen judges quietly working in Luxembourg, managed to transform the Treaty of Rome . . . into a constitution. They thereby laid the legal foundation for an integrated European economy and polity."[4]

But critics say the courts wield too much power over the courts of individual nations. Dutch law professor Henri de Waele of Radboud University in Nijmegen said a "visible attempt at more balanced interpretation [of European law] could do wonders."[5] Sir Patrick Neill, a leading British

in 1992, and its subsequent expansion to 27 members. The United States supported moves toward European political and economic integration after World War II, beginning with the 1957 Treaty of Rome. Following the Soviet Union's collapse, the United States favored inclusion of East European and Baltic countries into the European Union. Like NATO membership, EU membership helped speed up the restoration of democracy in such countries as Poland and Lithuania, because a democratic system was a prerequisite for membership in both institutions.

"Europe is more united, more democratic and more peaceful than it has ever been in history," said Daalder, the

U.S. NATO representative. "That is an accomplishment that NATO and the European Union and the countries [that make up these organizations] can be proud of."[44]

But the EU's plans for a Common Security and Defense Policy, including the creation of a European force parallel to NATO, drew strong U.S. opposition. John Bolton, the George W. Bush administration's U.N. ambassador, called the proposal "a dagger pointed at the heart of NATO." Madeleine Albright, President Clinton's secretary of state, warned that alliance members should avoid what she called the three "Ds" — decoupling, duplication and discrimination.

jurist, once famously called the Court of Justice "uncontrollable, skewed, and dangerous."[6]

In 2011 the Court of Justice completed 638 cases — a 10 percent increase over the previous year — and the General Court around twice that number.

Most corporate cases are on a smaller scale than the Microsoft antitrust action but can still have broad impact. In a famous 1979 ruling involving *Crème de cassis* (the French cordial), for example, the Court of Justice said a product approved for sale in one European country must be accepted by others. The so-called *Cassis de Dijon* case established the principle of Europewide product standards and was a cornerstone of the European single market.

Each EU member country appoints a judge to each of the three courts, but the full bench at plenary sessions consists of only 13 judges. Eight advocates-general deliver legal opinions on the cases, but the judges don't necessarily accept their interpretation.

Unlike in the U.S. Supreme Court, judges serve not for life but for six-year terms, and dissenting opinions are not made public. Yet, in the impact of its rulings, the European Court of Justice bears a strong similarity to its American counterpart.

Much of the court's work involves action against member states for failing to comply with regulations or treaty obligations. The European Commission (the EU's executive branch in Brussels) announced Feb. 28 that it was suing the French government in the Court of Justice for allegedly failing to prevent pollution of drinking water by agricultural chemicals in rural areas of France.[7]

The EU court's broad portfolio has given it a key role in the recent European social compact signed in March by 25 EU members and intended to bring national budgets under control. The compact mandates a maximum debt of less than 3 percent of the gross domestic product, and the court is charged with imposing fines of 0.1 percent of GDP on countries that fail to comply.

In the past few years the court has emerged from the shadows. "The (court's) accomplishments have long been the province only of lawyers," wrote Burley and Mattli more than a decade ago. No longer.

— *Roland Flamini*

[1]"Pub landlady Karen Murphy wins TV football court case," *BBC News*, Feb. 24, 2012, www.bbc.co.uk/news/business-17150054.

[2]Loek Essers, "Spain seek jurisdiction guidance from EU for Google privacy complaints," *Computer World*, March 6, 2012, www.computerworlduk.com/news/it-business/3342444/spain-seeks-jurisdiction-guidance-from-eu-for-google-privacy-complaints/.

[3]Oreste Pollicino, "Law Reasoning of the Court of Justice etc.," *German Law Journal*, Vol. 5, No. 03, 2004, www.germanlawjournal.com/article.php?id=402.

[4]Anne-Marie Burley and Walter Mattli, "Europe Before the Court: A Political Theory of Legal Integration," World Peace Foundation and Massachusetts Institute of Technology, 1993, www.seep.ceu.hu/alpsa/articles/burley.pdf.

[5]Henri de Waele, "The Role of the European Court of Justice in the Integration Process…," *Hanse Law Review*, 2010, www.hanselawreview.org/pdf9/Vol6No01Art01.pdf.

[6]"Biased Referee," *The Economist*, May 15, 1997, www.economist.com/node/149581.

[7]Helene Roques, "Dis-moi ce que tu peux depolluer, je te dirai ce que je vais fabriquer," *Le Monde*, March 13, 2012, www.lemonde.fr/idees/article/2012/03/13/dis-moi-ce-que-tu-peux-depolluer-je-te-dirai-ce-que-je-vais-fabriquer_1656463_3232.html.

As the European Common Market of the 1960s became the European Economic Community of the 1970s and then the European Union and the EU Single Market in the early 1990s, the continent's economic integration was at first seen as a rising challenge to U.S. industrial and commercial interests. Touring European cities in 1989, Carla Hills, the U.S. trade representative, expressed concern about "actions taken, threatened or merely implied that discriminate against American and other non-European firms, forcing them to locate in Europe or lose sales." Hills said she hoped the emerging EU Single Market would result in "a freer (market), not a fortress Europe."[45]

The New York Times warned that "through import quotas, antidumping actions and requirements of reciprocity, a fortress might just be taking shape, brick by brick."[46] But despite some remaining differences, the relationship was quickly perceived to be mutually beneficial.

The two economies represent 54 percent of the world's output or gross domestic product and nearly one-third of world trade. In 2010, nearly 93 percent of global foreign exchange holdings were in dollars, euros or pound sterling. In 2009, the two-way flow of goods, services and income receipts from investments totaled $1.25 trillion. In 2007, Washington and Brussels set up the Transatlantic

Once Spurned, 'Old Europe' Makes a Comeback

U.S ties shift away from Eastern Europe.

After France and Germany came out strongly against the use of force in the run-up to the U.S.-led Iraq War in 2003, U.S. Defense Secretary Donald Rumsfeld scornfully dismissed the two countries as anachronisms.

"You're thinking of Europe as Germany and France," he told journalists. "I don't. I think that's old Europe. . . . If you look at the entire NATO Europe today, the center of gravity is shifting to the East."[1]

The new Europe was Eastern Europe's former Soviet satellites, which joined President George W. Bush's "coalition of the willing" in the Iraq War, earning them praise from the president. In 2004, Poland deployed 1,700 troops to Iraq, Romania sent 700 and smaller numbers came from Bulgaria, Hungary and the Czech Republic.[2]

But eight years later, "Old Europe" is new again. The balance of U.S.-European ties has reverted to more traditional lines, with the larger and more important nations, such as the United Kingdom, Germany and France, again Washington's foremost allies. By contrast, U.S. ties to Eastern Europe have soured, largely because of what the East Europeans perceive as Washington's failure to live up to their expectations as allies.

Michael Rubin, a resident scholar at the American Enterprise Institute, a conservative think tank in Washington, recently wrote that "the Obama administration has, at various times, thrown Poland, the Czech Republic and Georgia under the bus." As a result, said Rubin, these countries "increasingly doubt the commitment of the United States to them."[3]

President Obama's decision in 2009 to cancel the Bush administration's agreement with Poland and the Czech Republic to deploy an anti-missile defense system on their territory was a major disappointment for Eastern Europe. The system's main purpose was to intercept missiles fired by a rogue state hostile to the United States — Iran or North Korea, for example. For the Eastern Europeans the plan would have meant enhanced security and a potentially useful bilateral link with Washington.

But the plan drew protests from Russia, which considered it a security threat.[4] The Obama administration denied that in canceling the plan it was kowtowing to Moscow's objections and said a more efficient system was being developed that did not require deployment in Eastern Europe.

But the Eastern Europeans saw the cancelation as the United States giving precedence to Moscow, their old nemesis.

And on the eve of Obama's visit to Poland in May 2011, the English-language *Warsaw Business Journal* said, "Relations between Poland and the United States are at a low point, as Warsaw has grown dissatisfied with Washington's level of commitment to Poland's security."[5]

Economic Council, a high-level body of government officials and economists who meet yearly to reduce non-tariff barriers and increase regulatory convergence.

The 2008 global financial meltdown shook this strong economic axis to its foundation. A collapse of the housing and banking sectors in the United States and Europe exposed huge government debts, threatening the eurozone economies of Spain, Portugal, Italy, Ireland, and Greece and even the viability of the European currency itself.

The close relationship made the United States vulnerable to the eurozone crisis, but differences over how to confront the crisis made it hard to adopt a coordinated response. Europeans rejected Treasury Secretary Timothy Geithner's calls for greater stimulus spending in preference for austerity programs.

CURRENT SITUATION

EU and Iran

The United States and Europe are struggling — together and separately — with a host of economic, military and national-security issues.

Both have imposed economic sanctions against Iran in hopes of halting what is widely suspected to be an effort by Tehran to develop nuclear weapons. The European Union, Iran's second-largest oil customer after China, halted all Iranian oil imports, effective July 1. (The United States has not imported oil from Iran for more than 30 years.)

In addition, U.S. and European leaders have sought to persuade Israel, which is considering a pre-emptive attack on Iran's nuclear facilities, to give the sanctions

U.S. relations with Hungary are strained following the election in 2010 of right-of-center Prime Minister Viktor Orbán, who, *The New York Times* said, is drifting "toward authoritarian government . . . in defiance of mounting criticism from Europe and the United States."[6]

In December, Secretary of State Hillary Rodham Clinton wrote to the Hungarian government to express concern "about constitutional changes under consideration in your country" and to push "for a real commitment to the independence of the judiciary, freedom of the press and transparency of government. . . . Our concerns are significant and well-founded."[7]

Orbán replied that all the changes were being made "in constant dialogue" with the European Commission, the executive body of the European Union, and interested parties in Hungary. But analysts pointed out that the European Union had been equally critical of what it considers the authoritarian drift of Orbán's government.[8]

— *Roland Flamini*

Former Secretary of Defense Donald Rumsfeld dismissed France and Germany in 2003 as remnants of "old Europe."

AFP/Getty Images

[1] "Outrage at 'Old Europe' remarks," *BBC News*, Jan. 23, 2003, http://news.bbc.co.uk/2/hi/europe/2687403.stm.

[2] Brookings Institution "Iraq Index," Nov. 21, 2005, "Non-U.S. troop deployment," www.brookings.edu/fp/saban/iraq/index20051121.pdf.

[3] Michael Rubin, "Afghanistan Exposes Old vs New Europe," *Commentary*, March 14, 2012, www.commentarymagazine.com/2012/03/14/afghanistan-exposes-old-vs-new-europe/.

[4] Douglas Lytle and Lenka Ponikelska, "Obama to drop Poland and Czech Missile Defense Proposal," *Bloomberg*, Sept. 17, 2009, www.bloomberg.com/apps/news?pid=newsarchive&sid=awZyw2fptKCQ.

[5] "Obama's visit to Poland," *Warsaw Business Journal*, May 27, 2011, www.wbj.pl/article-54714-stratfor-obamas-visit-to-poland.html?typ=ise.

[6] "Hungary," *The New York Times*, March 15, 2012, http://topics.nytimes.com/top/news/international/countriesandterritories/hungary/index.html.

[7] "Hillary Clinton letter to the Hungarian Government," *Scribd*, Dec. 23, 2011, www.scribd.com/doc/77009957/Letter-from-Hillary-Clinton-to-the-Hungarian-government.

[8] "Prime Minister Viktor Orbán's answer to Secretary of State Clinton's letter," *Hungarian Spectrum*, Feb. 25, 2012, http://esbalogh.typepad.com/hungarianspectrum/2012/02/prime-minister-viktor-orb%C3%A1ns-answer-to-secretary-of-state-hillary-clinton.html?cid=6a00e009865ae58833016762fbd947970b.

more time to work. In February, Israeli Defense Minister Ehud Barak bluntly warned that time quickly was running out for stopping Iran's nuclear program, which Israel appears convinced is weapons oriented.

After visiting Iranian nuclear sites, which Tehran claims are for peaceful energy-generation purposes, inspectors from the U.N. nuclear-monitoring organization, the International Atomic Energy Agency (IAEA), declared that the agency "continues to have serious concerns regarding possible military dimensions to Iran's nuclear program." But the IAEA stopped short of accusing the Iranians of planning to develop a nuclear arsenal.[47] U.S. intelligence officials say they remain unsure of Iran's intentions.

As 2011 ended, President Obama signed legislation barring foreign banks that did business with Iran's central bank from dealing with U.S. financial institutions. Afterward, the European Union froze the central bank's assets and halted Iranian oil imports.

The EU's oil cutoff represents a potentially significant hit to Iran's economy, which derives half its earnings from oil revenue. China, Japan and South Korea, which could conceivably cover the EU shortfall, have said they don't plan to increase oil imports from Iran. In response to Iranian threats to retaliate by closing the Strait of Hormuz — through which 20 percent of Gulf oil exports flow — Britain and France have sent warships to the Gulf to support the U.S. aircraft carrier *Abraham Lincoln*.

The Israelis argue that the sanctions, even if effective economically, will not halt Iran's nuclear program. Iran has been moving its nuclear enrichment program — the

Iran's first nuclear facility, the Russian-built Bushehr nuclear power plant, uses uranium fuel well below the enrichment level needed for weapons-grade uranium. Concern that Iran may be enriching fuel for nuclear weapons prompted the United States and Europe to impose strict economic sanctions on Iran. In January the European Union banned Iranian oil imports to Europe – aligning U.S. and European sanctions policies. The U.S. has not imported oil from Iran for 30 years.

key factor in its nuclear development — to a hardened underground facility in Fordow, near the holy city of Qom; Barak said that once the bunker-like site is finished, an attack on it could come "too late."

Debt Crisis

In an effort to neutralize the debt crisis, 25 members of the European Union in March signed a "fiscal compact" requiring governments to run balanced budgets and write the agreement into their nations' constitutions. The compact calls for capping annual deficits at 0.5 percent of each country's GDP and the tracking of their economies by the EU Commission in Brussels. The European court can impose fines on any country failing to observe that rule. The U.K. and Czech Republic refused to accept the pact.[48] Cameron, the British prime minister, said it meant giving up too much operational independence.

Many analysts, however, fear that the move came too late because the Europeans still have to dig out of their present fiscal plight. Greece, which is at the heart of the European debt crisis, was rescued from the brink of bankruptcy — at least for the moment — when its private creditors were persuaded to forgo 50 percent of their debt, thus opening the way for a second EU bailout of 130 billion euros. The debt reduction brought Greece's overall indebtedness down from 120 percent of GDP to 117

percent. Greece needed the money for a bond payment by March 30 to avoid defaulting. The slight improvement in Greece's situation had a salutary effect on Italy and Spain.

The United States has watched these developments warily. "For the longer term, analysts are concerned that economic difficulties in Europe could act as a brake on U.S. growth and the world economy," the Congressional Research Service stated. "A dawning age of austerity in Europe could also impact trans-Atlantic cooperation on international issues including defense and development assistance."[49]

But the EU is slowly coming around to the Obama administration's view that Europe needs to stimulate economic growth and create jobs rather than focusing exclusively on austerity measures, which have resulted in riots and protests across the continent from the United Kingdom to Greece — particularly in the latter.

Afghanistan Tensions

The U.S.-EU alliance in Afghanistan appears increasingly fragile. French President Sarkozy, reacting to the killings of four unarmed French soldiers by an Afghan soldier, threatened to pull France's contingent out of Afghanistan by the end of the year.

"If security conditions are not established clearly, then the question of an early return of the French army will arise," Sarkozy declared. Under the current plan, NATO began handing over security duties to Afghan forces last year, with the target date for completing the transition set for the end of 2014.[50]

Accomplishing the transition does not necessarily mean withdrawal from Afghanistan. In the view of Kamp, of the NATO Defense College, Obama was wrong to peg NATO's departure to 2014. This is "a myth" that helps the insurgents plan in advance and raises public expectations in alliance countries, Kamp argued. A long-term commitment needs to follow NATO's departure, both in terms of financial help and also physical presence on the ground, he said.[51]

"There is no question that the patience of America's NATO allies with the expensive, deadly Afghan war has been running out," *The New York Times* said. "They joined the war alongside the United States, which had been attacked by Al Qaeda on Sept. 11, 2001, from its sanctuaries in Afghanistan. But the Taliban government is long gone, Osama bin Laden is dead, and Al Qaeda has been diminished and mostly pushed into Pakistan."[52]

Should the NATO alliance continue?

YES
Xenia Dormandy
Senior Fellow, U.S. International Role, Chatham House, London

Written for *CQ Global Researcher*, March 2012

Among other factors, new technologies, diverse communications channels, more-integrated problems and a rising number of actors are all increasing the complexity and speed of change in the world today. Amid this cacophony and potential confusion, it would be only sensible to propose that the methods of responding to today's events need to be updated.

The United Nations will be 67 this year. NATO will be 63. While there are many valid questions regarding their constituent memberships, given their relatively broad inclusiveness and their long and respected histories, their activities invoke a certain legitimacy.

Nations will continue to choose, where possible, to undertake operations under the banner of these institutions according to the situation and their specific capabilities, responsibilities and strategic concerns. Recent efforts by European, Gulf and U.S. powers to gain a U.N. resolution on Syria are indicative of this. However, these efforts also demonstrate that such institutions, precisely because of their broad membership, can be dysfunctional. Different values and ideologies can stymie decisions and progress on vital issues.

If international institutions are to continue to be effective tools for multilateral action, they will have to find new ways of working. The likely path will mirror patterns already seen in structures like the Proliferation Security Initiative (PSI) or the post-2004 East Asian tsunami response, in which five countries came together to provide immediate relief as the U.N. mounted its operations and subsequently disbanded when its job was done. These are ad hoc groups of nations with the will, capabilities and interests to act to achieve specific objectives, which, when attained, break up. The future lies with such groups.

If current organizations like the U.N. and NATO want to continue to remain effective, they too will have to adopt similar mechanisms. We are already seeing this to be the case. The operation in Libya had NATO cover but involved only a subset of NATO members in its activities, in coordination with some non-NATO actors. The ISAF (International Security Assistance Force) operations in Afghanistan are another such example.

NATO is already finding ways to act effectively according to this new ad hoc method, within its more formal constructs. It is unlikely, however, that the members will formalize this methodology, instead letting it take place implicitly. One should not expect the current debate within NATO for all members to "pull their weight" to end anytime soon.

NO
Justin Logan
Director of Foreign Policy Studies, CATO Institute, Washington

Written for *CQ Global Researcher*, March 2012

The United States should form military alliances to fight wars. NATO was formed because after World War II Western Europe was devastated, and Washington feared that Moscow might be able to plunge into Western Europe and capitalize on the devastation.

In 1951, however, President Dwight D. Eisenhower remarked that "if in 10 years, all American troops stationed in Europe for national defense purposes have not been returned to the United States, then this whole project will have failed." According to Ike, the purpose of NATO was to help the Western European countries "regain their confidence and get on their own military feet."

NATO's broader purpose in Europe was summed up in an apocryphal quote attributed to Lord Ismay: The alliance was to keep "the Russians out, the Americans in and the Germans down." The Russians are out, and they are going to stay out. Poland faces no threat of Russian attack, to say nothing of countries to her west.

Instead, today NATO constitutes a system of transfer payments from U.S. taxpayers (and their Chinese creditors) to bloated European welfare states. It also serves as a make-work project for the think tankers, bureaucrats and journalists who make a living off the "trans-Atlantic relationship."

All of this might be waved off as harmless had the alliance not expanded eastward three times to include an array of countries that no major member has any intention of defending militarily, should it come to that. There simply aren't the funds in member-state accounts to cover the checks NATO has written.

In the past decades there has been talk in Europe of promoting autonomous European defense capabilities. (Indeed, talk of autonomous European cooperation goes back nearly to the founding of NATO.) However, Washington has consistently scuppered European attempts at creating a third force because it views NATO as a vehicle for controlling Europe's security policy. The result has been a militarily infantile Europe that found it impossible even to fulfill its desire to change the regime of Moammar Gadhafi without help from Washington.

Despite Washington's misgivings, a more powerful, more autonomous Europe would be a good thing for America. It would allow the United States to shrink its armed forces and save money. Sixty years after Eisenhower's admonition, surely it is time to declare the alliance a relic of the past and put NATO out to pasture.

> **"There is no question that the patience of America's NATO allies with the expensive, deadly Afghan war has been running out. They joined the war alongside the United States, which had been attacked by Al Qaeda on Sept. 11, 2001, from its sanctuaries in Afghanistan. But the Taliban government is long gone, Osama bin Laden is dead, and Al Qaeda has been diminished and mostly pushed into Pakistan."**
>
> — *The New York Times, Jan. 21, 2012*

The situation was not helped when on February 20 charred copies of the Quran were found in an incinerator at the Bagram Airfield, Afghanistan's largest military base. A military investigation found that the books were destined for disposal but that three U.S. service personnel on garbage detail inadvertently placed them in the incinerator before a decision had been made. President Obama publicly apologized for the incident amid an upsurge of protest demonstrations and attacks on NATO personnel, resulting in the death of 30 Afghans and six U.S. soldiers in separate attacks by Afghan security personnel.[53]

In a separate incident that further undermined the fragile relationship between the Afghans and NATO, a U.S. Army staff sergeant allegedly went on a dawn rampage and killed 16 Afghan villagers, mostly women and children, before giving himself up.[54]

OUTLOOK

NATO Summit

NATO's summit in Chicago in May will be the first in the United States in 13 years. The last one, in Washington in 1999, celebrated the alliance's 50th anniversary. Given the problems facing Europe, neither the NATO summit nor the G8 meeting is likely to be celebratory. Casting ominous shadows over the deliberations will be the war in Afghanistan and the European debt crisis.

What's more, the Iranian nuclear controversy could reach crisis proportions in the event of Israeli military action and the retaliatory closing of the Strait of Hormuz. In March, without going into detail, Obama told *The Atlantic* magazine that if sanctions failed, the United States itself would take

action. "I think that the Israel government recognizes that as president of the United States, I don't bluff," he said. It was, Obama went on, "unacceptable for Iran to have a nuclear weapon. We mean what we say."[55]

For now, however, NATO's top priority is spelling out in greater detail the Afghanistan exit strategy and its aftermath. In listing four main discussion areas for the Chicago summit recently, Daalder, the NATO representative, spoke of preliminary consultations currently under way to determine "how a shift in mission can occur most effectively." At the summit, he said, "President Obama and the other leaders will make a final decision on the transition and how the next phase will be implemented . . . and how we can support a sustainable and sufficient Afghan security force and how we can further strengthen our strategic partnership with Afghanistan in 2015 and beyond."[56]

All of which sounds like less of a done deal than Vice President Joseph Biden's "drop dead date" for a U.S. and allied withdrawal in 2014.[57]

Daalder also said NATO will be advancing plans for its long-proposed missile defense system or shield to protect Europe from a Middle East attack — a presumed reference to Iran. "New threats require new defense responses that are just as capable, just as immediate, just as agile as the ones that we had before," he said.

As a third summit issue, Daalder cited NATO'S Smart Defense program, designed to encourage allies to coordinate their defense spending better in an era of fiscal austerity. Daalder cited the example of Sweden paying for half of the purchase of three C-17 Globemaster transport planes and 11 other countries paying the rest. The arrangement entitles the Swedes to one-sixth share of the huge planes' flying time, he said.

NATO also will address the participation of non member countries in NATO operations, as has happened in both Libya and Afghanistan, Daalder said. "All these countries have come to recognize that NATO is a hub for building security; not that NATO is the world policeman, which it is not, but that it is a forum for dialogue and a forum for bringing countries together for collective action," he said.

Others see coalition-building as an effective way for the Atlantic alliance to stay in business. Says Dormandy of Chatham House: "You're going to see more and more coalitions because they answer problems more effectively. NATO will survive if it continues to show a willingness to move in this direction." The issue needs to be discussed, she says, because "the rhetoric is still behind the action. In people's minds they're not there yet."

Analysts say President Obama will also need to calm European anxiety about America's continued commitment to NATO. He will need to elaborate on whether America's first ever decision not to take the lead in a NATO action — in Libya — is to become an option in U.S. military planning, and if so, how that will change the geometry of the alliance.

By May, the leaders of the G8 industrialized nations may have to confront a fresh setback in Greece, Portugal on the edge and other aspects of the crisis in Europe. But on a more hopeful note, they are expected to discuss — and perhaps even agree on — a comprehensive, bilateral U.S.-EU trade agreement.

"Suddenly, there's a lot of support for an agreement," says the Atlantic Council's Burwell. "The United States and Europe have parallel economies, each is the other's main economic partner, and they have huge levels of investment," she says. A trade partnership will help resolve some of the pending issues, such as coordinating standards, she adds. "It's an achievable arrangement."

NOTES

1. "Remarks by President Obama and Prime Minister Cameron of the United Kingdom at Arrival Ceremony," *White House*, March 14, 2012, www .whitehouse.gov/the-press-office/2012/03/14/ remarks-president-obama-and-prime-minister-cameron-united-kingdom-arriva. For background, see the following *CQ Researcher* and *CQ Global Researcher* reports: Sarah Glazer, "Future of the Euro," *CQ Global Researcher*, May 17, 2011, pp. 237-262; Roland Flamini, "U.S.-British Relations," *CQ Researcher*, Nov. 5, 2010, pp. 917-940; Roland Flamini, "Future of NATO," *CQ Global Researcher*, January 2009, pp. 1-26; Brian Beary, "The New Europe," *CQ Global Researcher*, August 2007, pp. 181-210; Kenneth Jost, "Future of the European Union," *CQ Researcher*, Oct. 28, 2005, pp. 909-932; Philip M. Seib, "U.S. British Relations," *CQ Researcher*, Jan. 30, 1998, pp.73-96.

2. Deb Riechmann, "2 U.S troops are killed in Afghanistan: Quran backlash claims 6," *Detroit Free Press*, March 2, 2012, www.freep.com/article/ 20120302/NEWS07/203020383/2-U-S-troops-are-killed-in-Afghanistan-Quran-burning-backlash-claims-6.

3. Mirwais Khan and Sebastian Abbot, "Afghan official: Video shows soldier surrendering", *The Associated Press*, March 14, 2012, http://hosted.ap.org/ dynamic/stories/A/AS_AFGHANISTAN?SITE=AP &SECTION=HOME&TEMPLATE=DEFAULT.

4. European Commission, Trade, United States, http:// ec.europa.eu/trade/creating-opportunities/bilateral-relations/countries/united-states/.

5. "U.S. President Barack Obama addresses the Australian Parliament," Youtube, Nov. 17, 2011, www.youtube.com/watch?v=8_hSqLEtX_Y.

6. Jackie Calmes, "U.S. Marine Base in Australia Irritates China," *The New York Times*, Nov. 16, 2011, www.nytimes.com/2011/11/17/world/asia/ obama-and-gillard-expand-us-australia-military-ties .html?pagewanted=all.

7. David Ignatius, "Defense 'pivot' with big conse quences," *Commercial Appeal*, Jan. 7, 2012, www .commercialappeal.com/news/2012/jan/07/david-ignatius-defense-pivot-with-big/?print=1.

8. Judy Dempsey, "U.S. Sees Europe as Not Pulling Its Weight Militarily," *The New York Times*, Feb. 6, 2012, www.nytimes.com/2012/02/07/world/ europe/07iht-letter07.html?pagewanted=all.

9. "Military Capabilities available to the EU," *House of Lords Select Committee*, Nov. 3, 2011, www.iiss.org/ whats-new/iiss-experts-commentary/military-capa bilities-available-to-the-eu/.

10. Laurence Korb, "Invitation to a Dialogue: the Military Budget," *The New York Times*, Nov. 9, 2011, www.nytimes.com/2011/11/10/opinion/invitation-to-a-dialogue-the-military-budget.html?_r=1.

11. Robert Guttman, "Happy 60th Birthday NATO; Time to Go Out of Business?," *Huffington Post*, April 1, 2009, www.huffingtonpost.com/robert-guttman/ happy-60th-birthday-nato_b_181734.html.

12. Elizabeth Bumuller and Tom Shanker, "Obama Puts His Stamp on Strategy for a Leaner Military," *The New York Times*, Feb. 5, 2012, www.nytimes .com/2012/01/06/us/obama-at-pentagon-to-out-line-cuts-and-strategic-shifts.html.

13. "Obama's Remarks on Military Spending," *The New York Times*, Jan. 5, 2012, www.nytimes.com/2012/01/06/us/text-obamas-remarks-on-military-spending.html?pagewanted=all.

14. *Ibid.*

15. Simon Tisdall, "China Syndrome dictates Barack Obama's Asia-Pacific strategy," Jan. 20, 2011, *The Guardian*, www.guardian.co.uk/commentisfree/2012/jan/06/china-barack-obama-defence-strategy.

16. *Ibid*

17. Kevin Rudd, speech at the 48th Munich Security Conference, Feb. 2, 2012, www.securityconference.de/Activities.192+M52087573ab0.0.html.

18. Brian Knowlton, "Gates calls European mood a Danger to Peace," *The New York Times*, Feb. 23, 2012, www.nytimes.com/2010/02/24/world/europe/24nato.html.

19. "Sustaining Global Leadership," Department of Defense, January 2012, www.defense.gov/news/Defense_Strategic_Guidance.pdf.

20. Jonathan Masters, "The Pentagon points to Asia," Council on Foreign Relations, *Analysis Brief*, Jan. 6. 2012, www.cfr.org/united-states/pentagon-pivots-asia/p26979.

21. Christoph von Marschall, "Fear not, Europe!" *The German Times*, Feb. 2, 2012, www.german-times.com/index.php?option=com_content&task=view&id=41618&Itemid=25.

22. Thomas Wright and Richard Weitz, "The Transatlantic Alliance in a Multipolar World," *The Chicago Council of Foreign Affairs*, November 2010, www.thechicagocouncil.org/userfiles/file/task%20force%20reports/The%20Transatlantic%20Alliance%20in%20a%20Multipolar%20World.pdf.

23. T. Dotson Stamps and Vincent Esposito, "A Military History of world War II," Vol. 1, *U.S. Military Academy*, 1953.

24. "What Comes after Europe?" *The Wall Street Journal* online, Sept. 19, 2011, http://online.wsj.com/article/SB10001424053111904106704576580522348961298.html?mod=WSJ_Opinion_carousel_2.

25. "The North Atlantic Treaty, Washington, April 4, 1949," (text), *North Atlantic Treaty Organization*, www.nato.int/cps/en/natolive/official_texts_17120.htm.

26. Brookings Institution, "The Marshall Plan," http://www.brookings.edu/about/History/marshallplan.aspx.

27. *Ibid.*

28. Albrecht Ritschl, "The Marshall Plan, 1948-1951," EH.net, Feb 5, 2010, http://eh.net/encyclopedia/article/Ritschl.Marshall.Plan.

29. Ivo Daalder, "NATO and the Transatlantic Alliance: The American Perspective," speech at Chicago Council on Global Affairs, March 1, 2012, www.thechicagocouncil.org/files/Event/FY_12_Events/Transcripts/NATO_and_the_Transatlantic_Alliance_The_American_Perspective.aspx.

30. "NATO strategy of flexible response," *Bulletin of the Atomic Scientists*, April 1963, http://books.google.com/books?id=3QUAAAAMBAJ&pg=PA19&lpg=PA19&dq=nato+strategy+of+flexible+response&source=bl&ots=PNAGKyQ-zO&sig=3dp571exsYrlhnKAZdTzr4etkQs&hl=en&sa=X&ei=fyxRT8GpHePl0QHUzOjNDQ&ved=0CEAQ6AEwBjgo#v=onepage&q=nato%20strategy%20of%20flexible%20response&f=false.

31. Christian Nuenlist and others, "Globalizing de Gaulle: International Perspectives on French Foreign Policy 1958-1969," *Harvard Cold War Studies Book Series*, 2010; see introduction by Mark Kramer.

32. "U.S. will deploy Missiles if Soviets Balk," *Ocala Star-Banner*, Nov. 19, 1981, http://news.google.com/newspapers?nid=1356&dat=19811119&id=TbRPAAAAIBAJ&sjid=LgYEAAAAIBAJ&pg=2600,3550543.

33. "Clinton: 'We must act now,'" *BBC Online Network*, March 25, 1999, http://news.bbc.co.uk/2/hi/europe/303052.stm.

34. Richard K. Betts, "Compromised Command," *Foreign Affairs*, July/August 2001, www.foreignaffairs.com/articles/57062/richard-k-betts/compromised-command.

35. *Ibid.*

36. *Ibid.*

37. *Ibid.*

38. Ellen Hallams, "The Transatlantic Alliance Renewed: the United States and NATO since 9/11," *Journal of Transatlantic Studies*, Vol. 7, Issue 1, 2009, www.tandfonline.com/doi/full/10.1080/14794010802658823.

39. Derek E. Mix, "The United States and Europe: Current Issues," Congressional Research Service,

May 4, 2011, http://fpc.state.gov/documents/organ
ization/168024.pdf.

40. Barry D. Wood, "There is no clear line between 'Old' and 'New' Europe," *European Institute*, Spring 2003, www.europeaninstitute.org/20030302351/ Spring-2003/there-is-no-clear-line-between-qoldq-and-qnewq-europe.html.

41. Stefan Simons, "Sarkozy breaks with de Gaulle and tradition," *Spiegelonline*, March 13, 2009, www.spiegel .de/international/europe/0,1518,612840,00.html.

42. "Military Capabilities available to the EU," House of Lords Select Committee, Nov. 3, 2011, www.iiss .org/whats-new/iiss-experts-commentary/military-capabilities-available-to-the-eu/.

43. Karl-Heinz Kamp, "NATO Chicago Summit: A Thorny Agenda," *NATO Defense College*, November 2011, www.ndc.nato.int/research/series.php?icode=1.

44. Daalder, *op. cit.*

45. "Carla Hills Voices Concern on 'Fortress Europe,' " *Los Angeles Times*, Sept. 11, 1989, http://articles .latimes.com/1989-09-11/business/fi-1616_1_ fortress-europe.

46. Steven Greenhouse, "The growing fear of Fortress Europe," *The New York Times*, Oct. 23, 1988, www .nytimes.com/1988/10/23/business/the-growing-fear-of-fortress-europe.html?pagewanted=all&src=pm.

47. Scott Peterson, "IAEA report on Iran: 'serious con-cerns' about nuclear program," *The Christian Science Monitor online*, Feb. 24, 2012, www.csmonitor.com/ World/Middle-East/2012/0224/IAEA-report-on-Iran-serious-concerns-about-nuclear-program.

48. William Boston, "Fiscal Pact Huge Step Toward European Stability: Merkel," *The Wall Street Journal*, March 1, 2012, http://online.wsj.com/article/ BT-CO-20120301-708211.html.

49. Mix, *op. cit.*

50. Steven Erlanger and Alissa J. Rubin, "France Weighs Pullout After 4 of Its Soldiers Are Killed," *The New York Times*, Jan. 20, 2012, www.nytimes.com/2012/ 01/21/world/europe/sarkozy-weighs-afghan-withdrawal-after-4-french-troops-killed.html? pagewanted=all.

51. Kamp, *op. cit.*, November 2011.

52. Erlanger and Rubin.

53. Patrick Quinn, "Afghanistan Quran Burnings: Conflicting Accounts Emerge," *Huffington Post*, March 12, 2012, www.huffingtonpost.com/2012/03/03/ afghanistan-quran-burnings_n_1318297.html.

54. Richard Engel, "Soldier accused of killing 16 Afghans relocated," *NECN/NBC*, March 15, 2012, www.necn.com/03/15/12/Soldier-accused-of-killing-16-Afghans-re/landing_newengland.html?bl ockID=670288&feedID=4207.

55. Jeffrey Goldberg, "Obama to Iran and Israel: "As President of the United States, I Don't Bluff," *The Atlantic*, March 2, 2012, www.theatlantic.com/inter national/archive/2012/03/obama-to-iran-and-israel-as-president-of-the-united-states-i-dont-bluff/253875.

56. Daalder, *op. cit.*

57. "Joe Biden: 2014 Afghanistan Pullout is 'Drop Dead Date,' " *Huffington Post*, May 25, 2011, www.huffing tonpost.com/2010/11/19/afghanistan-2014-with drawal-biden_n_785904.html.

BIBLIOGRAPHY

Selected Sources

Books

Goldgeier, James, *The Future of NATO*, Council on Foreign Relations, 2010.
A professor of political science and international relations at George Washington University examines NATO's options for remaining relevant in the 21st century.

Lewis, Michael, *Boomerang: The Meltdown Tour*, Penguin Books, 2011.
A best-selling author and journalist examines develop-ments in the United States and Europe that led to the global debt crisis. He contends the Goldman Sachs investment bank helped the Greek government rig the books to hide the true nature of its economy from other European Union members.

Lundestad, Geir, ed., *Just Another Major Crisis? The United States and Europe Since 2000*, Oxford University Press, 2008.
Scholars on both sides of the Atlantic discuss the state of trans-Atlanticism; historian Lundestad is director of the Norwegian Nobel Institute.

Ross, Robert S., Tuosheng Zhang, *et al.*, *U.S.-China-EU Relations: Managing the New World Order*, Routledge, 2009.
A professor of political science at Boston College (Ross), the director of the Center for Foreign Policy Studies, Beijing, and other international scholars examine how U.S.-China-EU relations will shape the future of international politics, playing a key role in establishing and managing a new world order.

Sloan, Stanley R., *Permanent Alliance? NATO and the Transatlantic Bargain from Truman to Obama*, Continuum, 2012.
A longtime writer and lecturer on the Atlantic Alliance traces its development and reasons for its failures and successes.

Articles

Brezezinski, Zbigniew, "An Agenda for NATO: Toward a Global Security Web," *Foreign Affairs*, October 2009.
A former White House national security adviser, marking the Atlantic Alliance's 60th anniversary, notes that during its history NATO has united the West, secured Europe and ended the Cold War, and discusses its future role.

Hao, Li, "European Recession 2012: How would it affect the U.S. economy?" *International Business News*, March 7, 2012, www.ibtimes.com/articles/310705/20120307/european-recession-2012-exports-fdi-eu.htm.
In a recession, says the writer, bond investors will sell European debt, which would only exacerbate the current crisis.

Ifeany, K.C., "Euro debt crisis could cripple U.S. business travel," *Inc.*, Feb. 17, 2012, www.inc.com/kc-ifeanyi/european-debt-crisis-could-cripple-us-business-travel.html.
With Greece on the verge of bankruptcy and other European countries ailing, the economic climate abroad has potentially severe ramifications for U.S. business travel as executives lose interest in European business opportunities.

"European Debt Crisis: Recent Developments," *The New York Times*, March 2, 2012, http://topics.ny times.com/top/reference/timestopics/subjects/e/european_sovereign_debt_crisis/index.html.
The Times summarizes recent developments in the European debt crisis.

Soros, George, "How to Save the Euro," *The New York Review of Books*, Feb. 23, 2012.
A noted financier and philanthropist argues against Germany's austerity policy and says that what Europe needs to extract itself from the euro crisis is growth, not more belt-tightening.

Reports and Studies

Dewan, Selwa, and Christian E. Weller, "When Europe's Sovereign Debt Crisis Hits Home," Center for American Progress, Sept. 22, 2011, www.american progress.org/issues/2011/09/europe_debt.html.
Two economists at the liberal Washington think tank warn that the United States will not escape the backwash from Europe's sovereign debt crisis and outline ways in which America can minimize the impact.

"Economic Crisis in Europe: Causes, Consequences, and Responses," European Union, Directorate General of Economic and Financial Affairs, July 2009, http://ec.europa.eu/economy_finance/publications/publication15887_en.pdf.
This detailed and surprisingly frank official assessment of how the European Union got into its current fiscal mess explores the prospects for effectively resolving the crisis while offering useful background on the financial mechanisms of the EU.

Vasconcelos, Alvaro de, and Marcin Zaborowski, eds., "The Obama Moment," European Union Institute of Security Studies, 2009, www.iss.europa.eu/uploads/media/The_Obama_Moment__web_A4.pdf.
The election of Barack Obama occasioned this in-depth evaluation of European-American relations by leading analysts and political figures from both sides of the Atlantic; much of it is still relevant.

For More Information

Atlantic Council, 1101 15th St., N.W., 11th Floor, Washington, DC 20005; 202-463-7226; www.acus.org. Nonpartisan institution working to promote trans-Atlantic cooperation on such issues as security, business, energy and the environment.

Cato Institute, 1000 Massachusetts Ave., N.W., Washington, DC 20001; 202-842-0200; www.cato.org. Libertarian think tank advocating for U.S. troop reductions in Europe.

Chatham House, 10 St James's Square, London, England SW1Y 4LE; +44 (0) 20 7957 5700; www.chathamhouse .org. Non-governmental organization analyzing major international issues.

Council on Foreign Relations, 58 E. 68th St., New York, NY 10065; 212-434-9400; www.cfr.org. Nonpartisan think tank specializing in U.S. foreign policy and international affairs.

Court of Justice of the European Union, Boulevard Konrad Adenauer, Kirchberg, L-2925 Luxembourg; +352 4303 1; curia.europa.eu. Interprets laws of the European Union to ensure they are applied consistently across member nations.

European Union Delegation to the USA, 2175 K St., N.W., Washington, DC 20037; 202-862-9500; www .eurunion.org. European Union's representative body in the United States.

German Marshall Fund of the United States, 1744 R St., N.W., Washington, DC 20009; 202-683-2650; www.gmfus .org. Public policy institution promoting better understanding between North America and Europe on trans-Atlantic issues.

International Institute for Strategic Studies, 13–15 Arundel St., Temple Place, London, England WC2R 3DX; +44 (0) 20 7379 7676; www.iiss.org. Research institute specializing in political-military conflict.

North Atlantic Treaty Organization, Boulevard Leopold III, 1110 Brussels, Belgium; +32 (0) 2 707 41 11; www .nato.int. Intergovernmental military alliance of North American and European countries.arts.

6

Russia in Turmoil

Jason McLure

Vladimir Putin has led Russia as either prime minister or president for 13 years and won the 2012 presidential election with 64 percent of the vote amidst allegations of widespread fraud. His tenure was built on an implicit deal with voters: In exchange for a rising standard of living fueled by surging energy exports, citizens' legal and political rights have been curtailed.

AFP/Getty Images/Kirill Kudryavtsev

From *The CQ Researcher*,
February 21, 2012 (updated February 14, 2013).

When Vladimir Putin stepped into the ring at a Moscow stadium to congratulate the winner of an "anything goes" mixed martial arts bout in November 2011, he couldn't have been more at home.

During his time as head of Russia's government since 1999—first as president and then as prime minister—the 60-year-old former KGB agent has cultivated a macho image: allowing himself to be photographed practicing judo, shooting a tiger with a tranquilizer, and riding on horseback shirtless in Siberia. And Putin's harsh regime has exiled and imprisoned dozens of opposition supporters, journalists, and human rights activists, while others have died in suspicious circumstances.

So it came as a surprise that Putin was lustily booed by the fight fans, angered, like many other Russians, by the announcement in September that he would run for president again in 2012 to replace Dmitry Medvedev, the man he had handpicked to succeed him in 2008.[1]

The discontent erupted into the streets in three major protests in December of that year, after Putin's United Russia Party retained control of the Duma, Russia's lower house, after what was seen as rigged parliamentary elections.

Protesters turned out across Russia again on Feb. 4, 2012 despite sub-zero temperatures, just a month before the presidential elections and on March 5, after Putin's landslide win was announced amidst fraud allegations.[2] Smaller protests in Moscow occurred immediately before Putin's inauguration in May and continued in the capital as recently as January 2013, when thousands came out to protest the Kremlin's decision to ban adoptions by Americans in

131

A Giant on the World Stage

The world's largest country, Russia stretches across Asia from the Pacific Ocean to Europe. In recent years it has battled Islamic insurgents in the outlying republics of Ingushetia, Dagestan and Chechnya, situated in the southwestern Caucasus region. One of the world's largest oil producers, Russia recently completed a new oil pipeline to China and supplies much of Europe's natural gas. Many of Russia's neighbors — including Kazakhstan, Ukraine, Belarus and Estonia — were under Moscow's control during the Soviet era.

Russia and Surrounding Countries

Source: map by Lewis Agrell

response to a U.S. law targeting Russian human rights violators. The continuing unrest indicates deep divisions in Russian society and raises questions about the long-term viability of the political and economic system he has built. Putin's 13 years in power reflect an implicit deal with citizens: In exchange for a rising standard of living fueled by surging energy exports, citizens will have fewer legal and political rights than they enjoyed in the 1990s during the heady days that followed the collapse of the Soviet Union.

Already the world's largest source of natural gas, Russia under Putin expanded its oil production and now rivals Saudi Arabia as the world's largest oil producer. Increased production, combined with rising oil prices, has dramatically improved living standards, especially in Moscow and St. Petersburg—and oil and gas now provide about half of Russia's revenues.[3]

Yet authoritarian rule and record energy revenues have proven a recipe for corruption, which both reinforces Putin's control by providing a source of patronage while undermining his legitimacy. The spread of corruption into all facets of life—from hospital surgeries to kindergarten admissions—and the recent global economic turmoil have led to deep doubts about Russia's long-term survival as a one-party petro-state.

Meanwhile, the growing popularity of social media websites has enabled urban, middle-class Russians to circumvent state-censored media and share information about everything from corrupt local officials and ballot-box stuffing to protest plans.

The first public protests took many by surprise. Yet middle-class frustration with Putin gained momentum on Dec. 24, 2011 when some 80,000 people gathered in the streets of Moscow to call for an end to his tenure. "Putin should stand aside, he looks out of touch with reality," Alexei Frolov, a 26-year-old clothing shop manager, said, explaining that he decided to join the protests after he saw that the demonstrators were "normal, happy people who just wanted to defend their rights."[4]

They were joined by protesters in dozens of other cities, shocking many analysts with the scale of popular unrest. "No one really expected the middle class to protest so long as they had a solid, secure income," says Tamirlan Kurbanov, a Russian legal scholar researching Russian youth activism at the National Endowment for Democracy, a private, Washington-based, nonprofit foundation that supports democratic institutions around the world. "They came to protest not potential threats to their income but stolen votes—a purely political issue. This is a big shift in mentality."

The series of demonstrations have caused many to recall the throngs who took to Moscow's streets in March 1991, demanding the resignation of the last Soviet premier, Mikhail Gorbachev.[5] Gorbachev, who resigned nine months after those protests and is now 81, joined the calls for Putin to leave during the campaign, telling a Moscow radio station: "He has had three terms: two as president and one as prime minister. Three terms—that is enough."[6]

Russia at a Glance

Russia is nearly twice as big as the United States but has less than half the population. Its per capita income of $16,700 is about the same as Argentina's. Vladimir Putin, who has been in a leadership role for nearly 12 years, is expected to be elected president again in March.

Area: 6.3 million sq. miles (nearly twice as large as the U.S.)

Population: 138.7 million (July 2011 est.; slightly less than half the U.S. population)

Chief of state: President Dmitry Medvedev (since May 2008)

Head of government: Prime Minister Vladimir Putin (since May 2008; he served as president from 2000 to 2008.

Government type: Federation; president elected by popular vote for up to two four-year terms, but terms will increase to six years starting with 2012 election; legislative branch consists of the Federation Council (upper house) with members appointed for four-year terms by the top executives in the federal administrative units; members of the State Duma (lower house) are elected to four-year terms by popular vote.

Ethnic groups: Russian 79.8%, Tatar 3.8%, Ukrainian 2%, Bashkir 1.2%, Chuvash 1.1%, other or unspecified 12.1% (2002 census)

Religion: Russian Orthodox 15-20%, Muslim 10-15%, other Christian denominations 2%, other/agnostic 53-73% (2006 est.)

Infant mortality rate: 10.08 deaths/1,000 live births (147th in the world)

GDP: $2.373 trillion* (7th in the world, about the same as Brazil)

GDP per capita: $16,700* (similar to Argentina and a third of the United States)

Unemployment rate: 6.8%* (71st in the world, about the same as Indonesia)

Primary industries: complete range of mining and extractive industries producing coal, oil, gas, chemicals and metals; defense industries including radar, missile production and advanced electronic components, shipbuilding; road and rail transportation equipment; communications equipment; electric power generating and transmitting equipment

2011 estimate

Source: The World Factbook, *Central Intelligence Agency, 2012, https://www.cia.gov/library/ publications/the-world-factbook/geos/rs.html*

The Internet and the social media sites LiveJournal, Twitter, and Facebook have been key tools for the protesters. Even though state television removed the audio of Putin being booed in the martial arts ring, one version of the unedited video was viewed more than 449,000 times on YouTube.[7] Bypassing Russia's quiescent opposition parties, the largely leaderless movement has been shaped by up-and-coming activists, such as lawyer and anti-corruption blogger Alexei Navalny, who has more than 320,000 followers on Twitter and whose blog has more than 60,000 daily readers.[8]

Real Spies *Do* Use Invisible Ink and 'Sleeper Cells'

East-West espionage apparently is alive and well.

Messages written in invisible ink. Money buried in a field in upstate New York. Identical bags surreptitiously exchanged at a train station.

They sound like the makings of a good Cold War spy novel, but in fact such techniques were in the bag of tricks used by an alleged Russian spy ring broken up in the United States in 2010—nearly 20 years after the breakup of the Soviet Union.

Nor did these alleged spies use typical cover stories, such as claiming to be diplomats or representatives of vague-sounding Russian think tanks. In an effort to become culturally American, these so-called sleeper agents had come to the United States to live and work as ordinary middle-class people in suburban Boston, New York, and Washington, where they spent years developing American identities.[1] One worked for an accounting firm; another was a real estate agent; a third worked at a travel agency. All reportedly were part of a bizarre scheme that apparently gathered little information of value.

Moscow and the West may no longer fear nuclear war with each other, but the shadowy "spy vs. spy" dance between Russia and its Western counterparts has never slackened. President Vladimir Putin, a former KGB agent and director of its successor agency, the Federal Security Service (FSB), has ensured that Russia's intelligence agencies have played a large role in his government.[2] But at times, the nonstop spying has complicated post-Cold War diplomatic relations.

Indeed, the FBI uncovered the sleeper ring just as Presidents Barack Obama and former Russian President Dmitry Medvedev were discussing how to "reset" U.S.-Russia relations on more friendly terms. Instead of being prosecuted, 10 of the agents were sent back to Russia in exchange for four men accused of spying for Britain and the United States in Russia (the 11th slipped away after a court in Cyprus released him on bail).[3]

Not all alleged Russian intelligence operations have been so benign or inept. Three Chechen militants—two of them linked to a 2011 suicide bombing at Moscow's Domodedovo airport—were gunned down in the Turkish capital Istanbul last September. All were executed in daylight by an assailant who fired 11 shots in less than 30 seconds from a silenced pistol. The pistol, a night-vision camera, binoculars, and a Russian passport were later found in a Turkish hotel room. The Russian government officially denied any involvement in the killings.[4]

Russian operatives also are active in other Western countries. Former Russian agent turned dissident Alexander Litvinenko died a slow and excruciating death in London in 2006, after being poisoned with radioactive polonium shortly after meeting with Andrei Lugovoy, a former KGB bodyguard. Litvinenko blamed the Kremlin for his poisoning, and British police sought Lugovoy's extradition from Russia to face charges. The Kremlin has denied the extradition request, and Lugovoy is now a senior member of the Russian parliament representing the ultra-nationalist LDPR party.[5] Lugovoy denies the murder and has variously suggested that it was perpetrated by a dissident Russian oligarch, British security services, the Russian mafia, and unnamed people with links to Georgia.[6]

More recently, four Russian diplomats in Canada abruptly left their embassy in Ottawa after a Canadian

Yet the protesters fell short of their initial goal: preventing Putin from winning 50 percent of the vote in the March 5 election, an embarrassing result that would have forced a second round of voting. Though the ballot-rigging that was documented during the December parliamentary elections was less common, observers from the Organization for Security and Cooperation in Europe reported that Putin had faced no real competition and benefited from heavy government spending on his behalf during the campaign. "The point of elections is that the outcome should be uncertain," said Tonino Picula, a Croatian politician who led one team of election observers, according to the *New York Times*.[9] "This was not the case in Russia. There was naval intelligence officer was charged with passing secrets to a foreign entity.[7] However, a British court in November rejected efforts to deport a 26-year-old Russian woman who had an affair with a member of Parliament and was charged with being a Russian agent. The court said British intelligence officials had failed to prove she was an agent.[8]

But espionage is a two-way street. In January Jonathan Powell, former British Prime Minister Tony Blair's chief of staff, admitted that in 2006 British agents had been caught using a fake rock in a Moscow park to transmit and receive electronic signals. The embarrassing revelation led to Russian accusations that Britain was funding groups opposed to Putin.[9]

Still, the break-up of the alleged American sleeper cell last year was arguably even more embarrassing to Russia. State media gave heavy coverage to the 10 "suburban spies" being awarded medals by Medvedev upon their return home. But in a humiliating twist, it turns out the Moscow-based spymaster who operated the ring had been passing information to the Central Intelligence Agency since 1999. He was whisked out of Russia on the eve of the U.S. crackdown.[10]

"The activity of both intelligence services will not stop and never will," said Boris Solomatin, a retired KGB general, who spent two decades supervising Russian spy operations in the United States. "But the end of the Cold War gives us an opportunity to put an end to uncivilized methods."[11]

— *Jason McLure*

A courtroom drawing shows five members of an alleged Russian spy ring after their arrest in the United States in 2010—nearly 20 years after end of the Cold War

AFP/Getty Images/Shireley Shepard

[1]Scott Shane and Charlie Savage, "In Ordinary Lives, U.S. Sees the Work of Russian Agents," *The New York Times*, June 28, 2010, www.nytimes.com/2010/06/29/world/europe/29spy.html?pagewanted=all.

[2]Steven Eke, "KGB Influence 'Soars Under Putin,' " BBC News, Dec. 13, 2006, http://news.bbc.co.uk/2/hi/6177531.stm.

[3]Helena Smith, "Russian Spy Ring Suspect Jumps Bail in Cyprus," *The Guardian*, June 30, 2010.

[4]Lee Ferran and Rym Momtaz, "Payback? Istanbul Assassination Victims Linked to Moscow Bombing," ABCNews.com, Sept. 22, 2011, http://abc news.go.com/Blotter/payback-istanbul-assassination-victims-linked-moscow-bombing/story?id=14581977.

[5]"Zhirinovsky's New Sideman: Lugovoy," U.S. State Department Cable, Sept. 18, 2007. Released by Wikileaks and available at www.guardian.co.uk/world/us-embassy-cables-documents/122689.

[6]"Lugovoy Points to Possible Killers of Litvinenko," *RT*, Oct. 23, 2011, http://rt.com/news/lugovoy-litvinenko-court-hearing-509/.

[7]Steven Chase, Oliver Moore, and Tamara Baluja, "Ottawa expels Russian diplomats in wake of charges against Canadian," *The Globe and Mail*, Jan. 19, 2012, www.theglobeandmail.com/news/politics/ottawa-expels-russian-diplomats-in-wake-of-charges-against-canadian/article2308879/.

[8]John Fahey, "MI5 'Unfairly' Pursued Spy Accused Katia Zatuliveter," *The Independent*, Nov. 29, 2011, www.independent.co.uk/news/uk/home-news/mi5-unfairly-pursued-spy-accused-katia-zatuliveter-6269410.html.

[9]"UK Admits Spying With Fake Rock," BBC News, Jan. 18, 2012, www.bbc.co.uk/news/world-europe-16619623.

[10]Tom Parfitt, "Russian double agent sentenced in absentia to 25 years in prison," *The Guardian*, June 27, 2011, www.guardian.co.uk/world/2011/jun/27/russian-double-agent-tried-absence.

[11]Pete Earley, "Boris Solomatin Interview," truTV Crime Library, undated, www.trutv.com/library/crime/terrorists_spies/spies/solomatin/1.html.

no real competition, and abuse of government resources ensured that the ultimate winner of the election was never in doubt."

The upheaval comes on the heels of the 2011 Arab Spring—popular revolts that unseated dictators in Egypt, Tunisia, Libya, and Yemen, and it is difficult not to see parallels between those movements and Russia's unrest.[10] As U.S. Sen. John McCain, R-Ariz., tweeted in December 2011: "Dear Vlad, The Arab Spring is coming to a neighborhood near you."

When asked about McCain's comment during a televised call-in show, Putin responded sharply. "Mr. McCain fought in Vietnam," said Putin. "I think that he has enough blood of peaceful citizens on his hands. It must be impossible for him to live without these disgusting scenes anymore."[11]

But McCain wasn't the only American to draw Putin's wrath. Shortly after the protests erupted in December, Putin blamed U.S. Secretary of State Hillary Rodham Clinton for prompting the Russian protests by calling the 2011 parliamentary vote "neither free nor fair." Clinton's comment, he said, "sent a signal" to "some of our public figures inside the country. They heard this signal and launched active work with the U.S. State Department's support."[12]

The upheaval may be aggravating tensions between Russia and the West, but analysts debate whether it poses a threat to the underlying relationship, which warmed during a "reset" in 2010 between presidents Obama and Medvedev.

The State Department took a more cautious approach after the 2012 presidential election, issuing a statement endorsing the reports of observer groups that found the election flawed but praising the "government's efforts to reform the political system" and saying it "looks forward to working with the President-elect."[13]

That measured tone didn't stop Russian state media from producing a series of reports blasting the U.S. presidential campaign in 2012, including criticisms of Texas and Iowa for banning OSCE poll monitors and a report decrying the lack of polling stations on Indian reservations. Just before the U.S. election, Russia's electoral chief Vladimir Churov decried the U.S. elections system as "the worst in the world" in comments that were seen as fodder for Russian domestic politics—where the issue of voting remains sensitive for the government.[14]

"There is a very different agenda for inside Russia and outside of Russia," says Fatima Tlisova, a Russian journalist who has worked for the Russian newspaper *Novaya Gazeta* and The Associated Press. "Inside Russia [Putin] can play very anti-American populist games, and outside Russia he can be very sensitive. He tries to create a special image of Russia as being democratic."

The protests, however, reveal a Russian political and economic system more fragile than many analysts believed before the demonstrations. As policy experts gauge the recent upheaval on the streets of Moscow, here are some of the questions they are asking:

Could an Arab Spring-style revolt topple Putin?

Russia's recent uprising shares several similarities with the popular revolts that toppled autocratic regimes in the Arab world in the spring of 2011. In both instances, protesters objected to political stagnation, pervasive corruption, and the absence of democracy. And, as in the Arab world, the Russians have organized online, because television and radio are state-controlled.

But analysts differ strongly on whether such a movement could topple Putin's regime. Some say the system Putin built is far weaker than it appears, while others say popular protests and middle-class discontent hardly spell the end of a regime that has run the world's largest country for the last 13 years.

"Putin still enjoys the support of a large number of the population and is still the most popular leader," says Andranik Migranyam, an adviser to former President Boris Yeltsin and now director of the pro-Kremlin Institute for Democracy and Cooperation in New York. "It's not going to be something like what happened in Egypt or some other places."

"People who came out to rally don't want revolution, they want evolution," says Kurbanov, at the National Endowment for Democracy. "I don't think they were inspired by the Arab Spring."

Because many of the protesters have been middle-class city-dwellers, their demands are different from other revolutionaries. "They are mostly educated enough about the past to fear blood in the streets," Esther Dyson, a Swiss-born columnist, wrote recently in the *Prague Post*.[15] "They want Putin gone, not punished (mostly); they realize it is the system that produced Putin, who then reinforced the system. They want to reverse that cycle, putting an end to corruption, official impunity, and being treated like cattle."

In such a climate, Putin and his inner circle likely will resist surrendering power until the bitter end in order to avoid prosecution for corruption or other criminal behavior by a future Russian government, according to Michael Bohm, opinion page editor of the English-language *Moscow Times*. "The best, and perhaps only, guarantee of securing immunity for Putin—and dozens of his friends and colleagues who have become millionaires and billionaires over the past 10 years . . . is to remain in power," Bohm wrote recently.[16]

Others predicted the protests would continue to grow in size and passion, potentially toppling the regime. "My guess is that it's going to continue and radicalize," says Leon Aron, director of Russian studies at the American Enterprise

Institute (AEI), a conservative think tank in Washington, just before the election. "The first demonstrations were calling for new [parliamentary] elections. Then they were saying 'Putin is a thief, Putin is a dictator,' and it started to move into a critique of the regime itself."

However, many Russians now say the system can't evolve, says Stephen Blank, a Russia researcher at the U.S. Army War College. "Putin's gang, they basically tell people: 'You count for nothing; we're going to take power,'" says Blank. "It's a system that can't reform itself. It has to be transformed."

That hasn't happened yet. A year after the election, some who participated in protests now feel disillusioned with the protest movement, even if they remain more alienated than ever from Putin and the ruling party. "Suddenly we—a huge number of Internet hamsters—we decided that we had had enough, we got together and we went out," Yulia Fotchenko, an account director at a marketing agency told the *New York Times*. "And then, whoops! We turned back into Internet hamsters, the leaders and all the rest of us. Because nothing happened."

"And now I feel despair which is even stronger, deeper, worse than it was before we began these actions," she added.[17]

Will Putin's new government tackle corruption?

The scale of corruption in Russia is widely seen as staggering. Transparency International ranked Russia 143rd out of 182 countries in its 2011 corruption perceptions index, on par with Nigeria and more corrupt than international pariahs such as Syria, Iran, and Eritrea.[18]

Corruption costs Russia as much as $318 billion annually, or one-third of its total economic

Russia Ranks High on Corruption Scale

Russia is among the world's most corrupt nations, according to the corruption watchdog group Transparency International. Russia's corruption perception index score of 2.4 in 2011 was the same as Nigeria's, known worldwide for its rampant corruption. And Russia's corruption problem is more serious than countries with similar economic conditions such as China and India.

Corruption Perceptions Index Scores for Select Countries, 2001 and 2011
(on a scale from 0 to 10, with 10 being the least corrupt)

Country	2001	2011
Russia	2.3	2.4
Poland	4.1	5.5
Turkey	3.6	4.2
Indonesia	1.9	3.0
Nigeria	1.0	2.4
Estonia	5.6	6.4
India	2.7	3.1
China	3.5	3.6
Brazil	4.0	3.8
Mexico	3.7	3.0

Source: "Corruption Perceptions Index 2001," Transparency International, June 2001, www.transparency.org/policy_research/surveys_indices/cpi/2001; "Corruption Perceptions Index 2011," Transparency International, 2011, cpi.transparency.org/cpi2011/results/

output, according to the Moscow-based InDem Foundation, a nongovernmental organization that researches corruption and governance.[19] The average commercial bribe paid to a government or corporate official in the first half of 2011 was 293,000 rubles ($10,573). "Everyday" bribes to get children into kindergarten, avoid the military draft, or fix traffic tickets were 5,285 rubles ($191), according to Russian government figures.[20]

Although corruption has been a fixture under Putin's rule, some say he could still tackle the problem. Bribery already was rife before Putin came to power; in 2000 Transparency International ranked Russia 82nd out of 90 countries surveyed.[21]

By some measures corruption has declined in recent years. A survey by the PriceWaterhouse Coopers accounting firm found that 40 percent of businesses reported being victims of bribery and corruption in 2011, down from 48 percent in 2009. "There is reason to be hopeful that some effect is being felt from both the increased publicity and legal activities promoted by the Russian government," the report said.[22]

Putin launched his 2012 presidential campaign by addressing the need to crack down on corruption.[23] And after the Dec. 24, 2011 protest, he ordered managers at state-owned companies to declare their income and property and disclose the owners of all companies with which they do business.[24]

"To defeat systemic corruption, a line should be drawn to

Russia Leads World in Gas Reserves

With more than 1.5 quadrillion cubic feet of proven natural gas reserves, Russia has the world's largest gas deposits — about 50 percent more than Iran, which ranks second. Since Vladimir Putin came to power in 2000, Russia has increased its crude oil production by 50 percent, boosting the value of its oil exports more than fivefold. Critics say that by increasing Russia's dependence on lucrative energy exports, Putin has made the economy vulnerable to fluctuating world energy prices and fueled rampant corruption.

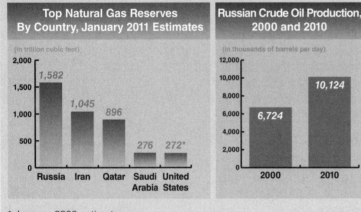

* January 2009 estimate

Source: "Natural Gas — Proved Reserves," The World Factbook, Central Intelligence Agency, 2012, https://www.cia.gov/library/publications/the-world-factbook/rankorder/2179rank.html; "Russia Country Analysis Brief," U.S. Energy Information Administration, November 2010, www.eia.gov/countries/cab.cfm?fips=RS; Bank of Russia

separate not only authority and property but also executive power and control over it," Putin wrote in *Kommersant,* a Russian business daily, in February 2012. In the same article, Putin promised a new system of administrative courts for corruption as well as online broadcasts and public transcripts of court hearings.[25]

"Authorities have adopted a number of steps indicating that they . . . are ready to act decisively," Migranyan, of the Institute for Democracy and Cooperation, wrote recently. "Both the prime minister and the president have spoken about important steps taken to combat corruption."[26]

In February 2013, Putin sent a bill to parliament that would ban public officials and their families from having overseas bank accounts, which are often used to hide ill-gotten funds overseas. Those caught with foreign bank accounts would be fired, under the legislation.[27]

Others say Putin cannot effectively tackle corruption because he and his closest allies are heavily implicated. "Putin himself is one of the biggest thieves," says Anders Aslund, a Swedish economist who advised former Russian President Boris Yeltsin and is now a senior fellow at the D.C.-based Peterson Institute for International Economics. "He has organized a set-up where he taps a number of government sources, and the money goes to his reliable friends."

Though such allegations are unconfirmed, anecdotal evidence abounds. In 2011, just hours after a Russian website patterned after Wikileaks published photos of a massive new mansion on the Black Sea reportedly owned by Putin, it suffered a cyber-attack that shut down the site.[28] And Vladimir Litvinenko, an economics professor who oversaw Putin's doctoral thesis, is now one of Russia's richest men and chairman of a phosphate mining company worth at least $350 million.[29]

"The fortune is raising eyebrows because Litvinenko, who has headed the state mining institute since 1994, was not previously known as a businessman," wrote Nikolaus von Twickel, a reporter for the *Moscow Times.* "Litvinenko's apparently rapid rise to riches speaks volumes in a country where who you know can be as important as what you know, if not more so."[30]

Some regime critics say Putin is worth up to $40 billion and controls hidden stakes in natural gas giant Gazprom, oil-explorer Surgutneftegaz, and oil-trader Gunvor.[31] Putin and the companies involved have denied this repeatedly, but the lack of transparency in Russian corporations makes verifying such assertions impossible.

Corruption also has become a core function of the Russian state itself, according to U.S. State

Department cables released by Wikileaks. Intelligence agencies use the Russian mafia to carry out arms trafficking, according to the cables, and police, prosecutors, and spy agencies operate a de facto protection racket. Bribery is so common, said the cables, it comprises a parallel tax system for the enrichment of security services.[32]

In a February 2010 cable released by Wikileaks, former U.S. ambassador to Russia John Beyrle wrote about the problem in Moscow's government. "The Moscow city government's direct links to criminality have led some to call it 'dysfunctional,' and to assert that the government operates more as a kleptocracy than a government," he wrote.[33] "Criminal elements enjoy a 'krysha' (a term from the criminal/mafia world literally meaning 'roof' or 'protection') that runs through the police, the Federal Security Service (FSB), the Ministry of Internal Affairs (MVD), and the prosecutor's office, as well as throughout the Moscow city government bureaucracy."

Reports of the links between criminal gangs and government security services are not exaggerated, says journalist Tlisova. Putin, who led the FSB before entering politics, restored the intelligence agency's pre-eminent role in the country after it had been greatly weakened in the decade following the fall of the Soviet Union. "When he came in, it grew and took over the whole country," she says. "If you're in with the FSB, you can get rich all over the country."

Are Russia's relations with the West worsening?

Putin's accusation that Secretary Clinton and the American government were behind the protests was not the only dent in U.S.-Russia relations during Russia's recent election season. There was also a nasty dispute over U.S. and European Union funding for Golos, the only independent Russian election-monitoring group to oversee the elections.

Putin accused the group of interfering in the elections on behalf of foreign powers. "Representatives of some states are organizing meetings with those who receive money from them, the so-called grant recipients, briefing them on how to 'work' in order to influence the course of the election campaign in our country," Putin said.[34]

During the parliamentary elections, the group documented 5,300 complaints of fraud and hosted an interactive map online for the public to post video and other evidence of irregularities.[35] In the run-up to the March presidential election, state television labeled the group a U.S. lackey, and it was ordered evicted from its Moscow offices.

Putin's criticism of the United States comes at a time when he may have determined that it's more useful for Russians to see America as a rival than as a friend. "There have been efforts to resurrect the image of an external enemy to unite the people," says Kurbanov, the legal scholar. "It distracts attention from the true and real problems."

The crackdown on Golos came as Russia increasingly was critical of U.S. plans to build a missile defense system in Eastern Europe. While the U.S. says the system, designed to shoot down enemy missiles, is being built to protect European allies from Iran, Russia views it as a threat to its own ballistic missiles.

The Russian military announced it would move missiles to within striking distance of European Union nations, and Putin's United Russia lambasted the new U.S. ambassador, Michael McFaul, for meeting with opposition groups. Meanwhile, Putin was ratcheting up opposition to Western efforts to isolate Syria over its crackdown on democracy protesters and Iran for its efforts to enrich uranium.[36]

"You can see that Putin is trying to pursue an anti-American campaign with his vicious attacks on McFaul and Clinton," says Aslund, of the Peterson Institute. "Putin is trying to mobilize his people. He's doing what it takes to win the presidential election."

That means a difficult future for relations. "The sides have exhausted the positive agenda, and the election-related political fervor in both countries will only emphasize areas of dissonance," said Fyodor Lukyanov, a foreign affairs columnist for Moscow-based Ria Novosti, a government-run news agency, in the run-up to Russia's presidential vote.[37]

Indeed, following the election the U.S. and Russia have butted heads over the civil war in Syria, where Russia has continued to ship arms to its ally President Bashar al-Assad even as rebels have steadily won territory and despite calls for his ouster by the U.S. and its regional allies.[38] In December 2012, Obama signed a law imposing visa and financial sanctions on Russian officials implicated in the death in prison of Sergei Magnitsky, a Russian tax lawyer who reported a plot by officials to steal $230 million from the country's treasury by filing a fraudulent tax return for a British-based private equity firm.[39] Russia responded with a new law banning Americans from adopting Russian children.[40]

Others see the harsh words as simply rhetoric that is unlikely to do lasting damage to the relationship between Russia and the West. "Typically, in moments like [elections], foreign policy issues disappear and the rhetoric and internal debate are focused on questions of power and the issues of legitimacy of the different political forces," says Sestanovich, of the Council on Foreign Relations. "I would be surprised if relations with the U.S. mattered a lot."

Indeed, some say the underlying relationship between Russia and the West is still strong, at least by historical standards, and could be much worse. During the U.S. presidential campaign, Russian officials repeatedly criticized Republican candidate Mitt Romney, who took a hawkish stance towards Putin and called Russia "our number one geopolitical foe."[41] Russia has been a key ally in the NATO operation in Afghanistan, primarily by providing an important corridor for shipment of supplies to the United States and its allies in Kabul, especially as U.S. relations with Pakistan have worsened. By the end of 2011, about 52 percent of cargo to allied forces in Afghanistan was shipped through Russia—a reflection of the fact that Russia wants NATO to succeed against the Taliban. Moscow fears the growth of radical Islam in Afghanistan and its neighbors.[42]

Other indications of a successful reset in U.S.-Russia relations in recent years include: the START nuclear arms reduction treaty signed by Medvedev and Obama in 2010; Russia's decision not to veto the U.N. Security Council vote allowing NATO missions against Libyan strongman Moammar Gadhafi; and cooperation in other areas ranging from cyber-security to the International Space Station.[43]

Though the warming of U.S.-Russia relations occurred under the presidencies of Obama and Medvedev, Putin's return to the presidency is not likely to herald a rolling back of previous agreements, some analysts say.

"Putin was involved with the reset from the very beginning," said Dmitry Suslov, of the Moscow-based Council on Foreign and Defense Policies.[44] "In fact, it would be weird to think that any major policy could have been developed in Moscow over the past four years without his leadership."

BACKGROUND

Revolutionary Dictatorship

From the 17th century to the early 20th century Russia was ruled as a feudal state by emperors known as tsars. Russia's entry into World War I and the massive suffering that ensued—with 4 million casualties in the first year-and-a-half alone—helped to trigger a communist revolution led by Vladimir Lenin, the iron-willed son of an education official.[45] With the country exhausted by six years of war and revolution, Lenin set about consolidating the Communist Party's control over what by then was called the Union of Soviet Socialist Republics (U.S.S.R.) and establishing a "dictatorship of the proletariat" led by factory workers and peasants.

However, by 1921, it was clear that all major decisions would be made solely by the party's leadership. Those opposed to centralized control were purged ruthlessly by Josef Stalin, a Georgia-born revolutionary who had become secretary of the party.[46]

After Lenin died following a series of strokes in 1924, Stalin used his power over the secret police and the party's bureaucracy to seize absolute control by 1929.

Leading a "revolution from above," he turned the Soviet Union into a totalitarian state infested with secret police in which citizens could not criticize the government and had few property rights. Millions of peasants starved as Stalin forced them from their land to join collective farms and systematically killed, starved, and imprisoned the wealthiest farmers, known as *kulaks*.[47]

Internationally, Stalin tried to protect his empire from a resurgent Germany by signing a nonaggression pact with Hitler in 1939. But when Hitler

CHRONOLOGY

1910s-1940s *Communist era begins after Russian Revolution ends Romanov dynasty and establishes Union of Soviet Socialist Republics (U.S.S.R).*

October 1917 Communist regime takes over Russia; Marxist Vladimir Lenin becomes first Soviet leader. . . . Czar Nicholas II and his wife and children are assassinated in July 1918.

1924 Lenin dies and within a few years is replaced by Josef Stalin, who will cause the deaths of tens of millions of peasants and potential dissidents.

1941 Soviet Union joins the Allies to help defeat Nazi Germany in World War II. After the war, Stalin negotiates with United States and Great Britain for control of Eastern Europe.

1950s-1980s *United States and Soviet Union vie for nuclear dominance and reach a Cold War standoff.*

1985 Mikhail Gorbachev becomes general secretary of the Communist Party and, as the Soviet Union's last leader, initiates political reforms.

1990s *Soviet Union disintegrates. Relations with the West warm.*

1991 Communist hard-liners fail to overthrow Gorbachev in August coup attempt, but he steps down four months later. . . . U.S.S.R. officially dissolves on Dec. 25. . . . Soviet Union eventually fragments into 15 republics.

1992 President Boris Yeltsin launches economic reforms. U.S. commits $24 billion in aid to Russia. Yeltsin and President George H. W. Bush sign Strategic Arms Reduction Treaty.

1994 Yeltsin starts war against separatist Chechen republic.

1997 Russia and NATO agree to cooperate on defense issues.

1999 Yeltsin resigns, designates Prime Minister Vladimir Putin as acting president. Putin restarts suspended Chechen offensive. . . . Former satellite states Poland, Hungary, and Czech Republic join NATO, despite Russian objections.

2000-Present *Economy benefits from high world prices for oil and gas exports; Putin rolls back democratic freedoms as he and a protégé trade leadership positions.*

2000 Newly elected Putin moves against oligarchs and independent media.

2001 After Sept. 11 terrorist attacks on New York and the Pentagon, Putin allows U.S. to use bases in Central Asia to launch Afghan war.

2004 Putin re-elected. . . . Freedom House downgrades Russia's rating to "not free."

2005 Yukos oil company founder and Putin critic Mikhail Khodorkovsky is convicted of financial crimes and sent to prison in Siberia.

2008 Putin is ousted by term limits; Dmitry Medvedev is elected president, vowing to crack down on corruption. Putin becomes prime minister. Duma extends presidential terms from four years to six.

2010 Medvedev and U.S. President Barack Obama sign a nuclear arms reduction treaty, as the two sides seek to reset relations that deteriorated under Putin and Bush. Russia decides not to veto U.N. decision to send NATO missions against Libyan strongman Moammar Gadhafi.

2011 Medvedev announces in September that he won't run for president in 2012, but Putin will. . . . Putin's party wins 49 percent of the vote—down from 64 percent in 2007—in December parliamentary elections roundly condemned as fraudulent, triggering weeks of anti-Putin demonstrations across Russia.

2012 Large anti-Putin demonstrations are held in Moscow in the months before the March 4 presidential election, despite frigid weather and the near-certainty that Putin will be re-elected. Russia blocks Western efforts at United Nations to condemn Syria's president, Bashar Assad, whose security forces have killed tens of thousands citizens in civil war. After Putin's election, Obama signs law sanctioning Russian officials implicated in human rights violations; Putin bans Americans from adopting Russian children.

2014 Russia scheduled to host Winter Olympics in the city of Sochi, which lies near the Caucasus republics of Dagestan, Ingusthetia and Chechnya, where rebels have battled Russian troops in recent years. Sochi is also less than 50 miles from Georgia, with whom Russia fought a brief 2008 war.

In Frigid Siberia, Warming Friendship With China

Cross-border trade and immigration are on the rise.

After the collapse of the Soviet Union, the military outpost of Mirnaya, along the border between Siberia and China, lost its garrison. To make enough money to survive, the Russian townspeople began selling what was left to buyers across the border in China.

First, villagers sold the garrison's prefabricated buildings and windows. Then the radiators and pipes went to scrap dealers. Finally even the stones that made up the outpost walls were sold.

The future of the tiny village, population 713, looked grim. More than two dozen people died in 2010, but not a single baby was born.[1]

The dismantling of the Soviet Union meant an end to subsidies that once encouraged people to settle in Siberia. Now China's huge population, combined with its booming economy's thirst for the raw materials found in abundance in Siberia, means the region is slowly drifting out of Moscow's orbit and into Beijing's.

The Far Eastern Federal District where Mirnaya is located stretches from the Pacific in the east to Lake Baikal in central Siberia. About 13 times the size of France, the area has only 6.3 million people—about the same as the Dallas-Fort Worth metropolitan area. And the region's population is declining: Its current census shows 21 percent fewer people than in 1992.[2] In contrast, the three Chinese provinces just across the border—Liaoning, Jilin, and Heilong—together have a total of about 110 million people.[3]

In cities like Novosibirsk, Siberia's largest, workers ride to work on Chinese buses, and Russian housewives use Chinese words to buy vegetables from Chinese traders. "Everything we have comes from China—our dishes, leather goods, even the meat we eat is from China," Vyacheslav Ilyukhin, head of the Building Department at Novosobirsk city hall, said.[4] "Siberia is becoming Chinese."

Once a feared destination for exiled political prisoners under the tsars and communists, Siberia boasts vast forests that stand atop massive reserves of minerals and petroleum needed by Chinese factories. China's demand for Siberian raw materials has made it Russia's largest trading partner.

abrogated the pact and invaded the Soviet Union in 1941, Stalin joined Great Britain and the United States against Hitler. The Soviets suffered catastrophically during the war: Cities and vast swathes of the countryside were destroyed, and an estimated 27 million soldiers and civilians died—about 14 percent of the population.[48]

After Hitler's defeat, Stalin sought to regain territory lost to Germany in World War I. He installed satellite regimes in Eastern European countries occupied by the Red Army—a plan formalized by Stalin, British Prime Minister Winston Churchill, and U.S. President Franklin D. Roosevelt at the 1945 Yalta summit. By the time he died in 1953, Stalin had lowered what Churchill called an Iron Curtain over Eastern Europe and had turned the Soviet Union into a nuclear superpower and foe of its former allies.[49]

Fraying Empire

After Stalin's death, a power struggle ensued in the Soviet politburo over who would succeed him. His top deputies were determined that no one would amass as much power as Stalin had during his three decades in power. In 1953, after a two-year internal struggle, Nikita Khruschev, a former coal miner and the son of peasants, emerged as the victor.[50]

Khruschev repudiated Stalin's "cult of personality" in a 1956 speech, but mixed reforms with hardline measures in the Soviet bloc, such as sending Soviet tanks to Hungary in 1956 to quell an anti-communist uprising. He was ousted in 1964 in a bloodless coup from within the party. In 1968, his successor, Leonid Brezhnev, sent Warsaw Pact troops into Czechoslovakia to halt reforms proposed by Premier Alexander Dubcek.[51]

Massive infrastructure projects abound in the region, often financed by Chinese banks. They include:

- The Kimkan open pit mine on the Russia-China border, thought to have enough iron ore to build hundreds of millions of cars.[5]
- The East Siberia Pacific Ocean Pipeline, a $25 billion project that opened last year to bring oil from eastern Siberia to the northeastern Chinese city of Daqing.[6]
- A 750-megawatt electricity transmission project, part of a Russian plan to export 60 billion kilowatt hours of electricity to China by 2020—an amount equivalent to Minnesota's annual electricity consumption.[7]

Besides stimulating trade and resource development, the Chinese investments also have been accompanied by some migration, but not the tens of millions of Chinese immigrants that Russians feared would pour across the border when it was opened in 1989. In fact, while there was some migration from China to Russia over the past two decades, much of the immigrant traffic has been from north to south. With China's economy vastly outperforming Russia's and Chinese urban professionals earning more than their Russian counterparts, many Russian businessmen have set up shop in border cities on the Chinese side.

Stanislav Bystritski, a Russian television producer living in the Chinese border city of Suifenhe, explained, "Many Russian businessmen say it's easier to work here. There is so much less corruption and bureaucracy."

—*Jason McLure*

[1]Matthias Schepp, "China's Growing Interests in Siberia," *Der Spiegel*, May 6, 2011, www.spiegel.de/international/world/0,1518,761033,00.html.

[2]Kataryzna Jarzynska, "The Results of the 2010 Census—A Deepening Demographic Crisis in Russia," Eastweek, Centre for Eastern Studies (Poland), Dec. 21, 2011, www.osw.waw.pl/en/publikacje/eastweek/2011–12–21/results-2010-census-a-deepening-demographic-crisis-russia. See also Vladimir Borisov, "Demographic Situation in Russia: The Role of Mortality in the Reproduction of Population," *Demographia*, 2005, http://demographia.ru/eng/articles/index. html?idR=68&idArt=1363.

[3]"Communiqué of the National Bureau of Statistics of People's Republic of China on Major Figures of the 2010 Population Census," National Bureau of Statistics of China, April 29, 2011, www.stats.gov.cn/english/newsandcoming events/t20110429_402722516.htm.

[4]Anna Nemtsova and Owen Matthews, "Fear and Loathing in Siberia," *Newsweek,* March 26, 2006, www.thedailybeast.com/newsweek/2006/03/26/fear-and-loathing-in-siberia.html.

[5]Andrew E. Kramer, "China's Hunger Fuels Exports in Remote Russia," *The New York Times,* June 9, 2010, www.nytimes.com/2010/06/10/business/global/ 10ruble.html?pagewanted=all.

[6]"Russia-China Oil Pipeline Opens," BBC News, Jan. 1, 2011, www.bbc.co. uk/news/world-asia-pacific-12103865.

[7]"China Completes Power Transmission Project With Russia," Xinhua, Jan. 2, 2012, www.china.org.cn/china/2012–01/02/content_24309649.htm. Also see "Electricity Consumption by State, 2009," University of Kansas Institute for Policy and Social Research, www.ipsr.ku.edu/ksdata/ksah/energy/18ener7.pdf.

By the 1970s Western capitalist economies clearly were far more prosperous than centrally planned communist countries. Fortunately for Brezhnev, the Soviet Union had become an oil exporter, and high oil prices in the 1970s had brought a large inflow of foreign cash. From 1973 to 1985, energy exports accounted for 80 percent of the country's hard-currency exports, allowing the Soviets to try to maintain near military parity with the United States.[52]

In the 1980s oil prices ebbed, as did the economy. The Soviet Union's "outer empire" in Eastern Europe also was fraying—most notably in Poland, where the Solidarity trade union movement had begun to challenge communist rule. Gorbachev, who had risen through the ranks of provincial Soviet officialdom to become general secretary in 1985, understood the decline of Soviet power and the weakness of the oil-based economy.

His *perestroika* (restructuring) and *glasnost* (opening) policies were designed to reduce the role of central planners in the economy and to check corruption by increasing freedom of speech and press. Better relations with the United States were meant to allow the Soviet Union to reduce its military budget and improve living standards. But greater openness only served to undermine Soviet authority, and resistance to Moscow's dominance grew in republics from Estonia to Uzbekistan.[53]

The Soviet empire began crumbling in June 1989, when Solidarity swept Polish elections that were considered free and fair. Hungary already had begun removing the fence along its border with non-communist Austria. By November thousands of German civilians, unmolested by authorities, were tearing down the infamous Berlin Wall between the communist East and capitalist

West Berlin. Peaceful revolutions would follow in Czechoslovakia and Bulgaria, along with the bloody toppling of Romania's communists.

The dissolution of the Soviet Union's "outer empire" had immediate ramifications for satellites in its "inner empire," such as Ukraine, Belarus, and Kazakhstan, which were governed directly by Moscow. By March 1990, the Communist Party in Lithuania had split from the Soviet Union, and within two years the nuclear superpower had fragmented into 15 independent republics.

Yeltsin and Putin

Like Gorbachev, Boris Yeltsin also had risen through the ranks of provincial Soviet officialdom. In 1985, when Gorbachev took power, Yeltsin quickly became a force for greater democracy within the party—so great that the KGB, the Soviet spy agency, conducted a public smear campaign against him.

As Gorbachev struggled to preserve Russia's links with its surrounding republics in 1991, Yeltsin resoundingly won a campaign for the newly created position of president of Russia—leaving two leaders in Moscow. In August Gorbachev agreed to devolve many government functions to individual republics. Yeltsin claimed that Soviet assets such as the oil and gas fields were now the property of the Russian republic, triggering an attempted coup by hardliners seeking to preserve Soviet power.[54]

Most of the members of the security services failed to back the coup, but four months later Gorbachev formally resigned. The red flag of the Soviet Union, with its iconic hammer and sickle, was lowered from the Kremlin and replaced with the red, white, and blue tricolor of Russia.[55]

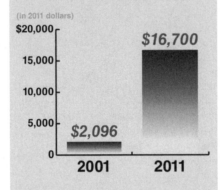

Per Capita GDP Soars

Russia's per capita gross domestic product (GDP) increased eightfold over the past decade, as production and export revenues at state-owned oil and gas companies skyrocketed along with rising energy prices. By comparison, per capita GDP in the United States is $48,100.

Russian Per Capita GDP 2001 and 2011

(in 2011 dollars)

$16,700 (2011)

$2,096 (2001)

Source: The World Factbook, *Central Intelligence Agency, 2012,https://www. cia. gov/library/publications/the-world-factbook/geos/rs.html*

As president, Yeltsin did not object when Ukraine and Belarus left the union, but when Chechnya, a Muslim region in the Caucasus Mountains, tried to break away in the early 1990s, he repeatedly sent in troops to try to quell the uprising, which has survived in varying forms to this day.

Meanwhile, Yeltsin had begun privatizing state assets. Often, former communist officials ended up owning state companies they previously had run, or state assets were bought up on the cheap by businessmen who had made their fortunes importing smuggled goods or changing money on the black market during Soviet times. The fire sale bred lawlessness: In 1994 alone, 600 businessmen, politicians, and journalists who were covering the scramble for assets were killed.[56]

A new class of so-called oligarchs emerged in the 1990s—businessmen who had excelled at buying up state assets cheaply. For instance, Mikhail Khodorkovsky, a former communist youth league official who operated an import-export business but had never seen an oilfield, was able to buy the vast assets that would become Yukos Oil for $350 million.

Though the chaotic breakup of the Soviet Union resulted in massive profits for some, the vast majority of Russians saw the government social safety net crumble and secure jobs in state-run factories vaporize. The resulting hyperinflation meant that an item that cost 100 rubles in 1990 cost 1.6 million rubles in 1999. By 1998, after a financial crisis and falling oil prices, gross domestic product had fallen 40 percent below 1991 levels.[57]

Yeltsin, weakened by alcoholism and illness, stepped down in late 1999, naming his last prime minister, former KGB director Putin, as his successor. The ascendance of Putin, who spoke nostalgically of the Soviet Union and was dismissive of press freedoms and other human rights, was greeted warily in the West.[58]

After several months as acting president, Putin won a lackluster presidential election that featured no presidential debates, fawning coverage of his campaign by progovernment television, and little discussion of the ongoing war in Chechnya.[59] The Kremlin soon began extinguishing the nation's few independent television channels and stepped up attacks on oligarchs who threatened to use their wealth to challenge Putin politically.[60]

Perhaps most notably, Yukos tycoon Khodorkovsky was arrested in 2003 and later convicted of tax evasion and embezzlement and sentenced to nine years in prison. His supporters said he was prosecuted for financing pro-Western opposition parties.[61] Even more worryingly, several critics of Putin have been killed or died under suspicious circumstances, including:

- Yuri Shchekochikhin, a journalist who had long campaigned against the Chechen war and who had investigated corruption in Moscow city government and in the military. His death in 2003 was described as an allergy attack; his family said he was poisoned.[62]
- Paul Klebnikov, founding editor of the Russian edition of *Forbes* and known for investigating corruption among business tycoons, was shot as he left his office in 2004.[63]
- Investigative journalist Anna Politkovskaya, who wrote about atrocities by Russian troops in Chechnya, was shot in the elevator of her apartment building in 2006.[64]
- Stanislav Markelov, a lawyer for the family of a Chechen woman murdered by a Russian army officer, was killed in 2009 after speaking out at a news conference in Moscow.[65]

Relations with the United States, which had warmed under Yeltsin, grew chillier as President George W. Bush announced plans to build an anti-missile system in Europe viewed by Russia as a threat. Meanwhile, Putin remained popular within Russia. By the end of his second term in 2007, Putin's popularity had been bolstered by rising living standards fueled by high oil prices, obsequious domestic television coverage, and his success at casting the liberal opposition as Western pawns.[66]

AFP/Getty Images/Jens Schlueter

Famed investigative journalist Anna Politkovskaya, who wrote about atrocities by Russian troops in Chechnya and about Russians' loss of civil liberties under Vladimir Putin, was shot to death in the elevator of her apartment building in 2006. She is one of several key anti-Putin dissidents to die of unnatural causes or in mysterious circumstances in recent years. Three men were tried for the murder, but they were aquitted in 2009.

Constitutionally barred from seeking a third consecutive term in 2008, Putin anointed Medvedev, a lawyer and former Putin campaign manager, to succeed him. Backed by Putin's United Russia Party, the little-known Medvedev won the election with 70 percent of the votes, while Putin became prime minister.

Medvedev took office vowing to fight corruption and to make the economy less dependent on oil and gas revenues.[67] He accomplished neither, and Russia's fragile, energy-dependent growth was shaken by the 2008 global financial crisis. Soon it became apparent that Medvedev was subservient to Putin, a fact most starkly illuminated when he announced that Putin would run for president to replace him in 2012.[68]

CURRENT SITUATION

Protesters and Polls

Most of the anti-Putin core are young, urban, and middle class. Many have traveled abroad and have seen how other political systems work.

"They realize there is a connection between politics and public life as a whole," says Kurbanov, of the National Endowment for Democracy. "If you don't participate in political life, then you cannot control many other things."

Many fear that Russia is beginning to resemble a Central Asian dictatorship, says Aron of the American Enterprise Institute.[69] With Russia's Duma extending presidential terms to six years and the constitution allowing two consecutive terms, Russians now face the prospect of Putin being in power for a total of 24 years.

Protest leader Navalny, 35, a former leader of the liberal Yabloko party, runs a small, corporate law firm in Moscow. Now enjoying a huge online following about government corruption, he has been a thorn in Putin's side since 2007, when he bought $40,000 worth of shares in Kremlin-owned Gazprom, the Rosneft oil company, and the pipeline company Transneft. As a shareholder, he began filing lawsuits seeking information about how the companies were run and where their profits were going.[70]

He soon found that Transneft had donated $300 million—the equivalent of 10 percent of its profits—to "charity" in 2007, but the company wouldn't reveal where it went and no major Russian charities had received any of the money. He later found that Gazprom had been buying gas from a supplier through a mysterious intermediary at a 70 percent markup and that the state-owned bank V.T.B. had purchased 30 oil rigs from China at a 50 percent markup, paid to a little-known intermediary registered in Cyprus.[71]

Navalny's website now posts government procurement orders and invites readers to contribute evidence of corruption, which has led to dozens of canceled contracts. More importantly, he has helped to galvanize a grassroots movement, one of the few civic organizations that provides young people with an alternative to their authoritarian government.

"If the swindlers and thieves continue robbing us and lying to us, we will ourselves get back what belongs to us," Navalny told the crowd during the Moscow protest on Dec. 24, 2011. "We don't want to scare anyone, but we believe that next year there will be a peaceful change of power, and power will belong to . . . the people."[72]

By focusing on corruption, Navalny has found an issue that unites both the right and the left in opposition to Putin's government—the right out of fear that their wealth can be stripped in a system without the rule of law, and the left out of anger at government officials who have enriched themselves while allowing social services for the elderly and poor to wither away.

"The new middle class is concerned they don't have enough legal security, and the left is concerned about justice," says Aslund of the Peterson Institute. "What you have now is the two sides . . . acting against the establishment."

Navalny's political criticism hasn't been without repercussions. In July 2012, Russian federal police charged him with embezzlement over a 2009 timber deal in which he was an unofficial adviser, a charge Navalny labeled "strange and absurd."[73] Five months later, federal authorities brought two other fraud charges against him—one for allegedly embezzling money from the postal service and a second for defrauding a defunct opposition party of about $4.2 million in 2007—a theft the leader of the party says never took place.[74]

Navalny is seeking to avoid the fate of Pussy Riot, a three woman feminist punk band whose members became famous for staging a high profile "punk prayer" in Moscow's main cathedral during anti-Putin demonstrations in February 2012. All three members were sentenced to two years in prison for "hooliganism motivated by religious hatred," a case that has become an international rallying point against Putin's repression of dissent.[75]

Economic Prospects

Russia's upheaval comes as its short-term economic prospects remain bright. Higher oil prices helped the economy grow 4.1 percent in 2011, and growth estimated at a still-healthy 3.6 percent in 2012 and 3.7 percent in 2013, according to the International Monetary Fund.[76] In December 2011, Russia joined the World Trade Organization (WTO) after 18 years of negotiations, ending its status as the only major economy not in the global commerce treaty.[77] A customs union with Belarus and Kazakhstan that began in January enlarged the market for Russian goods.[78] Domestic car sales rose 39 percent in 2011, unemployment stood at just 6.1 percent at the end of 2011 and there are plans to build a Disneyland-style theme park outside Moscow.[79]

The economy's longer-term outlook is decidedly darker, however, largely because of the nation's overreliance on energy production. Oil and gas shipments comprise nearly two-thirds of Russia's exports and about 40 percent of government revenues.[80] A deepening crisis in the European Union, Russia's largest trading partner, could darken the picture even further.

"Oil and gas are making Russia very dependent on foreign markets and external factors, which is not good for any country," says Migranyan of the Institute for Democracy and Cooperation. "When the price of oil goes down, the country is in a mess."

Russia has few globally successful non-extractive companies, and the World Economic Forum ranks it 66th—behind Vietnam and Iran—in its 2011 Global Competitiveness rankings, down three spots from 2010.[81] "Under Putin Russia has become almost a half petro-state," says Aron. "It needs to regain a semblance of technological prowess. Problems are not solved just by money anymore."

"The intellectual people are running away from Russia if they can," says journalist Tlisova. Four of the last five Russian-born Nobel Prize winners finished their careers at universities abroad. "You need to belong with the Kremlin. Otherwise you have two options: exile or jail."

That was the case for Yevgeny Chichvarkin, a flamboyant billionaire known for his mullet hairstyle and flashy clothes. Chichvarkin was 22 when he founded the mobile phone retailer Yevroset in 1997 with less than $5,000 in capital. By 2010 the company was valued at about $2.5 billion.[82]

But Chichvarkin was forced to sell his company and flee to London in 2008 after one of his employees was arrested and charged with kidnapping and extortion. Corrupt members of the Interior Ministry also were pursuing him, he said, although the charges against him were dropped this year.

Masked demonstrators, including one impersonating Russian Prime Minister Vladimir Putin with blood on his hands, protest at the United Nations on Jan. 24, 2012, against Russia's support for Syrian President Bashar Assad and his violent suppression of citizens. The demonstrators said they had delivered a petition to the U.N. containing signatures from 600,000 people demanding that the Security Council refer the Assad regime to the International Criminal Court for war-crimes prosecution.

The politicians "were the ones demanding bribes," Chichvarkin said in 2010. "If I'd paid off the people I was supposed to, I wouldn't be sitting here with you. I'd be sitting in Cantinetta Antinori on Denezhny Lane in Moscow."[83]

Putin has promised that—under the competitive framework of the WTO—Russia will become a leader in pharmaceuticals, composites, and aviation. In addition, he says, government control of the energy sector will continue, as will public financing of key sectors like technology.

Putin acknowledges the corruption problem. "The main problem is insufficient transparency and accountability on the part of state officials," Putin wrote in a recent editorial. "We are talking about systemic corruption." Yet he offered few specifics on how he will fix the problem. "Clearing the way for business that is ready to win in fair competition is a fundamental, systemic task. . . . We need to change the state itself—executive and judicial power."[84]

Few of his critics take such promises seriously. Meanwhile, the business climate for those without connections to the security forces or key government officials continues to be tenuous, says Kurbanov. "Smart people flee," he says.

Should the West give more support to Russia's protesters?

YES
Tamirlan Kurbanov
Fellow, National Endowment for Democracy, Washington, D.C.

Written for *CQ Global Researcher*, February 2012

The protests that erupted in December 2011 in Russia surprised the government, the official opposition in the Duma, and smaller opposition groups. It became clear that the protesters represented a broad group of citizens unhappy not only about fraud in the Dec. 4 parliamentary elections but also about Russia's political system in general.

The international community should support Russia's people in their aspirations to improve institutions such as the judiciary, the media, and civil society. People from across Russia took to the streets because they realized that the Putin regime cannot reform itself and Russians must seize their rights. To do that, the democracy movement must reach critical mass.

For the last decade the executive branch has subsumed legislative and judicial powers, while silencing dissent. Checks and balances have disappeared. Without real competition between political parties and oversight of government institutions, corruption has flourished.

International support for Russia's grassroots democracy movement should occur at the diplomatic level, through official support for pro-democracy institutions and international non-governmental human-rights and democracy organizations. The aid should include not only political and moral support but economic pressure to help Russia's citizens effect change. Russian officials may not be afraid of their own people's cries for democracy, but they crave the international community's respect.

Obviously, such aid is meaningless—even counterproductive—without the Russian people's genuine demand for change. Such indigenous support for new governance has been clearly established, given Russia's current environment. The government's effort to paint the protesters as U.S. pawns has failed, because much of the Russian public sees it as just another attempt to blame Russia's problems on an external force.

When the government abrogates human rights guaranteed by both the Russian constitution and international treaties, citizens have the right to exercise nonviolent resistance and public pressure against that government. International support for efforts to peacefully rebuild a democratic Russia should be strengthened, not weakened.

Ultimately, the world is interconnected, and a democratic Russia will provide greater opportunities for all of its citizens—at least all except those who have enriched themselves under the current corrupt system. The West must choose which side it will support.

NO
Andranik Migranyan
Director, Institute for Democracy and Cooperation, New York; Former Member, Russian Presidential Council

Written for *CQ Global Researcher*, February 2012

The answer lies in the recent history of Russian-American relations. They were tainted in the 1990s, when the economy and foreign policy were conducted by young reformers, such as Yegor Gaidar, Anatoly Chubais, and Andrey Kozyrev. The perception was widespread that all important decisions regarding personnel and key domestic and foreign policy matters were made with Washington's input and approval.

During that period, many Russians felt deeply humiliated by their de facto loss of sovereignty as the former superpower was undergoing an economic, social, and psychological catastrophe. Since the 1990s, therefore, many Russians have harbored an aversion toward U.S. meddling in Russian affairs—either directly or through American political and economic advisers.

Putin's presidency is widely seen as having restored Russian self-sufficiency domestically, resurrected Russian sovereignty, and reconstituted Russia as a strong partner of the West in foreign affairs.

Now Russia has entered a new phase in its domestic political development, which coincides with the start of a new electoral cycle. Putin, who will run for president again in March as a member of the party in power, retains a high level of trust among many Russians. But against this backdrop, there have been major societal divisions, mass protests and demands for more responsiveness and dialogue from the authorities.

In this context, the meeting of American diplomats, including Ambassador Michael McFaul, with representatives of the radical opposition appears to authorities in Moscow as an attempt by Washington to meddle in sovereign matters in order to push for regime change.

Now, throw in the fact that the record of both the United States and Ambassador McFaul provides a basis for such assumptions. McFaul is famous in both the United States and Russia as a supporter of the American policy of promoting democracy worldwide and is known to be close to those circles in Russia calling for regime overhaul.

Nobody is arguing the right of U.S. diplomats to meet with the opposition, but they should take into consideration the format, time, and venue for such meetings, as well as overall political context and possible reaction of Russian officials and the public at large. Otherwise such actions can harm Russian-American relations.

OUTLOOK

Bleak Future?

The confluence of long-term problems—rampant corruption, a shrinking population, the brain drain, over-dependence on oil exports, authoritarianism, and continuing conflict in the North Caucasus—prompts many analysts to paint a gloomy portrait of the country's future should Putin continue to lead the country.

"The country is facing huge problems: economic, social, demographic," says Aron of the American Enterprise Institute. "If Putin survives, 10 years from now you'll see a Russia totally dependent on oil revenue, declining across the board in social indicators, and losing its best and brightest. It will be a basket case."

If that happens, Putin would have to exercise even harsher repression in order to maintain control. "I hope we will be able to have a government that will meet the people half way, but I don't know how it will happen," says Kurbanov, of the National Endowment for Democracy. "The current group knows if they do one compromise, they won't be able to stop it, and they'll have to leave the country to avoid prosecution."

Regardless of who becomes president, Russia's population will continue to shrink, experts say. The population declined for 14 straight years before growing slightly in 2009, based largely on higher immigration numbers.[85]

Poor health contributes to Russia's demographic problems. Russian men can expect to live only to age 62 (compared to 78 in Germany), in part because of high rates of alcoholism.[86] The average 18-year-old Russian man has a 50 percent chance of living to retirement age, against a 90 percent probability in the West.[87]

The demographic challenges mean that Russia needs up to 1 million immigrants per year in order to maintain economic growth, says Migranyan, of the Institute for Democracy and Cooperation. But due to "the failure of multiculturalism" in Russia, he says, newcomers are not integrated into society and, in fact, face anti-immigrant hostility. In April 2011, an immigration service spokesman was fired after cautioning about "mixing bloods" of immigrants with Russian blood and warning that the "survival of the white race is at stake."[88]

Ethnic minorities and immigrants "don't feel like Russians, because there is such a strong message coming from the Kremlin and all these Russian nationalists," says journalist Tlisova, who herself is Circassian, a minority that is referred to as "blacks" in Russia. "The message is very clear: There is a black Russia and a white Russia, and black Russia does not have any rights."

Some of the ethnic tension stems from Russia's ongoing conflicts with separatist rebels in the North Caucasus, including Chechnya, Ingushetia, and Dagestan. Although the war in Chechnya officially ended in 2009, attacks by both Islamist rebels and Russian security forces have continued. Some fear the attacks will spike in the run-up to the 2014 Winter Olympics in Sochi, a southern city less than 250 miles from the hometown of an Ingushetian suicide bomber who killed 37 people at Moscow's airport in January, 2011.[89]

If Putin is ousted, the country's prospects improve, analysts say. "If the protesters do spark a political crisis that leads to a change of regime, then Russia goes back to around 2002 or 2003," says Aron. "It will be far less dependent on oil exports, it will be less corrupt, the courts will regain their independence, the political parties will be competing freely, and television will be uncensored."

Aslund, however, of the Peterson Institute and the author of 12 books about Russia and Eastern Europe, sees a better future ahead.

"No country that has been even half as wealthy as Russia has returned to authoritarianism after a democratic breakthrough," he says. "We will see a new democratic breakthrough this year. It will be peaceful, and new elections will be held for parliament and president, and Russia will start cleaning out corruption."

NOTES

1. David Remnick, "The Civil Archipelago," *The New Yorker,* Dec. 19, 2011, www.newyorker.com/reporting/2011/12/19/111219fa_fact_remnick.

2. Lidia Kelly and Alissa de Carbonnel, "Hundreds of Anti-Putin Protesters Detained in Moscow," Reuters, March 5, 2012, http://uk.reuters.com/article/2012/03/05/uk-russia-election-idUKTRE82300520120305.

3. Gleb Bryanski, "Russia's Putin Promises Change, Warns of New Crisis," Reuters, Jan. 16, 2012, www.reuters.com/article/2012/01/16/us-russia-putin-idUSTRE80F12020120116.

4. Miriam Elder and Tom Parfitt, "Russian Anti-Putin Protests Draw Thousands to Moscow Again," *The Guardian,* Dec. 24, 2011, www. guardian.co.uk/world/2011/dec/24/russia-eu rope-news.

5. Timothy Heritage, "Anti-Putin Protesters Show Staying Power in Russia," Reuters, Feb. 5, 2012, www.reuters.com/article/2012/02/05/us-russia-protests-idUSTRE8140D220120205. Also see Serge Schmemann, "100,000 Join Moscow Rally, Defying Ban by Gorbachev to Show Support for Rival," *The New York Times,* March 29, 1991, www.nytimes.com/1991/03/29/world/100000-join-moscow-rally-defying-ban-by-gorbachev-to-show-support-for-rival.html?pagewanted= all&src=pm.

6. Amanda Walker, "Mass Anti-Vladimir Putin Protest in Moscow Over Disputed Elections," Sky News, Dec. 24, 2011, http://news.sky.com/home/world-news/article/16136696.

7. "Putin Was Booed, Full Record From Sports Complex," YouTube, www.youtube.com/watch?v=ZxQslFifQBw.

8. Stephen Ennis, "Profile: Russian Blogger Alexei Navalney," BBC News, Dec. 20, 2011, www.bbc.co.uk/news/world-europe-16057045.

9. Ellen Barry and Michael Schwirtz, "After Election, Putin Faces Challenges to Legitimacy," *New York Times,* March 5, 2012, www.nytimes.com/2012/03/06/world/europe/observers-detail-flaws-in-russian-election.html?pagewanted=all.

10. For background, see Roland Flamini, "Turmoil in the Arab World," *CQ Global Researcher,* May 3, 2011, pp. 209–236.

11. Alex Spillins, "Vladimir Putin Calls John McCain 'Nuts' in Outspoken Attack," *The Daily Telegraph,* Dec. 15, 2011, www.telegraph.co. uk/news/world news/europe/russia/8958294/Vladimir-Putin-calls-John-McCain-nuts-in-out spoken-attack.html.

12. Kathy Lally, "Putin Lashes Back at Clinton Criticism," *The Washington Post,* Dec. 8, 2011, www.washingtonpost.com/world/putin-lashes-back-at-clinton-criticism/2011/12/08/gIQAQ51 YgO_story.html.

13. "Presidential Elections in Russia," U.S. Department of State, March 5, 2012, www.state.gov/r/pa/prs/ps/2012/03/185210.htm.

14. Julian Pecquet, "Russia Skewers U.S. Election as Undemocratic, "Worst in the World," *The Hill,* Nov. 4, 2012, http://thehill.com/blogs/global-affairs/russia/265689-russia-skewers-us-election-as-undemocratic-the-worst-in-the-world.

15. Esther Dyson, "Russia Protests Include a Broad Swath of Society," *Prague Post,* Feb. 1, 2012, www.praguepost.com/opinion/11928-russia-protests-include-a-broad-swath-of-society.html.

16. Michael Bohm, "Why Putin Will Never, Ever Give Up Power," *The Moscow Times,* Jan. 20, 2012, www.themoscowtimes.com/opinion/article/why-putin-will-never-ever-give-up-power/4513 32.html.

17. Ellen Barry, "As Putin's Grip Gets Tighter, a Time of Protest Fades in Russia," *New York Times,* Jan. 5, 2013, http://www.nytimes.com/2013/01/06/world/europe/in-russia-a-trendy-activism-against-putin-loses-its-moment.html?pagewanted=all.

18. "Corruption Perceptions Index 2011," Transparency International, http://cpi.transparency.org/cpi2011/results/.

19. Fred Weir, "Russia Corruption Costs $318 Billion—One-third of GDP," *The Christian Science Monitor,* Nov. 23, 2009, www.csmoni tor.com/World/Global-News/2009/1123/russia-corruption-costs-318-bil-lion-one-third-of-gdp.

20. Scott Rose, "Russia's Average Bribe Was $10,573 in First Half, Ministry Says," Bloomberg News, July 22, 2011, www.bloomberg.com/news/2011–07–22/russia-s-average-bribe-was-10–573-in-first-half-ministry-says.html.

21. "Corruption Perceptions Index 2000," Transparency International, www.transparency.org/policy_research/surveys_indices/cpi/previous_ cpi/2000.

22. "Russia: The Global Economic Crime Survey," PriceWaterhouseCoopers, November 2011, www.pwc.ru/en/forensic-services/crime-survey-2011.jhtml.

23. Lyubov Pronina, "Putin Orders Graft Probe at Utilities to Increase Transparency," Bloomberg News, Dec. 19, 2011, www.bloom berg.com/news/2011–12–19/putin-orders-graft-probes-at-utilities-to-increase-transparency.html.

24. "State Corporations Resist Putin Order," Vedemosti (reprinted in English by the *Moscow Times*), Jan. 17, 2012, www.themoscowtimes. com/business/article/state-corporations-resist-putin-order/451 133.html.

25. "Putin Ponders Corruption, Internet Democracy in New Article," *Ria Novosti,* Feb. 6, 2012, http://en .rian.ru/russia/20120206/171165740.html.

26. Andranik Migranyan, "Russian Protests Won't Stop Putin," *The National Interest,* Dec. 28, 2011, http://nationalinterest.org/commentary/russian-protests-wont-stop-putin-6312.

27. "Russia Tightens Bank Account Control," BBC News, Feb. 13, 2013, www.bbc.co.uk/news/world-europe-21446267.

28. Olga Razumovskaya, "Russia's Own WikiLeaks Takes Off," *The Moscow Times,* Jan. 21, 2011, www .themoscowtimes.com/news/article/russias-own-wikileaks-takes-off/429370.html.

29. Nikolaus von Twickel, "Putin's Old Teacher Mines a Fortune," *The Moscow Times,* April 5, 2011, www .themoscowtimes.com/news/article/putins-old-teacher-mines-a-fortune/434471.html.

30. Von Twickel, *op. cit.*

31. Luke Harding, "Putin, the Kremlin Power Struggle and the $40 Billion Fortune," *The Guardian,* Dec. 20, 2007, www.guardian.co.uk/world/2007/dec/21/russia.topstories3.

32. U.S. Ambassador John Beyrle, "The Luzkhov Dilemma," U.S. Department of State cable, Feb. 12, 2010, released by Wikileaks, http://wikileaks.org/cable/2010/02/10MOSCOW317.html.

33. *Ibid.*

34. Kathy Lally, "Russia Targets U.S. Linked Election Group," *The Washington Post,* Nov. 20, 2011, www .washingtonpost.com/world/russia-targets- us-linked-election-monitor/2011/11/30/gIQAl qzcDO_story.html.

35. "Russian PM Vladimir Putin Accuses U.S. Over Poll Protests," BBC News, Dec. 8, 2011, www.bbc.co .uk/news/world-europe-16084743. See also: "Russians Vote in Duma Poll Seen as Referendum on Putin," BBC News, Dec. 4, 2011, www.bbc .co.uk/news/world-europe-160 20632.

36. Daniel McLaughlin, "Putin Ratchets Up Anti-Western Rhetoric Before Presidential Poll," *Irish Times,* Jan. 27, 2012, www.irishtimes.com/newspaper/world/2012/0127/1224310807528.html.

37. Fyodor Lukyanov, "Uncertain World: Russia-United States—minimizing the damage," *RIA Novosti,* Dec. 29, 2011, http://en.rian.ru/columnists/20111229/170547384.html?id=170549753.

38. "Russia to Keep Supplying Syria Leader Bashar Assad's Regime With "Defensive" Weapons," CBS News, Feb. 13, 2013, www.cbsnews.com/8301–202_162–57569113/russia-to-keep-supplying-syria-leader-bashar-assads-regime-with-defensive-weapons/ .

39. Kathy Lally, "Magnitsky Law Sets Off Human Rights Fight Between Russia and U.S. Politicians," *Washington Post,* Dec. 7, 2012, http://articles .washingtonpost.com/2012-12-07/world/3567849_1_law-accountability-act-sergei-magnitsky-rule-hermitage-capital-management.

40. Anne Gearan, "Sour U.S.-Russia Relations Threaten Obama's Foreign Policy Agenda," *Washington Post,* Jan. 13, 2013, http://articles.washingtonpost.com/2013–01–13/world/36323155_1_putin-and-obama-missile-defense-russian-president-vladimir-putin.

41. "Romney: Russia Is Our Number One Geopolitical Foe," CNN, March 26, 2012, http://cnnpressroom .blogs.cnn.com/2012/03/26/romney-russia-is-our-number-one-geopolitical-foe/.

42. John Vandiver and Martin Kuz, "Military Looks at Supply Routes Away From Pakistan," *Stars and Stripes,* Nov. 28, 2011, www.stripes.com/news/military-looks-at-supply-routes-away-from-pakistan-1.161855.

43. Jim Wolf, "U.S. Russia Work to Expand Cyberspace Cooperation," Reuters, Dec. 9, 2011, www.reuters .com/article/2011/12/10/us-russia-usa-cyber-idUSTRE7B901N20111210.

44. Fred Weir, "As Putin Rises Again, Will the U.S.-Russia 'Reset' of Ties Hold?" *The Christian Science*

Monitor, Oct. 26, 2011, www.csmonitor.com/ World/Europe/2011/1026/As-Putin-rises-again-will-the-US-Russia-reset-of-ties-hold.

45. John Lawrence, *A History of Russia* (1960), pp. 240–241.

46. Lawrence, *op. cit.,* pp. 266–270.

47. Michael Kort, *The Soviet Colossus: A History of the USSR* (1985), pp. 171–177.

48. Kenneth Jost, "Russia and the Former Soviet Republics," *CQ Researcher,* June 17, 2005, pp. 541–564. See also Michael Ellman and S. Maksudov, "Soviet Deaths in the Great Patriotic War: A Note," *Europe-Asia Studies,* Vol. 46, Nov. 4, 1994, pp. 671–680, http://soviet info.tripod.com/ELM-War_Deaths.pdf.

49. Roland Flamini, "Dealing with the New Russia," *CQ Researcher,* June 6, 2008, pp. 481–504.

50. Kort, *op. cit.,* pp. 235–242.

51. Jan Velinger "The Soviet Invasion of Czechoslovakia and the Crushing of the Prague Spring," Radio Prague, Aug. 20, 2003, www.radio.cz/en/section/ czechs/the-soviet-invasion-of-czech oslovakia-and-the-crushing-of-the-prague-spring.

52. Stephen Kotkin, *Armageddon Averted: The Soviet Collapse 1970–2000* (2008), pp. 15–16.

53. Helene Carrere d'Encausse, *The End of the Soviet Empire: The Triumph of Nations* (1993).

54. Kotkin, *op. cit.,* pp. 92–99.

55. *Ibid.,* pp. 100–111.

56. *Ibid.,* p. 127.

57. Marshall Goldman, *Petrostate: Putin, Power and the New Russia* (2008), pp. 73–74.

58. Michael Specter, "Kremlin, Inc.: Why Are Vladimir Putin's Opponents Dying," *The New Yorker,* Jan. 29, 2007, www.newyorker.com/reporting/2007/01/ 29/070129fa_fact_specter. See also: "What Next, President Putin?" *The Economist,* March 30, 2000, www.economist. com/node/297415.

59. "A Russian Coronation," *The Economist,* March 23, 2000, www.economist.com/node/295952.

60. Michael Wines, "Russian Court Orders Dissolution of Independent TV Network," *The New York Times,* Jan. 12, 2002, www.nytimes. com/2002/01/12/ world/russian-court-orders-dissolution-of-independent-tv-network.html? pagewanted=all&src=pm.

61. "Yukos Ex-Chief Jailed for Nine Years," BBC News, May 31, 2005, http://news.bbc. co.uk/2/hi/business/ 4595289.stm.

62. Felix Corley, "Yuri Shchekochikhin," *The Guardian,* July 9, 2003, www.guardian.co.uk/news/2003/ jul/09/guardianobituaries.russia.

63. Otto Pohl, "The Assassination of a Dream," *New York,* May 21, 2005, http://nymag.com/nymetro/ news/people/features/10193/.

64. Anna Politkovskaya, "Her Own Death, Foretold," *The Washington Post,* Oct. 15, 2006, www.washington post.com/wp-dyn/content/article/2006/10/14/ AR2006101400805.html.

65. "Prominent Russian Lawyer Killed," BBC News, Jan. 19, 2009, http://news.bbc.co.uk/2/hi/europe/ 7838328.stm.

66. "Putin's Phoney Election," *The Economist,* Nov. 29, 2007, www.economist.com/node/102 17312.

67. Owen Matthews, "The Medvedev Doctrine," *Newsweek,* Nov. 21, 2008, www.thedailybeast. com/ newsweek/2008/11/21/the-medvedev-doctrine .html.

68. Christian Neef and Matthias Schepp, "The Puppet President: Medvedev's Betrayal of Russian Democracy," *Der Spiegel,* Oct. 4, 2011, www. spiegel .de/international/world/0,1518,789767,00. html.

69. For background, see Brian Beary, "Emerging Central Asia," *CQ Global Researcher,* Jan. 17, 2012, pp. 29–56.

70. Julia Ioff, "Net Impact: One Man's Cybercrusade Against Russian Corruption," *The New Yorker,* April 4, 2011, www.newyorker.com/re porting/2011/04/ 04/110404fa_fact_ioffe.

71. *Ibid.*

72. Sergei Loiko, "Tens of Thousands of Russian Protesters Want Vladimir Putin Out," *Los Angeles Times,* Dec. 24, 2011, http://articles.latimes.com/ 2011/dec/24/world/la-fg-russia-protest-putin-20111225.

73. "Russian Blogger Navalny Charged With Embezzlement," BBC News, July 31, 2012, www .bbc.co.uk/news/world-europe-19060444.

74. "Russian Opposition Leader Navalny Faces Third Inquiry," BBC News, Dec. 24, 2012, http://www.bbc.co.uk/news/world-europe-20836116.

75. "Pussy Riot Appeal Conviction to European Court," Associated Press, Feb. 7, 2013, www.npr.org/templates/story/story.php?storyId=171369539.

76. "World Economic Outlook Update," International Monetary Fund, January 23, 2013, http://www.imf.org/external/pubs/ft/weo/2013/update/01/index.htm.

77. David Jolly, "W.T.O. Grants Russia Membership," *The New York Times,* Dec. 16, 2011, www.nytimes.com/2011/12/17/business/global/wto-accepts-russia-bid-to-join.html?pagewanted=all.

78. Ilya Arkhipov and Lyubov Pronina, "Russia, Kazakhstan, Belarus Sign Accord on Economic Union," Bloomberg News, Nov. 18, 2011, www.bloomberg.com/news/2011–11–18/russia-kazakhstan-belarus-sign-accord-on-economic-union-1-.html.

79. "Russian Automotive Market is to Maintain a Consistent Growth in 2012," globalautoin dustry.com, Jan. 12, 2012, www.globalauto industry.com/article.php?id=7739&jaar=2012&maand=2&target= Euro. Also see "Site in Northwest Moscow Could Host 'Russian Disneyland'—Deputy Mayor," *RIA Novosti,* Oct. 14, 2011, http://en.rian.ru/business/201110 14/167680991.html.

80. "Key Economic Indicators in 2011," Bank of Russia, www.cbr.ru/eng/statistics. Also see James Brooke, "Russia Gets Giant Boost From Rising Oil Prices," Voice of America, March 11, 2011, www.voanews.com/english/news/europe/Russia-Gets-Giant-Boost-from-Rising-Oil-Prices-118258 659.html.

81. "Global Competitiveness Index 2011–2012 Rankings," World Economic Forum, www3.we forum.org/docs/WEF_GCR_Competitiveness IndexRanking_2011–12.pdf.

82. Anastasia Golisyna, Igor Tsukanov and Tatyana Romanova, "Yevroset Planning for IPO Next Year," *Vedemosti* (reprinted in English by the *Moscow Times*), Nov. 12, 2010, www. themoscowtimes.com/business/article/yevroset-planning-for-ipo-next-year/422383.html.

83. Shaun Walker, "The Whiz Kid Billionaire Who Says He Can't Go Home," *The Independent,* July 29, 2010, www.independent.co.uk/news/people/news/the-whiz-kid-billionaire-who-says-he-cant-go-home-2038006.html.

84. Douglas Busvine, "Putin Puts State Capitalism First for Russia," Reuters, Jan. 30, 2012, www.reuters.com/article/2012/01/30/us-russia-putin-economy-idUSTRE80T0PC20120130.

85. "Resident Population," Russian Federation Federal Statistical Service, 2011, www.gks.ru/wps/wcm/connect/rosstat/rosstatsite.eng/fig ures/population.

86. "Global Health Observatory," World Health Organization, 2009 statistics, www.who.int/countries/en/.

87. Grace Wong, "Russia's Bleak Picture of Health," CNN, May 19, 2009, http://edition.cnn. com/2009/HEALTH/05/19/russia.health/index.html.

88. Alissa de Carbonnel, "Russia Migration Official Fired in Racism Row," Reuters, April 2011, http://uk.reuters.com/article/2011/04/20/uk-russia-race-idUKTRE73J5CW20110420.

89. C. J. Chivers, "Author Q&A: The Insurgency in Chechnya and the North Caucasus," At War blog, *NYTimes.com,* Jan. 20, 2012, atwar.blogs.nytimes.com/2012/01/20/author-qa-the-insurgency-in-chechnya-and-the-north-caucasus/. Also see Clifford Levy, "Russia Faces 3-Year Race to Secure Site of Olympics," *The New York Times,* March 7, 2011. URL= www.nytimes.com/2011/03/08/world/europe/08sochi.html.

BIBLIOGRAPHY

Selected Sources
Books

Goldman, Marshall, *Petrostate: Putin, Power and the New Russia,* **Oxford University Press, 2010.**
Russia's expanding energy resources have been key to its recovery from the 1998 financial crisis, even as they've fueled corruption and harmed other parts of the economy.

Politkovskaya, Anna, Putin's Russia: *Life in a Failing Democracy,* **Metropolitan Books, 2005.**
Before the muckraking Russian journalist was assassinated in 2006, she authored this critical portrait of Putin's rule and the death of democracy in Russia.

Putin, Vladimir, Nataliya Gevorkyan, and Andrei Kolesnikov, *First Person: An Astonishingly Frank Self-Portrait by Russia's President,* **Public Affairs, 2000.**
The product of six interviews between Putin and Russian correspondents, the book may not be "astonishingly frank," but it does provide illuminating detail of the Russian politician's life and thinking when he first began to rule.

Satter, David, *Darkness at Dawn: the Rise of the Russian Criminal State,* **Yale University Press, 2003.**
A former Moscow correspondent for the *Financial Times* chronicles Russia's transformation from a communist state to a playground for organized criminal gangs.

Shevtsova, Lilia, and Andrew Wood, *Change or Decay: Russia's Dilemma and the West's Response,* **Carnegie Endowment for International Peace, 2011.**
Two decades after the fall of the Soviet Union, the West's relationship with Russia is still fraught, as revealed in a series of exchanges between a Russian scholar and a former British ambassador to Russia.

Articles

Anderson, Scott, "Vladimir Putin's Dark Rise to Power," GQ, **September 2009.**
Rare is a feature article so sensitive that a mainstream magazine refuses to post it on the Internet. But that was the case with this investigation challenging the provenance of a series of bombings in Moscow in 1999, officially blamed on Chechen separatists.

Eberstadt, Nicholas, "The Dying Bear," *Foreign Affairs,* **November/December 2011.**
Eberstadt examines the human, economic, and social costs of Russia's baby drought.

Freeland, Chrystia, "The Next Russian Revolution," *The Atlantic Monthly,* **October 2011.**
A Reuters editor describes Russia's efforts to create a Silicon Valley on the Volga, providing a glimpse of the country's peculiar form of capitalism.

Ioffe, Julia, "Net Impact: One Man's Cyber-Crusade Against Russian Corruption," *The New Yorker,* **April 4, 2011.**
Anti-corruption blogger Alexei Navalny is profiled, eight months before protests against Putin's government made him a democracy icon in Russia.

Knight, Amy, "The Concealed Battle to Run Russia," *New York Review of Books,* **Jan. 13, 2011.**
In reviewing a new book on the KGB's impact on Russian society, Knight's own reporting adds insight to a society dominated by security service strong-men.

Passell, Peter, "Why Putinomics Isn't Worth Emulating," *Foreign Policy,* **Jan. 27, 2012.**
Despite the glittering new buildings in Moscow and St. Petersburg, Russia's economy "is still a Potemkin façade" that runs on oil and weapons sales, the author argues.

Reports and Studies

"Georgia-Russia: Learn to Live Like Neighbors," International Crisis Group, Aug. 8, 2011.
Three years after Russia's war with Georgia over South Ossetia, the two sides are still preoccupied with bitter aspects of their relationship.

"2010 Human Rights Report: Russia," U.S. Department of State, April 8, 2011.
The U.S. government's annual list of human rights abuses in Russia—including the beating of a defense lawyer, an attack on a human rights activist, and the killing of seven journalists—makes for grim reading.

"Who Will Tell Me What Happened to My Son?" Human Rights Watch, Sept. 27, 2009.
The New York-based human rights group researched 33 cases of extrajudicial killings in Chechnya by Russian security forces or their allies. No one has been prosecuted, even though the alleged perpetrators have been named in European Court judgments.

Trenin, Dmitri, and Pavel Baev, "The Arctic: A View From Moscow," Carnegie Endowment for International Peace, September 2010.
As the Arctic ice cap melts, northern Russia—which might have twice the oil reserves of Saudi Arabia—may be transformed by oil exploration.

For More Information

Brookings Institution, 1775 Massachusetts Ave., N.W., Washington, DC 20036; 202–797–6999; www.brookings .edu. A nonprofit, centrist think tank providing research designed to "create a more open, safe, prosperous, and cooperative international system."

Carnegie Moscow Center, Carnegie Institute for International Peace, 16/2 Tverskaya, Moscow, 1250009, Russia; +7 495 935–8904; www.carnegie.ru. Russian branch of a Washington think tank that includes Russian and foreign researchers analyzing a range of policy issues.

Center for Russian and East European Studies, University Center of International Politics, 4400 Wesley W. Posvar Hall, University of Pittsburgh, Pittsburgh, PA 115260; 412–648–7404; www.ucis.pitt.edu/crees/. A clearinghouse for studies on Russia and its environs, with access to 400,000 volumes on Russia and Eastern Europe.

Center for Strategic and International Studies, 1800 K St., N.W., Washington, D.C. 20006; 202–887–0200; www.csis .org. Foreign policy think tank, founded in 1962, with experts that include academics, former politicians, and diplomats.

Institute for U.S. and Canadian Studies, 2/3 Khlebny per., Moscow 123995, Russia; +7 (0) 95 290–5875; www .iskran.ru/engl/index-en.html. Military and strategic research center offering research on U.S. and Canadian relations with Russia—from a Russian perspective.

Peterson Institute for International Economics, 1750 Massachusetts Ave., N.W., Washington, DC 20036; 202–328–9000; www.petersoninstitute.org. Think tank focused on international economic policy, with more than two dozen fellows focused on international economics, trade, and the international financial system.

Russia and Eurasia Program, Royal Institute of International Affairs, Chatham House, 10 St. James's Square, London SW1Y 4LE, England; +44 207 7957–5700; www.chatham house.org. Provides foreign and domestic policy analysis of Russia and other former Soviet states.

Voices From Abroad:

YELENA PANFILOVA

Director, Transparency International, Russia

A different corruption

"Unfortunately, in Russia we are dealing not with the traditional kind of corruption, which is observed all over the world at all times. Our corruption has acquired the features of forced corruption. That is when people in public offices treat their positions as sources of constant illegal [personal] enrichment."

RIA Novosti News Agency (Russia), December 2011

The Khaleej Times/UAE/Paresh Nath

VLADIMIR PUTIN

Prime Minister, Russia

Losing ground

"If you are saying that our elections were objective and fair, in my opinion, I have already said publicly that, beyond any doubt, the results of these elections reflect the actual line-up of forces in the country, as well as the fact that the ruling force—United Russia—has lost certain positions."

Philippine News Agency, December 2011

SERGEY PRIKHODKO

Presidential aide, Russia

Obstructionists

"The idea of a precipitous deterioration in Russo-American relations is being imposed by those that do not want to see real results of the work and do not want an improvement in relations."

Gazeta.ru (Russia), October 2011

DMITRY MEDVEDEV

President, Russia

Making progress

"We are prepared to develop full strategic relations with the United States. Our economic relations [still] trail the political relations considerably."

Rossiyskaya Gazeta (Russia), March 2011

SERGEI GURIEV

Rector, New Economic School, Russia

New demands

"Now, it seems, sufficient prosperity has arrived, calling forth a middle class solid enough to demand government accountability, the rule of law, and a genuine fight against corruption. . . . The political mobilization of the middle class will eventually lead to democratization."

Korea Times (South Korea), January 2012

GENNADIY GUDKOV

**Deputy Chairman, State Duma Security Committee
Russia**

A future at stake
"We are launching an anti-corruption march that will
continue until corruption has been eradicated in Russia.
Because of corruption, we may lose our future, our children, and our country."

Interfax News Agency (Russia), April 2011

ALEKSEY CHESNAKOV

**Chairman, United Russia General Council Presidium
Russia**

No Arabs in Russia
"Such a scenario [Arab Spring revolution] is impossible
in Russia, since we do not have enough Arabs for this."

Gazeta.ru (Russia), March 2011

ALESKO NEVLENI

Political opposition leader, Russia

"There is no sense in leading a life like mice, frogs, and
animals in stability and economic development. We
have the voice and the votes and the strength to utilize
them."

Jagran Post (India), December 2011

SERGEY MARKOV

Political analyst, Russia

Collapse leads to corruption
"The Soviet companies were the least corrupt. . . . Large-
scale corruption appeared with the collapse of the Soviet
Union, [its] system of social relations and work ethic and
[the] transition to rabid individualism."

RIA Novosti (Russia), November 2011

TATYANA YAKOVLEVA

First Deputy, One Russia party, Russia

Civil society's role
"The effectiveness of the fight against corruption depends
not only on the political will of the head of the state, not
only on correct legislative work . . . but, to a large extent,
on an active stance of civil society."

*Interfax News Agency (Russia),
February 2011*

7

Future of the EU

Brian Beary

Croatian President Ivo Josipović speaks at a ceremony at EU headquarters in Brussels on Dec. 9, 2011, marking the signing of a treaty allowing his country to join the European Union. The former Yugoslav republic has been seeking EU membership for nearly a decade. Croatians approved the treaty in a January referendum, paving the way for Croatia to become the union's 28th member on July 1, 2013. The accession process continues to be painstakingly slow for other Western Balkan nations and Turkey.

From *The CQ Researcher*, April 17, 2012 (updated February 14, 2013).

With doomsayers predicting the European Union's (EU) imminent demise, German Foreign Minister Guido Westerwelle insists the union is not sliding into an abyss. As American humorist Mark Twain said of works by German composer Richard Wagner, he told a largely American audience at the Brookings Institution think tank in Washington in January 2012: "The music is better than it sounds."

Moreover, Westerwelle pledges Germany is not abandoning its struggling EU partners, such as Greece. In fact, he notes, Germany is contributing €200 billion to a European bailout fund. "That is the equivalent of the U.S. Treasury giving a guarantee of a trillion dollars," given that the German population is about one-quarter that of the United States. "Can you imagine Congress approving such an amount to help non-Americans?" The total bailout fund has since been raised to €800 billion, of which Germany will contribute more than any other EU country.

If Westerwelle sounds a tad defensive, it is because Germany has been under fire of late, accused of bullying its southern European partners into reforming their profligate ways. "Germany and the Nordic countries have totally different cultures to Mediterranean nations," says Pierre Lemoine, editor-in-chief of the Brussels-based EU affairs daily newspaper *Europolitics.*

"If you try to impose the German way on them too brutally, they won't survive," he adds. With Greece's jobless rate topping 20 percent, 150,000 public-sector jobs being slashed and the Greek economy expected to contract by 7 percent in 2011 and 2012, some question the wisdom of the austerity measures being heaped on Athens.[1] "You need to give them time to develop," says Lemoine, a Frenchman who lived in Germany for 16 years.

European Union Continues to Expand

The 27-member European Union (EU) is more than four times the size of its predecessor, the six-member European Economic Community, when it was established in 1957. Any European state that adheres to EU principles may become a member. Croatia will become the 28th member in July 2013. Eight other countries, including Turkey, have been designated as candidates or potential candidates for membership, but with leaders preoccupied with saving the euro, expansion is not the priority it was in the 1990s and early 2000s, when membership more than doubled, from 12 to 27.

Enlargement, by Year, 1957-Present*

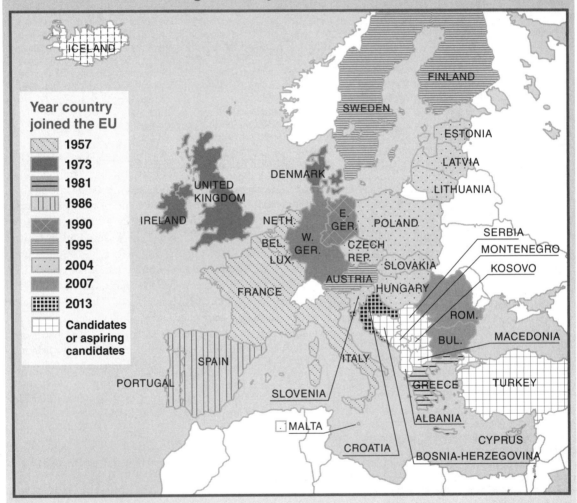

Year country joined the EU

- 1957
- 1973
- 1981
- 1986
- 1990
- 1995
- 2004
- 2007
- 2013
- Candidates or aspiring candidates

* Bosnia-Herzegovina has yet to apply. Kosovo cannot start the process because its independence has not yet been recognized by five EU nations. Macedonia's negotiations have been blocked by Greece over the name "Macedonia."

Source: "Enlargement," European Commission, February 2012, ec.europa.eu/enlargement/index_en.htm. Map by Lewis Agrell

Of the EU's 27 members, Greece is in the worst shape, but Portugal and Ireland also are struggling to implement austerity measures imposed as a condition for receiving massive bailout loans from the EU and International Monetary Fund (IMF) since 2010.[2] Meanwhile, Germany — the EU's most populous country with 82 million people — is performing strongly thanks to surging manufactured exports. Likewise, the former communist states of Central and Eastern Europe, which underwent massive reforms of their state-run economies in order to qualify for EU membership in 2004 and 2007, also are weathering the crisis reasonably well. In contrast, Spain and Italy, which did not have to undergo extensive economic scrutiny before joining the EU, are in the same debt-laden camp as veteran members Ireland, Greece and Portugal.[3] (*See map, p. 160.*)

Yet even the EU's most ardent defenders admit that the bloc, originally established after World War II to help keep the peace in Europe, has lost some of its luster. Opening a two-day conference in the Dutch city of Maastricht on Feb. 7, Theo Bovens, governor of Limburg province, explained that "for our young generation, war is only the nightmare of their parents. They have only known peace." While younger Europeans take peace for granted, he notes, they demand instead that the EU deliver economic prosperity and are growing disillusioned when it fails to do so.

Not surprisingly, support for the euro, has declined. In the spring of 2007, nearly 65 percent of Europeans supported the euro, the EU's single currency used by 17 of the 27 member states and considered a fundamental pillar of the union. By November 2011 support had slipped to 53 percent, and only 40 percent felt the euro had been good for their economy.[4] Anti-EU political parties are gaining in strength, such as France's National Front, whose candidate in this month's presidential elections,

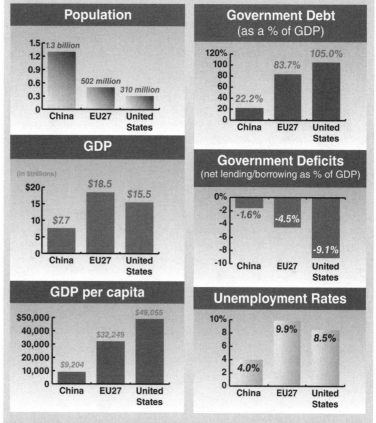

EU Has World's Biggest Economy

The 27 countries of the European Union (EU) together comprise the largest economy in the world, with an $18 trillion gross domestic product (GDP) that is slightly larger than America's and more than twice the size of China's. But since Europe's population exceeds the U.S. population by 200 million, the United States has the highest GDP per capita. However, the United States has worse debt and deficit problems than Europe, while the EU has higher unemployment. Although China's per capita GDP is less than a third of the EU's, its debt and deficits are lower.

Economic Data for EU27, the U.S. and China, 2011

Population

- China: 1.3 billion
- EU27: 502 million
- United States: 310 million

Government Debt (as a % of GDP)

- China: 22.2%
- EU27: 83.7%
- United States: 105.0%

GDP (in $trillions)

- China: $7.7
- EU27: $18.5
- United States: $15.5

Government Deficits (net lending/borrowing as % of GDP)

- China: -1.6%
- EU27: -4.5%
- United States: -9.1%

GDP per capita

- China: $9,204
- EU27: $32,249
- United States: $49,055

Unemployment Rates

- China: 4.0%
- EU27: 9.9%
- United States: 8.5%

Sources: Eurostat, European Commission, epp.eurostat.ec.europa.eu/portal /page/portal/eurostat/ home/; World Economic Outlook Database, International Monetary Fund, September 2011, www.imf.org/external/pubs/ft/weo/2011/02/weodata/index.aspx

Eurovision Songfest: Where Music and Politics Collide

Singing competition is older than the EU, and more beloved by many.

A gaggle of predominantly European expatriates is packed into a hot, airless room at the Goethe Institute in downtown Washington, D.C. Waving a variety of miniature European flags, they gulp down their beer, munch on bratwurst and burst into spontaneous renditions of kitsch classics such as "Volare" and "Waterloo."

A giant screen streams a live Internet feed of the 2011 Eurovision Song Contest, an annual singing competition as famous in Europe as it is unknown in America. The audience's spirits remain high, despite the transmission's frequent jamming under the weight of tens of millions of online viewers.

A year older than the EU's predecessor, the European Economic Community, the intensely competitive and hugely popular contest has been produced annually since 1956 by the European Broadcasting Union (EBU) in Geneva. It is built on a winning combination of campy pop songs, garish costumes and gimmicky performances. In the early years, the simultaneous broadcast of the taped competition in several countries was seen as a major technological coup. Today, the performances are broadcast live via satellite to 125 million viewers in 42 countries, and the votes are tallied and relayed in real time from dozens of capitals. And despite the occasional glitches — which usually only serve to add to the show's entertainment value — the EBU invariably acquits itself admirably.

Participating European countries hold national contests to select an original song to represent them. The songs are then sung live at a host venue and beamed into hundreds of millions of homes. Singers do not have to be from the country they are representing — famous singers from abroad can be recruited. Viewers and professional juries cast votes for the best song, using a graduated points system. The country with the most points wins, earning the right to host the next year's contest.

Previous winners have gone on to fame and fortune. ABBA's 1974 victory for Sweden set the group on the road to worldwide fame and fortune, and Canadian singer Celine Dion, whose French ditty "Ne Partez Pas Sans Moi" ("Don't leave without me"), composed by a Turkish and Swiss duo, took the title for Switzerland in 1988. The most famous "interval" act — the segment between the performances and the final vote tabulation — was Riverdance, an Irish dancing troupe that used its enthusiastic reception in 1994 as a launching pad for a series of highly profitable world tours.

Conceived as a unique way to unite millions of Europeans from diverse linguistic, cultural and ethnic backgrounds, the songfest has preserved its unifying philosophy, as evidenced by the 2010 contest motto, "Share The Moment." That year's interval act was conceived specifically to illustrate that, showing snippets of simultaneous "flash mob" dances from cities all over Europe, immortalized in a seven-minute Youtube video.[1]

But politics do enter the fray. This year, for instance, Armenia has withdrawn from the competition over a long-standing dispute with host-country Azerbaijan over the separatist enclave of Nagorno-Karabakh.[2]

The contest also sometimes serves as a microcosm of Europe's cultural cleavages. "The voting patterns follow regional lines," says Frank Rossavik, an editor at the Norwegian newspaper *Morgenbladet* and a devoted fan. "Only occasionally does someone break them."

For instance, Nordic nations stick together, as do the Balkans, and Cyprus and Greece raise collective groans by unfailingly awarding each other the maximum 12 points that each voting country can allot per song.

Regional animosities have hampered expansion of the show's audience into the Middle East. In 1978, many Arab broadcasters ran a commercial during the performance of the Israeli group Alphabeta, according to *The Guardian* newspaper. "When it became clear that Alphabeta were set to win, they simply pulled the plug," the paper said. "Jordan prematurely ended its transmission with a lingering still shot of a vase of daffodils." The EBU subsequently insisted that countries broadcast all of the show or none of it, essentially barring Arab countries from editing out Israeli performances. Many Arab countries chose to boycott Eurovision rather than allow their viewers to catch a glimpse of their arch-foe.

Israel caused a flutter again in 1998 when transsexual singer Dana International stole the show with her rendition of "Viva La Diva," performed in a Jean-Paul Gautier gown adorned with multicolored feathers. While Israel's perennial appearance is a testament to the EBU's liberal policy on which countries are allowed to compete, language can be a more sensitive matter.

In the past, singers had to perform in their country's national language, but today the EBU allows countries' singers to use any language they choose. To maximize their chances of winning, some contestants perform in "Eurovision-speak," a nonsensical vocabulary transcending linguistic boundaries. Thus, Spain won in 1968 with "La La La," and Britain later won with "Boom-Bang-A-Bang," the Netherlands with "Ding-A-Dong" and Sweden with "Diggy-Loo-Diggy-Ley." Indeed, Spain's "La La La" song originally was to be sung in Catalan, but Spain's dictator, General Franco, insisted it be performed in Spanish, worried it might rekindle the Catalan nationalist flame.[3]

"The music that Eurovision honors and enshrines is . . . [t]he stuff you hear in the back of Belgian taxis, on German radio, in Sicilian bars and in the lobbies of Danish hotels," wrote *New Yorker* writer Anthony Lane. "It was all created by the great god of dreck, and Eurovision is his temple."[4]

Eurovision's populist appeal leads the continent's culturally sophisticated to heap scorn and biting criticism at the contest. In 1982, for example, France's minister for culture ordered a boycott, calling the competition "nothing more than a monument to drivel."[5] The boycott did not last: by popular demand, France returned the following year — and every year since.

This May will mark a further milestone when Azerbaijan — last year's winner — hosts Eurovision. It will be the competition's easternmost venue, an indicator of how Europe's center of gravity continues to shift eastward. It is also a tribute to how phenomenally successful the contest has been, expanding from the seven countries that competed in the first contest to today's 42.

Political tiffs and kitschy costumes aside, with about 125 million people expected to tune in, it is clear that Europeans love to love their Eurovision.

— *Brian Beary*

Getty Images/Sean Gallup

Kitschy costumes, campy pop songs and gimmicky performances are hallmarks of the beloved, 56-year-old Eurovision Song Contest, which today draws 125 million viewers in 42 countries. Above, John and Edward Grimes of the Irish band Jedward rehearse for the finals of the 2011 contest, held last May 13 in Düsseldorf, Germany.

[1] Available at www.youtube.com/watch?v=wsuPqiCjyag.

[2] See Fareed Zakaria, "The Geopolitics of the Eurovision Song Contest," CNN, March 19, 2012, http://globalpublicsquare.blogs .cnn.com/2012/03/19/zakaria-the-geopolitics-of-the-eurovision-song-contest/.

[3] Sam Jones and Paul Lewis, "40 years on, congratulations may be in order: Sir Cliff demands trophy after film claims Franco plot denied him Eurovision win," *The Guardian* (U.K.), May 6, 2008, www.guardian .co.uk/music/2008/may/06/news.spain.

[4] Anthony Lane, "Only Mr. God Knows Why; The meaning of the Eurovision Song Contest," *The New Yorker*, June 28, 2010, www.new yorker.com/reporting/2010/06/28/100628fa_fact_lane.

[5] Tim Moore, "Eurovision's rallying might: We may laugh at the spangled catsuits. But this contest matters, in its own daft way," *The Guardian* (U.K.), May 11, 2011, www.guardian.co.uk/commentisfree/2011/may/10/eurovision-song-contest-diplomacy-matters.

ΑΠΟ ΤΟ ΧΙΤΛΕΡ
ΣΤΗ ΜΕΡΚΕΛ

ΕΝΩΣΗ ΠΟΛΙΤΩΝ "ΠΟΡΤΑ - ΠΟΡΤΑ"
Πέμπτη 6 Οκτωβρίου

Reuters/Yannis Behrakis

A Greek demonstrator on Oct. 28, 2011, displays a flyer depicting German Chancellor Angela Merkel wearing a Nazi uniform. Merkel has led the effort to bail out the troubled Greek economy, but many Greeks resent German "meddling" in their affairs because it revives memories of the wartime Nazi occupation of Greece, when 300,000 Greeks starved to death. The text says "From Hitler to Merkel" and "Citizens Movement Porta-Porta."

largest candidate for EU membership, with 80 million people — has watched with dismay as its accession bid has foundered.[8] The official reason given for the snub is its dismal relationship with EU member Cyprus, which has blocked Turkey's accession.* But many Turks believe larger EU nations such as Germany are happy to see Cyprus obstruct Turkey's membership, because they fear that Muslim Turkey would soon supplant the largely Christian Germany as the EU's largest country.

Accession hopes also have been hindered in the Balkans. For instance, before Greece will support membership for neighboring Macedonia, it wants the country to change its name, because Macedonia is also the name of a region in Greece. In Bosnia, disputes between Bosniak, Serb and Croat leaders have blocked the country's EU membership bid. And the fact that each of the EU's 27 members can veto any country's entry makes enlargement increasingly difficult.

Poor political leadership is a major reason Europe is in the doldrums, says Michael Geary, a professor of European integration at the University of Maastricht. "They lack the vision thing. In the past we had German Chancellor Helmut Kohl holding hands with French President François Mitterrand when the Berlin Wall came down," he says. "Today we have Angela Merkel and Nicolas Sarkozy, who do not have the same personal bond or vision for Europe."

"The financial crisis has caused people to think more deeply about the EU," says veteran EU reporter Blake Evans-Pritchard, a British freelance writer living in The Hague. "Before, it was viewed as a dry and irrelevant institution, but now you see pockets of euro-skepticism in places like Germany, where there were none before."

Wolfgang Wessels, an EU studies professor at the University of Cologne, notes how "some Germans complain a lot about Greece, saying, 'let's kick them out, forget about them, they don't deserve better if they cannot work decently, etc.' But German politicians argue that it is better to keep Greece in, because Germany's reputation is at stake. After all, if we cannot manage a country that is only 3 percent of the eurozone's economy, how can we manage anything?"

The European Commission, the union's executive arm, has been a relatively marginal player in the crisis,

ultraconservative Marine Le Pen, wants France to leave the EU. In Finland, the True Finns party — which opposes EU bailouts for indebted countries like Greece — created shockwaves in April 2011 when it won 19 percent of the seats in parliamentary elections.[5]

EU defenders believe the bashers are losing sight of the bigger picture. Indermit Gill, the World Bank's chief economist for Europe and Central Asia, said that throughout its history "the EU has been a great convergence machine. It takes in poor countries and makes them high-income countries. There is something very remarkable about that."[6]

With EU leaders preoccupied with saving the euro, enlargement of the organization is not the priority it was in the 1990s and early 2000s, when membership more than doubled from 12 to 27.[7] Turkey — the

---

*Turkey supports the separatist enclave of northern Cyprus, which has resulted in the partition of the island nation.

overshadowed by Merkel and other EU leaders who have cobbled together the various bailouts. "The commission does not have the same swagger that it did," says Bruce Stokes, senior trans-Atlantic fellow for economics at the German Marshall Fund of the United States (GMF), in Washington, D.C.

The United States, which has championed European integration since the end of World War II, seems more sympathetic to Berlin than Athens. George Soros, the Hungarian-born billionaire philanthropist, railed against Greece in a recent opinion article, saying "the Greeks atrociously abused the advantages of European Union membership."[9]

The average German retires at age 67 on 50 percent of salary while Greeks retire at 48 with 93 percent of their salary, pointed out Anne Krueger, a professor of international economics at the School for Advanced International Studies (SAIS) at Johns Hopkins University in Washington, D.C. "Greece is so far out of whack that there has to be austerity for a period," she said.[10]

As the world watches to see what kind of Europe will emerge from the crisis, here are some of the key questions being asked:

Has the euro crisis endangered the EU?

With the sovereign debt crisis in the euro area putting a huge strain on the EU's Economic and Monetary Union, some wonder whether the longstanding goal of integrating Europe has suffered irreparable damage.*

"The crisis is endangering the EU," says Geary of the University of Maastricht. "The euro's fate is linked to the EU because the EU was founded on the single market, part of which is the single currency. If the euro collapses, it will be a big step backwards."

---

* Sovereign debt is government debt accrued over a period of years as a result of having spent more money than the government collects.

Europeans Still Favor the EU

Trust in the European Union among citizens of member states has declined 40 percent since 2007, although 71 percent still say they view the union favorably, and nearly that proportion says membership has been good for their respective countries. Moreover, 60 percent want their countries to contribute to the EU's new bailout fund, established to help troubled economies pay off their debts. The fund, which stood at €500 billion when the poll was taken last summer, was raised to €800 billion on March 30.

Citizen Views on the EU in Member States

Do you tend to trust the EU?	Has EU membership been good or bad for your country's economy?
Yes (2007) 57%	
Yes (2011) 34%	Good.............................. 67%
What is your view of the EU? (2011)	Bad 24%
Favorable 71%	**Should your EU member state contribute to the EU bailout fund?**
Unfavorable 25%	Yes................................... 60%
	No.................................... 36%

Sources: "Eurobarometer 76 — Public Opinion in the EU," European Commission, December 2011, ec.europa.eu/public_opinion/archives/eb/eb76/eb76_first_en.pdf; "Transatlantic Trends 2011 — Topline Data July 2011," German Marshall Fund of the United States, July 2011,

---

But Geary does not think the euro will collapse, because most EU members are in better fiscal shape than Spain, Italy, Portugal, Ireland and Greece. For instance, Eastern Europe's former communist countries are better prepared for monetary union than their Mediterranean counterparts, he points out, because they had to undergo a more rigorous pre-accession vetting process, instituted in the 1990s.

Euro-skeptic Martin Callanan, a British member of the European Parliament and president of the European Conservatives and Reformists Group, says, "the crisis is fracturing the EU. Resentment is building between blocs of states, the north and south." Callanan believes the EU's future "depends on Germany and whether it will allow fiscal transfers to other countries." If not, he says, the union's future "is in peril."

Likewise, Frank Rossavik, an editor at the Norwegian newspaper *Morgenbladet* who previously reported on EU affairs from Brussels, thinks the crisis has done lasting damage. "The EU has always been an elite project, but that was broadly accepted, even supported, to some extent, because ordinary citizens saw that the integration process contributed visibly toward stability and prosperity," he says. "Over the last years, the EU has lost this magic touch. If the euro crisis is not solved comprehensively, it may disintegrate."

Even ardent supporters of EU integration, such as former Irish Prime Minister John Bruton (1994-1997), concede the EU "has been endangered by the crisis." That's because Europeans think the choice is between austerity or no austerity, rather than being a choice of "faster or more gradual austerity," he says. "There was a consensus that creating a single market was good. But that consensus is not there yet [regarding] tax and spending issues."

Still others, such as Jacques Delors, president of the European Commission from 1985 to 1994, believe the crisis ultimately will deepen EU integration. "The sovereign debt crisis has imparted a fresh thrust to the strengthening of the Economic and Monetary Union, fostering the kind of progress that would have been unthinkable until only shortly before the crisis," he has written.[11]

"Things have stabilized in recent months," says Ireland's Minister of EU Affairs Lucinda Creighton. "The EU is pretty strong and will probably emerge stronger," she predicts, adding that it is "absolutely necessary that the level of EU integration increases."

Poland's Minister for European Integration, Mikotaj Dowgielewicz, predicts the eurozone will not only survive but will expand from 17 to about 20 countries. "We are just before the corner of the tunnel and when we turn it, we will see the light," he says.

Italy's under secretary for foreign affairs, Marta Dassù, is similarly upbeat. "We did not waste the crisis," she says. "The euro is still there, and we have improved our economic governance. We were late, but in the end we are getting results."[12] As evidence, she cites the EU fiscal treaty designed to tighten budgetary discipline, signed in March 2012, and the radical economic reforms that Italy's new prime minister, Mario Monti, is pushing through.

The crisis in Greece does not spell disaster for the whole continent, however, said Jean Pisani-Ferry, director of Bruegel, a Brussels-based think tank on international economics. "The depth of Greece's woes should not obscure the fact that its economy is small and, in many respects, an extreme, special case," he wrote. "No other country flouted the EU's budget rules the way Greece did, or has accumulated as large a public debt burden,"

The euro's survival will not be determined by Greece but rather by whether the much larger economies of Italy and Spain can "rebuild competitiveness, foster growth, restore fiscal soundness and clean up banks' balance sheets."[13]

Desmond Dinan, a public policy professor at George Mason University in Arlington, Va., and a renowned specialist on EU integration, says: "The crisis does not jeopardize the existence of the EU but endangers it by damaging trust, weakening solidarity, sapping political and bureaucratic energy and saddling many member states with crippling debt, which hugely hinders prospects for economic growth."

Should the EU continue to expand?

The recent slowdown in EU expansion is a cause for concern, especially for the applicants, experts say. Even Turkey's failure to advance thus far has not dampened that government's enthusiasm for joining the union.

"It will take time for Europeans to wake up and smell the coffee. But they will. We are a very patient nation," said Egemen Bağiş Turkey's EU affairs minister.[14]

Bağiş, contends that the accession process has encouraged Turkey to improve its record on democracy and human rights by abolishing the death penalty and easing restrictions on the use of the Kurdish language among Turkey's minority Kurds. Further, argues Turkey's undersecretary for EU affairs, Burak Erdenir, Turkish accession would promote global stability.

"We are a bridge between cultures and regions," he says. "The EU can benefit from this because they need good relations with countries in the Middle East."

Apart from Turkey, three other countries with large Muslim populations — Albania, Bosnia and Kosovo — also want to join the EU. Anti-Muslim sentiment in the EU has increased significantly in recent years, much of it predicated on fears of Islamism among Muslim immigrants in Western Europe, who are mostly North African.*[15] Davor Kunc, a Croatian working on sustainable development issues at the World Bank, believes Muslims from southeast Europe "are more secular" and thus do not pose an Islamist threat.

Ajla Delkic, a Bosnian who is executive director of the Washington-based Advisory Council for Bosnia and Herzegovina, says that while Bosnians want to join the EU, they still must overcome some challenges and adopt certain reforms before being allowed in. For example, she

---

* Islamism — or political Islam — is a political ideology that advocates legal systems constructed in strict adherence with fundamental Islam.

CHRONOLOGY

Pre-20th Century *The earliest incarnations of a unified Europe emerge; World War II horrors create a new impetus for unity.*

27 B.C. Roman Republic transitions to Roman Empire; it will eventually expand to encompass much of Europe.

800 Charlemagne, King of the Franks, becomes Roman emperor and conquers most of Western Europe.

1804 Napoleon becomes Emperor of France; he rules over large swathes of Europe, including Spain, Italy and Austria, until his empire's demise in 1815.

1950-1989 *Western Europe integrates economically through the European Economic Community (EEC).*

1950 French Foreign Minister Robert Schuman proposes common market for coal and steel between France, Germany, Italy, Belgium, the Netherlands and Luxembourg. A year later, the European Coal and Steel Community is established.

1957 The Treaty of Rome is signed, creating the EEC, which lays the foundation for a common market in Europe.

1965 French President Charles de Gaulle refuses to allow majority voting in EEC; single-nation vetoes block measures until the early 1990s.

1973 In the EEC's first enlargement, Denmark, Ireland and the United Kingdom join the organization.

1979 The European Parliament for the first time is directly elected by the citizens.

1981 Greece joins the EEC.

1986 Portugal and Spain join.

1989 Communist regimes begin to collapse, opening the way for Eastern and Western Europe to forge closer ties.

1992-2007 *The EEC transforms itself into the European Union (EU) — a political union as well as a common economic market — with harmonized social, environmental, monetary and foreign policies. Former communist-bloc countries in Eastern European become free-market democracies and join the EU.*

1992 The Maastricht Treaty is signed, opening the way for a common foreign policy, a single currency and full lawmaking powers for the European Parliament.

1995 EU membership expands to 15, as Austria, Finland and Sweden join.

2002 A single currency becomes a reality as euro notes and coins replace national currencies for 12 of the 15 EU members. Denmark, Sweden and the U.K. opt out.

2004 Ten countries — eight formerly communist — join the EU: Cyprus, the Czech Republic, Estonia, Hungary, Latvia, Lithuania, Malta, Poland, Slovakia and Slovenia.

2007 Bulgaria and Romania join, pushing EU membership up to 27.

2008-2013 *A severe recession plunges Europe into recession as sovereign debt levels soar; the euro's existence is threatened.*

September 2008 Bankruptcy of the U.S. investment bank Lehman Brothers triggers a banking crisis that plunges Europe into deep recession and gradually causes EU governments to sink ever-deeper into debt.

2010-2011 EU leaders — fearing a Greek default could create a domino effect in the EU and potentially lead to the euro's collapse — give Greece a €120 billion bailout package. Similar rescue packages are subsequently given to Ireland and Portugal.

2012 Member countries — except for the U.K. and the Czech Republic — sign fiscal treaty tightening EU controls over national budgets. Greek parliamentary elections are scheduled for May 6.

July 2013 Croatia is to become 28th EU member. Eight other countries have been designated as candidates or potential candidates for EU membership, including Turkey, Albania, Serbia and Iceland.

June 2012 The seventeen eurozone nations agree that the €500 billion European Stability Mechanism can be used to bail out banks directly. In December, they approve the release of €39.5B to save four Spanish banks.

December 2012 The Nobel Prize Committee in Norway awards the Peace Prize to the European Union in recognition of its longstanding efforts to promote peace, democracy and human rights.

January 2013 United Kingdom Prime Minister David Cameron pledges that if he is re-elected, he will hold a referendum on Britain's EU membership.

February 2013 The 27 EU leaders agreed on an almost €1 trillion budget for the EU for 2014–2020. They reduce the budget by 3.5%, the first such cut in the EU's six-decade history.

Foreign Policy Unity Remains Elusive

Will Europe ever speak with one voice?

During the 2011 Arab Spring, as Libyan leader Moammar Gadhafi's forces stood on the verge of crushing a popular rebellion, Europe faced a dilemma. Should it let events unfold on their own or intervene militarily and help the rebels?

In essence, it chose both: France and the United Kingdom teamed with the United States and launched a successful NATO-backed military assault on Gadhafi's forces, while Germany stood on the sidelines.

The dual response confirmed the skepticism of those who doubted the ability of the European Union (EU) to forge a common position on critical global security issues. Moreover, the foreign ministers of 12 EU countries recently accused Catherine Ashton, the EU's foreign policy chief — known as the high representative for foreign affairs and security — of neglecting security policy concerns. Others say she doesn't provide strategic direction.[1]

For instance, in March 2012, Israel's government called for her resignation after she seemed to compare a shooting spree by an Islamist extremist in Toulouse, France, to Israel's assault on the Palestinian enclave of Gaza in late 2008 and early 2009. Israeli Defense Minister Ehud Barak called the comparison "outrageous [with] absolutely no grounding in reality."[2] In December 2011, Ashton, who is also vice president of the EU Commission, "placed last in a survey by European parliamentarians on the performance of 11 EU commissioners. Nearly one in two said she was ineffective," an article in the *New Zealand Herald* noted.[3]

Many EU watchers, however, sympathize with Ashton's predicament. Despite her lack of foreign policy experience (she previously was a member of Britain's unelected upper chamber, the House of Lords), Europe's leaders in December 2009 catapulted Ashton into a position requiring her to speak on behalf of 27 sovereign governments and the EU Commission.

All the while, says Pierre Lemoine, editor-in-chief of *Europolitics*, a Brussels-based EU affairs newspaper, she was being undermined by national governments. "Whenever she goes somewhere, other major EU capitals quickly let us journalists know, off the record, that their position is different. They will not let her negotiate for them," he says.

As Justin Vaïsse and Hans Kundnani, authors of the "Foreign Policy Scorecard 2012," noted, "in order to make a difference, she must be proactive. But when member states are divided . . . or fail to commit resources . . . her scope for action is severely limited."[4]

Ashton isn't the only problem, however, say observers. First, the EU often has no unified foreign policy position on an issue. Plus, the European External Action Service, the diplomatic corps established in 2010 that Ashton manages, "has no real power, because the common foreign policy has not been defined," Lemoine says.[5]

Ashton also must umpire turf wars between the commission and individual EU members. In February 2010, for example, she incurred the wrath of Swedish Foreign Minister Carl Bildt for allowing EU Commission President José Manuel Barroso to appoint his former chief-of-staff, João Vale de Almeida, as the new EU ambassador to the United States.[6]

"Ashton must sometimes feel she is in the middle of a jungle," says Michael Smith, a professor of European politics at Loughborough University in the U.K.[7]

John Bruton also faced challenges in presenting a common EU position when he served as EU ambassador to the United States (2004-2009). Thus, he says, "I focused on trade and regulatory issues." Bruton believes that military/defense policy underpins all foreign policy. "As long as the

says, the Bosnian constitution splits the country into two separate political units and does not allow ethnic minorities other than Bosniaks, Serbs and Croats to run for the country's top political posts.[16]

Farther east, Ukraine hopes to join the EU, even though it is not a formal candidate. "One day we should be a member," says Pavlo Klimkin, Ukraine's deputy foreign minister responsible for EU relations. Ukraine is negotiating a free-trade agreement with the EU, with the ultimate goal of "full integration into the EU market," he said.[17]

But some, like French member of the European Parliament Pervenche Berès, are less sure of the need to

EU does not have a common defense policy, it will not have a common foreign policy," he says.

But Bruce Stokes, senior trans-Atlantic fellow for economics at the German Marshall Fund of the United States, says the EU is proving "more decisive than I expected" on some issues, such as imposing sanctions against Iran to prevent it from acquiring nuclear weapons. The bloc also continues to lead the world on environmental issues, he says. Ashton also has successfully mediated newly resumed talks between Serbia and Kosovo after the latter unilaterally seceded from Serbia in 2008.

Daniel Hamilton, director of the Center for Transatlantic Relations at the Johns Hopkins University School of Advanced International Studies in Washington, D.C., believes Europe needs to achieve concrete results from its joint diplomacy. "Yes, the EU is united on Iran," he says, "but whether it will succeed in preventing it from acquiring a nuclear weapon is another matter."

For Blake Evans-Pritchard, a British freelance journalist in The Hague who has covered the EU for several years, Europe can achieve unified results if it consistently promotes its core values: democracy and human rights; opposition to the death penalty and torture; and pacifism, born out of the traumas Europe endured in two world wars.

— *Brian Beary*

AFP/Getty Images/John Thys

Catherine Ashton, the EU's new high representative for foreign affairs and security, has found it difficult to craft a unified foreign policy for the European Union. The group is often divided on foreign issues, and many of Ashton's peers lack confidence in her leadership.

[1] See Justin Vaïsse and Hans Kundnani, "European Foreign Policy Scorecard 2012," European Council on Foreign Relations, January 2012, p. 20, www.ecfr.eu/page/-/ECFR_SCORECARD_2012_WEB.pdf.

[2] Tim Shipman, "Baroness Ashton called on to resign after likening shooting at Toulouse school to troubles of Palestinian children in Gaza," *Mail Online*, March 20, 2012, www.dailymail.co.uk/news/article-2117715/Toulouse-shooting-likened-troubles-Palestinian-children-Gaza-Baroness-Ashton.html.

[3] Catherine Field, "Ministers have Ashton lined up in crosshairs," *New Zealand Herald*, Jan. 12, 2012, www.nzherald.co.nz/world/news/article.cfm?c_id=2&objectid=10778119.

[4] Vaïsse and Kundnani, *op. cit.*

[5] See Rosa Balfour, Alyson Bailes and Megan Kenna, "The European External Action Service at work — How to improve EU foreign policy," European Policy Centre, Paper No. 67, Jan. 25 2012, www.epc.eu/pub_details.php?cat_id=2&pub_id=1399&year=2012.

[6] Toby Vogel, "Swedish minister criticizes Washington appointment," *European Voice*, Feb. 22, 2010, www.europeanvoice.com/article/2010/02/swedish-minister-criticises-washington-appointment/67223.aspx.

[7] Comments made during a conference, "The Maastricht Treaty: Taking Stock After 20 Years," Maastricht University, Feb. 7-8, 2012.

expand the EU's borders. "There has been tension for many years now about enlargement," she says. "There is no longer political momentum for it. The public in most member states thinks the EU needs to be consolidated first."

Europolitics editor Lemoine agrees. The French public is "very negative" toward Turkish enlargement, and "if you were to have a referendum in France even on Croatia's membership, it probably wouldn't pass." Croatia's membership was approved by the EU in December.

Some also say religion plays a role in Europe's reluctance to let Turkey join. "There is a feeling across Europe that we are a Christian community," says the

University of Cologne's Wessels. "When we see women in Islamic headscarves, it feels strange — we don't know what to do."

Others don't want to rush enlargement. Better to let countries join "once they are ready," says former Irish Prime Minister Bruton, adding that "certain countries" were allowed to join in the past, when neither the EU or the eurozone were ready.

However, some want to hit the gas pedal rather than the brakes. "I don't think we need to take a break," says Irish EU minister Creighton. "We should focus on the Balkans in the short term" but should also "seriously consider" membership for countries in the southern Caucasus, Armenia and Georgia. "By opening our borders, we open up trade and attract more investment. Besides the economics argument, there is the political stability and democracy that the EU brings."

Polish minister Dowgielewicz supports membership for Turkey, Moldova, Belarus and Ukraine. There may be limits to EU expansion, he says, "but we have not reached them so far."

It is best to be open to flexible arrangements regarding enlargement, says Daniel Hamilton, director of the Center for Transatlantic Relations at the School for Advanced International Studies (SAIS). "Who is to say what the EU will look like in 20 years? Who would have guessed in 1989 that the EU would look the way it does now? You gain nothing by shutting the door today."

Is public support for the EU declining?

The EU's image has taken a battering during the economic downturn. But the drop in support has not been as precipitous as press coverage might suggest, says the German Marshall Fund's Stokes.

"There is a general commitment to Europe and the single market," he says, based on opinion polls. "People still support the euro. They do not want to return to national currencies."

Guy Verhofstadt, Belgium's prime minister from 1999 to 2008 and currently a member of the European Parliament, argues that the crisis has shifted public opinion toward greater EU integration. "Pro-European parties could win the 2014 European Parliament elections. We are using the word 'federalism' and the term 'United States of Europe' again," he said.[18]

But George Mason University's Dinan is not convinced. "The EU used to be associated with peace and prosperity, but since the euro crisis it's been associated with angst and austerity," he said.[19]

Likewise, British journalist Evans-Pritchard says that in the Netherlands, where he lives, "people openly question the EU. That is new." He cites the meteoric rise of the anti-EU Party for Freedom — led by right-wing, anti-Muslim politician Geert Wilders — which won 15.5 percent in the 2010 elections and now forms part of the coalition government.

Meanwhile, the British public is consistently the most anti-EU, he says, because "the U.K. has an island mentality. It does not see itself as part of Europe. It is a former colonial power trying to adjust to its new place in the world."

British Euro-skeptic Callanan agrees that "we have always seen ourselves as separate. We accept the EU as a single market but not as a political union."

By contrast, neighboring Ireland remains more pro-EU. "For Britain, the EU entails a loss of sovereignty," says Professor Dinan, who is Irish, while for Ireland, it means a gain. "Not strictly legally speaking, of course. Rather, think how much more independent and self-confident Ireland has become as a result of EU membership."

As for aspiring European Union members, Croatia's Kunc feels the crisis has tarnished the EU's image in the Balkans. Countries such as Italy and Greece, which joined the union during the early years, before strict new economic criteria were imposed on applicants, "got away with flouting the rules in order to join the eurozone," he says. "Many in Southeast Europe think the EU cannot get its own house in order." Thus, he continues, "Although the goal of governments in the region still is to join the EU, there is increasing public skepticism over the value of being in the union."

But Elmina Kulasic, chief political analyst and director of policy at the Post-Conflict Research Centre in Sarajevo, says, "The euro crisis has not registered much in Bosnia. I do not think it has hurt our view of the EU as being good for our well-being."

Turks, on the other hand, have grown disillusioned with the EU, according to Erdenir, the Turkish EU affairs undersecretary. "We have been trying to get in for 52 years," he says. "Turkish people do not believe the EU is sincere, so it is difficult to keep them on board."

"Indisputably, public support is slipping," says *Europolitics'* Lemoine. He cites a 43 percent turnout rate for the 2009 European Parliament elections, which he believes happened "because, as [former European Commission President] Jacques Delors once said, you can't ask citizens to fall in love with a single market. When we emphasize the euro so much, we forget about deeper values. It is time to re-center the European project around the citizen," he says. For example, the organization's original appeal was its unflinching commitment to peace, democracy and human rights.

SAIS's Hamilton believes that the different life experiences of the older and younger generations lie at the root of the drop in support. "Anyone who has grown up since the end of the Cold War has no knowledge of borders," he says. "They take the EU's construction for granted and assume it's reality. They are not galvanized to do more with it."

Anne Rasmussen, a Dane who teaches EU decision-making at Leiden University in the Netherlands, said, "It is hard to measure the EU's popularity. If you ask people about boring bureaucrats in Brussels you might get a negative opinion, but you might get a more positive one if you ask about whether the EU should be dealing with bread-and-butter issues."

BACKGROUND

Origins

At various points in its history, Europe has been dominated by a single political power. From 27 B.C. to A.D. 476 it was the Roman Empire. Then from 800 to 814 Charlemagne, king of the Franks, became a latter day Roman emperor, albeit with a smaller domain, centered on France and Germany.

From 962 until 1806, a loose alliance of states — the Holy Roman Empire — spanned much of modern-day Germany, Austria and Italy, ruled nominally by the Hapsburg family. French Emperor Napoleon ruled large swaths of Europe from 1806 to 1815, including Spain, Italy and Austria.[20]

After World War I (1914-1918) some political leaders and intellectuals began conceiving of a form of European unification that did not involve military conquest. In September 1929, France's foreign minister, Aristide Briand, proposed a "Europe Federal Union." The idea failed to garner much support.[21]

But after World War II (1939-1945), Europeans vowed never again to allow their continent to be ripped apart by bloody conflict. Frenchman Jean Monnet was perhaps the most influential of a handful of European integrationists who were pivotal in the early years. A cognac salesman by profession, Monnet was an internationalist by background and disposition, having worked for governments in London, Geneva, Washington, Shanghai and Algeria in a variety of capacities, including coordinator of military supplies and economic policy adviser.[22]

Another major figure was France's foreign minister, Robert Schuman, who came from Alsace, the disputed province that France and Germany fought over for centuries. Britain's wartime leader, Winston Churchill, in a speech at the University of Zurich on Sept. 19, 1946, called for a United States of Europe, to be led by France and Germany, with the United States and the U.K. as close allies.

With the onset of the Cold War in the late 1940s, the U.S. government began to promote European integration, believing a united Europe would be a bulwark against the communist Soviet Union, which was tightening its grip over Eastern Europe. On May 9, 1950, Schuman proposed a common market for coal and steel between France, Germany, Italy, Belgium, the Netherlands and Luxembourg. His idea culminated in the signing of the Treaty of Paris in April 1951, which set up the European Coal and Steel Community (ECSC), the EU's forerunner.[23]

Simultaneously, plans were hatched to create a European Defense Community (EDC) that would include a 100,000-strong European army. The United States was especially enthusiastic about the plan, thinking it would help dissuade the Soviet Union from sponsoring an East German-led invasion of West Germany.*

An EDC treaty was signed in May 1952, but the French parliament declined to ratify it, so it never took effect.

---

* This U.S. fear had been triggered in June 1950 when the Soviets provided military aid to communist North Korea in the latter's invasion of U.S.-supported South Korea during the Korean War (1950-53). After World War II, Germany had been divided into two parts: U.S.-supported West Germany and communist East Germany, supported by the Soviet Union.

Other organizations promoting European unity emerged, notably the North Atlantic Treaty Organization (NATO), a defense alliance between Western Europe, the United States and Canada established in April 1949. The Council of Europe was created in November 1949 in Strasbourg, the capital of the Alsace region in France, to symbolize Franco-German rapprochement. The council's mission was to support democracy and human rights in Europe.[24]

Common Market

Monnet became the first president of the Luxembourg-based ECSC. It proved very successful, with iron ore production increasing from 62 million to 92 million tons between 1952 and 1962. New patterns of trade also developed, and working conditions were harmonized.

The ECSC model was extended to other economic sectors, notably agriculture, with the Treaty of Rome in March 1957, which established a European Economic Community (EEC), based in Brussels. A European Atomic Community, or Euratom, which evolved into a research agency, was set up at the same time. Crucially, during the 1960s, the EEC abolished tariffs and quantity restrictions for goods traded between members, triggering strong economic growth.

Politically, however, the sailing was not so smooth. In 1965 French President Charles de Gaulle blocked an effort to introduce majority voting in EEC meetings, as he did not want to give up France's power to veto proposals. His stance resulted in many important decisions being blocked until the 1990s, slowing the pace of integration. For instance, De Gaulle vetoed Britain's application to join the EEC in 1963 and 1967, believing it would threaten French dominance of the organization.

The first proposal to create a single European currency was floated at an EU summit in The Hague in 1969, but the idea was put on hold after the 1973 oil crisis, because leaders felt it untimely in such a turbulent economic climate. It was relaunched in 1979, when a European Exchange Rate Mechanism (ERM) was created, allowing exchange rates to fluctuate within a narrow band. The ERM gradually became vulnerable to attacks from market speculators, and in September 1992 one such attack forced the U.K. to drop out of the ERM.

De Gaulle's resignation as French president in 1969 unblocked Britain's EEC membership bid. The first EEC enlargement occurred in 1973, when Denmark, Ireland and the U.K. joined. The demise of authoritarian regimes and successful transitions to democracy in Greece, Portugal and Spain in the 1970s opened the door to membership: Greece in 1981, Spain and Portugal in 1986.

European integration accelerated in the mid-1980s after leaders signed the Single European Act in 1986, which set 1992 as a deadline for removing outstanding barriers to intra-EEC trade.[25] In May 1989, as the Soviet Union was relaxing its grip on Eastern Europe, Hungary decided to open its border with Austria, triggering events that culminated in communism's collapse across Eastern Europe. The former communist bloc reemerged in the 1990s as free-market democracies and aspiring EU members. East Germany, which had never been part of the union before, was able to join before the others by unifying with West Germany in 1990, a year after the fall of the Berlin Wall.

In February 1992, European leaders signed the Maastricht Treaty, which changed the organization's name to the European Union (EU), mandated a common foreign policy, granted lawmaking powers to the European Parliament, extended the EU's power to new areas such as social policy and the environment and sowed the seeds for a single currency.

"There was a strong will to move to the next step after completing the single market, and creating a single currency was it," said Wim Kok, Dutch finance minister at the time.[26]

Henning Christophersen, a Dane who was commission vice president during the talks, said, "At first we thought Maastricht would be [just a] Treaty on Economic and Monetary Union," but when the Cold War suddenly ended, "we also had to decide what to do with Eastern Europe."

Enrique Barón Crespo, parliament president from 1989 to 1992, said the collapse of autocratic regimes around the world — from East Germany to Poland to South Africa and Chile — impressed on everyone the need to democratize the EU and provided an impetus for strengthening parliament's powers.

Political Union

The EU expanded from 12 to 15 members when Austria, Finland and Sweden joined in 1995 — no longer worried that EU membership would compromise their neutrality now that the Cold War was over. Norway was due to join in 1973 and 1995, but on each occasion Norwegians said no in an accession referendum.

"We have nothing substantial to gain in the EU," says Norwegian journalist Rossavik. "Our economy is very strong because of the oil and gas wealth, and at the moment we have no security issues where the EU could be of any help."

In 2004, eight ex-communist bloc nations from Central and Eastern Europe joined, along with Cyprus and Malta, to be followed in 2007 by Bulgaria and Romania. As restrictions on the free movement of labor between east and west were lifted, millions of East Europeans migrated westward, in search of higher-paid jobs. Between May 2004 and April 2007, for example, 630,000 arrived in the U.K. alone — mostly Poles, Lithuanians and Slovaks taking jobs in factories, warehouses and restaurants.[27] The migration touched off anti-immigrant sentiment in countries such as France and Belgium, where some feared it would result in lower wages and weaker worker protections, but the fears proved mostly unwarranted.

To prepare for the single currency, EU members pledged to keep their current-account deficits — caused by outspending revenue — below 3 percent of GDP and their national debts under 60 percent of GDP. By late 1990s most had met those pledges, so that when euro notes and coins were introduced in 2002, the only members not part of the euro area were Denmark, Sweden and the U.K., which kept their own currencies. Even before Greece adopted the euro, however, EU economists were warning that the country's debt and deficit figures were not trustworthy. The alarms went unheeded, however.

In the early 2000s, low interest rates triggered a borrowing and spending boom, especially in peripheral EU countries such as Ireland, Greece and Spain.[28] Core EU countries such as France and Germany were exporting large quantities of manufactured goods to the new markets.[29] With the EU enjoying steady economic growth overall, many were willing to ignore the euro membership rules about public deficits in some slower-growing countries. For example, in 2003, France and Germany's public deficits had exceeded 3 percent, but their EU counterparts chose not to penalize them.

Fiscal Compact Creates Greater EU Oversight

The European Union's fiscal treaty — signed in March by all EU member states except the Czech Republic and the U.K. — strengthens European Commission oversight over national budgets by allowing it to impose automatic corrective steps or sanctions (including fines) on overspending member states.

Key Components of Fiscal Compact

- Annual structural deficits* must not exceed 0.5% of gross domestic product — the so-called Golden Rule.

- The European Commission can impose automatic sanctions or other corrective actions on member states that do not keep spending within established limits. Only a veto by a "qualified majority" of members can prevent the sanctions from going into effect.**

- Only countries that ratify the treaty can access the European Stability Mechanism (the €800 billion bailout fund).

*A structural deficit occurs when a government spends more than it collects in tax revenue, even during periods when the economy is performing well. It differs from "cyclical deficits" that typically occur during a recession, when tax revenues decline and governments tend to spend more for social programs, such as unemployment benefits.

** A qualified majority is 258 out of 345 votes (or 74.8 percent) in the EU Council of Ministers. EU votes are weighted: more populous countries have more votes.

Source: Valentin Kreilinger, "The Making of a New Treaty: Six Rounds of Political Bargaining," Notre Europe, February 2012, www.notre-europe.eu/uploads/tx_publication/NewTreaty_V.Kreilinger_NE_Feb2012.pdf

---

Between 1997 and 2012, the EU concluded five treaties that amended its constitutional framework, ceding more national sovereignty to the EU. With more members, treaty talks became progressively more protracted and acrimonious as new fault lines emerged. For example, smaller members disagreed with larger ones over how their votes should be weighted in the EU lawmaking process.[30]

Ratification also became a problem, given that all member countries had to approve a treaty — either by a parliamentary vote or popular referendum — before it could enter into force. For example, in May and June 2005 voters in France and the Netherlands rejected the Constitutional Treaty that had been approved by governments in 2004.[31] In response, EU leaders signed the Lisbon Treaty in 2007, which included most of the same provisions and created an EU diplomatic corps, the European External Action Service.[32]

Financial Crisis

The global recession that followed the near collapse of the U.S. banking system in autumn 2008 put the EU through the greatest test of its history. And, according to Jacques Delacave, former chief economist at the Belgian Banque de Bruxelles, the creation of the euro was a contributing factor.

"The euro deprived banks of the profits they used to make from currency exchanges," he notes. "They needed to find new ways to make money," he said, so they devised new financial products such as credit default swaps and mortgage-backed securities that were not managed by the banks but simply sold on to other buyers. "There was no regulation of these products, which got us into trouble."[33]

With European banks battered by the crisis, EU governments came to the rescue, often by lending the banks billions of euros. Between 2009 and 2011, declining tax revenues precipitated by the recession, combined with large-scale government spending on bank bailouts and economic stimulus packages, caused sovereign debt levels to skyrocket.

In Ireland, for instance, the economy — known as the "Celtic Tiger" during the real estate boom in the 1990s and early 2000s — nosedived as its housing bubble burst. By 2011 half Ireland's homeowners owed more on their mortgages than their homes were worth.[34]

Anxious to prevent eurozone countries from defaulting and creating global panic, the EU and IMF intervened in 2010 and 2011 to provide bailout loans to the most indebted countries — Greece, Ireland and Portugal.[35] In return for the bailout money, recipient governments agreed to painful austerity measures to reduce debt levels — such as slashing public spending on pensions and public-sector employment. In addition, the EU in May 2010 created a €440 billion EU bailout fund, to which the IMF added €250 billion, for financially troubled eurozone countries that might need rescuing.

The EU also adopted reforms in September 2011 aimed at improving Europe's overall economic governance, and which called for automatic fines if members breached EU rules on debt limits.[36]

The economic downturn and resulting spike in joblessness caused many of the Central and East European migrants who had moved to the West to return home. Ireland, for instance, saw a 64 percent drop in immigration from 2006-2009.[37]

CURRENT SITUATION

Building a Firewall

Significant steps by EU leaders were taken in early 2012 to address the EU's grave financial problems, but the situation remained tenuous. In January the IMF forecast that the EU would slip back into recession in 2012 because of the sovereign debt crisis.[38] Olivier Blanchard, an IMF economics counselor and director, warned that if the EU reduced debt levels too quickly it could kill growth and further derail the recovery.[39]

Mass protests erupted in Greece, as its government appeared ready to default on its debts and the public began to feel the full impact of austerity measures, such as sharp cuts in government employment and social welfare entitlements.[40] Anti-German sentiment reached a fever pitch, with cartoonists depicting German politicians in Nazi uniforms and newspaper reports recalling how 300,000 Greeks died of starvation during Nazi occupation in World War II.[41]

"Most Greeks do not believe the austerity measures being imposed by the EU and IMF are working," said Alexis Papahelas, managing editor of the Greek daily newspaper *Kathimerini*. "They believe [the measures] are creating a vicious circle," with Greece now in its fifth successive year of recession.[42]

In this climate, extremist, anti-EU nationalist parties are expected to do well in Greece's parliamentary elections on May 6, raising the possibility of a future Greek government reneging on the bailout-for-austerity deal.

Despite the Greek situation, some EU politicians claim the worst of the crisis is over. "Whatever happens to Greece now is less relevant than six months ago, because we have set up a firewall to prevent contagion spreading to other eurozone states," said Luxembourg's finance minister, Luc Frieden.[43] He was referring to the EU bailout fund, which EU finance ministers increased by €200 billion — to €800 billion (about $1 trillion) — at a meeting in Copenhagen on March 30.[44]

In addition, 25 EU leaders on March 1 signed a fiscal treaty tightening budgetary discipline in member countries.[45] It limits annual structural deficits to 0.5 percent of

Should the EU control member states' budgets?

YES **Markus Ferber**
German Member of the European Parliament and Member, Economic and Monetary Affairs Committee

Written for *CQ Global Researcher*, April 2012

Recent debt problems in the eurozone have shown the need for more central European Union (EU) control and influence over national budgets. Eurozone countries cannot continue to pile up deficits and then launch desperate rescue attempts. EU member states that violate the EU's debt criteria have to be punished more quickly than in the past — and with tougher penalties. The recently adopted fiscal pact provides national debt brakes and automatic sanctions. This means a tightening of fiscal controls in the eurozone.

Since the establishment in 1997 of the Stability and Growth Pact, the European Commission has monitored the development of the budgetary situation in eurozone countries. Under the pact, each EU member state must submit an updated stability program annually to the commission, providing information on medium-term budget planning. The commission must also be notified twice per year of the projected deficit and the expected total debt. The Stability and Growth Pact clearly says that member states must limit the amount of their annual budget deficit to 3 percent of their gross domestic product (GDP) and their overall public debt to 60 percent of GDP.

Even before the current financial and economic crisis hit Europe, the institutional weaknesses of the pact became clear. Even major economies such as Germany and France did not adhere to its criteria, which led to the weakening of the pact.

The new "six-pack" is a legislative package that includes six reports that toughen European borrowing and debt-reduction rules. In the negotiations, the European Parliament fought for a hard line on the measure. Until now, sanctions against an EU member violating Stability and Growth Pact rules had to be decided by a majority of EU member states. Under the six-pack, the sanction process starts automatically and can only be stopped by a majority of EU finance ministers. Thus, in the medium term EU members are forced to keep to a balanced budget, without resorting to new borrowing.

As a next step, the European Parliament is working on the so-called two-pack, which would further improve the control and coordination of national budgets. Euro countries should adopt far-reaching domestic and economic reforms only after the EU Commission and the remaining members of the euro-zone have been consulted.

Recent history has clearly taught us that allowing member states to go it alone in setting budgetary policy is not sustainable once you have a monetary union.

NO **Nikolaos Chountis**
Greek Member of the European Parliament and Member, Economic and Monetary Affairs Committee

Written for *CQ Global Researcher*, April 2012

With the outbreak of the dept crisis in the eurozone, the dominant political forces (the social democrats and the conservatives) decided to minimize public spending and impose austerity policies all over Europe. To more closely coordinate fiscal policies and control national budgets, the EU recently adopted an "Austerity Treaty" [known as the fiscal treaty], called for European Commission control of national budgets and strengthened the Stability and Growth Pact through penalties to member states.

Fiscal policy is a very important tool for the implementation of economic and development policy. Especially, after the introduction of the eurozone, fiscal policy is the only macroeconomic instrument that member states have.

The suffocative coordination of fiscal policies under this austerity policy eliminates the capability and the flexibility of EU member states to pursue an effective and counter-cyclical stabilization policy, geared toward redistribution of wealth, sustainable development and maintaining adequate public services and infrastructure.

Tighter fiscal discipline and closer coordination of fiscal policies along the lines of dominant economic policies will not help member states recover from this crisis or prevent a future one. Instead, this kind of coordination exacerbates the effects of a crisis, increases social inequalities, poverty and unemployment and eventually leads to the impoverishment of Europe.

Unfortunately, the EU has decided practically to cancel the role of national parliaments, which are elected by the people, in order to give superpowers to bureaucratic institutions, such as the European Commission and the European Central Bank.

The tightening of the Stability Pact, the institutionalization of austerity and the limitation of democracy and national sovereignty are the new components of the European Union. The results of this change and of EU control of national budgets are more than obvious in Greece. The economic program to be implemented by Greece has nothing to do with the vision of a united Europe. It is incompatible with the European social model, with the ideas of solidarity and economic and social convergence of member states with the values — of democracy and social justice.

The experiment conducted in Greece is not confined to Greece. On the contrary, what we live today in my country, Greece, is the future of Europe and the euro.

GDP — and allows only countries that ratify the treaty to access the EU bailout fund.[46] (*See box, p. 173.*) The U.K. and Czech Republic didn't sign the treaty, fearing it would erode national sovereignty.[47]

German Foreign Minister Westerwelle said he regrets their decision. "I would like to have Britain on board. We have to work to build this bridge over this troubled water," he said.[48]

Berès, the EU Parliament member from France, says, "The U.K.'s refusal to even discuss the treaty showed bad form. It is in Britain's own interest to save the euro because the single market's survival depends on it." The U.K. does not use the euro.

By this spring, however, the biggest threat to the euro's existence arguably was not Britain — or even Greece — but Spain, whose fiscal situation had deteriorated dramatically. There was growing concern of a Spanish financial meltdown, with interest rates on government bonds rising to 5 percent, unemployment at nearly 24 percent, the public deficit forecast to hit 5 percent of GDP in 2012 and public debt at 80 percent of GDP.[49]

Spain's EU Commissioner, Joaquín Almunia, said, "We are not out of the woods yet." Stressing the need for EU members to continue with painful fiscal adjustments, he said, "if public debt continues to grow, there is no firewall that can be sufficient" to prevent contagion spreading across the eurozone.[50]

Germany's Dominance

German Chancellor Merkel has been the dominant figure in the crisis, with Germany contributing the most, by far, to the EU bailout fund.[51]

"Germany used to be in the passenger seat. Now it is in the driving seat," says the University of Maastricht's Geary. "With Germany the paymaster, it is not meek and mild anymore. It is finally getting over its World War II legacy," he says.

Westerwelle said confidently of his country's relationship with the EU: "Europe is the answer to the darkest chapter in our history and our life insurance in these times of globalization. For us, this is not a technical question, it's a historical one."[52]

But British journalist Evans-Pritchard feels Germany's dominance is beginning to be resented. "I feel sorry for the Greeks. They are being dictated to from Berlin. The

austerity solutions imposed on them benefit Germany the most," he says. "Germany is determined to make Greece get its fiscal house in order, keenly aware of the domino effect a disorderly Greek default could have on other eurozone countries such as Spain, to which German banks are even more heavily exposed.

The University of Cologne's Wessels feels criticisms of his country are inevitable. "Germany is the leader, and leaders are always criticized. The U.S. knows this well."

Hans-Gert Pöttering, former president of the European Parliament (2007-2009), admits that Germany must "be careful about the public perception that we are too dominant." Pöttering — who chairs the Konrad Adenauer Stiftung, the political foundation of the center-right German Christian Democrat party — praises Merkel, his party leader, as a person of substance, adding that "it is good she is taking the lead."[53]

While anti-German sentiment is strong in Greece, the mood in Ireland, where austerity measures are also biting, has not evolved into violent demonstrations as in Greece. Asked if she resents Germany laying down the law, a Dublin office worker who asked not to be named, jokes, "We have to do what we are told — the Germans are paying our unemployment benefit." She adds, "It had to be done. We were living beyond our means."

Europolitics' Lemoine is similarly philosophical. "Germany is the economic heavyweight, so it is normal that it imposes its views. But it also listens to others."

Stokes, of the German Marshall Fund, notes that Merkel "remains remarkably popular outside of Germany," with 80 percent of the French, 64 percent of British and 69 percent of Spanish expressing confidence in her leadership.[54]

Some believe the Franco-German marriage, the post-World War II engine behind EU integration, has changed fundamentally: that it is no longer a marriage of equals. "France is seen as having lost both economic and political parity with Berlin," Reuters journalist Paul Taylor has written. "French cartoonists have illustrated cruelly the increasingly unequal relationship. Plantu of *Le Monde* depicted Merkel as a uniformed matron pushing a battered Sarkozy in a wheelchair."[55]

French EU Parliament member Berès regrets that the European Commission, which she would like to act as a go-between for France and Germany, appears to be weakened. Commission President José Manuel Barroso "acts like a secretary general of the European Council, taking his orders from Berlin — followed by Paris," she says.

Pöttering notes that the 2007 Lisbon Treaty gave EU heads of state and government greater powers to set EU policy, leaving the commission sidelined to some extent in the current crisis.

Enlargement Fatigue

The expansion process, although going through a period of inertia, is not at a standstill. In December 2011 Croatia signed an accession treaty, which Croatians approved by 66 percent in a January referendum, paving the way for Croatia to become the union's 28th member in 2013. To qualify for membership, Croatia had to make many sacrifices, such as ending shipbuilders' subsidies, radically reforming its judiciary and handing over Gen. Ante Gotovina — seen by many Croats as a hero of Croatia's War of Independence (1991-1995) — to a war crimes tribunal in The Hague.[56] Croatia also had to cede some disputed territory to neighboring Slovenia, an EU member that had blocked Croatia's accession until the issue was resolved.

For other Western Balkans nations, the accession process continues to be painstakingly slow. Miroslav Lajčák, a Slovak who is a managing director of the new EU External Action Service, contrasts the situation in the Balkans with the accession of Central and Eastern European countries a decade ago. "Back then there was strong support in the EU for enlargement, and the candidate countries were willing to make the necessary reforms. But in the Western Balkans, the politicians are bickering with each other over borders and countries' names and are not focused solely on EU membership."[57]

Turning to Nordic Europe, after the collapse of Iceland's banking sector in 2008, the government decided it would be better off inside the EU tent and applied for membership. Should Iceland's accession proceed smoothly, it would become the EU's 29th member state — and the least populous, with just 317,000 people. It also would leave Norway as the only non-EU country in Scandinavia.

However, there are obstacles in Iceland's path, such as disputes with neighboring countries over fishing rights and a row over whether Iceland should be required to compensate British and Dutch investors who lost money in Iceland's banking collapse. In addition, many doubt that Icelanders would ratify an accession treaty.[58]

OUTLOOK

Declining Europe?

As Europe struggles with its chronic debt and double-dip recession, some are wondering if the continent is entering a more sustained period of decline.[59]

The Marshall Fund's Stokes warns that "if this current crisis presages a 'lost decade' of slow growth and introspection — and the chances are very high, given its financial problems — we will look to Europe less and less as a partner. The U.S. drift toward Asia, which we see under President Barack Obama, will only accelerate." Already more than 75 percent of Americans born after the Vietnam War (1955-1975) think Asia is more important than Europe, he points out.[60]

Apart from its economic woes, Europe also must contend with longer-term demographic challenges. The World Bank's Gill notes that "Europe has 10 percent of the world's population but accounts for 58 percent of world spending on social protection." For example, the French are living six years longer than in the 1960s but are retiring nine years younger — 15 years of additional dependence on social services.

"When you get more prosperous, you can shorten your working week, but not your working lifetime," Gill said. In addition, the EU's chronically low fertility rate — currently 1.6 children per woman — is well below the replacement rate of 2.1, which will place an increasing burden on the working-age population.[61]

Meanwhile, public support for the EU appears somewhat fragile, with some believing that the very process of EU integration is partly responsible for current economic problems. "It will be very, very difficult for the EU to be popular," given all the austerity measures so closely associated with it, said Tom De Bruijn, former Dutch ambassador to the EU.[62]

Some experts see different groups of countries integrating at different paces. "Variable speeds are inevitable and not a bad thing," George Mason University's Dinan says. "The more areas the EU gets involved with, the more we will have to do that kind of differentiated integration," he says.

But given the growing internal pressures on the EU, could the whole project collapse? Maastricht University's Geary thinks not. "It is too big to fail. We will find a way out of our problems whatever it takes because no leader wants to be blamed for it falling apart," he says.

Former Belgian Prime Minister Verhofstadt said the EU today is at the same point where the United States stood in 1781, when its leaders realized that the Articles of Confederation were too weak to hold the country together. "We need to create a federal state," Verhofstadt said. "There is no third way. Either you move toward a federal model or you lose the euro."[63]

He even goes so far as to want the EU to be allowed to raise taxes instead having its budget financed by contributions from member states. "A real democracy is based on taxation. There is no representation without taxation," he said.

Democratizing the EU is vital if the union is to survive, says former Irish Prime Minister Bruton. "We have reached the outer limits of what can be achieved by bureaucratic integration. We need more democratic legitimization," he says.

For instance, he says, the EU Commission president could be elected directly — by European citizens — rather than the 27 EU governments nominating him or her and then having the European Parliament approve the nominee, as currently happens.

Asked what direction she thinks Europe is headed, Krueger at the School for Advanced International Studies said, "So far, every time the EU has had a crisis in its history, it has integrated more. An EU fiscal union in the future is a possibility."

EPILOGUE

Can Europe Thrive Again?

When this report was first published on April 17, 2012, the EU was at its lowest ebb. There were widespread fears that Greece's debt contagion would spread to Italy and Spain and that the EU would be unable to bail out these large economies. Some were predicting the euro's collapse, which would have been a devastating blow to the EU. But over the past year EU leaders have shown a steely resolve to save the euro and have put their feet on the accelerator of closer economic integration. By early 2013 the situation had stabilized. According to Olivier Blanchard, chief economist for the International Monetary Fund (IMF), although debt levels remained worryingly high in many countries, a total meltdown had been averted, and Europe was set to recover if it proceeded with its structural reform plans.[64]

In June 2012, the seventeen eurozone nations agreed in principle that the €500 billion bailout fund they created back in 2010, the European Stability Mechanism (ESM), could be used to inject capital directly into banks, rather than going to national government coffers.[65] This was done to avoid the situation recurring where a governments intervenes to save a failing bank only to then need rescuing itself, as had happened with Ireland. The EU in December 2012 approved Spain's request for €39.5B from the ESM to save four failing Spanish banks.[66] The approval was made conditional upon those banks loaning less to real estate developers—a practice that contributed to a massive property market crash in 2008—and more to small businesses.

Meanwhile, the Frankfurt-based European Central Bank (ECB) continued to flex its muscles to bolster the euro. On July 5, 2012 it cut interest rates to historically low levels to encourage banks to loan to one another.[67] In September it started buying back sovereign bonds from secondary markets to boost investor confidence.[68] By early 2013 EU leaders and lawmakers were proceeding with plans to put the ECB in charge of supervising the eurozone's 6,000 banks. The ECB's star was in the ascendant and so too was the European Council's, the arm of the EU government comprising the leaders of the 27 members, which emerged as the dominant force in responding to the crisis. The European Commission, supposedly the EU's executive arm because it enjoys sole right to propose new EU laws, has been partially sidelined. The European Parliament—the only directly-elected EU body—has also struggled to assert itself.

A major piece of EU business was concluded on February 8, 2013 when the European Council agreed on an EU budget of almost €1 trillion for 2014–2020.[69] For the first time ever, the EU budget was cut—by 3.5%—a move precipitated by the depleted state of national coffers. Farm subsidies were slashed by 13%. The pressure to pare back the budget came from northern European states like the Netherlands and Germany who pay the most into it.

While public confidence in the EU remained low, national elections in two countries suggested that citizens were still keen for it to survive. In April 2012 the Dutch government collapsed due to one coalition partner's opposition to EU bailouts. In September's ballot, however, voters elected a pro-EU government, while the euro-skeptic party that quit the government suffered heavy losses.[70] Elections in Greece created a coalition government that supported the EU-IMF bailout-for-austerity program, leaving the anti-bailout parties, leftist Syria and neo-Nazi Golden Dawn, in opposition.[71] "The Greek people today voted for the European course of Greece and that we remain in the euro," said the new Prime Minister Antonio Samaras in June.

The main threat of an exit from the EU came from the United Kingdom, which has already opted out of the euro. In January 2013 British Prime Minister David Cameron announced that if re-elected, he would hold a referendum on Britain's EU membership.[72] Further complicating matters, less euro-skeptic Scotland plans to have a referendum in 2014 on whether to secede from the UK. In France, the victory of socialist François Hollande over incumbent center-right president Nicolas Sarkozy in the April/May 2012 elections shifted Europe's political center of gravity leftward. Whereas austerity had been the buzzword, the new mantra became 'jobs and growth' as political elites mulled over how to shake Europe out of its economic slump. At an EU summit in June 2012, they steered €120 billion of the European Investment Bank's funds to help the most troubled economies.[73]

Amidst all the stress generated by the crisis—indeed possibly in response to it—the Nobel Prize Committee in Norway awarded its annual Peace Prize to the European Union for its contribution to promoting peace, democracy and human rights. The award ceremony in Oslo on December 10 was attended by leaders from 20 European governments. Detractors of the decision—and there were many—noted that the EU had failed to prevent wars in the Balkans erupting in the 1990s.[74]

With such a strong focus on the economy, the EU had little time to think about foreign affairs. However, the process of admitting its 28th member state, Croatia, in July 2013, stayed on track. Croatia's Balkan neighbors Albania, Bosnia, Kosovo, Macedonia, Montenegro, and Serbia continued to knock on the EU's door, as did Turkey and

Iceland. On trade, after months of nudging by EU leaders keen for the U.S. to 'pivot' back to Europe, in February 2013 President Barack Obama agreed to start talks for a comprehensive trade and investment pact with the EU.[75]

On global security, in July 2012 the EU imposed the most severe economic sanctions ever against Iran to dissuade it from developing nuclear weapons. By late 2012 the EU's oil embargo and freeze on banking activities with Iran was inflicting real pain and Iran's currency was in a tailspin.[76] By early 2013 the focus shifted to Mali, where Al Qaeda-affiliated Islamist militants had seized control of large swathes of the north of the country. France took the lead in deploying combat troops to take back control of the north, while the EU deployed a mission to train Mali's army.[77]

NOTES

1. "World Economic Outlook Database," International Monetary Fund, September 2011, www.imf.org/external/ns/cs.aspx?id=28.

2. Croatia's membership has been approved, but not yet finalized. See Current Situation. For background, see Sarah Glazer, "Future of the Euro," *CQ Global Researcher*, May 17, 2011, pp. 237-262.

3. "World Economic Outlook Database," *op. cit.*

4. "Eurobarometer 76: Public Opinion in the EU," European Commission, December 2011; also see "Transatlantic Trends 2011: Topline Data July 2011," German Marshall Fund of the United States, http://trends.gmfus.org/transatlantic-trends/topline-data/.

5. See Bruce Stokes, "What Europeans Think about the Eurocrisis," German Marshall Fund of the United States, Feb. 1, 2012, www.gmfus.org/wp-content/files_mf/stokes_whateuropeansthink_jan12.pdf.

6. Gill was speaking at the European Institute in Washington, D.C., on Feb. 13, 2012, presenting the key findings of his report, co-authored with Martin Raiser, entitled "Golden Growth: Restoring the Luster of the European Economic Model," World Bank, Jan. 24, 2012, http://web.worldbank.org/WBSITE/EXTERNAL/COUNTRIES/ECAEXT/0,,contentMDK:23069550~pagePK:146736~piPK:146830~theSitePK:258599,00.html.

7. For background, see Kenneth Jost, "Future of the European Union," *CQ Researcher*, Oct. 28, 2005, pp. 909-932.

8. CIA World Fact Book.

9. George Soros, "Merkel is Leading Europe in the Wrong Direction," *Spiegel Online*, Feb. 13, 2012, www.spiegel.de/international/europe/0,1518, 814920,00.html.

10. Krueger was speaking at a discussion on the euro-zone crisis, School for Advanced International Studies, Johns Hopkins University, Washington, D.C., on Nov. 8, 2011.

11. Jacques Delors, in forward to Sofia Fernandes and Eulalia Rubio, "Solidarity within the Eurozone: how much, what for, for how long?" *Notre Europe*, Feb. 14, 2012, www.notre-europe.eu.

12. Dassu was speaking at "Europe in Crisis: The Impact on Foreign Policy," Brookings Institution, Feb. 22, 2012.

13. Jean Pisani-Ferry, "The Eurozone's strategy of survival is also one of pain," *The Daily Star* (Lebanon), Feb. 15, 2012, www.dailystar.com.

14. Bağiş was speaking at the School of Advanced International Studies, Johns Hopkins University, March 18, 2011.

15. For background, see Sarah Glazer, "Radical Islam in Europe," *CQ Global Researcher*, Nov. 1, 2007, pp. 265-294.

16. The Bosnian constitution divides the country into the Republika Srpska (with a predominantly ethnic Serbian population) and the Bosniak-Croat Federation. For background, see Brian Beary, "Separatist Movements," *CQ Global Researcher*, April 1, 2008, pp. 85-114.

17. Speaking at a conference on Ukraine at The Peter G. Peterson Institute for International Economics, Washington, D.C., July 7, 2011.

18. Speaking at a conference, "The eurozone crisis, and why the United States of Europe remains the only answer to Europe's sovereign debt crisis," Center for Strategic and International Studies, Washington, D.C., Feb. 28, 2012.

19. Rasmussen, Wessels and Dinan were speaking at "The Maastricht Treaty: Taking Stock After 20 Years," Maastricht University, Feb. 7-8, 2012.

20. See Jost, *op. cit.*

21. Unless otherwise noted, the material in this section is from Martin Dedman, *The Origins and Development of the European Union 1945-2008: A History of European Integration* (2009).

22. See Sherrill Brown Wells, *Jean Monnet: Unconventional Statesman* (2011).

23. B. W. Patch, "European Economic Union," *Editorial Research Reports*, March 27, 1957, available at *CQ Researcher Plus Archive*.

24. For background, see Roland Flamini, "U.S.-Europe Relations," *CQ Researcher*, March 23, 2012, pp. 277-300.

25. Jost, *op. cit.*

26. The comments of Kok, Christophersen and Crespo were made during "The Maastricht Treaty: Taking Stock After 20 Years," *op. cit.*

27. For background, see Brian Beary, "The New Europe" *CQ Global Researcher*, Aug. 1, 2007, pp. 181-210.

28. Glazer, *op. cit.*

29. Fernandes and Rubio, *op. cit.*

30. Dedman, *op. cit.*, p. 166.

31. Jost, *op. cit.*

32. See Rosa Balfour, Alyson Bailes and Megan Kenna, "The European External Action Service at work — How to improve EU foreign policy," European Policy Centre, Jan. 25 2012, www.epc .eu/pub_details.php?cat_id=2&pub_id=1399& year=2012.

33. Presentation, "The Maastricht Treaty: Taking Stock After 20 Years," *op. cit.*

34. See Glazer, *op. cit.*

35. *Ibid.*

36. "EU adopts 'six-pack' fiscal reform plan," *Business World*, Sept. 28, 2011, www.businessworld.ie/livenews .htm?a=2839524.

37. "Demography Report 2010: Older, more numerous and diverse Europeans," Eurostat, European Commission, March 2011, p. 103, http://ec.europa .eu/social/main.jsp?catId=738&langId=en&pubId= 5936&type=2&furtherPubs=no.

38. "World Economic Outlook Update," International Monetary Fund, Jan. 24, 2012, www.imf.org/external/ pubs/ft/weo/2012/update/01/index.htm.

39. Press briefing, International Monetary Fund, Feb. 24, 2012.

40. Ambrose Evans-Pritchard, "Greek economy spirals down as EU forces final catharsis," *The Telegraph* (U.K.), Feb. 14, 2012, www.telegraph.co.uk/finance/financialcrisis/9082843/Greek-economy-spirals-down-as-EU-forces-final-catharsis.html.

41. Steve Kroft, "An Imperfect Union: Europe's debt crisis," "60 Minutes," CBS News, April 8, 2012, www.cbsnews.com/8301-18560_162-57410910/an-imperfect-union-europes-debt-crisis/?tag=contentMain;contentBody.

42. Remarks made during conference call discussion organized by The Atlantic Council, April 9, 2012, www.acus.org/event/austere-life-changing-nature-europes-politics-and-societies.

43. Frieden was speaking at The Atlantic Council, Washington, D.C., Feb. 13, 2012.

44. Sarah Collins, "Finance ministers announce trillion-dollar firewall," *Europolitics*, March 30, 2012, www.europolitics.info//europolitics/finance-ministers-announce-trillion-dollar-firewall-art330522-46.html.

45. Gavin Hewitt, "EU Summit: all but two sign EU fiscal treaty," BBC News, March 2, 2012, www.bbc.co.uk/news/world-europe-17230760.

46. A structural deficit occurs when a government spends more than it collects in tax revenue. It differs from "cyclical deficits" that typically occur during a recession, when tax revenues decline and governments tend to spend more for social programs, such as unemployment benefits.

47. See David Král, "Why the Czechs did not sign up to the fiscal treaty," Centre for European Policy Studies, Feb. 7, 2012, www.ceps.eu/book/why-czechs-did-not-sign-fiscal-treaty.

48. Presentation, Brookings Institution, Washington, D.C., Jan. 20, 2012.

49. Ilan Brat and David Roman, "Spain Jobless Claims Continue To Rise," *The Wall Street Journal*, April 3, 2012, http://online.wsj.com/article/SB10001424052702304023504577321123755918522.html.

50. Almunia made his remarks at an "EU Rendezvous" talk, organized by the EU Delegation to the United States, at DAR Constitution Hall, Washington, D.C., March 28, 2012.

51. Fernandes and Rubio, *op. cit.*

52. Presentation, Brookings Institution, *op. cit.*

53. Pöttering's remarks were made at a dinner reception organized by the Konrad Adenauer Stiftung, at the Hay-Adams Hotel in Washington, D.C., March 22, 2012.

54. Stokes, *op. cit.*

55. Paul Taylor, "Merkozy fights to prevent Merkollande," Reuters, Feb. 2, 2012, www.reuters.com/article/2012/02/07/us-eurozone-merkozy-idUSTRE8151EY20120207.

56. Suzanne Daley and Stephen Castle, "As European Union Beckons, Allure Fades for Wary Croatia," *The New York Times*, Jan. 17 2012.

57. Lajčák was speaking at a conference on EU and U.S. Balkans policy, Center for Strategic and International Studies, Nov. 22, 2011.

58. See Cristian Dan Preda, "Iceland, 29th Member State of the EU?" In Focus (European Peoples Party blog), March 12, 2012, www.eppgroup.eu/infocus/iceland_120312_en.asp.

59. See "World Economic Outlook Update," *op. cit.* The IMF says eurozone economies will contract by 0.5 percent in 2012.

60. "Transatlantic Trends 2011," *op. cit.*

61. See "Demography Report 2010," *op. cit.*, p. 59. For background, see Alan Greenblatt, "The Graying Planet," *CQ Global Researcher*, March 15, 2011, pp. 133-156.

62. Comments from "The Maastricht Treaty: Taking Stock After 20 Years," *op. cit.*

63. Verhofstadt was speaking at "The eurozone crisis, and why the United States of Europe remains the only answer to Europe's sovereign debt crisis," *op. cit.*

64. Brian Beary, "IMF: Despite slow recovery, 'optimism is in the air,'" *Europolitics*, Jan. 24, 2013, www.europolitics.info//economy-monetary-affairs/imf-despite-slow-recovery-optimism-is-in-the-air-art347431–29.html.

65. Carsten Volkery, "Monti's Uprising: How Italy and Spain Defeated Merkel at EU Summit," *Spiegel Online*, June 29, 2012, www.spiegel.de/international/europe/

merkel-makes-concessions-at-eu-summit-a-841663.html.

66. Emma Rowley, "Spain requests €39.5bn bank bail-out, but no state rescue" *The Telegraph* (UK), Dec. 3, 2012, www.telegraph.co.uk/finance/financial crisis/9719875/Spain-requests-39.5bn-bank-bail-out-but-no-state-rescue.html.

67. Sakari Suoninen, "ECB cuts rates to new low, no move on bolder measures," Reuters, July 5, 2012, http://www.reuters.com/article/2012/07/05/us-ecb-rates-idUSBRE86405K2012070.5

68. Ian Traynor, "ECB introduces unlimited bond-buying in boldest attempt yet to end euro crisis," *The Guardian* (UK), Sept. 6, 2012, www.guardian.co.uk/business/2012/sep/06/debt-crisis-mario-draghi

69. "Q&A: EU Budget Battle" BBC News, Feb. 8, 2013, www.bbc.co.uk/news/world-europe-20392793.

70. "Dutch election: Pro-Europe VVD and Labour parties win," BBC News, Sept. 13, 2012, http://www.bbc.co.uk/news/world-europe-19566165.

71. Helena Smith, "Greek election: scramble to form coalition to steer country through crisis," *The Guardian* (UK), June 17, 2012, www.guardian.co.uk/world/2012/jun/17/greek-election-coalition-crisis.

72. Andrew Grice, "Handbagged! David Cameron's promise of EU referendum by 2017 provokes storm of controversy," *The Independent* (UK), Jan. 24, 2013, www.independent.co.uk/news/uk/politics/handbagged-david-camerons-promise-of-eu-referendum-by-2017-provokes-storm-of-controversy-8463417.html.

73. Rebecca Christie, EU Approves Jobs, Growth Plan With 10 Billion-Euro EIB Boost, Bloomberg, June 28, 2012, http://www.bloomberg.com/news/2012–06–28/eu-approves-jobs-growth-plan-with-10-billion-euro-eib-boost.html.

74. "EU receives Nobel Peace Prize," CBC News, Dec. 10, 2012, http://www.cbc.ca/news/world/story/2012/12/10/nobel-peace-prize.html.

75. Philip Blenkinsop and Ethan Bilby, "EU, U.S. to start free trade talks," Reuters, Feb. 13, 2013, www.reuters.com/article/2013/02/13/us-eu-us-trade-idUSBRE91C00C20130213.

76. Saeed Kamali Dehgan and Julian Borger, "Iran's currency hits all-time low as western sanctions take their toll," *The Guardian* (UK), Oct. 1, 2012, www.guardian.co.uk/world/2012/oct/01/iran-currency-rial-all-time-low.

77. Judith Crosbie, "Irish, UK troops to deploy to Mali," *Irish Times,* Feb. 13, 2013, www.irishtimes.com/newspaper/breaking/2013/0213/breaking38.html.

BIBLIOGRAPHY
Selected Sources
Books

Dedman, Martin, *The Origins and Development of the European Union 1945-2008: A History of European Integration*, Routledge, 2009.
A former senior lecturer at Middlesex University (1970-2007) gives a succinct, easy-to-read account of how European integration developed following World War II.

Dinan, Desmond, *Ever Closer Union: An Introduction to European Integration*, Lynne Rienner Pub, 2010.
A public policy professor at George Mason University outlines how the European Union (EU) came about and how it functions.

Geary, Michael, *The European Commission and the First Enlargement of the European Union: Challenging for Power*, Palgrave Macmillan, 2012.
A history professor at Maastricht University in the Netherlands examines the history of the EU's executive arm, the European Commission, as well as the EU's early efforts at enlargement.

Hamilton, Daniel S., and Robert M. Solow, eds., *Europe's Economic Crisis — Transatlantic Perspectives*, Center for Transatlantic Relations, School of Advanced International Studies (SAIS), Johns Hopkins University, 2011.
Edited by the director of the Center for Transatlantic Relations at SAIS (Hamilton) and a Nobel Prize-winning professor of economics at the Massachusetts Institute of Technology (Solow), this collection of essays charts the origins of Europe's current economic crisis, which has imperiled the future of the single currency — one of the cornerstones of European integration.

Articles

Kral, David, "Why the Czechs did not sign up to the fiscal treaty," Centre for European Policy Studies, Feb. 7, 2012, www.ceps.eu/book/why-czechs-did-not-sign-fiscal-treaty.

The director of EUROPEUM (the Institute for European Policy in Prague) explains why the Czech Republic chose to team up with the United Kingdom to become the only two EU member states not to sign the fiscal treaty adopted by EU leaders in December.

Krellinger, Valentin, "The making of a new treaty: Six rounds of political bargaining," *Notre Europe*, Policy Brief No. 32, February 2012, www.notre-europe .eu/uploads/tx_publication/NewTreaty_V.Kreilinger_ NE_Feb2012.pdf.

A researcher at Notre Europe, a pro-EU integration think tank, explains how the fiscal treaty signed by 25 EU member states in March 2012 ended up taking the form that it did.

Pisani-Ferry, Jean, "The Eurozone's strategy of survival is also one of pain," *The Daily Star* (Lebanon), Feb. 15, 2012, www.dailystar.com.lb/Opinion/ Commentary/2012/Feb-15/163307-the-eurozones-strategy-of-survival-is-also-one-of-pain.ashx#axzz1n3 Okeh6t.

The director of Bruegel, an international economics think tank, argues that Greece's financial problems are exceptional and ultimately will not bring down the entire European economy.

Stokes, Bruce, "What Europeans Think About the Eurocrisis," German Marshall Fund of the United States, Feb. 1, 2012, www.gmfus.org/wp-content/files_mf/ stokes_whateuropeansthink_jan12.pdf.

A senior fellow at a German government-funded foundation that promotes transatlantic relations charts how the European public has recently lost some of its enthusiasm for EU integration as the economic crisis has shaken their confidence in the union.

Reports and Studies

"Demography report 2010 — Older, more numerous and diverse Europeans," Eurostat, European Commission, May 20, 2011, http://ec.europa.eu/social/main.jsp?cat Id=738&langId=en&pubId=5936&type=2&furtherP ubs=no.

The European Union's statistical agency provides a comprehensive report on the present demographic makeup of the EU.

"Eurobarometer 76 — Public Opinion in the European Union — First Results," European Commission, December 2011, http://ec.europa.eu/public_opinion/ archives/eb/eb76/eb76_en.htm.

The EU Commission's unit responsible for public opinion analysis publishes one of its regular surveys on what Europeans' current attitudes are toward the EU.

"World Economic Outlook Update," International Monetary Fund, Jan. 24, 2012, www.imf.org/external/ pubs/ft/weo/2012/update/01/index.htm.

The latest IMF forecasts predict a brief recession for the EU in 2012, following its modest economic recovery in 2010 and 2011.

Gill, Indermit, and Martin Raiser, "Golden Growth: Restoring the Lustre of the European Economic Model," World Bank, Jan. 24, 2012, http://web .worldbank.org/WBSITE/EXTERNAL/COUNTRIES/ ECAEXT/0,,contentMDK:23069550~pagePK:146736 ~piPK:146830~theSitePK:258599,00. html.

The authors argue that despite its lack of competitiveness in particular regions, the EU overall has been an economic success story.

For More Information

Center for Transatlantic Relations, School of Advanced International Studies (SAIS), Johns Hopkins University, 1717 Massachusetts Ave., N.W., #525, Washington, DC 20036; 202-663-5880; http://transatlantic.sais-jhu.edu. One of the leading centers for European Union (EU) integration studies in the United States.

Center on the United States and Europe, Brookings Institution, 1775 Massachusetts Ave., N.W., Washington, DC 20036; 202-797-6000; www.brookings.edu/cuse. The European studies division of Brookings, a Washington think tank.

Centre for European Policy Studies (CEPS), Place du Congres 1, B-1000 Brussels, Belgium; +32 2 229 3911; www.ceps .be. One of the leading EU policy think tanks in Brussels.

Delegation of the European Union to the USA, 2175 K St., N.W., Washington, DC 20037; 202-862-9500; www.eurunion .org/eu. The EU's American office, responsible for fostering good relations between the EU and the U.S. government and public.

The European Institute, 1001 Connecticut Ave., N.W., Washington, DC 20036; 202-895-1970; www.european institute.org. The leading Washington-based public policy organization devoted solely to trans-Atlantic affairs.

Friends of Europe, Bibliotheque Solvay, Parc Leopold, rue Belliard 137, B-1040 Brussels, Belgium; +32 2 737 9145; www.friendsofeurope.org. A European think tank that aims to stimulate thinking about the future of the EU.

German Marshall Fund of the United States, 1744 R St., N.W., Washington, DC 20009; 202-683-2650; www.gmfus .org. An organization established by the German government in 1972 to promote trans-Atlantic relations.

Margaret Thatcher Center for Freedom, The Heritage Foundation, 214 Massachusetts Ave., N.W., Washington, DC 20002; 202-546-4400; www.thatchercenter.org. The trans-Atlantic relations division of the conservative think tank; provides a more euro-skeptic outlook than Brookings or SAIS.

Robert Schuman Foundation, 29, Boulevard Raspail, F-75007 Paris, France; +33 1 53 63 83 00; and at 40 rue des Drapiers/Lakenweversstraat 40, B-1050 Brussels; +32 2 5024713; www.robert-schuman.eu. A reference research center that researches the EU and its policies from its offices in Brussels and Paris.

Voices From Abroad:

ALEXANDER STUBB

Foreign Minister, Finland

Forgetfulness amid crisis

"I think the Western Balkans is one of the most strategic and important enlargements that we have in the EU. We just have a tendency to forget the importance of enlargement in the midst of the financial crisis."

DPA News Agency (Germany), February 2012

CATHERINE ASHTON

Vice President, European Commission and EU High Representative for Foreign Affairs and Security

Commitment to democracy

"The European Union was the first to offer a serious response to the Arab Spring. This new set of decisions is the result of the new and ambitious European Neighborhood Policy, launched in May, and it confirms that the EU has made it one of its main priorities to support 'deep' and sustainable democracy, but also economic recovery, in North Africa and the Middle East."

Trend News Agency (Azerbaijan), September 2011

ANGELA MERKEL

Chancellor, Germany

Crisis leading to renewal

"This [establishing central fiscal authority] is the breakthrough to the stability union. We are using the crisis as an opportunity for a renewal."

New Zealand Herald, December 2011

IVO JOSIPOVIĆ

President, Croatia

Only a first step

"The news that the European Commission has concluded that Croatia meets European Union membership

Sweden/*Svenska Dagbladet*/Riber Hansson

requirements and that it should become a member on 1 July 2013 is excellent news for Croatia and all its citizens. . . . We also need reforms that go beyond the European Union's demand, and we will also need to adjust to the new standards of the European Union, which is constantly upgrading and changing."

HINA News Agency (Croatia), June 2011

AHMET DAVUTOGLU

Foreign Minister, Turkey

Double jeopardy

"If the Greek Cypriot side stalls negotiations and takes over the presidency of the EU in July 2012, this means not only a deadlock on the island, but also a blockage, a freezing point in Turkey-European Union relations."

Daily Star (Lebanon), July 2011

SONY KAPOOR

Managing Director Re-Define (think tank), England

Austerity abounds

"In the absence of sufficient public support, troubled EU economies continue to face gut-wrenching austerity.... While austerity may help restore competitiveness for small, open economies — as it did for Sweden in the early 1990s — it will fail when applied to an economic area the size of the EU."

The Observer (England), December 2011

JOSCHKA FISCHER

Foreign Minister, Germany

Lacking leadership

"For the first time in its history, the very continuance of the European project is at stake. And yet the behavior of the European Union and its most important member states has been irresolute and dithering. This is owing to national egotism and a breathtaking absence of leadership."

Daily Star (Lebanon), July 2011

PAWEL SWIEBODA

President demosEUROPA (think tank), Poland

Addressing legitimacy

"The legitimacy question is the issue that will come back to haunt EU leaders if they don't address it properly. Getting citizens on board for these new fiscal solutions won't be easy."

The Guardian (England), September 2011

8

Rising Tension Over Iran

Roland Flamini

Two Iranian protesters try to pry a British coat of arms from the wall surrounding the British Embassy in Tehran, as rioters stormed the facility on Nov. 29, 2011. The assault recalled the 1979 attack and hostage-taking at the American Embassy in the same city. The November mob was protesting Britain's agreement to support beefed-up Western sanctions on Iran over its disputed nuclear program.

From *The CQ Researcher*,
February 7, 2012 (updated February 14, 2013).

In August 2012, the Saudi Arabian state-owned oil company Aramco was temporarily put out of action by one of the most destructive computer sabotage actions on a company to date. A cyber virus which experts said was named Shamoon wiped out the data on more than 30,000 of Aramco's corporate PCs, replacing all the e-mails and information with an image of a burning American flag.[1]

Then in January 2013, the website services of Capital One, a Mclean, Va.-based bank were blocked for more than a day after self-proclaimed Islamist hackers put the site out of action. Hackers calling themselves al-Qassam Cyber Fighters said they had attacked Capital One – as they had earlier claimed responsibility for attacking a string of U.S. financial institutions, including Bank of America, JPMorgan Chase, and U.S. Bank. But U.S. intelligence officials said Iran had sponsored the bank attacks and was also behind the Aramco operation.[2]

One reason Iran was blamed for Aramco: the most destructive element in Shamoon—the memory-erasing mechanism—was called Wiper. But Wiper was also the name given to the similar agent in Flame, a computer virus that had been siphoning off data from Iran's oil industry for years, before Iranians finally discovered it in May, 2012.

Because both Flame and Stuxnet, a cyber virus that destroyed 1,000 centrifuges in an Iranian nuclear facility in 2010, are widely believed to have been launched by the United States and Israel, experts suspect that the Aramco attack was Iran's retaliation.[3]

The United States and Iran have been bitter rivals for influence in the Middle East since the 1979 embassy hostage crisis when hard line

Tensions Rise in Volatile Gulf Region

The wars in Iraq and Afghanistan have garnered most of the world's attention in the past decade. But with the fighting in those countries winding down, the spotlight is turning to their neighbor — Alaska-size Iran. The Western powers worry that Iran is developing weapons at its numerous nuclear facilities, some buried deep underground, which Iran says are strictly for peaceful purposes. In an effort to force Iran to halt its nuclear program, the European Union on Jan. 23 voted to join with the United States in embargoing Iranian oil exports. Iran responded by threatening to close the crucial Strait of Hormuz, located in the Persian Gulf on Iran's southern border, through which nearly 40 percent of the world's seaborne oil is shipped.

Types of Nuclear Facilities in Iran

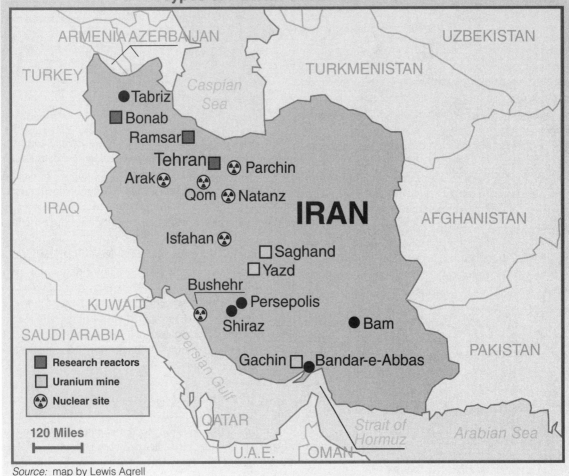

Source: map by Lewis Agrell

supporters of Iran's new Islamic Revolution stormed the American Embassy in Tehran and took 52 staffers and Marines hostage for 444 days. The U.S. has imposed increasingly crippling sanctions on Iran and suspects that

Iran is seeking to produce weapons of mass destruction. Now decades of animosity have escalated into cyber attacks.

At the same time, Iran has escalated "a kind of insidious interference" in Iraq, Lebanon, and Syria, says

Alanoud Al Sharekh, Bahrain-based senior research fellow of the International Institute of Strategic Studies (IISS), a leading London think tank. In the Gulf, it competes for dominance with Saudi Arabia. "Iran is pushing itself as an alternative Islamic leader," she says. In Iraq, the Iranians support the country's Shi'ite majority; in Lebanon, Tehran operates through Hezbollah, the fundamentalist Shiite military and political organization which the U.S. State Department lists as a terrorist group, and in the Syrian uprising, President Bashar al-Assad has active Iranian support in the shape of weapons and—it's said — fighters.

But the dominant question remains whether the ruling ayatollahs of the Iranian clerical regime plan to arm themselves with nuclear weapons, and what the West can do about it. "Iran almost surely does not possess nuclear weapons, and there is no evidence Iran has made a decision to produce nuclear weapons," says Mark Fitzpatrick, who follows nuclear disarmament issues at IISS. But "it seems clear that Iran aims to possess the capability to quickly produce nuclear weapons should it make the fateful decision to do so," adds Fitzpatrick who also points out that Iran's spiritual leader, Ayatollah Ali Khamenei, has said nuclear weapons are *haram*, meaning sinful and therefore forbidden, but it's not clear whether the prohibition extends to nuclear capability.

After keeping the Iranian nuclear conundrum on the back burner during the presidential campaign, President Barack Obama starts his second term facing a defiant regime still locked in a course of nuclear expansion, and impervious to threats, coercion, and diplomacy. This defiance continues in spite of escalating U.S.-led economic sanctions imposed by an exceptionally unified West. Ayatollah Khamenei recently rejected any prospect of direct bi-lateral talks with the United States while America was "pointing a gun at Iran." The Obama Administration mistakenly thinks "that the nation has been exhausted by the sanctions," he said.[4]

While Iran's talks with the United States, China, Russia, Britain, France, and Germany (known in

Iran at a Glance

The Islamic Republic of Iran is the size of Alaska but with a population that is three times that of Texas. It has a predominantly Persian population and a Shiite theocracy, surrounded by mostly Sunni-dominated countries with Arab populations. Iran's per capita income is on a par with South Africa's.

Quick Facts About Iran

Area: 636,371 sq. miles (about the size of Alaska)

Population: 77,891,220* (about the same as Turkey, or three times the population of Texas)

Chief of state: Supreme Leader Sayyid Ali Khamenei (since June 1989)

Head of government: President Mahmoud Ahmadinejad (since August 2005)

Government type: Theocratic republic; Supreme Leader appointed for life by the Assembly of Experts; president elected by popular vote for up to two four-year terms; legislative members elected by popular vote for four-year terms

Ethnic groups: Persian 61%, Azeri 16%, Kurd 10%, Lur 6%, Baloch 2%, Arab 2%, Turkmen and Turkic tribes 2%, other 1% (2008 est.)

Religion: Muslim (official religion) 98% (Shiite 89%, Sunni 9%), other (includes Zoroastrian, Jewish, Christian and Baha'i) 2%

Infant mortality rate: 42.26 deaths/1,000 live births (60th in the world)

GDP: $818.7 billion**

GDP per capita: $10,600** (about the same as South Africa)

Unemployment rate: 13.2%**

Industries: petroleum, petrochemicals, fertilizers, caustic soda, textiles, cement and other construction materials, food processing, metal fabrication, armaments

* *July 2011 estimate*

** *2010 estimate*

Source: The World Factbook, Central Intelligence Agency, 2012, https://www.cia.gov/library/publications/the-world-factbook/geos/ir.html.

Iranian Women Lost Rights Under the Mullahs

One Million Signatures Campaign seeks major changes.

During the Arab Spring uprisings last year, Iranian women's groups circulated a cautionary video, "Message from Iranian Women for Tunisian and Egyptian Women." The film depicted how Iranian women's lives changed dramatically after the Islamic Revolution of 1979 and warned Tunisian and Egyptian women that the same thing could happen to them if the religious party, the Muslim Brotherhood, gained majorities in their countries.[1]

During the reign of Shah Reza Pahlavi, Iranian women had made progress in the traditionally male-oriented region. They wore whatever they wanted in public and have been allowed to vote since 1963.

Under the ayatollahs, however, the *hijab* — the headscarf worn by Muslim women — immediately became mandatory, and Islamic law was introduced and strictly enforced.[2] For example, the minimum age of marriage for women was changed from 18 to nine — although it has since been raised to 13 after protests by activists.

Polygamy has increased, as has the so-called temporary marriage (*mut'a*), a verbal, short-term relationship for a predetermined period, with no divorce necessary to end it. Permitted under Shiite Muslim law, the *mut'a* is seen by many as prostitution under another name, because a dowry is one of its prerequisites.*[3]

The changes helped to spark the One Million Signatures Campaign, a grass-roots Iranian feminist effort to convince Iran's parliament to change marriage, divorce, custody, and inheritance laws that discriminate against women.

The movement also wants to improve the legal position of women who are sex-crime victims. A married Iranian woman who is raped is considered to have committed adultery and can be stoned to death. If she kills her aggressor, she can be

---

* Depending on the culture, a dowry is the money or property that a bride's family pays to the groom's family or that a groom pays to a bride.

tried for murder. If she is unmarried, she could end up being killed by a male family member to avoid bringing shame on the family name. Such so-called honor killings are more a patriarchal custom than a practice condoned by the Quran.[4]

But that's not the full picture, according to Sussan Tahmasebi, an American-born Iranian who helped launch the campaign. "We have female doctors, we have politicians, MPs (members of parliament)," she said. "It's paradoxical that, despite these achievements, discrimination against women is embedded in the legal system, and that lawmakers justify it by saying it's based on religion."[5]

However, CNN broadcaster and columnist Fareed Zakaria says Iranian women fare better than women in Saudi Arabia. He was struck while on a recent visit, he writes, "by how defiantly [Iranian] women try to lead normal and productive lives. They wear the headscarves and adhere to the rules about covering their bodies, but do so in a very stylish way. They continue to go to college in large numbers, to graduate school and to work."[6]

Iranian women can vote, he added, while women in Saudi Arabia —"another country . . . run along strict Islamic lines" — cannot. And in Saudi Arabia, he noted, women "are not well integrated into the workforce or mainstream life."[7]

Even so, Iranian women face a litany of constraints. A daughter still needs her father's permission to marry; a wife must obtain her husband's written permission to travel abroad or get a passport. An Iranian woman can't sing in public or attend sports events where men are present.

In 1979, thousands of women protested in the streets against the shah — only to be repressed by Ayatollah Ruhollah Khomeini as soon as he assumed power. In 2009, women were a strong presence in the "Green" protests against the disputed re-election of President Mahmoud Ahmadinejad. Neda Agha Soltan, a 26-year-old music student, was shot dead in a Tehran street during the demonstrations. The bloody video of her death went viral on the

---

diplomatic parlance as the 5+1) continue periodically, though with little progress to show for them, the International Atomic Energy Agency, which monitors nuclear proliferation on behalf of the United Nations, said in February that Tehran had refused a request to allow an on-site inspection of one of Iran's nuclear sites.

Iran has consistently claimed that its nuclear development is for peaceful purposes, and if the Iranians develop a nuclear weapon, it would violate the U.N. Nuclear Nonproliferation Treaty (NPT), which Tehran signed in 1968. It would also change the strategic equation in the Middle East, an unstable

Internet, making her what *The New York Times* called "the public face" of those who died in the protests.[8]

In 2002, the European Union lobbied to help persuade the Iranian courts to declare a moratorium on death by stoning, of either gender. The moratorium was extended in 2008 — although according to reports, four men and one woman were executed by stoning, a method usually reserved for convicted adulterers. In 2008, a spokesman for the judiciary confirmed that two of the men had been stoned, saying that the moratorium had no legal weight, and judges could ignore it. However, draft legislation to abolish death by stoning is being considered.[9]

The United Nations also has pressured Iran to reform its discriminatory laws, most of which violate the U.N.'s 1979 Convention of the Elimination of All Forms of Discrimination Against Women, which the mullahs say undermines Islamic teaching.[10]

The regime is particularly vigilant with regard to cultural activities. In 2011, the Iranian actress Marzieh Vafamehr was sentenced to a year in jail and 90 lashes for her role in the film "My Tehran for Sale," an internationally acclaimed underground movie about life in Tehran. She was never lashed, however, and was released after serving three months.[11]

It was a case of life imitating art. Vafamehr played a young theater actress trying to pursue her career against the backdrop of Iran's repressive regime. But the film's director, the Australian-Iranian poet Granaz Moussavi, says the movie, which was filmed in Iran, actually had the regime's approval.

"Nobody can deny that we are working with restrictions when it comes to writing and film making," she says. "But in Iran, and especially in Tehran, everything can be risky, even crossing the road."

— *Roland Flamini*

Female supporters of Mir Hossein Mousavi, Iran's reformist candidate in the 2009 presidential election, show off their fingers and nails — painted green, the color of Mousavi's campaign — during a Tehran rally on June 9, 2009. Iranian women, who have been able to vote since before the 1979 Islamic Revolution, played a big part in the so-called Green Movement — anti-government demonstrations that challenged Mousavi's defeat by President Mahmoud Ahmadinejad. The movement was brutally suppressed by the government.

[1] Dina Sadek, "Women in Egypt Heed Warning From Iranian Women on Rights," Global Press Institute, Jan. 10, 2012, www.globalpressinstitute.org/global-news/africa/egypt/women-egypt-heed-warning-iranian-women-rights.

[2] For background, see Sarah Glazer, "Sharia Controversy," *CQ Global Researcher*, Jan. 3, 2012, pp. 1-28.

[3] Donna M. Hughes, "Women in Iran: A look at President Khatami's first year in office," *Z Magazine*, October 1998, www.uri.edu/artsci/wms/hughes/khatami.htm.

[4] For background, see Robert Kiener, "Honor Killings," *CQ Global Researcher*, April 19, 2011, pp. 183-208.

[5] "Fighting for Women's Rights," Human Rights Watch, Oct. 11, 2011, www.hrw.org/news/2011/10/31/fighting-women-s-rights-iran.

[6] Fareed Zakaria, "Zakaria: Comparing the status of women in Iran and Saudi Arabia," CNN.com, Dec. 27, 2011, http://globalpublicsquare.blogs.cnn.com/2011/10/27/zakaria-comparing-the-status-of-women-in-iran-and-saudi-arabia% E2%80%A8/.

[7] *Ibid.*

[8] Nazla Fathi, "In a death seen around the world, a symbol of Iranian protests," *The New York Times*, June 22, 2009, www.nytimes.com/2009/06/23/world/middle east/23neda.html.

[9] "Chaknews" (Iranian human rights blog), undated, www.chaknews.com/Eng lish/print.php?type=N&item_id=365.

[10] Christina Hoff Sommers, "Feminism by Treaty," American Enterprise Institute, June 1, 2011, www.aei.org/article/society-and-culture/race-and-gender/feminism-by-treaty/.

[11] "Concerns Iran film star Marzieh Vafamehr 'to be lashed,' " BBC News, Nov. 11, 2011, www.bbc.co.uk/news/world-asia-pacific-15262071.

region on which the industrialized world depends for its oil lifeline.

"This is not a question of [Middle Eastern] security," declared German Foreign Minister Guido Westerwelle. "It is a question of the whole world." Israel, the Middle East's sole nuclear power, strongly opposes Iran joining the nuclear club, given Tehran's open hostility to the Jewish state. Indeed, Israel sees a nuclear-armed Iran as an existential threat, and an Israeli strike against Iran's nuclear sites has been openly discussed in Israel for more than two years; but the Obama administration has pressed a seemingly reluctant Israeli Prime Minister

Most Iranian Oil Ends Up in Asia

Nearly two-thirds of the 2.2 million barrels of oil exported daily by Iran goes to Asia, with one-fifth of it destined for China. Asian buyers have not signed onto new, tougher sanctions against Iranian oil purchases — imposed by the European Union on Jan. 23. For that reason, some observers doubt that the new restrictions will succeed in forcing Iran to halt its uranium enrichment program, seen as a possible precursor to the development of nuclear weapons.

Destinations of Iranian Oil Exports, 2010

Other 28%
China 20%
Japan 17%
India 16%
Italy 10%
South Korea 9%

Source: U.S. Energy Information Administration, November 2011, www.eia.gov/countries/cab.cfm?fips=IR

Benjamin Netanyahu to give sanctions a chance to work. Last summer, the Jerusalem Post quoted Netanyahu as saying that an Israeli action against Iran was worth considering even if it did not completely destroy the Iranian nuclear program. The attack would buy time that could perhaps bring change in Iran.[5]

Moreover, the United States apparently hasn't ruled out a strike of its own. Concerned for the stability of the region and pressured by Israel and its supporters in Congress, two successive U.S. presidents have repeatedly said a nuclear Iran was "unacceptable" and that — as President Obama warned during his Jan. 24, 2012, State of the Union address —"no options" are off the table.

Going nuclear would boost Iran's ambition to be a major international player. Some argue that it also would enable Iran to wreak havoc, by, for instance, giving a portable nuclear device to one of its proxies, such as the Lebanese Shiite fundamentalist movement, Hezbollah or the radical Palestinian Sunni party, Hamas, which controls the Gaza Strip. Both groups are yet listed as terrorist organizations by Washington.

Neighboring Arabs aren't crazy about the idea of the region's two non-Arab countries having the only nuclear weapons in the Middle East. If Iran gets the bomb,

warned Prince Turki Al-Faisal Al Saud, former head of Saudi Arabian intelligence, it would "unleash a cascade of [nuclear] proliferation that would significantly destabilize the region."[6]

But while the Sunni Saudis would certainly want to match the nuclear capability of their Shiite regional rival, most experts believe an arms race would be unlikely. "No countries went nuclear after Israel went nuclear, so why would they want to now?" asks Iran specialist Vali Nasr, a professor of international politics at the Fletcher School of Law and Diplomacy at Tufts University in Medford, Mass.

Iran insists it is enriching uranium for only peaceful purposes, such as power generation. According to an IAEA Nov 2012 report, Iran has stockpiled 134 kg of uranium enriched to 20 percent level that can relatively quickly be further enriched to weapons grade—90 percent. This is considerably short of the 220 – 250 kg of 20 percent enriched uranium required to produce one bomb, leading the Washington-based, nonpartisan Arms Control Association to conclude that "Iran remains years, not months away from having a workable nuclear arsenal, if it were to choose to pursue that capability."[7]

But Frederick W. Kagan, a defense and security specialist at the conservative American Enterprise Institute, a Washington think tank, contends there is no question Iran wants the bomb. "The Iranian regime intends to acquire nuclear weapons," he says, "and it's bizarre that we continue to say, 'Well, maybe they don't mean it.'"

Still, others aren't so sure. David Aaron, who tracks Iran developments for the RAND Corporation think tank in Palo Alto, Calif., says, "The picture is one of a country that has technology and some physical capacity to produce nuclear weapons, but they still haven't taken the next step of stockpiling material capable of being turned into nuclear weapons. There seems to be internal disagreement in the Iranian leadership on the issue."

In February 2013, the U.S. further tightened sanctions, making it even harder for Iran to receive its oil revenues: metal producers were also barred from doing business with Iran to hit Iran's automobile and other industries. The previous July, the 27 members of the European Union had put into effect a ban on Iranian oil imports. The EU also froze the Iran central bank's assets in Europe and banned transactions involving gold, precious metals, and diamonds. The measures amounted to "an unprecedented package of sanctions on Iran," said a joint statement issued by the British, German, and French leaders.

The regime's insistence that its program is for peaceful purposes has "helped to build up support domestically for the nuclear program, and everyone is committed as a matter of national pride," says Riccardo Alcaro, a foreign policy analyst at the Italian Institute of International Affairs in Rome. "If the regime was now seen to be producing nuclear weapons, it would lose credibility with its own people. Crossing that threshold would be difficult — unless Iran were attacked. In that case, Iranians would be much more understanding."

As the West and Iran's neighbors fret over the nuclear threat posed by the Iranian regime, here are some of the questions being debated:

Can economic sanctions stop Iran from building a nuclear weapon?

The United States first launched sanctions against Iran in 1979 and has been tightening the economic screws ever since. In 2006, in an effort to force fuller compliance with the IAEA, the U.N. Security Council adopted the first of four economic sanctions resolutions. (*See sidebar, p. 196.*) Iran's oil and gas exports, the mainstay of its exports which once accounted for three-quarters of its foreign revenue, have been hard hit by the sanctions. Iranian oil revenue has been slashed from 2.2 million barrels a day in 2011 to 1 million barrels in Feb 2013 at a cost of $40 billion in lost revenue, the Iranian rial dropped two-thirds of its value against the U.S. dollar. Unemployment has risen as demand for consumer goods has fallen and workers were laid off in the manufacturing sector.[8]

Iran today finds it increasingly difficult "to do business with any reputable bank internationally" or to conduct transactions in either euros or U.S. dollars,

said White House national security official Tommy Vietor.[9] But author Robin Wright, an Iran specialist, says, "There is no indication that all these pressures, tight as they are, have yet forced a fundamental change in the thinking of the Iranian Republic. And there's the question, "At what point does the cost become too high?"

Despite the economic pressure, Iran's nuclear program is well advanced, and progress — while slow at times — has never halted for very long. "Sanctions haven't failed in squeezing Iran and making it suffer, but they have failed in their objective" to halt Iran's enrichment program, says Middle East specialist Nasr of Tufts University.

But Iran's sanctions net is still riddled with Asian holes. For example, China imported a fifth of Iran's oil exports in 2010, and Japan bought 17 percent of Iran's oil in 2010. India bought another 16 percent and South Korea, 9 percent. By comparison, Italy bought 10 percent in 2010.[10]

Hence the skepticism is rife that the sanctions won't work. "Sanctions tend to punish citizens more than they do the regime," observes Kuwait-based Alanoud Al Sharekh. But that's partly the point, said a senior administration official. "The question is whether people in the government feel pressure from the fact that there's public discontent," the unnamed official told *The Washington Post* recently.[11]

That isn't happening, according to Al Sharekh. "In spite of the problems, there's belief in the [Iranian] leadership and the ideology," she says.

Russia, which opposes the sanctions, called the latest EU action a mistake. "Under this kind of pressure, Iran will not agree to any kind of concessions or change in its policies," the Russian Foreign Ministry said in a statement.[12]

Would a nuclear Iran trigger an arms race in the Middle East?

Last year, President Obama said "It will not be tolerable to a number of states in that region for Iran to have a nuclear weapon and them not to have a nuclear weapon." The outcome, he predicted, would be "a free-for-all in the Middle East."

The U.S. National Intelligence Council expressed the same concern in its "Global Trends 2025" report. A

Demonstrators hold portraits of assassinated Iranian nuclear scientist Majid Shahriari during a protest in front of the British Embassy in downtown Tehran on Dec. 12, 2010. At least five Iranian nuclear scientists have been killed in recent years in an apparent effort to slow Iran's nuclear program. Iranians have blamed the killings on British, U.S., or Israeli intelligence services.

nuclear Iran, it said, could well encourage other nations "to consider their own nuclear ambitions."[13]

Shmuel Bar, director of studies at the Institute of Policy Studies think tank in Herzliya, Israel, asked the question: Could "a polynuclear Middle East be avoided in the wake of Iran's acquisition of nuclear weapons?" The answer, he concluded, "seems to be clearly negative." Rather, he wrote, a nuclear Iran would "undoubtedly intensify the drive of other states in the region for nuclear weapons."[14] Those who agree with this scenario more frequently mention Egypt, Turkey, and Saudi Arabia as the most likely countries in the region to want to arm themselves with nuclear weapons.

But there's an opposite view that fear of a nuclear free-for-all are unfounded. The threat of nuclear proliferation is "more a talking point than a reality," says Tufts University's Nasr. "No Middle East countries went nuclear when Israel went nuclear. Egypt and Turkey would have no motivation to follow suit. Besides, it takes time to build up a nuclear arsenal of say 20 to 30 nuclear warheads — perhaps 10 years or more."

Some experts point out that when Communist China went nuclear in the 1950s, Beijing's neighbors were dissuaded from following suit because the United States offered to protect them from a nuclear attack.

The same thing happened after North Korea developed nuclear weapons.

But that approach was less likely to work in this instance, argues Bar, because of "the decline of American stature in the region after the withdrawal from Iraq" — and Washington's apparent failure, at least so far, to keep Iran from developing nuclear weapons.

A new report refutes this, arguing that the new Muslim Brotherhood government in Egypt was not likely to view a nuclear Iran as a threat, and moreover was "highly unlikely to divert scarce financial resources, put its peace agreement with Israel at risk, and invite the ire of the international community by pursuing nuclear weapons."[15] Turkey could probably afford a nuclear deterrent, the report goes on, but as a member of NATO is more likely to rely on the alliance's nuclear umbrella.[16]

However, many think the predominantly Sunni Saudis would likely want to assume a more responsive posture to a nuclear-armed Shiite Iran. In June 2012, Prince Turki told NATO officials that if Iran developed nuclear weapons, Saudi Arabia would have no choice but to do likewise, according to a British press report.[17] If the Saudis engaged in a race to produce the bomb "it could make the kingdom's strategic commitment worse," says the report, and "complicate the kingdom's national security, risk a strategic rupture with the United States," and harm Saudi Arabia's world reputation.[18]

But there's another alternative for Saudi Arabia, which does not involve having to its own bombs, says Kagan of the American Enterprise Institute, quoting a long-standing (but never confirmed) belief. "It could order them from Pakistan," he says. "The Saudis financed the Pakistani stockpile," which amounts to having "purchased" them.

Is military action against Iran inevitable?

"No doubt there is a danger there, but the Obama administration doesn't want to go there," says Iran expert Nasr, at Tufts University. And anyway "we may have passed the point" when attacking the Iranian nuclear facilities will make any lasting difference. The danger, he says, is from "the chances of war happening as a result of escalating the sanctions."

Both the Obama administration, with its action against the Iran central bank, and the European Union with its Iran oil embargo, have ratcheted up the sanctions to a level that might cause too much economic pain, potentially forcing the Iranians to take military action.

Tehran's threats to close the Strait of Hormuz are one result, says Nasr. Not that the Iranians would deliberately take on the U.S. Navy: Some covert action through surrogates in Afghanistan or Pakistan is more likely. But an incident in the strait could spark a shooting war; and mines and small gunboats could do a lot of damage before American warships asserted their superiority.

Furthermore, U.S. spy chiefs warned Congress in Jan. 2012 that, if pushed hard enough, Iran might launch terrorist attacks inside the United States. They said an alleged plot, uncovered October, 2012, to assassinate the Saudi Arabian ambassador in Washington might foreshadow other attempts.

"Sanctions were once enthusiastically embraced because they were free and stable, but they have become a factor of instability," Nasr says.

Others recommend more aggressive action by the West. The United States should "conduct a surgical strike against Iran's nuclear facilities, pull back and absorb the inevitable round of retaliation and then seek to quickly de-escalate the crisis," says Matthew Kroenig, an assistant professor of government at Georgetown University and a fellow of the Council on Foreign Relations. Prior to the attack, he adds, the United States would embark on a diplomatic effort to assure the Iranians that the strike was not an attempt to destroy the regime.

But even he concedes that military action is unlikely to halt Iran's nuclear program. At best it will "significantly" set it back from three to 10 years, "buying a lot more time for diplomacy."

For the Israelis, however, waiting for sanctions to succeed means time is running out for a pre-emptive strike. "It is still possible from the Israeli point of view to launch an attack within a few months," says Israeli military commentator Ron Ben-Yishai. While the nuclear facility in Natanz is vulnerable to air assault with penetration bombs, a newer facility near the holy city of Qom — built up to 450 feet deep inside a mountain —"is not so susceptible to air strike," he says, even with bunker-busting bombs. And the Iranians are moving their main uranium-enrichment operation to that underground site.

Unlike the Iraqi or Syrian nuclear facilities — both of which the Israelis bombed out of existence — a unilateral attack on the Iranian facilities would not be "an easy option," says Nasr, because Iran's facilities are widespread and would require "sustained aerial bombing."

Indeed, Iran's nuclear program is spread across a country the size of Britain and Germany combined, says Alcaro, of the Institute of International Affairs in Rome. Thus, no one thinks an attack will destroy the program, he says. Rather than deterring the Iranians, "The program is more likely to go forward underground," he contends.

Should the United States and/or Israel attack Iran, they likely would become locked into "a cycle of facing the same problem every three to 10 years," Alcaro adds. The only reason to attempt an attack would be to weaken the regime so as to create the conditions for a coup or insurrection that would install a government more responsive to U.S. demands, he says. But that probably won't happen, he adds, because, "the nuclear program is an issue of national pride; even a reformist government acceptable to the West would still want one."

Thus, a surgical strike, says Nasr, would probably only "encourage the Iranians to accelerate their program."

And Denis Bauchard, Middle East specialist at the French Institute of International Relations, points out that Iran's determination to establish its "nuclear sovereignty" is total, leaving little hope for a negotiated solution.

"History teaches that engagement and diplomacy pay dividends that military threats do not," Thomas R. Pickering and William H. Luers, two former senior U.S. diplomats, wrote last year. "Deployment of military force can bring the immediate illusion of 'success' but always results in unforeseen consequences and collateral damage that complicate further the achievement of America's main objectives."[19]

Decades of Sanctions, But No Surrender

Some companies still find ways to get around them.

"*A nation boycotted is a nation that is in sight of surrender. Apply this economic, peaceful, silent, deadly remedy, and there will be no need for force.*"

The speaker was not President Obama grappling with the Iran conundrum, or even one of his immediate predecessors. It was President Woodrow Wilson, who believed "no modern nation could resist" the power of economic sanctions.[1]

But in reality, sanctions have a poor record of bringing recalcitrant nations to heel. Sanctions failed to topple the late Iraqi leader Saddam Hussein, former Serbian President Slobodan Milosevic, or longtime Libyan dictator Moammar Gadhafi. And although the West has been piling on sanctions against Iran for more than 30 years, the regime doesn't seem to be in sight of surrender — at least not yet.[2] Some say sanctions worked in ending apartheid in South Africa because they hurt the middle class, which was able to pressure the government. But there were other factors at playas well, such as frustration at being excluded from international sporting events, a younger generation more sensitive to the injustices of the system, and political pressure from the British Commonwealth.

The Obama administration retains its faith in sanctions, coupled with diplomacy, to convince the Iranians to halt their uranium enrichment effort and agree to more transparency for their nuclear program. "The path we're on — the economic sanctions and the diplomatic pressure — does seem to me to be having an effect," Gen. Martin Dempsey, chairman of the Joint Chiefs of Staff, said recently. "It's premature to be deciding that the economic and diplomatic approach is inadequate."[3]

Sanctions also have been imposed on Iran by the U.N. Security Council, Canada, and the 27-member European Union.

After the American Embassy in Tehran was seized along with 52 hostages more than 30 years ago, President Jimmy Carter froze all Iranian assets in U.S. banks. In 1984, after Iran was implicated in bombings of French and U.S. military bases in Beirut that killed 299, export controls were imposed on dual-use products and a long list of products, from helicopters to scuba gear.[4]

Tougher U.S. trade restrictions were imposed when Iran appeared interested in developing nuclear weapons: the Iran-Iraq Arms Non-Proliferation Act of 1992 and the Iran, North Korea, and Syria Nonproliferation Act of 2000. Taken together, they banned the transfer of equipment or technology that could be used to "make a material contribution to the development of weapons of mass destruction."[5]

In 1995, President Bill Clinton banned U.S. trade and investment with Iran, making it virtually impossible for American companies to do business in Tehran. Then the Iran and Libya Act (ILSA) of 1996 banned energy investments in either country by foreign companies. Libya was removed from ILSA after it renounced its nuclear program in 2003.

The U.S. Treasury Department administers the American sanctions program. Its website lists sanctions covered by successive laws, executive orders, and other decisions, right down to a ban on importing Persian carpets. It also lists scores of banks and other organizations affected by the sanctions.[6]

Many companies have figured out ways to get around the sanctions, even though the United States imposes prison sentences and fines of up to $100 million on convicted "sanction busters."

The United States recently listed four shipping companies in the Mediterranean island-state of Malta that allegedly fronted for the Islamic Republic of Iran Shipping Lines.[7] The Gulf emirate of Dubai has long been a transit point for goods to Iran, legal and otherwise, but Dubai calls the process "re-exporting" rather than "sanctions busting." Iranian firms open offices in Dubai and import the prohibited goods ostensibly to the emirate. But then cargo planes and Gulf freighters transport the goods across the water to nearby Iran.[8]

In one of the highest-profile cases against sanction violators, Britain's Lloyds TSB Bank paid the U.S. government

$350 million in 2009 to settle a case involving cash transfers out of the country for clients in Iran, Libya, and Sudan.[9] Sanctions were imposed on Sudan in 1997 for its alleged support of terrorism and persecution of its Christian minority.

The United States also has frozen the financial assets and property of members of the elite Iranian Revolutionary Guard Corps, Quds commando forces and several leading military officers. On Dec. 31, the United States went one step further and banned financial institutions from doing business with the Iran central bank.

International Sanctions

Since 2006, the U.N. Security Council has passed four resolutions imposing sanctions on Iran — each tied to requests for better access for IAEA inspectors and the halting of Iran's uranium enrichment. The first banned the shipment of arms, nuclear materials, or technology to Iran. The second and third — in 2007 and 2008, respectively — froze the assets of organizations and some individuals involved in Iran's nuclear program.

But the toughest sanctions came in 2010, when the Security Council tightened the arms embargo, banned international travel for those involved in Iran's nuclear program, and froze the funds, businesses, and other assets of the Iranian Revolutionary Guard and the Islamic Republic of Iran Shipping Lines.[10] The Security Council listed 41 Iranian individuals subject to travel bans and assets freeze and of 75 entities subject to assets freeze.[11]

As for the European Union, in June 2008 it moved away from a policy of negotiation with Iran and froze the assets of 40 individuals and entities doing business with Bank Melli, Iran's biggest bank. This began what the Congressional Research Service, Congress' nonpartisan research arm, called "a narrowing of past differences between the United States and its allies on the issue."[12]

By June 2010, the EU had adopted many of the major U.S. sanctions, including a ban on investment in the Iranian oil and gas industries and doing business with the Iran central bank. It also published the names of 442 entities on its sanctions list.

Then in January the EU embargoed crude oil, petroleum and petrochemical products from Iran, starting in July. Contracts concluded before Jan. 23, 2012, were allowed to be executed — but only until July.[13]

Given that the EU is Iran's second-largest trading partner — some observers ask: If European sanctions don't bring the Iranians to the table, what will?[14]

— *Roland Flamini*

[1]Barry C. Hufbauer, "Economic Sanctions: America's Economic Folly," Council on Foreign Relations, Oct. 10, 1997, www.cfr.org/trade/economic-sanctions-americas-folly/p62.

[2]Simon Jenkins, "Why is Britain ramping up sanctions against Iran?" *The Guardian*, Jan. 3, 2012, www.guardian.co.uk/commentisfree/2012/jan/03/britain-ramoing-sanctions-against-iran-washington.

[3]Elad Benar, "Obama: Our Sanctions on Iran 'Had a Lot of Bite,' " Israel NationalNews.com, Jan. 27, 2012, www.israelnationalnews.com/News/News.aspx/152169#.TybRi9VLaf8.

[4]Greg Bruno, "The Lengthening List of Iran Sanctions," Council on Foreign Relations, Nov. 22, 2011, www.cfr.org/iran/lengthening-list-iran-sanctions/p20258.

[5]"Iran, North Korea and Syria Nonproliferation Act Sanctions," www.state.gov/t/isn/inksna/index.htm.

[6]"An Overview of OFAC Regulations Governing Sanctions against Iran," U.S. Treasury, www.treasury.gov/resource-center/sanctions/Programs/Documents/iran.pdf.

[7]"Malta companies on Iran sanctions busting list," *Times of Malta*, Aug. 27, 2010, www.timesofmalta.com/articles/view/20101027/local/us-lists-malta-based-companies-individuals-involved-in-iran-sanctions-busting.333387.

[8]Raymond Barrett, "Sanctions busting is in Dubai's DNA," *The Guardian*, April 20, 2010, www.guardian.co.uk/commentisfree/2010/apr/20/iran-sanctions-busting-dubai.

[9]Gil Montia, "Lloyds TSB settles US sanctions case with $250 million," *Banking Times*, Jan. 11, 2009, www.bankingtimes.co.uk/tag/sanctions/.

[10]Kenneth Katzman, "Iran Sanctions," Congressional Research Service, Jan. 6, 2012, www.fas.org/sgp/crs/mideast/RS20871.pdf.

[11]"Individuals and entities designated as subject to travel ban and assets freeze, etc.," United Nations Security Council, August 2010, www.un.org/sc/committees/1737/pdf/1737ConsolidatedList.pdf.

[12]Kenneth Katzman, "Iran Sanctions," Congressional Research Service, April 9, 2010, http://fpc.state.gov/documents/organization/141587.pdf.

[13]"EU publishes updated list of sanctions on Iran," Kuwait News Agency, Jan. 30, 2012, www.kuna.net.kw/ArticleDetails.aspx?id=2217118&language=en.

[14]Najimeh Bozorgmehr and Geoff Dyer, "China overtakes EU as Iran's top trading partner," *Financial Times*, Feb. 8, 2010, www.ft.com/intl/cms/s/0/f220dfac-14d4-11df-8f1d-00144feab49a.html#axzz1l6Bbzi00.

C H R O N O L O G Y

1950s-1960s *U.S. consolidates influence in Iran by helping to remove nationalist leader and installing pro-Western monarch.*

Aug. 20, 1953 After Prime Minister Mohammed Mossadegh nationalizes Iran's oil industry, he is overthrown with help of U.S. and British intelligence agencies. . . . Shah Mohammed Reza Pahlavi is put in power.

January 1963 Shah launches campaign to modernize Iran, including land and economic reform and improving conditions for women — which alienates religious clergy.

1970s-1980s *Rising discontent forces shah from office. Shiite Islamic theocracy is established. Hostage-taking at U.S. Embassy sours U.S.-Iran relations for decades. Iraq and Iran go to war.*

1978 Civil unrest against shah's dictatorial rule breaks out, inflamed by taped sermons by exiled Shiite clergyman Ayatollah Ruhollah Khomeini. Shah imposes martial law.

1979 Shah leaves Iran on Jan. 16. . . . Khomeini returns, and Islamic republic is established following referendum.

Nov. 4, 1979 Iranian militants storm U.S. Embassy in Tehran, demanding shah's return to Iran to stand trial. Fifty-two Americans are taken hostage and held for 444 days, leading to ongoing animosity.

September 1980 Iraq attacks Iran, triggering eight-year war.

Aug. 20, 1988 U.N. brokers peace in Iran-Iraq war.

1990s-2000s *Iran resumes abandoned nuclear program. West suspects Iran wants to develop nuclear weapons and imposes sanctions to pressure Iran to accept U.N. inspections. Iranian regime suppresses reform.*

Aug. 25, 1992 Iran re-starts nuclear program begun under shah's rule.

1995 U.S. imposes oil and trade embargo because of Iran's efforts to acquire nuclear arms, hostility toward Israel, and alleged sponsorship of "terrorism." Iran denies the charges; says its nuclear program is for peaceful use.

Aug. 15, 2002 Iranian exiles say Iran is building two secret nuclear sites — a secret uranium-enrichment plant at Natanz and another in Arak.

Nov. 12, 2003 Iran agrees to suspend uranium enrichment, allows tougher U.N. inspections. International Atomic Energy Agency (IAEA) finds no evidence of weapons program.

Nov. 14, 2004 Britain, France, Germany, and Iran sign Paris accord, reaffirming Iran's commitment not to acquire nuclear weapons.

Nov. 16, 2005 Iran reverses course and resumes enrichment program, breaking IAEA seals at Natanz nuclear facility.

Dec. 23, 2006 U.N. Security Council imposes sanctions on Iran's trade in nuclear materials and technology.

Oct. 25, 2007 U.S. slaps toughest-yet sanctions on Iran.

2009 Five Security Council members plus Germany offer to enrich Iran's uranium. Iranians refuse. Government cracks down on protests over disputed presidential election.

2010-Present *Despite persistent U.N. requests for more transparency in its nuclear program, Iran remains defiant and evasive. West increases sanctions. Danger rises of possible military intervention to halt Iran's uranium enrichment.* **U.S.-Israeli cyber virus Stuxnet in Iranian nuclear causes malfunction of 1,000 centrifuges at Natanz nuclear facility.**

2011 Iran strongly denies IAEA report saying it could be secretly trying to develop nuclear weapons. . . . United States bars any foreign bank that does business with Iran Central Bank from dealing with U.S. financial institutions.

2012 European Union agrees on Jan. 23 to embargo Iranian oil imports, starting in July. . . . Tehran threatens to block critical Strait of Hormuz oil-shipping lanes if Europeans put sanctions in place.

Feb. 6, 2013 President Obama follows his re-election for a second term by tightening the sanctions. Latest round prohibits payment for Iranian oil with either cash or gold – only using barter system.

BACKGROUND

Persian Roots

Persia was the center of Sunni learning until the rise of the conservative Safavid empire, a militant Shiite theocracy that governed the country from 1501-1732 and established a Shiite branch of Islam as the official religion. The predominantly Sunni population had no choice but to convert or leave.[20]

When the empire ended in the 18th century, Shiism survived as the dominant religion. For the next 200 years the country "lay in decay" as "[b]andit chiefs and feudal lords plundered it at will, [and] people yearned for strong central rule and stability."[21]

In 1921 Reza Khan Pahlavi, a Persian army officer, overthrew the reigning house, set up secular dynastic rule and — to differentiate his people from their Arab neighbors — changed the name of the country to Iran, which means Land of the Aryans.

The Shiite clergy "accepted the legitimacy of the rule of monarchs so long as they did not violate religious law [or] harm Shiism," explains Tufts' Nasr.[22]

The discovery of oil in Iran early in the 20th century drew the interest of the British and Americans. Until the early 1950s, the dominant Western presence in Iran was British. The Anglo-Iranian Oil Co. gave the British a majority interest in Iran's oil, and London exercised considerable political influence in Tehran. But in 1951, Iran's popular, newly elected liberal-democrat prime minister, Mohammad Mossadegh, nationalized the oil industry, at considerable financial loss to British interests.[23] Two years later, he was ousted in a coup organized jointly by the CIA and British Intelligence, mainly to safeguard Anglo-American oil interests.[24] America's role in Mossadegh's removal generated anti-American feeling in the region for the first time.

Shah Mohammad Reza Pahlavi gained control over the country, with growing U.S. support. During the 1950s, Iran was a frontline state in America's Cold War with the Soviet Union and the most important U.S. ally in the Middle East. About the size of Alaska, Iran shared a 1,200-mile border with the Soviet Union and served as an Allied listening post into the Soviet bloc. It also was one of the few Muslim countries to recognize Israel and to sell it oil. U.S. military aid to Iran increased from $10 million in 1960 to its highest level of just over $5 billion in 1977.[25]

But the Pahlavi regime was autocratic and tightly controlled by SAVAK, the nation's hated, CIA-trained, national security organization, notorious for its arrests and torture of political opponents and dissidents. The shah did introduce some reforms — agrarian reform, increased literacy, greater participation by women in society — but corruption was rife, and most citizens did not benefit from the country's oil wealth.

Shiite Radicalism

Social unrest grew, fomented by the Shiite clergy, which opposed Iran's secularization. Cassettes of anti-government sermons by exiled cleric and spiritual leader, Ayatollah Ruhollah Khomeini, were sold in the bazaars. Khomeini's violent rhetoric called the shah "the Jewish agent, the American serpent whose head must be smashed with a stone."[26]

By 1978, mosques had become centers of opposition to the regime. Huge anti-regime demonstrations erupted across the country, and up to a million protesters swarmed the streets of Tehran, including many women in chadors, the head-to-toe black covering mandated by the mullahs.

President Jimmy Carter pressured the shah to avoid bloodshed, so the army did not intervene. Even after some demonstrations turned into violent clashes with security forces, the Carter administration continued to urge the shah to try to ease tensions by bringing moderate opposition figures into the government and calling for elections.

On Jan. 16, 1979, the shah left Iran — ostensibly to seek medical treatment abroad. He would never return. Instead, Khomeini came home in triumph less than a month later, and Iran was declared an Islamic republic, with Khomeini as its supreme leader. Within less than a year, all members of the secular government had been purged, and the clerics were in control. A new age of Shiite radicalism had begun.

On Nov. 4, 1979, a group of student followers of Khomeini stormed and occupied the U.S. Embassy in Tehran, in retaliation for President Carter allowing the deposed shah to enter the United States for cancer treatment.[27] Khomeini publicly approved the takeover, calling the embassy "a nest of spies."

Eventually, 52 American diplomats, staff, and Marine guards were held captive for 444 days, despite a failed rescue attempt in April 1980.[28] Negotiations to free the hostages — mediated by Algeria — continued, even as the Carter administration froze $8 billion in Iranian assets in U.S. banks and embargoed Iranian oil exports — the first of a long series of sanctions. The United States has not bought Iranian oil since.

On Jan. 20, 1981, the hostages were released within minutes of President Ronald Reagan's inauguration as Carter's successor, a move designed to cause Carter the most humiliation. In return, the United States agreed not to interfere in Iranian politics.[29] By then, the shah was dead, and Iran had been attacked by Iraq in a conflict that was to last eight years.

War With Iraq

The previous September, Iraqi leader Saddam Hussein had taken advantage of Iran's domestic turmoil to take possession of Shatt al-Arab, a waterway disputed by both countries that flows into the Persian Gulf, and some adjacent oil fields. Centuries-old Sunni-versus-Shia and Arab-versus-Persian religious and ethnic tensions contributed to the outbreak of hostilities, as did a personal animosity between Saddam and Khomeini. Ten years earlier, Saddam had expelled the ayatollah after he had taken refuge in Iraq.[30]

Iran threw waves of young men and boys against Saddam's heavy armor in a conflict that developed into trench warfare reminiscent of the bloody fighting in World War I. And, like the Germans in WWI, Saddam even used mustard gas against the Iranians. In Tehran, fountains ran water dyed red to symbolize the blood of martyred Iranian soldiers.

In 1988, exhausted, economically battered and deadlocked, both sides agreed to a U.N.-brokered cease fire. Iraq's territorial gains were returned to Iran. More than a million soldiers and civilians perished in what was essentially an exercise in futility.

As the war was winding down, two incidents served to further sour U.S.-Iranian relations. In 1988, the *USS Samuel B. Roberts*, an American frigate, hit an Iranian mine in the Strait of Hormuz. In retaliation, U.S. forces destroyed two offshore oil platforms, sank two Iranian frigates, and damaged a third. "The aim was to teach the Iranians a lesson," the BBC recalled in a recent analysis. "The conclusion was clear — Iran's conventional naval forces were no match for U.S. sea power in a straight fight."[31]

Weeks later, the *USS Vincennes*, a guided missile cruiser, shot down an Iranian commercial jet carrying 290 passengers and crew. Washington said the *Vincennes* mistook the plane for a military aircraft, and refused to apologize or admit any wrongdoing.[32]

Driven by anti-U.S. sentiment and its perceived mission to spread Shiism, Iran between 1980 and 1996 strongly supported Islamist terrorist groups such as Hezbollah (in Lebanon), Hamas, Palestinian Islamic Jihad, the Supreme Council for Islamic Revolution in Iraq (SCIRI), the Afghan Northern Alliance and its precursors and groups in Bahrain, Saudi Arabia, Kuwait, Egypt, Algeria, and elsewhere. But since then, as Iran's revolutionary fervor has dissipated somewhat, Tehran's support for terrorist organizations has become more focused on its own strategic interests. By the mid- and late-1990s, the Iranians had reduced their support to Hezbollah and Hamas.[33]

That may have been in part because Iran was at a kind of political cross-roads. In the summer of 1989, Ayatollah Khamenei had succeeded Khomeini as supreme leader, and progressives were making inroads in Iranian politics. In 1997, the moderate Mohammad Khatami won the presidential election with 70 percent of the vote, beating the conservative ruling elite.

Stronger Sanctions

Beginning in the mid-1990s, Iran's efforts to resume its stalled nuclear program would escalate tensions between Tehran and the West.

In 1995, President Bill Clinton imposed new, stricter sanctions on Iran, arguing that Iran supported international terrorism, was trying to undermine the Middle East peace process, and was acquiring weapons of mass destruction.[34] The new restrictions blocked trade in technology, goods, or services to or from Iran and prohibited U.S. citizens from investing in Iranian projects.

In August 1996, Congress tightened the screws even further by passing the Iran-Libya Sanctions Act (ILSA), which extended restrictions on energy-related investments to foreign-owned companies. The new law, said a report by Chatham House, a British foreign affairs think tank, was designed to force foreign companies to decide whether they wanted to "do business with Iran and Libya or the United States."[35]

Despite the sanctions, U.S.-Iran relations appeared ready to thaw a bit in September 2000, when Iranian President Khatami remained in the hall at the annual opening of the U.N. General Assembly to listen to President Clinton address the body.[36] Later, Clinton reciprocated, breaking a tradition since 1979 of U.S. officials leaving the chamber when an Iranian leader spoke. Some American import restrictions were removed, including on Iranian carpets, but not on oil. And Secretary of State Madeleine Albright met with the Iranian foreign minister Kamal Kharrazi — the first such meeting since the United States broke off diplomatic ties with Tehran in 1979.

Then, after the Sept. 11, 2001, terrorist attacks in the United States, Iran quietly offered support for the U.S. campaign in Afghanistan, for example, by blocking the retreating Taliban from crossing into Iranian territory. That November, Secretary of State Colin Powell shook hands with Kharrazi — a simple yet historic gesture.

But in his Jan. 29, 2002, State of the Union address, President George W. Bush declared Iran a member of "an axis of evil" (along with North Korea and Syria) that was "arming to threaten the peace of the world."[37] Two days later, National Security Adviser Condoleezza Rice said, "Iran's direct support of regional and global terrorism and its aggressive efforts to acquire weapons of mass destruction belie any good intentions." Her statement was reinforced by a CIA report claiming that Tehran was "attempting to develop a domestic capability to produce various types of weapons — chemical, biological, and nuclear — and their delivery systems."[38]

Nuclear Program

Iran has always claimed it needed nuclear power in order to shift from its over-reliance on oil for domestic energy. With oil exports accounting for 50–76 percent of the Iranian government's revenues, the country prefers to sell as much oil as possible rather than burn it for electricity.[39]

With the help of the Germans and the Americans — before the revolution — and the Russians after it, Iran built a nuclear power station in Bushehr on the Persian Gulf. Enriched uranium is needed to run a nuclear power station, but only enriched to single-digit percentage levels. To make a nuclear weapon, uranium must be enriched to 90 percent or higher. Although Iran has not yet enriched uranium to weapons-grade levels, it has enriched some up to 20 percent of the strength needed, according to the IAEA.

In short, for nearly a decade Western governments have tried using negotiations, threats, and U.N. sanctions to persuade the Iranians to either import their enriched uranium from elsewhere or make their enrichment operation more transparent. So far, the Iranians have refused to comply.

Talks between Iran and Britain, France, and Germany got off to a promising start in 2004, when the Iranians agreed to suspend all uranium enrichment activities while negotiations continued and to allow the IAEA to inspect its nuclear sites. Some observers linked Tehran's concessions to the U.S. invasion of Iraq the previous year. The Iranian leadership had been cowed into cooperating by the proximity of a strong U.S. fighting force across the border, they said.

The most optimistic moment came in March 2005, when the United States joined the negotiations, and the Western team became known as 3+1 (and eventually as 3+2 when Russia was added, and then 5+1 with the inclusion of China). As a goodwill gesture, the United States offered to supply spare parts for Iran's civil aviation fleet. Then the Iranians insisted on resuming uranium enrichment as a condition for continuing negotiations, and the talks collapsed.[40]

The election of Ahmadinejad, then mayor of Tehran, as president in 2005 — when negotiators had hoped for the more pragmatic Akbar Hashemi Rafsanjani — further hardened Iran's position.

The battle then moved to the U.N. Security Council, which between 2006 and 2010 passed four resolutions, starting with an IAEA resolution demanding more inspections. Each subsequent resolution piled on more economic sanctions and restrictions, including freezing the assets of the Republic of Iran Shipping Lines and the powerful Iranian Revolutionary Guard Corps and authorizing the inspection and seizure of shipments violating the sanctions.

The Iranian facilities in question included the nuclear plant at Bushehr, the Isfahan plant, where "natural" uranium is converted into uranium hexafluoride — a gas used in centrifuges to create weapons-grade uranium — and Natanz, an enrichment facility where the Iranians were said to be installing centrifuges. In 2009, Iran revealed the existence of another heavily fortified plant near the holy city of Qom, where the Iranians told the IAEA it was transferring its operations to enrich uranium to 20 percent levels.

In 2009, the world reacted with shock when the Iranian regime brutally suppressed huge "Green" protest demonstrations that erupted after Ahmadinejad, who had trailed badly in the polls, somehow won an overwhelming re-election victory over his progressive challenger, Mir Hussein Mousavi.[41] Youthful supporters of Mousavi called for a more stable economy, greater freedom at home, and a friendlier foreign policy.

The Obama administration had remained aloof from the international chorus of criticism of the regime. "We do not interfere in Iran's internal affairs," Obama said at the time. But in December 2011, as his re-election campaign began heating up, Obama's GOP challengers criticized him for not supporting the Iranian protesters in 2009. The White House promptly issued sanctions against two senior members of the Iranian military for their part in "the violent crackdown in the summer of 2009."[42]

Inevitably, Iran's nuclear ambitions have spurred war talk. Both the United States and Israel are rumored to have contingency plans for a military strike against Tehran's nuclear facilities. For some years the accepted version of events was of Washington restraining an increasingly apprehensive Jerusalem and urging that sanctions be given a chance to work.

EU Trade with Iran Rose, Despite Sanctions

Even though the United States and the U.N. had imposed sanctions on trade with Iran, the European Union (EU) increased its trade with Iran more than 17 percent between 2009 and 2010. In January, the EU adopted its own sanctions against trade with Iran, increasing international pressure designed to stop the regime from enriching uranium, considered a precursor to the production of nuclear weapons.

Value of EU Trade (Imports and Exports) with Iran, 2009-2010

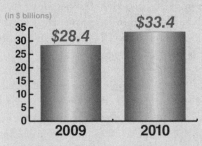

Source: "Iran: EU Bilateral Trade and Trade With the World," Directorate General for Trade, European Commission, January 2012, trade.ec.europa.eu/doclib/docs/2006/september/tradoc_113392.pdf

"Everybody says a military attack should be a last resort," says Ben-Yishai, the Israeli military affairs expert. "The question is, 'When is the last resort?'" The notion of a nuclear Israel and a nuclear Iran creating a system of mutual deterrence doesn't wash in Israel because of Iran's declared hostility to the Jewish state's very existence.

"Deterrence worked during the Cold War, because both sides were rational and responsible centers with fresh memories of World War II," argues Ben-Yishai. "The Iranian leaders are fanatic clerics with visions of martyrdom. We don't know what they'll do, and we can't live under the threat of doomsday."

Tensions rose again in November, when the IAEA reported for the first time that the Iranians could be working on a nuclear explosive device — although the agency did not say they were already capable of producing a bomb.[43]

If Israel and the United States have so far opted not to use military force against Iran's network of nuclear facilities, that has not stopped them from choosing another form of attack – cyber warfare. In 2010, the U.S. and Israel succeeded in infecting the nuclear facilities with a cyber worm called Stuxnet, which was only discovered after it had destroyed 1,000 of the 5,000 centrifuges in operation at the time. Stuxnet appears to be the first time the United States has repeatedly used cyber weapons to cripple another country's infrastructure. "The Americans and the Europeans . . . have succeeded in turning Iran's nuclear program into an issue of international security,"

Is Iran planning to build nuclear weapons?

YES — Frederick W. Kagan
Resident Scholar and Director Critical Threats Project American Enterprise Institute

Written for *CQ Global Researcher*, February 2012

Iran's leaders are seeking the ability to produce an arsenal of atomic weapons. No other explanation fits their behavior. Claiming that Iran needs nuclear power to meet its energy needs in order to strengthen its economy and raise its people's quality of life, the Iranian leadership has brought crushing sanctions on its country.

In addition to constraining Iran's economy, the sanctions have badly undermined its currency and harmed its population. The international community — including Russia, one of Iran's most trusted allies — has offered to provide Iran with nuclear fuel, yet the regime persists in its enrichment program. If the regime sought to improve Iran's economic well-being, it would have abandoned the nuclear program long ago.

The regime claims it has a right to the full nuclear fuel cycle, however, and insists that its program is nothing more than the pursuit of that right. Indeed, Iran could develop a nuclear program in accord with the international laws its leaders cite — if it complied fully with the inspections regime established by those laws and embodied in the International Atomic Energy Agency (IAEA).

Instead, the regime has consistently refused to answer questions from the IAEA, let alone provide the agency with full access and transparency to its program, which other signatories do.

The Iranian regime is not only pursuing a nuclear program to the enormous detriment of its people but it is doing so in violation of the very treaties it claims allow it to pursue the program in the first place.

One could add the disturbing fact that Iran has buried an enrichment facility (which it did not declare until others discovered it) under a small mountain — not the behavior of a regime seeking peaceful nuclear power. Numerous reports also show that Iran has tried to acquire and build atomic weapons devices, detonators, and testing facilities and already has a large arsenal of ballistic missiles ready to have atomic warheads fitted.

But the reality already should be clear. The facts support only one rational explanation: Iran's leaders are building a nuclear program to support an arsenal of atomic weapons. All other explanations are rationalizations.

NO — Riccardo Alcaro
Research Fellow, Istituto Affari Internazionali, Rome and Fellow, European Foreign and Security Policy Studies Program

Written for *CQ Global Researcher*, February 2012

It is true that Iran has gone the extra mile to divert international checks on its nuclear program, but uncertainty still clouds its ultimate objective. Meanwhile, there simply is not enough evidence to argue that Iran is determined to leave the Nuclear Non-Proliferation Treaty, test a nuclear device, and declare itself a nuclear state.

If Iran were to go openly nuclear, it would have a hard time persuading its mostly opportunistic partners (like China) to resist American and European demands to isolate it. In theory, Iran could go nuclear without telling anyone. In practice, however, keeping the construction of a nuclear arsenal secret is an increasingly difficult, costly, and risky option, and Iran is under almost unprecedented scrutiny from the International Atomic Energy Agency (IAEA) and Western powers.

Iran's behavior so far has seemed to fit the strategy of approaching but not crossing the nuclear threshold. While resisting what it considers excessive intrusions into its nuclear program, it has avoided severing ties with the IAEA. Defiance of Western pressure — as well as of IAEA and U.N. Security Council resolutions — seems to have paid off for the Iranian leadership. Domestically, it has given the regime a narrative around which popular support could coalesce. Internationally, it has forced a re-appraisal of Iran's role in the strategic calculus of the United States. And thanks to the nuclear dispute, Iran potentially is in a better position to extract concessions from what Ayatollah Ruhollah Khomeini labeled the "Great Satan" than it was before the nuclear standoff.

From that point of view, the nuclear program is more a means to get U.S. acceptance of the clerical regime and recognition of Iran's regional interests than an end in itself. If that is the case, there still is room for settling the nuclear dispute, as Iran may decide that compromise rather than continued defiance can ultimately deliver its strategic objective of climbing the region's hierarchy.

However, if it has no way out but bowing to U.S. demands or — worse — if attacked by the United States and/or Israel, Iran might instead calculate that isolation with an H-bomb is better than isolation without it. Grownup diplomacy, not teenage muscle flexing, can spare the world another unnecessary crisis.

says Alcaro of the Italian Institute of International Affairs. What happens next, he adds, will depend largely on whether the Americans and Europeans can maintain a united front with Russia and China.

"Under pressure from all the major powers, Iran may be willing to give in on the question of enriching uranium — provided a mechanism can be found to save appearance," Alcaro says.

CURRENT SITUATION

Tightening Sanctions

By the IAEA's count, Iran has a stockpile of about 6,000kg of up to 5 percent low enriched uranium (LEU), which may be sufficient for five nuclear weapons if further enriched to 90 percent. In addition, Iran also produced 230kg of 20 percent enriched product, uranium hexafluoride—not far off from the 240kg that may be sufficient for a weapon if brought to the 90 percent level. But late in 2012, Iran reduced that capability by converting about 100kg of the 20 percent enriched uranium hexafluoride to an oxide form for use in fuel rods for the Tehran Research Reactor (TRR).

"This conversion gave Israel a justification for delaying the deadline for military action," says mark Kennedy of the IISS, "because the enriched uranium in oxide form cannot immediately be further enriched." It would take two months or more to re-convert.

In the summer of 2012, tension escalated in the Persian Gulf as Iran threatened to mine the Straits of Hormuz in retaliation for stepped up U.S. and European sanctions. The U.S., Britain, and France moved ships to the waterway to ensure the safety of shipping routes through which 40 percent of the world's seaborne exports flow.

But in the fall, the naval standoff eased, and the United States withdrew one of its two aircraft carriers deployed in the Gulf even as the campaign for Barak Obama's re-election got under way. One of Obama's first actions on returning to the White House for a second term was to increase the sanctions.

According to the IAEA, Iran increased the number of centrifuges at Fordow, its newest plant built deep underground, by 644 to 2,784 since mid-August. The agency says that so far the Iranians are only using 696 centrifuges.

Experts say it could significantly step up enrichment at Fordow by using more centrifuges, but so far has not done so.[44]

A new round of talks between Iran and the so-called 5+1 (Britain, Germany, France, the European Union, and China, plus the United States) aimed at persuading the Iranians to halt enrichment and agree to more inspections was scheduled for late February at Almaty, Kazakhstan. According to a French official, the six would make the Iranians "an undated offer that will contain new elements of substance."[45]

Meanwhile, Ahmadinejad played down the impact of the EU oil embargo: "Today, we have attained a status that we need not sell oil to Europe, and we are following our path determinedly," he said. And the freezing of the Iran central bank's European assets, he continued, would have minimal effect, because only $24 billion of Iran's $200 billion in foreign exchange are in Europe.[46]

Economic Pain

The Iranian economy is in shambles because sanctions block outside investment and development. In the last three months, the value of the Iranian rial has plunged 40 percent against the dollar, according to the French newspaper *Le Monde*.[47]

Several European countries had been worried that an embargo would cause oil prices to spike, exacerbating the EU's serious economic problems. But the EU governments fell into line, in part because they have good prospects for alternative supplies.

"The French strategy is to confront Iran with a choice: The future of the regime, or the nuclear bomb," said *Le Monde*.[48]

But will it work? Turkey, China, and India — major importers of Iranian oil — say they will not honor the embargo, although Japan agreed to cut back its Iranian oil purchases. While Beijing "adamantly opposes Iran developing and possessing nuclear weapons," Prime Minister Wen Jiabao declared recently, it will continue to import Iranian oil.[49]

Ray Takeyh, a senior fellow at the Council on Foreign Relations, said skepticism abounds regarding Tehran's sincerity. "By threatening the disruption of global oil supplies, yet dangling the prospect of entering talks," he wrote recently, "Iran can press actors such as Russia and China to be more accommodating." But any concessions made by Iran at a negotiating table "are bound to be symbolic and reversible."[50]

Israel says the window of opportunity for a successful military operation is rapidly closing. "There's a very vivid and very bitter dispute going on between the Israeli and U.S. governments" over timing, says the Israeli commentator Ben-Yishai. "It is still practicable, from an Israeli point of view, to launch an attack, but the Americans say, 'Give sanctions time to work.'"[51] But in February, Prime Minister Netanyahu was quoted as saying that even a partially successful strike against Iran's nuclear complex might be worth considering because it would buy time and perhaps create the circumstances for a regime change in Iran.[52]

Some say a covert war to derail Iran's nuclear program already is underway. The computer worm Stuxnet created by the U.S. and Israel in 2010 caused more than a 1,000 centrifuges to malfunction at the Natanz nuclear facility, causing production delays. On Jan. 11, 2012, Iranian chemist Mostafa Ahmadi Roshan, head of the Natanz enrichment facility, was killed after a motorcyclist attached a magnetic bomb to his car in Tehran's rush-hour traffic. He was the fifth Iranian nuclear scientist killed in the past two years. The Iranians blame his killing on U.S. and/or Israeli intelligence agents, but the United States adamantly denied any role in the killing.

OUTLOOK

Diplomacy and Provocation

"The next few months will look pretty much like the last few months," predicts Takyeh, at the Council on Foreign Relations. "There'll be diplomacy, incremental gains and, occasionally, a degree of provocation, with all parties invested in not having full-scale conflict." But once started, the cyber war is likely to escalate, with the Iranians attempting further Aramco-type cyber attacks, and the United States and Israel using more Stuxnets to try to slow down Iran's progress towards a nuclear weapon, experts say.

However, he believes Iran would be open to "an arrangement with the United States," under "certain circumstances." For instance, if Iran were allowed to join the World Trade Organization, it could mean a quantum leap in the Iranian economy.[53]

As for the effectiveness of the oil embargo, experts say the international oil market is too complex, with too many options. "History is littered with failed oil embargoes ranging from Cuba, Rhodesia [today's Zimbabwe], and South Africa to the Arab oil embargo [of 1973], and the embargo against Iraq in 1990," Paul Stevens of London's Chatham House wrote recently.[54]

Moreover, he continued, "some form of [Iranian] retaliatory action against the EU countries . . . could also be expected. There could even be a Lockerbie-type response prompted by elements from within Iran," he continued, referring to Libya's 1988 bombing of a Pan American jet liner over Scotland.[55]

The endgame, according to Julian Lee, an energy expert at the London-based Centre for Global Energy Studies, is to get the Iranians to agree to "proper monitoring of their nuclear industry. The sanctions aren't an end in and of themselves."[56]

Meanwhile, Israel's intentions are unclear, and there is uncertainty about how the Iranian regime will respond to the latest sanctions. The more immediate concern is a renewed threat by Iran to close the Strait of Hormuz, which could easily spark a broader conflict. As for hopes of a breakthrough in the negotiations, "No amount of sanctions can pressure Iran into U-turning on its nuclear program," The *Arab News* commented recently.[57]

"Iran knows where the whole world stands; we know where Iran stands; the situation will continue that way," Saudi Prince Turki said recently. "None of us want to engage in military conflict, and I think the Iranians themselves . . . fear that they will be the target of military strikes either by Israel or the United States or both."[58]

In Israel, meanwhile, talk of war rises and subsides. "There's no realistic hope in Israel that the Iranians will suspend their enrichment program altogether," says commentator Ben-Yishai. "If the sanctions work, they might say, 'We suspend enrichment at 20 percent.' That, in itself, would be a big gain."

NOTES

1. Nicole Perlroth, "In Cyberattack on Saudi Firm, U.S. Sees Iran Firing Back," New York Times, Oct. 23, 2012, http://www.nytimes.com/2012/10/24/business/global/cyberattack-on-saudi-oil-firm-disquiets-us.html?pagewanted=all&_r=2&#h.

2. Nicole Perlroth and Quentin Hardy, "Bank Hacking Was the Work of Iranians, Officials Say," New York Times, Jan. 8, 2013, http://www.nytimes.com/2013/01/09/technology/online-banking-attacks-were-work-of-iran-us-officials-say.html.

3. Nicole Perlroth, Oct 23, 2012, Op. Cit.

4. Thomas Erdbrink, "Ayatollah Says Iran Will Control Nuclear Aims," New York Times, Feb. 16, 2013, http://www.nytimes.com/2013/02/17/world/middleeast/supreme-leader-says-iran-not-seeking-nuclear-arms.html.

5. Herb Keinon, "Iran strike worthwhile, even to delay nuke program," Jerusalem Post, Aug. 16. 2012, http://www.jpost.com/DiplomacyAndPolitics/Article.aspx?id=281573.

6. Ghazanfar Ali Khan, "Attack on Iran would have 'calamitous' consequences, says Prince Turki," *Arab News*, Dec. 13, 2011, http://arab news.com/saudiarabia/article547026.ece.

7. Kelsey Davenport, Darryl G. Kimball, Greg Thielmann, "The Nov. 2012 IAEA Report on Iran and its implications," Arms Control Now, Nov. 16, 2012, http://armscontrolnow.org/2012/11/16/the-november-2012-iaea-report-on-iran-and-its-implications-2/.

8. Andrew Torchia, "Analysis: Iran economy far from collapses as sanctions tighten," Reuters, Feb. 20, 2013, http://uk.reuters.com/article/2013/02/20/uk-iran-economy-sanctions-idUKBRE91J0SO20130220.

9. V. Vera, *et al.*, "Sanctions on Iran: Reactions and Impact," *AEI Iran Tracker*, Nov. 1, 2011.

10. "Iran exports by country, 2010," United States Energy Information Administration, www.eia.gov/countries/country-data.cfm?fips=IR.

11. Karen de Young and Scott Wilson, "Public ire is one goal of sanctions against Iran, U.S. official says," *The Washington Post*, Jan.11, 2012, www.washingtonpost.com/world/national-security/goal-of-iran-sanctions-is-regime-collapse-us-official-says/2012/01/10/gIQA0KJsoP_story.html.

12. Castle and Cowell, *op. cit.*

13. "Global Trends 2025: A Transformed World," National Intelligence Council, November 2008, www.dni.gov/nic/PDF_2025/2025_Global_Trends_Final_Report.pdf.

14. Shmuel Bar, "Can Cold War Deterrence Apply to a Nuclear Iran?" *Strategic Perspectives*, Jerusalem Center for Public Affairs, November 2011, www.jcpa.org/text/cold_war_deterrence_nuclear_iran.pdf.

15. Colin H.Kahl, Melissa G. Dalton, Matthew Irvine, "If Iran Builds the Bomb, Will Saudi Arabia Be Next?" Center for a New American Security,Feb. 2013, http://www.cnas.org/files/documents/publications/CNAS_AtomicKingdom_Kahl.pdf.

16. Ibid.

17. "Saudi Arabia may need nuclear weapons to fend off threat from Iran and Israel, says former intelligence chief," *op. cit.*

18. Ibid.

19. William H. Luers and Thomas R. Pickering, "Military action isn't the only solution to Iran," *The Washington Post*, Dec. 30, 2012, www.washingtonpost.com/opinions/military-action-isnt-the-only-solution-to-iran/2011/12/29/gIQ A69sNRP_story.html.

20. "History of Iran, Persian Empire," http://doc mv.co.uk/Documents/History%20of%20iran.pdf.

21. See "Safavid Empire (1501-1722)," "Religions," BBC online, www.bbc.co.uk/religion/religions/islam/history/safavidempire_1.shtml.

22. Quoted in Mike Shuster, "Shia Rise Amid Century of Mideast Turmoil," Part 2 of the series, "Partisans of Ali," NPR, Feb. 13, 2007, www.npr.org/templates/story/story.php?storyId=7371280.

23. David Painter, "The United States, Great Britain, and Iran," Georgetown University Institute for the Study of Diplomacy, 1993, www.princeton.edu/~bsimpson/Hist%20725%20Summer%202006/The%20US%20and%20Mossadegh%201951-1953.pdf.

24. Mark Gasiorowski and Malcolm Byrne (eds.), "Mohammed Mossadeq and the 1953 Coup in Iran," National Security Archive, June 2004, www.gwu.edu/~nsarchiv/NSAEBB/NSAEBB126/index.htm. "The CIA, with help from British intelligence, planned, funded and implemented the operation."

25. "Arms exports to Iran," Stockholm International Peace Research Institute, http://arm strade.sipri.org/armstrade/page/values.php.

26. "Ruhollah Mousavi Khomeini, Part 3: Life in Exile," Medlibrary.org, http://medlibrary.org/medwiki/Ruhollah_Mousavi_Khomeini#Life_in_exile.

27. "The American Experience: The Iranian Hostage Crisis," PBS, www.pbs.org/wgbh/americanexperience/features/general-article/carter-hostage-crisis/.

28. "On This Day, 1980: Tehran Hostage Rescue Mission Fails," BBC, April 25, 2005, http://news.bbc.co.uk/onthisday/hi/dates/stories/april/25/newsid_2503000/2503899.stm.

29. "Timeline: U.S.-Iran Contacts," Council on Foreign Relations, March 9, 2007, www.cfr.org/iran/timeline-us-iran-contacts/p12806.

30. "Iran-Iraq War (1980-1988)," Global Security, Nov. 7, 2011, www.globalsecurity.org/military/world/war/iran-iraq.htm.

31. Jonathan Marcus, "Is a U.S.-Iran maritime clash inevitable?" BBC News, Jan. 10, 2012, www.bbc.co.uk/news/world-middle-east-16485842.

32. Lionel Beehner, "Timeline: U.S.-Iran Contacts," Council on Foreign Relations, March 9, 2011, www.cfr.org/iran/timeline-us-iran-contacts/p1 2806#p5.

33. Mark Gasiorowski, "Evidence to the National Commission on Terrorist Attacks Upon the United States: Iranian Support for Terrorism," National Commission on Terrorist Attacks Upon the United States, July 2003, www.9-11 commission.gov/hearings/hearing3/witness_ gasiorowski.htm.

34. B. J. Rudy, "The Future of U.S. Unilateral Sanctions and the Iran-Libya Sanctions Act," Chatham House, Feb. 12-13, 2001, www.google.com/search?q=chatham%20house%3A%20clin ton%20adminis-tration%20imposes%20sanctions%20on%20iran&ie=utf-8&oe=utf-8&aq=t&rls=org.mozilla:en-US:official&client=firefox-a& source=hp&channel=np.

35. *Ibid.* Libya was removed from ILSA after Libyan leader Moammar Gadhafi renounced the development of nuclear weapons.

36. Scott McLeod, "Diplomacy: Clinton and Khatami Find Relations Balmy," *Time*, Sept. 18, 2000, www.time.com/time/magazine/article/0,9171,997984,00.html.

37. "Bush State of the Union Speech," CNN transcript, Jan. 20, 2002, http://edition.cnn.com/2002/ALLPOLITICS/01/29/bush.speech.txt/.

38. "How Iran entered the Axis," PBS "Frontline," undated, www.pbs.org/wgbh/pages/frontline/shows/tehran/axis/map.html.

39. "Firms Reported in Open Sources as Having Commercial Activity in Iran's Oil, Gas, and Petrochemical Sectors," Government Accountability Office, April 22, 2010, www.gao.gov/products/GAO-10-515R.

40. "Iran 'ready for nuclear talks,' " BBC News, June 8, 2006, http://news.bbc.co.uk/2/hi/middle_east/5059322.stm.

41. "Ahmadinejad wins Iran presidential election," BBC News, June 12, 2009, news.bbc.co.uk/2/hi/8098305.stm.

42. Joel Gehrke, "894 days: Now Obama stands up for the Greens," *The Examiner*, Dec. 14, 2011, http://campaign2012.washingtonexaminer.com/blogs/beltway-confidential/894-days-now-obama-stands-green-revolution/257116.

43. "Q and A: Iran nuclear issue," BBC News, Nov. 9, 2011, www.bbc.co.uk/news/world-middle-east-11709428.

44. Ashad Mohammed, "Exclusive: Big powers to offer easing gold sanctions at Iran nuclear talks," Reuters, Feb 15, 2013, http://www.reuters.com/article/2013/02/15/us-iran-nuclear-gold-idUSBRE91E0TP20130215.

45. "'5+1' group to make updated offer to Iran – Paris," Kuwait News Agency, Feb. 21, 2013, http://www.kuna.net.kw/ArticleDetails.aspx?id=2294485&language=en.

46. *Ibid.*

47. "Le EU décide de geler les avoirs de la Banque Central d'Iran," *Le Monde*, Jan. 18, 2012, www.lemonde.fr/proche-orient/article/2012/01/18/l-ue-

decide-de-geler-les-avoirs-de-la-banque-centrale-d-iran_1631366_3218.html.

48. Natalie Nougayrede, "Paris redoute des frappes sur Iran pendent l'ete," *Le Monde*, Jan. 19, 2012, www.lemonde.fr/proche-orient/article/2012/01/19/paris-redoute-des-frappes-sur-l-iran-pendant-l-ete_1631865_3218.html.

49. "Chinese Premier Wen Jiabao defends Iran oil imports," *Daily Telegraph*, Jan. 19, 2012, www.telegraph.co.uk/news/worldnews/middleeast/iran/9024517/Chinese-Premier-Wen-Jiabao-defends-Iran-oil-imports.html.

50. *Ibid.*

51. *Ibid.*

52. Jerusalem Post Op. Cit.

53. "The Manama Dialogue," Fifth Plenary Session, International Institute of Strategic Studies, Dec. 4, 2010, www.iiss.org/conferences/the-iiss-regional-security-summit/manama-dia logue-2010/plenary-sessions-and-speeches/fourth-plenary-session/fourth-plenary-qa-session/.

54. Paul Stevens, "An Embargo on Iranian Crude Oil Exports: How likely and with what Impact?" Chatham House, January 2012, www.chathamhouse.org/sites/default/files/public/Research/Energy,%20Environment%20and%20Development/0112pp_stevens.pdf.

55. *Ibid.*

56. Stephen Mufson, "Oil prices, Iran are increasingly sources of concern," *The Washington Post*, Jan. 14, 2012, www.washingtonpost.com/business/economy/increasing-concern-over-oil-prices-iran/2012/01/13/gIQAP98PzP_story.html.

57. Linda Heard, "U.S. and Iran: Wheels within wheels," *Arab News*, Jan. 17, 2012, http://arabnews.com/opinion/columns/article564103.ece.

58. "Fifth Plenary Session — HRH Prince Turki Al Faisal: The Changing Nature of Regional Security Issues," 7th IISS Regional Security Summit, The Manama Dialogue, The International Institute for Strategic Studied, Dec. 4, 2010, www.iiss.org/conferences/the-iiss-regional-security-summit/manama-dialogue-2010/plenary-sessions-and-speeches/fifth-plenary-session/hrh-prince-turki-al-faisal/.

BIBLIOGRAPHY
Selected Sources
Books

Brumberg, David, *Reinventing Khomeini: The Struggle for Reform in Iran*, University of Chicago Press, 2001.
An associate professor of government at Georgetown University examines Ayatollah Khomeini's often contradictory ideas about government and how they led to competing institutions and ideologies in today's Iranian leadership.

Kamrava, Mehran, *Iran's Intellectual Revolution*, Cambridge University Press, 2008.
The director of Georgetown University's Qatar-based Center of International Studies examines the strengths and weaknesses of the three major intellectual currents in Iran — religious conservative, religious reformist and secular modernist.

Nasr, Vali, *The Shia Revival: How Conflicts Within Islam Will Shape the Future*, W. W. Norton, 2006.
A noted authority on the Arab world and a professor of international politics at the Fletcher School of Law and Diplomacy at Tufts University argues that Operation Iraqi Freedom set the scene for a "new" Middle East fueled by the sectarian struggle between the majority Sunnis and minority Shiites.

Takeyh, Ray, *Hidden Iran: Paradox and Power in the Islamic Republic*, Times Books, 2006.
A senior fellow for Middle Eastern studies at the Council on Foreign Relations in Washington explains why we fail to understand Iran and offers a new strategy for redefining this crucial relationship.

Wright, Robin, ed., *The Iran Primer: Power, Politics and U.S. Policy*, United States Institute for Peace Press, 2010.
A distinguished American foreign correspondent well versed in Middle Eastern affairs pulls together 50 seasoned experts from around the world to compile a comprehensive primer on Iran today — its politics, society, military, and nuclear program.

Articles

Bergman, Ronen, "Will Israel Attack Iran?" *The New York Times Magazine*, Jan. 29, 2012, p. 22.
An Israeli journalist and author of *The Secret War With Iran* concludes, along with several other Israeli politicians, that Israel will attack Iran in 2012.

Escobar, Pepe, "The Myth of 'Isolated' Iran," *Le Monde Diplomatique*, Jan. 24, 2012, http://mondediplo.com/openpage/the-myth-of-isolated-iran.
An Al Jazeera analyst says Tehran, which is adept at "Persian shadow play," has no intention of provoking a suicidal Western attack.

Esfandiary, Dina, "It's Time to Deal With Nuclear Iran," The Huffington Post, Nov. 16, 2011, www.iiss.org/whats-new/iiss-experts-commentary/its-time-to-deal-with-nuclear-iran/.
A research analyst and project coordinator at the Non-Proliferation and Disarmament Programme at London's International Institute for Strategic Studies warns against jumping to conclusions about a 2011 IAEA report on Iran's nuclear ambitions.

Gelb, Leslie H., "Leslie H. Gelb on How President Obama Should Handle Iran," *The Daily Beast*, Jan. 30, 2012, www. thedailybeast.com/articles/2012/01/30/leslie-h-gelb-on-how-president-obama-should-handle-iran.html.
A former strategic arms reduction negotiator during the Carter administration says President Obama should offer a robust peace proposal now that toughest-ever sanctions are pressuring Iran to halt its nuclear program.

Kahl, Colin, "Not Time to Attack Iran," *Foreign Affairs*, Jan. 17, 2012, www.foreignaffairs.com.
An associate professor in security studies at Georgetown University explains why a military intervention to halt Iran's nuclear program would be ill-judged.

Kroenig, Matthew, "Time to Attack Iran," *Foreign Affairs magazine*, Jan/Feb 2012, www.foreignaffairs.com.
A nuclear security fellow at the Council on Foreign Relations says attacking Iran is the "least bad option."

Reports and Studies

Fitzpatrick, Mark, "Iran's Nuclear, Chemical, and Biological Capabilities —A Net Assessment," Institute of International Strategic Studies, Feb. 3, 2011, www.iiss.org/publications/strategic-dossiers/irans-nuclear-chemical-and-biological-capabilities/.
The London-based institute's detailed technical assessment of Iran's weapons of mass destruction programs concludes that Iran does not have a nuclear weapon and, "won't have one tomorrow, or next week, or next month or a year from now."

Kerr, Paul, "Iran's Nuclear Program: Tehran's Compliance with International Obligations," Congressional Research Service, Dec. 21, 2011, http://fpc.state.gov/documents/organization/180686.pdf.
A specialist reviews Iran's nuclear program and details the legal basis for actions taken by the IAEA and U.N. Security Council.

Pletka, Danielle, *et al.*, "Containing and Deterring a Nuclear Iran," American Enterprise Institute, December 2011.
Experts from the conservative think tank contend that Iran already is a nuclear state and outline a containment strategy.

For More Information

Chatham House, The Royal Institute of International Affairs, 10 St. James's Square, London SW1Y4LE, United Kingdom; 44 207 957 5710; www.chathamhouse.org. A leading source of independent analysis on global and domestic issues.

Council on Foreign Relations, The Howard Pratt House, 58 East 68th St., New York, NY 10065; 212-434-9400; www.cfr.org. An independent think tank that "promotes understanding of foreign policy and America's role in the world."

International Atomic Energy Agency, P.O. Box 100, 1400 Vienna, Austria; 431 2600-0; www.iaea.org. The U.N. agency charged with promoting the development of "safe, secure, peaceful nuclear science and technology."

King Faisal Center for Research and Islamic Studies, P.O. Box 51049, Riyadh 11548, Saudi Arabia; 966 1 465 2255; www.kff.com. Furthers Islamic civilization by supporting continuing research and cultural and scientific activities in a variety of fields.

National Iran-American Council, 1411 K St., Washington, DC 20005; 202-386-6325; www.niacouncil.org/site/PageServer?pagename=NIAC_index. A nonprofit, nonpartisan organization dedicated to furthering the interests of the Iranian-American community and providing information about Iran.

University of Tehran, 16 Azur St., Tehran 14174, Iran; 9821 664 05047; www.ut.ac.ir/en. Offers courses in most academic fields, including foreign policy.

Voices From Abroad:

BENJAMIN NETANYAHU

Prime Minister, Israel

A threat to all

"The significance of the (IAEA) report is that the international community must bring about the cessation of Iran's pursuit of nuclear weapons, which endangers the peace of the world and of the Middle East."

Al Jazeera (Qatar), November 2011

ALI AKBAR SALEHI

Foreign Minister, Iran

A peaceful program

"We have repeatedly announced that we are just after a peaceful use of the nuclear energy and we consider production or use of nuclear bombs as Haram (religiously banned). The European Union should think about the real threat of the atomic bombs stockpiled in Europe instead of presenting a deceitful and unreal image of Iran's peaceful nuclear program."

Fars News Agency (Iran),
October 2011

MAHMOUD AHMADINEJAD

President, Iran

Building other things

"The Iranian nation is wise. It won't build two bombs against 20,000 [nuclear] bombs you (the West) have. But it builds something you can't respond to: ethics, decency, monotheism, and justice."

National televised speech, November 2011

Riber Hansson/Sweden

caglecartoons.com

VLADIMIR EVSEYEV

Center for Public Policy Research, Russia

Japan's footsteps

"Iran is likely to follow Japan's way now, that is, it creates the opportunities for the production of nuclear weapons, but it does not produce it. It creates technical potential, which can allow it this. But it is difficult to restrict the creation of this potential."

Trend News Agency (Azerbaijan), May 2011

JOSCHKA FISCHER

Former Vice Chancellor Germany

Endangering balance

"An Iran armed with nuclear weapons (or one political decision away from possessing them) would drastically alter the Middle East's strategic balance. At best, a nuclear-arms race would threaten to consume this already-unstable region, which would endanger the NPT, with far-reaching global consequences."

Korea Times (South Korea), December 2011

AFZAL BUTT

President, National Press Club, Pakistan

Double standards

"Iran will go ahead with its nuclear activities which are the country's right. They (the United States) cannot see a Muslim state following independent policy and not paying any attention to American threats. They must stop adopting dual standards against Iran . . . [the] U.S. knows that Iran is not developing a weapon-oriented nuclear program."

Philippine News Agency February 2011

MEHDI GHAZANFARI

Minister of Industries, Mines and Commerce Iran

Meaningless sanctions

"Some people think that sanctions have reached a damaging point and if the sanctions include the Central Bank, Iran will be finished off. But we think differently because

this is their last ploy and test, and after this, sanctions will become meaningless."

Mehr News Agency (Iran), January 2012

UZI EILAM

Senior Research Fellow Institute for National Security Studies, Israel

Uncertainty

"If they have enough . . . enriched uranium, they (Iran) will have to come up with a good design for the bomb. Then again, nobody knows how far they went in this field."

Trend News Agency (Azerbaijan), December 2011

AYATOLLAH SEYED AHMAD KHATAMI

Senior cleric, Iran

The U.S. is finished

"Today Iran is mighty, strong, and powerful and retaliates against any plot so powerfully that it would become a lesson for others. . . . [T]he United States is a finished superpower . . . an empty drum."

Sermon during the Muslim Feast of Sacrifice, November 2011

9

Millennium Development Goals

Danielle Kurtzleben

Pakistani children in a Karachi slum area que up for safe drinking water from a public faucet. The U.N. announced that in 2010 the world had met the MDG target of halving the proportion of people without access to safe water and sanitation, the cause of many childhood and other diseases.

From *The CQ Researcher*,
September 4, 2012.

Jan Vandemoortele used to get glassy stares when he told family and friends he worked on "good governance and capacity development" at the United Nations — international development jargon for helping governments improve the lives and health of their constituents.

But after he helped craft the U.N.'s landmark Millennium Development Goals (MDGs) in 2000, he could tell people, simply, "I am working to get all girls in school and reduce maternal mortality."

That's how the former U.N. official explains the value of the framework he helped to create to boost economic growth and well-being in developing nations. The MDGs were adopted in 2001 after the U.N.'s 2000 Millennium Summit, when world leaders agreed to establish eight specific goals — with measurable targets — for reducing poverty and relieving related barriers to economic development. Each of the organization's 189 members pledged to meet the targets by 2015, with help from roughly two dozen international organizations.

Those leaders, presumably, were able to go home and succinctly explain to their neighbors and families about the good they were hoping to accomplish in the world. Now the question is whether, in three years, they'll be able to give another succinct summation: "We did it."

Judging by progress over the last 12 years, they may be able to do just that — at least on some of the goals. Two key targets — slashing by half the 1990 levels of extreme poverty and the proportion of people without access to safe drinking water — were both met by 2010, five years ahead of the 2015 deadline.[1] Girls' primary school enrollment has reached parity with boys, and the living conditions for more than 200 million slum dwellers have been ameliorated — double the target for 2020.[2]

213

Progress Has Been Made, but Obstacles Remain

India and China — representing nearly half of the developing world's population — have made the most progress toward meeting the U.N.'s eight ambitious Millennium Development Goals (MDGs) by 2015, largely due to their rapid economic growth. But sub-Saharan Africa, which was far behind the rest of the developing world at the outset, has farther to go to meet the goals. Worldwide, significant strides have been made in reducing extreme poverty and making safe drinking water more accessible to all, but obstacles remain in attaining the rest of the goals: achieving universal primary education and gender equality, improving child mortality rates and maternal health, fighting HIV-AIDS, malaria and other diseases, ensuring environmental sustainability and creating a global partnership for development.

Progress in Achieving MDGs, as of 2011

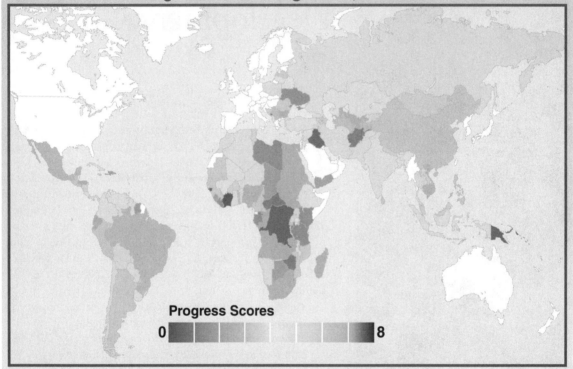

Source: "MDG Progress Index: Gauging Country-Level Achievements," Center for Global Development, www.cgdev.org/section/topics/poverty/mdg_scorecards. Map by Lewis Agrell

There has been marked progress on the other goals as well. The death rates for children under age 5 fell by 35 percent between 1990 and 2010. And by 2010, 90 percent of children in developing nations were enrolled in primary school, up from 82 percent in 1999.[3]

"These results represent a tremendous reduction in human suffering and are a clear validation of the approach embodied in the MDGs," U.N. Secretary-General Ban Ki-moon wrote in releasing the 2012 report on MDG progress. "But, they are not a reason to relax." Rather, he continued, "We must also recognize the unevenness of progress within countries and regions, and the severe inequalities that exist among populations, especially between rural and urban areas."[4]

Progress has indeed been uneven, with most gains occurring in economically vibrant India and China — which together represent 46 percent of the developing world's population. Achievements in eradicating poverty and hunger, for instance, have been due largely to rapid improvements in East Asia. "Over a 25-year period, the poverty rate in East Asia fell from nearly 60 percent to under 20 percent," the U.N. noted in 2010, and by 2015 poverty rates are expected to fall to around 5 percent in China and 24 percent in India.

But sub-Saharan Africa's extreme poverty rate declined far less dramatically — from 56 percent to 47 percent — during the 18-year period between 1990 and 2008.[5] In fact, the region has experienced remarkably slow progress — even declines — on many of the targets that the world as a whole has met.

In many cases, simple tactics led to progress. For instance, eliminating primary school fees helped to boost enrollment in several African countries; setting up tent schools brought education to children in remote areas of Mongolia; and using indigenous languages helped educate Bolivian children in outlying tribal regions.[6]

Routine immunizations have helped reduce child mortality in Africa, Vietnam and Bangladesh, and the distribution of insecticide-treated bed nets, particularly in Africa, has dramatically reduced the spread of malaria.

There have also been disappointments. Gender equality remains largely out of reach by several measurements, such as representation in classrooms, workplaces and government, and child

Most Rich Countries Miss Global Aid Target

Since 1970 developed nations have promised — and mostly failed — to provide foreign aid equivalent to at least 0.7 percent of their gross national incomes (GNI). Only five developed countries — all in Northern Europe — met the target in 2009 (bottom). Although the United States contributed far more foreign aid in total dollars than any other country in 2009 (top), it ranked 19th among the top 20 industrialized countries in the percentage of national income contributed in foreign aid.

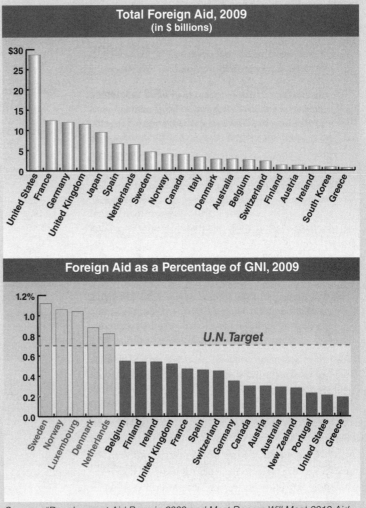

Source: "Development Aid Rose in 2009 and Most Donors Will Meet 2010 Aid Targets," Organisation for Economic Co-operation and Development, April 2010, www.oecd.org/investment/aidstatistics/developmentaidrosein2009andmostdonorswillmeet2010aidtargets.htm

Tackling Poverty Using Simple Techniques

Inexpensive strategies can be keys to progress.

After a dozen years fighting poverty through the Millennium Development Goals (MDGs), aid groups have learned new tactics for improving the lives of the world's poorest. Here are several:

Use low-cost strategies. Swooping in with lots of money and advanced technology can lead to improvements, but other methods often work better.

"The most effective health technologies are very cheap and very simple," Charles Kenny, a senior fellow at the Washington-based Center for Global Development, wrote in his 2011 book *Getting Better: Why Global Development Is Succeeding and How We Can Improve the World Even More.* For example, he noted, one-third of the 10 million annual child deaths in impoverished countries could be prevented with just three inexpensive, straightforward approaches: oral rehydration therapy, breast feeding and insecticide-treated bed nets.[1]

Even large-scale improvements to a nation's health-care system need not be massively expensive, he noted. Malaysia and Sri Lanka have virtually eliminated maternal mortality by making midwives available in rural areas. The dramatic improvement, he notes, has occurred even though spending on maternal and child health services in those countries is less than 0.4 percent of gross domestic product.[2]

Change social norms. Development is not just about aid organizations creating new institutions or services. The public also must have a genuine desire to use new programs.

More girls are attending school worldwide today not only because more schools have been opened but also because "it became normal to send girls to school," Kenny says, a cultural shift that occurred over decades.

Sanitation is another area where changing social norms provides benefits. To encourage pit latrine use and help people understand the health implications of defecating in the open, one specialist does a demonstration in which he puts excrement next to a plate of food so people can see how flies cross from one to the other.[3]

Use mobile phones. Mobile phones can open a world of economic possibilities to villagers in a developing country. "Poverty results from the lack of access to markets, to emergency health services, access to education, the ability to take advantage of government services and so on," Jeffrey Sachs, director of Columbia University's Earth Institute, told CNN in 2011. The mobile phone and IT technology can end "that kind of isolation in all its different varieties."[4]

Farmers in poor nations can use phones to find out where they can sell grain for the best price, and people can pay bills and send money to each other using cell phones, the World Bank notes.[5]

Still, mobile phones are no panacea. A recent study showed that 60 percent of the poorest one-fourth of Kenyans did not use the country's mobile phone service, *Slate* reported this year. "Telecom companies have relatively

deaths are not declining as quickly as hoped. Maternal mortality also has remained "unacceptably high."[7]

Limited women's empowerment is a major barrier to meeting some of the goals, according to Francesca Perucci, lead author of the U.N.'s 2012 MDG report. "[Gender equality] is slow to come in many settings, and then, of course, it's a big obstacle to reaching most of the other goals," she says. "Through women's empowerment you can achieve progress in other areas — child health, education, the economy."

And because women's empowerment is often difficult due to cultural norms, success is slow going. "It's not a matter of big donor initiatives or intervention," says Perucci. "It's a much broader policy issue."

Other far-reaching issues can restrict a country's MDG progress, she notes. If a country has a deeply troubled health-care system, for instance, change can require significant political action and a long time before maternal health and child mortality will improve. In addition, she adds, maternal and child health goals haven't received as much attention in recent years as other goals have.

As 2015 rapidly approaches, here are some of the questions development experts and political leaders are asking:

Will the goals be successful?

The answer to that question depends on how one defines "successful," say development experts.

little incentive to build out infrastructure, especially in poorer, rural markets," the online magazine said. Moreover, the cost of mobile phone service can be prohibitive for the poorest Kenyans, it said.[6]

Still, there is something to be said for a tool that can boost poor countries' economies and that people seek out on their own, as New York University economist and former World Bank official William Easterly pointed out in his 2006 book *The White Man's Burden: Why the West's Efforts to Aid the Rest Have Done So Much Ill and So Little Good.*

"The explosion of cell phones shows just how much poor people search for new technological opportunities, with no state intervention, with no structural adjustment or shock therapy to promote cell phones," he wrote, adding that the phones can provide services that would otherwise be "logistical nightmares in societies without good landline phones, functional postal services or adequate roads."[7]

— *Danielle Kurtzleben*

A South African shop owner displays her mobile phone on May 5, 2011, in a township near Cape Town. Development economists say cell phones can inexpensively increase people's access to markets, emergency health services, education and government services. "If you had to wire up Africa with land lines for telephones, it could never have been done," says Barry Carin, a senior fellow at the Canadian think tank, the Center for International Governance Innovation.

[1]Charles Kenny, *Getting Better: Why Global Development Is Succeeding and How We Can Improve the World Even More* (2011), p. 126.

[2]*Ibid.*, pp. 126-127.

[3]"West Africa: Smoothing the way for more pit latrines," IRIN [U.N. news agency], Aug. 31, 2011, http://irinnews.org/Report/93621/WEST-AFRICA-Smoothing-the-way-for-more-pit-latrines.

[4]Kevin Voigt, "Mobile Phone: Weapon Against Global Poverty," CNN, Oct. 9, 2011, http://articles.cnn.com/2011-10-09/tech/tech_mobile_mobile-phone-poverty_1_mobile-phone-cell-phone-rural-villages?_s=PM:TECH.

[5]Shanta Devarajan, "More Cell Phones Than Toilets," The World Bank, April 12, 2010, http://blogs.worldbank.org/africacan/more-cell-phones-than-toilets.

[6]Jamie M. Zimmerman and Sascha Meinrath, "Mobile Phones Will Not Save the Poorest of the Poor," *Slate*, Feb. 9, 2012, www.slate.com/articles/technology/future_tense/2012/02/m_pesa_and_other_ict4d_projects_are_leaving_behind_the_developing_world_s_poorest_people_.html.

[7]William Easterly, *The White Man's Burden: Why the West's Efforts to Aid the Rest Have Done So Much Ill and So Little Good* (2006), pp. 103-104.

The goals provide simple, clear numerical measurements of "success." By that definition all of the MDG targets won't be met by 2015, particularly on health-related goals such as maternal and child mortality.

But that view obscures the fact that three of the targets — on poverty, slum conditions and clean water — already have been met. And despite sizable hurdles, "Meeting the remaining targets, while challenging, remain[s] possible," the U.N. said in releasing its 2012 MDG report.[8]

In addition, the MDGs helped focus attention on certain development problems and boosted international cooperation on important global issues, according to Sam Worthington, president and CEO of InterAction,

an alliance of development nongovernmental organizations (NGOs). "The MDGs have played an essential role for the U.S. nonprofit community by organizing the billions of dollars of private giving around concrete themes and giving nonprofits targets," says Worthington.

The "concrete-ness" of the MDGs has been their strength, argues Vandemoortele, and having a manageable number of clear, specific goals has given the MDGs remarkable staying power. "Those are the main reasons why the MDGs are still talked about," he says. "So many things come and go, so many acronyms, and either they don't take off or after two years they are gone," he says. The MDGs "are still measurable, and we live in a world where numbers do matter."

Poverty Fell, Especially in China

The first Millennium Development Goal — cutting in half the proportion of people in the developing world living in extreme poverty in 1990 — has been achieved. However, much of the progress stemmed from China's phenomenal economic growth. When China is excluded, the proportion living on less than $1.25 per day was only cut by one-third.

Percentage Living on Less Than $1.25 Per Day, 1990-2008

Source: "The Millennium Development Goals Report: 2012," United Nations, 2012, p. 6, mdgs.un.org/unsd/mdg/Resources/Static/Products/Progress2012/ English2012.pdf

However, others question whether setting the goals spurred the improvements in individual targets or the success was due to other factors. For instance, the first MDG was halving the proportion of people living on $1.25 or less per day. Preliminary World Bank estimates say that target was met in 2010.[9]

But the lion's share of progress toward that goal occurred in China and, to a smaller extent, India, both of which saw stunning economic growth in recent years. In those two countries alone, the number of people in extreme poverty declined by 455 million between 1990 and 2005, according to the U.N.'s 2011 MDG report.[10] Without China in the equation, the proportion of people in developing regions living on less than $1.25 per day fell only from 41 percent in 1990 to 28 percent in 2008, so the target hasn't yet been met if China is not counted.[11] And in sub-Saharan Africa, the proportion living in poverty declined modestly, from 58 to 51 percent, and in the Caribbean, from 29 to 26 percent. In the Caucasus and Central Asia, the poverty situation worsened — from 6 to 19 percent.

"There's no causal chain whatsoever between MDGs and poverty reduction. And I say that as a fan of the MDGs and as a big cheerleader for the reduction in poverty," says

Laurence Chandy, a fellow in the Global Economy and Development program at the Washington-based Brookings Institution think tank. "It was this rapid increase in economic growth in many developing countries that brought about this big reduction in poverty."

All in all, the MDG "success" question is easy to answer on a numerical, success-or-failure basis, but the picture becomes fuzzier the deeper one looks, as the Bill and Melinda Gates Foundation — whose work in areas like global health and agriculture supports MDG progress — noted in its recent MDG assessment.

"While the MDGs provide a helpful quantitative framework for assessing broad-based progress in development, they do not in themselves adequately capture the distribution of progress across society, the sustainability of progress over time or subjective conceptions of progress itself."[12]

Progress in achieving universal primary education presents another clear example of this phenomenon. Abolishing primary-school fees has helped spur a surge in school enrollment in sub-Saharan Africa, but how much good are those schools doing?

"Getting children into school . . . isn't very useful if they learn little or nothing once they're there," wrote Abhijit Banerjee and Esther Duflo in their 2011 book *Poor Economics.* "The Millennium Development Goals do not specify that children should learn anything in school, just that they should complete a basic cycle of education."[13]

Development experts stress that the MDGs are only a stepping stone. Halving the poverty rate still leaves hundreds of millions in poverty. In other words, for every signpost passed, there is another in the distance for the world to strive toward — and the opportunity to ask, "What now?"

Were the goals unfair to some countries?

Countless news articles and U.N. reports have predicted that some countries — mostly in sub-Saharan Africa — would "fail" or "fall short" in meeting the MDGs. Likewise, India is "in a race against time" to achieve the MDGs by 2015, Noeleen Heyzer, executive secretary of the U.N. Economic and Social Commission for Asia and the Pacific, said in February.[14]

Indeed, U.N. monitoring reports show wide disparities in poverty reduction and other MDG indicators. The World Bank's 2012 report on food prices, nutrition and the MDGs notes that 105 of the 144 countries being monitored are not expected to reach the MDG goal for reducing child mortality, and 94 are unlikely to hit the target for improving maternal health.[15]

New York University economist William Easterly says in some cases those comparisons are unfair, particularly with regard to sub-Saharan African countries. For instance, said the former World Bank economist in a 2007 paper, by choosing 1990 as the base year for most measurements, such as the goal to halve extreme poverty rates by 2015, the MDGs set African nations up for failure.[16]

"African economic growth was very poor in the 1990s," he wrote. "Hence, it began the MDG campaign in 2000 already 'off-track' to meet the poverty goal."[17]

In addition, the method used to measure some goals meant that African nations would miss the targets, he said. Citing data from a 2005 World Bank analysis of MDG progress, Easterly pointed out that Africa was behind in reducing the share of its population without access to clean water. However, Africa would have been "catching up if it had been measured the conventional way, [using the] percent *with* access to clean water," he wrote, concluding that "the choice of *with* and *without* is arbitrary."

Big Rise in Children Attending School

The number of children not attending school dropped from more than 100 million in 1990 to just over 60 million in 2010 — a 42 percent decline. Sub-Saharan Africa has made the least progress — and Asia the most — toward the key U.N. goal of making primary education available to all by 2015.

Number of Out-of-School Children by Region, 1990 and 2010

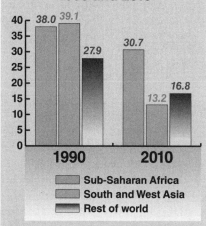

Sub-Saharan Africa
South and West Asia
Rest of world

Source: "Reaching Out-of-School Children Is Crucial for Development," United Nations Educational, Scientific and Cultural Organization, June 2012, p. 2, www.uis.unesco.org/ Education/Documents/fs-18-OOSC-2.pdf

Aside from such technical, statistical problems with the MDGs, others say it is unfair to dwell on individual countries' progress on what were meant to be global targets. The goals "were never formulated as targets for individual countries," says Jon Lomoy, director of the Development Co-operation Directorate at the Paris-based Organisation for Economic Co-operation and Development (OECD). "They were formulated as global targets."

"The misinterpretation of the MDGs as one-size-fits-all targets has set the bar for sub-Saharan Africa countries unrealistically high," wrote former U.N. official Vandemoortele in 2009. For example, Africa has made significant progress in curbing the spread of HIV-AIDS and in putting more children in primary schools, but because many African countries have so far to go before meeting some of the goals, it is easy to ignore the successes, he wrote.[18]

If the world fails to meet the MDGs, he argued, "it's not going to be because Africa has failed, [but] because Asia has failed to contribute its fair share" toward global poverty reduction.

Still, others say, taking a country-by-country look at poverty reduction highlights those parts of the world needing the most help and which tactics are working in particular countries. In a 2000 paper setting out guidelines for creating the MDGs, then-U.N. Secretary-General Kofi Annan pointed to deeply impoverished regions that desperately needed assistance, such as parts of southern Asia and sub-Saharan Africa.[19] In other words, while the goal may have been global poverty reduction, the drafters acknowledged that some had further to go than others.

A Chinese woman washes clothes at a slum across from new, subsidized, government-built apartments in Shenyang, China, on March 11, 2009. Achievements in eradicating poverty and hunger — key Millennium Development Goals — have been accelerated by rapid economic growth in East Asia, where the poverty rate fell from nearly 60 percent to less than 20 percent in the past 25 years. Poverty rates in China are expected to fall to around 5 percent 2015.

Country-level measures of "success" and "failure" also can reveal a government's commitment to achieving the goals. Highly indebted countries applying for debt relief from the International Monetary Fund (IMF) must be aware of their MDG progress and submit periodic updates on their poverty-reduction strategies. While countries do not have to achieve the MDG targets to gain debt relief, they must take "ownership" of their strategies by presenting a vision of how they will reach the goals.[20]

"In terms of country-level objectives, we need to leave that much more to the country," says Lomoy. Rather than aiming for global-level goals, he says, individual nations should be allowed to shoot for their own bar, asking themselves, "What's an ambitious but still realistic target we can set for our country?"

Having country-level aspirations also helps invest smaller countries in the outcome, says Homi Kharas, former World Bank chief economist for East Asia and the Pacific and currently a senior fellow at the Brookings Institution. "If it's just a global target dominated by what happens in China, India and maybe Brazil, it's not motivating for small countries," he says.

Is the progress achieved under the goals sustainable?

While the answer to that question is "unknowable," says Barry Carin, a senior fellow at the Center for International Governance Innovation, a Canadian think tank, many trends are bolstering MDG sustainability.

For instance, innovations in science and technology are helping to achieve the health-related goals. Vaccines reduce child mortality and the spread of diseases such as diphtheria and pertussis, and scientists are working on vaccines that could halt the spread of meningitis and malaria.

Advances in communication also boost local and national economies, says Carin. "Just look at the question of connectivity and telephones," he says. "If you had to wire up Africa with land lines for telephones, it could never have been done. Now, cell phones allow everybody to be connected."

Jeffrey Sachs, a poverty expert and director of Columbia University's Earth Institute, has called cell phones "the single most transformative technology for development," noting that even a limited number of cell phones can greatly boost economic activity.

"It doesn't take more than a few phones to make a transformative difference in an area," he told the news website AllAfrica in 2008. "We're seeing small businesses develop by virtue of people having phones, being able to find clients, make purchases, get supplies."[21]

If technology were the only factor, the outlook might be sunnier. Unfortunately, the world faces significant problems that threaten local economies — both rich and poor.

Climate change — and the world's inaction in curbing it — is a major threat to MDG progress, says Charles Kenny, a senior fellow at the Center for Global Development, a Washington think tank. "If Bangladesh is under water in 50 years, that's going to have an effect on Bangladesh's development process," he says.

Another challenge is the ongoing economic crisis, which has brought global GDP growth to a crawl and led many wealthy countries to cut foreign aid to impoverished countries.

"The financial crisis has had a direct impact on development assistance and flows of resources to poor parts of the world," says InterAction's Worthington. Yet, he adds, "at the same time, many developing countries have continued to see significant growth."

In fact, says the Brookings Institution's Chandy, during the 2007-08 recession developing countries fared "a lot better than the West did, and there are many reasons why that might be the case." For one thing, he says, their financial markets "are much less developed" and less exposed to the problems that roiled places like Europe and the United States.

That news would likely come as cold comfort to factory workers in those countries. A 2010 study from the London-based aid organization Oxfam found that many export-dependent workers and industries in countries such as Ghana and Indonesia were devastated by the global downturn, "even when national economies seem[ed] to be weathering the storm."[22]

More recently, however, some developing countries' economies are slowing, partly because of Europe's ongoing debt crisis.[23] "Developing countries should prepare for a long period of volatility in the global economy," the World Bank warned in June. The organization's "Global Economic Prospects" report noted decelerating GDP growth in Latin America and the Caribbean, the Middle East and North Africa, South Asia, and East Asia and the Pacific.[24]

Even if many developing countries remain strong, the fate of the world's largest nation looms as a major threat for the global economy.

"Frankly, so far, the developing world has weathered the global recession comparatively well," says Kenny. "That won't go on forever. If China crashes, we're all in trouble."

Indeed, the list of clear and present dangers that could shut down MDG progress at times seems endless. Still, the question of whether progress is sustainable may largely boil down to one factor.

"A lot of it depends on growth. If you have dramatic population growth and poor economic growth, things will get worse," says Carin.

BACKGROUND

Unmet Goals

Although the U.N. formally introduced the world to MDGs in 2001, the goals had, in fact, been decades in the making.

The world has a long, if not successful, history of setting human development targets. U.S. President Franklin D. Roosevelt, for example, crafted his own ambitious goals for fighting poverty. In his 1941 State of the Union address he laid out "four freedoms," including "freedom from want," that he believed would be foundational to rebuilding the world after World War II.[25]

Likewise, in the U.N.'s Universal Declaration of Human Rights in 1948, the fledgling organization's 58 members agreed that human beings were entitled to 30 fundamental civil, political, economic, social and cultural rights. The declaration gave birth to the Commission on Human Rights, which has promoted those rights via international treaties.[26]

At the suggestion of U.S. President John F. Kennedy, the U.N. in the 1960s declared the first "Development Decade," setting a minimum goal of 5 percent growth in aggregate national income in all less-developed countries, with developed nations contributing 1 percent of their incomes in economic aid and private investment.[27]

In a 2009 history of the MDGs, David Hulme, executive director of the Brooks World Poverty Institute at Great Britain's University of Manchester, described this period as one of "a rash of goal-setting," in which "enthusiasm to set targets ran ahead of commitment to action."[28]

When it became clear in the mid-1970s that the world would not meet the targets, the U.N. went on in 1970 and 1980 to declare its Second and Third Development Decades, which also became decades of largely unfulfilled goals.

During the Second Decade, developed nations agreed to provide 0.7 percent of their GDPs in foreign aid — a benchmark that remains in effect but that most developed countries fail to hit.

In 1974 the United Nations resolved to establish a New International Economic Order to improve developing countries' role in international trade and narrow the gap between them and developed nations. But this, too, would be unfruitful. In 1984, the General Assembly acknowledged the lack of progress and that the targets for the decade remained unmet.[29]

During the second half of the 20th century, developing countries racked up heavy debts, both to private banks and international institutions such as the World Bank and the IMF. By the early 2000s, payments on many of those debts would become larger than the indebted countries' domestic budgets for health, education and other basic needs.[30]

C H R O N O L O G Y

1960s-1980s *World experiments with development goal-setting.*

1961 U.N. declares 1960s the Decade of Development, later known as the First Development Decade. Developing countries are to accelerate growth by 5 percent annually.

1970 U.N. sets 0.7 percent of gross national product as a goal for rich nations to give in foreign aid.

1971 U.N. establishes Second Development Decade, with annual GDP growth target of 6 percent for developing nations.

1973 World Bank President Robert McNamara announces goal of eradicating poverty by close of 20th century.

1981 With the Second Development Decade goals still "largely unfulfilled," U.N. establishes Third Development Decade.

1990s *World grows more optimistic in fight against poverty; holds more development summits.*

March 5-9, 1990 World Conference on Education for All in Jomtien, Thailand, establishes a goal of universal primary education by 2000.

June 3-14, 1992 At U.N. Conference on Environment and Development (the Rio Earth Summit), more than 100 heads of state agree to strive for "achieving sustainable development in the 21st century."

1995 Organisation for Economic Co-operation and Development (OECD) establishes International Development Goals (IDGs), the precursors to the Millennium Development Goals (MDGs). . . . U.N.'s Fourth World Conference on Women in Beijing establishes 12-point Platform for Action in areas such as women's education and reproductive health.

2000s *World sets new development and anti-poverty goals.*

2000 At U.N.'s Millennium Summit, 189 countries adopt Millennium Declaration, which encourages

tolerance and solidarity and asserts that each individual has the right to dignity, freedom, equality and a basic standard of living — including freedom from hunger and violence.

2001 Millennium Development Goals are formally adopted; U.N. Secretary-General Kofi Annan releases "road map" toward implementing Millennium Declaration.

March 18-22, 2002 At a summit in Monterrey, Mexico, developed nations reaffirm their commitment to giving 0.7 percent of their national incomes to poor nations.

2005 At G8 summit in Gleneagles, Scotland, developed nations agree to provide debt relief to qualifying countries (July 6-8); world leaders agree to spend additional $50 billion annually to fight poverty and reaffirm their commitment to the MDGs (Sept. 14-16).

Jan. 1, 2008 Four new MDG targets go into effect: achieving full and productive employment, universal access to reproductive health services, universal access to HIV-AIDS treatment and reducing loss of biodiversity.

2010 At U.N. World MDG Summit in New York leaders pledge $40 billion toward a Global Strategy for Women's and Children's Health. . . . The first MDG target — halving the global extreme poverty rate — is met.

2012 World reaches two more targets: halving the proportion of people without access to clean drinking water and improving the lives of the world's slum dwellers. . . . U.N. Secretary-General Ban Ki-moon names three co-chairs of a high-level panel to advise on post-2015 goals: President Susilo Bambang Yudhoyono of Indonesia; President Ellen Johnson Sirleaf of Liberia; and Prime Minister David Cameron of the U.K. (May 9). . . . At the Rio+20 Summit, world leaders agree to move ahead with conceptualizing sustainable development goals (SDGs) as post-2015 MDG replacements (June 20-22).

2013 World leaders will hold summit in May to evaluate MDG progress and look ahead to the 2015 MDG deadline. In September, U.N. General Assembly will discuss including the disabled in new development goals.

2015 Deadline for reaching MDG targets.

Do MDG Targets Mask Failure?

Critics say some goals are set too low.

Since their inception, the Millennium Development Goals (MDGs) were seen as providing strong, concrete targets for measuring progress — or lack thereof — in meeting the goals. But critics say some of the targets are set so low that the success they indicate is sometimes illusory.

For example, the first goal — halving of the proportion of people living on less than $1.25 per day — was met in 2010. However, simply boosting average earnings to $1.26 per day, or even $2 per day, still leaves a person remarkably poor.

Substantial progress also was logged in education. As measured by the MDGs, 90 percent of primary school-age children were enrolled as of 2010, and gender parity was achieved in primary school education in 2012.[1]

However, "Enrollment and learning are two notably different things," as Charles Kenny, a senior fellow at the Center for Global Development, wrote in his 2011 book, *Getting Better: Why Global Development Is Succeeding and How We Can Improve the World Even More.* He points to a recent survey showing that, of Indian students who had completed lower primary schooling, 31 percent could not read a simple story. Only one-quarter of Ghanaian 15- to 19-year-olds scored more than 50 percent on tests of 1- or 2-digit math problems.[2]

Judging from such statistics, it's no wonder that kids in some of the poorest nations aren't learning. School days in some countries are as short as two hours.[3] In addition, just because the kids are in school doesn't mean that the teachers are. In fact, teacher absenteeism is rampant in some parts of the world. One new study found that teachers in five South African provinces were absent for more than one month in the year, or more than 20 school days.[4] A 2011 World Bank study showed that most primary school teachers in Ghana spend only 76 of 196 school days in the classroom.[5]

In other words, improving the quantity of children in the classrooms has achieved progress — statistically — toward the target. Measuring the quality of that education, however, is another story. This is just one example of the need to be careful about focusing too much on a goal and not on broader outcomes, says Homi Kharas, former chief economist in the East Asia and Pacific Region of the World Bank and currently a senior fellow at the Brookings Institution. That principle extends beyond education and to the other goals as well, he says.

Although 90 percent of primary school-age children were enrolled in schools as of 2010, experts warn that that statistic does not indicate how much the children are learning or whether there is a teacher present at all times. Above, children attend class at the Friendship Primary school in Zinder, Niger, in West Africa on June 1, 2012.

He likens the link between targets and outcomes to the link between carbon dioxide (CO_2) levels and global temperature change.

"We obviously have studies that link those two together, so it may well be that there's an intermediate target [such as CO_2 emissions] that you want to monitor," he says. "But at the end of the day, it's important to be very clear what that real outcome is" — temperature change — "so that we avoid just focusing on that one intermediate target."

— *Danielle Kurtzleben*

[1] "The Millennium Development Goals Report 2012," United Nations, pp. 16, 20, http://mdgs.un.org/unsd/mdg/Resources/Static/Products/Progress2012/English2012.pdf.

[2] Charles Kenny, *Getting Better: Why Global Development Is Succeeding and How We Can Improve the World Even More* (2011), p. 91.

[3] Larry Elliott and Decca Aitkenhead, "It's Payback Time: Don't Expect Sympathy — Lagarde to Greeks," *The Guardian,* May 25, 2012, www.guardian.co.uk/world/2012/may/25/payback-time-lagarde-greeks.

[4] Carol Paton, "SA Outdoes Poor Neighbours on Absentee Teachers," *Business Day,* May 17, 2012. www.businessday.co.za/articles/Content.aspx?id=171942.

[5] "High Teacher Absenteeism Hindering Inclusive Education in Ghana — World Bank," *Modern Ghana,* April 17, 2011, www.modernghana.com/news/325303/1/high-teacher-absenteeism-hindering-inclusive-educa.html.

International UNICEF ambassador Orlando Bloom, a British actor, visits the Kaule Community Organization in Kalika, Nepal, on Jan. 10, 2008. The UNICEF-supported organization has helped to boost school enrollment and encouraged the consumption of iodized salt, which prevents goiters. Maternal mortality and child deaths in Nepal have declined since 1996, putting the country on track to reach those two Millennium Development Goals by 2015.

New Beginning

As the Cold War ended in the late 1980s, industrialized countries began to cut their foreign aid budgets, which had been used in part to curry favor in the ideological superpower struggle between communism and capitalism. Between 1985 and 1995, U.S. government spending overall rose 15 percent, but U.S. foreign aid declined by 32 percent.[31]

International development organizations, worried about cuts in aid, rallied to consider how to attack global problems.[32] The World Bank's "World Development Report 1990" and the U.N. Development Programme's (UNDP) "Human Development Report" both stressed the importance of addressing global poverty. The U.N. held four international conferences in 1990, kicking off what would be a decade of international meetings and discussions about global development.

"In the '90s, almost every year we had a summit," remembers MDG architect Vandemoortele. "We had Copenhagen. We had Cairo, reproductive health in 1994, human rights in 1993, we had settlements in 1996, a food summit in 1996."

Although the summits suggested a renewed international vigor for development, says Hulme of the Brooks World Poverty Institute, summits often have one chief outcome: hot air. "First, national ministers declare a grand

goal," he says. "Subsequently this goal has some general influence on activity, but it is not systematically pursued. At the next U.N. summit or conference, the minister (or his/her successor) agrees to the same or a reduced goal for a later date."[33]

Still, the Christian relief organization World Vision described the 1990s as a time of optimism for the biggest international aid contributors. The U.S. economy, the world's largest, was humming along strongly, and two of the world's most powerful leaders, U.S. President Bill Clinton and U.K. Prime Minister Tony Blair, were beginning to work toward reducing poverty. As World Vision noted in a 2011 paper on the MDGs, the World Bank was switching its *modus operandi* in developing countries from imposing structural adjustment programs — which focused on establishing free-market economies and eliminating protectionism — toward poverty reduction strategies.[34]

Ultimately, many of the summits helped to establish the MDG policy framework.[35]

Amid this atmosphere of hopeful global cooperation a group of international development ministers in 1995 commissioned the OECD to predict how the next century of development would look. The organization's 1996 report, "Shaping the 21st Century," stressed the need for governments, international organizations and financial institutions to cooperate on economic development.

More important, the report laid out six "ambitious but realizable goals," which came to be known as the International Development Goals (IDGs). They were prototypes for some of the MDGs, with many of the same aims. For example, the OECD set the goal of halving the rate of "extreme poverty" in developing countries by 2015, achieving universal primary education, making progress toward gender equality and reducing infant and maternal mortality.

'We the Peoples'

The MDGs were born in part out of this atmosphere of goal-setting and summit-holding, but they were also, in former U.N. official Vandemoortele's opinion, a product of timing.

"Then came the Millennium and everyone had to do something special," he says. "The U.N., for lack of imagination called together another summit, the Millennium Summit."

In preparation, Secretary-General Annan — in an effort to help U.N. countries craft the declaration that would result from that summit, produced a report, released in early April 2000, entitled, "We the Peoples: The Role of the United Nations in the 21st Century." It emphasized many of the topics that would become part of the MDGs: eliminating extreme poverty, better educational and employment opportunities, promoting better health care and combating HIV-AIDS.

In advance of the Millennium Summit the mood was particularly ambitious, with leaders ready to make good on all of the past U.N. development shortcomings. "They kind of looked back at all these declarations and promises that were made in the past decades, and they made the mother of all declarations by summarizing the key promises the world leaders had made in terms of human development," says Vandemoortele.

However, drafting the final goals was controversial, as individuals and organizations jockeyed for their causes to be included in the MDGs. "If your goal was in the Declaration, then you could put it on the agenda at national and international meetings for years to come," wrote Hulme. "Websites buzzed, email campaigns piled up in ministers' accounts and large and small meetings were convened, especially in the rich world."[36]

Meanwhile, the goals had to have unanimous international backing — no small feat for a group of nearly 200 countries. While the process ultimately yielded eight goals, it also made for some very unhappy organizations.

For instance, Steven Sinding, director general of the International Planned Parenthood Federation in London, wrote in 2005 about the challenge of getting women's reproductive health onto the MDG agenda. At a 1994 International Conference on Population and Development in Cairo, participants agreed that women in least-developed countries needed basic reproductive rights, particularly the freedom to determine the number of children they would bear. These reproductive freedoms would be foundational for broader progress in areas such as public health, education and the environment, Sinding says.

But not everyone supported reproductive health as a global development goal, and in the minds of some women's health advocates, politics won out over women's — and some say society's — best interests. Annan's "We the Peoples" report notably made no mention of reproductive health. The developing nations were split on the issue of reproductive

A young Somali refugee is vaccinated against polio and measles at the Dadaab refugee complex in northeastern Kenya on Aug. 1, 2011. Vaccines are inexpensive ways to achieve health-related MDGs worldwide. Vaccines reduce child mortality and the spread of diseases such as diphtheria and pertussis, and scientists are working on vaccines that could halt the spread of meningitis and malaria.

AFP/Getty Images/Tony Karumba

health, and ultimately opted to appease the more conservative member countries, said Sinding's federation.[37]

"I think the calculation of the Secretariat was, 'Let's not sacrifice the greater coherence and get involved in these highly controversial topics,'" said Ambassador Gert Rosenthal of Guatemala, one of the Millennium Declaration's co-authors.[38]

As a result, according to women's health advocates, the issue would be ignored for 15 years on the international stage. As Sinding succinctly put it: "If you're not an MDG, you're not on the agenda."[39]

Similarly, other issues — such as economic growth and clearer targets for rich countries' assistance — did not make it into the MDGs, Hulme wrote.

Determining the numerical targets themselves was also a matter of some debate, according to Vandemoortele. Leaders eventually settled on what seemed to be a simple, diplomatic solution: The numerical goals should sustain recent development trends.

"Political leaders were asking themselves, what should be a reasonable target?" he says.

The only way to answer that question was to ask "What have we done over the past two or three decades?"

For instance, for under-age 5 mortality, Vandermoortele explained, "We had a rate of decline of the 1970s and

AFP/Getty Images/Pierre Verdy

Irish anti-poverty activist and singer Bono (right), former British Prime Minister Tony Blair (center) and billionaire American philanthropist Bill Gates (left) are leading intensified efforts to reduce global poverty. In 2005 they lobbied for multilateral institutions to forgive the external debt of highly indebted poor countries so they could afford to pursue the Millennium Development Goals. Today, countries with annual per-capita incomes of $380 or less can have their debt wiped clean if they have a satisfactory poverty-reduction strategy.

'80s of such a magnitude that if you extrapolate it, you would achieve a reduction of two-thirds." The same process was carried out for other targets as well. "On poverty it only says halving, because decline was much more modest in those areas."

Following Through

But if the MDGs were simply to follow existing poverty-reduction trends, what purpose did they really serve?

Perhaps the goals' most immediate achievement was to organize international donors, recipients and aid organizations around the MDGs as logical thematic areas of concentration. "Before the MDGs, we didn't have nicely organized communities focused on reducing malaria or increasing maternal health or decreasing infant mortality," says InterAction's Worthington.

"The shift from goals to results greatly accelerated the progress of human well-being in a number of areas," he adds. "The rapid drop in malaria happened because of this focus on results under the goals. All of these things had been happening at a certain pace, but they were accelerated once we had a set of indicators and a desire to increase results. And the goals were the frame that made that possible."

Indeed, malaria deaths, which had doubled between 1980 and 2004, reversed direction, falling from 1.8 million in 2004 to 1.2 million in 2010, largely because of the wider use of insecticide-treated mosquito nets.[40]

Developing countries, led by the IMF, also organized themselves around the new targets. They produced poverty-reduction strategy papers, updated regularly, describing the long-term structural and social policies and programs they would follow to promote overall growth and reduce poverty.[41] Although the papers force countries to assess their current and future situations, Sachs described the poverty-reduction plan process as backwards.

In his 2005 book *The End of Poverty*, Sachs outlined the typical steps in producing a policy-reduction strategy paper. "Ethiopia is told, for example, 'You can expect around $1 billion next year. Please tell us what you plan to do with that aid,'" Sachs wrote.[42]

Instead, he argued, the process should be "turned around. The first step should be to learn what the country actually needs in foreign assistance," he wrote. Then the IMF and World Bank could "go out to raise the required amount from the donors!"[43]

But obtaining the necessary aid is not easy. Donor countries have failed to meet their foreign aid commitments since before the goals were implemented. And in 2002, more than 50 heads of state signed the Monterrey Consensus, which urged developed countries to make "concrete efforts" to donate at least 0.7 percent of gross national income as foreign aid, known as official development assistance (ODA). Then again at the Gleneagles G8 Summit in 2005 in Scotland, donor countries pledged to boost ODA. But as of 2011, only Norway, Luxembourg, Denmark, the Netherlands and Sweden had hit the 0.7 mark in terms of ODA as a share of gross national income (GNI), a figure roughly comparable to GDP in many countries.[44] In 2011, the United States contributed 0.2 percent of its GNI in foreign aid.[45]

Still, since 2000, nations have taken several momentous steps forward. At Gleneagles the G8 countries agreed to forgive the debt of highly indebted poor countries — a cause championed by Sachs, Pope John Paul II and anti-poverty activist Bono, the lead singer of the Irish rock band U2. Under the Multilateral Debt Relief Initiative, the IMF, World Bank and African Development Fund (a branch of the African Development Bank that provides very low-interest loans to Africa's poorest countries) would forgive

100 percent of the debt of countries with unsustainable debt burdens. But they had to first "demonstrate satisfactory performance" in macroeconomic policies, implementing a poverty-reduction strategy and managing government expenditures.[46]

So far, of 39 eligible or potentially eligible nations, 33 are receiving full debt relief, according to the IMF. Former U.N. official Vandemoortele calls debt relief a lifesaver for citizens in the world's poorest nations. "The evidence is very clear that the savings that these countries made on their national budgets were [largely] allocated to the areas that matter for reducing poverty," he says.

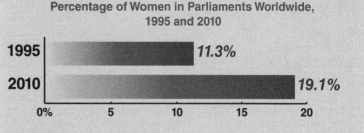

More Women Serving in Parliaments

Women hold about 20 percent of the seats in parliaments worldwide, nearly double the percentage in 1995. The third Millennium Development Goal calls for parity with men.

Percentage of Women in Parliaments Worldwide, 1995 and 2010

1995	11.3%
2010	19.1%

Source: "Women in Parliament in 2010: The Year in Perspective," Inter-Parliamentary Union, 2011, p. 4, www.ipu.org/pdf/publications/wmnpersp10-e.pdf

In 2005, member states agreed to pursue four new MDG targets to fill in gaps not addressed by the original goals: achieving full and productive employment, providing access to reproductive health and HIV-AIDS treatment and preserving biodiversity. These four targets went into effect in January 2008. And in 2010, a $40 billion initiative on women's and children's health was implemented.

In a 2010 op-ed in *The Financial Times*, Sachs criticized the series of headline-grabbing donor meetings and promises in the 2000s as a showcase for their lack of accountability. Taken together, he said, wealthy donor countries have fallen short on every big headline pledge they made during the decade, including at:

- Monterrey in 2002, to reach 0.7 percent of GNP in development aid;
- Gleneagles in 2005, to double African aid by 2010;
- L'Aquila in 2009, to direct $22 billion over three years to raise productivity of small farmers; and
- Copenhagen in 2009, to add $30 billion over three years for climate change adaptation and mitigation.

Promises were easily made but not delivered, he said, because the commitments had no clear mechanisms for fulfillment.[47]

The economic crisis of 2008-09 also threatened international aid, but the effects seem to have been muted thus far. A 2012 World Bank report notes that total disbursements by OECD donor countries increased by 4.3 percent from 2008 to 2010. The report also found that developing nations fared well by another key measure: "Despite the financial crisis, . . . debt service ratios continued to fall in most developing regions."[48]

Still, the crisis delivered a blow to MDG progress on some targets. The U.N. has estimated that there were 50 million more working poor in 2011 than was projected by pre-crisis trends.[49] And the crisis slowed the growing share of women in non-agricultural paid employment.[50]

Oxfam, the Christian relief organization, found that some companies in Thailand and Cambodia took advantage of the crisis to institute wage freezes, reduce work hours or pressure workers into less-secure contracts.[51]

Interestingly, the crisis boosted progress on one goal dealing with environmental sustainability. According to the 2012 U.N. MDG report, world greenhouse gas emissions dipped slightly in 2009, from 30.2 billion to 30.1 billion metric tons, due to slowing economic activity.

CURRENT SITUATION

Mixed Progress

Although progress has been rapid and even impressive on some of the eight Millennium Development Goals, on others it has been slow. Here is a rundown on progress made

Have developed countries done enough to help achieve the MDGs?

YES Jan Vandemoortele
Former official at UNICEF and U.N. Development Program; Co-Architect of the MDGs

Written for *CQ Global Researcher*, August 2012

To further the last of the eight MDG goals — building a global development partnership — developed countries promised significant progress in four areas: debt relief, foreign aid, global governance and global trade. Despite the absence of clear, quantitative targets on these points, one can draw a proxy scorecard for their performance since 1990.

First, developed countries can rightly claim to have kept the promise on debt relief. The debt burden of the developing world has become less crippling over the past two decades. Not only has this freed money for essential services, it has contributed to an economic revival in the developing world where the confidence of international partners and domestic actors was undermined by excessively high debt burdens.

Second, developed countries have increased foreign aid, currently about $133 billion a year. The increase was steepest in the early 2000s, in the wake of the adoption of the MDGs. Since the mid-2000s, however, foreign aid has leveled off. Only five countries — Denmark, Luxembourg, the Netherlands, Norway and Sweden — consistently reach the target of allocating 0.7 percent of national income to foreign aid. Most large countries spend less than 0.35 percent on foreign aid.

Third, developed countries have maintained undue influence over global institutions. This is best exemplified by the World Bank and International Monetary Fund (IMF). An unwritten rule dating to the 1940s prevails: that the former is headed by an American and the latter by a European. Still, the choice of leaders for these institutions is gradually changing, in favor of women and ethnic diversity.

Finally, the global trading system and patent laws have not become more MDG-friendly. The Doha round of trade negotiations remains in the doldrums, largely because developed countries try to keep the system rigged in their favor, in essence, trying to "kick away the ladder" they themselves climbed. Developed countries all used subsidies and tariffs and seldom honored patents, but they now say free trade and copyrights are essential for fostering development.

So, developed countries have contributed to MDG progress. But a partnership among equals will come about only if the MDG discourse focuses on "ideas changing minds" rather than "money changing hands." The British economist John Maynard Keynes once argued: "The power of vested interests is vastly exaggerated compared with the gradual encroachment of ideas."

NO Gabriele Köhler
Visiting Fellow, Institute of Development Studies, Brighton, U.K.

Written for *CQ Global Researcher*, August 2012

No! For more than 50 years, developed countries have committed to transferring 0.7 percent of gross national income (GNI) to developing countries in the form of official development assistance, or foreign aid. The target was conceived by the World Council of Churches during the 1960s, when organized development cooperation was first introduced. It has been reiterated ever since and is integral to MDG goal No. 8 — building a global development partnership. It was reaffirmed at European Union and G8 summits in 2005 and at the high-level U.N. General Assembly MDG review in 2010.

Despite those commitments, the average foreign-aid-to-GNI ratio for 23 of the world's most industrialized countries in 2011 was 0.31 percent — less than half the promised rate. Only five countries complied with the target. So on the whole, the developed world has not done enough to help developing countries achieve the MDGs.

However, other measures would have a more systemic impact on MDG achievement than meeting the 0.7 threshold, such as making deep structural reforms in international trade rules and revamping the international finance system. Preferential market access for developing countries' products and services, freer intellectual property rights, freedom of migration at properly remunerated wages and predictable international financial markets are preconditions for the MDGs to halve poverty, increase employment and decent work and assure access to affordable food, nutrition or medication.

Moreover, financial flows from outside cannot solve domestic structural inequities. Many low-income countries display rising income and wealth inequalities. They also have deteriorating health and education systems and tolerate exploitative work conditions and weak social-protection provisions for poverty, unemployment, childhood and old age.

If, however, developing countries' governments would adopt a higher tax-to-gross-domestic-product (GDP) ratio and better control their expenditures, they could afford more public goods, services and social assistance payments. In many low- and middle-income countries, taxes are only 15 percent of GDP — compared to an average of 40 percent in developed countries. More equitable tax systems could rebalance income inequality while ensuring that food price supports, education, health, water and sanitation, infrastructure and environmental protection are generously funded. Such reforms are a precondition for equitably achieving the MDGs.

thus far on key targets for each of the eight MDGs, based on the U.N.'s 2012 report on the status of the goals:[52]

- **Eradicate extreme poverty and hunger** — The first target, to cut in half the proportion of the world's inhabitants living on less than $1.25 a day, was met in 2008, driven largely by explosive economic growth in Asia's emerging economies. In July 2012, the U.N. reported that "for the first time since poverty trends began to be monitored, both the number of people living in extreme poverty and the poverty rates have fallen in every developing region — including sub-Saharan Africa, where rates are highest." Another poverty-reduction target, achieving "full and productive employment and decent work for all," has been more difficult to achieve during the global economic crisis. However, since 2000 the number of working poor — those earning less than $1.25 a day — has declined by 233 million people, again driven largely by Asia.

- **Achieve universal primary education** — Primary enrollment in developing regions reached 90 percent in 2010, up from 82 percent in 1999. But at this rate, the goal of universal primary school enrollment will not be reached by 2015.[53] More than half of the 61 million children who still are not in school live in sub-Saharan Africa, and 42 percent of those live in poor countries that are experiencing conflict. And being a girl is also a liability, though decreasingly so: in 1999, 58 percent of out-of-school kids were girls; today the share is 53 percent.[54]

- **Promote gender equality and empower women** — The developing world did not eliminate gender gaps in primary and secondary education by 2005, as the U.N. had originally set out to do, but it is now within striking distance of that goal. In 2010, there were 97 girls to every 100 boys enrolled in primary school, within the three-point margin-of-error range to equal parity. However, the developing world is just shy of parity in secondary education (with 96 girls to every boy). Developing regions achieved parity in tertiary, or university, education in 2010. Another indicator for this goal — having more women in the workplace — is falling short. Worldwide, only 40 percent of non-agricultural jobs are held by women, a figure that dips as low as 19 percent in western Asia and North Africa.[55]

- **Reduce child mortality rates** — Progress is "significantly off-track" on reducing by two-thirds the 1990 under-age 5 mortality rate of 97 deaths per 1,000 live births.[56] By 2010, under-5 deaths in developing regions had been reduced by only about one-third, to 63 per 1,000 worldwide, with sub-Saharan Africa making substantial progress — down from 174 in 1990 to 121 in 2009, still the world's highest.

- **Improve maternal health** — So far, the world appears likely to miss its target of reducing 1990 maternal mortality rates by three-quarters by 2015. As of 2008, the rate had been reduced only by about one-third, from 440 deaths per 100,000 live births to 290. Progress has been slowest in Oceania, southern Asia and sub-Saharan Africa. The second target — achieving universal access to reproductive health — also remains well out of reach, largely due to low rates of contraception use, high teen pregnancy rates and insufficient medical care for pregnant women. In 2010, only 55 percent of pregnant women in developing regions saw a doctor four or more times.

- **Fight HIV-AIDS, malaria and other diseases** — Remarkable progress has been made in halting and beginning to reverse the spread of HIV-AIDS. Between 2001 and 2010 the rate of new cases among 15- to 49-year-olds in developing regions declined by 22 percent, largely due to improvement in sub-Saharan Africa, where rates fell by nearly one-third. Still, treatment hasn't expanded quickly enough to hit another target: universal access to HIV-AIDS treatment. As of 2010, only 48 percent of people living with HIV in developing countries were receiving anti-retroviral treatment.[57]

Meanwhile, progress on many other serious diseases has been mixed. Malaria deaths have declined 20 percent since 2000, largely attributable to expanded use of insecticide-treated mosquito nets. However, new diagnoses of tuberculosis in the developing world are holding steady, as they have been for nearly two decades.

- **Ensure environmental sustainability** — This goal has four targets and 10 indicators covering a variety of environmental problems, some of which cannot be measured, such as integrating sustainable development principles into country policies and reversing the loss of biodiversity by 2010. According to the U.N., the world's total acreage of protected areas has increased by 48 percent since 1990, and more species are surviving than would have without conservation, but the gains have not been significant enough for this goal to have been declared as "met." However, the U.N. declared in 2012 that the world

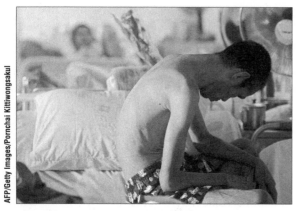

AFP/Getty Images/Pornchai Kittiwongsakul

HIV-AIDS patients are treated at a medical facility at a Buddhist Temple in Lopburi province, north of Bangkok on Nov. 27, 2011. Expanded access to treatment worldwide has meant remarkable progress in halting and beginning to reverse the spread of HIV-AIDS. Between 2001 and 2010 the rate of new cases among 15- to 49-year-olds in developing regions declined by 22 percent, much of that in sub-Saharan Africa, where rates fell by nearly one-third. Yet, treatment hasn't expanded quickly enough to hit another MDG target: universal access to HIV-AIDS treatment. As of 2010, only 48 percent of people living with HIV in developing countries were receiving anti-retroviral treatment.

has met the goal of halving the proportion of people without access to safe water and sanitation, and 200 million slum dwellers have either improved water and sanitation access or better housing.[58]

• **Develop a global partnership for development** — The last MDG has no clear targets. Rather, it calls for improving international trade, addressing poor countries' debt and providing access to pharmaceuticals and technology. Nevertheless, there has been some measurable progress. Development aid continues to grow, even though it has fallen as a share of donor countries' income. Least developed countries are benefiting from preferential trade agreements, and debt-servicing ratios for those countries are trending downward. However, given the goal's vague wording, exactly what "success" will look like when it is achieved is somewhat of a mystery.

Lessons Learned

After 12 years, the world has learned several lessons about meeting the Millennium Development Goals, most important that they are interconnected. Universal primary

education for instance, implies gender equality at least in schooling.

It also has become clear that improving the lot of women can improve a country's economy and health. Likewise, the U.N. noted in its 2011 MDG progress report, growing up in rural settings, living in poor households and having a less-educated mother all increase a child's risk of dying at a young age. And making measles vaccinations more available has helped to reduce child deaths due to measles by 78 percent since 2000.

According to former UNDP head Kemal Dervis, it is important to understand the inter-connectedness of the goals in order to make sustainable progress. For instance, he points out, improving health and education in the poorest countries is critical, but economic growth is necessary to reinforce those benefits. Unfortunately, no MDG explicitly targeted economic growth.

"It is true that if you don't have a healthy and educated labor force, you're not likely to grow," says Dervis. "But, on the other hand, if you produce a lot of high school graduates and have a very good health-care system, if your financial system doesn't work, there's not enough investment." When people are then left poor and jobless, "it's difficult for the country to break out of the trap of being poor."

Others point out that the strongest MDGs were those with specific, quantifiable targets. The weakest goals were those that were less clear, said UNDP poverty practice director Selim Jahan. For instance, the last goal about developing a global partnership for development was rarely assessed because it did not have any deadlines, said the goal.

"It will be useful if, in the post-2015 period, there is an initial assessment of . . . how improvements in development cooperation . . . would positively impact other MDGs," he wrote in 2009.[59]

OUTLOOK
Future Planning

Regardless of whether the goals will be met by 2015, world leaders are looking ahead to what comes next. U.N. Secretary-General Ban Ki-moon is creating a high-level panel to prepare for a new set of development goals. The panel will have three co-chairs: Prime Minister David

Cameron of the U.K., Liberian President Ellen Johnson-Sirleaf and President Susilo Bambang Yudhoyono of Indonesia.

To supplement the panel's work, the U.N. will gather information through three wide-ranging initiatives, including a national consultation process taking place through January 2013 in more than 50 countries. A series of meetings will be held to discuss key development issues with representatives from various sectors, including academia, trade unions, civil society and the private sector. And finally, the U.N. is creating a web portal to allow "open interaction and information exchange," according to Thangavel Palanivel, UNDP chief economist for the Asia-Pacific region.

Some had hoped that the Rio+20 Earth Summit in June 2012 would foster progress toward new "sustainable development goals." Yet the summit adjourned without defining new goals and without approving a proposed $30 billion fund for promoting a green economy.[60] Leaders did agree, however, to develop "sustainable development goals" that would address the intertwined issues of economic and environmental sustainability.[61]

Palanivel says that key issues under discussion include food security, income inequality, governance and conflict. In addition, a high-level meeting of the U.N. General Assembly has been planned for September 2013 to address a "disability-inclusive development process," to ensure that the world's disabled people, who are disproportionately poor, are considered in any new development goals.[62]

While those may be admirable topics to tackle, says the Center for Global Development's Kenny, they must also be measurable so progress can be tracked, which could prove difficult. "The measure has to be agreed on by 180-odd world leaders," Kenny says. "On child mortality, everyone agrees what child mortality is. On maternal mortality, everyone agrees what maternal mortality is. On democracy, not everyone agrees what democracy is," he says. "How do you measure it on a scale of 0 to 10?"

Likewise, he notes, while some want a goal addressing failed states, countries would have to agree on the definition of a "failed" state — a label most countries would not want applied to them. As Carin, of the Center for International Governance Innovation, succinctly puts it, "What's the use of an aspirational statement like 'life should be wonderful' if you can't measure progress?"

Carin's organization has proposed 12 goal options, which include new concepts such as "universal connectivity" and "disaster reduction."[63] Likewise, the UK-based think tank IDP advocates a fundamental reshaping of the MDGs to make sure they are "more explicitly rights-based and participatory." For instance, the group said in an April 2012 paper, the goals should recognize countries' rights to undertake "bolder" or unorthodox policies in areas such as land reform and hunger reduction.[64]

As with the MDGs, scores of players are ready to dive in and have their voices heard in the debate over the new goals. But while having more voices yields a more comprehensive view, it could ultimately lead to a more confusing set of targets. "Ultimately, if too many threads get woven into this and the goals lose their ability to be concrete, they will no longer be effective," says InterAction's Worthington.

And, says former World Bank chief economist Kharas, it should be emphasized amid all of the planning and maneuvering around the new goals that it is not 2015 yet.

"I think that's all healthy; people should be discussing these issues," he says. "But we've still got three years, and it's important that focus be kept on the implementation of the MDGs and not just, say, 'OK, let's now switch to the post-MDG planning.'"

NOTES

1. "A Fall to Cheer," *The Economist*, March 3, 2012, www.economist.com/node/21548963.

2. "Millennium Development Goal Drinking Water Target Met," March 6, 2012, www.who.int/media centre/news/releases/2012/drinking_water_20120306/en/index.html. Also see "The Millennium Development Goals Report 2012," United Nations, http://mdgs.un.org/unsd/mdg/Resources/Static/Products/Progress2012/English2012.pdf.

3. *Ibid.*, p. 26.

4. "MDG Goal 2 Fact Sheet," United Nations, www.un.org/millenniumgoals/education.shtml.

5. "The Millennium Development Goals Report 2012," *op. cit.*, p. 6.

6. "MDG Goal 2 Fact Sheet," *op. cit.*

7. "MDG Goal 5 Fact Sheet," *op. cit.* Also see "We Can End Global Poverty," United Nations Summit, Sept. 20-22, 2010, www.un.org/millenniumgoals/pdf/MDG_FS_5_EN_new.pdf.

8. "Millennium Development Goals Report 2012," press release, Department of Economic and Social Affairs, United Nations, July 2, 2012, www.un.org/en/development/desa/publications/mdg-report-2012.html.

9. "The Millennium Development Goals Report 2012," *op. cit.*, p. 7.

10. "The Millennium Development Goals Report 2011," United Nations, p. 7, www.un.org/millenniumgoals/11_MDG%20Report_EN.pdf.

11. "The Millennium Development Goals Report 2012," *op. cit.*, p. 6.

12. "Mapping Progress: Evidence for a New Development Outlook," Overseas Development Institute, 2011, p. 14.

13. Abhijit Banerjee and Esther Duflo, *Poor Economics* (2011), p. 74.

14. Hari Kumar, "India in a 'Race Against Time' to Meet Millennium Goals," *The New York Times*, Feb. 22, 2012, http://india.blogs.nytimes.com/2012/02/22/india-in-a-race-against-time-to-meet-millenium-goals/.

15. "Global Monitoring Report 2012: Food Prices, Nutrition, and the Millennium Development Goals." World Bank, 2012, p. 1.

16. William Easterly, "How the Millennium Development Goals Are Unfair to Africa," Brookings Global Economy and Development, Brookings Institution, November 2007, p. 2.

17. *Ibid.*, p. 5.

18. Jan Vandemoortele, "Taking the MDGs Beyond 2015: Hasten Slowly," Beyond 2015.org, May 2009, p. 2, www.eadi.org/fileadmin/MDG_2015_Publications/Vandemoortele_PAPER.pdf.

19. Kofi A. Annan, "We the Peoples: The Role of the United Nations in the 21st Century," United Nations, 2000, www.un.org/millennium/sg/report/full.htm.

20. "Factsheet — Poverty Reduction Strategy Papers (PRSP)," International Monetary Fund, April 19, 2012, www.imf.org/external/np/exr/facts/prsp.htm.

21. Cindy Shiner, "Africa: Cell Phones Transform Continent's Development," AllAfrica, Sept. 18, 2008, http://allafrica.com/stories/200809180986.html.

22. Duncan Green, Richard King, May Miller-Dawkins, "The Global Economic Crisis and Developing Countries: Impact and Response," January 2010, p. 9, www.iadb.org/intal/intalcdi/PE/2010/04613.pdf.

23. For background, see Sarah Glazer, "Future of the Euro," *CQ Global Researcher*, May 17, 2011, pp. 237-262.

24. "WB Urges Developing Countries to Strengthen Domestic Fundamentals, to Weather Economic Turmoil," press release, June 2, 2012, http://web.worldbank.org/WBSITE/EXTERNAL/NEWS/0,,contentMDK:23216493~pagePK:64257043~piPK:437376~theSitePK:4607,00.html.

25. For background, see Peter Katel, "Ending Poverty," *CQ Researcher*, Sept. 9, 2005, pp. 733-760.

26. "A United Nations Priority: Universal Declaration of Human Rights," United Nations, www.un.org/rights/HRToday/declar.htm.

27. "UN," Political Handbook of the World (2012).

28. David Hulme, "The Millennium Development Goals (MDGs): A Short History of the World's Biggest Promise," Brooks World Poverty Institute, University of Manchester, September 2009, p. 8.

29. Peter Jackson, "A Prehistory of the Millennium Development Goals: Four Decades of Struggle for Development in the United Nations," *U.N. Chronicle*, Jan. 12, 2007, www.un.org/wcm/content/site/chronicle/home/archive/issues2007/themdgsareweontrack/aprehistoryofthemillenniumdevelopmentgoalsfourdecadesofstrugglefordevelopmentintheunitednations.

30. Katel, *op. cit.*, p. 741.

31. "The politics of poverty: Aid in the new Cold War," Christian Aid, p. 11, www.un-ngls.org/orf/politics%20of%20poverty.pdf.

32. Todd Moss, "Crying Crisis," *Foreign Policy*, Sept. 20, 2010, www.foreignpolicy.com/articles/2010/09/20/crying_crisis.

33. Hulme, *op. cit.*, p. 8.

34. "Reaching the MDGs 2.0," World Vision, September 2011, p. 3.

35. *Ibid.*

36. Hulme, *op. cit.*, p. 25.

37. "Reproductive Health and the MDGs," International Planned Parenthood Foundation, April 24, 2012, www.ippf.org/news/blogs/reproductive-health-and-mdgs.

38. *Ibid.*

39. *Ibid.*

40. Christopher J. L. Murray, *et al.*, "Global Malaria Mortality Between 1980 and 2010: A Systematic Analysis," *The Lancet*, Feb. 4, 2012, www.thelancet.com/journals/lancet/article/PIIS0140-6736%2812%2960034-8/abstract.

41. "Factsheet — Poverty Reduction Strategy Papers (PRSP)," *op. cit.*

42. Jeffrey D. Sachs, *The End of Poverty* (2005), p. 271.

43. *Ibid.*

44. "Net ODA in 2011," Organisation for Economic Co-operation and Development, http://webnet.oecd.org/oda2011/.

45. *Ibid.*

46. "Factsheet —The Multilateral Debt Initiative," International Monetary Fund, June 26, 2012, www.imf.org/external/np/exr/facts/mdri.htm.

47. Jeffrey Sachs, "Pool Resources and Reinvent Global Aid," *Financial Times*, Sept. 20, 2010, www.ft.com/intl/cms/s/0/4c510f34-c4fb-11df-9134-00144feab49a.html#axzz20pxJ2uiS.

48. Global Monitoring Report 2012, *op. cit.*, p. 26.

49. The Millennium Development Goals Report 2012, *op. cit.*, p. 8.

50. *Ibid.*, p. 21.

51. The Global Economic Crisis and Developing Countries, *op. cit.*, p. 5.

52. The Millennium Development Goals Report 2012, *op. cit.*, p. 4.

53. *Ibid.*, p. 16.

54. *Ibid.*, p. 17.

55. *Ibid.*, p. 24.

56. Global Monitoring Report 2012, *op. cit.*, p. 12.

57. *Ibid.*, p. 42.

58. "Fact Sheet — MDG 7," United Nations, www.un.org/millenniumgoals/environ.shtml.

59. Selim Jahan, *The Millennium Development Goals Beyond 2015* (2009), p. 5.

60. Brian Clark Howard, "Rio+20 Brings Hope and Solutions Despite Weak Talks," *National Geographic*, June 21, 2012, http://news.nationalgeographic.com/news/2012/06/120621-rio-20-hope-solutions-official-talks/.

61. "The Future We Want: Rio+20 Outcome Document," earthsummit2012.org, June 19, 2012, www.earthsummit2012.org/resources/useful-resources/1157-the-future-we-want-rio20-outcome-document.

62. "High-Level Meeting of the General Assembly on Disability and Development, Sept. 23, 2013, www.un.org/disabilities/default.asp?id=1590.

63. "Conference Report: Post-2015 Goals, Targets, and Indicators," Centre for International Governance Innovation, p. 5, www.cigionline.org/publications/2012/5/post-2015-goals-targets-and-indicators.

64. Gabriele Köehler, *et al.*, "Human Security and the Next Generation of Comprehensive Human Development Goals," Institute of Development Studies, April 2012, pp. 5, 8.

BIBLIOGRAPHY

Selected Sources

Books

Duflo, Esther, and Abhijit Banerjee, *Poor Economics*, PublicAffairs, 2010.
Two MIT economics professors examine the factors behind poverty and what to do about it, exploring everything from the minutiae (the buying habits and parenting choices of the poor) to broader systemic factors (markets and governance).

Kenny, Charles, *Getting Better*, Perseus Books, 2011.
A senior fellow at the Center for Global Development in Washington, D.C., traces the giant leaps the world has made in development, focusing on advances other than income metrics, while acknowledging that plenty more can and should be done for the world's poorest.

Sachs, Jeffrey, *The End of Poverty: Economic Possibilities for Our Time*, Penguin Books, Feb. 28, 2006.
The director of Columbia University's Earth Institute lays out in depth a remarkable wealth of personal and statistical information on fighting poverty, plus a framework for ending it by 2025.

Easterly, William, *The White Man's Burden: Why the West's Efforts to Aid the Rest Have Done So Much Ill and So Little Good*, Penguin Books, Feb. 27, 2007.
A New York University economist delivers a scathing rebuke to the developed world's efforts to aid the developing world, pointing out the unintended consequences of development aid.

Articles

"Reproductive Health and the MDGs," International Planned Parenthood Federation, April 24, 2012, www.ippf.org/news/blogs/reproductive-health-and-mdgs.
The federation provides a fascinating insight into the political fight to get reproductive health into the Millennium Development Goals.

"WEST AFRICA: Smoothing the way for more pit latrines," *IRIN* [humanitarian news and analysis], Aug. 31, 2011, http://irinnews.org/Report/93621/WEST-AFRICA-Smoothing-the-way-for-more-pit-latrines.
Aid workers talk frankly about the dirty business of changing societal attitudes toward basic sanitation.

Moss, Todd, "Crying Crisis," *Foreign Policy*, Sept. 20, 2010, www.foreignpolicy.com/articles/2010/09/20/crying crisis.
A senior fellow and vice president for programs at the Center for Global Development in Washington, D.C., argues that paying more attention to MDG successes instead of continually begging for aid might "strengthen the policymakers, teachers and health workers in poor countries" and inspire more aid donations.

Shiner, Cindy, "Africa: Cell Phones Transform Continent's Development," *allAfrica*, Sept. 18, 2008, http://allafrica.com/stories/200809180986.html.
In this Q-and-A, economist Jeffrey Sachs explains how cell phones are revolutionizing life in the world's poorest countries.

Reports and Studies

"Global Monitoring Report 2012: Food Prices, Nutrition, and the Millennium Development Goals," World Bank, 2012.
The bank's MDG monitoring report assesses progress in attaining the goals while casting a critical eye on how global economic growth, food prices and international trade play into the fight against poverty.

"The Millennium Development Goals 2012," United Nations, 2012.
The latest official U.N. reckoning of MDG progress, this comprehensive report lays out where the world started, how far it has come and which regions are making more or less progress than others.

Annan, Kofi, "We the Peoples," United Nations, 2000.
This report set the tone for development of the Millennium Development Goals in 2000 and provides fascinating insight into the political jockeying that went into the process.

Easterly, William, "How the Millennium Development Goals Are Unfair to Africa," Brookings Global Economy and Development, November 2007.
A New York University economist lays out a thorough, statistic-by-statistic analysis of how MDG measures of "success" might be unfair — particularly to sub-Saharan Africa.

Hulme, David, "The Millennium Development Goals (MDGs): A Short History of the World's Biggest Promise," University of Manchester, Brooks World Poverty Institute, September 2009.
A professor in the school of environment and development at the University of Manchester in the U.K. provides a thorough and critical chronology of how the MDGs came into being, putting them into a longer-term context of the ongoing global fight against poverty.

On the Web

La Trobe University, "Millennium Development Goals," Podcast series, 2010.
In this 20-episode series, leading experts discuss how the goals were created, the challenges to meeting them and the future of global development targets.

For More Information

The Bill and Melinda Gates Foundation, 500 Fifth Ave., North, Seattle, WA 98102; 206-709-3100; www.gatesfoundation.org. A philanthropic organization that works on a variety of issues, including global health and development.

Center for Global Development, 1776 Massachusetts Ave., N.W., Suite 301, Washington, DC 20036; 202-416-0700; www.cgdev.org. A think tank that works to reduce global poverty and inequality.

The Earth Institute, Columbia University, 405 Low Library, #MC 4335, 535 West 116th St., New York, NY 10027; 212-854-3830; www.earth.columbia.edu. An institute, headed by famed economist Jeffrey Sachs, that seeks to address a host of global poverty, with a focus on sustainability.

Institute for Development Studies, Library Road, Brighton, BN1 9RE, UK; +44 1273 606261; www.ids.ac.uk. A research and educational institution that promotes social justice, sustainable growth and ending poverty.

United Nations Development Programme, One United Nations Plaza, New York, NY 10017 USA; 212-906-5000; www.undp.org. The U.N.'s primary development organization.

World Bank, 1818 H St., N.W., Washington, DC 20433; 202-473-1000; www.worldbank.org. Provides technical and financial support to help countries boost their citizens' standards of living.

World Health Organization, Avenue Appia 20, 1211 Geneva 27, Switzerland; +41 22 791 21 11; www.who.int. A U.N. agency that works to improve global public health.

World Vision, 34834 Weyerhaeuser Way So., Federal Way, WA 98001; 888-511-6548; www.worldvision.org. A Christian humanitarian organization that fights poverty worldwide.

Voices From Abroad:

GORDON BROWN

Former Prime Minister, United Kingdom

Gender equality not reached

"We know tragically it's impossible, despite all the changes, to change a situation where 350,000 mothers are dying each year from maternal mortality. It will not change quickly enough even if the figures go down, to meet that Millennium Development Goal. We know we have not achieved the Millennium Development Goal on gender equality."

This Day (Nigeria), November 2011

OLU AKEUSOLA

Provost, Michael Otedola College of Primary Education, Nigeria

Not attainable

"The MDGs are not attainable or achievable. Look, we are just deceiving ourselves in this country [Nigeria]. For over 40 years, the United Nations had said that for every nation to develop, it must accrue a minimum 25 percent annual budgetary allocation to its education sector. Malaysia gave it a trial and today it is working for them. That's why Malaysia, which gained independence with Nigeria during the same period, has outsmarted us in terms of growth and development."

Vanguard (Nigeria), August 2012

JUSTIN YIFU LIN

Chief Economist World Bank, Lebanon

Food prices causing problems

"High and volatile food prices do not bode well for attainment of many MDGs, as they erode consumer purchasing power and prevent millions of people from escaping poverty and hunger, besides having long-term adverse impacts on health and education. Dealing with food price volatility must be a high priority, especially as nutrition has been one of the forgotten MDGs."

Daily Star (Lebanon), April 2012

SERGEY LAVROV

Foreign Minister, Russia

Efforts must be strengthened

"Faced with the acute crisis in the financial/economic sphere, and limited funds for international development assistance, it is a relevant and urgent task to coordinate and increase the effectiveness of international efforts in critical areas. This is necessary if we [Russia] are to achieve the timely realization of the Millennium Development Goals, which are defined in the Millennium Declaration and other fundamental documents of the United Nations."

Russian Ministry of Foreign Affairs, October 2011

KING ABDULLAH

Jordan

Jordan advancing

"Today, due to the work of thousands of Jordanians, in schools, in healthcare, in communities across the country, we are in the process of achieving many of our millennium goals. Goal two, for example, has effectively been achieved: ensuring that all children enroll in primary school and stay in school, ending youth illiteracy, and giving our students the foundation they need to advance in life."

Jordan Times, September 2010

WEN JIABAO

Premier of the State Council, China

China's commitment

"China has always responded positively to U.N. initiatives and made unremitting efforts to realize the Millennium Development Goals. China has lowered the number of people living in absolute poverty by more than 200 million since 1978, accounting for 75 percent of the number of people lifted out of poverty in developing countries. We pay attention to protecting and improving the people's livelihood by institutional means."

Xinhua News Agency (China), September 2010

GEORGE CHICOTY

State Secretary for Foreign Affairs, Angola

A reassessment

"2015 is the deadline, and so far we are assessing issues related to half of the journey and all countries are already thinking that we will have to re-assess and see how we will manage to achieve the Millennium Development Goals."

Angola Press Agency, September 2010

10

Booming Africa

Jason McLure

A young mineworker in South Kivu province in the Democratic Republic of Congo (DRC) helps to extract cassiterite and coltan, valuable minerals used to manufacture sophisticated electronics. More than 90 percent of the DRC's export income comes from diamonds, minerals and oil, leaving the economy vulnerable to fluctuations in global prices. Many African countries are trying to become less dependent on such commodity exports.

From *The CQ Researcher*, November 20, 2012.

Just two decades ago, destitute Mozambique could have been the poster child for the economic basket case that was much of sub-Saharan Africa. More than a million people had died in a 17-year civil war, and up to a third of its 15 million people had fled their homes. With much of its farmland sown with landmines, the country had to import grain to feed itself. And the war's $15 billion cost — about seven times Mozambique's annual economic output — had virtually bankrupted the country.[1]

Today, the Texas-sized country bordering the Indian Ocean is rising from the ashes. Newly built resorts offer $600-a-night rooms along the 1,550-mile coastline. Vast coal deposits and the discovery of natural gas reserves twice the size of Saudi Arabia's could make Mozambique one of the world's largest energy exporters in the next decade, and a new aluminum smelter is one of the biggest in the world.

Mozambique's turnaround has been mirrored across much of sub-Saharan Africa, where per capita income has risen 132 percent over the past 15 years. Seven of the world's 10 fastest-growing economies currently are in sub-Saharan Africa, which is projected to grow by 5.3 percent next year, compared with 2.1 percent in the United States and 0.2 percent in eurozone countries, according to the International Monetary Fund (IMF).[2]

Yet many outside of Africa still think of the continent as it was 20 years ago. As recently as 2000, *The Economist* labeled Africa "the hopeless continent." The misperception "represents . . . a chasm between perception and reality," said a report this year from Ernst & Young, an international accounting firm.[3] "The facts tell a different story — one of reform, progress and growth."

239

A Continent on the Rise

In the past 20 years, 17 sub-Saharan countries are experiencing what some are calling an African Renaissance. These "emerging" countries have embraced democracy and economic reforms — such as slashing regulations, tariffs and the cost of starting a business — and saw per capita income rise more than 2 percent per year between 1996 and 2008, according to Steven Radelet, chief economist at the U.S. Agency for International Development. In his 2010 book Emerging Africa, Radelet also identified six "threshold" economies, with growth rates under 2 percent but showing signs of a turnaround. Ten oil exporting countries have economies and politics that are heavily influenced by oil revenues, and 16 others are neither oil exporters nor considered "emerging." according to Radelet.

Economic Status of Sub-Saharan Africa

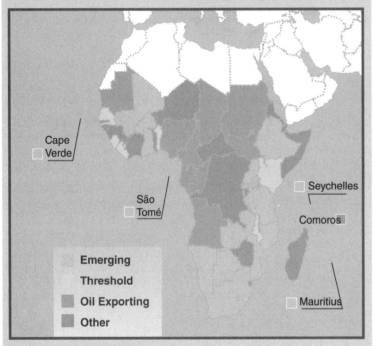

Cape Verde

São Tomé

Seychelles

Comoros

Mauritius

Emerging
Threshold
Oil Exporting
Other

Source: Steven Radelet, Emerging Africa: How 17 Countries Are Leading the Way (2010). Map by Lewis Agrell

The fruits of Africa's recent growth are visible across the continent: in the polished marble floors of the 205,000-square-foot Accra Mall, an American-style complex in Ghana's capital city featuring Apple and Nike stores and a five-screen cinema; in the high-tech, deep-water oil drilling platforms off Angola's coast; and in the sharp reductions in infant mortality in countries such as Ethiopia and Rwanda.

Analysts bullish on the continent's future see indications that sub-Saharan Africa is set for a sustained period of economic growth that could raise many of its countries to middle-income status. "Africa could be on the brink of an economic takeoff, much like China was 30 years ago and India 20 years ago," said a recent World Bank report.[4]

The growth is attributable in part to a boom in oil revenues stemming from high global prices and increased production in petro-states such as Angola, Chad and Equatorial Guinea. Yet, significantly, between 1996 and 2008 a star group of 17 emerging African economies produced per capita income growth of more than 2 percent per year — and another seven nearly reached that milestone, which economists say is a significant measure of rapidly rising living standards. None of the 24 countries were oil exporters.

"Thailand in 1960 looks a lot like Ethiopia or the Democratic Republic of Congo today," says Susan Lund, director of research at the McKinsey Global Institute, a subsidiary of the international consulting firm. "South Korea in 1965 looks like Senegal, Tanzania or Ghana. When you look backwards you think Africa could capture this potential."

And while it may seem far-fetched to compare Africa's rise to that of emerging economic giants like India, China or Brazil, consider the following:

• Between 2010 and 2020, some 122 million young people will enter Africa's labor force, providing a massive "demographic dividend" that will give the continent a larger labor force by 2035 than any country or region, including China or India.[5] By 2040, 1.1 billion Africans will be of working age, according to McKinsey.

- Although most of Africa is viewed as corrupt, 28 sub-Saharan nations are considered less corrupt than Russia, and six score better than India on Transparency International's Corruption Perceptions Index.[6]
- Africa's income per capita is greater than India's, and six sub-Saharan countries have greater income per capita than China.[7]
- While African countries are considered more difficult to do business in than other developing nations, eight sub-Saharan countries rank ahead of Russia on the World Bank's "ease of doing business" index; 12 were ahead of Brazil and 13 ahead of India.[8]

Several changes have fueled sub-Saharan Africa's growth since the dark days of the 1970s and '80s. First, countries across the continent have significantly improved governance and expanded democracy. Though many countries are still dominated by a single party or governed by authoritarian rulers — such as Rwanda's Paul Kagame or Uganda's Yoweri Museveni — corrupt, unaccountable despots like Zimbabwe's Robert Mugabe are an increasingly rare species. Major civil wars such as those that damaged the economies of Sudan, Angola, Mozambique and Liberia in the 1980s and '90s have ended or quieted significantly.

"Africa has reached the point that the Scandinavians got to 100 years ago, when they decided they are tired of fighting each other and said: 'Let's put everything down and work towards a more peaceful region,'" says Ifediora Amobi, director of the African Institute for Applied Economics in Enugu, Nigeria. "More stability will translate into growth."

Second, African central banks and finance ministries have become better economic managers. In the late 1970s and '80s, Ghana was hit by low prices for cocoa, its main export, and high prices for oil, which it imported. The government responded by controlling consumer prices, paying artificially low prices to cocoa farmers and expanding the civil service nearly 10-fold. As a result, the budget deficit ballooned, inflation reached 120 percent and cocoa production plummeted. Since the reversal of some of the harmful policies, Ghana's economy has become one of the

Africa Among Fastest-Growing Regions

Africa's gross domestic product (GDP) — a measure of economic output — grew at an average rate of 5.1 percent from 2000 to 2010, second only to emerging Asia (top). Angola, which has been exploiting its newfound oil reserves, had the world's fastest-growing GDP during the decade ending in 2010. For the current five-year period, seven of the world's fastest-growing economies (below, in red) are expected to be in Africa, with Ethiopia ranked just behind booming China and India.

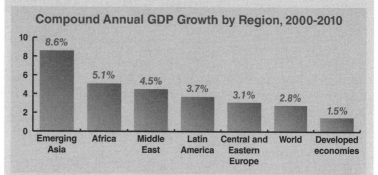

Compound Annual GDP Growth by Region, 2000-2010

Region	Growth
Emerging Asia	8.6%
Africa	5.1%
Middle East	4.5%
Latin America	3.7%
Central and Eastern Europe	3.1%
World	2.8%
Developed economies	1.5%

World's Fastest-Growing Economies, by Annual Average GDP Growth

2001-2010		2011-2015	
Angola	11.1%	China	9.5%
China	10.5%	India	8.2%
Myanmar	10.3%	Ethiopia	8.1%
Nigeria	8.9%	Mozambique	7.7%
Ethiopia	8.4%	Tanzania	7.2%
Kazakhstan	8.2%	Vietnam	7.2%
Chad	7.9%	Congo	7.0%
Mozambique	7.9%	Ghana	7.0%
Cambodia	7.7%	Zambia	6.9%
Rwanda	7.6%	Nigeria	6.8%

Sources: "Africa's Impressive Growth," The Economist, January 2011, www.economist.com/blogs/dailychart/2011/01/daily_chart; David Fine, et al., "Africa at Work: Job Creation and Inclusive Growth," McKinsey Global Institute, August 2012, p. 1, www.mckinsey.com/insights/mgi/research/africa_europe_middle_east/africa_at_work

Miners' Strike Deepens South Africa's Woes

Vast gulf between rich and poor bedevils the economy.

Even now, exactly how the trouble started in a dusty, brush-strewn field in Marikana, South Africa, on Aug. 16 isn't entirely clear. In the end, though, the clash between about 3,000 South African police and a similar number of striking platinum miners left 44 people dead, including 34 miners.

Video of the confrontation showed police opening fire with automatic rifles after tear gas failed to disperse the crowd, some of whom were armed with clubs and spears. Police said they came under fire first and initially charged 270 strikers with murder.[1]

The charges were dropped after a public outcry, and the government has opened an official inquiry into the incident. Whatever the outcome, the clash exposed deep divisions in South Africa and frustration with a democracy that has allowed wide disparities in income to persist 18 years after the end of the country's hated apartheid government.

"Nothing, nothing, nothing has changed," a Marikana man told the BBC after the bloodshed. "Democracy is just a word like a bird flying up in the sky."

South Africa is the largest economy in sub-Saharan Africa but has one of the most unequal distributions of income anywhere in the world. The top 10 percent of the population accounts for 58 percent of income, while bottom 50 percent earns just 8 percent.

The legacy of apartheid is seen as a major reason for the inequity, because blacks were largely denied the opportunity to gain education, land and capital. Economic growth has averaged 3.2 percent annually since 1995, a modest rate for a middle-income country.[2] And it has not been rapid enough to resolve inequalities or quell discontent among a growing population, where unemployment stands at 25.2 percent.

The strike, which ended after the mine operator, U.K.-based Lonmin, agreed to raise wages by up to 22 percent, has served as a catalyst for other labor actions. By early October an estimated 70,000 miners were on strike around the country, nearly a quarter of the total and a figure that included iron, gold and coal miners. An additional 28,000 truck drivers also went on strike seeking better pay and conditions.[3]

"Down with monkey salaries — down," said Buti Manamela, president of the Young Communist League, during a march near the offices of global mining giant AngloGold Ashanti in Orkney. "Divided we fall, united we stand. . . . We can never achieve Nelson Mandela's rainbow nation if we are unequal in terms of wages."[4]

The actions have led some mining companies to threaten to close mines and lay off workers, dampening the outlook for an economy hit by the eurozone crisis and slowing growth in China.[5] In late September, the Moody's credit rating agency downgraded South African debt, citing the government's "reduced capacity to handle the current political and economic situation and to implement effective strategies that could place the economy on a path to faster and more inclusive growth."[6]

strongest in Africa, with growth averaging more than 5 percent over the past 25 years.[9]

In addition, Africans have benefited enormously from technological advances, particularly in communications and information technology. The Internet provides more information — ranging from scientific research to engineering designs to financial data — than the continent's largest research libraries, and it is increasingly available, even in rural areas. Moreover, on a continent where phone service was once rare and expensive, mobile phones have become ubiquitous, even in remote areas of the Sahara Desert.

"Africa had no connectivity, and now everyone is connected by mobile phone. That has just changed things everywhere," said Jacko Maree, chief executive officer of South Africa-based Standard Bank Group.[10]

Finally, international lending institutions have forgiven many African countries' foreign debt, which has freed up government revenues to be spent on education, health care and infrastructure. Interest on foreign debts fell from 16 percent of Africa's export earnings in 1995 to 8 percent today.[11]

To be sure, growth has not occurred evenly across the continent, and even some of Africa's fastest-growing

The move reflects doubts about President Jacob Zuma's leadership and that of his ruling African National Congress (ANC), which has run the country since its transition to democracy in 1994 under President Mandela. The country's major unions have long been key allies of the ANC, but this year's strikes have largely been wildcat labor actions undertaken without the support of union leadership — and reflect the popular perception that ANC leaders are more focused on their own enrichment than improving the lives of the poor.

That perception has been buttressed by reports that the government is paying for $27 million in improvements to Zuma's private home, ostensibly to improve security. "In 1994 there were massive problems, but there was also a massive amount of hope," William Gumede, a political analyst, told *The New York Times*.[7] "Now people feel hopeless. People have lost confidence in all of these institutions they trusted will make a difference, like the unions and the ANC. The new institutions of democracy — Parliament, the courts — people have also lost confidence that those can protect them and help them."

— *Jason McLure*

AFP/Getty Images/Alexander Joe

Striking gold miners in Carletonville, South Africa, demand better pay and working conditions on Oct. 18, 2012. The placards read "We demand 18,500 rands — silicosis the cause of death in mines" and "Don't let police get away with murder."

[1] "South Africa's Lonmin Marikana Mine Clashes Killed 34," BBC News, Aug. 17, 2012, www.bbc.co.uk/news/world-africa-19292909. See also, Faith Karimi and Nkepile Mabusi, "South African Commission Probing Miners' Deaths Starts Proceedings," CNN, Oct. 1, 2012, www.cnn.com/2012/10/01/world/africa/south-africa-mine-unrest/index.html.

[2] "South Africa Economic Update: Focus on Inequality of Opportunity," World Bank, July 2012, p. vii, http://documents.worldbank.org/curated/en/2012/01/16561374/south-africa-economic-update-focus-inequality-opportunity.

[3] Devon Maylie, "South Africa's Labor Woes Worsen," *The Wall Street Journal*, Oct. 3, 2012, http://online.wsj.com/article/SB10000872396390443768804578034271819419406.html.

[4] Rodney Muhumuza, "Facing Pressure to End Strikes, South African Miners Find Strength in Numbers, Tough Words," The Associated Press, Oct. 4, 2012, *Calgary Herald*, www.calgaryherald.com/business/facing+pressure+strikes+SAfrican+miners+find+strength+crowd+numbers/7344234/story.html.

[5] For background, see Christopher Hack, "Euro Crisis," *CQ Researcher*, Oct. 5, 2012, pp. 841-864.

[6] "Moody's Downgrades South Africa's Government Bond Rating to Baa1; Outlook Remains Negative," Moody's Investors Service, Sept. 27, 2012, www.moodys.com/research/Moodys-downgrades-South-Africas-government-bond-rating-to-Baa1-outlook--PR_256159.

[7] Lydia Polgreen, "Upheaval Grips South Africa as Hopes for Its Workers Fade," *The New York Times*, Oct. 13, 2012, www.nytimes.com/2012/10/14/world/africa/unfulfilled-promises-are-replacing-prospects-of-a-better-life-in-south-africa.html?pagewanted=all.

economies still face corruption, inequality and ethnic strife. Long-running conflicts continue in Somalia and the Democratic Republic of Congo, discouraging foreign investment, hindering efforts to build infrastructure and prolonging instability.

In addition, outside of South Africa and a handful of small countries such as Mauritius, nearly all sub-Saharan economies depend heavily on exports of raw materials such as oil, gas, minerals or agricultural commodities. And while many commodity prices are high at the moment, export-driven economies remain vulnerable to fluctuations in global prices.

"A lot of this [growth] is still being driven by natural resources," says Vijaya Ramachandran, a senior fellow at the Washington-based Center for Global Development. "Africa has not diversified into manufactured exports. It has not been able to compete with Asian countries."

Moreover, while exports of minerals, oil and gas generate high revenues for governments, they have so far provided few jobs for Africans. Many of the jobs in these industries are filled by foreign workers trained by multinational companies. The failure to develop labor-intensive manufacturing has left many countries with high unemployment. Although the official unemployment rate for the continent is 9 percent, only 28 percent of Africa's labor force is in formal, wage-paying jobs, according to McKinsey. The remainder are in subsistence farming or informal trades such as hawking wares on the street — jobs the consulting firm describes as "vulnerable employment."[12]

"A lot of people in the West are so impressed with our growth, but in Sierra Leone a lot of the growth has come from the exploitation of iron ore," says Omotunde Johnson, Sierra Leone country director for the London-based International Growth Centre, a think tank. "The miners are all foreigners, so that is going to create a new set of problems when these African youth who are not trained and educated are not getting work."

As analysts examine Africa's economic expansion, here are some of the questions they are asking:

Can African economies diversify away from natural resource production?

Africa's recent growth has been driven largely by production of oil, gas and minerals. The so-called extractive industries account for more than 25 percent of exports in about half of the sub-Saharan countries, and in some cases the share is much higher.[13] In Equatorial Guinea, oil production brings in 98 percent of export earnings; in the Democratic Republic of Congo more than 90 percent of export income comes from diamonds, minerals and oil. In petroleum-rich Gabon, oil exports account for 60 percent of export earnings.[14]

The gushing revenues are due to both increased exploitation of resources and higher world prices. Between 2000 and 2009, oil production in Africa rose 24 percent. The continent now has about 10 percent of the world's oil reserves and 8 percent of its gas.[15]

Meanwhile, world oil prices shot from around $20 per barrel in the 1990s to around $100 this year — after having reached as high as $148 per barrel in 2008. African commodity exports such as gold, copper and coltan (a critical component in manufacturing electronics) saw similar increases.

"Technology is changing rapidly, and there will be more natural resource discoveries in Africa going forward," says Ramachandran, of the Center for Global Development. "Almost all of Africa will be an oil or mineral exporter. The question is how will they manage this?"

In the past, rising natural resource earnings have not been used to lift large numbers of people out of poverty. Paradoxically, developing countries rich in natural resources generally do not perform as well economically as countries without oil, gas or mineral wealth — a phenomenon known in economic circles as the "resource curse."[16]

"They have grown more slowly, and with greater inequality — just the opposite of what one would expect," Joseph Stiglitz, a Nobel Prize-winning economist, wrote recently in Britain's *The Guardian*.

"After all," he continued, "countries whose major source of revenue is natural resources can use them to finance education, health care, development and redistribution."[17]

The "resource curse" is blamed on several factors, including:

- Rapidly rising energy and mineral earnings tend to boost the value of the exporting country's currency, making foreign imported goods cheaper for the local population but making it harder for local exports of commodities or manufactured goods to compete with countries that have cheaper currencies.

- Governance may suffer as political leaders focus on capturing ballooning export revenues rather than taxing citizens for public services. Corruption abounds when a relatively small number of government officials control access to lucrative extraction licenses and contracts.

- Booms caused by high world prices often spur high levels of government spending and borrowing, which can lead to busts and debt crises when commodity prices tumble, as happened in the early 1980s in many African countries.

To enable continued growth and boost employment and productivity, African nations must expand their manufacturing and farming sectors, say analysts. But building internationally competitive industries will be a major challenge for many African nations, given their small size and lack of roads, electricity and other infrastructure. In fact, Africa's manufacturing sector has declined as a share of the continent's gross domestic product, falling from 15.3 percent of GDP in 1990 to 10.5 percent in 2008.[18]

"Manufacturing has started on a small scale, but that has to pick up," says Johnson, the Sierra Leonean economist. "Education and training are not there. And there is a general inefficiency in investment," he says, referring to poor investment returns due to systemic problems such as low productivity, corruption and lack of infrastructure that are "keeping a lot of investors out."

African economies are not well integrated, part of the continent's colonial legacy. Many countries on the arbitrarily divided continent are so small they cannot generate economies of scale large enough to compete globally, as China and India have been able to do, with their billion-person domestic markets. Landlocked Burkina Faso, for instance, has a population of 17 million — slightly smaller than Florida — and few roads to connect it to neighboring economies.

And larger African nations must compete with Chinese and other highly efficient Asian manufacturers.[19] In Ethiopia, a large, landlocked country with 91 million people, it is cheaper to buy a wooden chair made in China than one made domestically, even after transportation costs are factored in. That's because Ethiopian workers manufacture 0.3 pieces per day, compared to 4.9 in China.[20]

Even South Africa has trouble competing with Asia, despite having a highly developed infrastructure and established access to export markets in Europe and elsewhere. Willie Van Straaten, a chief executive officer of South Africa's Inventec, a company that designs exercise equipment and games, says his products are made in China because the scale of its integrated manufacturing sector makes it difficult for South Africa to compete.

Poor Governance Hinders Africa's Progress

Some foreign investors are wary of investing in sub-Saharan Africa's industrialization, largely because of corruption and the lack of infrastructure. The region is the most poorly governed in the world (top) and trails the emerging BRICs (Brazil, Russia, India and China) in the development of infrastructure (bottom).

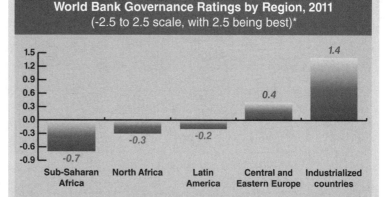

World Bank Governance Ratings by Region, 2011
(-2.5 to 2.5 scale, with 2.5 being best)*

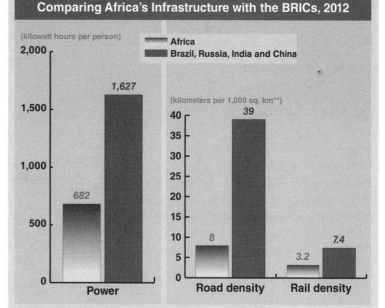

Comparing Africa's Infrastructure with the BRICs, 2012

* Based on government accountability, stability and effectiveness; regulatory and legal systems and corruption levels

** A kilometer is about six-tenths of a mile. A square kilometer is 0.39 of a square mile.

Sources: "Is Africa About to Take Off?" Societe Generale, May 2011; and David Fine, et al., "Africa at Work: Job Creation and Inclusive Growth," McKinsey Global Institute, August 2012, p. 43

African Workforce to Surpass All Others

Africa's working-age population is expected to exceed 1 billion by 2040, giving the continent a larger labor force than any country or region, including China or India. Experts say the burgeoning labor force will attract outside investors because of the growing consumer market they represent, but others warn that all those workers will need jobs.

Size of the Working-Age Population (ages 15 to 64), 1970-2040

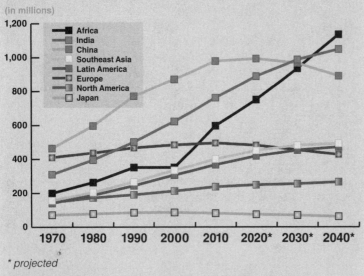

(in millions)

Legend: Africa, India, China, Southeast Asia, Latin America, Europe, North America, Japan

* projected

Source: David Fine, et al., "Africa at Work: Job Creation and Inclusive Growth," McKinsey Global Institute, August 2012, p. 13, www.mckinsey.com/insights/mgi/research/africa_europe_middle_east/africa_at_work

2006, with the exception of nine oil-exporting countries, the ratio of the cost of imported food and other goods rose as fast or faster than income from exports. In other words, higher prices for African exports cannot explain Africa's growth because the prices consumers paid for imports also rose.

Others say Africa has an opportunity to develop labor-intensive industries — such as horticulture, leather-working and textiles — especially once labor costs in China and other Asian manufacturing countries begin to rise. In Lesotho about 40,000 people now work in the garment industry for companies that export textiles to the United States under the African Growth and Opportunity Act, which allows duty-free access to the U.S. market.[23]

"It's not quite as dire as you might think," says Lund, of the McKinsey Global Institute. "We think the dynamics might be changing. There are two opportunities: the changing wage dynamics and higher transport costs (because of oil prices) both work against production in China."

"A lot of your Chinese factories have got very good vendor networks around them, so they may manufacture just one-third of the product, but two-thirds will come from the vendor network around them, and those vendors specialize in just one item," he recently told the television station African Business News. "So in South Africa you have to go and manufacture almost every item at low volume which makes it very, very expensive."[21]

Some analysts say Africa's growth is not all due to rising commodity export earnings. Steve Radelet, chief economist at the U.S. Agency for International Development, wrote that although rising commodity prices "have helped in some cases, the turnaround in the emerging countries is not solely the result of favorable commodity prices."[22] He found that between 1980 and

Can Africa provide enough jobs for its fast-growing population?

Sisay Asrat, a 27-year-old from the Ethiopian town of Debre Zeit, is happy to have a job at one of the dozens of flower farms that have sprung up in her country over the past decade. Even though she is only earning a little over a dollar a day, working in the farm's cold room packing roses to be shipped to Europe is better than having no job at all.

"There are no alternatives for those of us who don't have an education," she says. "I was dependent on my family. Now I cover my children's food, clothing and school fees."

Generating jobs for burgeoning populations is one of the most vexing challenges facing sub-Saharan economies. The continent's 9 percent official unemployment rate belies the fact that only 28 percent of the labor force has stable, wage-paying employment. Although that figure is up from 24 percent in 2000, 63 percent of the workforce is still in "vulnerable employment" — a category that includes subsistence farming or other informal sector jobs such as selling goods from market stalls and working as day-laborers.[24]

"The key thing is, are people getting wage-paying employment?" says Lund, of the McKinsey Global Institute. "Are they getting out of subsistence agriculture and street-hawking?"

Analysts say agricultural productivity could be boosted to make farming a more stable long-term job for millions. Expanding large-scale commercial farming on uncultivated land and moving from low-value grain production to labor-intensive crops such as flower farming could add up to 14 million stable jobs in the region by 2020, according to McKinsey.

Given the strong demand for African natural resources, employment and income could be boosted by processing more of those raw goods before exporting them, analysts say. "If you add more value to the resource, then you can generate more jobs," says Ramachandran, of the Center for Global Development.

For instance, Ghana and Côte d'Ivoire (Ivory Coast) together produce 69 percent of the world's cocoa, which can only be grown in tropical and subtropical climates.[25] Yet, Switzerland and Belgium are famous for making expensive chocolates from that African cocoa. Starbucks Corp. pays Ethiopian coffee farmers as little as $1.42 per pound, and sells some specialty beans — which the company roasts, grinds and markets — for as much as $26 per pound.[26] And Africa's largest crude oil exporter, Nigeria, imports gasoline because it lacks refining capacity.[27]

African manufacturers are on pace to generate 8 million new jobs by 2020, and could add an additional 7 million over that period, if governments improve infrastructure, cut unnecessary regulation and ease access to finance. The retail sector could add up to 14 million more jobs; currently Nigeria has only six shopping malls for 19.5 million people who live in its four largest cities, according to McKinsey. In total, the consulting firm forecasts that the continent will add 54 million stable jobs by 2020.

AFP/Getty Images/Issouf Sanogo

Getty Images/Per-Anders Pettersson

Changing Economies

Generating jobs for burgeoning populations is one of the most vexing challenges facing sub-Saharan governments, since only 28 percent of the region's labor force has stable, wage-paying jobs. Given the strong worldwide demand for Africa's natural resources and commodities — such as the cocoa beans being sorted by a farm worker in Côte d'Ivoire (top) —African governments want more of the continent's raw goods to be processed before they're exported, creating more domestic jobs. In Gaborone, Botswana, for instance, raw diamonds now are being sorted and polished before export (bottom).

Yet, expanding employment comes with costs. For instance, a wave of new, large commercial farms has displaced many existing smallholders. In 2009 alone, 77 million acres of African farmland were transferred to commercial investors — many of them foreigners.

Often, the land was sold out from underneath small farmers who lacked clear title to the land that their families had been tilling for generations.[28]

"All we want before they break our houses and take our fields is for them to show us the new houses where we will live, and the new fields where we will work," said Sekou Traoré, a 69-year-old villager in Mali, about plans to transfer land farmed by his family to Libyan investors.[29]

"They have to modernize agriculture, but when you modernize agriculture it's a double-edged sword because you kick out a lot of people from the agriculture sector," says Johnson, the Sierra Leonean economist.

Others say that despite Africa's recent growth, the rate of job growth is far too slow for the continent's growing workforce. While 54 million stable jobs may be added by 2020, the number of people in vulnerable employment is expected to grow by 67 million — and at current trends, the absolute number of people in "vulnerable" work will not decline until 2080.

Thus, at current rates, many African nations will have large numbers of underemployed young people, which can lead to political instability.

"The crisis of unemployment is a ticking time bomb, and if we are not careful in dealing with it we will see another Egypt and Tunisia," said Buti Manamela, secretary of South Africa's Young Communist League, referring to the legions of young people who took to the streets in 2011 and toppled Arab governments.[30]

Is Africa about to undergo an East Asia-style boom?

During the early 2000s, many sub-Saharan African governments adopted economic reforms, such as curbing deficits, privatizing banks, freeing exchange rates and slowing inflation. The private sector expanded rapidly, fueling support for additional reforms. Growth averaged 5 percent a year during the decade before the 2007-08 financial crisis but actually accelerated to 6 percent between 2006 and 2008. The growth wasn't solely attributable to oil: 22 non-oil exporters enjoyed 4 percent or higher annual growth during the decade.

"Then the global economic crisis hit, and everyone including myself panicked," says Shanta Devarajan, the Sri Lankan-born chief economist for Africa at the World Bank, "because now the payoffs for the reforms have disappeared."

> **"The crisis of unemployment is a ticking time bomb, and if we are not careful in dealing with it we will see another Egypt and Tunisia."**
>
> **— Buti Manamela Secretary South Africa's Young Communist League**

In the United States and Europe, some countries took measures to stave off depression, such as nationalizing banks and expanding deficits to as high as 10 percent of gross domestic product (GDP). With the global economy in free fall and Western governments intervening to prop up ailing financial and industrial firms, it would have been understandable if African governments had run-up large budget deficits and incurred foreign debts. Instead, sub-Saharan budget deficits widened by only 2 percent of GDP in 2009, and economies continued to grow by an average of 2.8 percent, even as European and North American economies were shrinking.

By 2010 economic growth in the region had rebounded to 5.3 percent. The resilience in the face of the financial crisis indicates that even stronger growth lies ahead, says Devarajan. He predicts that the region, with the exception of fragile or failed states such as Somalia, are on the brink of a sustained economic takeoff, with annual growth rates of more than 7 percent. Since the 1980s such growth rates have been commonly associated with China, and from the 1960s to the 1990s with the East Asian "tiger" economies of South Korea, Taiwan, Hong Kong and Singapore.

Better economic governance is not the only thing Africa shares with the East Asian tigers prior to their takeoff. Like the tigers, Africa's growth will be propelled in the coming decades by a "demographic dividend," according to some analysts.

The median age on the continent is 18, and there are 70 million more people under age 14 than there were a decade ago. The latter figure will rise by 76 million over the next decade.[31] Meanwhile, by 2035 the number of retirees and children that each worker supports, a figure known as the "dependency ratio," will fall from the highest in the world to about the same level as that in Western countries. As a result, each worker will have more disposable income to invest or spend on non-essential items.[32]

"This is what happened in East Asia in the 1970s and '80s, and if we can manage it right Africa has the demographic characteristics to experience the dividend," says Devarajan.

But others are more pessimistic about the prospects for a sustained boom, because corruption and unpredictable legal systems discourage foreign investment. "Africa is still not very good at things like corruption and efficiency of government," says Johnson, the Sierra Leonean economist. "Even some of the so-called diaspora [Africans working overseas] who might have $100,000 here and $200,000 there and together can come up with a million, even they are reluctant to go back and invest. The legal systems are awful. There are delays, there is corruption."

High transportation costs, which can be up to six times those in southern or eastern Asia, also block industrial growth in Africa. A 2009 World Bank study blamed monopolies and anti-competitive practices by trucking companies, which operate with high profit margins at the expense of other industries.[33] Reforms to prevent such problems may be adopted over time, but in the interim they are slowing growth.

"I'm not saying they'll stand still over the next 20 years; there will be progress," says Johnson. "But when you look at the population growth, that progress will be too slow."

Others see growth being dampened in the near future by the European debt crisis and a weakening of Chinese demand for African exports like oil, copper and coal.

Isabella Massa, a France-based researcher for the Overseas Development Institute, an international development think tank in the United Kingdom, says Europe's debt crisis will slow foreign direct investment and aid from Europe to Africa. Remittances to Nigeria from expatriate Nigerians fell by more than half in 2011, and Kenya's tourism and horticulture industries, which depend on European markets, also declined. Businesses in countries such as Angola, Rwanda and Cameroon are receiving fewer loans from European banks as well, she adds.

"The escalation of the Eurozone crisis and the fact that growth rates in the emerging BRIC [Brazil, Russia, India and China] economies, which have been the engine of the global recovery after the financial crisis, are now

Chinese workers construct a new railway near Luanda, Angola. Chinese companies have invested heavily in African mines and oil wells and have provided concessional loans to African governments to build roads, railways and electricity plants. Thousands of Chinese workers have come to Africa in recent years to build infrastructure projects.

slowing down make the current situation particularly worrying for African countries," says Massa.

BACKGROUND

Colonialism

Beginning in the 15th century, contact with Europeans had a profound impact on the economy of Africans. The Portuguese, English, French and Dutch initially sought to extract gold and ivory from the continent, but by the 17th century they had shifted their interest to a more lucrative trade: human beings.[34] Between 1600 and 1870 as many as 11.5 million Africans — mostly from Africa's western coastal states — were brought to work as slaves in North and South America.[35]

The impact of the slave trade on the region varied. The area near today's West African nations of Senegal and Gambia provided many of the slaves in the early years of the trade.[36] In the 1700s civil wars in the area around modern-day Nigeria provided a large number of slaves, who were shipped out via ports in Benin and from British slave forts in Ghana. After the Portuguese banned the slave trade north of the equator in 1815, the trade shifted further south toward Angola and the Democratic Republic of Congo.

CHRONOLOGY

1400s-1700s *Europeans begin trading with Africa, eventually shifting from buying gold and ivory to slaves, taking an estimated 11.5 million people from Africa and undermining local economies.*

1800s Europeans begin colonizing Africa.

1807 Slave trade is banned in the British Empire, but not slavery.

November 1884-January 1885 European powers meet in Berlin to establish rules for colonizing Africa; "scramble for Africa" begins.

1950s-1970s *Era of independence begins. Optimism turns to stagnation.*

1956 Substantial oil reserves are discovered in southern Nigeria.

1957 Britain grants independence to Ghana. Most British colonies become independent by 1965, including Nigeria, Uganda, Kenya, Zambia, Malawi and Gambia.

1958 Guinea becomes independent. Most French African colonies gain independence by 1960, including Mauritania, Nigeria, Senegal, Gabon, Republic of Congo, Central African Republic, Chad, Niger, Benin, Mali, Cameroon, Togo and Ivory Coast (now called Côte d'Ivoire).

1960 Mineral-rich Katanga province secedes from newly independent Democratic Republic of Congo with Belgium's support, sparking six years of political crisis and civil war.

1973-1979 Skyrocketing oil prices hit oil-importing African countries hard; World Bank counsels spending cuts by African governments, fueling poverty. Oil producers such as Gabon and Nigeria see revenues jump.

1980s-1990s *Heavy borrowing and economic mismanagement lead to high rates of debt; end of Cold War spurs reforms.*

1981 World Bank economists warn that many of its loans to poor countries cannot be repaid and should be canceled.

1991 Collapse of Soviet Union heralds end of Cold War and diminishing superpower support for African dictators.

1994 End of apartheid in South Africa ends international isolation of continent's largest economy.

1995 Foreign debt owed by sub-Saharan governments tops $340 billion, up from $11 billion in 1970.

1996 Chinese President Jiang Zemin visits six African countries promising aid "without political strings." . . . IMF and World Bank launch debt relief program for heavily-indebted poor countries.

2000s-Present *Improved economic governance along with spread of democracy and new communications technology spur growth.*

2000 United States passes African Growth and Opportunity Act, eliminating tariffs on hundreds of African products.

2005 International debt relief is expanded, freeing African governments to spend more on economic development.

2006 Forty-eight African nations attend meeting on cooperation with China in Beijing. President Hu Jintao promises to increase Sino-African trade to $100 billion by 2010.

2009 Global financial crisis slows growth in Africa but continent avoids recessions experienced in United States and Europe. Relative isolation of African banks helps them avoid global financial contagion; continuing Chinese demand for African commodity exports helps fuel growth.

2010 Number of Africans with mobile phones tops 500 million as Internet and mobile technology spread.

2011 Oil-producer South Sudan gains independence from Sudan. African oil production tops 417 million barrels per day, up from 328 million in 1991.

2012 More than 40 South African miners and police are killed during unrest over wages and benefits; anger over income inequality grows in Africa's biggest economy.

The High Cost of Nigeria's Fuel Subsidy

Love of low-cost fuel costs government dearly.

Most mornings, enterprising young Africans along Togo's coastal border with Benin harvest a surprising catch: jerry cans full of fuel. Wooden boats carry the contraband gasoline on a 13-hour trip from Nigeria through the Gulf of Guinea. Then, when they are close to the coast, young men swim out with empty jerry cans and fill them with gasoline and then haul them back to shore.

The fuel is then poured into large blue barrels and distributed as far as Ghana, Mali and Burkina Faso, where it is often sold on the street in liter liquor bottles at a steep discount from the price charged by licensed filling stations. The smuggling is profitable because fuel is heavily subsidized in Nigeria, selling for just 97 naira ($.62) per liter, or about $2.33 per gallon.[1]

Such subsidies are roundly criticized for a variety of reasons. Not only have price supports fueled the smuggling boom to other West African nations, but a disproportionate share of the subsidy benefits the wealthy and upper-middle-class Nigerians who can afford to own cars.

Moreover, the subsidy has discouraged local companies from building refineries, which has forced Africa's largest exporter of crude oil to import much of its gasoline and diesel from refineries overseas. The subsidy system also is hugely expensive and riddled with corruption. In 2011, the fuel subsidy accounted for 30 percent of government spending. In a country where more than half the population lives in poverty, the government spent $8 billion on fuel subsidies compared with $2 billion on education.[2]

Long-associated with misrule and public corruption, Nigeria in recent years has won praise from the International Monetary Fund and others for its economic management. High crude prices have helped the economy grow more than 7 percent for the past three years, and oil revenue helped cushion the economy during the 2008 global crisis. President Goodluck Jonathan's government has launched efforts to build electricity generation plants and increase lending to small businesses and agriculture to generate employment.

The government is well aware of the costs to the economy of the subsidies. But there's a major hurdle to reducing or eliminating them: Nigerians love low-priced fuel, and for many it's the only government benefit they see. When Jonathan attempted to end the subsidies in January, unions

AFP/ Getty Images/ Pius Utomi Ekpei

Protesters in Lagos, Nigeria, demonstrate during a nationwide strike after the government tried to abolish decades-old fuel subsidies in January. President Goodluck Jonathan partially restored the subsidies two weeks later, citing a " near-breakdown of law and order" in parts of the country.

called a nationwide strike, and thousands of people poured into the streets of Lagos, Kano and other cities to protest.

"The doctors are going on strike, the lawyers are not going to court, teachers are on strike, everybody is joining this because the only aspect where we feel government is in the area of subsidy," a protester told the Al Jazeera news network. "If you remove it, then the government can as well resign."[3]

Two weeks after eliminating the subsidies Jonathan partially restored them, citing a "near-breakdown of law and order in certain parts of the country."

— Jason McLure

[1]Jaime Grant, "On the Road With West Africa's Fuel Smugglers," ThinkAfricaPress, March 20, 2012, http://thinkafricapress.com/economy/road-west-africa-fuel-smugglers-inevitable-spread-nigeria-fuel-crisis.

[2]Vera Songwe, "Removal of Fuel Subsidies in Nigeria: An Economic Necessity and a Political Dilemma," Brookings Institution, Jan. 10, 2012, www.brookings.edu/research/opinions/2012/01/10-fuel-subsidies-nigeria-songwe.

[3]"Nigerian Fuel Protests Turn Deadly," Al Jazeera, Jan. 10, 2012, www.aljazeera.com/news/africa/2012/01/201219132749562385.html.

Bans on the slave trade in the early 19th century fueled European exploration of Africa's interior. By the late 19th century the major colonial powers — Britain, France, Belgium, Portugal and Germany — were in a "scramble for Africa," competing for huge tracts of land to secure access to natural resources such as gold and timber. In the process, they sent Christian missionaries, established large administrative bureaucracies and built railroads and other infrastructure — primarily to facilitate the export of raw materials. In the process, millions of Africans died from disease, starvation, overwork and war.[37]

In November 1884, Africa's main European colonizers sought to formalize their conflicting commercial, missionary and diplomatic efforts at a conference in Berlin.[38] At the time, the moral justification for the conquest of Africa was underpinned by pseudo-scientific ideas of European racial superiority, a desire to "civilize" technologically primitive African societies and the hope that Europe might gain from utilizing Africa's raw materials while selling manufactured goods to its inhabitants.[39]

On the eve of World War I, Europeans ruled virtually all of sub-Saharan Africa except Ethiopia.[40] In the late 1800s up to 10,000 independent African political and ethnic groups had been consolidated into 40 European colonies, often with scant regard to ethnic and language groups. The French colonial empire alone claimed 3.75 million square miles of African territory, an area more than 12 times the size of France.[41]

The colonial powers met with armed resistance virtually everywhere and maintained authority only by possessing superior arms and forming strategic alliances with traditional rulers. Financial self-sufficiency was the main goal of European colonial governments; public services such as education, sanitation and healthcare were largely left to missionaries. European-owned companies controlled most commerce and focused on producing cash crops such as coffee, cocoa and rubber or raw materials like minerals and timber. The legacy of that commodity-based economic model still exists in much of Africa today.

World War II had a profound, long-term impact on Africa. Nearly 400,000 Africans joined the British army, and African units helped defeat the Italians in Ethiopia and restore the rule of Emperor Haile Selassie. Africans fighting overseas also witnessed the independence movements in other colonies such as India and Burma, which had won pledges of self-governance from the British Crown.[42]

The war also crippled European economies and led to the rise of the United States and Soviet Union — emerging superpowers that opposed colonialism. Under the 1941 Atlantic Charter between President Franklin D. Roosevelt and British Prime Minister Winston Churchill, Britain and the United States vowed to "respect the right of all peoples to choose the form of government under which they would live."[43] Anti-colonialism was also a key facet of Soviet communism, which sought to replace colonial governments in Africa with pro-communist nationalist ones.

Independence and Stagnation

Reform efforts by colonial administrations — ending slave labor, investing in infrastructure and social services and offering Africans a larger governance role — were made grudgingly. Independence came to the region first in 1957, in Ghana, which had a relatively well-educated elite and plentiful cocoa, timber and gold. By 1960 France had granted independence to most of its colonies in West and Central Africa, and by the mid-1960s Belgium had exited its territories.

In 1963, some 32 independent African states (including those of North Africa) gathered in Ethiopia to form the Organization of African Unity (OAU), with a mandate to support the freedom of Africa's remaining colonies and foster continental political and economic integration.

Many of the newly independent countries faced enormous challenges: Some were landlocked, most had largely illiterate and uneducated populations and lacked basic infrastructure. Independence would come later in southern Africa, where colonial or white-dominated governments ruled in Mozambique and Angola until 1975, in Zimbabwe until 1980, in Namibia until 1990 and in South Africa until 1994.

Still, economic optimism ruled in the 1960s. A leading development textbook at the time foresaw Africa as having greater growth potential than East Asia, and the World Bank's top economist ranked seven African countries with potential to top 7 percent annual growth rates.[44] Yet efforts at economic integration were abortive — with consequences for the continent's long-term development.

For example, Côte d'Ivoire — France's wealthiest former West African colony — rejected a plan to unify with the seven other Francophone states in the region. As a result, the Ivoirians did not have to share their lucrative coffee and cocoa revenues with their poorer neighbors. The region remained divided into many small, weak states susceptible to foreign economic domination.[45]

The region's economies also were hampered by the legacy of colonial economic management. Between 1945-1960, as Western Europe practiced full-blown capitalism, Britain, France and other powers shackled their colonies with wage and price controls, agricultural marketing boards, state-owned industrial companies and other trappings of centrally planned economies.[46]

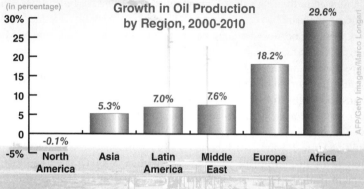

Rapid Oil Exploitation Fuels Africa's Boom

African oil production rose by about 30 percent between 2000 and 2010, faster than in any other region. The increase is due to higher global demand for oil and a surge in oil exports from Africa, which has about 10 percent of the world's reserves.

Growth in Oil Production by Region, 2000-2010 (in percentage)

- North America: -0.1%
- Asia: 5.3%
- Latin America: 7.0%
- Middle East: 7.6%
- Europe: 18.2%
- Africa: 29.6%

AFP/Getty Images/Marco Longari

Source: "Oil Production," BP Statistical Review, 2012, www.bp.com/sectiongenericarticle800.do? categoryId=9037169&contentId =7068608

The Soviet Union influenced many post-independence African leaders in an effort to export communist ideology to the developing world. Some African leaders saw the relatively stable communist economies of 1950s Eastern Europe as good models for development. In the three decades after Ghana's independence, at least 16 countries in sub-Saharan Africa would adopt socialist policies or mold their economic systems along socialist lines, according to World Bank economist John Nellis. Yet the Soviet Union was hardly the only force pushing Africa's newly independent states away from the free market. In many countries, government ownership of resources was seen as a way to prevent an elite few from dominating the economy.

Additionally, without capital markets to finance large businesses or educated business classes to run them, African leaders as well as Western donors saw a need for governments to fill the gap. In some cases, resentment of colonial domination led to nationalization of some foreign-owned companies. Revenues from state-owned companies were considered a source of funds for building infrastructure and other parts of the economy.[47]

Foreign business interests often fueled resentment because their economic practices were viewed by some as neo-colonialist. After the Democratic Republic of Congo

gained independence in 1960, the copper-rich Katanga region, backed by Belgian troops and European business interests, tried to secede from the new state.[48] After two years of fighting, the effort failed, however, and the United Nations sent troops to fight on the side of the Congolese government.

In fact, conflict and bad governance played no small role in stifling economic growth. And the two problems were exacerbated by ethnic tensions and Cold War rivalry. The United States and the Soviet Union often backed rival armed factions in sub-Saharan Africa, which helped to extend civil wars. It also led to support for authoritarian "Big Men," such as Zaire's [now the Democratic Republic of Congo (DRC)] Mobutu Sese Seko, who relied on foreign aid and support to buttress his corrupt rule rather than good governance and democracy. During the period between independence and the fall of the Berlin Wall, many of Africa's large countries experienced horrific civil wars or interstate conflicts, including Mozambique, Angola, Nigeria, DRC, Zimbabwe, Chad, Sudan, Ethiopia, Somalia, Uganda and Tanzania. These protracted conflicts stifled investment and infrastructure development and kept living standards low.

By the 1980s, bad governance and ongoing conflicts had fueled massive external borrowing by governments and state-owned companies. Foreign debt in sub-Saharan Africa had increased from around $11 billion in 1970 to $340 billion in 1995. Many countries had borrowed heavily during a period of high interest rates in the 1970s, much of it from multilateral institutions such as the African Development Bank and IMF, but when commodity prices plummeted in the 1980s the fall undermined their ability to repay the loans.

Often, the borrowed money was diverted for private use. For instance, the Mobutu regime in Zaire may have stashed up to $18 billion in foreign banks, a significant portion of which likely came from external loans to the government.[49] Other borrowing was used for consumption or white elephant development projects, such as the administrative capital city of Yamoussoukro, built by Côte d'Ivoire's late President Félix Houphouët-Boigny in his birthplace — complete with a $300 million Catholic basilica.

As a result, many countries found themselves in a "debt trap," in which they could not even pay the interest on their foreign debts, causing them to spiral ever higher. In oil-exporting Nigeria, for example, a disastrous four-year period of borrowing in the 1980s during a period of low world oil prices has haunted the country for more than 20 years. As late as 2003, its external debt was equivalent to 71 percent of its gross domestic product, and interest payments on government debt alone were equivalent to 7 percent of the country's entire economic output.[50]

The combined effects of corruption, conflict, poor economic policies, over-borrowing and unfair trade practices by wealthy nations — which subsidize their domestic farming and light-manufacturing industries — left sub-Saharan economies in tatters by the early 1990s.

From 1965 to 1987, as Asia's economies were growing annually by 4 percent and Latin America's by 2.1 percent, African per capita GDP grew by only 0.6 percent. The differences in growth rates had dramatic effects over time. For instance in 1965, Zambia's per-capita income was higher than that of South Korea. But by 1998 South Korea's was more than 17 times larger.[51]

A host of other statistics detailed the stagnation. Food production in the 1980s was 20 percent lower than in 1970, even as population soared. Per capita incomes fell by almost 2 percent a year. Primary school enrollment declined from 79 percent to 67 percent.

By the 1990s, widespread pessimism about sub-Saharan Africa's prospects abounded. "The economic failure is undercutting a drive for political liberalization, raising ethnic rivalries to a dangerous level and forcing countries to impose politically inflammatory austerity programs, often under the dictates of Western financial institutions," John Darnton, a foreign correspondent, wrote in *The New York Times* in June 1994, as Rwanda was convulsed by a genocide that left at least 800,000 dead.

African "Renaissance"

Such gloomy assessments didn't give a full picture of some of the changes underway in sub-Saharan Africa.

After the collapse of the Soviet Union in 1991, the continent embraced economic reforms — particularly in 17 countries now classified as "emerging Africa" by Radelet, the chief USAID economist. Countries slashed regulations and tariffs and cut the costs of starting a business.[52]

Democratic reforms slowly advanced as well. After decades of struggle, South Africa's apartheid government permitted multiracial elections in 1994. And in a "second liberation," long-serving autocrats such as Benin's Mathieu Kérékou, Zambia's Kenneth Kaunda and Malawi's "Life President" Hastings Banda were voted out of office. The number of African leaders leaving office due to coups, assassination or other violent means declined sharply.

By the late 1990s, reforms in Radelet's 17 emerging countries — a group that excludes oil exporters — had begun to pay off. Per capita income began to rise at more than 2 percent per year, an important threshold for sustained growth. Farm productivity in the emerging countries rose 50 percent between 1996 and 2006, and investment and trade nearly tripled.[53] Meanwhile, a series of debt-relief measures by Western banks and governments in the 1990s and early 2000s freed up cash for education, health and infrastructure.

The political and economic gains of the late 1990s and early 2000s weren't universal. The Democratic Republic of Congo, Sudan, Sierra Leone and Liberia spent parts of that period embroiled in horrific civil wars. Life expectancy in parts of southern Africa declined during the period amid an AIDS epidemic. A number of countries, such as Somalia, the Central African

Republic and Eritrea remained fragile states with limited growth prospects. Others, such as Angola, the Republic of Congo and Equatorial Guinea enjoyed rapid increases in their GDP, fueled by oil exports and rising global petroleum prices — but the gains were not shared by the majority of the population.

Despite these setbacks, by the late 1990s South Africa's then-Deputy President Thabo Mbeki had heralded the dawn of an "African Renaissance" built on popular government, economic growth and poverty alleviation.[54] By 2009 the idea had gained such currency that Senegal began work on a "Monument to the African Renaissance," a 170-foot sculpture (taller than the Statue of Liberty) of a man, woman and child meant to symbolize Africa's rise.[55]

CURRENT SITUATION

Hope and Change

With 49 countries in sub-Saharan Africa as diverse as South Africa and Somalia, it is difficult to make generalizations about the vast region. Here are overviews of African economies by sub-region:

East Africa

Cars are banned on the cobblestoned streets of Lamu, a medieval stone city on Kenya's Indian Ocean coast. The town, a UNESCO World Heritage Site where tourists mingle with load-bearing donkeys and souvenir salesmen, may soon lose some of its tranquil atmosphere.

Construction began this year on a $23 billion port project and oil refinery — the jewel of a new transport corridor meant to link landlocked South Sudan and Ethiopia to the sea via Kenya. "I am proud to say this is one of the biggest projects that we are carrying out in Africa," Steven Ikuwa, a manager of the project, told the BBC.[56]

With economic growth of more than 7 percent from 2003 to 2008, East Africa was one of the world's fastest-growing regions prior to the global financial crisis. Growth dipped in 2009, partly due to post-election violence in 2007-08 in Kenya — the region's business and transport hub — and the effects of the global slowdown. But since then growth has bounced back, and the region is expected to grow by 5.1 percent this year and 5.6 percent in 2013.[57]

A power plant rises near Libreville, Gabon, on Oct. 11, 2012, part of a $20 billion infrastructure plan financed in part by the country's abundant oil revenues. But critics complain that much of the country's oil wealth has been diverted to the family of President Ali Bongo, who owns dozens of houses around the world. By one estimate, the Bongo family has stolen up to 25 percent of the country's gross domestic product during its four-decade rule.

AFP/Getty Images/Steve Jordan

However, East Africa is marked by political instability and wide disparities in development among countries. The skyscrapers and landscaped office buildings of Kenya's capital, Nairobi, house the local offices of multinational firms such as Google, Samsung and Pfizer. In Rwanda, the economy is roaring ahead, 18 years after genocide left 800,000 people dead. Economic growth lifted more than 1 million people — nearly 10 percent of the population — out of poverty between 2006 and 2011, while Kenya's investments in an advanced fiber optics network has attracted such companies as Visa, along with top-flight educational institutions like Carnegie Mellon University.

Meanwhile, much of Somalia has not had a stable central government since 1991, and investment has been deterred by an Islamist insurgency. Nevertheless, the economy has managed to stave off collapse — nine mobile phone companies compete for business, and demand in neighboring Kenya is strong for Somali exports such as meat and the widely used narcotic leaf khat, which is

Is Africa poised for an East Asia-style economic boom?

YES G. Pascal Zachary

Professor of Journalism, Arizona State University; Author, Hotel Africa: The Politics of Escape

Written for *CQ Global Researcher,* November 2012

When I visited Ghana in June, I met dozens of former U.K. residents — well-educated offspring of Ghanaian immigrants to Britain — who'd recently returned to their ancestral home in West Africa in pursuit of better opportunities. With Britain's economy contracting and Ghana's expanding, thousands from the African diaspora are now working in Africa, in jobs and companies that need their professional skills.

What an historic reversal. Throughout much of sub-Saharan Africa, economic conditions are better than at any time in more than 50 years and have been excellent since the beginning of the 21st century. The obsession of the U.S. media and foreign-aid lobby with disaster, disease and mayhem in Africa has long distorted the continent's image. But with commodity prices high, low levels of debt by global standards, expanding domestic markets and near-record levels of foreign investment, Africa's economic strength is impossible to dismiss.

From 2000 to 2010, six of the world's 10 fastest-growing countries were in sub-Saharan Africa: Angola, Nigeria, Ethiopia, Chad, Mozambique and Rwanda. In eight of the past 10 years, sub-Saharan Africa has grown faster than Asia. While many of the region's growth stars rely in part on oil exports, Ethiopia — which has no oil — saw its economy grow 7.5 percent in 2011. In 2012, the International Monetary Fund expects Africa to grow at 6 percent — about the same as Asia.

And Africa's boom is benefiting a broad swath of African society — reversing the continent's brain drain, reducing rural poverty, enabling governments to broaden access to free education and improving Africans' technological sophistication.

Will the boom continue? With robust commodity prices, tangible productivity gains due to the mobile communications revolution and the fledgling expansion of African agriculture, the answer is surely yes. Meanwhile, an astonishing 50 percent of Africa's under-25 population is fueling household formation and growth in personal consumption unmatched in the world.

The problems aren't those touted by Afro-pessimists: That Africa remains dependent on imported goods, corruption flourishes and women are unempowered. While these concerns are considerable, they co-exist with an Africa that's generating wealth at an unprecedented rate. The challenge for African leaders is no longer coping with the scourge of scarcity, but rather managing prosperity by reducing inequality and expanding opportunity, especially for women. The big political question is how to ensure that all Africans benefit from the boom.

NO Omotunde E. G. Johnson

Sierra Leone Country Director, International Growth Centre London

Written for *CQ Global Researcher,* November 2012

If Africa is to embark on an East Asian-style economic take-off, it needs drastic improvement in economic governance and management. This in turn requires much better leadership and cooperation than exists at the present time. The prospect of this happening in the near future is not good.

African countries now face three overarching policy challenges: raising investment, boosting the efficiency of investment and increasing technological change and innovation. To do that, African citizens must be willing and able to design and implement appropriate economic policies.

As everyone knows, investment — in equipment, research and development and education and training — is good for growth. Such investment, relative to domestic product, is currently low in Africa, on average, compared to what Asian countries were able to attain during their years of rapid growth, as well as today.

The efficiency of investment in Africa is low by world standards — a symptom of underlying factors, such as government inefficiency, low education and training, poor operation of markets, weak institutions (rules), corruption and political instability.

The policy failings in Africa come mainly from weaknesses in governance arrangements (rules, processes and organization) which in turn come from weaknesses in leadership and cooperation. The role of institutions in the development process has come to be greatly appreciated over several decades now. Institutions are rules governing behavior in human interaction. But institutions are themselves outcomes of cooperation. In other words, they are elements of the order that cooperation brings about. Hence, countries succeed in the development process when they are able to cooperate to bring about appropriate political, legal and social institutions that favor economic development and growth.

To embark on an East Asian-style economic take-off, African countries need more cooperation. Trust and self-interest will play major roles in bringing that about. Leadership is also crucial. The vast majority of African countries can benefit from transforming leadership at all levels: political, civil society and business.

In building institutions, legitimation processes matter. Indeed, one of the operational requirements for institutions to be effective is legitimacy. Institutions that are not legitimated by the populace at large will not be willingly obeyed and promoted by the people; there will be no sense of loyalty to the institutions.

chewed.[58] In September, the economy's long-term prospects brightened after African Union peacekeepers and Kenyan soldiers captured Kismayo, the last city held by al-Shabaab, a radical Islamist militia.[59]

South Sudan, which gained independence from Sudan in 2011, has only 100 miles of paved roads in an area larger than France.[60] Ethnic conflict and sporadic cross-border clashes with Sudanese soldiers have left South Sudan as one of the world's least-developed countries. Yet the new port in Kenya — and a pipeline that will connect South Sudan's oilfields to it — is cause for hope. The project will ease South Sudan's dependence on export pipelines through Sudan, with which it fought two destructive wars.

Central Africa

Gabonese President Ali Bongo doesn't lack for places to sleep. The president, who took power in 2009 after the death of his father Omar, owns dozens of houses around the world, including three in Beverly Hills, one on the French Riviera, and a $120 million, 14-bedroom mansion in Paris. By one estimate, the Bongo family has siphoned off as much as 25 percent of the oil exporter's gross domestic product during the family's four-decade rule.

"There's absolutely no shame," said Jack Blum, a United Nations' consultant and expert on offshore banking. "The people running the country are guilty of grand theft nation."[61]

Indeed, oil has been a blessing for the leaders of Central African nations such as Gabon, Equatorial Guinea and Chad. But, for ordinary people, it has brought fewer benefits. Wealth began flowing into Equatorial Guinea in the late 1990s as it expanded offshore oil production. Today the country is the eleventh most corrupt in the world, according to Transparency International. Just 0.7 percent of its GDP is spent on education, compared to the average elsewhere in Africa of 3.9 percent, and more than half the population lacks access to basic services such as clean water and electricity.[62]

Still there is cause for hope. The Democratic Republic of Congo, central Africa's most populous nation, is gradually recovering from two wars, the last of which officially ended in 2003. Though conflict simmers in the eastern Kivu region, the DRC's economy will grow by more than 7 percent this year and 8.2 percent in 2013, according to the IMF.[63] Foreign direct investment increased more

> Oil exporter Angola grew by an average of more than 14 percent per year in 2003-2008. Yachts in the harbor of the capital, Luanda, must steer through garbage and debris as they come and go. A one-bedroom apartment in the center of Luanda rents for $12,000 a month, leading one British tabloid to declare it "the most expensive city in the world."

than fourfold from 2010 to 2011, fueled by telecom companies seeking to expand mobile communications in the heavily populated country.[64]

Southern Africa

In August the De Beers diamond consortium announced it had begun sorting rough diamonds in Botswana's capital, Gaborone, a process it had previously done in London. The move to Botswana, the world's largest producer of diamonds, will transform the southern African nation into a major gem-trading hub, with about $6 billion in gems handled annually.[65]

The shift is emblematic of Botswana's rise from being one of the world's poorest nations at independence to a middle-income nation today, with per capita income of $14,560. Experts attribute the rise to political harmony and wise management of the country's diamond reserves.

Botswana and other southern African nations comprise sub-Saharan Africa's wealthiest region. They also are the most economically integrated, through the 15-nation free-trade bloc known as the Southern African Development Community. Their economies are closely linked with that of South Africa, the regional giant.

However, integration can also have disadvantages. South Africa's advanced economy is heavily reliant on exports to Europe. The European Union is South Africa's largest trading partner and buys one-third of its manufacturing exports — making South Africa vulnerable to the eurozone crisis, as Europe's slowing economies buy fewer South African goods.[66]

Fortunately, strong demand from Asia has helped counteract some of the slowing demand in Europe. South African exports to China alone were worth $12.4 billion last year, although the South African goods China buys are different from those exported to the European Union.

"While South Africa's export profile to Europe is fairly balanced, the same cannot be said for China and other large emerging market partners," said Simon Freemantle, an economist with Johannesburg-based Standard Bank.[67] In 2011, 90 percent of South Africa's exports to China were made up of commodities, he says.

Strong demand for commodities has fueled growth elsewhere in southern Africa. New oil exporter Angola grew by more than 14 percent per year on average between 2003 and 2008. Its economy slowed during the downturn, when oil prices fell but is expected to grow again by 8.2 percent this year and 7.1 percent next year.[68] The rest of the country's economy has struggled to keep up with the tide of petrodollars pouring in. Yachts in Luanda's harbor must steer through garbage and debris as they come and go. A one-bedroom apartment in the center of the capital rents for $12,000 a month, leading one British tabloid to declare it "the most expensive city in the world."[69]

Meanwhile, Zimbabwe's economy is slowly recovering from a spectacular swoon, when it shrank by half between 1998 and 2008 after President Robert Mugabe began seizing land mainly from white farmers and held onto power through violence-riddled elections. The United States and Europe responded with sanctions, further crippling the economy.

After a national unity government was forged in 2009 between Mugabe's ruling party and the opposition, the economy began slowly growing. Zimbabwe dropped its devalued currency and replaced it with the dollar. But growth has been stunted by a government directive last year that all foreign-owned companies cede 51 percent ownership to black Zimbabweans.[70] This year the economy is projected to grow 4.4 percent, according to the African Development Bank, rising to 5.5 percent next year. The 88-year-old Mugabe remains president, though he is in frail health, and the country is slated to hold elections next year.

West Africa

Niger is among the world's poorest countries, ranking 186th of 187 nations on the U.N.'s Human Development Index. One in eight children dies before age 5, and 60 percent of the population lives in poverty, according to the World Bank.

Yet shoots of hope are sprouting. The country's economy may expand as much as 15 percent this year on higher production of uranium from the country's mines and the beginning of its first oil production. Foreign aid and government efforts have helped increase life expectancy from 42 in 1992 to 54 in 2010, while the percentage of children in primary school has doubled to 71 percent over the last decade.[71]

Niger's growth is emblematic of a transformation underway in West Africa. The region is expected to grow by 6.9 percent this year and 6.4 percent next year, led by strong growth in regional powers Nigeria and Ghana and a rebound in Côte d'Ivoire following a decade of political instability and civil war. (*See sidebar, p. 251.*) Oil discoveries in the Gulf of Guinea, which stretches from Ghana to Sierra Leone, also have boosted growth expectations. Nigeria had been the region's only major oil exporter until 2007, when U.K.-based Tullow Oil made a large discovery in Ghana.

"What you've had since then was an increasing number of finds showing that there are oil systems in the region," British oil analyst John Marks told a reporter, after the announcement of discoveries off Sierra Leone and Liberia. "Announcements like this will only raise the excitement."[72]

Political instability continues to pose risks for growth, however. In Mali, soldiers ousted the democratically elected president in March, and radical Islamists have taken control of the northern part of the country, where they have instituted Islamic law.[73] In October, the United Nations' Security Council declared its "readiness" to aid the government in a military effort to dislodge the Islamists. "There is no alternative," Jack Christofides, an official in the U.N.'s Department of Peacekeeping Operations, told *The New York Times*. "It's going to take military force.[74]

In addition, a decade-long political crisis that divided Côte d'Ivoire between north and south ended in a brief civil war last year after disputed elections. Once one of Africa's wealthiest countries, Côte d'Ivoire has seen foreign investors flee and development of its all-important cocoa sector stall. The economy shrank by 5.9 percent in 2011, as forces loyal to President Alassane Ouattara battled those of former President Laurent Gbagbo. Projected economic growth of 8.2 percent this year and 6.2 percent next year could be hindered by further unrest when members of Gbagbo's government are put on trial for alleged atrocities committed during the civil war. In September the government briefly closed its borders with Ghana after attacks by Gbagbo loyalists based in Ghana left at least 10 dead.[75]

OUTLOOK

Chinese Challenges

As sub-Saharan African countries strive for an East Asian-style transformation in the coming decades, much will depend on their relationship with the world's most important emerging economy: China. Africa's trade with China has risen from $10 billion in 2000 to $160 billion in 2011. This year China is expected to become the continent's largest export destination.[76]

In addition, Chinese companies have invested heavily in African mines and oil wells and have provided concessional loans to African governments to build roads, railways and electricity plants. "Their investment ideas are backed by finance," says Ifediora Amobi, director of the Nigeria-based African Institute for Applied Economics. "Even when the Chinese say we'll come build it and put it together, it still is a good model for most countries."

Chinese companies have provided African governments with an alternative to foreign aid and multinational corporations. The competition has allowed African governments to strike better deals than they otherwise would have obtained, say some experts.

"You're finding the big Chinese state-owned companies competing very aggressively on the continent," said Maree, of South Africa's Standard Bank, which is 20 percent owned by a Chinese state bank. "Our view is that generally China has been a huge force for good and for growth and development in Africa."[77]

Others see the relationship as carrying risks as well as reward. Even on concessional terms, African governments could risk being overburdened by debt. In addition, China's authoritarian government's willingness to do business with unsavory regimes such as Zimbabwe and Sudan can undermine needed governance reforms, says Massa, the France-based economist for the Overseas Development Institute.

The Chinese economic juggernaut is a challenge for Africa as its economies seek lift-off in a more competitive global economy than other emerging countries faced in previous decades. "The East Asian countries didn't have

to face competition from China," says the World Bank's Devarajan. "China didn't have a China to compete with in global markets."

Others worry that China will continue to dominate manufacturing — discouraging the development of African manufacturing — and that Africans aren't benefiting enough from the commodities-for-infrastructure deals with Chinese firms. "The stream of cheap Chinese exports to Africa may reduce incentives for African firms to build productive capacity or make their products less competitive in foreign markets," says Massa. "Finally, there is a risk that African countries endowed with natural resources are seeing their resources drain slowly away without profiting enough from Chinese deals."

The lack of strong growth in high-employment industries such as manufacturing will lead to deepening political tensions and instability in countries with growing numbers of underemployed and "vulnerable" employed people, says Johnson, the Sierra Leonean economist. Such instability will make it difficult for many countries to enjoy the sustained period of growth needed to improve living standards.

"What will change is the nature of the conflict," he adds. "Right now a lot of conflict is for control of the state. The fight [in the future] will be over jobs and income."

Africa's wealthiest economies may be able to avoid such an outcome, says Lund, of McKinsey. "For the most diversified economies you are seeing this tipping point," she says. "But then for the rest of the African countries, they're in the opposite situation, where the number of vulnerable [people] employed will continue to grow."

Others see the challenges to industrialization for African nations — small size, lack of regional integration and poor infrastructure — as major stumbling blocks. Natural resource wealth may also prove a hindrance if revenue management does not improve. As Chinese labor costs rise, rival developing nations, such as India, could emerge as the next low-cost center of manufacturing.

"I would find it hard to envision" an East Asia-style takeoff for Africa, says Ramachandran, of the Center for Global Development. "The Asian cost advantage will still be significant. Ten years from now I can see better management of resources that could translate into more service [jobs] and back-office operations."

The fact that hundreds of millions of workers in sub-Saharan Africa will still be doing subsistence agriculture or other vulnerable types of work in the decades to come does not necessarily mean their economies will not attain annual rates of 8 percent growth or more, says Devarajan.

"We have to accept the fact that even under the best of circumstances, a large number are going to go into the informal sector," he says. "So we have to acknowledge that rather than fight it. Informal is normal, at least for the next 20 years. Then we should ask the question about how we can improve their productivity."

Devarajan predicts that by 2025 all of sub-Saharan Africa, except fragile states such as the DRC, Somalia and South Sudan, will be middle-income countries with per capita income above $5,000. Development will no longer be measured by the percentage of children completing primary school but secondary education and college. Some sub-Saharan countries, in his view, may even become "manufacturing powerhouses."

"In 2025 it will look like what East Asia looks like today," he says.

NOTES

1. "Landmines in Mozambique," Human Rights Watch, February 1994, www.hrw.org/sites/default/files/reports/MOZAMB943.pdf.

2. "Africa's Impressive Growth," *The Economist*, Jan. 6, 2011, www.economist.com/blogs/dailychart/2011/01/daily_chart. Also see "Sub-Saharan Africa Maintains Growth in an Uncertain World," International Monetary Fund, Oct. 12, 2012, www.imf.org/external/pubs/ft/survey/so/2012/CAR101212B.htm. See also "World Economic Outlook: Coping With High Debt and Sluggish Growth," International Monetary Fund, October 2012, www.imf.org/external/pubs/ft/weo/2012/02/index.htm. For background, see Christopher Hack, "Euro Crisis," *CQ Researcher*, Oct. 5, 2012, pp. 841-864; and Sarah Glazer, "Future of the Euro," *CQ Global Researcher*, May 17, 2011, pp. 237-262.

3. "Building Bridges: Ernst & Young's Attractiveness Survey 2012: Africa," Ernst & Young, www.ey.com/ZA/en/Issues/Business-environment/2012-Africa-attractiveness-survey.

4. "Africa's Future and the World Bank's Role in It," World Bank, Nov. 15, 2010, http://web.worldbank.org/WBSITE/EXTERNAL/COUNTRIES/AFRICAEXT/0,,contentMDK:22765606~pagePK:146736~piPK:226340~theSitePK:258644,00.html.

5. "Africa at Work: Job Creation and Inclusive Growth," McKinsey Global Institute, 2012, www.mckinsey.com/insights/mgi/research/africa_europe_middle_east/africa_at_work.

6. "2011 Corruption Perceptions Index," Transparency International, 2011, http://cpi.transparency.org/cpi2011/results/.

7. "GNI Per Capita Ranking, Atlas Method and PPP based," World Bank, 2012, http://data.worldbank.org/data-catalog/GNI-per-capita-Atlas-and-PPP-table. Also see Vijay Mahajan, *Africa Rising: How 900 Million African Consumers Offer More Than You Think* (2009), p. 29.

8. "Doing Business 2012: Economy Rankings," World Bank, Oct. 20, 2012, www.doingbusiness.org/rankings.

9. Steven Radelet, *Emerging Africa: How 17 Countries Are Leading the Way* (2010), pp. 71-72.

10. "The Economic Rise of Mozambique," Al Jazeera English, Aug. 18, 2012, www.aljazeera.com/programmes/countingthecost/2012/08/201281714514039254.html.

11. Radelet, *op. cit.*, p. 96.

12. "Africa at Work: Job Creation and Inclusive Growth," *op. cit.*, p. 2.

13. "Natural Resources Can Spur Growth But Need Good Management," International Monetary Fund, March 30, 2012, www.imf.org/external/pubs/ft/survey/so/2012/POL033012A.htm.

14. Data on oil exports from U.S. Energy Information Administration database, www.eia.gov/countries/. See also "Democratic Republic of Congo," *Revenue Watch*, www.revenuewatch.org/countries/africa/democratic-republic-congo/overview.

15. "What Has Contributed to Growth?" Societe Generale Groupe, May 10, 2011, www.societegenerale.com/en/node/11823.

16. For background, see Jennifer Weeks, "The Resource Curse," *CQ Global Researcher*, Dec. 20, 2011, pp. 597-622.

17. Joseph Stiglitz, "Africa's Natural Resources Can Be a Blessing, Not an Economic Curse," *The Guardian*, Aug. 6, 2012, www.guardian.co.uk/business/economics-blog/2012/aug/06/africa-natural-resources-economic-curse.

18. "Economic Development in Africa: 2011," United Nations Conference on Trade and Development, July 11, 2011, http://unctad.org/en/docs/aldcafrica2011_en.pdf.

19. For background, see Karen Foerstel, "China in Africa," *CQ Global Researcher*, Jan. 1, 2008, pp. 1-26.

20. "Africa at Work: Job Creation and Inclusive Growth," *op. cit.*, p. 34.

21. "South Africa: Challenges in Manufacturing," *African Business News*, Nov. 9, 2011, www.youtube.com/watch?v=hGxlz89ADd8.

22. Radelet, *op. cit.*, p. 44.

23. Caswell Tlali, "U.S. Saves 40,000 Jobs in Lesotho," *Sunday Express* (Lesotho), Aug. 5, 2012, http://sundayexpress.co.ls/?p=7152.

24. "Africa at Work," *op. cit.*

25. Isis Almeida, "Ghana, Ivory Coast's Cocoa Areas Seen Getting Improved Rainfall," Bloomberg News, Sept. 13, 2012, www.bloomberg.com/news/2012-09-13/ghana-ivory-coast-s-cocoa-areas-seen-getting-improved-rainfall.html.

26. Marianne Stigset, "Yirgacheffe Has Starbucks' Number in Coffee Brand Row (Update 1)," Bloomberg, April 17, 2008, www.bloomberg.com/apps/news?pid=newsarchive&sid=aLB6drYEOTF8&refer=home.

27. Jessica Donati, "Nigerian Fuel Shortages Loom as Suppliers Drop Out," Reuters, June 1, 2012, www.reuters.com/article/2012/06/01/nigeria-fuel-subsidies-idUSL5E8GV9WI20120601.

28. For background, see Jina Moore, "Resolving Land Disputes," *CQ Global Researcher*, Sept. 6, 2011, pp. 421-446.

29. Neil MacFarquhar, "African Farmers Displaced as Investors Move In," *The New York Times*, Dec. 21, 2010, www.nytimes.com/2010/12/22/world/africa/22mali.html?pagewanted=all.

30. "Unemployment a 'Ticking Time Bomb," *The Times* (South Africa), May 27, 2012, www.timeslive.co.za/local/2012/05/27/unemployment-a-ticking-time-bomb-ycl. For background, see Roland Flamini, "Turmoil in the Arab World," *CQ Global Researcher*, May 3, 2011, pp. 209-236.

31. Linah Moholo, "Africa's Millions of Young People Must Add Up To Demographic Dividend," *The Guardian*, July 17, 2012, www.guardian.co.uk/global-development/poverty-matters/2012/jul/17/africa-young-demographic-dividend.

32. "Africa at Work," *op. cit.*, p. 2.

33. Supee Teravaninthorn and Gaël Raballand, "Transport Prices and Costs in Africa: A Review of the International Corridors," World Bank, 2009, www.infrastructureafrica.org/system/files/WP14_Transportprices.pdf.

34. Basil Davidson, *The African Past* (1964), pp. 176-177.

35. Philip Curtin, *The Atlantic Slave Trade: A Census* (1969).

36. Roland Oliver and Michael Crowder (eds.), *The Cambridge Encyclopedia of Africa* (1981), pp. 146-148.

37. Foerstel, *op. cit.*

38. Thomas Pakenham, *The Scramble for Africa: White Man's Conquest of the Dark Continent from 1876 to 1912* (1991), pp. 239-255.

39. Jason McLure, "Sub-Saharan Democracy," *CQ Global Researcher*, Feb. 15, 2011, pp. 92-94.

40. Parts of South Africa were under independent white rule at the time. Liberia, established as a homeland for freed U.S. slaves in the 1840s, was functionally a U.S. protectorate despite being granted independence.

41. Martin Meredith, *The Fate of Africa* (2005), p. 2.

42. *Ibid.*, p. 8.

43. "The Atlantic Charter," Aug. 14, 1941, U.S. National Archives, www.archives.gov/education/lessons/fdr-churchill/images/atlantic-charter.gif.

44. William Easterly and Ross Levine, "Africa's Growth Tragedy: Policies and Ethnic Divisions," *World Bank Policy Research Working Paper*, August 1995, http://papers.ssrn.com/sol3/papers.cfm?abstract_id=569226.

45. Meredith, *op. cit.*, p. 64.

46. John R. Nellis, "Public Enterprises in Sub-Saharan Africa," *World Bank Discussion Paper*, 1986.

47. For background see: J. McChesney, "Privatization: Third World Moves Slowly," *Editorial Research Reports*, 1988, available at *CQ Researcher Plus Archive*.

48. Oliver and Crowder, *op. cit.*, p. 260.

49. "Debt Sustainability: Oasis or Mirage," United Nations Conference on Trade and Development, 2004, pp. 5-16, http://archive.unctad.org/Templates/WebFlyer.asp?intItemID=3246&lang=1.

50. "The Burden of Debt," PBS Online News-hour, July 2003, www.pbs.org/newshour/bb/africa/nigeria/debt.html.

51. Malcolm McPherson, "Restarting and Sustaining Growth and Development in Africa: A Framework for Improving Productivity," U.S. Agency for International Development, http//:pdf.usaid.gov/pdf_docs/pnack931.pdf.

52. Radelet, *op. cit.*, pp. 71-79.

53. *Ibid.*, pp. 27-38.

54. Thabo Mbeki, "The African Renaissance: South Africa and the World," Speech at the United Nations University in Japan, April 9, 1998, http://archive.unu.edu/unupress/mbeki.html.

55. "Dakar's African Renaissance Monument Project Has Detractors," Voice of America, Nov. 1, 2009, www.voanews.com/content/a-13-2008-08-22-voa64/405373.html.

56. "Lamu Port Project Launched for South Sudan and Ethiopia," BBC News, March 2, 2012, www.bbc.co.uk/news/world-africa-17231889.

57. "African Economic Outlook 2012: Eastern African Countries," African Development Bank, 2012, www.africaneconomicoutlook.org/en/countries/.

58. Damina Zane, "Somalia: 20 Years of Anarchy," BBC News, Jan. 26, 2011, www.bbc.co.uk/news/world-africa-12278628.

59. Lucas Barasa, "Kibaki Commends Kenyan Forces Over Kismayo Victory," *Daily Nation* (Kenya) Sept. 28, 2012, www.nation.co.ke/News/Kibaki+commends+KDF+over+Kismayu+victory/-/1056/1520274/-/10jb9e2z/-/index.html.

60. "One-Year Old South Sudan: Potential to Be Harnessed," NPR, July 9, 2012, www.npr.org/2012/07/09/156491044/1-year-old-south-sudan-potential-to-be-harnessed.

61. Brian Ross and Anna Schecter, "Obama Invites Ali Bongo to White House," ABC News, June 8, 2011, http://abcnews.go.com/Blotter/obama-invites-ali-bongo-white-house/story?id=13791159#.UGYPwhiy83Q.

62. Joseph Kraus and Jonathan Hershon St. Jean, "Equatorial Guinea No Place to Hold a Human Rights Summit," *The Guardian*, Aug. 24, 2012, www.guardian.co.uk/global-development/poverty-matters/2012/aug/24/equatorial-guinea-human-rights-summit.

63. "DR Congo Economic Growth Seen at 8.2 Percent in 2013 — IMF," Reuters, Sept. 28, 2013, http://af.reuters.com/article/commoditiesNews/idAFL5E8KS75820120928. For background, see Josh Kron, "Conflict in Congo," *CQ Global Researcher*, April 5, 2011, pp.157-182.

64. "African Economic Outlook 2012: Central African Countries," African Development Bank, 2012, www.africaneconomicoutlook.org/en/countries/.

65. "Botswana: De Beers Moves Diamond Sorting to Gaborone," BBC News, Aug. 14, 2012, www.bbc.co.uk/news/business-19268851.

66. "South Africa Urges G20 Summit to Tackle Eurozone Crisis," Xinhua, June 17, 2012, http://news.xinhuanet.com/english/world/2012-06/18/c_123295579.htm.

67. "South Africa Must Protect Competitive Advantages as BRICs Build Ties With Africa," Standard Bank, March 29, 2012, www.standardbank.com/Article.aspx?id=-177&src=m2012_34385466.

68. "African Economic Outlook 2012: Southern African Countries," African Development Bank, 2012, www.africaneconomicoutlook.org/en/countries/.

69. Barbara Jones, "Luanda: The Capital of Angola, the Most Expensive City in the World," *The Daily Mail*, Aug. 4, 2012, www.dailymail.co.uk/news/article-2183616/Luanda-The-capital-Angola-expensive-city-world.html.

70. "Zimplats Happens," *The Economist*, March 17, 2012, www.economist.com/node/21550289.

71. Philip Baillie, "Niger Economy to Grow 15 Percent in 2012 — President," Reuters, June 12, 2012, www.reuters.com/article/2012/06/12/britain-niger-growth-idUSL5E8HCGC120120612.

72. Alphonso Toweh and Simon Akam, "UPDATE 2 — New Discoveries Raise West African Oil Hopes," Reuters, Feb. 21, 2012, http://af.reuters.com/article/liberiaNews/idAFL5E8DL1DE20120221?sp=true.

73. "Northern Mali Islamists Reopen Schools With Girls in Back," The Associated Press, Sept. 28, 2012, www.usatoday.com/story/news/world/2012/09/28/mali-islam-women/1600117/.

74 Adam Nossiter, "The Whiff of Conflict Grows in Mali," *The New York Times*, Oct. 23, 2012, www.nytimes.com/2012/10/24/world/africa/an-aura-of-conflict-grows-in-a-divided-mali.html?pagewanted=all.

75. Ange Anboa, "Ivory Coast Closes Frontier With Ghana After Border Attack," Reuters, Sept. 21, 2012, http://uk.reuters.com/article/2012/09/21/uk-ivorycoast-attacks-idUKBRE88K1AS20120921.

76. "Africa and China's Growing Partnership," Africa Progress Panel, April 2012, www.africaprogresspanel.org/index.php/download_file/view/1754.

77. Al Jazeera English, *op. cit.*

BIBLIOGRAPHY

Selected Sources

Books

Ayittey, George, *Africa Unchained: The Blueprint for Africa's Future*, Palgrave MacMillan, 2006.
A prominent Ghanaian economist is unsparing in his criticism of modern African governance, 50 years after the end of colonialism. Freeing African economies from their governments' shackles would raise living standards for the continent's poorest, he argues.

Easterly, William, *The White Man's Burden: Why the West's Efforts to Aid the Rest Have Done So Much Ill and So Little Good*, Oxford University Press, 2007.
In this seminal critique, a development economist examines why the tens of billions in aid spent in the past 50 years have done so little to alleviate poverty in the world's poorest nations. Easterly was fired by the World Bank for his earlier critiques of the ineffectiveness of Western aid.

Mahajan, Vijay, *Africa Rising: How 900 Million African Consumers Offer More Than You Think*, Pearson Education Inc., 2011.
A marketing professor offers a detailed argument for greater private-sector investment in Africa. Mahajan says the continent is richer than most people outside Africa realize, and its rapidly growing population is the next big market for multinational companies.

Miguel, Edward, *Africa's Turn?* Massachusetts Institute of Technology, 2009.
A University of California economist argues that the end to major civil wars and trade with China has bolstered African growth, though the continent still faces threats from climate change and fragile states. Nine guest experts also critique his narrative of African growth.

Radelet, Steven, *Emerging Africa: How 17 Countries Are Leading the Way*, Center for Global Development, 2009.
Now the top economist for the U.S. Agency for International Development, Radelet says that since 1995 a group of 17 African countries has plowed ahead economically without the benefit of oil. From South Africa to Tanzania to Ghana, these countries are raising living standards due to better governance, improved technology and international debt relief.

Articles

Fox, Killian, "Africa's Mobile Economic Revolution," *The Guardian*, July 23, 2011.
From mobile banking to dissemination of agricultural prices, the rapid spread of mobile technology in Africa is revolutionizing the continent's economies.

French, Howard, "The Next Asia Is Africa: Inside the Continent's Rapid Economic Growth," *The Atlantic*, May 21, 2012.
A former *New York Times*' Africa correspondent travels to Zambia to see how African societies are changing as they grow wealthier.

Grant, Jaime, "On the Road With West Africa's Fuel Smugglers," ThinkAfricaPress, March 20, 2012.

The trade in smuggled fuel from Nigeria has led to the creation of what the author calls "micro-petro-states" in Benin and Togo, where local officials and enterprising teenagers alike profit from sneaking subsidized Nigerian gasoline into other West African countries.

Smith, David, "Wikileaks Cables: Shell's Grip on Nigerian State Revealed," *The Guardian*, Dec. 8, 2010.
Royal Dutch Shell's top executive in Nigeria, where the company produces about 800,000 barrels of oil per day, told U.S. officials the company had placed company loyalists in relevant ministries within the Nigerian government so the company could keep tabs on its deliberations.

Straziuso, Jason, "Unexpected: Africa's Hotel Boom," The Associated Press, Oct. 1, 2012.
Marriott, Hilton and Radisson are scrambling to build hotels on a continent they have long ignored. The hotel boom is a symbol of the growth of African trade and wealth.

Reports and Studies

"Africa At Work: Job Creation and Inclusive Growth," McKinsey Global Institute, August 2012.

Africa's recent growth record is good, but the continent will have to produce many more salaried jobs to reduce the share of its fast-growing population that remains in subsistence agriculture and other vulnerable forms of employment.

"African Economic Outlook: 2012," African Development Bank, Organisation for Economic Cooperation and Development, U.N. Development Program and U.N. Economic Commission for Africa (joint publication), 2012.
The annual publication synthesizes economic statistics and forecasts from a range of international agencies to describe the current and future economies of Africa.

"Building Bridges Africa: 2012 Attractiveness Survey," Ernst & Young, 2012.
Many international businesses have outdated perceptions of Africa's economies, leaving many opportunities for investment on the continent as yet unexplored. To accelerate growth, however, African governments must invest more in roads, ports, electricity generation and other infrastructure.

For More Information

African Economic Research Consortium, P.O. Box 62882 00200, Nairobi, Kenya; +254 20 2734150; www.aercafrica.org. Researches management of sub-Saharan economies.

African Institute for Applied Economics, 54 Nza St., Independence Layout, Enugu, Nigeria; +234 706 209 3690; www.aiaenigeria.org. Think tank that provides research and policy advice with a West African focus.

African Union, P.O. Box 3243, Addis Ababa, Ethiopia; +251 11 551 77 00; www.africa-union.org. Mediates election disputes and seeks economic and political cooperation among 53 member nations.

Center for Global Development, 1800 Massachusetts Ave., N.W., Third Floor, Washington, DC 20036; www.cgdev.org. Independent think tank studying aid effectiveness, education,

globalization, health, migration and trade in developing nations.

McKinsey Global Institute, 1200 19th St., N.W., Suite 1000, Washington, DC 20036; 202-662-3100; www.mckinsey.com/insights/mgi. International economics research arm of the McKinsey consulting firm.

Overseas Development Institute, 203 Blackfriars Road, London SE1 8NJ, United Kingdom; +44 20 7922 0300; www.odi.org.uk. A leading think tank that seeks to shape policy on economic development and poverty alleviation in the developing world.

South African Institute of International Affairs, P.O. Box 31596, Braamfontein 2017, South Africa; +27 11 339 2154, www.saiia.org. Think tank that studies African governance, parliamentary performance and natural resources governance.

Voices From Abroad:

BEN SEAGER-SCOTT

Analyst, BestinvestEngland

Economic potential

"The continent sits on huge natural resources and has a young and growing population, which can drive demand as economic development progresses. Major problems remain over governmental integrity and political interventions, as well as the lack of infrastructure, both of which are vital for supporting economic growth."

Daily Telegraph (England), April 2012

MTHULI NCUBE

Vice President, African Development Bank Tunisia

Unacceptable stagnation

"The continent is experiencing jobless growth. That is an unacceptable reality on a continent with such an impressive pool of youth, talent and creativity."

New Times (Rwanda), May 2012

KATHRIN TRUMPELMANN

Executive manager, DAV Professional Placement Group, South Africa

The search continues

"African companies are battling to find suitably qualified people who are the cream of the crop in their chosen fields. They are actively recruiting these skills internationally — and that includes South Africa."

Sunday Times (South Africa), October 2012

CLIFFORD SACKS

CEO, Renaissance Capital, South Africa

The next success story

"The emerging markets, and Africa in particular, are attracting unprecedented attention as capital shifts from

The Khaleej Times/UAE/Paresh Nath

developed to growth markets. With the highest concentration of fast-growing economies, Africa will be the investment success story of the next decade."

Accra Mail (Ghana), May 2012

RICHARD JENKINS

Chair, Black Creek Investment Management Canada

Questions remain

"The big question is if I'm going to invest in South Africa and deal with some of the economic and political issues there, and I'm going to buy a gold mining stock, why wouldn't I own one in Australia or Canada instead?"

Financial Post (Canada), July 2012

NOEL DE VILLIERS

CEO, Open Africa South Africa

Unleashing potential

"We don't just need new jobs. We need new kinds of jobs in new niches innate to the indigenous potential of South Africa's people and assets. . . . New niches for new products in new markets have to be found, and these should be aligned with our indigenous skills and strengths. We have to invent new Africa-sourced products, and fast."

Sunday Times (South Africa), March 2012

PETER ESELE

President General, Trade Union Congress, Nigeria

Jobs for a growing population

"[African] governments at all levels should embark on core principles that can create the much-needed business environment for our indigenous companies to thrive and generate employment opportunities for the teeming populace."

This Day (Nigeria), June 2012

ANTHONY JONGWE

Principal consultant Global Workforce Solutions Zimbabwe

The youth opportunity

"With over 40 percent of the population below 15 years, Africa is by far the continent with the largest global youthful population. Sixty percent of Africa's population is below 24 years. If managed well, this demographic represents Africa's best development asset over the coming decades."

Financial Gazette (Zimbabwe), February 2012

ROB DAVIES

Trade and Industry Minister South Africa

The next frontier

"It's widely and increasingly recognised that Africa is the next growth frontier. The whole world is being battered by the headwinds of the global economic crisis and (also) battered by the headwinds from the slowdown in Asia."

WeekendPost (South Africa), August 2012

11

Euro Crisis

Christopher Hack

President Obama visits informally with German President Angela Merkel and French President François Hollande following a G-8 summit meeting on May 19 at Camp David, the presidential retreat in rural Maryland. With the U.S. presidential election just weeks away, the Obama administration is urging European leaders to intensify efforts to resolve their economic problems. Many experts agree that if troubled nations, such as Greece, exit the eurozone, the effect on the U.S. economy could be disastrous.

From *The CQ Researcher*,
October 5, 2012.

R iots overseas don't usually cause jitters on Wall Street, but when civil unrest in late September in Greece and Spain led to sell-offs in the world's major stock markets U.S. exchanges suffered too.

More than 100,000 Greeks marched through downtown Athens, some throwing Molotov cocktails at police. In Madrid, truncheon-wielding Spanish riot police fired rubber bullets as tens of thousands of Spaniards gathered near parliament to protest government austerity measures. The demonstrations were only the latest protests at government efforts to balance their books, including drastic spending cuts and tax hikes.

The protests worried Wall Street because Greece's debt crisis has dragged down the European economies that share the single euro currency, and some analysts fear that the troubles in the eurozone could knock the weak U.S. recovery off course — or even put the country back in recession.

The European Union is the second-largest purchaser of American exports, and many U.S. banks do a large portion of their business either in Europe or in conjunction with European banks. The problems in Europe already have hit U.S. export income and forced banks to retrench. But, in an increasingly globalized world, and one in which the economies of Europe and the United States are often said to be joined at the hip, many economists worry that Europe's problems could undermine Americans' fragile confidence in the U.S. economic recovery — even for individuals and companies that don't deal directly with the continent.

The strong economic ties between the United States and Europe are well known. With mutual investments worth $2.71 trillion, the

Five Eurozone Members Face Crises

Seventeen of the 27 European Union (EU) members — representing a population of about 330 million — have adopted the euro currency. Seven others are scheduled to join the eurozone by 2017. Sweden, Denmark and the United Kingdom have declined to join the eurozone. Portugal, Ireland, Italy, Greece and Spain are experiencing sovereign debt crises, largely because of profligate government borrowing and spending during the early 2000s.

The European Union and the Eurozone

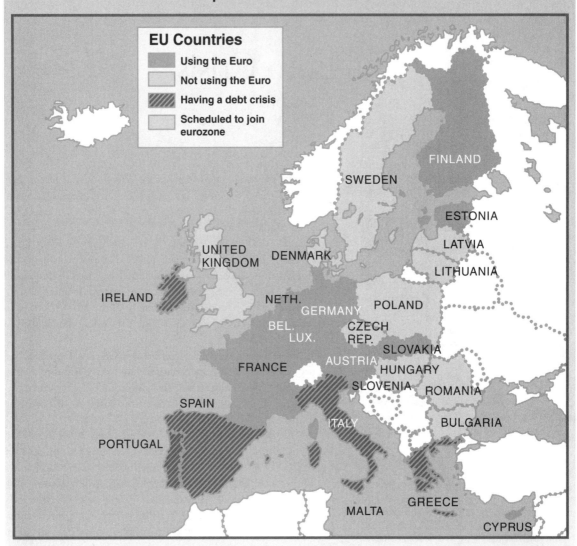

Source: European Commission. Map by Lewis Agrell

United States and the 27-member European Union (EU) have the world's most integrated economic relationship. The "transatlantic economy" supports 15 million jobs and accounts for 45 percent of the world's annual output, or gross domestic product (GDP), according to the U.S. Chamber of Commerce. In trade terms alone, the EU bought 18 percent of all U.S. exports last year, second only to Canada's 19 percent.[1]

But the relationship is deeper than just trade, with many large companies investing and operating on both sides of the Atlantic, says Jacob Kirkegaard, a research fellow at the Peterson Institute for International Economics in Washington, who says up to 70 percent of U.S. foreign investments are in Europe.

EU Is America's Second-Biggest Customer

The 27-member European Union (EU) was the second-largest buyer of U.S. products in 2011, just behind Canada. Exports to all the major U.S. trading partners increased between 2002 and 2011, led by China, where U.S. exports nearly quintupled.

Most Important Destinations for U.S. Exports
(2002-2011)

U.S. Exports
(in $ billions)

Legend: 2002, 2011

Categories: Canada, European Union, Mexico, China, Japan, Korea, Rest of world

Source: U.S. Department of Commerce, 2012

In 2002, 17 EU members gave up their individual currencies to create a shared currency, the euro. The move was part of a long-term plan to create a "united states of Europe" that would lead to a greater sense of cohesion after two world wars tore the continent apart. It was also designed to boost business, trade and prosperity, just as adopting a central currency shared by all the states aided America's fledgling economy at the end of the 18th century.

Initially, the euro was credited with creating solid growth and lower costs, as companies saved up to $33 billion per year just by not having to exchange currencies.[2]

But the euro also created massive problems, unforeseen by most proponents at the outset. By joining the 17-nation eurozone, some less-prosperous countries — notably Greece, Ireland, Portugal, Spain and Italy — suddenly had access to cheap credit. Greece's borrowing costs, for instance, dropped from about 8 percent to less than 4 percent.[3] The governments and people from those countries went on borrowing sprees, racking up huge debts.

Meanwhile, the poorer countries' less-efficient economies could not compete with the productivity of powerhouses such as Germany. German workers, for instance, produce on average about $55 worth of output per hour, compared to $34 in Greece.[4] And social benefits are higher

in the poorer states. Germans typically retire at age 67 on 50 percent of their former salaries, while Greeks retire at 65 with 93 percent of their salaries.[5] With such diverse countries now locked together in a single currency, business and wealth began to shift from the poorer countries in the south to wealthier nations in the north.

After the global recession hit in 2007-2008, international lenders sharply raised lending rates for the weaker euro countries, pushing them to the verge of bankruptcy. EU authorities and the International Monetary Fund (IMF) offered cheap loans to rescue the indebted countries, provided they cut spending, raised taxes and increased productivity.[6]

After three years of such austerity, affected countries are seeing massive job and wage cuts and sharply rising taxes. Official figures show average unemployment in the eurozone reached 11.4 percent in August, compared to 8.1 percent in the United States for the same month. With unemployment comparatively low in the prosperous countries such as Germany, the averages reflect very high levels in the periphery countries. Greece, for instance, has 24.4 percent unemployment, while Spain is at 25.1 percent.[7] The Greek economy is expected to shrink 4.7 percent in 2012, after contracting 6.9 percent last year.[8]

Austerity is provoking anger, demonstrations, riots and swings toward extremist political parties. Some economists question whether slashing spending and jobs is the right way to dig the continent out of its troubles. "There has been so much austerity that in most of those countries being hit, there is going to be absolutely no growth in 2013," says Scheherazade Rehman, director of the European Union Research Center at The George Washington University in Washington.

Meanwhile, in the euro's wealthier countries, bailouts for nations viewed as spendthrift and feckless are unpopular. German voters especially feel they are picking up the tab for others. An opinion poll in Germany in June found that 51 percent thought the country would be better off leaving the euro, while 71 percent wanted Greece out.[9] In addition to the German public's anger over bailouts, the German economy is being dragged down by the European recession. The IMF forecasts that the economy will grow by just 1 percent in 2012, and some analysts fear it may slip into recession.

International investors remain skeptical, continuing to demand high interest rates despite the austerity programs. Spain — seen as financially well managed but with high debt levels — saw its borrowing costs on 10-year debt rising to 7.5 percent, from about 4 percent. That triggered a bold move in early September by the European Central Bank (ECB). It promised to buy up any eurozone country's debt that could not be sold in the international financial markets. Effectively, this meant the ECB was agreeing to bail out the indebted nations, which angered the Germans. To placate them, the ECB said it would agree to buy the debt only if the marginal countries stuck to their austerity plans — but few believed that.[10]

All these measures have affected U.S. exports to Europe, which were down 4.8 percent as of April, and undermined the earnings of U.S. companies.[11] U.S. multinational companies such as GM, Ford, Dow and IBM are attributing lower earnings this year to Europe's debt crisis. "The majority of global holdings or global subsidiaries of U.S. companies are in Europe, which means it's not so much U.S. exports that are hurt, but it's the earnings of U.S. multinationals," says Kirkegaard.

Analysts also say the crisis is hitting confidence at home, with some suggesting that the U.S. recovery is being held back by Europe's troubles. With a presidential election only weeks away, the Obama administration is urging European leaders to move more quickly to get the crisis under control. "People in the administration and the Treasury want to see more aggressive action by the Europeans to resolve this in an orderly manner, rather than this slow unraveling of the crisis," says Ethan Ilzetzki, a professor of economics at the London School of Economics. "But the influence any administration has is limited."

Experts say the euro crisis will end either with the weaker economies being reformed and returned to growth or with one or more being forced out. Some suggest the latter could be achieved in a managed way, to limit the fallout, but almost all agree that if forced exits lead to panic — as was the case in 2008 with the collapse of the giant American investment bank Lehman Brothers — the effect on the U.S. economy could be disastrous.

"A meltdown in European financial markets would — because of the role of European banks in American money markets and the role of the U.S. banks in European money markets — be quite significant for some time, but you're talking here about a pretty extreme event," explains Martin Wolf, chief economics commentator at London's *Financial Times*.

As efforts continue to focus on keeping the weaker economies afloat, attention is turning to upcoming political events — notably parliamentary elections in Italy next April. Some fear that the unpopularity of Italy's austerity program could lead voters to choose extremist parties advocating a break-up of the euro, with potentially devastating effects on the United States and the world.

"Everybody has their eye on Italy . . . we are tied in so many ways to them, either through interest rates, trade, exchange rates, credit threats, borrowing costs. There is no way around it," says George Washington University's Rehman.

As American leaders, economists and consumers watch developments in the eurozone, here are some of the questions being debated:

Is the euro crisis slowing the U.S. recovery?

U.S. exports, banking, investment and economic confidence are feeling the effects of the European debt crisis, although experts disagree on the extent of the impact on American businesses, investors and consumers.

The EU bought 18 percent of all American exports last year, much of it from the aircraft, computer and pharmaceutical industries.[12] With Europe in recession and its economies shrinking, Europeans are expected to buy fewer American goods this year. How that will affect the U.S. economy, however, is a matter of debate.

Rehman, of the European Union Research Center at George Washington University, foresees trouble for the American economy. "The U.S. and the EU growth patterns — if you look at them over time — have mirrored each other," he says. "Clearly any slowdown or crisis or worsening of what's happening in the euro is going to slow us down."

But others suggest that, even if exports take a hit in Europe, U.S. companies can look to wider markets. "The world's emerging economies, led by China and India, account for half of the global economy and will continue to expand . . . , keeping the global economy — including the United States — churning for some time," said Fred Bergsten, director of the Peterson Institute for International Economics in Washington.[13] Indeed, the United States sold $1.48 trillion worth of goods and services overseas in 2011, up 15.8 percent over the previous year. All of Europe only accounted for about 20 percent of that total.

Ilzetzki, at the London School of Economics, says the domestic side of the U.S. economy is so big that a slowdown in global trade would not have as large an impact as some might expect. "The U.S. is a relatively closed economy," he says. "Total trade — exports plus imports — is approximately 30 percent of [the economy], which is very, very low compared to most other economies." Instead of focusing on increasing or maintaining European trade, U.S. policymakers should concentrate on the "real problem" of creating jobs at home, he says.

But others say the European crisis is worrisome for exporters such as the United States. They note that European banks, which often finance foreign purchases of U.S. goods, are contracting, raising the specter of a major slowdown in foreign trade — not just to Europe but to emerging markets such as Asia and Africa. "European banks, which have traditionally been the main financiers of emerging-market trade and are a huge presence in the global economy, are retrenching," says David Smick, a global economic policy strategist in Washington

and publisher of the journal *International Economy*. "So, that's not great for the U.S. export sector."

European banks financed about three-fourths of Boeing's $40 billion in international sales in 2011, and the euro crisis could undermine sales this year, the company says.[14] That is because many international sales of big-ticket U.S. exports such as commercial aircraft are financed by European banks, which are more willing to lend to purchasers such as the governments of developing countries. And now, with the European banks retrenching, those governments can't get financing to buy the U.S. exports.

The euro crisis also could hurt U.S. banks because, as Rehman says, American and European banks have large investments in one another. If those on either side of the Atlantic are having financial trouble, it immediately affects those on the other side. And while American banks have taken measures to recover from the 2008 financial crash, they are still exposed to problems in the eurozone through their links to European banks.

U.S. multinational corporations also have major investments, including manufacturing and services subsidiaries, in Europe. "The majority of global subsidiaries of U.S. companies are in Europe, which means it's not so much U.S. exports that are hurt but the earnings of U.S. multinationals," says Kirkegaard at the Peterson Institute. "The economic relationship between the U.S. and Europe is closer than just trade. It's investments; it's companies like General Motors." Reduced earnings at such U.S. multinationals have a greater impact on the U.S. economy than lower exports, he says. This problem is hidden in companies' lower earnings figures rather than being in published trade data, he adds.

Ordinary American investors are also on the hook, some say, because their savings are invested in pension and hedge funds that often invest heavily in European companies, many of which have seen lower returns as a result of the euro crisis.

Economic confidence may be among the biggest casualties of Europe's troubles. "It used to be that most Americans really didn't understand or didn't worry about these issues," says Uri Dadush, director of the International Economics Program at the Carnegie Endowment for International Peace. "But in the last two years — and in the last year particularly — the euro crisis has become very, very present in the minds not

Euro's Path: Promise to Uncertainty

Creation of the euro in 1999 spurred economic growth in the eurozone. The euro-to-dollar exchange rate — showing the strength of the euro against the dollar — peaked in 2007. But the sovereign debt crisis that began in 2008 has sent the exchange rate down, reflecting a weaker euro and concern about struggling European nations.

**Euro-to-Dollar Exchange Rate,
January 1999-present**

Dollars needed to purchase 1 euro (exchange rate)

Source: "Exchange Rates," European Central Bank, September 2012, www.ecb.int/ stats/exchange/eurofxref/html/eurofxref-graph-usd.en.html

Would a euro collapse be as bad as doomsayers predict?

If the euro collapses, it could be another "Lehman moment" for the United States, say some analysts — referring to the 2008 bankruptcy of the giant U.S. investment bank Lehman Brothers, whose fall helped push the United States into its steepest recession since the 1930s.

To prevent the U.S. and global financial system from collapsing in the wake of Lehman's failure, the U.S. Treasury Department, Federal Reserve and central banks and governments around the world undertook an unprecedented multitrillion-dollar rescue effort. Doomsayers predict a financial collapse in Europe today would similarly threaten the global financial system, including American banks.

just of business people and investors but families and consumers" as well. Lack of confidence in the economy affects people's decisions to spend and invest.

That is especially noticeable in the corporate sector, Kirkegaard says. U.S. businesses have at least $1 trillion on their balance sheets "just sitting there that they could be investing," he says, but many are holding back on hiring new workers and making sizeable capital investments. "I think it has to do with the uncertainty in the global economy — linked to Europe," Kirkegaard says. "Rightly or wrongly, a lot of U.S. businesses are worried about the euro. And you don't need to be a multinational to be affected."

In one area — interest rates — the euro crisis is helping the U.S. economy, analysts agree. European anxiety is encouraging global investors to put their money into U.S. government bonds, which are seen as one of the world's safest currencies. Because demand is up for those bonds, authorities don't have to offer high interest rates to get investors to buy them. So global investors effectively are lending money to the U.S. government at a cheaper rate, and interest rates for American borrowers thus remain low.

"This is a little bit of a positive effect that should not be ignored," says Dadush.

But things have changed since 2008, insist U.S. banks, the Fed and the Obama administration. Wall Street institutions have built a financial firewall by increasing the amount of capital set aside to cover bad loans and by reducing their exposure to loan risk in the eurozone. In other words, bankers and policy makers say, the U.S. economy would be protected from a euro collapse because Wall Street firms have cut their lending to European institutions.[15]

Economist Ed Yardeni, an independent analyst who previously worked for the Federal Reserve and U.S. Treasury, agrees. "My sense is that the U.S. banks are not greatly exposed to the European banks. U.S. banks have been able to issue a lot of the bonds and raise money in the equity markets since early 2009, and the money markets are still open to U.S. banks."

Some analysts say it is important to be clear on what a financial "collapse" means. In a much-discussed scenario, Greece would become either unwilling or unable to keep paying interest on its debts. This "default" would prevent it borrowing money, so it would leave the eurozone and print a new currency in order to keep paying employees — a chain of events dubbed "Grexit."

The Carnegie Endowment's Dadush says that if this were a well-managed, "not too messy" divorce, then the effect on the United States could be limited.

Ilzetzki, at the London School of Economics, says Europe would suffer, but the United States could ride it out. "This would not be a shock of the magnitude of Lehman Brothers to the United States," he says. "For the U.S. the exposure would be big enough, given the already weak recovery, to tip the scales towards another recession. There could be political ramifications — the presidential race is close enough that any economic bad news could tip the scales — but it would not be another Lehman for the U.S."

Much would depend on the mechanics of a "Grexit." Analyst say the Greek government could introduce a new currency "virtually overnight."[16] That currency would then fall against the euro and the dollar, allowing Greece to start growing again.[17] But the devaluation would decimate the wealth of Greek individuals and companies — and European banks that hold Greek debt.

What would happen next is unclear. The markets could restabilize or an international financial panic could ensue. The latter scenario could lead investors to withdraw their money from banks across Europe and force larger countries, such as Spain and Italy, into default — by which time the crisis could be too big to stop.

This worst-case scenario, dubbed "contagion," would bankrupt even heavyweight European banks, a crisis that in turn could hit U.S. banks in a domino effect, since many of these European banks owe large sums of money to American banks. "If the exit of Greece was very messy and disputed, the first impact would be on the rest of Europe, Spain and Italy, and the contagion could become very serious," says Dadush. "The effect on the U.S. would be huge and disastrous," undermining thousands of businesses and consumers and eventually putting the country "back into recession."

The key is whether the exit of one or two smaller countries could be contained, the Peterson Institute's Kirkegaard says. "Direct U.S. exposure to Greece, Ireland and Portugal is very, very small; maybe $10

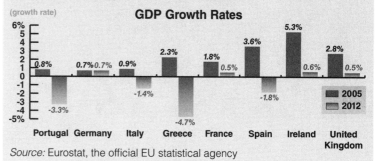

Euro Crisis Devastated EU Growth

Declining growth in Europe's biggest economies in the last seven years reflects the impact of the euro crisis across the European Union (EU). Greece's gross domestic product (GDP) growth rate has fallen the furthest, followed by Spain and Ireland.

GDP Growth Rates
(growth rate)

	2005	2012
Portugal	0.8%	-3.3%
Germany	0.7%	0.7%
Italy	0.9%	-1.4%
Greece	2.3%	-4.7%
France	1.8%	0.5%
Spain	3.6%	-1.8%
Ireland	5.3%	0.6%
United Kingdom	2.8%	0.5%

Source: Eurostat, the official EU statistical agency

billion. But U.S. exposure to Spain and Italy is in the multi-hundred billions of dollars," he says. "In the worst-case scenario, it would destroy large parts of the euro area financially, and that would have an immediate effect on the United States, reminiscent of what happened after Lehman. And that is something U.S. authorities should be worried about."

American banks say their net exposure to the troubled countries of Europe — Portugal, Ireland, Italy, Greece and Spain, known collectively as the "PIIGS" — is limited. In June filings to the Securities and Exchange Commission, Bank of America put its exposure at $9.7 billion (down from $16.7 billion in June last year), Citigroup was at $17.5 billion, and JPMorgan Chase at $6.2 billion.

But Dadush says all the firewalls erected by the banks could amount to nothing in the event of contagion. "I never bought the idea that the U.S. banks are insulated from the euro crisis," he says, explaining that American banks only report their "net exposure" to the eurozone. Banks across the world lend each other billions of dollars on a daily basis as part of their routine transactions. But instead of saying, for example, that an American bank owes a European bank $100 million, and that the European bank owes them $100 million, they cancel the figures out and say that they have a "net exposure" of zero. In a global financial crisis, however, if a European bank can't pay the $100 million it owes, the fact that an American bank owes it some money in

Students demonstrate in Rome on Sept. 28 against spending cuts by the Italian government aimed at bringing Italy back from the brink of economic collapse. Some experts fear that the unpopularity of Italy's austerity program could lead voters in parliamentary elections next April to choose extremist parties advocating a breakup of the eurozone, which could have devastating effects on the United States and the world.

return becomes meaningless, because both debts could be left unpaid. So measuring this "net exposure" becomes meaningless.

"A lot of exposures that you read about are concluded on the 'net basis' . . . but in a systemic crisis, gross exposures matter a lot," explains Dadush. "The fact that people owe you money cannot be offset against the fact that you owe them money, because you cannot be sure that you are going get your money back."

Bank analyst Christopher Wolfe, a managing director at Fitch Ratings, a New York-based credit-rating agency, says there are always risks. "You can look at the published numbers, in terms of who holds what sovereign [government] and corporate debt in the eurozone, and come up with the numbers and gross and net, but that's not the concern. It's what happens if there are some very disorderly actions in the eurozone. No one can predict that."

Smick, the global economic policy strategist in Washington, says there also are questions about how strong the big European banks are. "Nobody believes the balance sheets of the European banks," he says. "So much of the stuff on the balance sheets is junk." Many loans recorded as assets may be worthless, because a

borrower has either stopped making repayments or is close to stopping repayments, he says. "That's a lot of concern."

While American banks are well protected in the current situation, Yardeni says, if the euro crisis leads to contagion, then all bets are off. "If there is a financial meltdown in Europe, the trouble at Lehman will seem like just a warm-up act."

Should the United States provide more aid to help Europe?

Given the risks the euro crisis poses to the U.S. economic recovery, some economists say Washington should do more to rescue Europe.

For instance, the administration could pledge more money to the IMF to ensure that it has sufficient funds to prevent another global crisis. "The U.S. is running a big risk in Europe," says the Carnegie Endowment's Dadush, who criticizes Congress for blocking an expansion of IMF funding. "Their response has not been adequate. By not contributing to the expansion of IMF resources, they have let everybody else off the hook — China and others."

Since the Lehman collapse, the IMF has sought to increase its funding in case there is a new international crisis. At the beginning of 2012, for example, Christine Lagarde, the new IMF managing director, sought to raise $500 billion and urged the United States to play a role, saying: "If the European economy falters, the American recovery and American jobs would be in jeopardy."[18]

The United States, which provides about one-fifth of the IMF's funding, already underwrites part of the euro bailout program, which is jointly financed by the IMF and the EU. But so far Congress has refused to approve a proposed temporary boost in the U.S. share of the institution's funding by $63 billion. In addition, in May 2010 Congress blocked IMF funds from being used to directly bail out debtor nations.[19]

When Washington said no, much of the money to increase the IMF's emergency funding reserve came from European and emerging nations, with $43 billion from China.[20]

"It is a tremendous mistake by Congress to not have authorized the IMF capital expansion," says the Peterson Institute's Kirkegaard. "It is in very strong American interest to make sure the IMF is strong and well capitalized."

It is also a strategic mistake at a geopolitical level, he says, for Washington to allow China to play a bigger role. "The IMF was essentially designed by the U.S. and has been run by the United States and Europe since inception and is more dominated by the United States and Europe than any alternative organization that could be created today. If the Asian countries decided to create an Asian monetary fund, U.S. influence on that would be a lot smaller. So it is in the direct U.S. national interest to ensure the IMF remains the indispensable, unambiguous global body. Congress has made a huge mistake. The Chinese can [now] put a lot of money into the IMF, and say 'Look, give us a lot more influence.' And that influence is going to come at the direct expense of Europe and the U.S."

But former Federal Reserve official Yardeni says the United States is right to limit its role: "If you start going down that road, you may find that it's a black hole and you have committed yourself to being involved in a rescue that is not in our interest. The Europeans got themselves into this mess; they're going to have to work themselves out."

Policy strategist Smick says he is surprised that the euro issue has not featured more in the presidential campaign. "If I were running as a Republican, I'd be talking about Greece every day. I would be quoting European policy officials who said not that long ago that this kind of massive debt is manageable. You would say, 'Here is a group who thought they could finance their way around it using central-bank tricks. Has it worked? We risk going into that at some point.' "

Ilzetzki at the London School of Economics says the policy will be largely unchanged no matter who is in the White House. "There tends to be continuity in international affairs, and even more so in international economic affairs," he says. "So I would not expect a big change. And even if there was the desire, it's not clear that there is much that the United States could really do."

BACKGROUND

Dreams of a United Europe

Merging Europe's economies and currencies has been a dream for centuries. But after World War II, which devastated Europe for the second time in less than 40 years, policymakers increasingly saw economic integration as the best way to end centuries of bloodshed on the continent.

Part of the pressure came from the United States, which launched its four-year Marshall Plan in 1947 to reconstruct the continent's war-torn economies.[21] Another step came in 1951, when France, Germany, Italy, the Netherlands, Belgium and Luxembourg agreed to operate their coal and steel industries under a common umbrella organization called the European Coal and Steel Community. The idea was that none of the six countries could then go to war against a fellow member because steel is essential for the manufacture of weapons. War would be "not only unthinkable, but materially impossible," France's foreign minister said at the time.[22]

In a precedent-setting move, the six nations agreed to surrender some sovereignty to the new organization. Six years later they signed the Treaty of Rome creating the European Economic Community (EEC), which aimed to remove trade barriers and allow the free movement of goods, services and people across borders.[23]

Over time, trade and cooperation grew in this "Common Market," and more European countries joined, with Britain, Denmark and Ireland signing up in 1973, Greece in 1980 and Portugal and Spain in 1985.

While many proponents saw the EEC as merely a vehicle to boost trade, others — notably French leaders, European intellectuals and, increasingly, EEC officials and advisers — had an unwavering desire for an "ever-deeper union," which became the EU motto. France sought to reinforce its own political status while weakening Germany's economic dominance and saw a merging of political and economic sovereignty as a means to that end. In 1986, the Single European Act committed member states to "economic and monetary union" — but with no deadline, since some countries — especially Britain — preferred to maintain the EEC as little more than a trading bloc.

In 1989, the fall of the Berlin Wall separating East and West Germany raised the prospect of a reunified Germany for the first time since World War II.[24] But German reunification required the consent of the four post-war occupying powers: France, Britain, the United States and Russia. France seized the opportunity to advance its dream of a unified Europe, agreeing to German reunification in exchange for an unwavering pledge by

CHRONOLOGY

1950s-1970s *European nations cooperate after World War II to prevent future conflicts and foster growth.*

1951 To prevent future weapons build-ups, France, Germany, Italy, the Netherlands, Belgium and Luxembourg agree to operate coal and steel industries under a common pact.

1957 The six nations create the European Economic Community (EEC) allowing free movement of goods and people.

1968 EEC members remove all customs duties between themselves; trade and prosperity accelerates.

1973 Denmark, Ireland and United Kingdom join EEC.

1980s *EEC membership grows; Berlin Wall falls; Germany agrees to monetary union in exchange for national reunification.*

1981 Greece becomes 10th nation to join EEC, followed five years later by Portugal and Spain.

1988 Single Market Act commits members to "monetary union" — creating a single European currency — but resistance slows setting final date.

1989 Collapse of communism leads to fall of Berlin Wall; France reluctantly approves reunification of East and West Germany in exchange for German agreement to push for creation of euro.

1990s-2003 *Euro is established; economies enjoy strong growth as huge credit bubble develops.*

1992 Maastricht Treaty, signed in the Netherlands, commits countries to monetary union by 1999. Stability Pact later sets debt and budget targets but is not enforced.

1999 Eleven countries abandon their currencies and adopt euro; Britain balks. Greece joins currency two years later, but its financial qualifications turn out to have been falsified.

2002 Euro currency is introduced, national currencies phased out. Cheap credit lifts heavily borrowing poorer countries, but real estate and debt bubbles grows.

2003 Germany and France override EU budget rules, join others in running large budget deficits; rules are eventually abandoned.

2008-2012 *World financial crisis leads investors to withdraw funds; indebted nations face crisis.*

2008 Lehman Brothers collapses in wake of U.S. subprime crisis; financial panic spreads to Europe as investors run from highly indebted banks, companies and nations. European governments pour money into local banks to keep them afloat, incurring even more so-called sovereign debt.

2009 Greece reveals its budget deficit is twice what it previously reported, prompting fear the country will go bankrupt and bring down the euro.

2010 EU and International Monetary Fund (IMF) bail out Greece and Ireland and set up European Financial Stability Facility. Across Europe, countries pledge to end credit binge, cut spending and raise taxes.

2011 EU and IMF bail out Portugal and agree to second bailout for Greece (May). . . . European leaders persuade banks that lent money to Greece to accept 50 percent cut in value of loans (October); European rescue fund is raised to €1 trillion ($1.3 trillion, at today's exchange rate).

2012 Voters across Europe, angry at cuts and higher taxes, elect anti-austerity politicians (May); socialist François Hollande becomes French president, and Greeks choose extremist parties offering utopian solutions. But the parties are unable to form a government, leading to new elections. As fears grow afresh for the euro, Greek voters elect centrists who back the austerity program. . . . Pressure grows on larger economies, such as Spain and Italy. . . . In September, the European Central Bank calms nerves when it pledges to bail out any eurozone state that adopts strict austerity measures.

German officials to support monetary union — and to end Germany's powerful deutschemark currency.

"Now that Germany's land area, population and economic capacity were set to expand at a stroke, it became even more urgent to lock it into Europe," writes Barry Eichengreen, a University of California economist.[25] Germany, in effect, sacrificed the deutschemark for reunification.

On Feb. 7, 1992, a new treaty was signed at Maastricht, in the Netherlands, by members of the renamed European Union. It established rules for a single currency and a 1999 deadline for introducing the "euro." Because of strong domestic resistance — in part because of British nationalism and fears of continental socialism — Britain refused to join and retained its pound currency.[26] After a referendum on the issue in 2000, Denmark also chose to stay outside the eurozone.[27]

Adopting the euro offered many economic benefits, including a massive trade boost, much as the creation of the original EEC had done in 1957. But creating a single currency for independent nations with different political and economic systems also raised the prospect of intra-continental tension. To ensure that one country did not drag the others down, politicians reluctantly agreed that member countries would need similar economic policies. Germany, which had the strongest economy, insisted that all members maintain debt and budget deficits similar to its own stringent standards.

Euro countries adopted a set of "Maastricht criteria" stipulating that countries seeking to join the euro maintain deficits of no more than 3 percent of the country's annual income [or gross domestic product (GDP)] and public debt of no more than 60 percent of GDP. For Germany, the biggest hurdle was the need to abandon the iconic deutschemark.

But Germany also recognized a huge potential economic reward from joining a single currency: a vast market for its famed industrial goods, made by BMW, Mercedes, Bosch, Braun and others, without having to deal with constantly fluctuating exchange rates.

Although a single European currency was created for economic reasons, it was also done as a political move. Many European political figures and intellectuals rode roughshod over dissenting voices, urging them to believe in the single currency as the embodiment of the European

ideal, as something almost mythical. Skeptical economists and center-right politicians who opposed the euro were portrayed as narrow-minded Luddites.[28] Pro-euro politicians insisted that "political will" would overcome any economic problems.[29]

However, the new eurozone rules for how European economies should be managed were routinely broken, even by Germany. After reunification, the high cost of rebuilding East Germany drove up Germany's borrowing, leading to a budget deficit of 4 percent in 2004, and forced the government to ask the EU for permission to break the rules it had itself demanded.

That left the rules in tatters, but politicians across the continent were swept up in the desire to expand the eurozone. "Policymakers wanted the new currency to succeed . . . allowing weaker economies to join without due scrutiny," writes Mary Elise Sarotte, a professor of international relations at the University of Southern California.[30] "Such laxness allowed the entry of members [Belgium and Italy] with debt-to-GDP ratios well in excess of 60 percent but also applicants such as Greece, which not only flouted the rules but also falsified its records."[31]

The Golden Years

In 1999 the euro was introduced as the currency for commercial transactions in 11 countries. Then three years later, with great fanfare, bank teller machines were stocked with new euro notes for the first time on Jan. 1, 2002.

The "European dream" became real. Aside from promoting more trade, growth and wealth, the single currency created a new sense of oneness, or social integration, on the continent. Rather than the EU being about distant meetings of ministers, or a new law, it was something physical, in Europeans' pockets.

The early European integration period is forever linked to the emergence of an elite group of young, highly educated, multilingual graduates from across the continent who had participated in the "Erasmus program," a university-level European student-exchange program.[32] This "Erasmus generation" effortlessly crossed borders and language barriers, taking well-paid white-collar jobs in Brussels, the capital of the EU. It was seen as the embodiment of the new Europe and the rootstock of a new generation of leaders on the continent.

How Wall Street Helped European Nations Cheat

New economic problems may reveal more scandals.

When economic times turn bad, it's not hard to spot the investors with poor judgment or those who took excessive risks. As billionaire investor Warren Buffett colorfully puts it, "After all, you only find out who is swimming naked when the tide goes out."

Buffett could have been describing the fallout from the current euro crisis. In one of his legendary annual letters to his investors, Buffett illustrates how unacceptable practices and nefarious deals in the eurozone came to light only after the crash — many involving Wall Street investment banks.[1]

In 2000, for example, euro membership was seen as a symbol of success, modernity and pride, and the Greek government was desperate to join. But EU rules stipulated that government debt be no more than 60 percent of a country's economy, or gross domestic product (GDP), or at least "approaching" that figure. Greece's debt was 94 percent of GDP that year, and with state funds pouring into preparations for the 2004 Olympics in Athens the debt figure was going in the wrong direction.[2]

But Goldman Sachs, the Wall Street investment bank, came to the rescue in 2001, lending Greece €2.80 billion ($3.64 billion) disguised in a complicated foreign-currency transaction.[3] The secret loan made Greece's debt ratio appear to be improving enough to allow it to join the euro.

As Buffet essentially predicted, the full details of the transaction came to light in 2010, only after the euro debt crisis began.[4] The already indebted Greek government had indeed agreed to pay Goldman €600 million ($540 million at the time) in fees and interest for the deal. But by 2005, the total cost had risen to €5.1 billion ($6.1 billion) — contributing towards Greece's downfall. Martin Wolf, the chief economics commentator at London's *Financial Times*, described the deal as "completely legal and completely scandalous."[5]

Greece was not alone in cooking its books to meet the euro entry criteria. Italy in 1996 engaged in a similar transaction with JP Morgan, another Wall Street bank.[6] Similar deals have come to light across the continent, from Portugal to France. As recently as 2009 — as the euro crisis was unfolding — Goldman was back in Athens offering the troubled government a way to stretch its health-care costs over a longer period to make debt figures look better.[7] This time Greece declined.

Through the mid-2000s, a huge wave of prosperity spread across the continent, especially in once-marginalized Ireland, Greece, Portugal and Spain. Ireland, which became known as the "Celtic Tiger," enjoyed mushrooming manufacturing and service industries and a massive housing boom. Greece poured money into new infrastructure, roads, railways and airports in preparation for hosting the 2004 Olympics. Spain and Italy enjoyed boom years previously unimagined.

The new investments were the product of a little-discussed factor. Before the creation of the euro, international banks lent to each government in Europe at different exchange rates, charging risky governments the most. With the arrival of the euro, all European economies were considered as safe as the safest nation: Germany. As

a result, borrowing costs fell for the more marginal nations. Like a teenager getting his first credit card, once countries were accepted into the union, they could borrow vast amounts at very low interest rates. Greece, for example, had previously paid about 8 percent to borrow money using a 10-year bond. After the introduction of the euro, that rate fell below 4 percent.[33] National spending sprees ensued. With few countries sticking to the rules, many borrowed vast amounts during the 2000s, and some countries became hugely indebted.

The single currency also exacerbated another perennial problem: imbalances among nations. German workers are very productive, receive few pay rises, retire late on a relatively low pension and enjoy low inflation rates. Workers in southern Europe typically have low productivity levels,

Banks also have manipulated the international interest rates on which much European debt is calculated. Again, the shenanigans only emerged this summer, "when the tide went out," as Buffett would say. The issue concerns the London interbank offer rate, or "Libor," which is used to set the interest rate on millions of international loans.

Libor is announced daily, by drawing together data from many banks on the interest rate they are charging and being paid in loans between themselves. Many consumer, auto and housing loans, for example, charge interest at the current "Libor rate" with the addition of a fixed percentage, such as "Libor + 4 percent." So if Libor goes down, a consumer's repayments go down, and vice versa. But in July it emerged that this rate for years had been artificially fixed so that banks could profit from it, with the finger pointing at Bank of America, Citigroup, JPMorgan Chase, the Swiss bank UBS and Barclays in the U.K.[8] Moreover, knowledge of the scandal went right to the top. It was revealed, for example, that Treasury Secretary Timothy Geithner knew about the scandal as far back as 2008, but did little.[9]

Despite American bankers' claims that they are now "fully protected," should the euro collapse, the Libor scandal highlights how little is known of their real exposure to European markets.

With fears growing that the euro crisis could get dramatically worse in coming months — possibly forcing one or more countries out of the single currency — it's likely that still other bankers were "swimming naked."

— *Christopher Hack*

[1]Warren E. Buffet, "Chairman's Letter," Berkshire Hathaway, Feb. 28, 2002, www.berkshirehathaway.com/2001ar/2001letter.html.

[2]See Christopher Hack, "Hosting the Olympics," *CQ Global Researcher*, July 3, 2012, pp. 305-328.

[3]Nicholas Dunbar and Elisa Martinuzzi, "Goldman Secret Greece Loan Shows Two Sinners as Client Unravels," Bloomberg, March 6, 2012, www.bloomberg.com/news/2012-03-06/goldman-secret-greece-loan-shows-two-sinners-as-client-unravels.html.

[4]Beat Balzil, "How Goldman Sachs Helped Greece to Mask its True Debt," *Der Spiegel*, Aug. 2, 2010, www.spiegel.de/international/europe/greek-debt-crisis-how-goldman-sachs-helped-greece-to-mask-its-true-debt-a-676634.html.

[5]Aaron Task, "Greece-Goldman Sachs Deals Were 'Completely Scandalous' — And Perfectly Legal: Martin Wolf," *The Huffington Post*, May 2, 2010, www.huffingtonpost.com/2010/03/02/greece-goldman-sachs-deal_n_482001.html.

[6]Louise Story, Landon Thomas Jr. and Nelson D. Schwartz, "Wall St. Helped to Mask Debt Fueling Europe's Crisis," *The New York Times*, Feb. 13, 2010, www.nytimes.com/2010/02/14/business/global/14debt.html?pagewanted=all.

[7]Robert Scheer, "It's Greek to Goldman Sachs," *The Huffington Post*, Feb. 17, 2010, www.huffingtonpost.com/robert-scheer/its-greek-to-goldman-sach_b_465134.html.

[8]Mark Gongloff, "Citigroup Manipulated Libor More Than Any Other U.S. Bank: Reports," *The Huffington Post*, July 20, 2012, www.huffingtonpost.com/mark-gongloff/libor-scandal-citigroup_b_1689853.html.

[9]Margaret Hartmann, "With Release of 2008 Memo, Focus Shifts to Geithner in Libor Scandal," *New York Magazine*, July 13, 2012, nymag.com/daily/intel/2012/07/focus-shifts-to-geithner-in-libor-scandal.html.

retire early on high pensions, receive frequent pay rises and are accustomed to high inflation rates. Before the euro, such trends were unimportant when it came to their respective economies and the effect on exports, because each country had its own currency, and the weaker currencies usually fell in value compared to the deutschemark. As a result, the price of an item made in Greece, for instance, continued to rise steadily measured in the drachma. But when exported, the steady devaluation of the drachma meant that when the price of the item converted into deutschemarks, it had not gone up. So Greek exports remained affordable in Germany, despite steadily rising wages and inflation at home.

The arrival of the euro changed all that. The Greek government could no longer allow a steady decline in the exchange rate of its currency against its neighbors. Wages, costs and inflation rose in Greece, but rose more slowly in Germany. So with every passing year, Greek exports became more expensive in Germany and elsewhere in Europe, progressively destroying the country's economy.

During the same early period, roughly from 2002-2007, many peripheral countries, such as Ireland, Spain and Greece, experienced massive real estate booms, fed by the lower borrowing costs. In Ireland, for example, average house prices nearly doubled between 2000 and 2006, and the Irish economy became increasingly dependent on the construction sector. When the mortgage bubble burst and the Irish government bailed out its banks, it took over all of their debts, undermining Ireland's position in the euro.[34]

Sovereign Debt Crisis

In early 2007, when it became clear that home loans had been made to millions of people who could not afford to pay them back, the U.S. subprime mortgage crisis went largely unnoticed in Europe, where it was seen as an "Anglo-Saxon problem" — standard EU jargon for the free-market economics embraced by the United States and Britain.

But in 2008, after the situation morphed into a global banking crisis, European banks began to look hard at how much they had lent to individuals, companies and governments across the continent and began asking questions about heavily indebted countries such as Greece and Ireland.

Europe's government — or "sovereign" — debt crisis emerged at the end of 2009, when Greece's new prime minister, George Papandreou, revealed that his country's budget deficit was nearly four times worse than reported by his predecessor. Instead of being 3.7 percent of GDP, he said, the deficit was 12.7 percent.[35] And worse, government debt was an astounding 120 percent of GDP in 2010.[36] Global financial markets panicked as investors began to demand higher interest rates on government bonds to keep lending to Greece.

Bond rating agencies downgraded Greek government debt to "junk" status, in essence advising clients that lending to Greece was a gamble with no guarantee the money would ever be repaid.[37] Although the government desperately cut spending and raised taxes, it wasn't enough. High interest costs on government debt were beginning to swallow up a larger proportion of state income. Declaring Greece "a sinking ship," Papandreou asked the EU for help.[38]

Countless summits between the governments of Europe, senior figures in the European Union, the European Central Bank and IMF resulted in a series of bailouts, in which the EU and IMF agreed to lend the indebted countries enough to keep them afloat while they sorted out their financial problems. Greece initially received €110 billion ($146 billion), Portugal €78 billion and Ireland €85 billion. With the IMF involved in the lending, some of the money was effectively being put up by U.S. taxpayers.

But when governments desperately cut spending and raised taxes to balance their books, a backlash erupted across Europe, with demonstrations, strikes, riots and — in some countries — a swing towards extreme leftist politics. The chaos in Europe has had pronounced economic effects on the United States. Exporters sending goods to Europe have seen their order books shrink, affecting jobs at home. American banks, worried about how much they have already lent to European countries, have tightened up their lending, and fears have grown about what would happen to the U.S. recovery if the crisis in Europe gets worse.

CURRENT SITUATION

Hoping for Salvation

Almost three years after the euro debt crisis began, the situation today seems little changed, although the mood is brighter in Brussels — the EU capital — where a new plan to buy bonds from heavily indebted countries has lifted spirits.

Still, the situation in the peripheral countries — Greece, Portugal, Ireland, Spain and Italy — remains grim. To be able to continue making payments on their huge amounts of debt, governments are cutting spending, raising taxes and trying to improve competitiveness. But the austerity measures are slashing economic growth and personal incomes. The Greek economy is expected to shrink by "only" 4.7 percent in 2012, according to the IMF, an improvement from 2011, when it dropped 6.9 percent.[39]

And popular anger is growing. In Athens, protesters took to the streets again in September, with demonstrations that in some cases descended into widespread rioting. But the anger was not just coming from rebellious youth. In one week in September alone, for example, doctors and teachers took to the streets to protest funding cuts;[40] 2,000 retired military officers marched through Athens against pension cuts;[41] local government workers announced a two-day strike;[42] and pensioners stormed the health ministry protesting reductions to spending on pharmaceuticals and plans to reduce their benefits.[43]

Darker forces also are emerging. In the same week, surveys showed that support for Golden Dawn, a neo-fascist party, reportedly had climbed to 10.5 percent, making it the third most popular political party in the country.[44] Greek President Karolos Papoulias summed

Preparing for the Worst in Greece

Many American firms are staying but hedging against a euro crash.

The shaky euro has American companies operating in Greece preparing for the worst. To protect their funds if Greece suddenly abandons the euro, U.S. and other international companies routinely sweep money out of Greek banks every evening and into accounts in countries outside the eurozone, such as the U.K. and Switzerland. Then, every morning, they transfer it back in so that they can do business.

"These sorts of measures are expensive, but American and other foreign companies are nervous now," says a Greek business journalist in Athens, who asked not to be named. He says many U.S. companies also are simply pulling up stakes. "They have been leaving for about four or five years now, and it is continuing. Every now and then you hear that another company has gone."

Analysts warn that a Greek exit from the euro would temporarily freeze all bank accounts in the country. Funds in euro accounts would then be converted into a new national currency, which would then plummet in value by at least half, they predict. And a euro exit would affect even dollar accounts in Greece, because the government would be expected to impose "capital controls" to prevent a hemorrhage of wealth out of the country, thus trapping all moveable foreign assets.

"It is irrational for anyone, whether a corporation or an individual, to be leaving money in Greek financial institutions, so long as there is a credible prospect of a eurozone exit," said Ian Clark, a London attorney.

Meanwhile, American firms across the eurozone are subtly changing their business practices. When negotiating new contracts, for example, some seek payment in dollars or British pounds instead of the euro; others are storing dollars in eurozone countries to pay local workers in case of a breakdown in the currency union.[1]

Sandra Cohen, an assistant professor in the Department of Business Administration at the Athens University of Economics and Business, who is Greek, says such moves are to be expected. At the same time, she notes, many American companies are staying and doing good business: "Some are leaving, but many companies have chosen to stay and keep trading here, including big American firms like Proctor & Gamble and Johnson & Johnson.

"Of course, they are making contingency plans — it is their money, and they want to be prepared," she continues.

A gas mask-wearing protester runs from tear gas fired by riot police in Athens on Sept. 26 during a 24-hour general anti-austerity strike that turned violent.

"But they still see opportunities." Since parliamentary elections in June brought a pro-reform coalition to power, she says, "there is a much more optimistic feel in the country," noting for example that the General Index of the Athens Stock Exchange has almost doubled in three months, from 476 at the beginning of June to 770 in mid-September. "The Greeks are a proud people, and we take any opportunity to be positive and hopeful."

The business journalist adds that despite the generally negative international view of the country's finances, plenty of investment opportunities exist. "Salaries have gone down, labor laws have been reformed, assets are very cheap, rents are low. This can be a good place to do business now, but there are still risks, and funding of course is difficult." He says that some markets for foreign goods also are being tested by a shift in favor of domestically produced products — a consumer initiative to "buy Greek."

"Some American brands are suffering, but that is not deliberate," he says. "It is the German brands that are being deliberately left on the shelves."

— *Christopher Hack*

---

[1]Heidi N. Moore, "U.S. firms prep for Greece exit from euro," American Public Media, Sept. 7, 2012, www.marketplace.org/topics/business/european-debt-crisis/us-firms-prep-greece-exit-euro.

A Boeing 787 Dreamliner undergoes finishing touches in Everett, Wash., on Feb. 17. European banks financed about three-fourths of Boeing's $40 billion in international sales in 2011, but the euro crisis could undermine sales this year, the company says. European banks finance many purchases of big-ticket U.S. exports, especially to developing countries. With European banks retrenching, it is harder for Boeing's customers to buy U.S.-made planes.

up the national mood: "The Greek people have suffered great sacrifices. I think they have reached their limit. . . . We have sustained merciless whipping. I think we have paid for our mistakes enough."[45]

In Brussels, however, officials are more optimistic. Mario Draghi, the new president of the European Central Bank (ECB), announced in September that the bank would start buying unlimited quantities of the most indebted euro countries' government bonds, which had become increasingly unattractive to investors.[46] The announcement has reassured analysts that, no matter how bad things get, no European government will be allowed to go bankrupt because it cannot sell bonds. Investors are reassured, stock markets have risen and the interest rates indebted governments must pay to raise money have eased.

Rehman, of George Washington University, welcomes Draghi's move. "It is calming the markets, easing the pressure and stating that they will do anything to keep Spain and Italy solvent," she says. "That is exactly what we need to hear, because there is a crisis in confidence."

Economic policy strategist Smick echoes her sentiment. "The fact that the ECB is now going to buy everything

probably takes some of the threat away," he says. "Now they feel like they have probably bought some time."

But the move has triggered fresh anger in Germany, where it is perceived as letting the peripheral countries avoid tackling their profligate spending habits. Although Draghi has said the purchases will occur only if the indebted governments stick to their austerity programs, many Germans are skeptical.

The ECB move is "tantamount to financing governments by printing bank notes," railed the head of the German central bank, which for nearly half a century had built the deutschemark into a powerful currency by acting cautiously and avoiding inflation.[47] His comment echoed the popular opinion among many Germans that the ECB move would lead to rampant inflation and decimate the wealth of hardworking German savers, while letting work-shy spendthrifts off the hook.

U.S. Reverberations

While EU politicians and bankers struggle to keep the euro alive, Europe's economies continue to stagnate, which is damaging the American economic recovery, say some analysts. Although there are no reliable indicators of how the crisis is affecting American business, investor and consumer confidence, published figures indicate that exports and corporate investments in Europe are down.

During the year that ended in April, U.S. exports to the EU dropped 4.8 percent, according to the U.S. Commerce Department, the worst performance in three years. The effects are being felt in sectors such as auto, aircraft, chemicals and pharmaceutical manufacturing. And analysts say the decline in European demand is only just beginning to show up in trade data because it typically takes three to six months for goods to be shipped after an order is placed.[48]

U.S. manufacturing subsidiaries in Europe also are seeing lower profits and returns on investment. "Anecdotally, companies in the second quarter did blame some of their earning disappointments on Europe. And investors weren't surprised to hear that," says economist Yardeni.

The auto industry is a classic case. GM Europe and Ford Europe have manufacturing plants in Germany, Spain, Belgium and the U.K. With demand in Europe down due to the euro crisis, many subsidiary plants on

Should the U.S. bail out Europe's financial system?

YES
Uri Dadush
Director, International Economics Program, Carnegie Endowment for International Peace

Written for *CQ Global Researcher*, September, 2012

The United States is running a big risk in Europe, and the American response so far has been inadequate. Even given the European Central Bank's recent decision to buy the bonds of troubled countries, the euro's survival is far from assured. It is in America's interest for Congress to increase U.S. contributions to the International Monetary Fund (IMF) for a contingency fund to support countries in the European periphery and across the world.

A collapse of the euro would be a calamity for Europe but also a disaster for the United States. A failure of banks in the core European countries could have implications for U.S. banks similar to the failure of Lehman Brothers. Other U.S. financial institutions would be hit, including money market funds and insurance and pension companies.

A crisis that called into question the existence of the euro would also generate the mother of all flights to the dollar, causing a big dollar appreciation. Global demand for U.S. goods would plummet. The Organisation for Economic Co-operation and Development (OECD) calculates that disorderly sovereign defaults in some euro countries could cut U.S. gross domestic product (GDP) by more than 2 percent. But in a systemic crisis, official projections cannot be trusted, because they tend to shy away from the direst possibilities.

The IMF has about $250 billion in unused lending capacity, but it needs it to support the whole world and may need another $1 trillion in the event of a generalized European crisis. The U.S. share would be about $160 billion, if the United States took the lead. It would be a loan that may never be disbursed, but it would help restore confidence and contain the crisis. By deciding not to support a large IMF expansion, Congress let everybody else off the hook, including China.

But the message to Congress remains. This is not a question of whether the United States will pay for the euro crisis. It will. The question is how. Congress needs to be convinced that a failure to act could have catastrophic implications. If the euro breaks apart and Europe becomes politically unstable, that could induce Congress to act. But it would be better to act well in advance, in the interest of stability, rather than take that risk. If not, we may well have a Lehman repeat, or perhaps worse. The debts are much bigger, and so much fiscal and monetary ammunition has been spent already.

NO
Rep. Ron Paul, R-Texas
U.S. House of Representatives

Written for *CQ Global Researcher*, September, 2012

The United States should not consider bailing out the European financial system. The economic establishment in this country has come to the conclusion that it is not a matter of "if" the United States must intervene, but "when" and "how." Newspapers are full of assertions that the breakup of the euro would result in a worldwide depression and that economic assistance is the only way to prevent this.

These assertions are yet again more scaremongering, just as we witnessed during the 2008 crisis. The real cause of economic depression — and every boom and bust — is loose monetary policy. Yet it is precisely what political and economic elites, in both Europe and the United States, are prescribing as a resolution for this crisis, with a multitrillion-dollar bailout.

The euro was built on an unstable foundation. Its creators tried to establish a dollar-like currency for Europe while forgetting that it took nearly two centuries for the dollar to devolve from a defined unit of silver to so-called fiat currency completely unbacked by a commodity such as gold. The euro had no such history. Europe's economic depression is the result of the euro's very structure, a fiat money system that allowed member governments to spend themselves into oblivion and expect someone else to pick up the tab.

A bailout of European banks by the European Central Bank and the Federal Reserve would only exacerbate the crisis. What is needed is for bad debts to be liquidated. Banks that invested in sovereign debt need to take their losses rather than socializing these and prolonging their balance-sheet adjustments. If this were done, the correction would be painful but quick. Bailing out profligate European governments will only ensure that no correction will take place.

The Federal Reserve already has pumped trillions of dollars into the U.S. economy with nothing to show for it. Just considering Fed involvement in Europe is ludicrous. The U.S. economy is in horrible shape precisely because of too much government debt and too much money creation; the European economy is destined to flounder for the same reasons. We have an unsustainable amount of debt at home; it is hardly fair to U.S. taxpayers to take on Europe's debt as well. That will only ensure an accelerated erosion of the dollar and a lower standard of living for all Americans.

the continent are reducing capacity, which is hitting the companies' global profits.

For example, General Motors in August attributed a 38 percent drop in net global profits in the second quarter of 2012 to losses in Europe.[49] Industry analysts expect GM Europe to spend at least $1 billion shutting some of its 11 European factories.[50] At Ford, which gets a quarter of its sales from Europe, net global income was down 57 percent in the second quarter of 2012 due in part to losses in Europe.[51]

European losses also are having an effect on U.S. operations, the analysts add. "The European market has been dragging everyone's balance sheets down," said Rebecca Lindland, a research director for IHS Automotive, a forecasting company. "Ford and General Motors are feeling that just as much as anyone else," with fewer profits reinvested in American jobs, new models or more efficient factories.[52]

Similar gloom clouds the chemical sector in Europe. Dow Chemical, which has several plants in Europe that manufacture Styrofoam, reported a 34 percent fall in overall profits for the second quarter due to falling sales in Europe and currency conditions. The company says it will close or idle five factories in Europe. Closing plants overseas has ripple effects in the United States: The company needs fewer support staff back in the United States, and it brings back fewer profits from abroad, so it can't hire or invest at home.[53]

In the technology sector, similar trends are emerging. IBM, with plants across Europe, reported a 3 percent fall in global sales for the second quarter, blaming conditions in Europe, where sales were down 9 percent.[54]

Meanwhile, pharmaceutical companies such as Pfizer and Bristol-Myers Squibb say European governments are cutting back on buying drugs for health care, which could force companies to consolidate European operations.

It is difficult to calculate other potential effects on the U.S. economy. Kris Bledowski, a senior economist at the Virginia-based Manufacturers Alliance for Productivity and Innovation, said the effects extend to the U.S. supply chain, because Europe supplies important components, such as car engines and plastic parts, to many U.S. manufacturers.

"The feedback I'm getting is a concern over the logistical issues that may arise in Europe due to labor issues or economic paralysis there," said Bledowski.[55]

Other analysts discount these effects, saying that most events in the European economy have only a limited impact on the United States. "Demand in Europe is clearly weak. There is no question of that, but it hasn't collapsed," says Wolf, at London's *Financial Times*. Moreover, he says, U.S. exports to Europe represent only about 2 percent of U.S. GDP. "As long as the crisis is contained, and you don't have a real meltdown, then the effect on the U.S. of the eurozone crisis is pretty small."

The effect on U.S. confidence is limited as well, he contends. The eurozone crisis will be near the bottom on a "top 20" list of "things Americans might not be confident about," he says. At the top of the list, he says, are future U.S. tax policy, who will be running U.S. economic policy and the health of the domestic financial system. "These are all obviously vastly more important."

OUTLOOK

Eyeing Italy

In the long term, the euro debt crisis can be resolved in only one of two ways: Either the economic problems in the marginal countries are fixed and the eurozone returns to growth and prosperity, or the eurozone disintegrates, one or more countries leaves the single currency and the European Union fragments.

Optimists suggest that due to the ECB's recent promise to buy all marginal countries' government debt — coupled with the existing bailouts of Greece, Portugal and Ireland — the countries will remain solvent as they cut spending, raise taxes and improve competitiveness. Antonis Samaras, the Greek prime minister, who is committed to the country's austerity program, has predicted that Greece will return to economic growth in 2014.

"Over this year we will begin to contain the recession, and by the beginning of 2014 we will be able to move towards recovery. . . . We will prove that Greece can pleasantly surprise both friends and opponents, and even itself," he said.[56] His optimism is supported by the Organization for Economic Co-operation and Development, which represents the world's industrialized countries. It says Greece's efforts to cut wages and make exports more competitive will see results by 2013, and lead to a return to positive growth.[57]

However, the World Bank's new chief economist thinks the European debt crisis could adversely affect the world economy for years, prompting policy makers to consider new approaches to restarting growth and creating new jobs.

The global economy "is not doing well," said Kaushik Basu, a former top Indian government official who went on leave from Cornell University to take the bank's top economics post on Oct. 1. "The difficult phase will live with us for a while."[58]

Meanwhile, the EU is pushing for a new treaty that will bind member states into a tighter economic union, allowing Brussels to more directly control spending so as to avoid the problems that precipitated the current crisis. But some countries are resisting the loss of yet more sovereignty.[59] And in Greece, criticism is taking on a nationalist edge, portraying the EU austerity program as German colonialism by another name.[60]

More rational skeptics of the EU plan say the ECB move only buys time, and that the Greeks and citizens of other marginal countries are not prepared to suffer the growing poverty required to return their countries to growth. Citigroup has predicted, for example, a "90 percent" chance that Greece will leave the eurozone before 2014.[61]

If that occurs, the question is: Will it be a managed exit, or will it be messy, leading to the destruction of many European banks, and possibly some in the United States? The key is what happens in Spain and Italy. EU authorities believe they can cope with the financial fallout from a default by Greece, Ireland or Portugal, but not if it spreads to the larger troubled European economies — Spain and Italy.

Thus, attention is focused on next April's parliamentary elections in Italy. If populist politicians are elected, they could tear up the austerity program, potentially bringing down the whole eurozone. "Italy is too big to fail, and it is too big to save," says Rehman of George Washington University. "If Italy starts to go south then we are in real trouble, and if you thought that the Greek election [June 2012] was bad for the market, I want to hide under the bed for the Italian elections."

Her concern stems from Italy's history of electing politicians "who are not taken very seriously," she continues. "And if you look at the Italian economy, we know it is contracting. We know they have a terrible year ahead of them, and you look at the aging population, and you look at the way Italians vote. You could get another

Berlusconi-type figure, and that would a death sentence for Italy," she said, referring to Italy's former populist prime minister, Silvio Berlusconi, who was widely blamed for allowing the country to fall into high levels of debt by avoiding tough economic policies that were needed.

The United States, she says, is basically powerless. "Our hands are tied. We can try to assure ourselves that the best possible way is to make sure there is enough liquidity in our system and try to get job growth going," she says. "But other than that, you really can't do much against what happens in Europe."

NOTES

1. "Why Europe matters: facts and figures," U.S. Chamber of Commerce, www.uschamber.com/international/europe/facts-and-figures-why-europe-matters.

2. "The euro — Business Benefits," *EUBusiness.com*, Oct. 1, 2009, www.eubusiness.com/topics/euro/business.

3. "Greece Government Bond 10Y," *Trading Economics*, www.tradingeconomics.com/greece/government-bond-yield.

4. "Labour productivity levels in the total economy," Organisation for Economic Co-operation and Development, http://stats.oecd.org/Index.aspx?DatasetCode=LEVEL.

5. For background, see Brian Beary, "Future of the EU," *CQ Global Researcher*, April 17, 2012, p. 188; and Roland Flamini, "U.S.-Europe Relations," *CQ Researcher*, March 23, 2012, pp. 277-300.

6. "Troika demanding increase to working week, retirement age," *Ekathimerini* (newspaper), Sept. 12, 2012, www.ekathimerini.com/4dcgi/_w_articles_wsite1_1_12/09/2012_460867.

7. David Jolly and Raphael Minder, "Unemployment in Euro Zone at Record High," *The New York Times*, Oct. 1, 2012, www.nytimes.com/2012/10/02/business/global/unemployment-in-euro-zone-rose-to-new-high-in-august.html?_r=1&emc=eta1.

8. "Greece and the IMF," International Monetary Fund, Aug. 30, 2012, www.imf.org/external/country/GRC/index.htm.

9. "Germans say they're 'better off without euro': poll," France24.com/AFP, July 29, 2012, www.france24

.com/en/20120729-germans-say-theyre-better-off-without-euro-poll.

10. Robin Wigglesworth, "Spanish borrowing costs reach record level," *The Irish Times*, July 24, 2012, www.irishtimes.com/newspaper/finance/2012/0724/1224320708393.html.

11. Ian Katz and Cheyenne Hopkins, "Europe Imperils U.S. Sales from Chemicals to PCs: Economy," Bloomberg, June 18, 2012, www.bloomberg.com/news/2012-06-18/europe-crisis-imperils-u-s-sales-from-chemicals-to-pcs-economy.html.

12. "Trade in Goods with European Union," U.S. Census Bureau, September 2012, www.census.gov/foreign-trade/balance/c0003.html.

13. Fred C. Bergsten, "Five myths about the euro crisis," *The Washington Post*, Sept. 7, 2012, www.washingtonpost.com/opinions/five-myths-about-the-euro-crisis/2012/09/07/9b8d1412-f6db-11e1-8253-3f495ae70650_story.html.

14. Peter Whoriskey, "U.S. exporters brace for cutbacks in European bank lending," *The Washington Post*, Dec. 22, 2012, www.washingtonpost.com/business/economy/us-exporters-brace-for-cutbacks-in-european-bank-lending/2011/12/21/gIQA3n8KAP_story.html. Also see Andrew Parker, "Banks withdraw from aircraft financing," *Financial Times*, Dec. 6, 2011, www.ft.com/cms/s/0/097a515c-2003-11e1-8462-00144feabdc0.html#axzz25XNdCt9s.

15. Dan Fitzpatrick and Victoria McGrane, "Stress Test Buoys US Banks," *The Wall Street Journal*, March 14, 2012, http://online.wsj.com/article/SB10001424052702304537904577279720671471152.html. Also see Craig Torres and Josh Zumbrun, "Fed says 15 of 19 banks pass stress tests," *The Washington Post*, March 13, 2012, www.washingtonpost.com/business/economy/fed-says-15-of-19-banks-pass-stress-tests/2012/03/13/gIQAIdg99R_story.html; and Richard Wolf, "Five ways the European debt crisis could affect the U.S.," *USA Today*, Oct. 28, 2011, www.usatoday.com/money/world/story/2011-10-27/eurozone-crisis-deal/50963370/1.

16. "Who, What, Why: How would Greece switch currencies?" BBC News, June 12, 2012, www.bbc.co.uk/news/magazine-18279522.

17. Shawn Tully, "Greece: The anatomy of a default," *CNN Money*, May 16, 2012, http://finance.fortune.cnn.com/2012/05/16/greece/.

18. "IMF chief Christine Lagarde urges US to give more cash to fight European debt crisis," *The Telegraph*/AFP, April 3, 2012, www.telegraph.co.uk/finance/financialcrisis/9183884/IMF-chief-Christine-Lagarde-urges-US-to-give-more-cash-to-fight-European-debt-crisis.html.

19. Ambrose Evans-Pritchard, "Congress blocks indiscriminate IMF aid for Europe," *The Telegraph*, May 18th, 2010, http://blogs.telegraph.co.uk/finance/ambroseevans-pritchard/100005734/congress-blocks-indiscriminate-imf-aid-for-europe/.

20. "IMF wins pledges of $456bn for crisis fund," *The Telegraph*, June 19, 2012, www.telegraph.co.uk/finance/financialcrisis/9340480/IMF-wins-pledges-of-456bn-for-crisis-fund.html.

21. "The Marshall Plan," National Archives, www.archives.gov/exhibits/featured_documents/marshall_plan/. Also see F. Van Schaick, "Conditions for American Aid," *Editorial Research Reports*, Aug. 17, 1947, available at *CQ Researcher Plus Archive*.

22. Robert Schuman, "The Schuman Declaration — 9 May 1950," European Union, europa.eu/about-eu/basic-information/symbols/europe-day/schuman-declaration/index_en.htm.

23. For background, see B. W. Patch, "European Economic Union," *Editorial Research Reports*, March 27, 1957, available at *CQ Researcher Plus Archive*.

24. For background, see Mary H. Cooper, "A Primer on German Reunification," *Editorial Research Reports*, Dec. 22, 1989, available at *CQ Researcher Plus Archive*.

25. Barry Eichengreen, *Exorbitant Privilege* (2011), pp. 88-89.

26. Under Conservative Prime Minister John Major, Britain had participated in an earlier version of monetary union, the European Monetary System. But after a speculators' attack on the pound, Britain took its currency out of the joint system in 1992. "Tony Blair could credit his victory in the 1997 general election to the damage done to the Conservative government of John Major by the 1992 crisis," Eichengreen writes.

27. The €110 billion package, formally agreed to May 10, 2010, consists of €80 billion from euro area countries and €30 billion from the IMF.

28. Daniel Hannan, "Black Wednesday: Britain was free, but we Tories were done for," *The Telegraph*, Sept. 11, 2012, www.telegraph.co.uk/news/politics/9535659/Black-Wednesday-Britain-was-free-but-we-Tories-were-done-for.html.

29. Roger Bootle, "Unraveling an economy with an interlinked crisis," *The Telegraph*, Oct. 16, 2011, www.telegraph.co.uk/finance/comment/roger-bootle/8830079/Unravelling-an-economy-with-an-interlinked-crisis.html.

30. Mary Elise Sarotte, "Eurozone Crisis as Historical Legacy," *Foreign Affairs*, Sept. 29, 2010, www.foreign affairs.com/print/66715?page-2.

31. *Ibid.*

32. "The ERASMUS Program — studying in Europe and more," The European Commission, http://ec.europa.eu/education/lifelong-learning-programme/erasmus_en.htm.

33. "Greece Government Bond 10Y," *op. cit.*

34. "Irish Construction output at 23 percent of GNP in 2007; 416,000 employed in construction related activity — 19 percent of workforce; Up to 30,000 job losses by 2009," *Finfacts Ireland*, Sept. 25, 2007, www.finfacts.ie/irishfinancenews/article_1011255.shtml.

35. Dan Bilefsky and Niki Kitsantonis, "Greek Statistician Is Caught in Limelight," *The New York Times*, Feb. 13, 2010, www.nytimes.com/2010/02/14/world/europe/14greek.html. Also see William L. Watts, "Greece's revised 2009 deficit tops 15 percent of GDP: Eurostat lifts reservations over Greek methodology," MarketWatch, Nov. 15, 2010, 6:36 a.m. EST, www.marketwatch.com/story/greeces-revised-2009-deficit-tops-15-of-gdp-2010-11-15.

36. "Greek debt to reach 120.8 pct of GDP in '10 — draft," Reuters News Agency, Nov. 5, 2009, www.reuters.com/article/2009/11/05/greece-budget-debt-idUSATH00496420091105. Also see "A very European crisis: The sorry state of Greece public finances is a test not only for the country policymakers but also for Europe," *The Economist*, Feb. 4, 2010, www.economist.com/node/15452594?story_id=15452594.

37. "Greek bonds rated 'junk' by Standard & Poor's," BBC News, April 27, 2010, news.bbc.co.uk/1/hi/business/8647441.stm.

38. Jessica Pressler, "Greece's Economy Is a 'Sinking Ship,' Prime Minister Says in Asking for Aid," *The New York Times*, April 23, 2010, nymag.com/daily/intel/2010/04/greeces_economy_is_a_sinking_s.html.

39. "Greece and the IMF," *op. cit.*

40. Nicholas Paphitis, "Greece faces more anti-austerity strikes, protests," The Associated Press, Sept. 12 2012, www.google.com/hostednews/ap/article/ALe qM5gpnG2yszLfyfOf3DqbSdfqlpJG_A?docId=15e e557e881c4a0d8a9a09ffe9de0344.

41. "Athens: Members of Greek Armed Forces Protest Wages and Pensions Cuts," keeptalkinggreece.com, Sept. 12, 2012, www.keeptalkinggreece.com/2012/09/12/athens-members-of-greek-armed-forces-protest-wages-and-pensions-cuts/.

42. "Municipalities to begin two-day strike on Wednesday," *Ekathimerini* (newspaper), Sept. 12, 2012, www.ekathimerini.com/4dcgi/_w_articles_wsite1_1_11/09/2012_460666.

43. "Pensioners storm Health Ministry," *Ekathimerini* (newspaper), Sept. 4, 2012, www.ekathimerini.com/4dcgi/_w_articles_wsite1_1_04/09/2012_459616.

44. "Support for Golden Dawn rises, poll shows," *Ekathimerini* (newspaper), Sept. 12, 2012, www.ekathimerini.com/4dcgi/_w_articles_wsite1_1_06/09/2012_459953.

45. " 'Enough merciless whipping' of Greece, says president," *Ekithimerini* (newspaper), Sept. 11, 2012, www.ekathimerini.com/4dcgi/_w_articles_wsite1_1_11/09/2012_460758.

46. Michael Steen, "ECB signals resolve to save euro," *Financial Times*, Sept. 6, 2012, www.ft.com/cms/s/0/b70ff9a8-f84c-11e1-b0e1-00144feabdc0.html#axzz263MhkteO.

47. Gavin Hewitt, "Eurozone crisis: From deutschmark to lira?" BBC News, Sept. 7, 2012, www.bbc.co.uk/news/world-europe-19516810.

48. Ian Katz and Cheyenne Hopkins, "Europe Imperils U.S. Sales From Chemicals to PCs: Economy," Bloomberg, June 18, 2012, www.bloomberg.com/news/2012-06-18/europe-crisis-imperils-u-s-sales-from-chemicals-to-pcs-economy.html.

49. Jeff Bennett, "Europe's Woes Hamper GM," *The Wall Street Journal*, Aug. 2, 2102, http://online.wsj.com/article/SB100008723963904436875045775 64694275806410.html.

50. Mathew Phillips, "How Europe's Contagion May Hit the U.S. Economy," Bloomberg, June 7, 2012, www.businessweek.com/articles/2012-06-07/how-europes-contagion-may-hit-the-u-dot-s-dot-economy#p2.

51. Dee-Ann Durbin, "Ford's second quarter earnings hobbled by European losses," *Denver Post*, www.denverpost.com/business/ci_21159253/fords-second-quarter-earnings-hobbled-by-european-losses.

52. Richard Wolf, "Five ways the European debt crisis could affect the US," *USA Today*, Oct. 28, 2011, www.usatoday.com/money/world/story/2011-10-27/eurozone-crisis-deal/50963370/1.

53. Jack Kaskey, "Dow Chemical to Close Five Plants on Slower European Economy," Bloomberg, April 2, 2012, www.bloomberg.com/news/2012-04-02/dow-chemical-to-close-five-plants-on-slower-european-economy-2-.html. Also see Viktor Puskorius, "Weakness in Europe Leads to Weak Earnings for Dow Chemical," *Benzinga*, July 26, 2012, www.benzinga.com/news/earnings/12/07/2779225/weakness-in-europe-leads-to-weak-earnings-for-dow-chemical.

54. Erin Kim, "IBM sales fall, dragged down by Europe," *CNN Money*, July 18, 2012, http://money.cnn.com/2012/07/18/technology/ibm-earnings/index.htm.

55. Matthew Philips, "How Europe's Contagion May Hit the U.S. Economy," *Bloomberg Business Week*, June 7, 2012, www.businessweek.com/articles/2012-06-07/how-europes-contagion-may-hit-the-u-dot-s-dot-economy.

56. "Greek PM Samaras Predicts Economic Growth by 2014," *VOA News*, July 24, 2012, blogs.voanews.com/breaking-news/2012/07/24/greek-pm-samaras-predicts-economic-growth-by-2014.

57. "OECD sees Greek recession lasting through 2013," *Ekathimerini* (newspaper), Sept. 13, 2012, www.ekathimerini.com/4dcgi/_w_articles_wsite2_1_22/05/2012_443265.

58. Sudeep Reddy, "World Bank Sees Long Crisis Effect," *The Wall Street Journal*, Oct. 2, 2012, p. A9, http://online.wsj.com/article_email/SB100008723 96390443862604578030841318692174- lMy QjAxMTAyMDAwMjAwODI3Wj.html?mod=wsj_valetleft_email.

59. Luke Baker and Mark John, "Europe moves ahead with fiscal union, UK isolated," Reuters, www.reuters.com/article/2011/12/09/eurozone-idUSL5E7N900120111209.

60. "Greeks brand Germans 'Nazis' for driving through painful cuts and 'taking control of their economy,'" *Daily Mail*, Feb. 15, 2012, www.dailymail.co.uk/news/article-2101614/Greece-debt-crisis-Greeks-brand-Germans-Nazis-taking-control-economy.html#ixzz26LfVRlq6.

61. Cheyenne Hopkins, "Citigroup Sees 90 percent Chance That Greece Leaves Euro," Bloomberg, July 26, 2012, www.bloomberg.com/news/2012-07-25/citigroup-sees-90-chance-that-greece-leaves-euro.html.

BIBLIOGRAPHY

Selected Sources

Books

Lewis, Michael, *Boomerang: The Meltdown Tour*, Penguin, 2011.
The co-author of *Barbarians at the Gate* and other bestsellers about the financial world explains entertainingly and clearly how the global financial crisis spread to Europe.

Manolopoulos, Jason, *Greece's Odious Debt: The Looting of the Hellenic Republic by the Euro, the Political Elite and the Investment Community*, Anthem, 2011.
A Greek investment banker offers a detailed analysis of Greece's experience with the euro, from birth to bailout.

Marsh, David, *The Euro: The Battle for the New Global Currency*, Yale, 2011.
A business consultant who has written extensively on European finance analyzes the birth and plight of the euro.

Soros, George, *Financial Turmoil in the United States and Europe: Essays*, PublicAffairs, 2012.

The global financier looks at what went wrong with the euro and the global economy, and ruminates on how the financial system can be fixed.

Van Overtveldt, Johan, *The End of The Euro: The Uneasy Future of the European Union*, Agate, 2011.

A Belgian economic journalist analyzes what has happened with the single currency and where it is heading.

Articles

Dadush, Uri, Shimelse Ali and Zaahira Wyne, "What Does the US Election Mean for the World Economy?" *Carnegie Endowment for International Peace*, Aug. 2, 2012, www.carnegieendowment.org/2012/08/02/what-does-u.s.-election-mean-for-world-economy/d5mp.

The director of Carnegie's International Economics Program and two writers contemplate the implications of the U.S. presidential election for the euro crisis and other global issues.

Eichlers, Alexander, "The European Debt Crisis: A Beginner's Guide," *The Huffington Post*, Dec. 21, 2011, www.huffingtonpost.com/2011/12/21/european-debt-crisis_n_1147173.html.

A business reporter explains the euro crisis and its importance.

Elliott, Douglas, "What the Euro Crisis Means for Taxpayers and the U.S. Economy," Brookings Institution, Dec. 15, 2011, www.brookings.edu/research/testimony/2011/12/15-euro-crisis-elliott.

A former investment banker testifies before the House Subcommittee on TARP, Financial Services and Bailouts of Public and Private Programs.

Gongloff, Mark, "Eurozone Crisis Explainer That Will Finally Make You Care," *The Huffington Post*, June 12, 2012, www.huffingtonpost.com/2012/06/12/eurozone-crisis-explainer_n_1590446.html.

The Huffington Post's chief financial writer offers a readable account of how the continuing euro crisis can affect the U.S. economy.

McNamara, Kathleen R., "Can the Eurozone be Saved?" *Foreign Affairs*, April 7, 2011, www.foreignaffairs.com/articles/67710/kathleen-r-mcnamara/can-the-eurozone-be-saved.

The director of Georgetown University's Mortara Center for International Studies says the eurozone has failed to create the kind of unified federal government necessary for a monetary union to work.

Tankersley, Jim, "How the Euro Crisis Could Destroy the U.S. Economy," *The Atlantic*, Dec. 2, 2011, www.theatlantic.com/business/archive/2011/12/how-the-euro-crisis-could-destroy-the-us-economy/249392/.

An economics correspondent explains how America could be dragged into the euro crisis.

Wolf, Richard, "Five ways the European debt crisis could affect the US," *USA Today*, Oct. 28, 2011, www.usatoday.com/money/world/story/2011-10-27/eurozone-crisis-deal/50963370/1.

A financial journalist examines the specific threat from the euro crisis to various aspects of the U.S. economy.

Reports and Studies

"Europe Will Work," Nomura, March 2011, www.nomura.com/europe/resources/pdf/Europe%20will%20work%20FINAL_March2011.pdf.

An Asian investment bank concludes that the euro zone probably will not break up but needs to strengthen its governance.

Bergstein, Fred, and Jacob Kirkegaard, "The Coming Resolution of the European Crisis," Peterson Institute for International Economics, June 2012, www.iie.com/publications/interstitial.cfm?ResearchID=2158.

Two leading academics examine the factors driving the European sovereign debt crisis.

Tilford, Simon, "How to Save the Euro," Centre for European Reform, September 2010, www.cer.org.uk/about_new/about_cerpersonnel_tilford_09.html.

The gap between the rhetoric of economic integration in Europe and the reality of national interests is proving lethal to the eurozone, argues the chief economist for a London think tank.

For More Information

Centre for Economic Policy Research, 77 Bastwick St., London EC1V 3PZ, U.K.; +44 20 7183 8801; www .cepr.org. A network of more than 700 European researchers who study economic issues, such as the future of the euro.

European Council, Rue de la Loi 175, B-1048 Brussels, Belgium; +32 2 281-6111; www.european-council.europa .eu. Composed of the heads of member states of the European Union; defines the political directions and priorities of the EU.

European Policy Centre, Résidence Palace, 155 rue de la Loi, B-1040, Brussels, Belgium; +32 2 231-0340; www.epc .eu. An independent Brussels think tank devoted to European integration.

European Union, http://europa.eu/index_en.htm. Web portal that links to all EU agencies.

European Union Delegation to the United States of America, 2175 K St., N.W., Washington, DC 20037; 202-862-9500; www.eurunion.org/eu. Provides information about the EU for Americans.

European Union Research Center, The George Washington University, 2121 Eye St., N.W., Washington, DC 20052; 202-994-1000; www.business.gwu.edu/eurc. Promotes research and analysis on the EU and EU-US relations.

European-American Business Council, 919 18th St., N.W., Suite 220, Washington, DC 20006; 202-828-9104; www .eabc.org. Promotes investment, innovation and integration between the U.S. and EU business communities.

Open Europe, 7 Tufton St., London SW1P 3QN, U.K.; +44 207 197 2333; www.openeurope.org.uk. An independent think tank with offices in London and Brussels.

Peterson Institute for International Economics, 1750 Massachusetts Ave., N.W. Washington, DC 20036-1903; 202-328-9000; www.iie.com. A private, nonprofit, nonpartisan research institution devoted to the study of international economic policy.

Trans-Atlantic Business Dialogue, 1717 Pennsylvania Ave., N.W., Suite 1025, Washington, DC 20006; 202-559-9299; hwww.tabd.com. Works to improve economic relations between the United States and Europe.

12

China in Latin America

Kenneth J. Stier

A street peddler in Mexico City sells sneakers made in China. While inexpensive Chinese imports are good for Latin American consumers, they harm local manufacturers, who must compete with lower-wage Chinese companies. Central American textiles and low-tech manufacturing in Mexico have been especially hard hit. As China ratchets up the sophistication of its exports, it is undercutting a wider and wider swathe of Latin American businesses.

AP Photo/Marco Ugarte

From *The CQ Researcher*,
June 5, 2012.

From a control center at a Venezuelan military base, President Hugo Chávez watched as his country's first satellite blasted off into space. But Chávez had to watch it on a TV screen — the launch occurred half a world away in Sichuan, China. At his side for the Oct. 29, 2008, event was Bolivian president Evo Morales, another leftist leader who also has developed strong ties with Beijing in recent years.

The $400 million Simón Bolívar satellite (Venesat-1) relays Internet and television transmissions, including TeleSUR — the TV network Chávez hopes will rival CNN in the Caribbean and Central and South America. It was built by the China Great Wall Industry Corp., one of China's biggest space contractors, with 110,000 employees. A second Venezuelan satellite — to be constructed jointly in Venezuela by Chinese and Venezuelan firms — will carry out surveillance and strategic reconnaissance.[1]

Both satellites are part of China's roughly $40-billion investment in Venezuela, which helps to prop up the virulently anti-American leader. But it is only a fraction of the expanding profile China has been quietly carving out for itself throughout the region in the past decade.

China's trade with Latin America has been growing at an astonishing 30 percent or more per year, mostly driven by the Asian giant's voracious demand for metals, oil and food. In 2011, Chinese-Latin American trade reached $237 billion, up from $180 billion just the year before.[2] China's share of the region's trade reached 20 percent in 2010, up from just 1 percent in 1995.[3] China today is the top trading partner for Brazil, Argentina and

Latin America Is Biggest Investment Target for China

Chinese companies invested more than $73 billion in Latin America and the Caribbean between 2005 and 2011 — more than in any other region. Sub-Saharan Africa, with just over $67 billion, received the second highest amount. Australia received more than any other individual country, while the United States and Canada together ranked sixth, with about $50 billion.

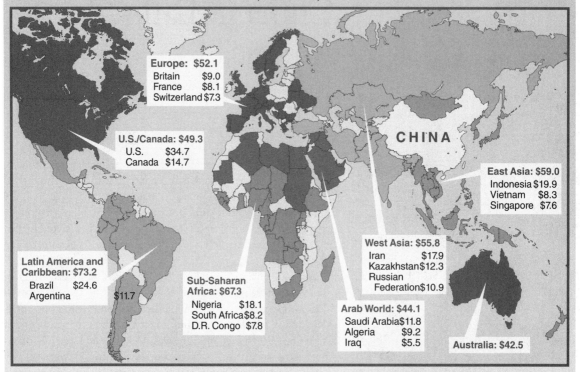

Chinese Investment Worldwide, by Region, as of January 2012*
(in $billions)

Europe: $52.1
Britain $9.0
France $8.1
Switzerland $7.3

U.S./Canada: $49.3
U.S. $34.7
Canada $14.7

CHINA

East Asia: $59.0
Indonesia $19.9
Vietnam $8.3
Singapore $7.6

West Asia: $55.8
Iran $17.9
Kazakhstan $12.3
Russian
Federation $10.9

Latin America and Caribbean: $73.2
Brazil $24.6
Argentina $11.7

Sub-Saharan Africa: $67.3
Nigeria $18.1
South Africa $8.2
D.R. Congo $7.8

Arab World: $44.1
Saudi Arabia $11.8
Algeria $9.2
Iraq $5.5

Australia: $42.5

* Does not include Chinese government loans or bond investments

Source: "China's Worldwide Reach," The Heritage Foundation, January, 2012, www.heritage.org/research/projects/china-global-investment-tracker-interactive-map. Map by Lewis Agrell

Chile, and a leading partner for many other countries in the region.*

China's dramatic arrival in the region has triggered a flood of U.S. congressional hearings and think-tank reports — not to mention hand-wringing — about

the potential erosion of American influence in its own hemisphere. Chinese diplomats repeatedly affirm that Beijing is only interested in "peaceful development," a mantra designed to divert U.S. and other powers from trying to thwart China's rise.[4] To that end, China scrupulously has avoided being linked to Chávez's anti-Washington rhetoric, even as it angles for a favored position in the rush for Venezuela's massive oil reserves.

---

* This report deals with South America, Mexico, Central America and the Caribbean countries.

China has tried to soft-pedal its activities in the area. But a Chinese policy paper on Latin America and the Caribbean — released the day after Barack Obama was elected U.S. president — clearly indicates that China has launched a full-court press in the region, including cultivating military ties with nearly half of the area's more than 40 countries.[5]

Meanwhile, because of its mammoth size, China's demand for imported resources has driven up world prices for Latin America's commodities such as oil, soybeans and copper, spurring dramatic growth. Between 2002 and 2010, the number of Latin Americans living in poverty — those earning less than $2 a day — dropped from 221 million people to 180 million, or from 44 percent of the population to 32.1 percent.[6]

China is also becoming a significant regional investor and banker. Its direct investment surged from a mere $48.9 million in 2008 to a total of more than $73 billion by the end of 2011.[7] In 2010 Chinese development banks extended $37 billion worth of credit in the region — more than the World Bank, the Inter-American Development Bank and the U.S. Export-Import Bank, combined.[8]

The Chinese now seem to be everywhere in Latin America — doing everything from building highways, dams and bridges to opening restaurants and retail shops. Beijing is also funding Confucian Institutes, which teach Mandarin language and Chinese culture, adding to the existing private and university-based language programs.

And the Chinese immigrant population is swelling with newcomers from the mainland. In Argentina, the Chinese population doubled between 2005 and 2010, to 120,000. Buenos Aires alone has some 10,000 Chinese-owned grocery stores.[9]

Metals Dominate Exports to China

Metals — including base metals, iron and copper alloys from Brazil, Chile and Peru — accounted for nearly 50 percent of Latin America's commodity exports to China in 2009. Soybeans and other seeds — mostly from Brazil and Argentina — represented nearly 17 percent of the total.

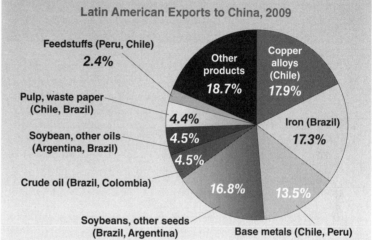

Latin American Exports to China, 2009

Feedstuffs (Peru, Chile) **2.4%**
Pulp, waste paper (Chile, Brazil) **4.4%**
Soybean, other oils (Argentina, Brazil) **4.5%**
Crude oil (Brazil, Colombia) **4.5%**
Soybeans, other seeds (Brazil, Argentina) **16.8%**
Other products **18.7%**
Copper alloys (Chile) **17.9%**
Iron (Brazil) **17.3%**
Base metals (Chile, Peru) **13.5%**

Four Countries Are China's Biggest Suppliers

Nearly 90 percent of Latin America's exports to China in 2008 came from four countries.

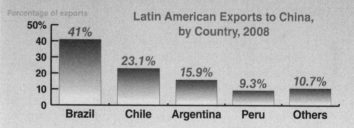

Latin American Exports to China, by Country, 2008

Percentage of exports

- Brazil: **41%**
- Chile: **23.1%**
- Argentina: **15.9%**
- Peru: **9.3%**
- Others: **10.7%**

Source: Katherine Koleski, "Backgrounder: China in Latin America," U.S.-China Economic & Security Review Commission, May 2011, p. 6, www.uscc.gov/Backgrounder_China_in_Latin_America.pdf

However, the rosy glow associated with China's expansion into Latin America is beginning to fade. The recent windfall trade income, for example, threatens to return the continent to an over-dependence on commodity exports, the prices of which fluctuate wildly.

This is not the first time Latin America has tried to escape the commodities trap. As occurred in past

Troubled Copper Mine in Peru Teaches China a Lesson

Firms are now more sensitive to improving their image.

Chinese firms are flocking to Peru for its large copper deposits — the second-largest in South America, behind Chile. China is the world's largest consumer of copper, prized for its electrical conductivity and essential in computers, cars and air conditioners — all important Chinese exports.

China's first mining investment in Latin America — by the Shougang Group, a major steel company — started off promisingly but soon became a case study in all that can go wrong in the extraction industry.

In 1992 the Beijing-based firm acquired the Marcona Mine, an open-pit iron operation on Peru's southern coast, in what was the first privatization of a Peruvian mining company under then President Alberto Fujimori. The mine had been opened by Americans in the 1950s before being nationalized by the leftist military regime in the 1970s. Besides paying $118 million, the state-owned Shougang agreed to assume $42 million in debt and invest an additional $150 million over the next three years in the community.[1] The company won extra points for entering a remote area still contested by the Shining Path, a violent Maoist-inspired guerrilla group.

But the honeymoon did not last long, particularly for the miners, whose ranks were promptly slashed by nearly half. The company set wages at $14 a day, less than half the industry average of $33, according to Peru's National Society of Mining, Petroleum and Energy. Living conditions deteriorated, particularly housing. Instituto de Peru director Miguel Santilla called them "a disgrace." There was minimal investment in the nearby town, San Juan de Marcona, home to some 13,000 miners.

"We quickly realized that we were being exploited to help build the new China, but without seeing any of the rewards for doing so," union official Honorato Quispe told a *New York Times* reporter in 2010, when there were repeated strikes and clashes with police.[2]

Shougang was repeatedly fined for breaches of health, safety and environmental regulations, including pumping waste water into a port and contaminating water supplies. But the fines levied often seemed inadequate ($30,000 for contaminating water supplies) and it's unclear whether the fines were actually paid. A national government commission found the company had only spent $35 million of the $150 million it had committed to spend. Instead, it opted to pay a fine of $14 million.[3]

"At the local level, Shougang has had a significantly negative impact on development," concluded Ruben Gonzalez-Vincente, whose doctoral dissertation examined Chinese mining in Peru.[4] Peruvian authorities were reluctant to get tougher on Shougang, he found, because it was owned by the Chinese government, and Lima did not want to impair bilateral relations or discourage further Chinese investments.

"Nonetheless, as China's regional policy has been progressively drawn, and as Peru has increasingly democratized, Shougang's developmental impact has begun to show signs of improvement," said Gonzalez-Vincente.

By 2008 Shougang's investment had been dwarfed by the $2.1 billion purchase of the Peruvian Toromocho copper mine by Chinalco (Aluminium Corporation of China), one of the world's largest aluminium firms. For two years Chinalco left intact the Canadian management of the firm, Peru Copper, including the Canadian president. The new Chinese owners conducted an environmental impact assessment and held public hearings with the local community, something Shougang had never countenanced. Chinalco is

trading relationships with Western partners, Latin America is trading its raw commodities for manufactured goods. While inexpensive Chinese imports are good for Latin consumers, the cheap imports hurt Latin competitors of Chinese manufacturers. And as China ratchets up the sophistication of its exports, it is undercutting a wider and wider swathe of Latin American businesses. Hardest hit have been Central also improving the local community's infrastructure and working with nongovernmental organizations to help the local community.

The difference between the operation of the two mines stems from improved worldwide industry standards, stronger enforcement by local governments and the fact that Chinalco is a public company listed on the New York Stock Exchange and others. Investor-owned companies must withstand more scrutiny, so they tend to adopt defensible standards or face reputational risk, said a report by the Peterson Institute for International Economics.

In addition, China is now much more sensitive to the need to improve its image, particularly following widespread criticism of its performance in Africa.[5] Some changes have emanated from the Beijing-based Assets Supervision and Administration Commission (SASAC), which manages more than 100 key state-owned enterprises.[6] China's Export-Import Bank, which is backing Chinalco, has offered guidelines.

Although China seems increasingly mindful of risks to its reputation, it appears determined to raise standards on its own — not at the bidding of others. For instance, China has not signed on to either of the two most important international initiatives aimed at improving mining standards and preventing government corruption in resource-rich countries — the International Council on Mining and Metals and the Extractive Industries Transparency Initiative.[7] Shougang and Chinalco also are not members of either.

"The rationale seems to be that [the Chinese] don't like other bodies telling them what to do, particularly those they think are dominated by the U.S.," says Barbara Kotschwar, one of the authors of the Peterson report.

There may be some justification for concern about Western influence in these industry groups. Developed countries account for 80 percent of the accumulated foreign direct investment in Peru's mining sector in 2010, led by the United Kingdom (45 percent), the United States (19 percent) and Brazil (15 percent).

China accounts for just 3 percent.[8]

— *Kenneth J. Stier*

Peruvian workers for China's Shougang mining company protest job cuts in the capital, Lima, on April 25, 2007. Shougang, China's first mining venture in Latin America, slashed its local workforce by nearly half and paid substandard wages when it first took over the mine, and has since been repeatedly fined for health, safety and environmental violations.

[1] Information in this section comes largely from Barbara Kotschwar, Theodore H. Moran and Julia Muir, "Chinese Investment in Latin American Resources: The Good, the Bad and the Ugly," Peterson Institute for International Economics, February 2012, www.piie.com/publications/wp/wp12-3.pdf.

[2] Simon Romero, "Tensions over Chinese Mining Venture in Peru," *The New York Times*, Aug. 14, 2010.

[3] Kotschwar, Moran and Muir, *op. cit.*

[4] Ruben Gonzalez Vicente, "The Developmental Impact of China's Investment in South America's Extractive Industries," (in partial fulfillment of the requirements for the degree of master of philosophy), Department of Asian and International Studies, City University of Hong Kong, September 2009.

[5] For background, see Karen Foerstel, "China in Africa," *CQ Global Researcher*, Jan. 1, 2008, pp. 1-26.

[6] For background, see Jason McLure, "State Capitalism," *CQ Global Researcher*, May 15, 2012, pp. 229-256.

[7] For background, see Jennifer Weeks, "The Resource Curse," *CQ Global Researcher*, Dec. 20, 2011, pp. 597-622.

[8] Kotschwar, Moran, and Muir, *op. cit.*

American textiles and low-tech manufacturing in Mexico, where wages are substantially higher than in China.[10] But even regional powerhouse Brazil is suffering losses.

"They're beating the pants off the Brazilians all over the planet, and the longer-run danger is that it could kick a country like Brazil back to the 19th century," says Kevin Gallagher, an international relations professor at

Boston University and co-author of *The Dragon in the Room: China and the Future of Latin American Industrialization.* "Brazil basically spent the past 200 years trying to move away from having a handful of commodities be the rudder of its growth into diversifying, into manufacturing and services."

The situation has triggered powerful protectionist impulses in Brazil and elsewhere, which economists warn will only torpedo Latin America's long-term competitiveness and eventually trigger a fiscal crisis. But the problem goes beyond economics to its root in China's singularly mercantilist economic model, in which state-owned enterprises, enjoying robust government backing, control two-thirds of the country's economy.[11]

"Sometimes you don't know whether the investments are looking for Brazil as a market or whether they correspond to strategic purposes of the Chinese government," said Sergio Amaral, chairman of the China-Brazil Business Council, which promotes bilateral ties. Most Chinese firms investing in Brazil are state-owned but even private firms have close ties to the government, he noted.[12]

China's pursuit of Latin America's vast mineral and agricultural resources has touched a nerve. "The Chinese have bought Africa and now they are trying to buy Brazil," warned former finance minister, Antônio Delfim Netto, suggesting it would be a "grave mistake" to allow a foreign state to buy Brazil's natural resources.[13]

In addition to China's voracious resource appetite and vast language and cultural differences, there are other sources of friction. Mexican relations with China, for example, are the worst since diplomatic ties were established 40 years ago, according to Enrique Dussel Peters, coordinator of the Center for Chinese-Mexican Studies at the National Autonomous University of Mexico, in Mexico City.

The biggest irritant is Mexico's crushing trade deficit with China, running at more than 14 imports to one export — which has devastated Mexico's labor-intensive industries.[14] But there is also no binational agenda, which Dussel Peters blames on both the Mexican and Chinese leadership. "From a Mexican perspective, we are not well prepared for China — the best thing would be to say, look, give me a 10-year window and then we meet in 10 years. Unfortunately, that's not going to happen. China is not going to wait for anyone."

Likewise, Brazil is scrambling to develop a China policy. "For the past 150 or 200 years, Brazil has been used to three main economic, political and diplomatic partners — Latin American countries, the United States and Europe — with whom we have historical and cultural links," says Joao Augusto de Castro Neves, an analyst with the New York City-based Eurasia Group consultancy. "Then all of sudden there's this new actor in the region, and you don't quite know what this player wants, so Brazil is basically learning how to engage, to figure this out."

The timing of China's robust new engagement with Latin America also has set off some alarm bells in Washington, because it kicked into high gear just as the Sept. 11, 2001, terrorist attacks shifted U.S. attention to Afghanistan and global terrorism.

But China sees its rising presence in Latin America as part of the country's return to its natural global prominence after a "century of humiliation" suffered at the hands of foreign powers — the period from the mid-19th century until Mao Zedong's communist forces defeated the Kuomintang (Chinese Nationalists) in 1949. In 1820, China accounted for nearly 33 percent of the world's gross domestic product (GDP); by 1980 Latin America's collective GDP was seven times larger than China's. Now China's output is larger than all of the Latin American economies combined.[15]

As Latin America, China and the United States deal with the region's changing economic landscape, here are some of the issues being debated:

Is Latin America benefiting from China's new engagement in the region?

With China purchasing huge quantities of Latin American commodities, the region has enjoyed a giant windfall in recent years. About 90 percent of its exports — mostly copper, iron, petroleum and soy — originate in the so-called Southern Cone, which includes Argentina, Chile and Uruguay, as well as from Brazil.[16]

The sheer scale of China's imports has sent global commodity prices skyrocketing. That so-called China effect has boosted producers' incomes globally. And in 2007 alone, it increased earnings for Latin America's top 15 commodities by $56 billion — or 21 percent — according to Rhys Jenkins, a professor of international development at the University of East Anglia, Norwich, U.K.[17]

In addition to 40 million Latin Americans being raised out of poverty between 2002 and 2010, per capita income in the region could double by 2025 if annual growth rates continue at the current average of nearly 5 percent, said Luis Moreno, president of the Inter-American Development Bank.[18]

The timing of China's arrival helped Latin America weather the global financial crisis of 2008-2009. In 2009, as the value of Latin American and Caribbean exports plunged 28.5 percent, exports to China grew 12.4 percent, helping to consolidate an important structural shift in trade.[19] By 2015, experts say, China will likely displace the European Union (EU) as Latin America's second-most-important trading partner after the United States.

"That has reinforced the impression that China really matters in a way it did not before," says Peter Hakim, president emeritus of the Inter-American Dialogue, a Washington think tank.

However, as China was making inroads, much of Latin America was becoming dangerously dependent on a narrow range of mostly unprocessed, low value-added exports. Primary product exports to China, which accounted for 35 percent of Latin American exports in 1995, rose to 62.5 percent by 2006.[20] And that dependency could deepen, because China's foreign direct investment and much of the accompanying cheap financing from its state-owned development banks — both welcomed by the Latin Americans as net benefits — are focused primarily on exploiting Latin America's natural resources.[21] State-subsidized loans from China's development banks throughout the region reached $75 billion between 2005 and 2010.[22]

"China's economy is resource-intensive and relatively inefficient, and in order to protect employment and ease social tensions Chinese enterprises will in all likelihood intensify their resource imports from abroad," said Jiang Shixue, former vice president of the Chinese Association of Latin American Studies in Beijing.[23]

The imbalance in Sino-Latin American trade is another major concern. In exchange for Latin American commodities, China sends manufactured goods to Latin America. After a slow start, China's exports to the region are growing faster than its imports, creating a sizeable and growing trade deficit for the region.

China's exports also are clobbering Latin American manufacturers in both domestic and foreign markets, especially in the vital U.S. market. For instance, in 2001 China and Central America each had 12 percent of the U.S. market for labor-intensive, low-tech exports such as textiles and apparel. By 2009, China's share had risen to 38 percent while Central America's had dropped to 8.7 percent.[24] More than 80 percent of Mexico's manufactured exports to the United States — textiles, televisions, video recorders and industrial machinery — are competing with Chinese goods, which started taking market share when China joined the World Trade Organization (WTO) in 2001.[25] Membership in the WTO means reduced trade barriers among members, which includes most of the world's countries.

"Developments in China have seriously compromised Latin America's capacity to achieve export-oriented growth through the upgrading of its own light and medium manufacturing," laments Dussel Peters, the Mexican economics professor.

On the positive side, however, most Chinese exports to Latin America are cheaper intermediate, or capital, goods, such as steel or car engines, which enable local businesses to improve efficiency. In both Brazil and Mexico, less than 10 percent of Chinese imports are consumer goods; in Brazil close to 70 percent are equipment and other inputs for local businesses.[26]

"This reality has been effectively masked from public perception by the persistent efforts of Brazilian textile, toy, machinery and shoe producers to publicly blame their waning competitiveness on cheap Chinese manufactured imports," argued Rodrigo Tavares Maciel, a former executive secretary of the China-Brazil Business Council, in Rio de Janeiro, a lobbying and public relations campaign promoting protectionist measures. Such measures, he says now, would eventually harm local businesses' competitiveness and raise prices for local consumers.[27]

Does China threaten U.S. influence in Latin America?

The U.S. government has largely acquiesced to China's new engagement with Latin America, partly because there isn't much the United States can do about it and partly because officials don't think China's current economic focus is a threat — yet.

Chinese Imports Outpace Regional Purchases

China accounted for nearly 16 percent of all manufactured goods imported by Latin America in 2009, up sharply from 2 percent in 1996. During the same period, the share of manufactured goods imported by Latin American countries from within the region rose only two percentage points — to about 16 percent, the same as China's share.

Sources of Latin America's Manufactured Imports, 1996-2009

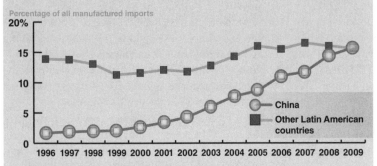

Source: Mauricio Mesquita Moreira, "Manufacturing — Shuttered," China Economic Quarterly, September 2011, p. 22

"At the conceptual level, the United States has tacitly accepted that China's evolving role in Latin America reflects the increasingly complex mosaic of international relationships that is a product of a globalized world," said Daniel Erikson, then director of Caribbean programs at the Inter-American Dialogue. He has since joined the State Department as policy adviser in the Bureau of Western Hemisphere Affairs.[28]

In short, Washington believes China's commercial relations are a net positive for the region. However, the U.S. belief that trade in Latin America is not a zero-sum game conflicts with *realpolitik* impulses that occasionally lead U.S. politicians to describe China's presence in the region as a threat to American interests.[29]

For its part, China emphasizes that its predominantly commercial engagement benefits the United States and Europe by reducing Latin America's need for more aid.[30] Beijing's policy paper on China's regional engagement was an attempt to reassure through transparency. In addition, Chinese academics continue to acknowledge that the region is Washington's "backyard."[31]

"Based on Chinese national interests, Beijing has no incentive to compete against the U.S. in the Western

hemisphere," argued Minxin Pei, director of the Keck Center for International and Strategic Studies at Claremont McKenna College in Claremont, Calif. "Such competition would be costly and have meager geopolitical benefits. It will divert precious resources from China's efforts to defend its interests closer to home — in East Asia."[32]

But, in a post-Cold War world, global competition is defined by economic might almost as much as by military strength. Thus, China's arrival in the region has strategic implications even if they can be only dimly perceived at this point.

America's economic stake in Latin America, developed over more than 200 years, is not easily displaced, even by such a vigorous newcomer as China. China's share of Latin American trade is still only about a quarter of the United States,' which currently is approaching $700 billion per year and growing. U.S. investment in Latin America, meanwhile, is $350 billion, second only to Europe's $620 billion. China's investment in the region — on the other hand — increased rapidly through 2011, but still is only $73.2 billion.[33]

Until recently U.S. and Chinese businesses in Latin America did not compete head-on, but that seems to be changing. The playing field, however, does not appear to be level. Chinese firms often benefit from cheaper, state-subsidized financing. Major U.S. firms lost their position in Argentina's telecommunication sector, for example, to Chinese firms offering larger, lower-cost loans through Chinese development banks.[34]

"Complacently watching as established markets are captured by others is inexplicable, particularly when some of those markets were originally developed by years of patient, taxpayer-financed efforts to reduce violence, build capacity and support democracy," complained Eric Farnsworth, vice president of the Council of the Americas, a New York City-based business organization, founded by David Rockefeller in 1965, that promotes free trade, open markets and democracy. "Just when the U.S. should be reaping the reward, others are swooping in to gain the advantage."[35]

After 15 years of effort, China finally was approved to join the Inter-American Development Bank (IDB) in 2008, enabling Chinese firms to bid on the multimillion-dollar contracts issued each year by the institution. In March 2009, shortly after formally joining the IDB, Beijing used the occasion of the IDB's annual meeting to announce a $10.2 billion loan for Argentina — denominated in *renminbi* — in a bold effort to promote use of the Chinese currency abroad.[36] In March 2012 China's Export-Import Bank launched a new $1 billion equity fund, in conjunction with the IDB, to promote Chinese investments in Latin America and the Caribbean.[37] And where Chinese firms are not particularly strong they set up alliances, such as with Spanish banks with long-established Latin American networks.[38]

The emergence of leftist regimes — notably in Venezuela, Ecuador and Bolivia — indicate some erosion of U.S. influence in the region, and China is deeply involved with leftist governments in Nicaragua and Cuba.[39] Although Beijing has been careful not to be seen as endorsing the anti-U.S. rhetoric popular in those capitals, its financing has been crucial for sustaining those governments. In return, China has won valuable investment positions. All of those countries except Nicaragua have substantial petroleum resources.

In 2008 Ecuador defaulted on $3.2 billion in government bonds held by international investors, and the country was effectively shut out of international credit markets. China quickly stepped in with billions in loans — totaling $7.25 billion by 2012 — to cover Quito's budget shortfall, often secured with access to future Ecuadorian oil.[40]

Chinese firms are now seeking contracts for four dams and hydroelectric projects in Ecuador worth more than $3 billion as well as part of a $12.5 billion refinery project.[41]

The scale and suddenness of China's rise has added to the mystique of China and the riches it can shower on compliant governments. As a result, Latin American governments may think twice about cooperating with the United States, even on police or security matters, if they think the American presence could jinx a major purchase or investment from China, argues R. Evan Ellis, an expert on China in Latin America at the Center for Hemispheric Defense Studies at the National Defense University in Washington.

That calculus may have been in play in 2009, he argues, when Ecuador decided to deny U.S. access to an airfield in Manta. American forces had used the airfield for decades to support anti-narcotics military operations and surveillance flights against Colombian drug cartels. They may have figured cutting off U.S. access was a "necessary step" before inviting China to develop an aviation hub for trans-Pacific flights, even if it was probably never demanded by the Chinese, Ellis suggests.[42]

China's growing influence could also dilute anti-corruption efforts, a key U.S. focus in the region for years. Financial aid from China is still, after all, strictly a state secret in China. For instance, when Costa Rica switched its diplomatic recognition from Taipei to Beijing in 2007, the Central American country received a substantial aid package (including an $83 million soccer stadium, a $300 million bond purchase and $650,000 to attend a Shanghai trade fair), details of which the governments tried to keep secret, according to a leaked diplomatic cable released by WikiLeaks.[43]

"China is not a democracy, and I don't think China has a particular interest in strengthening democratic institutions," says Charles S. Shapiro, a former U.S. ambassador to Venezuela. "It may be too strong to say they are thwarting democracy in Latin America, but they certainly aren't working to promote it. That's not what they're up to."

Does China threaten Latin America's current economic model?

China's new economic embrace of Latin America is reopening an old debate — last settled in 1950s — about the best economic model for the region. In particular, leaders and economists are discussing how much to depend on Latin America's bountiful natural resources.

For many, trade with China is uncomfortably reminiscent of old-style global trade in which Latin America exported raw commodities and imported increasingly expensive manufactured goods from industrialized countries. The model was discredited in the 1950s by Argentine economist Raúl Prebisch, the second director of the United Nation's Economic Commission for Latin America and the Caribbean (ECLAC). Prebisch's own country's history, he pointed out, exemplified why this model did not work: Argentina was once among the world's richest countries until commodity booms went bust.

CHRONOLOGY

1400s-1930s *Chinese explorers reportedly discover the New World. Indentured Chinese workers seed worldwide communities that still flourish.*

1405-1435 Chinese Adm. Zheng He discovers the Americas some 70 years before Columbus, according to a controversial interpretation of a 1418 Chinese book, *The Marvelous Visions of the Star Raft.*

1575-1815 A "silk-road by sea" nourishes China and Latin America, with 20-60 ships a year plying between Mexico and China.

1847 European ships carry unskilled Chinese workers to Cuba. By mid-19th century roughly half a million Chinese are scattered throughout Latin America and the Caribbean.

1890s-1930s Chinese laborers from the United States work on Mexican railroads. . . . Anti-Chinese backlash develops in Mexico during Great Depression. Many Chinese flee to Latin America during Chinese civil war and World War II.

1950s-1970s *Communist China takes new interest in developing countries; vies with Cuba for influence, especially in Africa; pursues relations with newly independent military regimes.*

1954 Panama is first of many Latin American countries to recognize Taiwan as the rightful representative of the Chinese people.

1960 Cuba becomes first Latin American country to recognize People's Republic of China (Mainland China). The next year China establishes Institute of Latin American Studies at the Chinese Academy of Social Sciences in Beijing.

1970s-1980s *China widens relationships in Latin America with flurry of bilateral agreements.*

1970 Chile's socialist president Salvador Allende recognizes the communist government in Beijing, followed by other countries, including rightist military regimes.

1978 Chile and China form a binational commission to extend commerce, scientific, technical and cultural relations.

1980 Gen. Jorge Videla is the first Argentine president to visit China.

1988 China signs first of several agreements with Brazil on satellite development; launches occur in 1999, 2003 and 2007.

2000s *China steps up diplomatic engagements in Latin America. Trade soars. China boosts its investments in the region.*

2001 Chinese Premier Jiang Zemin visits Venezuela, Cuba, Brazil, Uruguay, Argentina and Chile during 13-day tour.

2004 President Hu Jintao visits Latin America and promises $100 billion in investment by 2010; the government later clarifies that he meant "trade" rather than "investment." China deploys peacekeepers for the first time in the Western Hemisphere, joining the United Nations in Haiti.

2005 China signs its first free-trade agreement in the region — with Chile. At least seven others follow and many more are under negotiations.

2008 Sino-Latin American trade soars to $143 billion pre-recession peak; Beijing releases a policy paper about its engagement with Latin America, with peaceful coexistence and "South-South" cooperation as underlying themes.

2009 As China is being inducted into the Inter-American Development Bank it signs $10.2 billion loan for Argentina.

2010 China becomes largest trading partner for several Latin American countries and an increasingly important investor, especially where there are rich lodes of natural resources. China becomes Brazil's largest investor for the year.

2011 Chinese state-owned firms increase their large investments in Latin American manufacturing and commodities to serve local markets, establish regional export platforms and secure long-term food sources.

In Clash Over Shipping, Brazil Backs Down

"This is a real tug-of-war, and China is playing very tough."

The complex, competitive dynamic being played out in Latin America can be seen in China's dealings with the Brazilian firm Vale, one of the world's largest metals and mining companies.

Vale embraced China after the Asian giant began buying large quantities of iron ore in the early 2000s. In 2004, Vale announced it would participate in a $3 billion joint venture with Shanghai-based BaoSteel, the world's second-largest steel company.

Brazilian-Chinese relations had never been better. In a speech that year before the Brazilian parliament, Chinese President Hu Jintao promised $100 billion in investments for the region, with Brazil as a key recipient.[1] At a dinner honoring Hu, Brazilian President Luiz Inácio Lula da Silva said that the $7 billion of Chinese investments targeted for Brazil "will help the country regain its competitiveness in strategic sectors such as infrastructure, energy, steel and telecommunication."[2]

But after five years of negotiations, the BaoSteel-Vale venture was abandoned, and Brazil morphed from being an enthusiastic supporter of Chinese investment to a disappointed partner to — today — a deeply skeptical doubter. Meanwhile, Vale has turned against potential Chinese competitors, particularly those challenging its commanding position in mining, and Brazil's parliament is considering a new law that would restrict land purchases by foreigners.[3]

Vale's troubles with China stemmed in part from a protracted tussle over shipping, which is a significant expense in the iron ore business. In 2008, in a cost-saving move, Vale ordered a fleet of super-large ore carriers that would allow it to cut shipping costs by about 25 percent.[4]

To the dismay of the Brazilian government, Vale decided to have the huge, 400,000-deadweight-ton Valemax ships built at Chinese and South Korean shipyards. But Chinese shippers then complained that Vale was out to monopolize the trade, although Vale said it was just trying to remain competitive against closer suppliers, such as Australia.

"We don't want to be a major freight operator or make money out of our shipping business. We just want to make sure that our freight cost doesn't shoot up," Vale's global marketing director Pedro Gutemberg told Reuters last September. "Whenever they understand better our strategy, we believe they will accept it and negotiations will be finalized."[5]

But Shouguo Zhang, vice executive chairman of the China Shipowners' Association, demanded that Vale "immediately stop its ambitious fleet expansion plan."[6] And on Jan. 31, China's Ministry of Commerce moved to protect the domestic freight industry, banning dry bulk carriers exceeding 300,000 tons from entering Chinese ports.[7]

Now, in a reversal, Vale intends to sell or lease its new fleet of carriers, most likely to Chinese state-run shipping companies with long-term charter contracts.

"This is a real tug-of-war, and China is playing very tough," said Bernardo Lobao, a steel and mining analyst at Studio Investimentos, a Rio de Janeiro-based investment fund. "China's attitude is pretty amazing when you consider that Vale went against its own government, which wanted the ships built in Brazil, and decided instead to build them in China to please its steelmaking clients."[8]

— ***Kenneth J. Stier***

---

[1]Chinese officials later claimed that President Hu was misquoted and had been speaking about trade (not investment) reaching $100 billion by 2010, a climb-down that caused consternation in a region that was eager to receive the investments. It did not help that Beijing took more than a year before offering this "correction." See Daniel Erikson, "Conflicting US Perceptions of China's Inroads in Latin America," in Adrian Hearn and Jose Luis León-Manríquez, eds., *China Engages Latin America: Tracing the Trajectory* (2011), p. 122.

[2]Quoted in Rodrigo Maciel and Dani Nedal, "China and Brazil: Two Trajectories of a 'Strategic Partnership,' " in Hearn and Leon-Manriquez, *ibid.*, p. 249.

[3]Mario Sergio Lima and Juan Pablo Spinetto, "Brazil Said to Require Local Content on New Mining Contracts," *Bloomberg Businessweek*, Feb. 6, 2012, www.businessweek.com/news/2012-02-14/brazil-said-to-require-local-content-on-new-mining-contracts.html.

[4]Silvia Antonioli, "Interview: Vale mega ships to cut freight costs by 20-25 pct," Reuters, June 17, 2011. More background is available at http://en.wikipedia.org/wiki/Valemax.

[5]Silvia Antonioli and Jonathan Saul, "Exclusive: Vale in talks to sell giant ships to China," Reuters, Sept. 5, 2011, www.reuters.com/article/2011/09/05/us-vale-shipping-idUSTRE78434U20110905.

[6]"China Shipowners' Association's Comment and View on Vale's Construction of Transshipment Hub and Distribution Centre in Philippines and Malaysia to Transport Iron Ore Imported by China," China Shipowners Association, http://eng.csoa.cn/Reports/201112/t20111206_1162695.html.

[7]"China bars Brazil's bulk carriers from its ports; clash over iron ore shipping rates," Mercopress, South Atlantic News Agency, Jan. 31, 2012, http://en.mercopress.com/2012/01/31/china-bars-brazil-s-bulk-carriers-from-its-ports-clash-over-iron-ore-shipping-rates.

[8]*Ibid.*

Prebisch's analysis prevailed and set the stage for the "import substitution" industrialization model popular from the 1950s through the '80s, which called for high import tariffs to protect local manufacturers from international competition. The strategy produced mixed success in Mexico and Brazil but eventually led to economic stagnation throughout the region. In the 1980s, after watching the celebrated "Asian Tigers" (Hong Kong, Singapore, South Korea and Taiwan) achieve dramatic growth by lowering tariffs and exporting value-added manufactured goods, Latin American countries adopted similar measures.

Then, along came China, whose relentless industrial policy and sheer size not only dwarfed the Tigers but also began chipping away at Latin Americans' new faith in market forces. Among China's implacable advantages: the 600,000 engineering graduates it churns out each year (compared to 60,000 in Brazil and 38,000 in Mexico). China also saves or reinvests 40 percent of its GDP — twice what Latin Americans muster.[44]

China threatens "to bury, once and for all, any promise of endogenous [home-grown] Latin American development," warned Alexandre de Freitas Barbosa, a professor of economic history at the Institute of Brazilian Studies of the University of São Paulo.[45] Thwarting this would require a return to state intervention, such as heavy protectionism, which didn't work very well over the long term. It's also anathema to the free-market "Washington Consensus" approach advocated by the IMF, World Bank and other international institutions, which still holds sway in most of the region.[46]

As hopes for regional manufacturing growth have dimmed, some are looking more hopefully again at commodities, which have enjoyed a "super cycle" of higher-than-normal prices since the early 2000s, when the huge emerging Chinese and Indian markets began buying large quantities of commodities.

"Argentina would do well to realize that in the economic environment of the future, it is not the buyer who should set the rules . . . it is Argentina and other exporters that control the supply of increasingly indispensable raw materials," argued Jorge E. Malena, director of the Contemporary China Studies Program at the Universidad del Salvador's School of Oriental Studies in Buenos Aires.[47] Others dream of establishing OPEC-like cartels among regional producers, such as a "Soybean Republic" of soy growers.[48]

But such an approach, experts point out, would mean incurring the ecological and social costs of significantly expanding the region's food and meat production. Brazil's soy production has more than quadrupled in recent years while employment shrank with mechanization, and more than 203,000 square miles of Amazon rain forest has been deforested.[49]

Such a commodities-led path could also suffer if China's economy cools. China's GDP growth is expected to dip below 8 percent this year for the first time since 1998. "Brazil must recognize that the era of easy growth in emerging markets and high commodity prices is ending," Ruchir Sharma, head of emerging markets and global macro at Morgan Stanley Investment Management, warned in a recent *Foreign Affairs* article.[50]

Developed economies with innovative industries built around a strong natural resource base — such as Canada or Australia — might be a middle path. "There is no reason why a company like Monsanto cannot emerge in the region, but that will not happen in an environment where good engineers are scarce and there is little incentive or resources for R&D," argues Mauricio Mesquita Moreira, an Inter-American Development Bank (IDB) economist promoting this path.[51]

BACKGROUND

Early Chinese Trade

During the late 16th century, a "silk road by sea" developed between China and Latin America. Some 20-60 ships traveled between China and the Spanish colony of Mexico (now the resort city of Acapulco) each year between 1575 and 1815. The Mexicans exported shoes, hats, wine, olive oil and other foods, while the Chinese sent gun powder, jewelry, food, cotton cloth and silk. Eventually, British exports displaced Chinese goods, and by 1815 China had shut down the trade.[52]

However, the New World's need for labor prompted the importation of large numbers of Chinese workers for the mines and plantations in Mexico, Cuba, Peru, Panama, Chile and Brazil. By 1873 nearly 500,000 Chinese were in the region.[53] The workers, who lived much like African slaves, were conscripted for eight years, but many stayed on; their descendants comprise the region's modern Chinese communities, mostly in Peru, Brazil and Cuba.[54]

Mixed Welcome

Although largely integrated into their host country populations, Chinese communities in Latin America retained a distinct, or at least mixed, identity. Havana's sprawling Chinatown (Barrio Chino), for instance is the largest in Latin America, rivaling those in San Francisco and New York.[55]

Thousands of Chinese fought in Cuba's war of independence against Spain.[56] And six weeks after Fidel Castro's 1959 revolution, the José Wong Brigade, a Mandarin-speaking Cuban military unit, cracked down on black-market trading, gambling, prostitution and opium trafficking in Barrio Chino. Cuba's revolutionary government recognized the People's Republic of China (instead of non-communist Taiwan). It also nationalized Chinese businesses, prompting many Chinese Cubans to emigrate to the United States.[57]

Today more than 100,000 mixed-race Chinese still live in Cuba. And while they may not speak Chinese, they retain connections to their culture. And since official discrimination is prohibited, Chinese-Cubans can advance.[58] In the mid-1990s, Brig. Gen. Moises Si Wong of the Cuban Revolutionary Armed Forces became a key interlocutor between the Chinese Embassy and the Cuban government in efforts to revitalize Chinatown and accommodate local Chinese business interests in developing ties with the motherland.

In Mexico, the first Chinese settlements were established by railroad workers imported from the United States during the 1890s. Laborers were later brought over from Hong Kong and Macao to cut sugarcane and pick cotton. In the 1920s Chinese-owned mining, construction and agriculture firms imported some 50,000 workers.

Chinese traders soon dominated the local economies in Baja, Calif., and later Mexico's Sonora and Sinaloa states. As light manufacturing developed, much of western Mexico's commercial infrastructure was created by the Chinese.

But their success engendered resentment, which peaked in the 1930s as the Great Depression compelled thousands of Mexicans workers to return home from the United States. A virulent anti-Chinese campaign emerged — using the slogan "Mexico for Mexicans" — led by then-President Plutarco Elías Calles and his son. It led to a ban on intermarriage, forced Chinese businesses to close and eventually expelled thousands. Hundreds were reportedly killed.

"Mexico has . . . fantastic conditions for xenophobia and Sino-phobia, as happens, by the way, in other countries of Latin America and . . . even in the U.S.," says Dussel Peters at the National Autonomous University of Mexico. "And this is what scares me."

Since 1978 Beijing has reached out to Chinese communities overseas as "connecting bridges" to the rest of the world, a policy initiated by then-Premier Deng Xiaoping.[59] In Latin America the effort has been complicated, because many Chinese immigrants fled the mainland during civil-war fighting and because of the 1949 victory by Mao Zedong's Communist Party, which continues its one-party rule.

"Overseas Chinese in Latin America are generally pleased to see China's rise on the world stage," said Jiang Shixue, a prominent Chinese Latin America expert. With their knowledge of local markets, language, business networks and long-established informal relationships with local governments, they have been "extremely useful for Chinese investors wishing to develop projects in Latin America."[60]

While Latin American officials generally appreciate the help their local Chinese communities provide in developing closer ties with China, many are ambivalent about whether and how to promote these connections. Often Chinese immigrant dealings with business partners in China are regarded as a threat to national interests. And the local media, particularly in Mexico, often stoke stereotypes and prejudices, sometimes triggering violence.[61]

"The stronger the hostility against Chinese communities, the more likely it is that they will defend themselves by strengthening internal loyalties and ethnic protectionism," write authors of a chapter on China and Mexico in *China Engages Latin America: Tracing the Trajectory.*[62] One of the authors, Adrian Hearn, who has studied Chinese communities in Mexico and Cuba, advises governments to harness local ambitions into culturally appropriate regulations. So far, said the University of Sydney anthropologist, the two governments are bungling their approach. "In both cases, national policy is out of step with local reality," he writes, "impeding genuine engagement with Chinese communities and neglecting potentially useful sources of economic growth and political support."[63]

Balancing U.S. Hegemony

China's relations with Latin America have been nothing if not pragmatic.

Economic relations got under way shortly after the Chinese Communist victory in 1949, but only simmered for the next decade. Then, when Castro's communist regime came to power in 1959, Cuba became the first Latin American country to establish diplomatic ties with the People's Republic.

Chile's socialist President Salvador Allende followed suit in 1970, but relations cooled after he was deposed in a military coup three years later. By 1978, China and Chilean military leaders were creating a commission to develop scientific, cultural, technical and commercial relations.

In 1974 Brazil's military dictatorship established diplomatic ties with China, and in 1978 China signed an economic and trade agreement with Argentina's military regime, whose relations with the United States soured after President Jimmy Carter's administration (1977-1981) adopted a tough pro-human rights foreign policy and began publishing annual reports on the status of human rights across the globe.[64] Latin America's military regimes were more comfortable with China's hands-off approach to human-rights issues.

Latin American leftists also welcomed China's political heft as a counter-balance to U.S. influence in the region. "The wide South American consensus on behalf of improved relations with China [in the early 2000s] owes much, therefore, to the patterns first set in the 1970s: There is a broad cross-ideological support to expand relations with China and, on the Latin American right as well as on the left, to use such relations to provide some balance to U.S. power," noted one of the first serious American studies about China's new engagement with Latin America, funded by the Japanese foreign ministry.[65]

Similarly, China was "indifferent to the form of the political regime so long as there were political and economic gains to be made," noted a report by the Inter-American Dialogue.[66]

Charm Offensive

China's modern era of engagement with Latin America is generally seen as having been kicked off by a 13-day tour of the region in April 2001, when then-Chinese premier Jiang Zemin visited Venezuela, Cuba, Brazil, Uruguay, Argentina and Chile.

A stream of high-level official visits soon followed, in both directions, a mutual courtship that — coming on the heels of the 9/11 attack in the United States — struck some U.S. observers as opportunistic, if not worrisome.

But well-timed and increasingly high-level diplomatic visits by Beijing officials had, in fact, begun in the early 1980s, when Beijing began training a core cadre of diplomats to manage regional relations.[67] China also invested in think tanks focusing on Latin American studies at the Chinese Academy of Social Sciences in Beijing and a Latin American department within the Communist Party's Department of Studies.

By contrast, Latin American countries are just now developing expertise on China — even after 30 years — and their efforts are less organized or systematic. Of the 55,251 foreign students studying at Chinese universities in 2010, only 771 were from South America, compared to 6,065 from North America, according to Chinese education ministry figures.[68]

The Chinese investment has yielded what the Inter-American Dialogue study called "an impressive systematic long-term strategy." When President Hu Jintao spent two weeks in the region in 2004, considered another high-water mark in relations, he "harvested the blossoms from the seeds planted in decades past."[69]

Nonetheless, there are growing signs that relations are not so sturdy. Beijing has consistently insisted that China's new global prominence is a "peaceful rise" aimed at developing a "harmonious world" based on mutually beneficial South-South relations.[70] These declarations were aimed at countering the specter of a "China threat," particularly as China aggressively invests overseas.[71]

But Latin Americans are "not buying" that argument any longer, says He Li, a Chinese political scientist at Merrimack College in North Andover, Mass. "It is ridiculous to call yourself a 'South' country when you are the world's second-largest economy, you are sending up satellites and hosting the Olympics."

Harvard professor Joseph S. Nye, Jr., author of the 2004 book *Soft Power: The Means To Success In World Politics*, says despite Beijing's $8.9 billion investment (in 2009-2010) in external publicity efforts — including a 24-hour cable news channel — the campaign has had "limited return on its investment" because its message is undermined by China's suppression of human rights and the private sector.

There is a more prosaic reason why China's charm offensive has lost its sheen. As Chinese investors deal with mundane local matters — such as regulations, taxation, militant labor, indigenous peoples' rights or environmental protection — the more potential there is for daily friction.[72]

"As China mixes it up in Latin America . . . you're going to have three simultaneous things going on: an acceleration of learning on both sides, an acceleration of conflicts and the acceleration of Chinese influence," says Ellis, of the National Defense University, "the net balance of which remains to be seen."

CURRENT SITUATION

Infrastructure Transformation

China's new presence in Latin America has produced an explosion of infrastructure projects in just about every country in the region. Tens of thousands of Chinese workers are building roads, rails, refineries, dams, ports, pipelines and power plants. And wherever there are legions of Chinese workers, Chinese traders and small businessmen are there to serve their needs.

An estimated 40,000 Chinese are in Suriname (formerly Dutch Guyana) — roughly 10 percent of the population — carving new highway and rail links through the jungle from Brazil's vast interior to a new Caribbean gateway at Suriname's deep-water port, also being built by China.[73] Similar avenues are being punched through the Amazon over the Andes to Pacific ports in Ecuador and Peru.[74]

The influx of Chinese workers has not occurred everywhere. Many Latin American governments have restricted the number of Chinese workers that can be imported, reflecting the region's much stronger, sometimes even militant, labor movements.

Most projects would enable China to exploit Latin America's natural resources. Ports and rail connections are being built, for instance, so copper can be exported from Chile and Peru.[75] Argentina received more than $10 billion to upgrade railways connecting Buenos Aires to key soybean producing areas.[76] Chinese firms in Venezuela are building infrastructure projects worth $25 billion, some of which will service Venezuela's bitumen deposits — the world's largest — to which China has favored access.[77]

About 600 Chinese engineers and workers helped to build Costa Rica's new National Stadium in the capital, San Jose. The Chinese paid for construction of the stadium, completed in 2011, after Costa Rica established diplomatic relations with China in 2007. China is building dozens of infrastructure projects in Latin America, with tens of thousands of Chinese workers helping to build roads, railroads, refineries, dams, ports, pipelines and power plants.

AFP/Getty Images/Yuri Cortez

Chinese firms also are building various national development projects — infrastructure and industrial projects designed to enhance long-term economic prosperity — often because of low-cost Chinese government financing.

After buying several Brazilian electric utility companies for nearly $1 billion, China's state-owned State Grid Corp. — the world's largest electric utility company — is expected to have a lucrative role in distributing the power generated from a series of 20 dams, including the Belo Monte Dam, the third-largest hydroelectric project in the world. The dams have been controversial because they are expected to flood an area of the Amazon River basin more than 100 times the size of Manhattan. Another 20 dams are on the drawing boards.[78]

Not everyone is thrilled about the projects. "There are so many reasons these dams don't make sense," said Celio Bermann, a University of São Paulo engineering professor and a leading critic of the projects.[79] His major criticism is that the dams reinforce the reshaping of Brazil's economy into an exporter of low-priced primary products, rather than of higher-value manufactured exports.[80]

Chinese companies are also bidding on regional projects, such as a $7.6 billion railroad link between the Atlantic and Pacific coasts in Colombia, and China wants to participate in the planned expansion of the Panama Canal.[81]

China's infrastructure improvements could significantly boost growth in the region, according to Barbara Kotschwar, a researcher at the Peterson Institute for International Economics in Washington, because inadequate transportation infrastructure has prevented Latin American countries from taking advantage of "the multitude of regional, bilateral and multilateral trade agreements signed in the past decade-and-a-half."[82]

Hardball Tactics

Even with huge, new infrastructure improvements, Latin America still must figure out how to leverage China's new engagement to achieve strong growth and sustainable prosperity — something that has eluded the Latin American and Caribbean region for more than a century.[83] Economists generally agree that the region needs to maximize earnings from natural resources while boosting technological sophistication.

But Latin America's record on making that transition is mixed so far: While its share of the world "worked" metals market has increased eightfold in about 30 years, the region's overall productivity growth — which was virtually zero from 1960-2000 — has begun to pick up only in the past decade.[84]

However, some worry that China's hardball trade tactics could throttle Latin America's growth. For example, in 2009 after Argentina filed 18 complaints against China with the WTO — claiming China was dumping cheap shoes, toys and steel pipes — China abruptly stopped ordering Argentina's soybean oil. The cancelled orders amounted to far more than the value of Chinese goods affected by the anti-dumping complaints.

Although Argentina was able to find other buyers for its soybean oil, the incident highlighted Argentina's growing dependence on China. The value of Argentina's soy exports had skyrocketed from $57.4 million in 1995 to $2.4 billion a decade later — largely on the strength of Chinese demand. And shortly after Argentina argued its case the Chinese vice minister of trade showed up in Buenos Aires to admonish officials to take a "more cautious approach dealing with trade issues."[85]

Two years later, the issue still rankles Argentines and appears to have reinforced China's determination to build up its own oilseed-crushing industry in order to capture more of the value-added market. To control costs and boost profits, China plans not only to grow its own food but also to process and ship it.

"The Chinese are systematically trying to decouple themselves from the international grain companies — as we have seen them do in other industries," says Mariano Turzi, a professor at Torcuato De Tella University in Buenos Aires.

The scale of China's ambitions — and needs — is staggering. A Chinese firm has leased about 740,000 acres of private farmland in Rio Negro province in Argentina's northern Patagonia — one of the last uncultivated temperate-climate valleys in South America.[86] The company, the Heilongjiang Beidahuang Nongken Group — or the Great Northern Wilderness Land Reclamation Co. — already farms nearly 5 million acres outside China and has said it wants to buy another 490,000 acres this year in Latin America.[87]

Although the land was privately owned, Great Northern cut the deal with the provincial government, prompting national legislation last December limiting land purchases to foreign individuals and companies.[88] Brazil is also working to close loopholes in land ownership rules.[89]

Many local residents worry about how the huge soy plantations will affect indigenous peoples' lands and habitat. "Soy and other industrial crops will not be welcomed under the conditions created by this agreement, which clearly jeopardizes the future of Rio Negro residents," said the provincial Pastoral Care Ministry of the Catholic Church.[90]

Likewise, the Foro Permanente por una Vida Digna (Permanent Forum for Dignified Life) calls the project a "land grab."

"We oppose the agricultural export megaproject . . . which jeopardizes 320,000 hectares [791,000 acres] of land and nature in our province by handing it over to . . . China to do with it as it sees fit," said the group. "This violates our sovereign laws, posits a future of farming without farmers, and contaminates us with pesticides. It is a project that does great harm to this generation and the ones to come."[91]

To ease such criticisms, Chinese investors have begun leasing land or forming joint ventures with local companies. Beidahuang formed a joint venture in 2011 with one of Argentina's top agricultural firms, Cresud S.A., which controls 2.47 million acres for grain, cattle and dairy production.[92] Chongqing Grain Group Co., Ltd. — a leading state-owned Chinese grain company — announced

Is China a threat to Latin America's manufacturing base?

YES Mauricio Mesquita Moreira
Principal Economist, Integration and Trade Sector, Inter-American Development Bank

Written for *CQ Global Researcher*, June 2012

Export-oriented manufacturing is no longer a viable growth path for most of Latin America. That door has been shut by China and other major exporting countries such as India.

The best option for South America is to make the most of its comparative advantages in natural resources, avoid the resource curse and promote alternative forms of employment. Resource-poor Mexico and Central America must take advantage of their proximity to the United States and other regional markets through massive investment in transport and logistics.

Given the size of Latin America's most industrialized economies, manufactured exports cannot be a major source of growth unless they capture a substantial share of world markets. That is not happening. Latin American manufacturers saw some gains in market share in the late 1990s, but their modest position deteriorated in the early 2000s.

Latin America's misfortunes contrast sharply with China's breakneck performance. In little more than a decade, China roughly tripled its market share in the United States and the world, helping to reduce manufacturing's share of GDP in Brazil and Mexico to less than 20 percent and accentuating a decline that began when trade was liberalized in both countries.

The sheer size of the Chinese economy and the strength of its comparative advantages — a vast, cheap labor pool, education levels comparable to those in Latin America and a relentless industrial policy — mean that the manufacturing road to development has become highly congested and particularly hazardous for countries that don't have an abundance of skilled workers. India, another populous, resource-scarce economy with even lower wages than China's, already exports more manufactured goods than Brazil.

If Latin America tries to force manufacturing growth by adopting the failed protectionist tools of the past, it will return to 1980s stagnation. Yes, economies specializing in natural resources are risky, but it's riskier to ignore market signals, comparative advantages and the limitations of government intervention.

As Latin America moves into uncharted waters, it must devise a new route to development that relies on natural resource exports, some manufacturing and reforms and investments to enhance the region's competitiveness. A glance at China and India's desperate need for land and natural resources suggests that the "super cycle" that commodities have experienced since the early 2000s may be more of a structural trend. So the risk of specializing in natural resource exports is not as high as history may suggest.

NO Dani Nedal
Research Fellow, University of Birmingham (U.K.) and Member, Inter-American Dialogue's Working Group on China and Latin America

Written for *CQ Global Researcher*, June 2012

There is a prevailing perception that China-Latin America trade endangers regional industrial development. But the impact of this trade on individual countries is markedly heterogeneous and not conclusively dire. In other words, the impact of China has been uneven, and the winners and losers within countries have varied greatly.

Generally, China's effect on domestic industries and exports varies according to the country's resources, labor and capital and whether the government hampers doing business or constrains labor markets and capital mobility.

Trade with China has clearly benefited extractive industries in Brazil, Peru, Venezuela, Argentina and Chile, but Chinese exporters have outcompeted those countries' manufacturers, especially in low-skill, labor-intensive sectors.

Increasingly, that is also true for more capital-intensive goods. However, while alarmists like to point out that Latin firms are losing market share to Chinese companies, they fail to mention that Latin firms often are producing and selling more, even though the Chinese exports are growing even faster.

These companies might eventually get pushed out altogether, but the data so far don't support such gloomy predictions. Brazil's machinery sector, for instance, generally cited as under threat from China, keeps posting export growth rates among the highest in the world (30 percent in 2011), with rising revenue and employment. Studies also have shown that in some countries — such as Costa Rica, Nicaragua and Brazil — losers in the low end of the value chain have moved onto higher value-added goods, partly because they have had access to cheap, Chinese capital goods. The few econometric studies that have looked for links between Chinese import growth and manufacturing job losses in Argentina and Brazil have found them to be negligible.

This more nuanced and optimistic account of China-Latin trade does not, however, negate the profoundly sound advice (offered by Mauricio Mesquita Moreira) that countries should make the most of their natural-resource endowments and leverage revenue from those resources to upgrade their infrastructure and human capital. However, that advice will likely go unheeded, especially in Brazil and Argentina, where changing course would entail steep political costs because the leaderships and societies are still enthralled with outdated theories of dependency and development and an obsession with manufacturing. China's success has only intensified that predicament.

plans in April 2012 to invest $1.2 billion to develop soybean, corn, and cotton farms in Argentina, part of $6 billion it plans to spend in overseas land acquisitions this year.[93]

Commodities produced by these Chinese-driven companies are expected to be cheaper than those purchased through international grain dealers. Great Northern's president explained why: "Under the guidance of the [Chinese] government, we plan to build a comprehensive industrial chain," which will offer financial services, storage, logistics, agricultural production and distribution.[94]

Meanwhile, Argentine farmers complain that their government treats the export sector as the country's golden goose, taxing exports up to 70 percent without investing in public infrastructure.[95] The government has collected $48 billion in export taxes over the past eight years, leaving precious little for farmers to invest in new processing technology, says Alberto Rubio, dean of the graduate school at the University of Belgrano in Buenos Aires.[96]

Coping with the Juggernaut

While reeling from hugely lopsided trade imbalances with China, Latin American countries continue to lag in their scramble to devise national strategies to cope with the Chinese economic juggernaut.

For instance, China and Brazil have been strategic partners since 1993, but a China-Brazil binational commission reconvened in early April for the first time in two years. And Brazil recently revived a dormant interagency working group created to devise a coherent national strategy for trade with China. Both are part of Brazilian President Dilma Rousseff's renewed focus on relations with China, its biggest trading partner and a growing investor.

"China's growth is so complex that if you don't have a well-defined strategy it can be a disaster," explains Maciel, the former executive secretary of the China-Brazil Business Council. "There are many different interests on the table, but no one is selecting which ones are more important and saying 'let's focus on this.' No, we are doing it by the moment, depending on which industry is being most affected from China, and then the agenda is built around this," he explains. "[But] Brazil has more to lose than China, so it's our duty to be more proactive in this relationship."

Instead, Brazil has given in to an old reflex — protectionism. Before liberalizing its trade in 1990s, Brazil's high import tariffs meant that only 5 percent of its consumer goods were imported. The protected local Brazilian car industry produced vehicles with nearly 90 percent local content, but at almost four times the prevailing international price.[97]

Chinese carmakers want to tap Brazil's market, which buys 3.5 million new vehicles a year. Last July China's state-owned Chery Automobile Co. — which assembles 1 million cars in 11 countries — broke ground on a $400 million plant near São Paulo. "This is our biggest investment outside China and will be the base of exports for all of South America," Chery President Yin Tongyue told reporters.

"This factory is a symbol of the quickly developing relationship between China and Brazil," added China's ambassador to Brazil, Qiu Xiaoqi.[98]

But soon afterward, the Brazilian government abruptly hiked taxes by 30 percent on cars with less than 65 percent local content, torpedoing Chery's plans to build an assembly plant using imported parts.[99] Eventually, Chery decided to set up a complete supply chain of components, using Chinese suppliers who will set up shop inside Brazil.[100]

However, the move still concerns free-marketers. "We are in favor of international trade, however, we reject unfair trade practices, as practiced by China, [and] China is not a market economy," said Paulo Skaf, president of the powerful Federation of Industries of São Paulo. In addition, he complained, the Brazilian government's recognition of China as a "market economy" undercuts the ability to impose sanctions against "unfair" Chinese imports.[101]

Some economists view Latin American governments' response to China's economic expansion as falling backwards on a slippery slope. "They seem to want to bring back the whole protectionist apparatus," says the IDB's Moreira, a Brazilian. "We need fresh thinking to deal with these challenges. But the pressure to expand protection to all sectors is huge. The end result is going to be another fiscal crisis like we've had before, no doubt about it."

OUTLOOK
Rivalry vs. Cooperation

As the global economic center of gravity shifts toward Asia, competing — and possibly adversarial — trade regimes are emerging.

As part of its global reorientation toward Asia, the Obama administration has been promoting the so-called Trans-Pacific Partnership, a free trade pact between Asia and the Americas. Trade barriers would be lowered, and China — should it decide to join — would have to open its economy to more imports and investment from Latin America.

Beijing has balked, however, because it would have to reduce the role of its state-owned enterprises, which dominate roughly two-thirds of China's economy. Instead, China has forged its own trade pact with Southeast Asia and has proposed another with its northeast Asian neighbors.

In Latin America, China has negotiated separate "free trade agreements" with individual countries.[102]

"Latin America has long talked about a collective response to China," but it has never really materialized, making them "easy pickings for the Chinese," says Ellis of the National Defense University. "China has everything to win by a divided global response to its rise."

To counter China's divide-and-conquer strategy in Latin America, he says, the United States should leverage its close ties with other Asian countries to help Latin America forge better trade ties with China. "We could really help Latin America best take advantage of the promises represented by doing business with Asia while avoiding some of the pitfalls," Ellis says. "And that would collectively give Latin Americans a stronger hand vis-à-vis their own negotiations with China."

Whether that comes to pass depends on improving relations between Brazil and the United States. Although the United States and Brazil are the two biggest economies in the Americas, they have not signed a major economic pact in two decades, during which time the United States signed trade deals with 11 other Latin American countries.

The main challenge is recalibrating bilateral relations to reflect Brazil's new stature as the world's sixth-largest economy — up from 12th in 2004 — which has happened while the United States was deeply distracted by the Middle East.[103]

Brazil complains the United States has not acknowledged this power shift and even tries thwarting it by, for instance, favoring India's bid for a U.N. Security Council seat but opposing Brazil's.[104] For its part, Washington feels that Brazil often goes out of its way to obstruct U.S. efforts on key global issues, just to assert its new influence.[105]

"Brazilians and American talk a great deal about the desirability of a 'strategic' relationship between their countries, but neither does much to achieve it," the Inter-American Dialogue's Hakim wrote in April, just before Brazilian President Rousseff visited Washington. "Still, it is time for the U.S. to consider dropping its ambivalence over Brazil's international ambitions and acknowledge — more than half-heartedly — its emergence as a powerful nation."[106]

Nevertheless, for better or worse, Latin America is not a vital strategic priority for either China or the United States, reducing the likelihood of Sino-U.S. conflicts in the region. In the resultant power vacuum, Brazil has become the region's economic heavy weight.

Nevertheless, Brasilia's relations with Beijing — and Washington — will be vital for the whole region, says Dani Nedal, a Brazilian research fellow at the University of Birmingham (U.K.), because, "Brazil has neither China's deep pockets and competitive edge nor U.S. strategic assets." Thus, he says, Brazil "would be hard pressed to compete on an equal footing to maintain a preeminent position in the region."

NOTES

1. Gonzalo Sebastian Paz, "China and Venezuela: Oil, Technology and Socialism," in Adrian H. Hearn and José Luis León-Manríquez, eds., *China Engages Latin America: Tracing the Trajectory* (2011), p. 229.

2. "Trade: China-Latin America," in "Direction of Trade Statistics," International Monetary Fund.

3. Enrique Dussel Peters, "China's Challenge to Latin American Development," in Hearn and León-Manríquez, *op. cit.*, p. 95

4. Eric C. Anderson and Jeffrey G. Engstrom, "China's Use of Perception Management and Strategic Deception," U.S.-China Economic and Security Review Commission, Science Applications International Corporation, November 2009, www.uscc.gov/researchpapers/2009/ApprovedFINALSAIC StrategicDeceptionPaperRevisedDraft06Nov 2009.pdf.

5. "China's Policy Paper on Latin America and the Caribbean," Ministry of Foreign Affairs, People's Republic of China, Nov. 5, 2008, www.fmprc.gov .cn/eng/zxxx/t521025.htm.

6. Luis Alberto Moreno, "The Decade of Latin America and the Caribbean: A Real Opportunity," Inter-American Development Bank, September 2011, pp. 35-36.

7. Mauricio Mesquita Moreira, "China, Latin America, and the United States: The New Triangle," Woodrow Wilson International Center for Scholars, January 2011, p. 12, www.wilsoncenter.org/sites/default/files/LAP_120810_Triangle_rpt.pdf. Also see "China Global Investment Tracker," The Heritage Foundation, January 2012, www.heritage.org/research/projects/china-global-investment-tracker-interactive-map. See also Derek Scissors, "Chinese Outward Investment: Slower Growth in 2011," The Heritage Foundation, Jan. 9, 2012, http://report.heritage.org/wm3445.

8. Kevin P. Gallagher, Amos Irwin and Katherine Koleski, "The New Banks in Town: Chinese Finance in Latin America," Inter-American Dialogue, February 2012, p. 1, http://ase.tufts.edu/gdae/Pubs/rp/GallagherChineseFinanceLatinAmericaBrief.pdf.

9. Janie Hulse Najenson, "Argentina's New Melting Pot," *Americas Quarterly*, Winter 2012, p. 87.

10. Mauricio Mesquita Moreira, "The Big Idea. China and Latin America: Manufacturing — Shuttered," *China Economic Quarterly*, September 2011, p. 23.

11. For background, see Jason McLure, "State Capitalism," *CQ Global Researcher*, May 15, 2012, pp. 229-256.

12. Solana Pyne, "China's Brazilian shopping spree," globalpost.com, Nov. 22, 2010, www.globalpost.com/dispatch/brazil/101118/china-foreign-investment-trade.

13. Tom Phillips, "Brazil's huge new port highlights China's drive into South America," *The Guardian*, Sept. 15, 2010.

14. According to Mexican statistics; Chinese statistics show a smaller deficit. Adrian Hearn, Alan Smart, Roberto Hernandez Hernandez, "China and Mexico: Trade, Migration and Guanxi," in Hearn and León-Manríquez, *op. cit.*, p. 140.

15. Jerome Cukier, "China: back to the future," OECD Factblog, Organisation for Economic Co-operation and Development, March 24, 2010. Also see Kevin Gallagher, "China and the Future of Latin American Industrialization," Issues in Brief, Frederick S. Pardee Center for the Study of the Longer-Range Future, October 2010, www.bu.edu/pardee/issues-in-brief-no-18/.

16. Mauricio Mesquita Moreira, "Ten Years After the Take-off: Taking Stock of China-Latin America and the Caribbean Economic Relations," Inter-American Development Bank, Integration and Trade Sector, September 2010.

17. Rhys Jenkins, "The 'China Effect' on Latin American Export Earnings," *CEPAL Review #103*, Economic Commission for Latin America and the Caribbean, April 2011, p. 82, www.eclac.cl/publicaciones/xml/1/44061/RVI103Jenkins.pdf.

18. Moreno, *op. cit.*, p. 36.

19. Moreira, "Ten Years After the Take-off: Taking Stock of China-Latin America and the Caribbean Economic Relations," *op. cit.*, p. 7.

20. The United Nations Economic Commission on Latin America and the Caribbean (ECLAC). In Spanish, www.cepal.org/comercio/serieCP/eclactrade/serie_spanish_110.html. (Roll cursor over the bar graph to get percentages.)

21. Gallagher, Irwin and Koleski, *op. cit.*

22. *Ibid.*

23. Jiang Shixue, "Ten Key Questions," in Hearn and Leon-Manriquez, *op. cit.*, p. 52.

24. Gallagher, *op. cit.*, p. 6.

25. Kevin Gallagher and Enrique Dussel Peters, "NAFTA's uninvited guest: China and the disintegration of North American Trade," submitted to CEPAL Review (*Economic Journal of the U.N. Economic Commission for Latin America and Caribbean*). Mexico's share of U.S. imports was cut in half from 13.22 percent in 2000 to 6.51 percent in 2010, during which China's share rose from 12 to 42 percent, according to U.S. International Trade Commission 2011 data.

26. Interviews with Dussel Peters and Rodrigo Maciel.

27. Rodrigo Maciel and Dani Nedal, "China and Brazil: Two Trajectories of a 'Strategic Partnership,'" in Hearn and León-Manríquez, *op. cit.*, p. 248.

28. Daniel Erikson, "Conflicting U.S. Perceptions," in Hearn and León-Manríquez, *op. cit.*, p. 133.

29. See Hilary R. Clinton's keynote address and town hall meeting, "Foreign Affairs Day," U.S. Department of State, May 1, 2009, www.state.gov/secretary/rm/2009a/05/122534.htm.

30. Zhang Mingde, "Much in Common," *Americas Quarterly*, Winter 2012, p. 78, http://americasquarterly.org/Mingde.

31. Jiang Shixue, "Three Factors in Recent Development of Sino-Latin American Relations," in Cynthia Arnson, Mark Mohr and Riordan Roett, eds., "Enter the Dragon? China's Presence in Latin America," Woodrow Wilson International Center for Scholars, undated, p. 48, www.wilsoncenter.org/sites/default/files/EnterDragonFinal.pdf.

32. Minxin Pei, "Ask The Experts: China's Global Rise," *Americas Quarterly*, Winter 2012, p. 115.

33. Monthly 2011 figures are at www.eclac.org/cgi-bin/getprod.asp?xml=/publicaciones/xml/3/46553/P46553.xml&xsl=/comercio/tpl/p9f.xsl&base=/comercio/tpl/top-bottom.xsl.

34. Janie Hulse, "China's Expansion into and U.S. Withdrawal from Argentina's Telecommunications and Space Industries and the Implications for U.S. National Security," Strategic Studies Institute, September 2007, www.strategicstudiesinstitute.army.mil/pdffiles/pub806.pdf.

35. Eric Farnsworth, "Memo to Washington: China's Growing Presence in Latin America," *Americas Quarterly*, Winter 2012, p. 81.

36. Hearn and León-Manríquez, *op. cit.*, p. 58. See also R. Evan Ellis, "Chinese Soft Power in Latin America: A Case Study," *Joint Force Quarterly*, First Quarter, 2011, p. 88, www.ndu.edu/press/chinese-soft-power-latin-america.html.

37. "China Eximbank further advances in the creation of equity investment platform for Latin America and the Caribbean," Inter-American Development Bank, March 19, 2012, www.iadb.org/en/news/news-releases/2012-03-19/china-latin-america-equity-investment-fund,9894.html.

38. "Spanish Banks: Embracing Globalization and Leveraging Latin America's Ties with China," Knowledge@Wharton, May 4, 2011, www.wharton.universia.net/index.cfm?fa=viewFeature&id=2062&language=english.

39. For background, see Roland Flamini, "The New Latin America," *CQ Global Researcher*, March 1, 2008, pp. 57-84.

40. Nathan Gill, Bloomberg, Jan. 24, 2012, www.bloomberg.com/news/2012-01-24/ecuador-borrows-from-china-seeks-bond-sale.html.

41. R. Evan Ellis, "The Expanding Chinese Footprint in Latin America: New Challenges for China, and Dilemma for the U.S.," *Asie Visions #49*, Center for Asian Studies, Institut Francais des Relations Internationales, February 2012, p. 12, www.ifri.org/?page=contribution-detail&id=7014.

42. For background see Joshua Partlow, "Ecuador Giving U.S. Air Base the Boot," *The Washington Post*, Sept. 4, 2008.

43. "Costa Rica and China Explore an Evolving Relationship," U.S. Department of State cable, http://wikileaks.as50620.net/cable/2009/12/09SANJOSE985.html.

44. Moreira, "The Big Idea. China and Latin America: Manufacturing — Shuttered," *op. cit.*

45. Alexandre Freitas Barbosa, "The Rise of China, Its Impacts on Latin America and the Main Challenges Faced by the Region's Labour Movement," www.global-labour-university.org/fileadmin/GLU_conference_Unicamp_2008/Submitted_papers/The_Rise_of_China....by_Alexandre_de_Freitas_Barbosa.pdf.

46. See John Williamson, "Is the 'Beijing Consensus' Now Dominant?" *Asia Policy 13*, National Bureau of Asian Research, January 2012, www.nbr.org/publications/element.aspx?id=571.

47. Jorge E. Malena, "China and Argentina: Beyond the Quest for Natural Resources," in Hearn and León-Manríquez, *op. cit.*, p. 275.

48. Mariano Turzi, "The Soybean Republic," *Yale Journal of International Relations*, Spring-Summer, 2011, pp. 59-68.

49. Gallagher, "China and the Future of Latin American Industrialization," *op. cit.*, p. 4. For background, see Doug Struck, "Disappearing Forests," *CQ Global Researcher*, Jan. 18, 2011, pp. 27-52.

50. Ruchir Sharma, "Bearish on Brazil: The Commodity Slowdown and the End of the Magic Moment," *Foreign Affairs*, May-June, 2012. See also "China Slows Down, and Grows Up," *The New York Times*, April 25, 2012.

51. Moreira, "Manufacturing — Shuttered," *op. cit.*

52. Jiang Shixue, "On the Development of Sino-Latin American Relations," Institute of Latin American Studies, Chinese Academy of Social Sciences, July 20, 2009, http://blog.china.com.cn/jiangshixue/art/915285.html.

53. Adrian H. Hearn, "Harnessing the Dragon: Overseas Chinese Entrepreneurs in Mexico and Cuba," *The China Quarterly*, 2012, Vol. 209, pp. 111-133.

54. Lisa Yun, *The Coolie Speaks: Chinese Indentured Laborers and African Slaves in Cuba* (2009).

55. Hearn, "Harnessing the Dragon," *op. cit.*

56. Shixue, "Ten Key Questions," *op. cit.*, p. 60.

57. Hearn, *op. cit.*

58. Brian Latell, *After Fidel: The Inside Story of Castro's Regime and Cuba's Next Leader* (2005).

59. Shixue, *op. cit.*, p. 60.

60. *Ibid.*, p. 61.

61. Hearn, *op. cit.*

62. Hearn, Smart and Hernandez, *op. cit*, p. 146.

63. Hearn, *op. cit.*

64. Jorge Dominguez, "China's Relations with Latin America: Shared Gains, Asymmetric Hopes," Inter-American Dialogue, June 2006.

65. *Ibid.*, p. 6.

66. *Ibid.*, p. 5.

67. *Ibid.*, p. 21.

68. Rachel Glickhouse, "Studying Abroad in China," *Americas Quarterly*, Winter 2012, p. 57.

69. Dominguez, *op. cit.*, p. 22.

70. Zheng Bijina, "China's Peaceful Rise to Great Power Status," *Foreign Affairs*, September/October 2005.

71. China's "Go Out Policy" (known as the Going Global Strategy) was initiated in 1999.

72. Ellis, "The Expanding Chinese Footprint in Latin America," *op. cit.*

73. Simon Romero, "With Aid and Migrants, China Expands Its Presence in a South American Nation," *The New York Times*, April 11, 2011, www.nytimes.com/2011/04/11/world/americas/11suriname.html.

74. R. Evan Ellis, "Strategic Implications of Chinese Aid and Investment in Latin America," *China Brief*, Vol. 9, Issue 20, Oct. 7, 2009, www.jamestown.org/single/?no_cache=1&tx_ttnews%5Btt_news%5D=35590.

75. "Sinopec finishes 1,377-km GASENE pipeline in Brazil," Alibaba.com, April 9, 2010, http://news.alibaba.com/article/detail/business-in-china/100274645-1-sinopec-finishes1%252C377-km-gasene-pipeline.html.

76. Neil Denslow, "China Backs $12 Billion Argentina Rail Projects to Ease Commodity Supplies," Bloomberg, July 14, 2010.

77. Cynthia Watson, "The Obama Administration, Latin America, and the Middle Kingdom," in Hearn and León-Manríquez, *op. cit.*, p. 106.

78. Michael Smith, "Brazil Be Damned," Bloomberg Markets, May 2012, pp. 90-102.

79. *Ibid.*, p. 95.

80. Francis McDonagh, "Brazil: Energy policies under spotlight," Latin America Bureau, Nov. 21, 2011, www.lab.org.uk/index.php?option=com_content&view=article&id=1137:brazil-energy-policies-under-the-spotlight&catid=66&Itemid=39.

81. Ellis, "The Expanding Chinese Footprint in Latin America," *op. cit.*

82. Barbara Kotschwar, "Going Places," *Americas Quarterly*, Winter 2012, p. 35.

83. Augusto de la Torre, "Latin America and the Caribbean's Long-term Growth — Made in China?" World Bank, September 2011.

84. *Ibid.*

85. Malena, *op. cit.*

86. Janie Hulse Najenson, "Chinese Want Strategic, Long-Term Ties to Argentina," *Americas Quarterly* blog, Oct. 4, 2011.

87. For background, see Jina Moore, "Resolving Land Disputes," *CQ Global Researcher*, Sept. 6, 2011, pp. 421-446.

88. Mark Keller, "Argentina's Land Law Seeks to Limit Foreign Ownership," *Americas Society*, Dec. 19, 2011, www.as-coa.org/article.php?id=3860.

89. Official records show foreigners own 10.6 million acres of Brazilian land, but it could be up to three times that, according to "Brazil to further limit foreign ownership of land, says local media," Mercopress, Nov. 21, 2011.

90. GRAIN, *The Great Food Robbery: How Corporations control food, grab and destroy the climate* (2012), p. 151. For more see "Land grab in Latin America: Meeting in Buenos Aires, social movements criticize a recent report on land-grabbing by the UN's Food and Agriculture Organisation (FAO)," Latin America Bureau, May 16, 2012. Also see Saturnino M. Borras Jr., *et al.*, "Land grabbing in Latin America and the Caribbean viewed from broader international perspectives," U.N. Food and Agriculture Organization, www.tni.org/sites/www.tni.org/files/download/borras_franco_kay__spoor_land_grabs_in_latam__caribbean_nov_2011.pdf.

91. *Ibid.*, p. 151.

92. Shane Romig, "Argentina limits farmland foreign ownership," Gateway to South America, Dec. 12, 2011, www.gatewaytosouthamerica-newsblog.com/2011/12/29/argentina-limits-farmland-foreign-ownership. Also see Alejandro J. del Corro, "China Invests billions in South American Farmland Improvements," Gateway to South America Newsblog, July, 19, 2011, www.gatewaytosouthamerica-newsblog.com/2011/07/19/china-to-invest-billions-in-south-american-farmland-improvements/.

93. "CCM International: Chongqing Grain Group Seeking More Overseas Investment in China," *China Business News*, April 14, 2012, www.cnchemicals.com/PressRoom/PressRoomDetail_w_1012.html.

94. *Ibid.*

95. Eugenio Aleman, presentation at "Intellectual Capital Conference 2012," Legg Mason Investment Council, May 2, 2012.

96. "A Numbers Game: Can Argentina's Government and Its Agricultural Sector Find Common Ground?" Knowledge@Wharton, Dec. 14, 2011, www.wharton.universia.net/index.cfm?fa=printArticle&ID=2146&language=english.

97. Mauricio Mesquia Moreira, interview.

98. Paulo Winterstein, "China's Chery Will Build Cars in Brazil," *The Wall Street Journal*, July 19, 2011.

99. "Brazil's trade policy: Seeking protection," *The Economist*, Jan. 14, 2012. The magazine called the tax increase "an unusually blatant act of protectionism" that probably violates WTO rules.

100. Joey Wang, "Chery: Brazil supply chain to aid local production," *Car News China*, April 9, 2012.

101. Ricardo Leopoldo, "Fiesp wants to exclude China as market economy," *O Estado de Sao Paulo*, Feb. 12, 2011, http://economia.estadao.com.br/noticias/economia,fiesp-quer-excluir-china-como-economia-de-mercado,55934,0.htm.

102. Osvaldo Rosales, "People's Republic of China and Latin America and the Caribbean: Ushering in a new era in the economic and trade relationship," Economic Commission for Latin America and the Caribbean, June 2011, pp. 29-32.

103. Peter Hakim, "A U.S.-Brazil Respect Deficit," *Los Angeles Times*, April 9, 2012, http://articles.latimes.com/2012/apr/09/opinion/la-oe-hakim-brazil-policy-20120409.

104. For background, see Brian Beary, "Brazil on the Rise," *CQ Global Researcher*, June 7, 2011, pp. 263-290.

105. Moises Naim, "Rousseff should leave the US with a trade deal," *Financial Times*, April 8, 2012, www.ft.com/intl/cms/s/0/9311c644-7da4-11e1-bfa5-00144feab49a.html#axzz1vWVaHk6t.

106. Hakim, *op. cit.*

BIBLIOGRAPHY

Selected Sources
Books

Ellis, R. Evan, *China in Latin America*, Lynne Rienner Publishers, 2009.

An assistant professor of National Security at the National Defense University in Washington — an expert on China's presence in Latin America — provides an acute, but not alarmist, analysis.

Gallagher, Kevin, and Roberto Porzecanski, *The Dragon in the Room: China and the Future of Latin American Industrialization*, Stanford University Press, 2010.

An associate professor of International Relations at Boston University (Gallagher) and a pre-doctoral fellow at the Global Development and Environment Institute at Tufts University analyze the economic threat China poses for Latin America.

Hearn, Adrian H., and Jose Luis León-Manríquez, *China Engages Latin America: Tracing the Trajectory*, Lynne Rienner Publishers, 2011.

A University of Sydney sociology professor (Hearn) and a professor of international and East Asian studies at the Metropolitan Autonomous University in Mexico argue that China has a coherent strategy in Latin America but the region's governments have no such plan.

Moreno, Luis Alberto, *The Decade of Latin America and the Caribbean: The Real Opportunity*, Inter-American Development Bank, 2011.

The president of the regional development bank offers a broad-based assessment of the most important trends buffeting the region.

Roett, Riordan, and Guadalupe Paz, eds., *China's Expansion into the Western Hemisphere*, Brookings Institution, 2008.

Drawing on lessons from China's presence in Africa and Southeast Asia, scholars examine what China's dramatic arrival in Latin America means for the region.

Subramanian, Arvind, *Eclipse: Living in the Shadow of China's Economic Dominance*, Peter G. Peterson Institute for International Economics, 2011.

A senior fellow at the Peterson Institute for International Economics says China's global dominance could soon match the reach of the British Empire at its peak, a transition that is further along than generally acknowledged.

Weitzman, Hal, *Latin Lessons: How South America Stopped Listening to the United States and Started Prospering*, John Wiley & Sons, 2012.

A *Financial Times* Andes correspondent says the United States must become a team player if it is to remain relevant in rapidly changing Latin America.

Articles

Romero, Simon, "With Aid and Migrants, China Expands Its Presence in a South American Nation," *The New York Times*, April 11, 2011, www.nytimes.com/2011/04/11/world/americas/11suriname.html.

Drawing on some of its $3 trillion in international reserves, China is building infrastructure and investing in Suriname.

Sharma, Ruchir, "Bearish on Brazil: The Commodity Slowdown and the End of the Magic Moment," *Foreign Affairs*, May-June 2012, www.foreignaffairs.com/articles/137599/ruchir-sharma/bearish-on-brazil.

A Morgan Stanley fund manager and financial columnist says that as the commodity boom winds down Brazil should open its manufacturing sector to global competition.

Turzi, Mariano, "The Soybean Republic," *Yale Journal of International Relations*, Spring-Summer 2011, www.ucema.edu.ar/conferencias/download/2011/10.14CP.pdf.

A political science professor at Torcuato Di Tella University in Buenos Aires says soybean growers should create a cartel to protect themselves from fluctuating prices.

Reports and Studies

Arnson, Cynthia, Mark Mohr and Riordan Roett, eds., "Enter the Dragon: China's Presence in Latin America," *Woodrow Wilson International Center for Scholars*, www.wilsoncenter.org/sites/default/files/EnterDragonFinal.pdf.

Seven leading scholars discuss the rapidly evolving economic and political relationship between China and Latin America.

Ellis, R. Evan, "The Expanding Chinese Footprint in Latin America: New Challenges for China, and Dilemmas for the U.S.," *Asie Visions 49*, Institut Francais des Relations Internationales, February 2012, www.ifri.org/?page=contribution-detail&id=7014.

A report by a Brussels-based think tank examines the implications of Chinese wealth transforming Latin American infrastructure.

Mesquita Moreira, Mauricio, "The Big Idea — China and Latin America: Manufacturing — Shuttered," *China Economic Quarterly*, September 2011.

Latin American policymakers should embrace the region's comparative advantage in natural resources rather than trying to compete with China's manufacturing juggernaut.

For More Information

Centro de Estudios China-México, Universidad Nacional Autónoma de México; Av. Universidad 3000, CU, Circuito Escolar Edificio B de la Facultad de Economía, C.P. 04510, México, D.F.; +52 56222195; www.economia.unam.mx/cechimex/. A comprehensive source for Mexican research about China.

China-Brazil Business Council, Seção Brasileira, Rua Araújo Porto Alegre, 36, sala 1201, Rio de Janeiro RJ 20030-902; +55 21 32.12.43.50; cebc@cebc.org.br. A nonprofit organization that promotes Brazil-China trade and investment.

China Institutes of Contemporary International Relations, A-2 Wanshousi, Haidian District, Beijing 100081, China; +10 68.41.86.40; www.cicir.ac.cn/english/. A think tank affiliated with China's intelligence community that has 11 institutes and 10 research entities staffed by 150 research professionals.

Chinese Academy of Social Sciences, Institute of Latin-American Studies, 5, Jianguomennei Dajie, Beijing 100732, China; +10 85.19.59.99; www.cass.net.cn. A key hub for China-based research on Latin America.

The Heritage Foundation, 214 Massachusetts Ave, N.E., Washington DC, 20002-4999; 202-546-4400; www.heritage.org/places/asia-and-the-pacific/china. A conservative think tank that tracks China's growing economic, military and diplomatic capabilities. Maintains an interactive map that tracks China's global investments at: www.heritage.org/research/projects/china-global-investment-tracker-interactive-map.

Institute of the Americas, China-Latin America Program, 10111 N. Torrey Pines Rd., La Jolla, CA 92037; 858-453-5560; www.iamericas.org/en/programs/china-latin-america. An independent think tank, dedicated to enabling dialogue among Western Hemisphere leaders, that is working with the China Institutes of Contemporary International Relations (above) to help strengthen relationships between China and Latin America.

Inter-American Dialogue, China and Latin America Program, 1211 Connecticut Ave., N.W., Suite 510, Washington, DC 20036; 202-822-9002; www.thedialogue.org. Engages and informs academics, policymakers and private-sector leaders on evolving themes in China-Latin America relations.

Voices From Abroad:

JOAO PEDRO FLECHA DE LIMA

Operations Director for Brazil, Huawei, Brazil

A learning curve

"They [Brazilian businessmen] are starting to get China, but still at a very preliminary level. Very few get to go there and visit the country, to spend time to understand the culture, the tradition, the history, the business practices."

The Washington Post, September 2011

GUSTAVO CISNEROS

Chairman, Cisneros Group, Venezuela

A second option

"What they're [Chinese government investments in Latin America] doing is gigantic, but it's only a small part. They have to put those dollars to work. I think and I believe they want to do it in Latin America because they believe in Latin America."

Bloomberg, September 2011

HONG LEI

Spokesperson, Chinese Foreign Ministry

Parallel paths

"China and Latin America have innovated ways of cooperation, realized rapid development of trade cooperation and robustly boosted their respective economic growth. . . . Trade and investment are equally valued when developing China-Latin trade relations."

Xinhua news agency (China), September 2011

ANTONIO BARROS DE CASTRO

Former President, Brazilian Development Bank, Brazil

A different continent

"They [Chinese businessmen] know that here they have to work mostly with Brazilian laborers, the government has made that clear. In places like Africa, they resolved work force problems by ignoring the problem, by working with Chinese workers."

The Associated Press, May 2011

DAVID FLEISCHER

Professor of Political Science, University of Brasília, Brazil

Filling a void

"After [George W.] Bush took over, Latin America was totally forgotten. A lot of Latin Americans thought that was great: better to be forgotten than be taken care of too much. The U.S. opened a void, and the Chinese came right in. . . . There are cases of Chinese imports wiping out Brazilian firms, then the Chinese came to Brazil and recruited the unemployed shoemakers and brought them to China."

Los Angeles Times, July 2011

ERNESTO FERNANDEZ TABOADA

Director, Argentine-Chinese Chamber of Production, Industry and Commerce Argentina

For the long term

"For China, this is a strategic, long-term investment. They're thinking in the future, not just in the moment.

These oil investments, for example, are for 15 to 20 years."

The Associated Press, June 2011

CHEN PING

Political Counselor Chinese Embassy Venezuela

Mutual help

"Venezuela has what we need. And we also have what they need, for example technology. . . . Therefore we can help each other mutually."

Los Angeles Times, June 2011

JULIO GUZMAN

Deputy Industry Minister Peru

Strengthening further

"From the step we have taken with the free trade agreement [with China], we are going to strengthen our relations in other areas, such as international cooperation, technical assistance and investment, and we look forward to diversifying exports of value-added products."

Xinhua news agency (China), November 2011

La Prensa, Panama/Arcadio Esquivel

RUBENS BARBOSA

Former Ambassador to the United States, Brazil

A principal partner

"With trade, we have a problem because the aggressiveness of Chinese companies is very strong. But the government still has a lot of interest in these relations with China. China is now the principal partner of Brazil."

The Associated Press, June 2011

13

State Capitalism

Jason McLure

AFP/Getty Images/Roosevelt Cássio

Some of the 4,270 workers dismissed by Brazilian aircraft manufacturer Embraer demonstrate in front of the city hall in Sao Jose dos Campos on March 11, 2009. Like workers elsewhere who lost their jobs during the 2008-2009 worldwide recession, the Embraer employees demanded that the company be nationalized.

From *The CQ Researcher*, May 15, 2012.

China's Huawei Technologies Co. Ltd. is among the world's most successful telecom equipment firms. Founded in 1987 with only $2,500 by Ren Zhengfei, a former director of a People's Liberation Army telecom research center, Huawei didn't make its first overseas sale until 1997.

But by 2010, the Shenzen-based company was the second-largest player — after Sweden's Ericsson — in the $78.6 billion global market for telecommunications network infrastructure. In 2011, Huawei had 110,000 employees and about $31 billion in revenues.[1]

However, Huawei is different than its Western competitors. Designated as a "national champion" by the Chinese government, Huawei has greatly benefited from easy access to government resources. Its customers — from Brazil to South Africa — can borrow from a $30 billion line of credit at the state-owned China Development Bank, which offers two-year grace periods on repayments and interest rates as low as 4 percent.[2] Huawei also receives tens of millions of dollars a year in research funding from the government.[3]

Such hand-in-glove relationships that Huawei and other quasi-private companies enjoy with the government helps explain the sudden rise of Chinese multinational companies on the world stage. It's also emblematic of the economic model known as state capitalism, in which the state owns or controls many of a country's largest economic entities and operates them, ultimately, for its own political advantage.

State capitalism is not new, but China's historic success along with the strong recent economic performance of Russia and several Persian

World's Freest Economies Are Hong Kong and Singapore

The two Chinese city-states have the most economic freedom, along with Australia, New Zealand and Switzerland, according to the conservative, pro-free-market Heritage Foundation's Index of Economic Freedom. The United States, Canada and Northern Europe are considered "mostly free," while China, Russia, India and Brazil are "mostly unfree." Countries rank high on the index if they have strong protections for property rights, low rates of corruption, efficient regulatory agencies and are open to global trade.

Levels of Economic Freedom, 2012

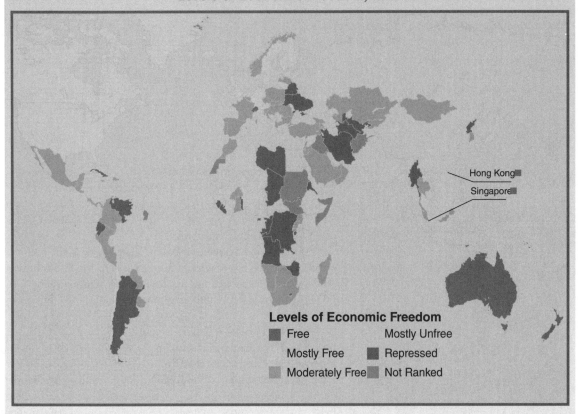

Source: "2012 Index of Economic Freedom," Heritage Foundation, 2012, www.heritage.org/index/ranking. Map by Lewis Agrell

Gulf states has renewed interest in the hybrid economic model.[4] The ongoing global financial crisis, attributed by many to the excesses of unfettered Western-style free-market capitalism, have further piqued interest in state-controlled economies.

While the economies of many industrialized Western nations contracted between 2008 and 2010, China's exploded, rising at an average of 9.7 percent per year.[5]

The country's equally breathtaking economic growth over the past three decades has lifted hundreds of millions of people out of poverty and into the middle class and set the stage for a new battle of ideas about how countries should run their economies.

As the economic failures of communist systems became apparent in the 1970s, U.S.-style free-market capitalism and democracy emerged triumphant. Large state-owned companies across Western Europe and Canada were privatized, and communism collapsed in the Soviet Union and Eastern Europe under the weight of its economic failures.[6]

In 1992, political scientist Francis Fukuyama famously argued in *The End of History* that representative democracy and liberal capitalism not only had defeated communism but also were the endpoint of centuries of clashes over political and economic ideologies.[7] Scholars such as Richard Barnet and John Cavanagh foresaw privately held corporations dwarfing the power of governments and controlling the global flow of money, goods and information.[8]

But Fukuyama and others did not foresee the rise of state capitalism and its potential impact on free markets and free politics. Instead of corporations subsuming the state, the reverse occurred. Governments in China, the Persian Gulf, Russia and other countries would develop economic systems that allowed their companies to grow and participate in world markets, but in a way that allowed the state to control major corporate decisions. In many cases, such as in China, Singapore and Russia, state capitalism was used to entrench authoritarian

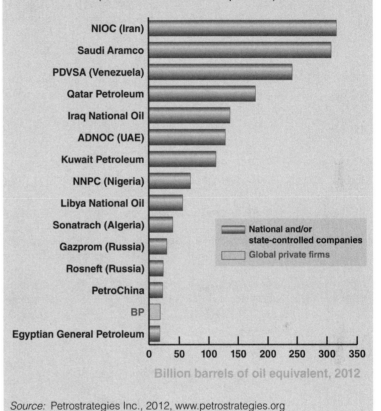

State Companies Control Oil, Gas Reserves

Of the world's 15 companies with the largest proven oil and/or gas reserves, only one is privately owned. About 96 percent of oil and gas reserves held by the world's 20 largest oil and gas entities are held by state-owned oil companies.

Owners of the World's Largest Oil and Gas Reserves, 2012
(in billion barrels of oil equivalent)

Legend:
- National and/or state-controlled companies
- Global private firms

Categories (top to bottom): NIOC (Iran), Saudi Aramco, PDVSA (Venezuela), Qatar Petroleum, Iraq National Oil, ADNOC (UAE), Kuwait Petroleum, NNPC (Nigeria), Libya National Oil, Sonatrach (Algeria), Gazprom (Russia), Rosneft (Russia), PetroChina, BP, Egyptian General Petroleum

X-axis: 0, 50, 100, 150, 200, 250, 300, 350

Billion barrels of oil equivalent, 2012

Source: Petrostrategies Inc., 2012, www.petrostrategies.org

governments. But democracies — such as Brazil, India and Indonesia — also have adopted some statist economic practices.

State capitalism is practiced differently around the globe. China is now the worlds' second-largest economy — after the United States — after developing a manufacturing export colossus. The oil-rich Gulf monarchies have used oil windfalls to buy up foreign assets and build "national champions" in industries ranging from television to airlines to logistics. Russia's Gazprom has been used as a lever in political disagreements with European

nations that rely on its gas exports and to purchase — and silence — domestic media outlets that criticize the government.

State capitalism's strength is evidenced in the growth of both state-owned companies, such as the United Arab Emirates' DP World, and privately held, state-aligned companies such as Huawei. Such companies have capitalized on Western technology, massive government financial backing and a newly educated workforce to challenge Western multinationals — and not just in emerging markets but also in the United States, Japan and Western Europe.

Corporate Spying by Russia and China 'Pervasive'

Western countries are warned to expect more espionage.

Three employees of American Superconductor Corp. (AMSC), a Massachusetts-based company that makes software to run wind turbines, recently climbed to the top of a shaft in a giant turbine in China's Gobi Desert. The turbine had been manufactured by the Sinovel Wind Group, a Chinese company that was once AMSC's biggest customer.

AMSC had sent the three men to China to find out why its software had failed to shut down the turbine at the end of a testing period several weeks earlier and why Sinovel had suddenly stopped buying new AMSC turbine controllers.

After sending a copy of the code from the turbine's computer to a company lab, AMSC discovered that Sinovel was using a stolen version of its software, according to *Bloomberg Businessweek*.[1]

The theft of corporate and trade secrets by China and Russia is pervasive and openly facilitated by the closely intertwined relationships between spy agencies and businesses in both countries, according to a 2011 report by U.S. intelligence agencies. And while corporate espionage is now increasingly conducted in cyberspace, much spying is still done the old-fashioned way, by people on the ground with access to information sources.

"China's intelligence services, as well as private companies and other entities, frequently seek to exploit Chinese citizens or persons with family ties to China who can use their insider access to corporate networks to steal trade secrets using removable media devices or e-mail," the report said.[2]

Russia's intelligence service not only engages in spying to help the country economically but also has been quite open about it.

"Intelligence . . . aims at supporting the process of modernization of our country and creating the optimal conditions for the development of its science and technology," said Mikhail Fradkov, director of Russia's SVR, the foreign intelligence successor to the KGB, in December 2010.[3] Six months earlier, 10 Russian spies trying to collect economic and technology information had been arrested in the United States. They were later returned to Russia as part of a spy swap.[4]

In the United States, FBI agents in July 2011 arrested a California couple accused of participating in a decade-long effort to steal trade secrets from Dupont Co. The investigation led the Justice Department to file charges against China's Pangang Group, the first time the United States has brought criminal charges against a foreign state-owned company.[5] And in 2010, David Yen Lee, a chemist with Minnesota-based Valspar Corp., pleaded guilty to the theft of trade secrets after downloading 160 secret formulas for paints and coatings before leaving for a job with a Chinese paint company.

China's so-called Project 863, launched in 1986, offers funding and advice to Chinese citizens on how to steal high-level technologies from foreign companies to help narrow China's gap in fields such as biotechnology and computers. In December, a Chinese scientist was sentenced to seven years in a U.S. prison after pleading guilty to stealing secrets from Dow AgroSciences and Cargill Inc. and passing it on to Project 863.

Rapid and sustained economic growth in state capitalist countries has lured imitators elsewhere in the developing world, from Ethiopia to Vietnam. "We're coming to the end of a historical period when the liberal capitalist model has been extremely dominant worldwide," says Mitchell A. Orenstein, a political scientist at the School of Advanced International Studies at Johns Hopkins University in Washington. "The state capitalist model is ascendant."

The 2008 global financial crisis, widely seen as the result of deregulation of the financial markets, hastened that shift. In the face of a worldwide recession, governments took on a larger role in running both their economies and private corporations. Even the U.S.

Estimates on how much economic espionage is costing U.S. industries in lost business and jobs range so widely — from $2 billion to $400 billion or more a year — as to be meaningless, said the intelligence report, reflecting the scarcity of data and the variety of methods used to calculate those losses. Cargill alone says it lost $12 million due to information recently stolen from the company.[6]

And the United States is hardly the only victim. Germany estimates its companies lose at least $28 billion a year to economic espionage, while South Korea puts the toll at up to $82 billion. A government survey of 625 Japanese manufacturing firms in 2007 found that 35 percent had reported some form of loss — more than 60 percent of the leaks involved China.[7]

Western companies should brace for additional threats, intelligence experts say, as more work is shifted to online networks and more data is stored through cloud computing.

"China and Russia will remain aggressive and capable collectors of sensitive U.S. economic information and technologies, particularly in cyberspace," the U.S. counterintelligence report says. "Both will almost certainly continue to deploy significant resources and a wide array of tactics to acquire this information from U.S. sources, motivated by the desire to achieve economic, strategic, and military parity with the United States."[8]

— *Jason McLure*

Sinovel Wind Group, a Chinese state-run company that manufactured these wind turbines at an offshore wind farm near Shanghai, was alleged to have stolen software from the Massachusetts-based American Superconductor Corp., according to Bloomberg Businessweek. Corporate espionage is often facilitated by state capitalist governments to benefit state-run companies.

[1]Michael Riley and Ashlee Vance, "Inside the Chinese Boom in Corporate Espionage," *Bloomberg Businessweek*, March 15, 2012, www.businessweek .com/articles/2012-03-14/inside-the-chinese-boom-in-corporate-espionage.

[2]"Foreign Spies Stealing US Economic Secrets in Cyberspace," Office of the National Counterintelligence Executive, October 2011, www.ncix.gov/ publications/reports/fecie_all/index.php.

[3]"Cyber Theft of Corporate Intellectual Property: The Nature of the Threat," *Economist Intelligence Unit*, 2012, www.boozallen.com/ media/file/Cyber-Espionage-Brochure.pdf.

[4] Mary Beth Sheridan and Andrew Higgins, "U.S. and Russia complete Spy Swap," *The Washington Post*, July 10, 2010, www.washingtonpost .com/wp-dyn/content/article/2010/07/09/AR2010070901956.html.

[5]Justin Scheck and Evan Perez, "FBI Traces Trail of Spy Ring to China," *The Wall Street Journal*, March 10, 2012, http://online.wsj.com/article/ SB10001424052970203961204577266892884130620.html.

[6]"Chinese Scientist Huang Kexue Jailed for Trade Theft," BBC News, Dec. 11, 2011, www.bbc.co.uk/news/business-16297237.

[7]"Foreign Spies Stealing US Economic Secrets in Cyberspace," *op. cit.*

[8]*Ibid.*

government — for a time — became the largest shareholder in General Motors, Citigroup and AIG. It also approved $787 billion in economic stimulus spending and authorized another $700 billion to purchase or insure troubled financial assets. In an effort to spur commercial bank lending, the Federal Reserve bought hundreds of billions in U.S. treasury bonds.[9] In the

U.K., banking giants RBS, Lloyds TSB and HBOS were all bailed out by the government and partially nationalized. In France, automobile giants Renault SA and Peugeot-Citroen survived only with the help of a $7.8 billion loan from the government.

Still, large government interventions in the United States, Europe, Japan and other market economies were

Getty Images/Bloomberg/Fabrice Dimier

Protesters in Paris call for nationalization of the country's banks on March 19, 2009. During the global financial crisis of 2008-2009 — widely seen as resulting from excesses in Western-style capitalism — many employees facing layoffs demanded that their governments take a greater role in running private corporations.

not intended to replace free-market capitalism but to save it. Major political parties in those countries largely agreed that industrial and financial companies that came under government-control during the crisis should be returned to private investors once stabilized.[10]

In mainland China, however, 37 of the 40 largest companies are owned outright by the government.[11] About 80 percent of the value of China's stock markets represent majority state-owned companies, according to research by *The Economist*, based on data from *Fortune* magazine and Deutsche Bank. In Russia the government's share is 62 percent and in Brazil, 38 percent.[12] (*See graph, p. 325.*)

The state's greater role in these economies allowed their governments to move much more quickly to head off the economic crisis. "In Brazil and China they can do fiscal stimulus very quickly," says Aldo Musacchio, a Mexican adviser to state-owned companies in Latin America who is also a professor at Harvard Business School. "They just tell state-owned companies to build stuff."

Unlike the stodgy, inefficient government-owned firms of past eras — often the repositories for political cronies — today's giant state-run companies are more likely to be professionally managed, globally competitive titans, says Musacchio. State-owned China Mobile, for example, has

more cellular phone subscribers than Verizon Wireless, AT&T, T-Mobile and Sprint combined.[13]

Meanwhile skyrocketing oil prices have led to windfall revenues for petroleum exporters with nationalized oil and gas resources. That wealth has helped to finance the global growth of state enterprises.

Today, 10 state-owned oil and gas companies have larger reserves than Exxon Mobil, the world's largest private oil company.[14] In addition, oil-rich states have made several splashy overseas real estate acquisitions: London's Harrods' department store is now owned by the government of Qatar, and New York's Chrysler Building is 90 percent owned by Abu Dhabi.

Yet state capitalism also creates problems. As China's cheap financing for Huawei's customers demonstrates, state capitalism tests the architecture on which global trade is built: the assumption that companies will compete on a level playing field.

"For the global trading system, one of the possible threats may be unfair advantages over non-state owned enterprises, such as the government's backing in financial resources or protection of market shares," says Li-Wen Lin, a Taiwanese corporate governance scholar at Columbia University in New York City.

Critics point out that even the most nimble state capitalist economies have not been able to innovate new products — largely because resources and talent are channeled to risk-averse government bureaucracies.

"To operationalize a new concept in a commercial setting, they don't do that very well, they're much better at acquiring the blueprints somewhere else," says Stefan Halper, a political scientist at the University of Cambridge in the U.K. "The mark of a highly mature capitalist economy is where wealthy individual investors can see the excitement and prospects of new innovation to invest in somebody like [Facebook's] Mark Zuckerberg."

State capitalism — often used to reinforce authoritarian governments — also can be particularly vulnerable to political shocks. Russia's stock market dropped 9 percent in one week after then-Prime Minister Vladimir Putin's rule was challenged by mass protests in December.[15]

State-run companies' links to governments also can limit growth prospects. Huawei missed out on telecom contracts in the United States and Australia last year over concerns that its links to the Chinese government could facilitate electronic eavesdropping.[16] Mongolia is considering capping the percentage foreign state-owned firms can purchase in local companies, after China's Aluminum Corp. announced plans to buy a Mongolian coal mine.[17] In 2006 DP World was forced to withdraw a bid to manage six major U.S. ports amid congressional concerns over national security, and China National Offshore Oil Co. dropped its bid to buy the U.S. oil company Unocal in 2005 for similar reasons.

Finally, state capitalism in China and other countries is seen as a means of supporting authoritarian governments that systematically violate democratic and human rights.

Unlike European social democracies, in which trade unions play a key role in governance and government-ownership of certain economic assets in order to provide political stability through wealth redistribution, state-run capitalist economies typically provide few labor rights or social safety nets. Because it is not a democracy, China does not have to address short-term discontent like Germany does. China can funnel profits toward longer-term investment goals, even at the expense of domestic living standards.[18]

As economists, political analysts and legal scholars survey state capitalism's rise, here are some of the questions they are examining:

Is state capitalism better at avoiding economic crises?

It was April 2009, and the wreckage of the financial crisis was still

State Firms Dominate Stock Markets in China, Russia

State-owned companies represent a majority of the value of the stock markets in China and Russia and nearly 40 percent of Brazil's.

Share of Value on MSCI* National Stockmarket Index, June 2011
(Percentage of market's total value)

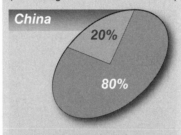

China
20%
80%

Russia
38%
62%

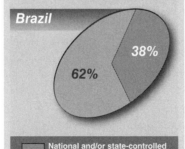

Brazil
38%
62%

National and/or state-controlled companies

Private firms

* A New York-based financial firm that creates indices for global stock markets.
Source: "The Visible Hand," The Economist, Jan. 21, 2012, www.economist.com/node/21542931

working its way through the economies of many countries. In the United States, the Dow Jones Industrial Average had lost a third of its value from the previous year. Unemployment was spiking across the industrialized world, and European Union (EU) member nations alone had committed $4 trillion to bail out the continent's banks.[19]

Against this backdrop, China's Vice Minister of Foreign Affairs He Yafei met with a group of Western academics in New York. Yafei had a provocative question: "Now that the free market has failed, what do you think is the proper role for the state in the economy?"[20]

The Chinese official had reason to sound smug. After all, the collapse of the global economy had been precipitated by Western banks borrowing heavily and making huge bets on opaque and lightly regulated financial products called derivatives, a practice China's state-owned banks had largely avoided.[21] Though Chinese unemployment was rising, a $586 billion stimulus — announced by the government less than two months after the collapse of the overleveraged American investment bank Lehman Brothers — was already pouring money into its economy.[22]

Analysts were soon touting China's resilience — and that of other state-run economies. "After the financial crisis, the countries that are doing the best out there economically — Saudi Arabia and the states of the Gulf, Russia and, most importantly, China. All of them share some interesting things in common," Ian

Fifty-four Chinese bullet trains, such as these used on a high-speed rail link between Beijing and Shanghai, were recalled because of "flaws," said state-owned train manufacturer China CNR Corp. in August 2011. Critics say state-run companies lack accountability.

Bremmer, president of the Eurasia Group political risk consultancy, said in a speech at London's Chatham House think tank in 2010.[23] "The state is the principal economic actor in those countries, and they use markets for ultimately political purposes." Indeed, the Chinese government was able to channel stimulus spending to businesses much more quickly than the United States because of its control over banks and industrial companies.

"The Chinese Communist Party, as the single-ruling party, has established comprehensive institutions to control the political and economic spheres," says Lin, the Taiwanese researcher. "This gives Chinese leaders tremendous power to channel resources to where they want."

By comparison, the U.S. government in 2008 authorized $700 billion to encourage private banks to increase lending and stimulate the stalled economy. Instead, many of the banks chose not to lend the money but to pay down debt, acquire other businesses or invest in government securities.[24]

"In the U.S. they were trying to get the banks to lend, but [the banks] were using it to buy Treasury bills," says Harvard's Musacchio. "In Brazil and China the stimulus happened very fast. Having state-owned banks that can deploy money really fast can help."

While there is broad agreement that state capitalist economies — in particular China — fared relatively well during the 2008-2009 financial crisis and have performed well during the current European debt crisis, there is no guarantee such economies will avoid future crises. Indeed, some experts argue that the boom in infrastructure and property spending in China after the financial crisis is inflating an economic bubble that may burst, with dire consequences.

"China today has the characteristics of a truly great bubble," Edward Chancellor, an asset manager at the British investment firm GMO, wrote in London's *Financial Times* last year. "The value of the housing stock is set to exceed 350 percent of GDP this year, the same level as Japan's at the height of its [1991] real estate bubble. Construction accounts for around one-quarter of economic activity in China, which by coincidence is the same level that Ireland attained before its dramatic implosion.[25]

"Ponzi finance proliferates in China," he continued. "Wasteful infrastructure projects are funded with bank loans and land grants from local governments, which themselves depend on land sales for the bulk of their income."[26]

Russia likewise rebounded quickly from its recession in 2009, when its economy shrank 7.8 percent, to grow by about 4 percent over the next two years, buoyed in part by rising oil prices. Still, the country's rapid growth — the economy doubled in size over the past decade — led the IMF to warn in April that it faces the risk of a "credit bubble" due to the blistering pace of consumer lending.[27]

China's Sovereign Wealth Tops $1.4 Trillion

China has by far more sovereign wealth than any of the world's top 15 funds — more than $1.4 trillion spread among three non-petroleum-based funds. The two biggest individual funds, in Abu Dhabi and Norway, are based on oil revenues.

The 15-Largest Sovereign Wealth Funds
(by assets under management, May 2012)

Country	Fund Name	Assets ($Billions)	Date Created	Origin
UAE — Abu Dhabi	Abu Dhabi Investment Authority	$627	1976	Oil
Norway	Government Pension Fund — Global	$611	1990	Oil
China	SAFE Investment Co.	$567.9*	1997	Non-Commodity
Saudi Arabia	SAMA Foreign Holdings	$532.8	n/a	Oil
China	China Investment Corp.	$439.6	2007	Non-Commodity
Kuwait	Kuwait Investment Authority	$296	1953	Oil
China — Hong Kong	Hong Kong Monetary Authority Investment Portfolio	$293.3	1993	Non-Commodity
Singapore	Government of Singapore Investment Corp.	$247.5	1981	Non-Commodity
Singapore	Temasek Holdings	$157.2	1974	Non-Commodity
Russia	National Welfare Fund	$149.7**	2008	Oil
China	National Social Security Fund	$134.5	2000	Non-Commodity
Qatar	Qatar Investment Authority	$100	2005	Oil
Australia	Australian Future Fund	$80	2006	Non-Commodity
UAE — Dubai	Investment Corp. of Dubai	$70	2006	Oil
Libya	Libyan Investment Authority	$65	2006	Oil

Estimate

** *Includes the oil stabilization fund of Russia.*

Source: Sovereign Wealth Fund Institute, www.swfinstitute.org/fund-rankings

Indeed, when a single entity — the state — controls the courts, the government treasury and major companies and banks, problems can be hidden longer, analysts say. But that doesn't mean they'll never surface, even in an economy as robust as China's.

"China's a bubble; I just think it's a very big bubble," said Bremmer, during his address at Chatham House. "The disadvantage of free-market systems, even regulated free-market systems, is that you have massive amounts of volatility in these bubbles that occur. People get hurt. The disadvantage of state capitalist systems is that you smooth that out, at the expense of a much larger bubble down the road."

Is state capitalism an effective model for developing nations?

State capitalist economies have demonstrated they can eliminate poverty. Between 1992 and 2008 China lifted nearly 600 million people out of extreme poverty — defined as living on less than $1.25 a day. Vietnam, another state capitalist economy, reduced the portion of its citizens living in extreme poverty from 64 percent in 1993 to 17 percent in 2008. Russia started from a higher base, but under Putin, the percentage of Russians living on less than $5 a day declined from 41 percent 2001 to 12 percent in 2009.[28]

Those figures outpace improvements in sub-Saharan Africa and parts of Latin America, where the so-called Washington consensus — the leading developmental model espousing liberal democracy and free markets — lifted fewer people out of poverty over the same period.

"For bringing countries out of extreme poverty we know that authoritarian capitalism has been more successful than democracy and liberal capitalism," says Azar Gat, an Israeli political scientist at Tel Aviv University. "We know in some stages it has been very effective."

Wei-Wei Zhang, a professor at the Geneva School of Diplomacy in Switzerland, says China's pragmatic approach to economic development offers several lessons for developing countries. First, he says, developing countries should reform gradually rather than rapidly privatizing, as post-Soviet Russia did in the early 1990s under American tutelage. That experiment ended with fire-sales of state assets to politically connected businessmen, a fraying social safety net and a boom in organized crime.

Secondly, Zhang says, before implementing economic reforms nationwide, countries should experiment with them on a small scale, as China did with its free-trade zones in southern cities in the 1980s. Chinese reforms also followed a certain sequence: easy reforms, followed by more difficult ones; rural reforms before urban; changes in coastal areas followed by inland, and economic reforms before political ones.

"In terms of eradicating poverty and helping the poor and the marginalized, the Chinese model, however imperfect, has worked far more effectively than what can be called the American model," he wrote in the *International Herald Tribune*.[29]

Even as it has joined the ranks of middle-income countries, the Chinese government is showing it can adapt to new challenges. Lin, the Taiwanese corporate governance researcher, says China is likely to reform its state-owned companies by hiring more outside directors, reducing fraud and adding more professional managers. "These changes do not require any ownership or political revolution," she says. "Many Westerners may be happy to see such reforms. But . . . if these technical reforms are successful, ultimately making state-owned enterprises efficient and profitable, why does China need to change state capitalism?"

Others say that once countries achieve middle-income status, state capitalism probably won't be so successful at raising living standards. As the population becomes wealthier, it will demand greater accountability as well as labor and environmental protections, thereby undermining state control — both politically and economically.

"China has proven it can move to this point with the low level of regulation that it has, but it hasn't entered the 20th century in Western terms," says Michael Santoro, a management professor who studies China at Rutgers Business School in New Jersey. "I can guarantee you they're not going to continue at this level without better regulation of their economic system: The rule of law, worker safety, the environment. There are so many aspects of China that are going to hold it back from getting to the next level."

In addition, say critics, state-run companies are unlikely to be able to innovate and produce new products and inventions that drive growth. Government-directed capitalism works when it is buoyed by revenues from oil or other natural resources, as in Russia or the Middle East, or is geared mainly toward producing products developed elsewhere, as in China and Vietnam.

China now accounts for 13 percent of global spending on research and development; the United States accounts for 34 percent. No Chinese company is among the top 20 R&D spenders in information technology.[30] More than 75 percent of patents granted in China are known as "utility model" patents — usually not for substantive new inventions or concepts but for products sometimes derided as "junk," according to Dieter Ernst, an economist for the Hawaii-based East-West Center think tank.

Because of barriers to entrepreneurship and research and development investment, "China's innovation policy is not a threat to U.S. leadership in science and technology," Ernst told a congressional commission last year.[31] "The U.S. retains a strong lead in overall innovative capacity, and China still has a long way to go to close the innovation gap."

Liberalizing their economies would help countries like Vietnam and China move beyond making products conceived and designed elsewhere, says Long Le, a professor at the University of Houston's C. T. Bauer College of Business. Yet, such a transition is not inevitable. "It's really hard, once you get politicians in the economy, to get them out," says Le.

Does state capitalism threaten free trade?

As companies in China, Russia and other state capitalist countries have grown, they have become increasingly competitive with Western multinationals across the globe, raising trade tensions, especially if state power is seen as clearly aiding "national champions."

For example:

• In 2006, Royal Dutch Shell was forced to sell a controlling stake in Russia's Sakhalin-2 oil and gas development to state-owned Gazprom at below-market value after months of pressure from Russian environmental regulators — pressure that evaporated once the sale was announced.[32]

• In 2009 state-owned Aluminum Corp. of China, known as Chinalco, tried to buy 18 percent of the Anglo-Australian mining giant Rio Tinto in an effort to assure a reliable supply of metals for China. The deal was scuttled, due in part to Australian opposition to turning over vast swathes of the country's natural resources to the Chinese government.[33]

• In March the United States, European Union and Japan complained to the World Trade Organization (WTO) about China's export restrictions on rare earth metals, which are needed to manufacture high-tech products such as flat-screen televisions, smart phones and hybrid car batteries. Because China produces more than 90 percent of the world's supply of rare earth metals, the move has sharply raised prices for the minerals, while boosting the prospects of China's own domestic technology industry. China has cited environmental risks in curtailing the exports.[34]

Some analysts say state capitalism is incompatible with the global trade architecture established under the WTO in the mid-1990s, before the recent rise of today's state capitalism giants. WTO rules are meant to level the competitive playing field between companies from member countries by restricting government subsidies and requiring members to treat foreign companies operating in their territory the same as domestic companies. China joined the WTO in 2001, while Russia became a member in January.

"The WTO was not set up with the premise of state capitalism, it was set up with the premise of open competition," says Rutgers' Santoro. "It's a walking violation

of international trade law to have state capitalism. It's certainly not what anyone bargained for when China was admitted to the WTO."

However, subsidies for favored industries are not solely the province of state capitalist economies. The WTO has ruled that the United States illegally subsidizes some products, including orange juice, passenger jets and cotton, and the EU, Canada and other free-market democracies have faced similar rulings.[35]

But in many cases China and Russia are doing more than just ensuring that their companies can participate in global markets. "In sectors as diverse as defense, power generation, telecoms, metals, minerals and aviation, a growing number of emerging market governments — not content with simply regulating markets — are now moving to dominate them," Eurasia Group's Bremmer wrote in a 2009 essay.[36]

"By manipulating markets to achieve political ends," he continued, "these governments have upended the assumption that they will no longer interfere in the free flow of ideas, information, people, money, goods and services."[37]

Such economic nationalism leads to political conflict. Xiaonian Xu, an economics professor at the China Europe International Business School in Shanghai, has compared China's economy to that of the tight industry-government links in Chancellor Otto von Bismarck's late 19th-century Germany, which Xu argues laid the groundwork for World War I.[38]

"I really worry about China," said Jeffrey Immelt, General Electric Co.'s chief executive officer, in a 2010 address to Italian businessmen in which he criticized China's protection of its domestic market.[39] "I am not sure that in the end they want any of us to win, or any of us to be successful."

Others say state capitalism does not pose a severe challenge to globalization, largely because state capitalist countries need global markets and investment at least as much as democratic capitalist countries do. They note, for example, that China is now the world's largest exporter and second-largest importer. State capitalists can adapt to international norms when they are forced to do so, they say.

One preliminary success in doing this has been the handling of sovereign wealth funds. In the early 2000s, the growth of such funds raised concerns that these giant

C H R O N O L O G Y

1960s-1970s *With communist and capitalist nations embroiled in the Cold War, a hybrid state capitalist model emerges in the Middle East and Asia.*

1965 Singapore becomes a "developmental state" under President Lee Kuan Yew, welcoming foreign investment but retaining firm control over the economy.

1973 State-owned oil company revenues skyrocket after the Organization of Petroleum Exporting Countries (OPEC) embargoes exports to the United States and its allies, causing world oil prices to quadruple.

1978 Chinese leader Deng Xiaoping initiates economic reforms in China, freeing agriculture from government control and gradually opening the country to global trade.

1980s *Soviet Union collapses; Western countries privatize state companies.*

1981 President Ronald Reagan initiates era of deregulation and lower taxes to spur private-sector growth. . . . British Prime Minister Margaret Thatcher pushes for privatization of state companies; other European countries later follow suit.

1986 Vietnam remains communist but begins to move away from centrally planned economy toward a socialist-oriented market economy.

1989 Berlin Wall falls; communism unravels in Eastern Europe. . . . U.S. scholar Francis Fukuyama asserts in an essay that free markets have permanently vanquished other economic ideologies. . . . China's Communist Party suppresses protesters demanding political reform.

1990s-2006 *Russian free-market reforms result in inequality, volatility and corruption, spurring disillusionment. China continues reforms.*

1991 Soviet Union collapses; new Russian President Boris Yeltsin begins rapid transition to free-market capitalism.

2000 Former KGB agent Vladimir Putin becomes Russian president, moves to limit power of oligarchs and reassert role of state in economy.

2001 After relaxing trade barriers, China joins World Trade Organization, triggering dramatic growth in exports.

2003 Russian oil tycoon Mikhail Khodorkovsky is arrested on tax-fraud charges; he is later convicted and remains in prison. His Yukos oil firm will be swallowed by state-owned Rosneft and Gazprom.

2005 State-owned Chinese oil company CNOOC drops $18.5 billion bid for U.S.-based Unocal after outcry in U.S. Congress.

2006 Amid security concerns, United Arab Emirates' state-owned DP World abandons its bid to manage six major U.S. ports.

2008-Present *Financial crisis and economic recession damage credibility of free-market economies, which experience turmoil, while Saudi Arabia, Russia, China and other state-capitalist economies grow rapidly.*

2008 Financial crisis strikes U.S. and European banks and corporations. . . . United States bails out 220 banks and other companies. . . . Chinese Premier Wen Jiabao credits China's economic success to "both the visible [and] invisible hand."

2009 United States bails out another 600 banks and other companies, including General Motors and Chrysler. . . . China, now Africa's largest trading partner, becomes an economic model for several African countries.

2010 China's economy surpasses Japan's to become world's second-largest. . . . Dilma Rousseff, soon to be Brazil's president, says state-owned enterprises saved Latin America's biggest economy during crisis.

2012 Reelected Russian President Putin vows to expand state businesses into pharmaceutical, information technology, chemical and other industries. . . . Australia bars Chinese firm Huawei from broadband project over security concerns. Argentina nationalizes Spanish-owned oil company YPF.

State Capitalism Flounders in Vietnam

Poor management of state companies is blamed.

For a time, state capitalism made Vietnam an economic poster child for developing countries. Under the Communist Party's so-called *doi moi* economic reforms, agricultural and industrial collectives were abolished in 1986. Spurred by export-oriented factories producing textiles and other low-cost goods, the economy has grown, on average, about 7 percent a year since 1995.

Now the economic party appears to be over. Inflation has spiked above 20 percent per year, real estate prices are in free-fall and government companies are loaded with debt they can't repay.[1]

Long Le, a business professor at the University of Houston, says Vietnam is at a crossroad. The country must decide whether it is "time to transition out of state capitalism," Le says. "In recent years the state enterprises have been poorly run and wasteful, and much of the investment they've received has been invested in non-core areas."

An emblem of that waste is the $1.2 billion skyscraper in Ho Chi Minh City (formerly Saigon) being built by state-owned PetroVietnam, whose 1,732-foot-high PVN Tower headquarters will become the tallest tower in Asia and would dwarf New York's Empire State Building.[2] In the banking sector, one in eight loans is not being repaid, according to Fitch Ratings.[3]

Like other fast-growing East Asian economies, Vietnam kick-started its early development by focusing on winning foreign investment in manufacturing industries, keeping its currency weak to spur export growth and protecting fledgling local industries from foreign competition.

Introducing further market reforms could help rebalance the economy. Yet transitioning from state capitalism to a free market economy may not be easy. Vietnam's per-capita income of $3,300 is less than half of China's, and the country does not have the human resources of some of its neighbors.

The $1.2 billion PVN Tower — a 1,732-foot-high skyscraper being built in Ho Chi Minh City by state-owned PetroVietnam — is a symbol of the wastefulness of Vietnam's faltering state capitalism.

http://nhatkybatdongsan.blogspot.com/

"Unlike Chinese state capitalism, Vietnam doesn't have any national champions [of manufacturing] or state industries that are globally competitive," says Le. "They're trying to follow the model of Singapore and China. But in terms of personnel and structure, they're really lagging behind. The people who run the state enterprises don't have technical or professional degrees, whereas in China or Singapore they have Ivy League degrees. Anybody with talent, either they moonlight or they get out."

Vietnam's state capitalism did help the economy recover from the 2008 financial crisis quickly. Still, it lags far behind nearby Malaysia and Thailand, which have both created much more market-oriented economies over the past decade. Malaysia's income per capita is more than four-times Vietnam's; Thailand's is more than twice as large.

Vietnam hasn't "been able to close the gap with Malaysia and Thailand, whose economic development has been accompanied by greater political freedom," says Le. "In Vietnam the state has increased economic competitiveness, but not at a rate that has allowed them to catch up."

— *Jason McLure*

[1]"Vietnam: Hero to Zero," *The Economist*, March 31, 2012, www.economist.com/node/21551538.

[2]"Vietnam to Build Second Tallest Tower in Asia," *Vietnam+*, July 21, 2010, http://en.vietnamplus.vn/Home/Vietnam-to-build-second-tallest-tower-in-Asia/20107/10769.vnplus.

[3]Jason Folkmanis, "Vietnam Yet to Fix Dire Situation of Weak Banks," *Bloomberg BusinessWeek*, March 13, 2012, www.businessweek.com/news/2012-03-13/vietnam-yet-to-fix-dire-situation-of-weak-banks-imf-says.

government-controlled pools of cash would be used to wield political influence by buying stakes in strategic overseas companies. Those concerns grew in 2007 when China's sovereign wealth fund bought minority stakes in two of the biggest Wall Street investment houses: investment bank Morgan Stanley and private equity giant Blackstone Group.[40]

Yet, in 2008, governments with the largest sovereign wealth funds — including the U.A.E., Kuwait, China, Russia, Qatar, Libya and Singapore — agreed on voluntary principles for how to use the funds. Under the guidelines the funds were to be invested based on economic returns and risk in a way that would help maintain a stable world financial system and in compliance with regulatory and disclosure requirements in foreign countries.[41]

"It basically deals with most of the concerns that people had back then about sovereign wealth funds, their corporate governance and transparency," says Debra Steger, a law professor specializing in international trade at the University of Ottawa.

But the guidelines aren't mandatory and don't govern the international investment activities of state-owned companies like Chinalco. Nor do they address state subsidies or resolve problems such as those encountered by Royal Dutch Shell in Russia or China's hoarding of rare earth minerals.

Experts predict that future trade disputes can be mitigated if governments develop similar multilateral rules on investment by state-owned enterprises, as they've done with sovereign wealth funds. In addition, Western nations concerned about foreign ownership of their natural resources or other assets should make sure to negotiate regulations on transparency and corporate governance before signing investment treaties with China and other state capitalist countries, Steger says.

"They don't necessarily conduct investment exactly the way we do" in Canada, says Steger. However, Canada wants China to invest in developing Canadian oil reserves. "We are going to see more investment from those countries, and that's going to be a good thing for us."

BACKGROUND

Corporate Colonies

Perhaps the most powerful state corporation in history was founded in 1600, when the British crown granted a group of noblemen and merchants — the fabled East India Co. — a monopoly over trade with the East Indies.[42]

What began as a way to pool private capital to undertake trade missions evolved into a de facto appendage of the British state. In 1757 a group of 3,000 East India Co. soldiers under Baron Robert Clive defeated up to 50,000 Bengalis in what is now northern and central India, ousting the Mughal emperor. Clive then appointed his own local administrator, who immediately shuttered factories operated by Britain's French rivals and awarded large new tracts of land to the East India Co. In one fell swoop, one of Asia's largest empires had come under the control of a British company.[43]

The firm's reach eventually extended to East Asia. In 1819 the company purchased Singapore, and in 1843 — in an effort to protect the East India Co.'s opium trade with China — Britain acquired Hong Kong after a joint force of company and government soldiers and warships defeated the Chinese.[44] The company was formally dissolved in 1874, long after its influence had begun to wane.[45] But for more than two centuries Britain's foreign policy in Asia and the Middle East had revolved around what trading privileges the company needed.

Dutch, French, Portuguese and other colonial powers operated similar companies that enjoyed broad governmental backing — ranging from monopoly grants and tariff exemptions to the exercise of military force. Such companies dominated the age of mercantilism, during which European powers tried to horde the greatest amount of gold and silver by discouraging imports through tariffs, acquiring monopoly trade rights over colonies and promoting exports of manufactured goods.

"It is clear that one country can only gain if another country loses," French philosopher Voltaire said in describing the philosophy behind the system.[46]

By the Enlightenment, such views were being challenged, most notably by the British economist Adam Smith. In his classic, *The Wealth of Nations*, published in 1776, Smith pointed out the flaws of an international economic system built on every major economic power trying to export more than it imported. The trade barriers that such a system required helped a few favored manufacturers but damaged the rest of society.

"In the mercantile system, the interest of the consumer is almost constantly sacrificed to that of the producer,"

Smith wrote.[47] "And it seems to consider production, and not consumption, as the ultimate end and object of all industry and commerce."

Smith instead argued that a free market's "invisible hand" could best create wealth and permit individuals and nations to specialize in producing goods to which they were best-suited. These ideas, along with the spread of industrialization and better transport methods, made it more difficult for governments to control trade, and gradually led to the decline of mercantilism.

In the 19th century Britain became the first major power to embrace free trade. Economic nationalism spiked in the years after World War I, deepening the Great Depression and fomenting the fascism that led to World War II. Protectionism would ebb and flow during the 19th and 20th centuries, but on the whole, most industrialized countries adopted free-market economies.

Capitalism vs. Communism

Liberal capitalism met a new challenger after the 1917 Russian revolution, when Bolshevik adherents to the communist principles of German philosopher Karl Marx took power. Under communism the new Soviet government nationalized industries and confiscated land and property from the wealthy to redistribute to the peasants.[48]

In theory, the workers owned the means of production and governed the state through the Communist Party, a system that supposedly would more fairly distribute the benefits of production. In practice, the party elite made all major decisions and embarked on radical schemes such as Stalin's effort to collectivize farms in the 1920s and '30s, which caused a famine that killed up to 9 million people.[49]

After World War II, the Soviets spread communism to Eastern Europe, while in Asia the communists emerged as victors in China's civil war. China soon embarked on a similarly devastating program of farm collectivization and industrial nationalization. At its height in the late 1970s, the communist world numbered 23 countries. In each country, the Communist Party established an authoritarian regime and repressed individual liberties.[50] Communism also failed economically. By the 1970s Western capitalist countries were enjoying vastly superior living standards.

After World War II, industrialized countries in Western Europe established social democratic economies with

Argentine President Cristina Kirchner lauds the nationalization of the Spanish-owned oil company YPF on May 4, 2012. Argentine lawmakers approved the nationalization by a wide margin.

market economies but strong labor unions, high taxation, expansive social safety nets and significant government ownership of large corporations. Many of the biggest companies were partially or wholly privatized in the 1980s and '90s, but the state still owns a controlling share in about one-fifth of the largest companies in Denmark, Finland, France, Germany, Norway and Sweden.[51]

Such social democratic systems were designed to establish greater stability and cushion against the economic shocks that had led to social unrest and fascism prior to World War II. A high degree of state ownership and management of the economy was seen as a key to protecting democracy. Conversely, as citizens demanded expanded rights and protections, multiparty democracy was seen as the key to establishing social democracy.[52] Eventually, some of these companies would become complacent and uncompetitive, inviting a wave of privatizations in the 1980s.[53]

Hybrid Economies

Unlike Western Europe after World War II, the city-state of Singapore was not industrialized and had little experience with democracy when it gained independence in 1965. Lacking natural resources or a large domestic market, the government set out to build export industries for manufactured goods.

Two Faces of State Capitalism

The ultra-luxurious interior of the headquarters of the state-owned Harbin Pharmaceutical Group Sixth factory in Harbin, China — with its inlaid floors and gold-tinted walls and chandeliers — has stirred popular outrage for its extravagance (top). Critics of state capitalism say it often results in waste and abuse in undemocratic societies where companies are not accountable to the electorate. Factory workers at the OAO AvtoVAZ factory in Togliatti, Russia, work on Lada Largus vehicles on April 11, 2012 (bottom). AvtoVAZ is owned partly by Russian Technologies, a state corporation.

Under the authoritarian hand of President Lee Kuan Yew and his People's Action Party, Singapore welcomed foreign investment from multinationals while the state itself invested in strategic government-owned companies.[54] U.S. giants such as General Electric and Hewlett-Packard soon built plants and began sharing their technology with their local workers and suppliers.[55] During the 1960s the state-owned giants Singapore Airlines, the Development Bank of Singapore and Neptune Orient Lines grew rapidly through government investment.

The hybrid public-private economic model seemed to work well. From 1965 to 1998, economic growth averaged between 7.7 and 10 percent per year. By then the country's economy had been transformed from a low-cost manufacturing center into a global finance and technology hub.[56] However the growth was accompanied by strict limits on individual liberties, symbolized by the government's infamous laws banning chewing gum and criminalizing failure to flush a toilet.

Today Singapore scores near the top of economic freedom indices published by groups such as the Heritage Foundation because of its openness to trade and investment, flexible regulatory environment and low taxes, though the government still plays a large role in guiding economic development and owns large stakes in firms in key industries.[57]

On the other side of Asia, a different strain of authoritarian state capitalism was taking root in the oil-rich monarchies of the Persian Gulf. After Arab oil producers in 1973 clamped an embargo on oil exports to the United States and its allies — to protest Western support for Israel during the 1973 Yom Kippur war — oil prices quadrupled. Producers such as the Gulf states were soon awash in billions of new petrodollars.[58]

The royal families in Saudi Arabia, Kuwait and the United Arab Emirates channeled proceeds from government oil companies into sovereign wealth funds, which have invested in both "national champions" and in foreign companies. In the U.A.E., which has about 7 percent of the world's hydrocarbons, the government was able to develop world-class companies such as DP World, the world's third-largest port operator, and Emirates, the globe's third-largest airline by capacity. Dubai, once a sleepy town with an economy that revolved around pearl diving, is now the most important financial and commercial city in the region — home to the world's tallest building, an indoor ski area and a shopping mall the size of 60 football fields.

After Communism

By the 1980s the growing wealth gap between the Western market economies and the Soviet Union and China led the two communist states to reexamine their economic models. Deng Xiaoping, who emerged as China's top leader in the late 1970s, initiated a series of gradual economic reforms in cities along China's east coast.

He established "special economic zones," where foreign companies were allowed to invest on advantageous terms in cities such as Shenzhen and Guangzhou to produce export goods. State industries meanwhile, were protected from foreign competition or were aided through foreign partnerships in which they acquired technologies. Manufacturing flourished in these cities, and the special zones grew in number. But city dwellers remained largely dependent on government-owned companies for housing, employment and health care. By the late 1980s, tension had developed within the Communist Party over the pace of the reforms and whether they should be accompanied by political liberalization.[59]

In 1989, as communist-totalitarian regimes were beginning to crumble in Eastern Europe, Chinese students began demanding more political freedom, and protests erupted in Beijing's Tiananmen Square. When Deng sent in tanks to crush the uprising, China's path was set: The country would reform economically under the guidance of the state, but there would be no meaningful political challenge to Communist Party rule.

Economic reforms accelerated in the 1990s under Jiang Zemin, who pushed the new business elite to become party members. One of Jiang's deputies, Zhu Rongji, was credited with modernizing, breaking up and privatizing thousands of state-owned companies and vastly increasing productivity.[60] In 2001 Rongji successfully negotiated China's accession to the WTO, paving the way for the rising manufacturing power to become the world's largest exporter and second-largest importer within a decade.[61]

In contrast to China's gradual economic reforms, Russia tried rapid economic liberalization — or "shock therapy" — under President Boris Yeltsin after the 1991 dissolution of the Soviet Union. State assets were quickly privatized, often bought at a fraction of their value by former communist *apparatchiks* who had previously managed them or by businessmen of questionable repute. A new class of so-called oligarchs emerged in the 1990s — Russian businessmen who got very rich by buying state assets cheaply.[62]

Russians had never enjoyed so much political freedom during their lifetimes. Opposition parties and independent media flourished. Yet, corruption and criminality thrived. In 1994, some 600 businessmen, politicians and journalists were killed.[63] The country's social safety net began to crumble, and a wave of organized crime swept across the country. By 1998, with world oil prices tumbling, the country was forced to default on its foreign debts; the value of the ruble plummeted.[64]

In 2000, Yeltsin's chosen successor, Putin, became president and quickly moved to restore stability and order, at the expense of political freedoms. He centralized power in the Kremlin and took control of state media and the oligarchs and their vast business empires. Those who opposed him quickly found that they or their businesses ran into legal trouble.

By the time Putin won re-election in 2004 with 71 percent of the vote, Russia was on the path back to authoritarianism, and most of its major companies were either directly controlled by the state or owned by its allies.[65] After four years as prime minister, Putin was re-elected to a new six-year term as president in March, amid protests over the conduct of elections. Some think he may run for another six-year term in 2018.[66]

CURRENT SITUATION

China Inc.

State capitalism's power as an economic model rests largely on the success of the two largest world powers that practice it — China and Russia. Yet, the system differs between the two countries.

Large swathes of China's economy are no longer under government control: retail, agriculture and most service sectors are now almost entirely privately run. But the largest and most important industries — banking, energy, metals, communications and transport — are dominated by state-run firms.[67] Controlling stakes in the 117-largest industrial groups are held by the State Owned Assets Supervision and Administration Commission (SASAC), a part of the central government. SASAC can appoint and remove executives, allocate capital between the different companies and oversee wages and worker safety, among other responsibilities.[68]

These firms are state-connected in several other ways as well. Government ministries often play an active role in managing the companies they nominally regulate. For

Is state capitalism a good model for the world's poorest countries?

YES
Aldo Musacchio
Associate Professor of Business Administration, Harvard Business School; Author, Experiments in Financial Democracy

Written for *CQ Global Researcher*, May 2012

Poor countries are usually plagued by a series of market failures that inhibit economic activity, such as high barriers to entry for new companies, a paucity of information about the market and lack of insurance to protect investors against risk. But the biggest failure is often the government's inability — or unwillingness — to deliver public goods such as roads, water, sanitation and education.

State capitalism grows out of the necessity to solve such market failures. Governments turn into entrepreneurs because the barriers to entry make it difficult for the private sector to thrive. States become entrepreneurs to fill in the infrastructure void left by the private sector. Even in Europe or Canada, large infrastructure projects, such as railways, were developed based on a system of state guarantees or the creation of state-owned rail lines. Thus, state capitalism can help poor countries out of poverty if it successfully alleviates the institutional voids that plague underdeveloped countries.

State capitalism is not an ideology and is not just a developmental stage. Nor is it a product of authoritarian regimes, because big democracies like India and Brazil are adherents. Neither is it exclusive to poor countries, because Sweden, Finland, France and other wealthy countries have a strong state-presence in their economies.

To be sure, it does have weaknesses. History shows one of the biggest problems with state capitalism is its proclivity to yield to clientelism, with politicians appointing managers based on political support or seeking to use state enterprises to influence short-term political objectives such as employment. This is true in both democracies and autocracies. When politicians use productive state-owned institutions for their own clientelistic and patronage purposes, the results are inefficient state-owned companies, failed banks and corruption.

Where this can be avoided, state capitalism can efficiently move countries out of poverty. The more the managers of state-owned enterprises and banks are isolated from the objectives of the politicians who oversee them, the more successful they are at creating efficient organizations that create growth. Countries such as Singapore and Malaysia are perhaps the best examples of this. State capitalism may not be the best system for getting every poor country out of poverty. But it can be a winning strategy for countries that can isolate the productive bureaucracy from politics and where leaders have the vision to alleviate institutional voids.

NO
Stefan Halper
Director of American Studies, Department of Politics and International Studies, University of Cambridge; Author, The Beijing Consensus

Written for *CQ Global Researcher*, May 2012

I argue the "No" side of this proposition with caveats. This question must be addressed in stages. State capitalism, or what I call "market authoritarianism," may be a viable model for the poorest countries for a limited time, but it eventually generates more problems than benefits. China demonstrates the strengths and weaknesses of "market authoritarianism," allowing us to see how tremendous growth and targeted social benefits lead to dysfunction that clouds the model over time. China's economy has grown by 10 percent a year for more than two decades, millions have been lifted out of poverty and China challenges the West economically, militarily and ideationally.

The ideational challenge is most worrisome. China proposes to legitimize authoritarianism. The public square is closed, freedom of religion and assembly are sharply restricted and political participation may be exercised only through the Communist Party. Bothersome legislatures and intrusive media are for other countries and other times.

The party, in turn, is closely linked to state enterprises (as well as many private enterprises) that dominate the exploitation of natural resources, infrastructure development, industrial production, trade and commerce in an arrangement that — in another era — would be termed "classical fascism." It's a system in which the state and large enterprises operate together to reach national goals most efficiently — but without the voice of working men and women or a broader civil society.

Does this produce rapid growth? Yes. Does it optimize individual potential, opportunity and growth? No. Does it allow plural politics that encourage a diversity of opinions? No.

So, for the poorest nations, authoritarian government may be necessary to develop a basic infrastructure, provide basic health and regulate agriculture. When such societies proceed from subsistence to distributing benefits for an emerging middle class, however, dysfunction is manifested in extensive corruption, a struggle to impose the rule of law, difficulty in achieving a national identity and control by a vast security apparatus.

So, yes, "market authoritarianism" works up to a point, but it suppresses the development of civil society, requires an ever-larger security apparatus and lacks the moral authority to exert leadership — an unexpectedly powerful dimension. In China's case, for example, its disgraceful repression of Tibet and other minorities has helped to deny China a seat at the "head table" in global affairs.

> **"The WTO was not set up with the premise of state capitalism. It was set up with the premise of open competition. It's a walking violation of international trade law to have state capitalism. It's certainly not what anyone bargained for when China was admitted to the WTO."**
>
> **— Michael Santoro**
> **Professor of Management**
> **Rutgers Business School,**
> **New Brunswick, N.J.**

instance, the Ministry of Industry and Information Technology nominates managers at China Mobile, the state-owned mobile network.[69]

In addition, several positions in elite government and party entities are reserved for leaders of state-owned companies. Fully one-third of the employees at government-owned companies are members of the Communist Party, which has party structures at every level of the company. Government-owned companies also are linked to each other through cross-ownership of shares, joint ownership of subsidiaries or by being organized into "business groups" with supplier firms.[70]

For example, the Agricultural Bank of China is the country's third-largest bank (by assets) and one of the world's 200 largest companies. In 2010, it raised $22.1 billion by listing shares on the Hong Kong and Shanghai stock exchanges in the largest initial public offering in history.[71] Yet 80 percent of the shares remain in the hands of the Ministry of Finance, China's sovereign wealth fund and the government's pension fund.[72] The bank's chairman, Jiang Chaoliang, 54, is a former deputy governor of Hubei Province, worked at China's central bank and the state-owned development bank and is a senior member of the Communist Party.[73]

The system often suffers from internal contradictions, analysts say. "The government's control over the top managers' careers is the most important mechanism to drive productivity and profitability," says Lin, the corporate governance researcher. "But at the same time, this mechanism itself may be a problem to productivity and profitability." For instance, she points out, "The best strategy to get promotions is not really seeking profits in a typical business sense but to implement the state's economic, political or social policies."

The commingling of state-private interests can be heavy-handed — sometimes comically so — such as when Hubei provincial officials in 2009 ordered teachers and government workers to smoke nearly a quarter-million packages of Hubei-branded cigarettes to boost the local economy and cigarette tax revenues.[74]

"Today, [state-owned enterprises] enjoy access to cheap loans from state banks and are first in line for government procurement contracts and foreign deals," wrote Grace Ng, China correspondent for Singapore's *Straits Times*, in March. "All this blocks new private entrepreneurs from entering industries and leads foreign investors to complain about unfair competition. And yet, such is Chinese pride in state giants like China Mobile, ICBC Bank and China National Petroleum Corp. — which top global rankings for market value, profits and branding — that resistance to major reform may get even stronger now."[75]

Indeed, despite state capitalism's shortcomings, many analysts now agree it is not just a way-station on the journey from communism to the free market but an endpoint in itself. There is even a nickname in Mandarin for the phenomenon: *guojin mintui*, which means "while the state advances the privates retreat."[76]

"We have one important thought," Wen Jiabao, China's premier, said during a CNN interview during the height of the 2008 financial crisis, "that socialism can also practice market economy. The complete formulation of our economic policy is to give full play to the basic role of market forces in allocating resources under the macroeconomic guidance and regulation of the government. We have one important piece of experience of the past 30 years: that is to ensure that both the visible hand and the invisible hand are given full play in regulating market forces."[77]

Russia's Revival

In Russia, Putin is reversing the process that began in the 1990s under President Yeltsin, in which many state assets were privatized. For example, Aeroflot, the state-owned airline dismantled under Yeltsin, re-acquired several regional airlines last year.[78] When Putin took power eight years ago, the state controlled 10 percent of Russia's oil production. Today it owns nearly 50 percent.[79]

AFP/Getty Images/Dmitry Kostyukov

Mikhail Khodorkovsky, former CEO of Russia's Yukos Oil Co., speaks from the glass-enclosed defendants' cage during a court session on Dec. 30, 2010, when he was sentenced to 14 years in prison for tax evasion. Critics said the trial was staged to punish Khodorkovsky for daring to oppose Russian President Vladimir Putin. Khodorkovsky's company, once Russia's largest oil firm, was swallowed by state-owned firms.

Putin's government wants the government to charge a retroactive "windfall tax" on those who profited from the privatizations of state assets during the 1990s.[80] And the president defends the establishment of large state companies — such as Russian Technologies, nuclear energy producer Rosatom, United Aircraft Corp. and United Shipbuilding Corp. — and vows to expand state control into pharmaceuticals, chemicals, metals and information technology.

"It is often argued that Russia does not need an industrial policy, since the government often selects the wrong priorities and gives preference to the wrong sectors, supports ineffective and inefficient producers and hinders innovations which would have emerged naturally in a free market environment," Putin wrote in an essay published during the campaign.[81]

These statements "are only true with all other conditions being equal," he continued. "Russia has gone through deindustrialization, which significantly damaged its economic structure. Large private capital is not flowing into innovative sectors because investors are reluctant to take the high risk. . . . Are we ready to risk Russia's economic future for the sake of pure economic theory?"

Nationalism has played a big role in bolstering state control. In 2008, Russia's parliament passed a law requiring foreign companies to seek permission to invest in 15 strategic sectors, such as media, fishing, mining, oil exploration, telecom and gas and oil transport.[82] Domestically, a larger portion of Russian industries are under private control than in China, but they are kept firmly in line. Business tycoons are expected not to use their wealth to challenge the state — as was starkly illustrated when oligarch Mikhail Khodorkovsky was arrested in 2003 on tax charges. Khodorkovsky has been jailed ever since, and the oil company he ran, once Russia's largest, has been swallowed by state-owned firms.[83] More recently, the state expanded its control over some privately held businesses by offering them loans during the financial crisis in return for minority stakes.[84]

Although China has successfully diversified its economy, Russia remains heavily dependent on hydrocarbons. Oil and gas shipments comprise nearly two-thirds of Russia's exports and about 40 percent of government revenues.[85] And while Putin's government retains a firm grip in Russia, there are more outlets for dissent and criticism.

"Russia's a one-trick pony, the core of its economy is the oil and gas that they provide to Europe," says Halper, of the University of Cambridge. "The Russians have also tried to embrace a form of democracy. They have political parties, and they have expectations about a different social contract than the Chinese."

Despite major protests against Putin's rule and electoral rigging during recent elections, high oil prices are helping to ensure stability in Russia — at least for the moment.[86] "Oil and gas are making Russia very dependent on foreign markets and external factors, which is not good for any country," says Andranik Migranyan, an adviser to former President Yeltsin. "When the price of oil goes down, the country is in a mess."

Experiments Elsewhere

China's economic success has bred imitators in other emerging markets. Authoritarian regimes in such countries as Ethiopia, Cuba, Myanmar (formerly Burma), Iran, Syria and Cambodia have all sent delegations to China to study how the country's economic dynamism might be exported without political liberalization.[87]

Such capitalism is already familiar to Saudi Arabia's ruling family, which has long tried to use its oil revenues to purchase stability. The state-owned oil company,

Saudi Aramco, has the largest proven crude reserves of any company and is the world's largest exporter. Nearly all of the kingdom's big companies are state-owned or owned by members of the royal family. In an effort to diversify the state has used some of its windfall oil revenues during the past decade to start building six new "economic cities," in which it plans to invest $500 billion.[88]

Similarly, neighboring Qatar, Bahrain, Kuwait and the seven city-states of the United Arab Emirates have successfully used state oil revenues to direct their economies. The emirate of Dubai, for instance, has been transformed into an international business hub, even though its largest business groups are controlled by the state or the royal family. But the financial crisis nearly bankrupted Dubai, leading to a collapse in property prices and fears that its state-owned companies would default on their bonds. However, state control came to the rescue, when neighboring Abu Dhabi used its own oil earnings to bail out Dubai's failing state firms.

"The thing about state capitalism is it's capitalism at the service of political power, and considering that a lot of these countries are in extractive industries, it may be possible for them to not be very efficient," says Orenstein, at Johns Hopkins University.

State capitalism also has thrived in parts of Southeast Asia, where Vietnam has transformed itself from one of the world's poorest nations to a middle-class economy in a quarter-century. Malaysia's state-owned oil company Petronas is the largest firm in the region.

Yet state capitalism's success isn't only attractive to authoritarian nations. In democratic South Africa, President Jacob Zuma wants to revive his country's economy along state capitalist lines by renewing the role of state-owned enterprises in major infrastructure projects, such as power stations, railroads and hospitals. Over the past decade, the government has founded both an oil and a mining company and flirted with the idea of nationalizing some of its biggest firms.

"The Chinese model of building infrastructure and growing jobs will be a key focus of the ANC's economic policy," Enoch Godongwana, head of the ruling African National Congress's Economic Transformation Committee, said in February.[89]

Similarly Brazil, which privatized many of its stodgy state companies in the 1980s, re-empowered government firms over the past decade under former President Luiz Inácio Lula da Silva and his Workers' Party successor Dilma Rousseff.[90] The 2007 discovery of a major offshore oilfield by state-run Petrobras has vastly expanded the state's economic role. During the 2008-09 financial crisis, Brazil's state-owned National Development Bank (BNDES) kept the country's economy from tanking by providing billions in credit to large businesses. By the end of 2010, BNDES accounted for more than one-fifth of all loans to the private sector.[91]

"During the crisis, after the failure of Lehman Brothers, it was [state-controlled] institutions like the Banco do Brasil, Caixa Econômica Federal and the National Development Bank that prevented the economy from being shipwrecked," Rousseff said in 2010. Her message: State capitalism succeeded where the private sector failed.[92]

OUTLOOK
Shifting Focus?

Many analysts agree that state capitalism is not likely to disappear in the short term — not least because of China's continuing economic success. That means Western countries will have to adapt to having companies owned by foreign governments playing an ever-increasing role in the global economy.

"Obviously, we're going to see more and more investment from state-owned enterprises," says Steger, the University of Ottawa trade law scholar. "I don't think they've been behaving in an anti-competitive or bad way, it's just that in China or other countries that's the form of enterprise they have, and that's something that we in the West have to get used to."

Others say the success of state-owned companies in the future will depend more on whether the rest of the world is comfortable with the governments that own the companies. "Would the level of U.S. resistance against foreign state-owned enterprises (SOEs) be the same when the buying entity is a Norwegian SOE as opposed to a Chinese SOE?" asks Lin, the Taiwanese corporate governance researcher. "Probably not. The level of suspicion and scrutiny would vary with the institutional quality of the state-owned enterprise's home country."

China must continue to grow at 8 percent a year or more, analysts say, in order for the Communist Party to maintain its legitimacy in the absence of democracy. "Unless the Chinese government can find an alternative mechanism to generate political and economic power like the 'national champions' do, it is hard to imagine the Chinese government significantly shifting away from state capitalism," says Lin.

Yet, other factors fueling China's growth — including low wages, high savings rates and an undervalued currency — are beginning to come under strain as living standards rise and trade partners become increasingly uncomfortable with the imbalances caused by China's undervalued currency and its export-dominated growth model. The next several decades will determine whether the country can transition from an economy that makes products invented elsewhere to one that builds wealth based on its people's own innovation.

"For the first step or early intermediate stages of development, we know authoritarian capitalism or state capitalism works," says Israeli political scientist Gat. "Whether they can succeed politically or economically in the next phase we don't yet know."

It will also determine whether states can sustain a large, educated middle class without being forced to democratize. "The Chinese have reached a crossroads, whether they're going to be ever more repressive to silence critics or whether they adopt some reform," says Halper, of the University of Cambridge. "They have been able to set ideology aside for the most part, so my sense is that this is not a straight line toward democratic governance. This is a highly tortured and difficult path that the reformers will have in China, because the established power will fight them at every step of the way."

The current fascination with state capitalism may also be a natural reaction to fatigue with three decades of hegemony for free-market capitalism — a model whose shortcomings were cruelly exposed during the recent financial crisis. Some also say it may be an attempt to provide a theoretical explanation for the rise of China, a country which has enormous human resources and other economic advantages and that acted pragmatically rather than ideologically in seeking to develop them.

"It probably was true that there was a lack of attention to the state side of development for the past 30 years, and this model corrects that," says Orenstein, the Johns Hopkins political scientist. "China grew partly because of its model, and for that country the model may have made a lot of sense. When you begin to communicate it and use it as a mechanism to spread to different countries, you create issues."

Inevitably as China becomes a stronger global power, it will attempt to restructure the global economic and political order in its own image. Yet, while its nationalistic and export-dependent economic model may work for an individual country within a larger trading system, it would be impossible for every country in the world to adopt such a system, some analysts say.

"The United States enabled China to get where it is today," says Santoro, of Rutgers Business School. "There would be no China growth if the U.S. wasn't there to buy Chinese products, to design Chinese products. What we need to be asking is, Where would the Chinese system take us? Where is the growth path for state capitalism? Where is the innovation going to come from?"

State capitalism is just one possible strategy for poor nations seeking to lift their economies from the lowest rung of the economic ladder, he points out. "China succeeded inside of free-market capitalism, and there are opportunities within the international economic order to do that, but it doesn't advance the system, it's just a way of gaming the system" he says.

"China will not be practicing state capitalism in 20 years," Santoro predicts. "It will either be closer to Western models of capitalism with a much more vibrant private sector and democratically elected government, strong regulatory system and predictable rule of law, or it will regress. It won't putter along like this."

NOTES

1. Kazunori Takada and David Lin, "China's Huawei Sees $100 Billion Revenue in 10 Years," Reuters, April 27, 2011, www.reuters.com/article/2011/04/27/us-huawei-idUSTRE73Q23420110427.

2. "Huawei's $30 Billion China Credit Opens Doors in Brazil, Mexico," Bloomberg, April 24, 2011, www.bloomberg.com/news/2011-04-25/huawei-counts-on-30-billion-china-credit-to-open-doors-in-brazil-mexico.html.

3. Bryan Krekel, Patton Adams and George Bakos, "Occupying the Information High Ground: Chinese Capabilities for Computer Network Operations and Cyber Espionage," U.S.-China Economic and Security Review Commission, March 7, 2012, pp. 69, 76-77, www.uscc.gov/RFP/2012/USCC%20 Report_Chinese_CapabilitiesforComputer_ NetworkOperationsandCyberEspionage.pdf.

4. For background, see Jennifer Koons, "Future of the Gulf States," *CQ Global Researcher*, Nov. 1, 2011, pp. 525-548.

5. "GDP Growth (Annual %)," World Bank, http://data.worldbank.org/indicator/NY.GDP.MKTP.KD.ZG.

6. For background, see Alex Kingsbury, "Communism Today," *CQ Global Researcher*, Aug. 2, 2011, pp. 367-394.

7. Francis Fukuyama, *The End of History and the Last Man* (1992).

8. Richard Barnet and John Cavanagh, *Global Dreams: Imperial Corporations and the New World Order* (1994).

9. For background, see the following *CQ Researchers*: Kenneth Jost, "Financial Crisis," May 9, 2008, pp. 409-432; Thomas J. Billitteri, "Financial Bailout," Oct. 24, 2008, pp. 865-888; Marcia Clemmitt, "Public-Works Projects," Feb. 20, 2009, pp. 153-176.

10. Ian Bremmer, *The End of the Free Market: Who Wins the War Between States and Corporations?* (2010), pp. 46-48.

11. See: Fortune Global 500: China 2011, http://money.cnn.com/magazines/fortune/global500/2011/countries/China.html and "List of Central State-Owned Enterprises," State Owned Assets Supervision and Administrative Commission of the State Council, People's Republic of China, www.sasac.gov.cn/n2963340/n2971121/n4956567/4956583.html.

12. "The Visible Hand," *The Economist*, Jan. 21, 2012, www.economist.com/node/21542931.

13. "China Mobile says total subscribers rose to 661.4 million in Feb," Reuters, March 19, 2012, www.reuters.com/article/2012/03/20/us-chinamobile-idUSBRE82J01A20120320.

14. Adrian Wooldridge, "New Masters of the Universe," *The Economist*, Jan. 21, 2012, www.economist.com/node/21542925.

15. Leon Lazaroff and Halia Pavliva, "World's Biggest Stock Drop Stoked by Protests: Russia Overnight," *Bloomberg News*, Dec. 11, 2011, www.bloomberg.com/news/2011-12-11/world-s-biggest-stock-drop-stoked-by-protests-russia-overnight.html.

16. Stephanie Kirchgaessner, "Huawei Goes on Attack Against U.S. Restrictions," *Financial Times*, Oct. 16, 2011, www.ft.com/intl/cms/s/0/ 2b1eaddc-f810-11e0-8e7e-00144feab49a.html#axzz1sKZUcA2v. See also: "China's Huawei Barred From Australia Broadband Deal," BBC News, March 26, 2012, www.bbc.co.uk/news/business-17509201.

17. "Mongolia Discussing Law to Cap Investment by Foreign State-Owned Firms in Strategic Assets-Sources," Dow Jones, April 30, 2012, www.foxbusiness.com/news/2012/04/30/mongolia-discussing-law-to-cap-investment-by-foreign-state-owned-firms-in/.

18. Mitchell Orenstein, "Three Models of Contemporary Capitalism," in Nancy Birdsall and Francis Fukuyama, eds., *New Ideas on Development After the Financial Crisis* (2011).

19. Elitsa Vucheva, "European Bank Bailout Total: $4 Trillion," Bloomberg/EUObserver.com, April 10, 2009, www.businessweek.com/globalbiz/content/apr2009/gb20090410_254738.htm.

20. Bremmer, *op. cit.*, p. 1.

21. Dennis McMahon, "China Creates Derivatives Clearinghouse," *The Wall Street Journal*, Nov. 29, 2009, http://online.wsj.com/article/SB10001424052748703300504574565532572813994.html.

22. Paul Maidment, "China Announces Massive Stimulus Package," *Forbes*, Nov. 9, 2008, www.forbes.com/2008/11/09/china-stimulus-economy-biz-cx_pm_1109notes.html.

23. Transcript of remarks by Ian Bremmer, James Crabtree and John Llewellyn, "The Rise of State Capitalism," Chatham House, July 12, 2010, www.chathamhouse.org/sites/default/files/public/Meetings/Meeting%20Transcripts/120710bremmeretal.pdf.

24. Mike McIntire, "Bailout Is a Windfall to Banks, If Not to Borrowers," *The New York Times*, Jan. 17, 2009,

www.nytimes.com/2009/01/18/business/18bank
.html. See also "Emergency Capital Injections
Provided to Support the Viability of Bank of
America, Other Major Banks and the U.S. Financial
System," Office of the Special Inspector General for
the Troubled Asset Relief Program, Oct. 5, 2009,
www.sigtarp.gov/reports.shtml.

25. Edward Chancellor, "Entranced by China's Bubbling
Economy," *Financial Times*, Feb. 6, 2011, www
.ft.com/intl/cms/s/0/13604674-3092-11e0-9de3-
00144feabdc0.html#axzz1sxVhj0Mx.

26. *Ibid.*

27. "IMF Warns Russia Over 'Credit Bubble,'" RIA
Novosti, April 20, 2012, http://en.ria.ru/business/
20120420/172932623.html.

28. "Poverty and Equity Data," The World Bank, http://
povertydata.worldbank.org/poverty/home.

29. Wei-Wei Zhang, "The Allure of the Chinese Model,"
International Herald Tribune, Nov. 1, 2006, www
.nytimes.com/2006/11/01/opinion/01iht-edafrica
.3357752.html.

30. Dieter Ernst, "Testimony to the U.S.-China
Economic Security Review Commission Hearing on
China's Five Year Plan, Indigenous Innovation and
Technology Transfers, and Outsourcing," East West
Center, June 15, 2011, www.eastwestcenter.org/news-
center/east-west-wire/testimony-of-dr-dieter-ernst.

31. *Ibid.*

32. Terry Macalister, "Thin Smile From Shell As It Sells
Sakhalin Stake," *The Guardian*, April 18, 2007, www
.guardian.co.uk/business/2007/apr/19/oilandpetrol
.news.

33. Dana Cimilluca, Shai Oster and Amy Or, "Rio
Tinto Scuttles Its Deal With Chinalco," *The Wall
Street Journal*, June 5, 2009, http://online.wsj.com/
article/SB124411140142684779.html.

34. Alan Beattie, Leslie Hook and Joshua Chaffin,
"Fight Against China on Rare Earths," *Financial
Times*, March 13, 2012, www.ft.com/intl/cms/
s/0/4c3da294-6cc2-11e1-bd0c-00144feab49a
.html#axzz1t40fRh7B.

35. For background, see Reed Karaim, "Farm Subsidies,"
CQ Global Researcher, May 1, 2012, pp. 205-228.

36. Ian Bremmer and Alexander Kliment, "State
Capitalism and the Future of Globalization," *World
Politics Review*, Nov. 24, 2009, www.worldpolitics
review.com/articles/4688/state-capitalism-and-
the-future-of-globalization.

37. *Ibid.*

38. Peter Coy, "China's State Capitalism Trap,"
Bloomberg Businessweek, Feb. 2, 2012, www.business
week.com/magazine/chinas-state-capitalism-
trap-02022012.html.

39. Guy Dinmore and Geoff Dyer, "Immelt Hits Out at
China and Obama," *Financial Times*, July 1, 2010,
www.ft.com/cms/s/0/ed654fac-8518-11df-adfa-
00144feabdc0.html#axzz1uIpoYKgl.

40. William Mellor and Le-Min Lim, "Lou Suffers
Blackstone's 'Fat Rabbits' in China Fund (Update 1),"
Bloomberg News, Feb. 26, 2008, www.bloomberg
.com/apps/news?pid=newsarchive&sid=at7tCLyl
bz2U.

41. Simon Wilson, "Wealth Funds Group Publishes
24-Point Voluntary Principles," *IMF Survey*, Oct.
15, 2008, www.imf.org/external/pubs/ft/survey/
so/2008/new101508b.htm.

42. Philip Lawson, *The East India Company: a History*
(1993), pp. 7-16.

43. Nick Robins, *The Corporation that Changed the
World* (2006), pp. 72-74.

44. *Ibid.*, p. 158.

45. Stephen R. Bown, *Merchant Kings: When Companies
Ruled the World* (2010), pp. 147-148.

46. Fernand Braudel, *The Wheels of Commerce:
Civilization and Capitalism 15th-18th Century, Vol. 2*
(1979), pp. 542-545.

47. Adam Smith, *The Wealth of Nations* (1776), p. 390
(2012 reprint).

48. Kingsbury, *op. cit.*

49. See also: Kenneth Jost, "Russia and the Former
Soviet Republics," *CQ Researcher*, June 17, 2005,
pp. 554-564.

50. *Ibid.*

51. Orenstein, *op. cit.*

52. *Ibid.*

53. For background, see R. C. Deans, "State Capitalism," *Editorial Research Reports,* April 7, 1971, available at *CQ Researcher Plus Archive.*

54. "Background Note: Singapore," U.S. Department of State, Dec. 2, 2011, www.state.gov/r/pa/ei/bgn/2798.htm.

55. Lee Kuan Yew, *From Third World to First: The Singapore Story: 1965-2000* (2000), p. 62.

56. "Economic History," Ministry of Trade and Industry Singapore, last updated June 24, 2010, http://app.mti.gov.sg/default.asp?id=545#2.

57. "Singapore: 2012 Index of Economic Freedom," Heritage Foundation, www.heritage.org/index/country/singapore.

58. Ron Chernow, "No Funeral for OPEC Just Yet," *The New York Times*, Jan. 5, 1999, www.nytimes.com/1999/01/05/opinion/no-funeral-for-opec-just-yet.html?scp=4&sq=1973%20embargo%20oil%20saudi%20arabia%20quadruple&st=cse.

59. Bremmer, "The End of the Free Market," *op. cit.*, pp. 128-130.

60. Keith Bradsher, "China Urged to Continue Reforms for Growth," *The New York Times*, Feb. 23, 2012, www.nytimes.com/2012/02/24/world/asia/china-urged-to-continue-reforms-for-growth.html.

61. "Ten Years of China in the WTO: Shades of Grey," *The Economist*, Dec. 10, 2011, www.economist.com/node/21541408.

62. Jason McLure, "Russia in Turmoil," *CQ Global Researcher*, Feb. 21, 2012, pp. 81-104.

63. Stephen Kotkin, *Armageddon Averted: The Soviet Collapse 1970-2000* (2008), p. 127.

64. Roland Flamini, "Dealing With the 'New' Russia," *CQ Researcher*, June 6, 2008, pp. 481-504.

65. Jost, *op. cit.*

66. Maria Tsetkova, "Russian Protest Leaders Held as Putin, Medvedev Swap," Reuters, May 8, 2012, www.reuters.com/article/2012/05/08/us-russia-idUSBRE84708A20120508.

67. Stefan Halper, *The Beijing Consensus* (2010), pp. 123-125.

68. "Main Functions and Responsibilities of SASAC," State-Owned Assets Supervision and Administration Commission of the State Council, the People's Republic of China.

69. Li-Wen Lin and Curtis J. Milhaupt, "We Are the (National) Champions: Understanding the Mechanism of State Capitalism in China," *Columbia Law and Economics Working Paper No. 409*, www.law.columbia.edu/center_program/law_economics/wp_listing_1/wp_listing/401-425.

70. *Ibid.*

71. "Agricultural Bank of China Sets IPO Record as Size Raised to $22.1 Billion," Bloomberg News, Aug. 15, 2010, www.bloomberg.com/news/2010-08-15/agricultural-bank-of-china-sets-ipo-record-with-22-1-billion-boosted-sale.html.

72. "2011 Annual Report," Agricultural Bank of China, p. 94, www.abchina.com/en/about-us/annual-report/.

73. "Appointment of the Chairman of the Board," Agricultural Bank of China, Jan. 16, 2012.

74. Peter Foster, "Chinese Ordered to Smoke More to Boost Economy," *The Telegraph*, May 4, 2009, www.telegraph.co.uk/news/newstopics/howaboutthat/5271376/Chinese-ordered-to-smoke-more-to-boost-economy.html.

75. Grace Ng, "China's State-Owned Giants Are Here to Stay; With the Firms' Market Share and Political Heft, Any Reform Will Be Small," *The Straits Times* (Singapore), March 2, 2012.

76. David Barboza, "Entrepreneur's Rival in China: the State," *The New York Times*, Dec. 7, 2011, www.nytimes.com/2011/12/08/business/an-entrepreneurs-rival-in-china-the-state.html?pagewanted=all.

77. "Transcript of Interview With Chinese Premier Wen Jiabao," CNN.com, Sept. 29, 2008, http://articles.cnn.com/2008-09-29/world/chinese.premier.transcript_1_financial-crisis-interview-vice-premier?_s=PM:WORLD.

78. "Aeroflot plans finalizing Rostechnologii assets' consolidation Nov.," Itar-Tass News Agency, Sept. 27, 2011, www.itar-tass.com/en/c154/234443.html.

79. Bremmer, *World Politics Review, op. cit.*

80. Henry Meyer, "Putin May Copy U.K.'s 5 Billion-Pound Windfall Tax on State Asset Sales," Bloomberg, Feb. 17, 2012, www.bloomberg.com/news/2012-02-17/putin-may-copy-u-k-s-5-billion-pound-windfall-tax-on-state-asset-sales.html.

81. Vladimir Putin, "Prime Minister Vladimir Putin Contributes an Article to the Vedemosti Newspaper," Government of the Russian Federation, Jan. 30, 2012, http://premier.gov.ru/eng/events/news/17888/.

82. Toby Gati, "Russia's New Law on Foreign Investment in Strategic Sectors and the Role of State Corporations in the Russian Economy," Akin Gump Strauss Hauer & Feld LLP, October 2008.

83. "Yukos Ex-Chief Jailed for Nine Years," BBC News, May 31, 2005, http://news.bbc.co.uk/2/hi/business/4595289.stm.

84. Bremmer, *World Politics Review, op. cit.*

85. "Key Economic Indicators in 2011," Bank of Russia, www.cbr.ru/eng/statistics. Also see James Brooke, "Russia Gets Giant Boost From Rising Oil Prices," Voice of America, March 11, 2011, www.voanews.com/english/news/europe/Russia-Gets-Giant-Boost-from-Rising-Oil-Prices-118258659.html.

86. McLure, *op. cit.*

87. "Ethiopia and China: Looking East," *The Economist*, Oct. 21, 2010, www.economist.com/node/17314616. See also Halper, *op. cit.*, pp. 128-130.

88. Jad Mouawad, "The Construction Site Called Saudi Arabia," *The New York Times*, Jan. 20, 2008, www.nytimes.com/2008/01/20/business/worldbusiness/20saudi.html?pagewanted=all.

89. Sharda Naidoo, Charles Molele and Matuma Letsoalo, "State of the Nation: Zuma Adopts Chinese Model," *Mail & Guardian*, Feb. 3, 2012, http://mg.co.za/article/2012-02-03-zuma-adopts-chinese-model/.

90. For background, see Brian Beary, "Brazil on the Rise," *CQ Global Researcher*, June 7, 2011, pp. 263-290.

91. Sergio Lazzarini, Aldo Musacchio, Rodrigo Bandeira-de-Mello and Rosilene Marcon, "What Do Development Banks Do? Evidence from Brazil, 2002-2009," *Harvard Business School Working Paper*, Dec. 8, 2011, www.hbs.edu/research/pdf/12-047.pdf.

92. "Falling in Love Again With the State," *The Economist*, March 31, 2010, www.economist.com/node/15816646.

BIBLIOGRAPHY

Selected Sources

Books

Bremmer, Ian, *The End of the Free Market: Who Wins the War Between States and Corporations?* Portfolio, 2010.
The president of the Eurasia Group political risk consultancy says China's economic rise is linked to the success of state-controlled economies elsewhere following the 2008 global financial meltdown.

Goldman, Marshall, *Petrostate: Putin, Power and the New Russia*, Oxford University Press, 2010.
Russia's rebirth as a major world economic power has been largely due to its expanded energy resources. even though they've fueled corruption and harmed other parts of the economy.

Halper, Stefan, *The Beijing Consensus: Legitimizing Authoritarianism in Our Time*, Basic Books, 2010.
A professor of political scientist at the University of Cambridge in the U.K says the Chinese economic and political model is gaining sway in the developing world.

Huang, Yasheng, *Capitalism With Chinese Characteristics: Entrepreneurship and the State*, Cambridge University Press, 2008.
A professor of international management at the MIT Sloan School of Management describes how China's agricultural reforms of the 1980s brought entrepreneurial and broad-based growth to the countryside, but how urban China gained the upper-hand in the next decade, with mixed results for human welfare.

Truman, Edwin, *Sovereign Wealth Funds: Threat or Salvation?* Peterson G. Institute for International Economics, 2010.
A former Treasury Department official examines the implications of governments controlling large cross-border holdings of international assets.

Articles

Barboza, David, "Wen Calls China Banks Too Powerful," *The New York Times*, **April 3, 2012, www .nytimes.com/2012/04/04/business/global/chinas- big-banks-too-powerful-premier-says.html.**

China's prime minister calls for the breakup of the country's biggest state-owned banks, saying they've become too powerful.

Betts, Paul, "EU wary as Russia puts velvet glove on iron fist," *Financial Times*, **Dec. 11, 2007, www .ft.com/intl/cms/s/0/e6100398-a81e-11dc-9485- 0000779fd2ac.html#axzz1tuYkSg3h.**

EU nations are concerned about state-run Russian companies investing in Europe.

Bremmer, Ian, "The Long Shadow of the Visible Hand," *The Wall Street Journal*, **May 22, 2010, http://online.wsj.com/article/SB1000142405274870 4852004575258541875590852.html.**

State-owned firms that control more than 75 percent of the world's oil production dwarf ExxonMobil and BP, a sign of the growing power in the world economy of state-run companies.

Ng, Grace, "China's State-Owned Giants Are Here to Stay: With the Firms' Marketshare and Heft, Any Reform Will Be Small," *The Straits Times* **(Singapore), March 2, 2012.**

Although Chinese state-capitalist companies are draining talent and money from the private sector, they are unlikely to be radically reformed.

Schuman, Michael, "Why China Will Have an Economic Crisis," *Time*, **Feb. 27, 2012, http://business .time.com/2012/02/27/why-china-will-have-an- economic-crisis/.**

China is heading for economic collapse because the state is distorting its economy with subsidies for export businesses.

Sender, Henny, "FT Analysis: Silence not necessarily golden for sovereign funds," *Financial Times*, **Jan. 17, 2008, http:// ftalphaville.ft.com/blog/2008/01/18/10265/ft-analysis- silence-not-necessarily-golden-for-sovereign-funds/.**

Wall Street bankers have mixed feelings about the foreign sovereign wealth funds that have taken stakes in U.S. financial giants.

Wooldridge, Adrian, "Special Report: State Capitalism," *The Economist*, **Jan. 21, 2012.**

The Economist's management editor concludes that state capitalism is unsustainable over the long term because it concentrates and corrupts power by applying political criteria in commercial decisions, and vice versa.

Reports

"China 2030: Building a Modern, Harmonious and Creative High-Income Society," World Bank, 2012, www.worldbank.org/en/news/2012/02/27/china- 2030-executive-summary.

China must transition to a market economy, accelerate innovation, reduce environmental stress and seek mutually beneficial relations with the world, according to a team from the World Bank and the Development Research Center of China's State Council.

Tordo, Silvana, Tracy Brandon and Noora Arfaa, "National Oil Companies and Value Creation," World Bank, 2011, http://siteresources.worldbank.org/ INTOGMC/Resources/336099-1300396479288/ noc_volume_I.pdf.

Three World Bank economists examine the advantages and drawbacks of state control of natural resources.

For More Information

Asia Pacific Foundation of Canada, 220-890 West Pender St., Vancouver, BC, V6C 1J9; +1 604 684-5986; www.asiapacific.ca. An independent think-tank specializing on economic, political and security issues involving Canada's relations with Asia.

The Emirates Centre for Strategic Studies and Research, P.O. Box 4567, Abu Dhabi, U.A.E.; +971 2 404-4444; www.ecssr.ac.ae. An independent research institution that studies public policy and Middle Eastern affairs.

Heritage Foundation, 214 Massachusetts Ave., N.E., Washington, DC 20002-4999; 202-546-4400; www.heritage.org. A conservative, free-market-oriented think tank that ranks countries on economic freedom, among other political and economic studies.

Shanghai Institutes for International Studies, 195-15 Tianlin Rd., Shanghai, China, 200233; +86 21 546-14900; www.siis.org.cn. A think tank that studies China's economics, security and foreign relations.

Sovereign Wealth Fund Institute, 2300 West Sahara Ave., Suite 800, Las Vegas, NV 89102; www.swfinc.com. A private research firm that collects information on the impact of sovereign wealth funds on global politics, financial markets and trade.

S. Rajaratnam School of International Studies, Nanyang Technological University, BlkS4, Level B4, Nanyang Avenue, Singapore 639798; +65 6790 6982; www.rsis.edu.sg. A leading graduate school and research institute on strategic and international affairs in the Asia-Pacific region.

World Bank, 1818 H St., N.W., Washington, DC 20433; 202-473-1000; www.worldbank.org. Provides financial and economic technical assistance to developing countries around the world.

Voices From Abroad:

DMITRIY MEDVEDEV

President, Russia

Manual control

"Any ambiguity in the law is a risk for the businessman, but not for the state. And the principle that the state is always right expresses itself either in corruption or in universal preferences for one's own companies, regardless of the form of ownership. In these conditions the economy is operating not by market institutions but on the principles of manual control."

Nezavisimaya Gazeta (Russia), June 2011

PRAKASH KARAT

General Secretary Communist Party of India, India

A false equation

"We tended to equate social ownership with state ownership, even when there are many forms of public ownership, be it like collective ownership and cooperative ownerships. Even within the state-run public sector, more diverse forms of holdings and wider shareholding are there, which allows a certain degree of competition."

The Times of India, April 2012

ROB THOMSON

Member Ceasefire Campaign Steering Committee, South Africa

Arming the state

"The rationale for state ownership [of an arms manufacturer] is the nature of its product: The purpose of arms production is not to arm the people but to arm the state, and that must be controlled by the state."

Business Day (South Africa), February 2012

La Prensa, Panama/Arcadio Esquivel

NICOLAS MADURO

Minister for Foreign Affairs, Venezuela

Oil nationalism welcome

"President Chávez welcomes and supports the decision announced by the government of President Cristina [Kirchner] to nationalise the main oil corporation of Argentina. Venezuela puts all the technical, operational, legal and political experience of [state oil company] Petroleos de Venezuela at the disposition of the government of Argentina and its people to strengthen the state oil sector."

Evening Standard (England), April 2012

GAVIN KEETON

Professor of Economics Rhodes University, South Africa

The price of nationalization

"Nationalisation usually occurs where institutions are weak and governments can ignore legal restrictions with impunity. This is not true for SA [South Africa]. SA has attracted billions in foreign capital since 1994 and has signed treaties guaranteeing foreign investors full repayment in the event of nationalisation. The price we would pay for nationalisation is therefore even higher. Investors would retreat, reversing foreign capital inflows, thereby undermining prosperity and condemning us to increased unemployment and poverty."

Business Day (South Africa), July 2011

BERNARD TABAIRE

Media consultant African Centre for Media Excellence, Uganda

Sovereignty vs. money

"African governments are asserting themselves, very justifiably, even if only at long last, against the super-oiled multinationals. It is a contest between sovereignty and hard cash. Sovereignty is just waking up to the fact it has power, but power that must be exercised as to not chase away hard cash."

The Monitor (Uganda), February 2012

HUGO CHÁVEZ

President, Venezuela

Gold's value

"We're going to nationalize the gold and we're going to convert it, among other things, into international reserves because gold continues to increase in value."

Reuters, August 2011

14

Women's Rights

Sarah Glazer

Legions of Arab women — like these university students in Tunisia — are earning college degrees today, as North African and Middle Eastern countries improve female literacy and education levels. Some of the biggest gains in closing the gender gap across the globe have been in educational attainment: In 22 countries women have reached parity with men in education, according to the World Economic Forum.

From *The CQ Researcher*,
April 3, 2012.

R eem, a Yemeni girl, was only 11 when her father forced her to marry a cousin almost 21 years her senior. Three days after her marriage, Reem tried to commit suicide by slitting her wrists. Eventually, she ran away to her mother, who helped her try to get a divorce.

"We don't divorce little girls," the judge told her.

"But how come you allow little girls to get married?" Reem retorted.[1]

Forced child marriage is widespread in Yemen, the poorest country in the Middle East, according to Human Rights Watch. Indeed, marrying off little girls remains common — especially in sub-Saharan Africa and South Asia — wherever bread-winners earn under $2 a day and maintaining a daughter's virginity until marriage is a point of family honor.

The consequences of involuntary child marriage — a practice that dates back to ancient Mesopotamia — are widespread in the developing world: interrupted education, high mortality in childbirth, domestic violence and lack of economic independence.[2] Yet, the continued prevalence of the practice is a stark reminder that women in many countries still lack basic human rights.

Indeed, women's rights around the globe often appear to take one step forward and two steps back. Many countries with traditional attitudes toward women, such as Yemen, have ratified international conventions aimed at guaranteeing women basic rights — such as not forcing children to marry. But signing a treaty doesn't necessarily mean the government will abide by it, especially if the convention

More Than 100 Countries Have Electoral Gender Quotas

Over the past 20 years, more than 50 countries have mandated gender quotas for elections requiring either that a certain percentage of assembly seats be reserved for women or that a minimum percentage of legislative candidates be female. In more than 50 other countries, at least one political party uses voluntary quotas to compile candidate lists. Quota advocates argue that female legislators are more likely than male lawmakers to promote laws beneficial to families, such as mandates for clean water and improved health care.

Countries with Electoral Gender Quotas

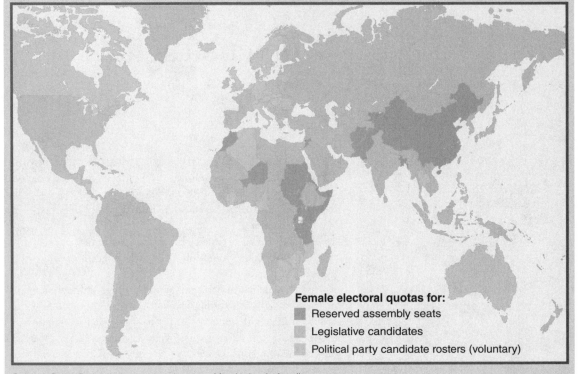

Female electoral quotas for:
- Reserved assembly seats
- Legislative candidates
- Political party candidate rosters (voluntary)

Source: Quota Project, www.quotaproject.org. Map by Lewis Agrell

conflicts with tradition.[3] In 2009, for instance, Yemeni religious conservatives blocked a bill requiring brides to be at least 17. Such a law went against Sharia, or Islamic law, they said, and would spread immorality.[4]

Women's rights remain precarious in countries such as Yemen that have overthrown repressive governments during the past year's so-called Arab Spring.[5] Conservative Muslim parties won major gains in recent elections in Egypt, Tunisia and Morocco, raising questions about whether liberal divorce, custody and other laws governing women's rights will be rolled back. New

political leaders in Libya and Tunisia recently extolled polygamy, for instance. (*See sidebar, p. 354.*)

While the Arab Spring's youthful revolutionaries — many of whom were women — often assumed a new era of democracy would bring them new freedoms, women's rights were not an explicit part of the protests or of recent election campaigns. After Egypt's recent parliamentary elections, for example, women now fill only 2 percent of the seats, fewer than the 12 percent mandated during the regime of ousted President Hosni Mubarak.

"The Arab Spring has definitely brought more attention to women's rights, but we haven't necessarily seen an improvement in practice," says Elena Zacharenko, a foreign-policy expert at Amnesty International's Brussels office. "The tendency in the region is to dismiss campaigning for women's rights as something imported from the West — not local or regional."

As these countries write new constitutions, some are considering introducing laws reserving a minimum percentage of parliamentary seats or candidate slots for women. More than 50 countries have such quotas, often advocated on the premise that female legislators are more likely to promote laws that benefit families, such as mandates for clean water and health care.[6]

But it's unclear whether such quotas are always successful. Tunisia's new parliament fell short of its mandatory quota when too few women ran for office. Egypt's transitional government abandoned Mubarak's 12 percent quota for women in Parliament, which was widely viewed as a ploy to install Mubarak supporters.[7]

In the Arab world, as around the globe, women are making some progress, according to the Geneva-based World Economic Forum. The gender gap is narrowing with regard to women's educational attainment and their safety and survival, the Forum says. But big gaps still exist between men and women on wages and political participation.[8] (*See graph.*)

While women in wealthier countries now command more than half of university degrees, they still earn less than men. In the United States, for instance, even in highly educated professional fields such as law, engineering and business, women on average earn $33,932 less than men — or about 70 percent of the average female salary.[9]

Gender Gap Narrows Slowly in Most Areas

The gender gaps in four categories — health, education, economic participation and political empowerment — have changed little since 2006, as measured by an index that reflects a wide range of socioeconomic factors. Nevertheless, the gaps between men and women in health and education have been nearly eliminated, while wide gaps still remain in economic and political participation. The study of 135 countries representing more than 90 percent of the world's population also found that the overall gender gap is largest in the Middle East and North Africa.

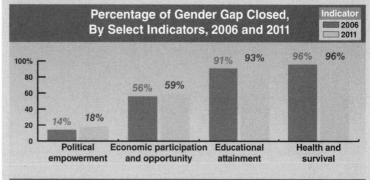

Source: Ricardo Hausmann, et al., "The Global Gender Gap Report 2011," World Economic Forum, 2011, p. 35, www3.weforum.org/docs/WEF_GenderGap_Report_2011.pdf

Women also are poorly represented in management positions. According to the World Economic Forum, slightly less than 5 percent of the CEOs of the world's largest employers in 20 major economies are female.[10] And over the past 20 years, gains in women's relative earnings have slowed, as has the pace of change in their share of the labor force.

Such statistics lead University of Massachusetts-Amherst economics professor Nancy Folbre to conclude that feminism "seems to be losing momentum." Gender

Women Lead in 16 Countries

Sixteen countries have elected female heads of state or government, including five who serve as both head of state and head of government.* Angela Merkel, chancellor of Germany since 2005, is the longest-serving female head of government. Swiss President Eveline Widmer-Schlumph, who assumed office in January, is the newest elected female world leader.

Elected Female World Leaders

Heads of State and Government

 Laura Chinchilla — President, Costa Rica, since 2010; vice president, 2006-2010

 Cristina Fernandez de Kirchner — President, Argentina, since 2007; former first lady; former president, Senate Committee on Constitutional Affairs

 Ellen Johnson Sirleaf — President, Liberia, since 2006; previously held finance positions with the government and World Bank

 Dilma Rousseff — President, Brazil, since 2011; minister of Mines and Energy, 2003-2005

 Eveline Widmer-Schlumph — President, Switzerland, since 2012; vice president, 2011

Heads of State

 Dalia Grybauskaite — President, Lithuania, since 2009; European commissioner for financial programming and the budget, 2004-2009

 Pratibha Patil — President, India, since 2007; governor of Rajasthan state, 2004-2007

* In a parliamentary system, the head of state (often called the president) has a largely ceremonial role, such as greeting foreign dignitaries and representing the country at state functions. The head of government (often the prime minister) supervises the bureaucracy and makes policy decisions. In parliamentary monarchies, the king or queen is often the head of state.

participation gaps would close," says Laura Liswood, secretary general of the Council of Women World Leaders in Washington, D.C., which represents current and former female presidents and prime ministers. "We're all just discovering there's nothing natural about it."

While the plight of a Yemeni woman who was forced to marry at a young age and a mother trying to break through the glass ceiling in an industrialized country may seem worlds apart, one common strand runs through the lives of all women, says Victoria A. Budson, founding executive director of the Women and Public Policy Program at the Harvard Kennedy School of Government. Women are "never free" without economic independence, she says. "If they don't have that, they can't freely move in and out of marriages or define what their own life looks like."

Some experts attribute the economic gaps to what they see as women's personal preference. Women are more likely than men to take time off to have children and work part time, which results in lower pay, says Catherine Hakim, a British social scientist and author of the 2000 book, *Work-Lifestyle Choices in the 21st Century*, which examines women's work preferences.

inequality in earnings "strongly reflects the penalty imposed on caregivers who take time out of paid employment," she has argued.[11]

The gap is even more pronounced with regard to political participation. With notable exceptions — such as Rwanda and Sweden — women don't come close to filling half the seats of representative bodies in most countries. (*See graph, p. 367.*)

"A lot of us thought if you close the education and health gaps, then naturally the economic and political

Now that legislation has removed barriers to workplace discrimination in such places as the United Kingdom and United States, she contends, women have gone as far as they want in the work world. Feminists had "widely exaggerated and unrealistic expectations of how much change would occur," Hakim argues. "It's simply not the case that the majority of women want full-time, lifelong, career-centered lives in the same way that men typically do."

Facebook CEO Sheryl Sandberg recently said that young women in the developed world have an "ambition gap" that explains their failure to rise up the corporate career ladder over the last 10 years, even as they have claimed a growing share of college and graduate degrees. She blamed this on societies' disapproval of female ambition; assertive little girls are often called "bossy," she observed, but forceful little boys are not.[12]

Some experts blame a motherhood gap — in which working mothers are penalized with lower pay, less promotion and ultimately smaller retirement benefits.[13] "In no country do men and women share household responsibilities equally," Liswood says. But in every country "women free up men's time and subsidize men's ability to be in the public sphere."

Some Scandinavian countries are trying to narrow that gap by requiring fathers to take leave upon the birth of a child. (*See sidebar, p. 360.*)

Still other experts are convinced that women continue to face discrimination — albeit subtle — when trying to rise to the highest ranks of management. On returning from maternity leave, according to Budson, women often are assigned less challenging tasks because it's assumed they're too busy with home responsibilities. But colleagues assume a new father will want to work more to support his growing family.

Norway has led the world in trying to break the glass ceiling by mandating that 40 percent of corporate board seats be filled by women. Seven other countries — Spain, Iceland, France, Italy, the Netherlands, Belgium and Malaysia — have followed suit, and European Union (EU) Justice Commissioner Viviane Reding is considering proposing an EU-wide quota for women on corporate boards, along with other measures to boost their membership.[14] But such a quota is likely to face an uphill battle from member countries: 24 of the 27 employment ministers have argued against corporate quotas.[15]

As women's rights are debated in government, academia and business, here are some of the questions being asked:

Do international agreements improve women's rights?

The U.N. Convention on the Elimination of All Forms of Discrimination against Women (CEDAW) is the international gold standard for gender equality. Since its approval by the U.N. General Assembly in 1979, it has been ratified by 187 member states; the United States is not among them.

However, the treaty has more "reservations" than any other international convention — conditions attached by signing nations specifying that they won't comply with certain provisions. Thirty countries' reservations

---

Elected Female World Leaders (Cont.)

Heads of Government

 Julia Gillard — Prime minister, Australia, since 2010; deputy prime minister, 2007-2010

 Sheikh Hasina Wajed — Prime minister, Bangladesh, since 2009; held same position, 1996-2001

 Angela Merkel — Chancellor, Germany, since 2005; parliamentary leader of Christian Democratic Union party, 2002-2005

 Kamla Persad-Bissessar — Prime minister, Trinidad and Tobago, since 2010; commonwealth chairperson-in-office, 2010-2011

 Iveta Radicova — Prime minister, Slovakia, since 2010; minister of Labor, 2005-2006

 Yingluck Shinawatra — Prime minister, Thailand, since 2011; member of the House of Representatives, since 2011

 Cisse Mariam Sidibé — Prime minister, Mali, since 2011; minister of Rural Development, 2002

Jóhanna Siguroardóttir — Prime minister, Iceland, since 2009; minister of Social Affairs and Social Security, 2007-2009

Helle Thorning-Schmidt — Prime minister, Denmark, since 2011; member of the European Parliament, 1999-2004

Women Fear Loss of Rights After Arab Spring

"As a woman and an artist, I'm scared."

To Egyptian novelist Ahdaf Soueif, participating in the first 18 days of protests in Cairo's Tahrir Square last year was like living a dream of equality and harmony between men and women, religious and secular.[1]

Soueif, who does not cover her hair with the headscarf worn by conservative Muslims, recalled men in Tahrir as being "chivalrous, helpful. You could smoke, sit together, whatever headgear you were wearing."[2]

But on March 9, the day after a women's rights protest was disrupted by angry men, the army violently cleared a rally in Tahrir Square and seven women who were arrested said they were subjected to a forcible, invasive "virginity test." Victim Samira Ibrahim, 25, said it amounted to a military doctor sticking his hand into her "chastity" for five minutes.[3]

Then in December, the military government's police beat women protesters, including some in religious garb, in clashes that left 14 people dead and hundreds wounded. The footage of soldiers stripping, beating and kicking one woman protester triggered international outrage when it was broadcast around the world.[4]

Now, after elections in January gave Islamist parties, led by the Muslim Brotherhood's Freedom and Justice Party (FJP), a majority of the seats in Egypt's parliament, Soueif's dream of an egalitarian utopia between the sexes has faded away for some women. Abeda Naguib, 35, a filmmaker who was active in the protests, is thinking of leaving the country.

"As a woman and an artist, I'm scared," she says. "We are expecting them [the Muslim Brotherhood] to make women put on the veil. It's definitely going to be less freedom. The Brotherhood has sold out the revolution."

Before the Tahrir protests led to the ouster of President Hosni Mubarak, Egypt had passed some of the Middle East's most progressive divorce laws. In 2000, Egyptian women gained the right to a divorce without a husband's consent or proof of maltreatment.[5]

Since Mubarak's fall, however, some Freedom and Justice members have vowed to revoke those reforms.[6] And although women's groups had helped to get the divorce reforms through parliament before the revolution, the groups now seem "very disorganized and have different agendas," says Nadia Sonneveld, author of a forthcoming book on Egypt's divorce law.

During the Arab Spring, "Despite women joining these protests and being very active, it was not necessarily as women's rights activists," adds Elena Zacharenko, a Middle East expert in Amnesty International's Brussels office. Women's rights "were downplayed. When they were mentioned, they were painted as a Western influence imposed from the outside world."

Feminists are also disappointed that in Egypt, the largest Arab Spring country, women won barely 2 percent of the new parliament's seats, far less than the 12 percent mandated during the 2010 election under the Mubarak regime. By comparison, Morocco, where religious parties won a landslide victory, now has a parliament that is 17 percent female, while Tunisia elected women candidates to 28 percent of its parliamentary seats — though still short of its 50 percent quota.[7]

Hania Sholkamy, an anthropologist at the American University in Cairo, blames the lack of female representation in Egypt's Parliament on the failure of women's rights groups to unite around any candidates.[8]

"State-sponsored feminism . . . harmed the popular perception of women's rights," Sholkamy writes, referring to Mubarak's gender quota, widely viewed as a way for the authoritarian leader to pack parliament with his supporters. "The state imposed an unpopular quota for women and implemented it in the most discredited and corrupt elections in Egyptian history."[9]

It remains unclear what the Muslim Brotherhood will try to do regarding women's legal status. Lawmakers from the Brotherhood and the ultraconservative Salafi parties voted on March 24 to give Islamists an overwhelming majority on the panel that will write the new constitution. Liberal lawmakers criticized the panel for excluding women and Christians.[10]

To date, the Brotherhood's official statements have tended to be more moderate than those of some of its most prominent members.[11] The group's English-language website speaks often of women while its Arabic websites almost never mention them.[12]

Such two-facedness is also a concern in Tunisia. During its October election campaign, the Islamist Al-Nahda party was careful not to state its position on the issue of women's rights, says Maaike Voorhoeve, a University of Amsterdam researcher studying Tunisian politics. Yet after Al-Nahda took the lead, party leader Rachid Ghannouchi declared polygamy was "possible."[13]

"So everyone who was already afraid something like this would happen saw this as some kind of bad omen that Al-Nahda will go even further," says Voorhoeve, speaking by telephone from Tunisia, which until now has enjoyed liberal family laws.

However, the new constitution being drafted in Tunisia will not call for Sharia to be the source of all legislation,

Al-Nahda announced on March 26, despite calls from extremist Salafis to implement Sharia.[14]

In Libya, women had triggered a revolution on Feb. 15, 2011, when the mothers, sisters and widows of prisoners killed in a 1996 massacre staged street demonstrations in Benghazi to protest the arrest of their lawyer.

But after the ensuing civil war there, interim leader Mustafa Abdel-Jalil shocked the West when he declared in October that Libya would be governed by Islamic law, allowing polygamy, which is legal now only if the first wife consents.[15] Still, "there's no appetite for an extreme law of Sharia in Libya," says BBC Libya reporter Rana Jawad, author of *Tripoli Witness*, a new book about the revolution.

The transitional Libyan government also decided months ago not to implement a quota that sets aside 10 percent of parliamentary seats for women in upcoming elections, even though it had originally promised to abide by the quota. Women "are shocked to discover that there is now no quota at all, leaving them at even greater risk of exclusion," according to the women's advocacy group Women 4 Libya, which had said the 10 percent quota was paltry.[16]

"This revolution was started by women. They captured the imagination of everyone, including sons and husbands," Libyan writer Faraj Najem said recently. Now, "they're taking a passenger seat. We need them to play a pivotal role."[17]

— Sarah Glazer

Egyptian women have been at the forefront of that country's Arab Spring protests. These women were demonstrating in Cairo on March 16, 2012, in support of Samira Ibrahim, who has sued an army doctor for allegedly conducting forced "virginity tests" on female protesters. He was acquitted on March 10, sparking outrage among Egyptian women.

[1]Ahdaf Soueif, *Cairo: My City, Our Revolution* (2012), p. 187. For background, see Roland Flamini, "Turmoil in the Arab World," *CQ Global Researcher*, May 3, 2011, pp. 209-236.

[2]Adhaf Soueif, speaking at the Jan. 19, 2012, launch of her book, *Cairo: My City, Our Revolution* (2012) at the South Bank Centre, London.

[3]Sarah A. Topol, "Virginity Tests: A Trial for Egypt," "Global Opinion blog," International Herald Tribune, http://latitude.blogs.nytimes .com/2012/03/15/acquittal-in-a-virginity-test-trial-in-egypt-is-a-setback-for-government-accountability/?scp=1&sq=virginity%20tests&st=cse.

[4]"Egypt: 10,000 March in Protest," *Telegraph*, Dec. 21, 2011, www .telegraph.co.uk/news/worldnews/africaandindianocean/egypt/8969555/ Egypt-10000-march-in-protest-at-woman-dragged-half-naked-through-street.html. Also see "Mass March by Cairo Women," *The New York Times*, Dec. 21, 2011, www.nytimes.com/2011/12/21/world/middleeast/ violence-enters-5th-day-as-egyptian-general-blames-protesters.html?_ r=1&scp=1&sq=Blue-bra%20girl&st=cse; and "Days of Shame in the Middle East," *Mail Online*, Dec. 19, 2011, www.dailymail.co.uk/news/ article-2075683/Egypt-violence-Female-protesters-brutally-beaten-metal-poles-vicious-soldiers.html.

[5]Vicki Langohr, "How Egypt's Revolution Has Dialed Back Women's Rights," *Foreign Affairs*, December 2011, www.foreignaffairs.com/ articles/136986/vickie-langohr/how-egypts-revolution-has-dialed-back-womens-rights.

[6]Monika Lindbekk, "A Revolution in Egypt's Family Law?" *Babylon*, No. 2, November 2011, pp. 22-35. Published in Norwegian as "En revolusjon i egyptisk familierett?" www.tidsskriftforeningen.no/index.php/nor/ Magasin/Babylon-2-11.

[7]Hania Sholkamy, "Egypt's Women Missing from Formal Politics," *Ahramonline*, Jan. 22, 2012, http://english.ahram.org.eg/News/32349.aspx.

[8]*Ibid.*

[9]*Ibid.*

[10]Kareem Fahim, "Tunisia Says Constitution Will Not Cite Islamic Law," *The New York Times*, March 26, 2012, www.nytimes .com/2012/03/27/world/africa/tunisia-says-constitution-will-not-cite-islamic-law.html?_r=1&ref=world.

[11]Essiam Arian, deputy leader of the Freedom and Justice Party, has declared that rolling back "personal status" laws — as divorce and family laws are known — is not a priority. See Lindbekk, *op. cit.*

[12]David Pollock, "Egypt's Muslim Brotherhood and Its Record of Double Talk," *The Washington Post*, Jan. 26, 2012, www.washingtonpost .com/opinions/egypts-muslim-brotherhood-and-its-record-of-double-talk/2012/01/26/gIQALhO4TQ_story.html.

[13]"Tunisia: Shaking the Foundations of Secularism," *Al-Akhbar English*, March 3, 2012, http://english.al-akhbar.com/node/4771/.

[14]Fahim, *op. cit.*

[15]For background, see Sarah Glazer, "Sharia Controversy," *CQ Global Researcher*, Jan. 3, 2012, pp. 1-28.

[16]"Women 4 Libya Says Draft Election Law Risks Failing Women," *Tripoli Post*, Jan. 20, 2012, http://tripolipost.com/articledetail .asp?c=1&i=7711.

[17]Faraj Najem, speaking at "Rebuilding Libya" forum, Feb. 15, 2012, Frontline Club, London, www.frontlineclub.com/blogs/theforum/ 2012/02/rebuilding-libya.html.

AFP/Getty Images/Mychele Daniau

Despite the success of women like Marie-Christine Lombard, CEO of TNT Express Division in the Netherlands, only about 3 percent of the presidents and board chairs of the EU's largest companies are female. To help break that glass ceiling, the Netherlands recently copied Norway's example by mandating that a certain percentage of corporate board seats be filled by women.

marriage, 14 percent of Yemeni girls are married before age 15, and 52 percent marry before 18, according to UNICEF. In fact, Yemen in 1999 repealed its law setting 15 as the minimum age, and religious conservatives in 2009 blocked an attempt to raise the marriage age to at least 17. Yemeni children today can be married at any age, and in some rural areas girls as young as 8 become brides.[19]

Although CEDAW signatory countries must submit status reports to a special committee every four years outlining their compliance with the treaty, there is no enforcement mechanism for the provisions, says Gerntholz. "It comes down to the willingness of national governments to comply with the obligations," she says.

During the perennially stalled debate in the U.S. Congress over whether to ratify CEDAW, opponents have often questioned the treaty's effectiveness. "Many of the signatories to CEDAW have deplorable human rights records, and these countries have not advanced women's human rights any faster after joining the convention," according to Grace S. Melton, an associate for U.N. social issues at the Heritage Foundation, a conservative think tank in Washington, D.C.[20]

"CEDAW is an ineffective and inappropriate instrument for advancing women's rights around the world," she has charged. "In the case of gross abuses of women's rights, such as sex trafficking or female circumcision, it has been less effective than targeted instruments to address [those activities]."[21]

Christina Hoff Sommers, a resident scholar at the conservative American Enterprise Institute in Washington, D.C., notes that, despite six committee reviews, Yemen still has a law exempting from prosecution any man guilty of a so-called honor killing — the murder of a female relative suspected of adultery, in the name of family honor.[22]

Yet human rights activists say CEDAW is useful in holding governments to an international standard. "Naming and shaming" helps to bring about reform, according to June Zeitlin, director of the CEDAW Education Project at the Leadership Conference on Civil and Human Rights in Washington, D.C. "But you can't expect it to work miracles."

Kuwait, for example, ratified CEDAW even though its female citizens did not yet have the right to vote.

deal with the article guaranteeing women's rights within marriage and the family.[16] Some Muslim countries contend the treaty's provisions calling for the elimination of polygamy and child marriage and for equal inheritance rights for women conflict with their conservative interpretations of Sharia.[17] As a result, some countries simply never incorporate the treaty's principles into domestic law.

"In Yemen, CEDAW seems to have little impact on the ground," says Liesl Gerntholz, director of the Women's Rights Division at Human Rights Watch.[18] Although the Yemeni government has signed CEDAW and at least four other conventions that condemn child

When Kuwait came up for review, the CEDAW committee raised the suffrage issue. "It's hard to prove cause and effect, but a year later [in 2005] Kuwait did give women the right to vote," Zeitlin says. "That kind of pressure makes a difference because clearly every country wants to look good before the world community."[23]

Nadia Sonneveld, a Dutch legal anthropologist, believes that without international pressure the Mubarak regime would never have passed its liberal divorce law allowing Egyptian women to divorce their husbands without consent. "I don't think it would have been put into effect if there had not been pressure from the CEDAW committee and the convention," says Sonneveld, author of a book on the law's passage.[24]

Of course, countries can pass laws under international pressure without really changing domestic practices. "That happens a lot," Sonneveld says. "There's international pressure and laws are issued, but they do not find a basis of support in society." For instance, in 2007, under pressure from outsiders, Egypt outlawed female circumcision. Yet, female genital mutilation — as it is also called — has been performed on more than 90 percent of Egyptian girls and women ages 14-49, according to the most recent estimate.[25]

Should governments impose electoral gender quotas?

More than 50 countries have legislated electoral gender quotas during the past 20 years, either reserving a percentage of legislative assembly seats for women or requiring that a minimum proportion of candidates be female. In another 50 countries, at least one

Women Make Gains on EU Corporate Boards

With women holding 27 percent of the board seats, Finland's largest corporations have the highest percentage of female directors than companies in any other European Union country and nearly twice the EU average (top). However, Finland lags behind non-EU member Norway, which since 2008 has mandated that women fill 40 percent of board seats. Since then seven other countries — Spain, Iceland, France, Italy, the Netherlands, Belgium and Malaysia — have legislated phased-in gender quotas for corporate boards, and other countries are considering quotas. Meanwhile, only about 3 percent of the presidents and board chairs of the EU's largest companies are female (bottom), double the percentage in 2003 but still far behind their male counterparts.

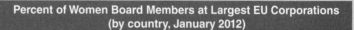

Percent of Women Board Members at Largest EU Corporations (by country, January 2012)

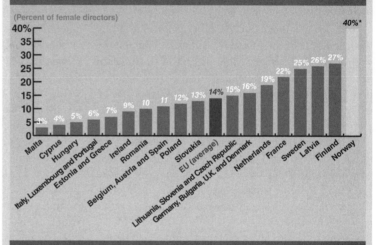

Percent of Male and Female CEOs, Board Chairs of Largest EU Companies, 2003 and 2012

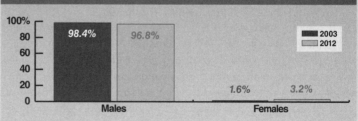

* Norway is not an EU member.

Source: "European Commission Weighs Options to Break the 'Glass Ceiling' for Women on Company Boards," European Commission, March 2012, europa.eu/rapid/pressReleasesAction.do? reference=IP/12/213&format=HTML&aged=0 &language=EN&guiLanguage=en

political party uses voluntary quotas to draw up candidate lists.[26] (*See map, p. 350.*) Global treaties such as CEDAW also support quotas, as do international foreign aid donors.

Nevertheless, women still represent less than 20 percent of parliamentary seats worldwide — compared to 13 percent a decade ago.[27] Only Rwanda, where 56 percent of lawmakers are female, has an elected body in which at least half of the legislators are women. In Sweden, with the second-highest female representation, women hold 45 percent of seats.[28] (*See graphic, p. 367.*)

The rapid spread of gender quotas in recent years has been spurred by countries writing new constitutions, often after conflicts. Rwanda, for example, instituted quotas after its 1994 genocide left the population 70 percent female, leading women to take on new roles as heads of households and community leaders.[29]

The new Rwandan constitution, adopted in 2003, was the result of three years of intensive lobbying by women's groups. It allocated 30 percent of seats in each house of Parliament to women. In the country's first post-genocide parliamentary elections in October 2003, women exceeded the quota by running not only for the 30 percent of reserved seats but also for seats available to male candidates, winning about half of the seats in the lower house. Rwanda's jump to a global high of 56 percent has resulted in part because early quotas served to "incubate" budding female politicians, who then ran in the general elections against men, say women's rights advocates.[30]

Establishing female quotas "is part of being a democratic . . . modern society now," says Drude Dahlerup, a professor of political science at Stockholm University, who tracks quota activity internationally for the Quota Project, a global database.[31]

Without quotas, advocates say, it would take forever to get parity in legislatures. "No country gets to critical mass in its representation in a parliamentary body [at least 30 percent] without some affirmative mechanism in place," says Liswood of the Council of Women World Leaders. There's a "persuasive argument" for quotas "overcoming some of the cultural barriers that kept us out of power."

The United States has supported constitution-writing efforts in Afghanistan that include gender quotas. But women's advocates concede that quotas conflict with the American notion of ensuring equality of opportunity rather than equality of outcomes. Lee Waldorf, human rights adviser at U.N. Women, the U.N.'s division that advocates for female equality, notes that CEDAW's philosophy supporting gender quotas is "about equality of results" rather than the "formal equality" guaranteed in the U.S. Constitution, which is more about "making sure people are treated on paper similarly."

Waldorf says quotas were envisioned as a stopgap designed "to speed up that cultural shift, and then you're supposed to get rid of them." So far no country has dropped their quotas.

Cristina Finch, policy and advocacy director for women's human rights at Amnesty International, says it's critical to make sure that the female candidates are "actually representatives" and not women "selected by party leaders to speak the party line. We want to make sure women's voices are actually being heard."

For example, Egypt's 2009 quota law was widely viewed as a way for the Mubarak regime to pack the parliament with female supporters. So there was little opposition when the transitional military leadership abandoned the quota in January's elections for the first post-Mubarak parliament.[32]

In India, under a 1993 law, villages are randomly selected during each five-year election cycle to institute a 33 percent quota for women in the village council, known as a *panchayat*. In the early years, many female candidates were criticized for being "proxy women" — voting the bidding of their husbands or other male relatives. Some openly campaigned that way. But recently more women council members appear to be acting independently, say researchers.

Bidyut Mohanty, who as head of women's studies at New Delhi's Institute of Social Science has studied the quota system for the U.N., visited her home state of Odisha in February during the recent election. She found women canvassing door-to-door without a male relative — unheard of in the state's first quota-based election in 1997.

Studies by her and others find that female officeholders in India are more likely than men to campaign for benefits important to women, such as clean water, child care, maternal health and education. But the scholarship on these findings is divided, says Ashutosh Varshney, a professor of international studies and director of the

C H R O N O L O G Y

1700s-1920 *Age of Enlightenment and Industrial Revolution lead to greater freedoms for women.*

1792 Mary Wollstonecraft publishes *A Vindication of the Rights of Women*, advocating greater equality for women.

1893 Women in New Zealand become first to win full suffrage.

1918 British women win the right to vote.

1920 U.S. women gain right to vote.

1940s-1980s *International conventions endorse equal rights for women.*

1944 French women gain right to vote.

1946 U.N. creates Commission on the Status of Women to address key issues affecting women's health, welfare and rights.

1947 Pakistan allows women to vote. India follows suit in 1950.

1951 U.N. International Labour Organization adopts convention promoting gender pay equality.

1952 U.N. calls for full women's suffrage.

1975 U.N. holds first World Conference on Women, in Mexico City, followed by similar conferences every five years.

1979 U.N. adopts Convention on the Elimination of All Forms of Discrimination Against Women (CEDAW). Called the gold standard for women's equality, it has been signed by 187 nations, but not the United States.

1990s *Atrocities in the former Yugoslavia and Rwanda trigger efforts to recognize violence against women as human rights crimes.*

1996 In first-ever prosecution of rape as a war crime, the International Criminal Tribunal for the Former Yugoslavia convicts eight Serb police and military officers for mass rapes during Bosnian conflict.

1998 International Criminal Tribunal for Rwanda, while prosecuting those responsible for the 1994 genocide, recognizes wartime rape and sexual violence as genocide and crimes against humanity.

2000s *Islamist election victories in post-Arab Spring countries raise questions about the future of women's rights; some European countries adopt corporate board gender quotas; Egyptian women protest military's sexual harassment.*

2000 Egypt gives women right to divorce without husband's consent.

2002 Rome Statute creating International Criminal Court codifies sexual violence as a crime against humanity and rape as a war crime; in last U.S. congressional action to date, Senate Foreign Relations Committee approves CEDAW but full Senate never takes action.

2009 Norway's major companies meet the country's new mandatory quota for females occupying 40 percent of corporate board seats.

2010 Tunisian fruit-peddler's self-immolation protest in December triggers anti-government revolutions — many of which include large numbers of women protesters — across the Arab world.

2011 Arab Spring protests continue and civil war breaks out in Libya after women-led demonstrations. Weeks after Egyptian President Hosni Mubarak is driven from office, men in Cairo attack women protesting sexual harassment. . . . France, the Netherlands, Belgium, Italy and Malaysia adopt mandatory gender quotas for corporate boards; EU Minister Viviane Reding urges companies to adopt voluntary quotas. . . . In December, female protesters in Egypt are stripped and beaten by soldiers, sparking mass protests.

2012 Muslim Brotherhood's Islamist party wins lead in Egyptian Parliament, raising questions about the future of women's rights. . . . Reding announces review of EU corporate board quotas. . . . Egyptian court acquits military doctor accused of performing forced "virginity tests" on female demonstrators.

Scandinavia's Male-Female Equality Has a Catch

Pay gap still victimizes women.

If you try to phone Norwegian economist Harald Dale-Olsen late on a weekday afternoon, he might not answer. He's probably busy caring for his 11-month-old baby and kindergarten-age daughter.

After Dale-Olsen and his wife had their second child, they decided to share their state-guaranteed 13-month parental leave. She took the first seven months off at 80 percent pay, then returned to her job as a social science researcher. Now Dale-Olsen, a research professor at the Institute for Social Research, is halfway through his six-month leave, also at 80 percent of his salary and also with his job guaranteed.

For Dale-Olsen, sharing child care is a no-brainer. "The first month the mom needs to be home due to breastfeeding and that sort of thing," he says, noting that the government reserves the first month after birth just for the mother. But from around six months of age on, he says, "there's less reason she has to be home, at least in my opinion." And because they both earn the same salary, there was less pressure for the lower income earner to stay home.

Dale-Olsen acknowledges his ideas about equal sharing are politically contentious, even in egalitarian Norway, which guarantees 47 weeks of parental leave at 100 percent pay or 13 months at 80 percent. Some of Norway's more conservative politicians think women should take most of the staying-home time.

It's often more expensive for the father to take time off, since men earn about 15 percent more than women in Norway, a pay gap that rises to about 30 percent when women's greater tendency toward part-time work is factored in, says Dale-Olsen.

Norway, Sweden and Denmark — with their generous guaranteed parental-leave policies — are often painted as Nordic nirvanas by American working women, who often get derailed from their careers when they have children. U.S. women face a stark choice between going right back to work to stay on their promotional track or committing to full-time motherhood, argues Sylvia Ann Hewlett, president of the Center for Talent Innovation, a New York City think tank.

As a result, even though the United States has a higher percentage of top female executives than Scandinavia, American female executives are less likely to have children than either U.S. men or Swedish women. Forty-two percent of American women executives ages 41-55 are childless compared to 12 percent of Swedish executives, ages 46-55, according to Hewlett.[1]

"The U.S. is much better at integrating women into the corporate world and as managers, but American women have to choose between motherhood and careers," says Anette Borchorst, a professor of political science at Denmark's Aalborg University. In Scandinavia, she says, "Since the '70s . . . you are able to combine both."

India Initiative, at Brown University in Providence, R.I. He reports that lower-caste leaders demonstrate similar sympathies, leading some researchers to argue that "which caste comes to dominate village *panchayats* is more important than whether it's a female or male head."

Critics of quotas often say they could constitute reverse discrimination against qualified males. However, Dahlerup argues that that ignores the latest diagnosis of why women are so poorly represented: clubby, all-male political parties traditionally select candidates who are just like themselves. "If the problem is middle-aged men

recruiting one another, then quotas are not unfair to men; it's a compensation for the disfavor women meet," Dahlerup says.

Perhaps the most powerful argument for quotas is what could be called the Maggie Thatcher effect, after the former British prime minister: When girls see a woman in power, they're more likely to harbor a similar ambition.

A new study in West Bengal villages found that having female leaders provided such powerful role models that Indian girls' aspirations were raised significantly; they soon caught up to boys in how long they stayed in

In 1974, Sweden introduced lengthy paid parental leaves that for the first time could be divided by the parents as they wished, and other Scandinavian countries soon followed suit.[2] But Borchorst says such long parental leaves can be "a double-edged sword" for women. The longer you stay out of a job, she says, the more "you lose career chances and wage increases, and that has implications for your pension."

And it was mothers — not fathers — who took more than 90 percent of the allowed parental leave in Nordic countries in the 1990s. The expectation that mothers could be legally absent for a year made employers less willing to invest in training women for a management track, experts say, and probably increased the pay gap.

To redress this gender imbalance, Norway introduced a "daddy month" in 1993 — parental leave for fathers only, available on a "use it or lose it" basis. Today most fathers who take leave take one month.[3] Other Scandinavian countries copied "daddy leave."

Today Iceland, where fathers take more parental leave than in any Nordic country, is the new nirvana for Scandinavian gender experts. Parental leave is divided into three 13-week chunks: one-third reserved for the father, one-third for the mother and the remaining to be divided as parents see fit. Almost as many men as women take leave, and fathers take 34 percent of the leave — generally the 13 weeks allocated to them.[4]

Norway is considering a similar proposal. "In my opinion, it's a good thing," says Dale-Olsen, "because very often you hear employers argue that women are so costly due to this parental leave. So by forcing fathers to stay home, it makes them recognize that men are equally costly."

Nevertheless, conservative politicians say parental leave meddles with family values and choices about who belongs home with the children. In Denmark, where the right-wing Danish People's Party has been gaining strength, a two-week "daddy leave" was abolished after a two-year experiment.

Although Scandinavia has the world's highest proportion of working women, many still carry the "second shift" of cooking and child care, which may explain why they make up only a fraction of top management positions — about 5 percent in Norway, for example. Scandinavian countries also still have a highly gender-segregated workforce, with women heavily concentrated in public sector jobs that have 9-to-5 workdays that track the hours of subsidized child-care centers. That's partly why Scandinavia's gender pay gap remains almost as large as the rest of Europe: Government salaries are lower than private sector wages.[5]

— Sarah Glazer

[1] Cited in Magnus Henrekson and Mikael Stenkula, "Why Are There So Few Female Top Executives in Egalitarian Welfare States?" *The Independent Review*, Vol. 14, No. 2, Fall 2009, pp. 239-270, www.ifn.se/eng/people/research_fellows/mh/publications_4/articles_in_english_1.

[2] In 1974, Sweden introduced a six-month parental leave, paid at 90 percent, that could be shared by the father and mother. See Kimberly Earles, "Child Care and Parental Leave in Sweden," *Cortona Colloquium*, 2008, p. 8, www.fondazionefeltrinelli.it/dm_0/FF/ . . . /0386.pdf.

[3] *Parental Leave, Care Policies and Gender Equalities in the Nordic Countries* (2010), p. 30. See graph p. 23 for Nordic countries' length of leave, www.norden.org/en/publications/publikationer/2010-539.

[4] "Nordic Statistical Yearbook, 2010," 2010, p. 67, www.norden.org/en/publications/publikationer/2010-001.

[5] See Maria Charles and David B. Grusky, *Occupational Ghettos: The Worldwide Segregation of Woman and Men* (2005), and Catherine Hakim, "Feminist Myths and Magic Medicine," Centre for Policy Studies, January 2011, www.catherinehakim.org.

school. One-third of randomly selected village councils were designated to have a woman chief councilor. Villages without a quota showed sizable gaps between girls and boys in educational ambition and school years completed, while in quota villages girls' ambitions were similar to those of the boys. After just two election cycles, girls in quota villages were more likely to say they wanted to wait until age 18 to marry and have a job that required an education.[33]

Noting that attitudes changed just as rapidly among parents as among the girls themselves, Harvard's Budson says, "In a blink of an eye they could remake who women thought they could be."

Should governments try to close the corporate gender gap?

It's been called the Norwegian paradox. Women in Norway are as highly educated as men, comprise half the workforce and hold nearly as many political posts as men. But until recently they occupied only 4 percent of corporate board seats and only slightly more of the top corporate management jobs.[34]

In a country that normally leads the world in its egalitarian treatment of women, some Norwegians consider the lack of female executives a cultural flaw. The effort to mandate a fix to that flaw, somewhat surprisingly, has been led by a conservative government minister of trade and industry, Ansgar Gabrielsen, who says mixed-gender boardrooms create better business results.[35]

In 2003 Norway became the first country to urge that large, publicly listed companies reserve 40 percent of board seats for women. Initially the target was voluntary, but when companies failed to meet it, the parliament in 2007-2008 made the quota mandatory and even authorized the government to dissolve noncompliant companies. By 2009, companies had reached the 40 percent target — up from less than 5 percent in 2000.[36] Researchers determined that the success in reaching the target was due mainly to the tough penalties.[37]

Experts point out that Norway is somewhat unusual in that its government holds a large stake in public companies, and only about 1,500 of Norway's 160,000 companies — generally its largest — are affected by the quota.[38]

While business leaders initially objected to the mandate, the criticism largely has faded away, according to a 2009 survey of board members conducted a year after the law's full implementation. A majority of the 990 members surveyed said they had seen no change, positive or negative, in their board's operation after the reform. Of the 6 percent who saw a negative effect, most said new female board members lacked "important competence and insight." But that complaint was counterbalanced by the finding that women directors tended to have more advanced degrees than men.[39]

Recently, some have complained that an elite handful of women, known as the "golden skirts," have captured too many of the female seats on multiple boards. But business professor Aagoth Storvik of Akershus University College says, "on average, men have the same number of board memberships as women."

Similar quotas have been passed by six European parliaments and in Malaysia and are being hotly debated in Germany, Sweden and Finland.[40] (See "Current Situation.") In March, EU Justice Minister Reding launched a three-month public review to consider an EU-wide mandate to boost the percentage of women sitting in directors' seats across the union. Research shows that companies with women at the helm tend to be more profitable than those with all-male leadership, she argued. Companies with more female board members outperformed their male-dominated rivals with a 66 percent higher return on invested capital, according to Catalyst, an international nonprofit that researches women in business.[41]

"In general, women tend to focus on the oversight functions, checking to make sure the company is not taking on too much risk," says Susan Ness, a senior fellow at the Center for Transatlantic Relations at Johns Hopkins University's School of Advanced International Studies, which holds an annual international conference on female directors. "They raise questions guys don't raise and that guys sometimes feel foolish asking."

However, a recent University of Michigan study found that Norwegian companies that took on more women to meet the quota became less profitable because women directors had less experience than male ones.[42]

A third study among a larger group of firms by Norwegian economist Harald Dale-Olsen at the Institute for Social Research, a private research foundation in Oslo, found no effect on profitability. From an equality point of view, he says, the mandate is "a tremendous success because this quota is dramatically increasing female representation and at the same time did *not* reduce the performance of these firms."[43]

Still, it's disappointing that the quota "has not had much more effect" on the executive suite, says Mari Teigen, a research professor at the Institute for Social Research in Oslo. Management, she says, is "just as male-dominated as before," with no more than about 5 percent women in top executive positions.

Perhaps that's because "when things are voluntary, women do not get those positions," suggests Storvik. The "extremely effective" mandatory quota shows that "if you want a rapid change, this is the way to go," she says.

Politicians and businesses in free-market Britain and the United States tend to recoil at the idea of mandatory quotas. "In the U.S., people seem to think quotas disadvantage one group and advantage another group," says Liswood of the Council of Women World Leaders. "The fact is there actually has been a quota; it's just been a very informal one: 'The person I play golf with' or 'the person who went to the same school as me.'"

In Britain, a government commission last year urged the boards of large British companies to voluntarily double their female representation by 2015 by reserving 25 percent of board seats for women.[44]

British business interests strongly oppose mandatory quotas. "Ultimately, it's up to companies to decide who suits them," says Simon Walker, director general of the Institute of Directors, an organization for British corporate board directors. While it's good to have a diversity of perspectives, he says, it's not clear that women necessarily provide that.

"Quite often, where firms do struggle to find people who look or sound different, they end up with people who all think the same," he says.

BACKGROUND

From Witches to Enlightenment

The idea that matriarchal societies such as the warlike Amazons once ruled over men has long held a grip on the artistic imagination — from Greek legends to the present day.[45] Yet, archeologists have found little hard evidence that such societies ever existed.[46]

Rather, the earliest written records from ancient Mesopotamia, in 2500 B.C., and later from ancient Greece and in the Old Testament describe women's enslavement through war and their subordination through marriage contracts. Christianity empowered women in some ways and weakened them in others.

A girl, betrothed against her will, could ask the local clergyman to intervene on her behalf, and a woman could appeal her husband's divorce plans. But unlike the the ancient Greeks, Romans and Hebrews, early Christian fathers, such as St. Jerome (347-420 A.D.), denounced contraception — such as coital withdrawal — as "murder" of "man not born."[47]

Long seen as having ties to the spirit world, women often were assumed to have supernatural powers and became a scapegoat for illness or misfortune. Between A.D. 1300 and the 17th century, at least 100,000 women throughout Europe were burned at the stake, drowned, strangled or beheaded in a wave of antiwitchcraft persecution, led by religious leaders struggling to cope with the Black Plague, the Hundred Years' War and conflicts between Catholics and reformers.[48]

AFP/Getty Images/Raveendran

Indian activists demonstrate in front of the Indian parliament in New Delhi on July 23, 2009, demanding that one-third of the seats be reserved for women. No such law has passed, but under a 1993 law villages are randomly selected during each five-year election cycle to institute a 33 percent quota for women selected to serve on each village council, known as a panchayat. In the early years, many female candidates were criticized for voting the bidding of their husbands or other male relatives. But recently more women council members appear to be acting independently, researchers say.

The 18th century's Enlightenment emphasized the political and civil autonomy of individuals, ideas that provided a philosophical platform for rejecting all kinds of legal dependency — from slavery to relations between men and women. In 1792 Mary Wollstonecraft published *A Vindication of the Rights of Women*, which has been hailed as the "feminist declaration of independence," although at the time many viewed the British writer and philosopher as a dangerous iconoclast. The book was heavily influenced by the French Revolution's notion of equality and universal brotherhood.

Paradoxically, French revolutionary leaders were unsympathetic to feminist causes and in 1789 the National Assembly rejected a Declaration of the Rights of Women. Jean Jacques Rousseau, one of the philosophical founders of the Enlightenment, wrote, "the whole education of women ought to be relative to men. To please them, to be useful to them, to make themselves loved and honored by them."[49]

The 19th century's economic shift from a largely agricultural society to the Industrial Revolution changed women's views of their own role and their relation to men. Women began to earn their own money working

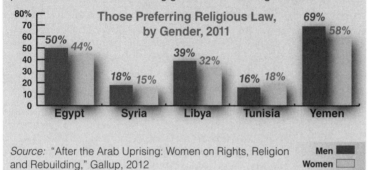

Most Arabs Want Secular Law

Among countries that experienced last year's "Arab Spring" revolutions, in only Yemen does a majority of both sexes favor having Islamic law as the sole basis for legislation. In most other Arab countries, a majority of men and women reject that approach, according to the latest Gallup poll. In Egypt half of men and 44 percent of women favor basing governance on religious law.

Those Preferring Religious Law, by Gender, 2011

	Egypt	Syria	Libya	Tunisia	Yemen
Men	50%	18%	39%	16%	69%
Women	44%	15%	32%	18%	58%

Source: "After the Arab Uprising: Women on Rights, Religion and Rebuilding," Gallup, 2012

Men ■ Women □

in textile mills, gained more education and were recruited as teachers, although they received a fraction of men's pay.

Starting in the 1830s, public campaigns in Britain agitated to "protect" working women: Their work hours were limited, and they — along with children — were barred from the mines under the British Mines Act of 1842. But the protectionists failed to provide alternative sources of income. In isolated mining districts, particularly in Scotland, women desperate to work dressed up as men and sneaked into the pits.[50]

Before 1800 there is no record of women's groups organizing to change women's rights or status, according to historian Janet Zollinger Giele.[51] After 1800, however, women around the world began establishing societies and movements to protest their subordinate status. They would eventually win new rights, from child custody to the right to vote.

In England, the women's movement began by organizing a campaign for the rights of married women to own property. In the 19th century, as soon as a woman married she was considered merely an extension of her husband, unable to own property — including what she brought into the marriage. And since a divorced woman had no legal rights to her children, a wife was little more than chattel, argued British philosopher John Stuart Mill. In his 1869 book *The Subjection of Women*, he argued that "no slave is a slave to

the same lengths, and in so full a sense of the word, as a wife is."[52]

In 1870, the Married Women's Property Act in England allowed women to keep their earnings, and the Act of 1882 gave married women the same property rights as unmarried women.[53] The emergence of universal male suffrage in Britain — allowing all men, including those in the working class, to vote — established a goal for the women's suffrage movement.[54]

Following a campaign promise by Mill to introduce a women's suffrage amendment when he ran for Parliament, British women formed their first suffrage group, presenting a petition to Parliament in 1866 seeking the right of women to vote. By 1910, Britain's suffrage movement was one of the world's largest.

From its early days, the movement was divided over tactics. In October 1912, Emmeline Pankhurst led a militant wing, advocating attacks on private property with the announcement, "I incite this meeting to rebellion." During the following two years her organization burned churches, unoccupied houses and a school and exploded a bomb.[55] British women finally won the right to vote in 1918.

In America, the growth of feminism was closely associated with the anti-slavery movement, as parallels were drawn between the slave as property and the woman as property. The 1840 World Anti-Slavery Convention in London was attended by American suffragists Elizabeth Cady Stanton and Lucretia Mott, although women were excluded from the discussion.[56]

In 1848, a small group of women and men met in a Wesleyan chapel in Seneca Falls, N.Y., and read a "Declaration of Sentiments" that paralleled the Declaration of Independence. Its list of grievances included not just the lack of women's right to vote but also unequal employment and education and married women's loss of property and child custody.[57]

In 1893 New Zealand became the first country to enfranchise women, followed by Western Australia in 1899 and the rest of Australia in 1902.[58]

Feminist activity first appeared in Japan in the 1860s, largely due to Western influence, but Japanese women would have to wait until 1945, during the post-World War II installation of a democratic regime, to gain the right to vote.

In 1920, only a handful of countries had female suffrage, including the United States, where women won the vote with passage that year of the 19th Amendment to the Constitution. By 1945 more than 40 countries had instituted women's suffrage, and by the 1970s women in more than 100 countries could vote.[59]

The first wave of women's suffrage between 1890 and 1922 occurred in Western democracies with a tradition of individualism. The second occurred in largely Catholic countries, such as France, where church officials had tried to block feminists' efforts. French women finally gained the right to vote in 1944. The third wave of reforms occurred in 1945-71 in newly independent developing countries such as Indonesia, which granted female suffrage in 1945, and Pakistan, in 1947.

A fourth group of countries, primarily Muslim, began debating women's voting rights only in recent decades. Since 1970 women in Jordan, Yemen and Kuwait have gained the right to vote, and last year Saudi Arabia promised to allow women to vote — starting in 2015.[60]

International Action

Women's issues received new visibility when the year-old United Nations established the Commission on the Status of Women in 1946 to address urgent problems facing the world's women. Then during the 1950s the U.N. adopted several conventions aimed at improving women's lives, including the 1952 Convention on the Political Rights of Women, ensuring the right to vote.[61] A year earlier, the International Labour Organization — a U.N. agency specializing in labor issues — had adopted a convention calling for equal pay for equal work.

But it wasn't until 1975 that the U.N. held its first World Conference on Women. Activists from around the world converged on the meeting, held in Mexico City, to demand a treaty to hold countries responsible for enforcing equal rights. The Commission on the Status of Women began drafting such a treaty, and four years later the U.N. General Assembly adopted the Convention on the Elimination of All Forms of Discrimination against Women (CEDAW).

Often described as an international bill of rights for women, CEDAW defines discrimination against women

Moroccan women protest outside the parliament in Rabat on March 17, 2012, demanding the repeal of a law, Article 475, that allows a rapist to avoid jail if he marries his victim with her parents' consent. The women blame the law for the recent suicide of Amina al-Filali, 16, who was forced to marry her rapist. The signs say, "Article 475 killed me," "Rest In Peace Amina . . . Rest In Peace Moroccan justice system."

as "any distinction, exclusion or restriction made on the basis of sex" that impairs or nullifies the recognition, enjoyment or exercise by women — irrespective of their marital status — of their human rights and fundamental freedoms "in the political, economic, social, cultural, civil or any other field."[62]

Ratifying countries are legally bound to end discrimination by incorporating gender equality into their legal systems, abolishing laws that discriminate against women, trying to end trafficking of women and ensuring that women have equal access to political and public life. Countries must submit reports every four years outlining the steps taken to comply with the convention.

The treaty also stresses "reproductive choice," urging signatory states to develop laws guaranteeing women's right "to decide freely and responsibly on the number and spacing of their children."[63] Although the treaty does not mention abortion, the United States has not ratified CEDAW in part because American conservatives fear it could undermine their efforts to restrict abortions in the United States.

The treaty, which also does not explicitly mention violence, has been used to stem gender-based violence against women. In 1992 the CEDAW committee charged with monitoring treaty compliance specified gender-based violence as a form of discrimination. For example, Mexico responded to an epidemic of violence against women in 2007 by incorporating CEDAW principles into a statute requiring states to punish domestic battering and other forms of violence against women. By 2009, the law had been adopted by all 32 Mexican states.[64]

In the 1990s new legal precedents were established to protect women against violence, including the use of rape as a weapon of war.[65] In 1993 the International Criminal Tribunal for the Former Yugoslavia, set up to try those accused of war crimes during the Bosnian War, declared that wartime rape is a crime against humanity. A series of landmark cases soon followed, recognizing sexual violence as a serious war crime. In 1996, a U.N. tribunal indicted eight Bosnian Serb police and military officers in connection with the mass rape of Muslim women during the war, marking the first time sexual assault was prosecuted as a war crime under international law.[66]

Likewise, in 1998, the International Criminal Tribunal for Rwanda — set up to try those responsible for the 1994 massacre of hundreds of thousands of mostly minority Tutsis in Rwanda — found that wartime rape constitutes genocide and a crime against humanity.[67] In 2002, the Rome Statute, which established the International Criminal Court, codified a broad range of sexual crimes as international crimes against humanity. Of the 23 indictments issued by the court so far, 12 have involved sexual violence.[68]

Meanwhile, high-profile women continued to work for gender equality. "Women's rights are human rights," first lady Hillary Rodham Clinton famously declared to women delegates from 189 countries gathered in Beijing in 1995 for the U.N.'s Fourth World Conference on Women. The blueprint for gender equality that emerged, the so-called Beijing Platform, addressed 12 critical women's issues, ranging from poverty and unequal education to inadequate health care and gender-based violence.[69]

But more than 15 years later, say some women's advocates, women's rights worldwide have fallen short of the Beijing platform.[70]

"To meet all the goals of the Beijing platform will take 50 years at least, but that doesn't mean there haven't been extensive changes," says the U.N.'s Waldorf. "There's been a sea change in the violence area: We've gone from 10 years ago, when there was almost no recognition of the evils of domestic violence and sexual harassment in the workplace, to a shift where governments are taking up responsibility for women's rights in the workplace and in the home," she says.

CURRENT SITUATION

Trouble Spots

Every year more than 10 million girls are forced into marriage, according to the U.N., perpetuating one of the oldest forms of gender oppression. Fifty countries have a lower legal marriage age for females than males, with grim consequences: Early pregnancy and childbirth are the leading causes of death for 15- to 19-year-old girls in the developing world.[71]

Tunisia, one of the first Arab countries to eliminate child marriage, demonstrates how progressive laws can quickly change centuries-old customs. In 1960, nearly half of Tunisian women ages 15-19 were married, but in 1964, the legal marriage age for girls was raised from 15 to 17. By 2004 only 3 percent of girls aged 15-19 were married. In 2007 the minimum age was raised again, to 18.[72] Tunisia also has some of the region's most liberal family laws affecting women (concerning divorce, polygamy, etc.).

Tunisia now ranks higher than most other Middle Eastern countries — including Yemen, which is dead last — on the World Economic Forum's gender gap ratings of 135 countries. Yet in Yemen, where child marriage remains widespread, few investments have been made in education and health for women, which would put them on a more equal footing.[73]

Wealthy Saudi Arabia, by contrast, shows how money invested in education and health can effectively erase the difference in the amount of schooling women receive compared to men and to their survival rates. Although it still ranks fifth from the bottom overall on the Forum's index, since 2006 Saudi Arabia has been one of the "highest climbers" on the women's education and health and survival indices. Women's university enrollment rates in Saudi Arabia are now higher than those of men, and the country now ranks in the top half of countries in women's health.[74]

But according to Saadia Zahidi, who directs the gender gap program at the World Economic Forum, Gulf countries such as Saudi Arabia haven't made the same commitment to women's political participation or economic opportunity, so they aren't "reaping the rewards of that investment" from their untapped pool of educated women.[75]

Although Saudi women were recently told they would be allowed to vote starting in 2015, guardianship rules bar them from acting independently in nearly every other aspect of their lives, including working and attending school. "In Saudi Arabia, women are perpetual minors. To make almost any decision in their life — whether [about] medical care or travel — requires the assistance of a male member of the family. It's degrading women to the legal status of children," says Gerntholtz of Human Rights Watch.

Last May and June, Saudi authorities arrested women who drove cars to protest the government's ban on female drivers. Shaima Jastaina was convicted in September for violating public order by driving and sentenced to a public lashing.[76] King Abdullah later canceled the judge's order for 10 lashes.[77]

Recently, Human Rights Watch argued that the International Olympic Committee should bar the Saudi delegation from the Summer Olympics in London unless the delegation includes female athletes.[78] Gerntholtz says barring women from sports is just the most recent visible aspect of Saudi guardianship rules.

"Sadly," she says, she does not expect the International Olympic Committee to follow her organization's recommendations.

Meanwhile, in the aftermath of the Arab Spring revolutions, fundamentalist Muslim parties have gained leading roles in new transitional governments in Egypt, Tunisia and Morocco. Prominent politicians in those countries and in Libya — where national assembly elections are scheduled for May or June — have suggested introducing more stringent forms of Islamic law.[79] Interpretations of Sharia can vary widely, from calling for the stoning of adulterous women in Iran to allowing liberal divorce laws in Tunisia. (*See sidebar, p. 354.*)

Experts say it is hard to predict whether women's rights will be threatened as a result of this turn toward religious conservatism. But there are some counter-intuitive trends

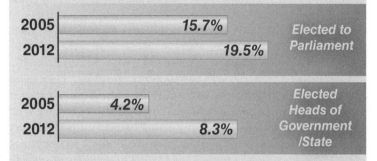

Women's Political Power Grows

About 20 percent of lawmakers worldwide are women, up from about 16 percent in 2005. More than 8 percent of elected heads of state and government are women, nearly double the percentage seven years earlier.

Women in Government, 2005 and 2012

	Elected to Parliament
2005	15.7%
2012	19.5%

	Elected Heads of Government /State
2005	4.2%
2012	8.3%

Sources: "Women in Politics: 2005," Inter-Parliamentary Union, January 2005, www.ipu.org/pdf/publications/wmnmap05_en.pdf; "Women in Politics: 2012," Inter-Parliamentary Union, January 2012,www.ipu.org/pdf/publications/wmnmap12_en.pdf

found in Gallup polls across the region, according to Dalia Mogahed, director of the Gallup Center for Muslim Studies in Abu Dhabi.

"We haven't found the link in our empirical research between religiosity and an anti-woman point of view," says Mogahed. In fact, she adds, "We've seen quite the opposite." A recent Gallup poll in Egypt shows that men who attend mosque regularly are more likely to favor equality for women, she notes.[80]

The growing level of higher education among women is another important trend, she says. "If you look across universities in the Arab world, the percentage of women will be at least as high as in the U.S. and in many cases higher in technical areas like engineering and computer science," Mogahed says. "But for some reason, when it comes to politics that representation goes way down. It's not clear why that is."

Developed Countries

The recent World Economic Forum report on closing gender gaps finds that 135 countries representing more than 90 percent of the world's population have closed almost 96 percent of the gap in health outcomes between women and men and almost 93 percent of the gap in educational attainment. However, gaps in economic opportunity remain wide (only 59 percent of the gap has closed) and the gap in political participation remains even wider (only 18 percent has closed).[81]

Not surprisingly, Nordic countries — topped by Iceland — lead the rankings. Voluntary electoral quotas for female candidates adopted by political parties in Denmark, Sweden and Norway in the 1970s have led to high levels of female participation in Parliament — with Sweden at 45 percent, the second highest in the world (Rwanda had the highest), followed by Iceland at 43 percent.[82]

Electoral quotas, together with new corporate gender quotas and concerted efforts to make parenting more of a shared responsibility through joint paid parental leave make the Scandanavian countries highly egalitarian places for women, according to the World Economic Forum report. (*See sidebar, p. 360.*)

Removing barriers to women working makes economic sense, the report contends. Countries that have not done so "have an untapped but educated talent pool and . . . much to gain through women's greater participation in the workforce," it says. In Japan, closing the gap between male and female employment would boost gross domestic product by up to 16 percent, according to one estimate.[83]

All 15 of the countries rated most competitive by the Forum — except for the United States — offer at least 14 weeks of paid leave to new parents. China offers 18, India, 12.[84] Paid parental leave and corporate gender quotas remain controversial in free-market economies such as the United States.

Norway's corporate board quota is being widely debated in the rest of Europe and Scandinavia. Spain committed to a 40 percent target in 2007 to be met in 2015; Iceland in 2010 adopted quotas to be met in 2013. The argument that the 2008 collapse of Iceland's economy was partly caused by an old-boys' business and government network helped pave the way for the quota law in that country.[85]

In 2011, France, the Netherlands, Belgium, Italy and Malaysia all adopted corporate board quotas. Most already had a tradition of quotas in their electoral politics, either as voluntary party quotas or legal mandates. But most of the board targets don't kick in until a few years down the road, and few governments have specified penalties for not complying — a crucial element to success, according to Norwegian expert Teigen.

Germany, Australia, Canada, Sweden and Denmark have all recently debated instituting corporate quota mandates. Denmark, Finland, Greece, Austria and Slovenia have adopted gender-balance rules for state-owned companies' boards.

On March 1, 2011, EU Justice Minister Reding urged EU companies to sign her voluntary pledge to have women fill 40 percent of their directorships by 2020. She warned that if companies did not take significant steps toward that goal within a year, "you can count on my regulatory creativity."[86]

Last month, after a disappointing number of companies had signed her year-old pledge, Reding announced that she would conduct a three-month review to look at potential measures, including legislation, to boost female representation on corporate boards. However, a mandated quota for all EU countries likely would face tough opposition, especially from the U.K.

Although British Prime Minister David Cameron has hinted that he might consider mandated quotas if British companies don't improve their representation, few experts see mandates in Britain's future.[87] A year after a government-commissioned report proposed a voluntary quota of 25 percent by 2015, a progress report released last month estimated that major companies were on track to hit that target, having already reached an average of 15 percent.[88]

Stalled Treaty

All but six of the U.N.'s 193 member countries have ratified CEDAW, the primary international convention banning discrimination against women. Those six include the United States, Sudan, Somalia, Iran and the two small Pacific nations of Palau and Tonga.[89]

President Obama supports ratification, but there has been no legislative action since 2002, when the Senate Foreign Relations Committee voted it out of committee. Ratification, which requires the approval of 67 senators, has never been brought to the Senate floor.

"Some ascribe the U.S. failure to ratify the treaty to one man: the late Senator Jesse Helms of North Carolina," writes Sommers, of the American Enterprise Institute. A conservative Republican and fierce opponent of abortion, Helms called CEDAW a treaty "negotiated by radical feminists with the intent of enshrining their radical anti-family agenda into international law." As chairman of the

Should government impose mandatory gender quotas on corporate boards?

YES
Mari Teigen
*Research Professor and Research Director,
Institute for Social Research Oslo, Norway*

Written for *CQ Global Researcher*, April 2012

Quota procedures have proved to be a very effective way of promoting gender equality. The strongest argument for gender quotas on corporate boards is that they are an efficient means for crashing the glass-ceiling, the invisible barrier for women to reach top positions in the business world. It's also about democracy. Since large companies influence and make decisions of central importance for business and society in general, gender quotas are a good way to expand democracy by allowing everyone to participate in the decision-making process.

In Norway the introduction of quota regulations has been successful; within a few years the presence of women board members increased eightfold — from less than 5 percent to 40 per cent. Within the Organisation for Economic Co-operation and Development region, only one in 10 board members of top companies is a woman. There are strong arguments for government imposition of quotas: Thus far, voluntary effort has only brought about slow changes, or none at all. In the countries where self-regulating procedures have been emphasized, only small changes in women's representation have come about.

Gender parity on corporate boards also provides women with role models. And quota reform questions the fairness of male dominance — and economic power — as being a predominantly male concern.

The Norwegian quota reform proves change is possible in an area that long appeared incapable of change. The Norwegian case proves that female candidates indeed are available, but election committees need to be pushed to identify them. The circles from which selectors normally search for candidates must be widened.

It has been argued that introducing a controversial reform is problematic, and that women newcomers may be stigmatized. Experience tells us that the opposite happens. Evidence from Norway indicates that gender quotas counteract negative gender stereotypes; exposure reduces biases. This may be why the initial fierce opposition to quota reform appears to have vanished into thin air after the Norwegian law came into effect.

The introduction of corporate board quotas in Norway was a response to the disparity between virtual gender parity in political decision making and the strong male dominance in top management in a country that prides itself on being the international leader in gender equality. The Norwegian experience tells us that gender quotas work in leveling out gender inequality.

NO
Baroness Mary Goudie
Member, British House of Lords

Written for *CQ Global Researcher*, April 2012

As a founding member of the 30% Club, which is a group of chairmen voluntarily committed to bringing more women onto U.K. corporate boards, I do not believe that governments should impose gender quotas.

On average, the boards of the 100 largest companies listed on the London Stock Exchange (FTSE 100) are less than 15.6 percent female. Increasing board diversity is the key to driving profitable growth. Having a better balance of at least 30 percent senior female leaders positively influences both a company's culture and the decision-making process.

However, government quotas are not the answer. If we maintain the present momentum we would see a record 27.7 percent female board representation by 2015. This is good news and demonstrates how a voluntary, business-led approach can work.

Helena Morrissey, CEO of the British firm Newton Investment Management, said, "The acceleration in the pace of change is especially pleasing, with the progress seen over the past 12 months becoming a dramatic improvement over the preceding three years. The rate of change is also likely to continue to accelerate as more companies embrace change, and that 30 percent female representation on FTSE 100 boards is well within reach by 2015."

The issue of women in the boardroom was addressed recently by Prime Minister David Cameron at the Northern Futures Forum summit in Stockholm, Sweden. He suggested that 30 percent quotas could be the answer to inequalities in Britain's boardrooms. He believes that more female representation on boards would be good for the overall effectiveness of boards and therefore good for business.

I believe it's a positive step to focus on this issue, but quotas are not the answer. The discussion needs to continue so people begin to be persuaded to the benefits. By illustrating that the movement is beginning to happen, we hope to see women over time playing a substantial role in the success of FTSE 100 companies.

Talking to people and being persuasive is the best way to deal with it. Women are now on the radar of headhunters and investors, who increasingly are pushing for women to fill board seats. This is already making a difference.

My view is that there will be an improvement. Once it starts to happen, everything else will have changed. Having more female board members is becoming a way of corporate life, not an exception.

Senate Foreign Relations Committee from 1995 to 2001, Helms refused even to hold hearings on the treaty.[90]

Since then, conservatives have continued to attack CEDAW and its governing committee for taking what they say is a liberal attitude toward abortion laws. The recent debate in the United States over health insurance coverage for contraception and the spate of state laws introduced aimed at limiting abortion strengthen the view of some skeptics that the United States will never ratify the treaty.

"International governance has been so highly politicized for you folks that I couldn't imagine you guys getting the votes together in support of this," says U.N. Human Rights adviser Waldorf. CEDAW is just one of several international agreements the United States has refused to sign because of concerns they would impinge on its sovereignty, she points out.

Finch of Amnesty International says the treaty is "abortion neutral" and calls the sovereignty and abortion concerns "red herrings." But the current debate in the United States over contraception and abortion has "its own special flavor," she says, one that doesn't seem to have the same grip on public debate in other countries.

Zeitlin, of the CEDAW Education Project campaigns, concedes that whether the United States will ever ratify the treaty is "the thousand dollar question." But she says that in recent hearings, "We're trying to keep it less polarized, less contentious and more concrete."

OUTLOOK

Continuing Pay Gap?

For years, women have struggled for equality as their ultimate goal. In Muslim countries in the Middle East, where traditional societies have kept women in subservient roles, all eyes are on the new post-Arab Spring governments to see if they will restrict women's legal status relative to men's.

"But what if equality isn't the endpoint?" asks author Hanna Rosin in her provocatively titled article, "The End of Men," in *The Atlantic* magazine. "What if modern postindustrial society is simply better suited to women?"[91]

In the future, males' physical strength in factory and construction jobs will no longer be as important as women's reputedly superior skills at communication,

empathy and the ability to sit still and focus, Rosin argues. Women in poor parts of India are learning English faster than men to meet the demands of new global call centers, she reports, and women own more than 40 percent of private businesses in China.

Washington Post reporter Liza Mundy, similarly, argues in her new book *The Richer Sex* that women will be the more fortunate sex. While women's salaries have been rising over the past three decades, men's salaries, often tied to dying industries like ship-building and manufacturing, have been stagnating. Wives in dual-earner families contributed on average 47 percent of family earnings. And in 2009, 38 percent of wives out-earned husbands.[92]

In developed countries such as the United States, women already earn 60 percent of the master's degrees and dominate 13 of 15 job categories scheduled to grow over the next decade, many of them related to traditional female duties: nursing, home health assistance, child care and food preparation.[93]

However, note other experts, such care-taking professions traditionally are poorly paid. And even in highly paid professions such as law — where women comprise 54 percent of the U.S. workforce — they still are paid far less across the board than men, according to a recent study.[94]

Looking broadly at white-collar professions — including law, architecture, business and education — men earn an average of $82,009 vs. $48,007 for women, according to a study by Richard Florida, director of Toronto University's Martin Prosperity Institute. Even when his study adjusted salaries to reflect lower pay from fewer hours worked or differences in education, it still found men out-earning women by $23,700 — or 49 percent of the average woman's salary in these professions.[95]

Some of this pay gap reflects the fact that women don't rise to the top of their professions in the same numbers as they enter them. Increasingly, worried government commissions in Europe and Britain — facing aging populations and labor shortages — see this as an economic brain drain.

Some European politicians agree governments can't afford to neglect half of the labor force. Leaders like EU Minister Reding are raising the alarm about a talent drain — women torn between family and work leaving the labor force in mid-career, just as they're developing the skills to lead companies.

"Getting more women into the labor market can be one of the ways to improve Europe's competitiveness," Reding said recently. Noting that women now account for 60 percent of EU university graduates, constituting a valuable talent pool, she added, it's "a responsibility of governments to help improve the equilibrium between family and working lives."[96]

Nordic countries seem to be doing just that. They consistently rank as the best countries for women, with their government-subsidized paid parental leave and excellent child care. But all of that comes at a cost — the notoriously high taxes of welfare-state societies. Given current economic stresses in most industrialized countries, will other governments be willing to spend as much as the Scandinavians to give women an equal part in the labor force?

In predicting the future for women, expectations may change in unimaginable ways as women move into once-unheard-of roles. Vigdís Finnbogadóttir, Iceland's president from 1980 to 1996, describes how after her first eight years in office, Icelandic children under the age of 8 had never known a male leader.

When she visited schools around the country, little boys would ask her, "Can a boy be president too?"[97]

NOTES

1. "How Come You Allow Little Girls to Get Married?" Human Rights Watch, December 2011, www.hrw.org/reports/2011/12/07/how-come-you-allow-little-girls-get-married.

2. Gerda Lerner, *The Creation of Patriarchy* (1986), p. 107.

3. "How Come You Allow Little Girls to Get Married?" *op cit.*, p. 38.

4. *Ibid.* For background, see Sarah Glazer, "Sharia Controversy," *CQ Global Researcher*, Jan. 3, 2012, pp. 1-28.

5. "Yemen Violence Mars Poll," BBC, Feb. 21, 2012, www.bbc.co.uk/news/world-middle-east-17108117. For background, see Roland Flamini, "Turmoil in the Arab World," *CQ Global Researcher*, May 3, 2011, pp. 209-236.

6. See Lori Beaman, *et al.*, "Female Leadership Raises Aspirations and Educational Attainment for Girls: A Policy Experiment in India," *Science*, Feb. 3, 2012, pp. 582-586, www.sciencemag.org/content/335/6068/582.full?sid=224be4e1-342e-4440-ae02-6cf1b5614d88.

7. Sarah A. Topol, "Egypt's Pro-Women Election Turns Ugly," *Foreign Policy*, Nov. 27, 2010, www.foreignpolicy.com/articles/2010/11/27/egypts_pro_women_election_turns_ugly?page=0,1.

8. "The Global Gender Gap Report 2011," World Economic Forum, 2011, http://reports.weforum.org/global-gender-gap-2011/.

9. Richard Florida, "The Income Disparity of Women in the Creative Class," *The Atlantic*, Nov. 2, 2011, www.theatlanticcities.com/jobs-and-economy/2011/11/income-disparity-women-creative-class/359. Overall, women's earnings in 2010 amounted to 86 percent of men's in the United States. Also see Nancy Folbre, "Feminism's Uneven Success," Economix, *The New York Times*, Dec. 19, 2011, http://economix.blogs.nytimes.com/2011/12/19/feminisms-uneven-success. A similar hourly pay gap, averaging 17.6 percent, is estimated in the EU. See European Commission, "Report on Equality between Women and Men 2010," 2011, pp. 17-18, http://europa.eu.

10. "The Corporate Gender Gap Report 2010," World Economic Forum, 2010, p. 5, www.weforum.org.

11. Folbre, *op. cit.*

12. "Sandberg Sees Global Ambition Gap for Girls," Bloomberg, Jan. 30, 2012, www.bloomberg.com/video/85189956/.

13. See Martina Viarengo, "The Closing of the Gender Gap in Education: Does it foretell the closing of the employment, marriage and motherhood gaps?" John F. Kennedy School of Government, Harvard University, March 30, 2011, www.hks.harvard.edu/centers/wappp.

14. "European Commission Weighs Options to Break the 'Glass Ceiling' for Women on Company Boards," press release, European Commission, March 5, 2012, http://europa.eu/rapid/pressReleasesAction.do?reference=IP/12/213&format=HTML&aged=0&language=EN&guiLanguage=en.

15. Stanley Pignal, *et al.*, "Commission to Push Quota for Women Directors," *Financial Times*, March 4,

2012, www.ft.com/cms/s/0/c519b44a-6633-11e1-acea-00144feabdc0.html#axzz1ou9yFmAj. Also see "Davies Calls Women Directors Quota a Mistake," *Financial Times*, March 4, 2012, www.ft.com/cms/s/0/b8b2be1c-6486-11e1-b30e-00144feabdc0.html#axzz1ou9yFmAj.

16. "2011-2012 Progress of the World's Women: In Pursuit of Justice," Executive Summary, U.N. Women (United Nations Entity for Gender Equality and the Empowerment of Women), 2011, pp. 2-3, http://progress.unwomen.org.

17. "CEDAW and Muslim Family Laws: In Search of Common Ground," 2011, Musawah, www.musawah.org.

18. "How Come You Allow Little Girls to Get Married?" *op. cit.*, pp. 38-40.

19. *Ibid.*

20. Grace Melton, "CEDAW and the New UN Gender Office: the US Can Do Better," Heritage Foundation, April 7, 2010, www.heritage.org/research/reports/2010/04/cedaw-and-the-new-un-gender-office-the-us-can-do-better.

21. Grace Melton, "CEDAW: How UN Interference Threatens American Women," Heritage Foundation, Jan. 9, 2009, www.heritage.org/research/reports/2009/01/cedaw-how-un-interference-threatens-the-rights-of-american-women.

22. Christina Hoff Sommers: "Feminism by Treaty: Why CEDAW is Still a Bad Idea," Policy Review, Hoover Institution, June 1, 2011, www.hoover.org/publications/policy-review/article/80191. For background, see Robert Kiener, "Honor Killings," *CQ Global Researcher*, April 19, 2011, pp. 183-208.

23. Kuwait's parliament passed a law in 2005 giving women the right to vote, effective in 2006. See "Kuwaiti Women Win Right to Vote," BBC, May 17, 2005, http://news.bbc.co.uk/1/hi/world/middle_east/4552749.stm. Also See, "Kuwaiti Women Vote for First Time," BBC, April 4, 2006, http://news.bbc.co.uk/1/hi/4874990.stm.

24. Nadia Sonneveld, *Khul' Divorce in Egypt* (forthcoming in 2012).

25. Jan Michiel Otto, *Sharia Incorporated* (2010), p. 81. However, the practice appears to be waning. Only 81 percent of young women ages 15-19 have been circumcised compared to 94 percent of women aged 25-29. See Fatma El-Zanaty and Ann Way, "Egypt Democratic and Health Survey, 2008," March 2009, www.measuredhs.com/pubs/pdf/FR220/FR220.pdf.

26. Drude Dahlerup and Lenita Freidenvall, "Judging Gender Quotas: Predictions and Results," *Policy & Politics*, 2010, pp. 407-425.

27. *Ibid.*

28. See www.quotaproject.org/uid/countryview.cfm?country=197.

29. Elizabeth Powley, "Case Study: Rwanda: Women Hold up Half the Parliament," Women in Parliament: Beyond the Numbers, International IDEA, pp. 154-163, 2004, www.idea.int/publications/wip2/upload/Rwanda.pdf.

30. Andrea Friedman "Looking to Rwanda for Lessons," *The Huffington Post*, Dec. 3, 2008, www.huffingtonpost.com/andrea-friedman/looking-to-rwanda-for-les_b_147833.html.

31. See www.quotaproject.org.

32. See Egypt profile at www.quotaproject.org.

33. Beaman, *et al.*, *op. cit.*, pp. 582-586.

34. In 2002 only about 4 percent of board members were women. See Aagoth Storvik, "Women on Boards: Experience from the Norwegian Quota Reform," CESifo DICE Report, 2011. Corporate management jobs have remained at about 5 percent. Also see Aagoth Storvik and Mari Teigen, "Women on Board: The Norwegian Experience," Friedrich-Ebert-Stiftung International Policy Analysis, June 2010, http://library.fes.de/pdf-files/id/ipa/07309.pdf.

35. Stefanie Marsh, "Women Never Work Past 5 pm in Norway . . . ," *The Times*, Jan. 19, 2012, www.thetimes.co.uk/tto/life/families/article3290983.ece.

36. Mari Teigen, "Gender Quotas on Corporate Boards: On the diffusion of a distinct national policy reform," *Comparative Social Research*, Vol. 29, 2012, pp. 114-146, www.emeraldinsight.com/books.htm?issn=0195-6310&volume=29&chapterid=17014609&show=abstract.

37. Storvik and Teigen, *op. cit.*

38. Teigen, *op. cit.*

39. Storvik, *op. cit.*

40. Teigen, *op. cit.*

41. Both studies cited in "Women On Boards," (The Davies Report), U.K. Department for Business, Innovation and Skills, February 2011, p. 7, www .bis.gov.uk/news/topstories/2011/Feb/women-on-boards. See Lois Joy, *et al.*, "The Bottom Line: Corporate Performance and Women's Representation on Boards," Catalyst, 2007, www.catalyst.org/publication/ 200/the-bottom-line-corporate-performance-and-womens-representation-on-boards, and "Women Matter: Gender Diversity, a Corporate Performance Driver," McKinsey & Company, 2007, p. 14, www .mckinsey.com/locations/paris/home/womenmatter .asp.

42. Kenneth R. Ahern and Amy K. Dittmar, "The Changing of the Boards: The Impact on Firm Valuation of Mandated Female Board Representation," *The Quarterly Journal of Economics*, 2012, Vol. 127(1), pp. 137-197, http://papers.ssrn.com/ sol3/papers.cfm?abstract_id=1364470.

43. The study has not yet been published.

44. "Investors Urged to Close Sex Gaps on British Boards," Reuters, Feb. 24, 2012. http://in.reuters.com/ article/2012/02/24/boardrooms-britain-women-idINDEE81N0F320120224. For the report itself, see "Women on Boards," *op. cit.*, and "Women on Boards-One Year On," BIS, March 13, 2012, www .bis.gov.uk/news/topstories/2012/Mar/women-on-boards-one-year-on.

45. According to Greek legend, the Amazons were a female-led tribe that was supposed to have besieged Athens around 1200 B.C. Novelist and antiquities scholar Robert Graves' *The White Goddess: A Historical Grammar of Poetic Myth* (1948), arguing for the worship of mother-goddesses and matriarchal society in early Europe, has been widely discredited. See "Matriarchy," *New Dictionary of the History of Ideas*, 2005, www.encyclopedia.com/topic/matriarchy .aspx.

46. Gerda Lerner, *The Creation of Patriarchy* (1986), pp. 28-29. Also see "Matriarchy" above.

47. *Ibid.*, p. 82.

48. *Ibid.*, p. 173.

49. Karen Foerstal, "Women's Rights," *CQ Global Researcher*, May 1, 2008, pp. 115-147.

50. Sheila Rowbotham, *Hidden from History: 300 Years of Women's Oppression and the Fight Against It* (1973), p. 48.

51. Janet Zollinger Giele, *Two Paths to Women's Equality* (1995), p. 4.

52. John Stuart Mill, *The Subjection of Women*, http:// ebooks.adelaide.edu.au/m/mill/john_stuart/m645s/.

53. "The Married Women's Property Act," HerStoria, www.herstoria.com/discover/marriedwp.html.

54. In the debate on the 1832 Reform bill, a petition was introduced to grant the vote to unmarried women who met the bill's property requirements. Parliament responded by passing legislation, which for the first time explicitly restricted suffrage to men. The Reform Act specified that it enfranchised "male persons."

55. Harold L. Smith, *The British Women's Suffrage Campaign 1866-1928* (1998), pp. 36-37.

56. Rowbotham, *op. cit.*

57. Giele, *op. cit.*, pp. 1, 55.

58. *Ibid.*, p. 177.

59. *Ibid.*, p. 5.

60. See "Women in Saudi Arabia to Vote and Run in Elections," BBC, Sept. 25, 2011, www.bbc.co.uk/ news/world-us-canada-15052030.

61. Foerstal, *op. cit.*, p. 130.

62. "Convention on Eliminating Discrimination of All Forms of Discrimination Against Women: Text of the Convention," U.N. Division for the Advancement of Women, www.un.org/womenwatch/daw/cedaw/ cedaw.htm.

63. "Convention on Eliminating Discrimination of All Forms of Discrimination Against Women: Full Text of the Convention in English," U.N. Division for the Advancement of Women, www.un.org/women watch/daw/cedaw/text/econvention.htm.

64. "Frequently Asked Questions: Why should the United States ratify CEDAW?" CEDAW 2012, www.cedaw2011.org/index.php/about-cedaw/faq. The General Law on Women's Access to a Life Free of Violence came into force on Feb. 2, 2007. Each

Mexican state also must adopt such a law for it to take effect within its territory. See www.unhcr.org/refworld/docid/48a3028817.html.

65. For background, see Jina Moore, "Confronting Rape as a War Crime," *CQ Global Researcher*, May 1, 2010, pp. 105-130.

66. "Progress of the World's Women: Executive Summary," *op. cit.*, p. 6. Also See Marlise Simons, "For First Time, Court Defines Rape as War Crime," *The New York Times*, June 28, 1996, www.nytimes.com/specials/bosnia/context/0628warcrimes-tribunal.html.

67. *Ibid.*

68. *Ibid.*

69. Hillary Clinton, "Remarks to the U.N. Fourth World Conference on Women Plenary Session," Sept. 5, 1995, www.americanrhetoric.com/speeches/hillaryclintonbeijingspeech.htm.

70. See Foerstal, *op. cit.*

71. "2011-2012 Progress of the World's Women," *op. cit.*, p. 29.

72. *Ibid.*

73. Saadia Zahidi, summarizing the 2011 Global Gender Gap Report, World Economic Forum, www.weforum.org/s?s=Saadia%20Zahidi.

74. "The Global Gender Gap Report 2011, *op. cit.*, pp. 17, 25.

75. Zahidi, *op. cit.*

76. Christoph Wilcke, "Lessons from the Saudi 'Spring,'" *Foreign Policy*, March 12, 2012, http://mideast.foreignpolicy.com/posts/2012/03/12/lessons_from_the_saudi_spring.

77. Michael Sheridan, "Saudi Arabia Woman, Shaima Jastaina, Spared 10 Lashes for Driving," *New York Daily News*, Sept. 29, 2011, http://articles.nydaily news.com/2011-09-29/news/30244714_1_lashes-ban-on-female-drivers-saudi-prince-alwaleed.

78. "IOC/Saudi Arabia: End Ban on Women in Sport," Human Rights Watch, Feb. 15, 2012, www.hrw.org/news/2012/02/15/iocsaudi-arabia-end-ban-women-sport.

79. "Libya," *The New York Times*, http://topics.nytimes.com/top/news/international/countriesandterritories/libya/index.html.

80. Dalia Mogahed, "What Egyptian Men and Women Want," *Foreign Policy*, March 10, 2011, www.foreign policy.com/articles/2011/03/10/what_egyptian_women_and_men_want?hidecomments=yes.

81. "The Global Gender Gap Report 2011," *op. cit.*

82. See www.quotaproject.org.

83. "The Global Gender Gap Report 2011," *op. cit.*

84. Alison Earle, *et al.*, "International Perspectives on Work-Family Policies: Lessons from the World's Most Competitive Economies," *Work and Family*, Fall 2011, http://futureofchildren.org/publications/journals/article/index.xml?journalid=76&articleid=557&sectionid=3856.

85. Teigen, *op. cit.* Also see U.K. BIS "Women on Boards," *op. cit.*

86. "EU Justice Commissioner Reding challenges busines leaders to increase women's presence on corporate boards with 'Women on the Board Pledge for Europe,'" Press Release, European Union, March 1, 2011, http://europa.eu/rapid/pressReleasesAction.do?reference=MEMO/11/124.

87. "Cameron Won't Rule out Women in Boardrooms Quota," BBC, Feb. 9, 2012, www.bbc.co.uk/news/uk-politics-16958852.

88. "Women on Boards — One Year On," *op. cit.*

89. "Frequently Asked Questions," CEDAW, www.cedaw2011.org/index.php/about-cedaw/faq.

90. Sommers, *op. cit.*

91. Hanna Rosin, "The End of Men," *The Atlantic*, July/August 2010, www.theatlantic.com/magazine/archive/2010/07/the-end-of-men/8135.

92. Stephanie Coontz, "It's a Woman's World — Almost," *The Washington Post*, March 25, 2012, p. B1.

93. Rosin, *op. cit.*

94. Florida, *op. cit.*

95. *Ibid.*

96. Speech by Vivian Reding, "Increasing Gender Balance on Company Boards: Good for Business and Good for the Economy," European Union, Feb. 17, 2012, http://europa.eu/rapid/pressReleasesAction.do?reference=SPEECH/12/110.

97. According to Laura Liswood, who cofounded the Council of Women World Leaders with Vigdís Finnbogadóttir.

BIBLIOGRAPHY

Selected Sources

Books

Anderson, Bonnie S., and Judith P. Zinsser, *A History of their Own: Women in Europe from Prehistory to the Present*, Oxford University Press, 2000.
This sweeping survey of women's roles, rights and work life from ancient times through the 20th century is considered a classic — thorough and readable. Anderson and Zinsser are emeritus historians at, respectively, Brooklyn College and Miami University.

Lerner, Gerda, *The Creation of Patriarchy*, Oxford University Press, 1986.
A professor emerita at the University of Wisconsin-Madison and founder of the women's history field traces the history of ancient patriarchal societies and laws.

Otto, Jan Michiel, ed., *Sharia Incorporated*, Leiden University Press, 2010.
Experts provide a thorough review of laws affecting women in 12 Muslim countries, including those in Egypt and Morocco, where women face threats from new governments.

Rowbotham, Sheila, *Hidden from History: Rediscovering Women in History from the 17th Century to the Present*, Random House, 1976.
A British feminist theorist summarizes 300 years of women's history in Britain, including the suffrage movement.

Soueif, Ahdaf, *Cairo: My City, Our Revolution*, Bloomsbury, 2012.
A prominent Egyptian novelist gives a moment-by-moment account of her participation in the Tahrir Square protests last year.

Articles

Beaman, Lori, *et al.*, "Female Leadership Raises Aspirations and Educational Attainment for Girls: A Policy Experiment in India," *Science*, Feb. 3, 2012, pp. 582-586.
Indian girls' ambitions and time spent in school caught up to boys in villages where legislative quotas installed female leaders, this study found, crediting female role models.

Folbre, Nancy, "Feminism's Uneven Success," Dec. 19, 2011, Economix, *The New York Times*.
Feminism seems to be losing momentum, says a University of Massachusetts economist.

Rosin, Hanna, "The End of Men," *The Atlantic*, July/August 2010.
In this much-discussed article, *Atlantic* writer Rosin suggests that women will have an advantage over men in the post-industrial work world of the future.

Sommers, Christina Hoff, "Feminism by Treaty: Why CEDAW is Still a Bad Idea," *Policy Review*, June 1, 2011, www.hoover.org/publications/policy-review/article/80191.
A resident scholar at the conservative American Enterprise Institute argues that the United States should not sign the U.N.'s treaty on discrimination against women.

Storvik, Aagoth, and Mari Teigen, "Women on Board: The Norwegian Experience," Friedrich-Ebert-Stiftung International Policy Analysis, June 2010, http://library.fes.de/pdf-files/id/ipa/07309.pdf.
Two Norwegian researchers analyze Norway's mandatory 40 percent gender quota for women on corporate boards.

Reports and Studies

"The Global Gender Gap Report 2011," World Economic Forum, 2011, http://reports.weforum.org/global-gender-gap-2011.
This annual report ranking 135 countries by their success in closing gender gaps places Iceland at the top and Yemen at the bottom.

"How Come You Allow Little Girls to Get Married?" December 2011, Human Rights Watch, Dec. 7, 2011, www.hrw.org/reports/2011/12/07/how-come-you-allow-little-girls-get-married.
Child marriage remains widespread in Yemen even though the government has signed several treaties condemning it, according to this human rights group's report.

"2011-2012 Progress of the World's Women: In Pursuit of Justice," UN Women, 2012, http://progress.unwomen.org.
This annual report from the United Nations looks at progress in legislation and litigation around the world to advance women's rights.

"Women On Boards," U.K. Department for Business, Innovation and Skills (BIS), February 2011, p. 7; and **"Women on Boards-One Year On,"** *BIS*, March 13, 2012.

A government-commissioned report recommended last year that British companies meet voluntary targets of 25 percent female board members by 2015. A one-year progress report projects they are on track to reach that goal.

Joy, Lois, *et al.*, **"The Bottom Line: Corporate Performance and Women's Representation on Boards,"** Catalyst, 2007, www.catalyst.org/publication/200/the-bottom-line-corporate-performance-and-womens-representation-on-boards.

Companies with more women on their boards have greater profits, a finding that is widely cited by politicians and women's advocates in Europe and the United States.

For More Information

American Enterprise Institute, 1150 17th St., N.W., Washington, DC 20036; 202-862-5800; www.aei.org . Conservative think tank where resident scholar Christina Hoff Sommers, a critic of the U.N. Convention on the Elimination of All Forms of Discrimination against Women (CEDAW), blogs about women's preferences for home over work at www.aei.org/scholar/christina-hoff-sommers.

Amnesty International, 1 Easton St., London WC1X 0DW, U.K.; +44 20 74135500; www.amnesty.org/en. Human rights group that tracks women's rights around the world and supports U.S. ratification of CEDAW.

CEDAW Education Project, The Leadership Conference on Civil and Human Rights, 1629 K St., N.W., 10th Floor, Washington, DC 20006; 202-466-3434; www.civilrights.org. Advocates U.S. ratification of CEDAW; is housed at a coalition of 200 civil rights advocacy groups.

Human Rights Watch, 350 Fifth Ave., 34th floor, New York, NY 10118-3299; 212-290-4700; www.hrw.org. An international human rights groups that tracks violations of women's rights around the world.

International Center for Research on Women, 1120 20th St., N.W., Suite 500 North, Washington, DC 20036; 202-797-0007; www.icrw.org. Independent organization

known for its research on the status of women in developing countries.

International Institute for Democracy and Electoral Assistance (International IDEA), Strömsborg, SE-103 34 Stockholm, Sweden; +46 8 698-3700; www.idea.int/index.cfm. Tracks electoral developments around the world including women's political participation.

International Parliamentary Union (IPU), 5 chemin du Pommier, Case postale 330, CH-1218 Le Grand-Saconnex, Geneva, Switzerland; +41 22 919-4150; www.ipu.org/english/home.htm. International organization of parliaments.

Quota Project, www.quotaproject.org. A collaborative effort of International IDEA, Inter-Parliamentary Union and Stockholm University that tracks electoral gender quotas worldwide.

UN Women, 405 East 42nd St., New York, NY 10017; 646-781-4400. Also known as the United Nations Entity for Gender Equality and the Empowerment of Women; the U.N. division that works to eliminate discrimination against women and helps member states achieve that goal.

World Economic Forum, 3 East 54th St., 18th Floor, New York, N.Y. 10022; 212-703-2300; www.weforum.org . Independent international organization that issues an annual report ranking countries on their "gender gaps."

Voices From Abroad:

FATMA EMAM

Director, Nazra for Feminist Studies, Egypt

Changing the discourse

"The Islamist movements had a very patriarchal and outdated discourse towards women. . . . This discourse needs to be contested from within the paradigm and from outside it as well. However, I see that if we managed to establish a new republic based on the full and equal citizenship, women rights should be granted and guarded by the power of law."

Daily News (Egypt), August 2011

WOMEN NEED TO STAND AND FIGHT AGAINST THIS MAN'S WORLD...

IN ANOTHER PART OF THE WORLD...

I WISH I COULD THINK THAT WAY...

Sweden/Olle Johansson

ARI RAFIQ

Director, Directorate of Following Up Violence Against Women, Iraq

All are accountable

"If we want to improve conditions for women, then all sides need to feel responsible. The educational foundations such as universities have to do research on women's issues. The media has to dedicate time to family education. Imams need to address the issues in their Friday sermons."

Kurdish Globe (Iraq), March 2012

MICHELLE BACHELET

Executive Director, U.N. Women, United Nations

Equality under the law

"The foundations for justice for women have been laid: In 1911, just two countries in the world allowed women to vote — now that right is virtually universal. But full equality demands that women become men's true equals in the eyes of the law — in their home and working lives, and in the public sphere."

Economic Times (India), July 2011

WANG XIUQUAN

Partner, Chang'an Law Firm, China

Panicking women

"We've had a lot of inquiries from women who are panicking. They think the [divorce] law means their husband can take a mistress without anything happening to him, because if the wife threatens him with a divorce he will keep the house."

Sunday Telegraph (England), October 2011

NANDITA SHAH

Co-director, Akshara Women's Resource Center, India

Growth isn't all-inclusive

"While there are some examples of women breaking the glass ceiling and making it to the highest corporate positions, the growth obviously hasn't created a space for all women."

Times of India, May 2011

HAJIYA ZAINAB MAINA

Minister of Women Affairs and Social Development, Nigeria

Anticipating a correlation

"Although having women in parliament and government does not in itself guarantee that policies will address the concerns and needs of women, it is anticipated that the numerical increase in the number of women would be followed by qualitative increase in the power and authority that women are given."

Daily Trust (Nigeria), November 2011

NOELEEN HEYZER

Executive Secretary Economic and Social Commission for Asia and the Pacific, United Nations

Committing to the MDGs

"The best celebration of International Women's Day on March 8 was a commitment to redouble our efforts in a final push on the MDGs [Millennium Development Goals] to 2015 — because confronting gender inequality and advancing the empowerment of women holds the key to accelerating regional development and meeting the goals."

Korea Times (South Korea), March 2012

THURYA ABED SHEIKH

Founding Member National Society for Human Rights, Saudi Arabia

No power in courts

"Women's rights are lost in courtrooms. Even when a woman receives a ruling in her favor, no executive power follows up on whether the ruling has been executed."

Arab News (Saudi Arabia), March 2011

15

Human Trafficking and Slavery

Robert Kiener

Children denounce child trafficking during a march in New Delhi, India, on March 22, 2007. According to the U.S. State Department, nearly 450,000 children were trafficked for labor in India in the past three years, but only 25,000 cases were prosecuted. The United States has urged India to pass a comprehensive anti-trafficking law and boost convictions, which reportedly are often blocked by "official complicity."

From *The CQ Researcher*, October 16, 2012.

As Walusungu Msondo and some friends were fishing near their village in the impoverished Southeast African country of Malawi, some strangers approached and offered them lucrative jobs. For 10-year-old Msondo, the offer was too good to refuse.

"They coaxed us with some money and told us that they had well-paying jobs for us in Tanzania," he remembers.[1]

Some of the boys backed out when the men warned them not to tell their parents about the job offers, but Msondo left with the men. After arriving in Tanzania, however, he realized he had made a big mistake. Surrounded by other children lured by the job offer, he learned he would have to fish for nine hours a day in crocodile-infested Lake Lukwa to earn less than 25 cents. When he asked to leave, the men refused. With no one to come to his aid, Msondo had become a slave, dependent on his traffickers for survival.

The traffickers held Msondo for 10 months. During that time, some children died from malnutrition or cholera; others were killed by crocodiles. Finally, without having been paid, Msondo and some other abducted children were driven to the Malawi border and abandoned. He eventually made his way back home.

Msondo is one of the lucky ones. The U.S. State Department has identified Malawi as "a source country for men, women and children subjected to forced labor and sex trafficking."[2] Each year more than 5,000 women and children are trafficked from Malawi for sex exploitation abroad.[3]

Although slavery was banned worldwide more than a century ago, millions of people are still victims every year. "People think slavery ended years ago," says Cambodian human rights activist Somaly Mam, winner of the department's "Heroes of

Slavery and Human Trafficking Trap 21 Million Victims

Although slavery was banned more than a century ago, forced labor and human trafficking are still thriving around the world. Modern slaves are lured to other countries with promises of a better life, only to find themselves forced into hard labor or prostitution. According to the U.N.'s International Labour Organization, 21 million people are "trapped in jobs into which they were coerced or deceived into and which they cannot leave." More than half are in Asia, nearly 20 per- cent are in Africa and about 10 percent are in Latin America. Up to 17,500 are in the United States.

Human Trafficking Touches All Corners of the Globe

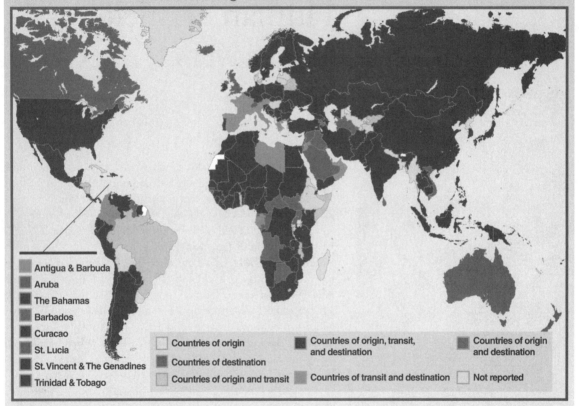

Antigua & Barbuda
Aruba
The Bahamas
Barbados
Curacao
St. Lucia
St. Vincent & The Genadines
Trinidad & Tobago

Countries of origin
Countries of destination
Countries of origin and transit

Countries of origin, transit, and destination
Countries of transit and destination

Countries of origin and destination
Not reported

Source: U.S. Department of State, Office to Monitor and Combat Trafficking in Persons, Trafficking in Persons Report 2012. Map by Lewis Agrell

Anti-Trafficking" award for her work in the field. "However, they are amazed to discover that slavery and trafficking exist today and are flourishing in countries all around the world."

Even the United States is not immune. (*See story, p. 382.*) The government estimates that up to 17,500 people are trafficked into the United States each year. And prosecutions are on the rise: In 2011 prosecutors filed 118 cases against traffickers in the United States — up 19 per- cent over 2010 and the most ever charged in a single year.[4]

In a powerful speech in September at the Clinton Global Initiative detailing his administration's new anti-trafficking program, President Obama called the crime "a debasement of our common humanity." He continued, "I'm talking about the injustice, the outrage, of human trafficking, which must be called by its true name — modern slavery."[5]

Slavery is defined as one person completely controlling another person, through violence or intimidation, and exploiting them without payment. "Slavery implies ownership," says Susu Thatun, a child protection specialist at UNICEF, the U.N. agency that oversees child welfare. Human trafficking, on the other hand, is the process of transporting someone for the purposes of enslaving them against their will. "Trafficking is about exploitation of others, not necessarily ownership." (*See story, p. 389.*)

"We often describe trafficking as 'compelled service,' " says Mary Ellison, director of public policy for the Polaris Project, an anti-trafficking organization in Washington, D.C.[6]

Finding reliable statistics on human trafficking is difficult. "Given the hidden, criminal nature of trafficking, it's difficult to get precise numbers," explains Louise Shelley, author of the 2010 book *Human Trafficking: A Global Perspective* and an expert on transnational crime at George Mason University, in Fairfax, Va.

Like Msondo, many modern slaves were lured to other countries with promises of a better life, only to find themselves forced into hard labor or prostitution. According to the U.N.'s International Labor Organization (ILO), 21 million victims of forced labor currently are "trapped in jobs into which they were coerced or deceived into and which they cannot leave."[7] More than half of them — 56 percent — are in Asia, 18 percent are in Africa and 9 percent are in Latin America.[8] (*See graph.*) However, developed countries are not immune: There are 1.5 million forced laborers and sex slaves in the European Union, the United States, Canada and other developed Western economies.[9]

Besides those who are promised a job, other victims are kidnapped — and not just in the developing world.

Forced Labor Most Prevalent in Asia

An estimated 20.9 million people are held in forced labor across the world, according to the International Labour Organization. More than half are in Asia and the Pacific region, where lax laws and weak government oversight have been blamed for high levels of trafficking. Most trafficked persons are exploited for labor, while nearly 5 million work as prostitutes.

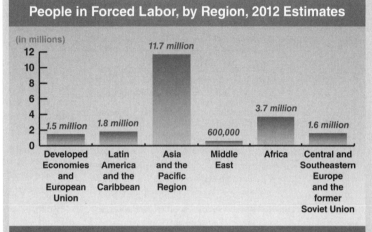

People in Forced Labor, by Region, 2012 Estimates

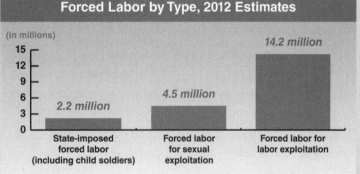

Forced Labor by Type, 2012 Estimates

Source: "ILO 2012 Global Estimate of Forced Labour," International Labour Organization, June 2012, www.ilo.org/wcmsp5/groups/public/@ed_norm/@declaration/documents/publication/wcms_181921.pdf

Homeless men reportedly have been abducted from U.K. streets and forced to work in Europe.[10] A staggering 2.5 million people — most of them children — have been kidnapped or forcibly conscripted into government or rebel military forces around the world.[11]

Many of today's slavery victims are bonded laborers: forced to work off their own or their relatives' debts. "In

Trafficking Exists in 90 U.S. Cities

Many "legitimate" businesses enable the trade.

Up to 17,500 people are trafficked into the Unites States each year and subjected to "forced labor, debt bondage, involuntary servitude and sex trafficking," according to the U.S. Department of State.[1]

In its annual "Trafficking in Persons Report," the department lists the United States as "a source, transit and destination country for men, women and children — both U.S. citizens and foreign nationals" — who are forced to work as prostitutes, maids, farm laborers, restaurant workers or in other jobs.

Most foreign trafficking victims in the United States come from Mexico, the Philippines, Thailand, Guatemala, Honduras and India.[2] They often end up in California, Florida, New York and Texas — all major international transit hubs — where they become "virtual slaves," owned and controlled by their traffickers. Slavery and human trafficking have been documented in at least 90 U.S. cities, according to the Washington, D.C.-based group Free the Slaves.[3]

According to the 2012 "Trafficking in Persons Report," recent U.S. trafficking convictions include:[4]

- Sex and labor traffickers who used threats of deportation, violence and sexual abuse to compel young, undocumented Central American women and girls into hostess jobs and forced prostitution in bars and nightclubs on Long Island, N.Y.
- A Mexican-U.S. sex trafficking ring that resulted in sentences of up to 37 years' imprisonment for three traffickers.
- A defendant in Chicago who used beatings, threats and sexual assault to force Eastern European women to work in massage parlors and prostitution.

Federal trafficking prosecutions are up significantly since 2000, when Congress passed the Trafficking Victims Protection Act, which beefed up penalties and protected trafficking victims in the country illegally, making them more likely to cooperate in prosecutions. While the Department of Justice prosecuted only two human trafficking cases in 1998, federal prosecutors last year filed 118 cases — the highest number in a single year and 19 percent more than in 2010.[5] The average prison sentence was 11.8 years.

Human trafficking in the United States also involves Americans who were not brought into the country from outside. American minors — especially homeless and runaway children — are prime targets for pimps, who are considered sex traffickers if their victims are working involuntarily or are under 18.

"Brianna" was just 12 when she ran away from her New York City home. She stayed with a friend's older brother, who refused to let her return home. "I tried to leave, and he said, 'You can't go; you're mine,' " she told *The New York Times*. She was beaten and sold for sex many times before being rescued.[6]

In June, the FBI's Operation Cross Country rescued 79 minors — 77 of them girls — being held as sex slaves in 57 cities. "The youngest kid was 13, while another told of being held as a sex slave since age 11," said Kevin Perkins, head of the FBI's Criminal Division.[7]

Despite such high-profile rescues, human rights activists say the United States is not doing enough to address the problem. "Only a tiny fraction of the nation's law enforcement

countries such as India, Nepal and Pakistan there are entire families kept like cattle, supposedly paying off their debts," says Paul Donohoe, spokesman for the London-based human rights group Anti-Slavery International. Although international law bans bonded labor, millions of laborers are working off debts across the globe.

Despite growing international awareness of the problem, increasing numbers of people are falling prey to what U.N. General Assembly President Nassir Abdulaziz Al-Nasser recently called "an appalling form of human rights abuse."[12]

Recent examples of rescued victims illustrate the scope of the abuse and exploitation:

- Siyathon, an 8-year-old in Burma taken by traffickers from his home near the Thai border, was forced to beg and sell flowers in Bangkok. For six months he was paid nothing but was regularly beaten by his captors before being rescued last April by human rights workers and Thai police.[13]
- Linda Muyimba* was lured from her home in Uganda by the promise of a job as a retail clerk in Asia.

resources are directed at slavery and trafficking in the U.S.," says Karen Stauss, director of programs for Free the Slaves.

The federal anti-trafficking budget, about $61 million a year since 2001, is 33 times less than the money the government spends to fight the war on drugs, according to Siddharth Kara, a fellow on human trafficking at Harvard University's Kennedy School of Government.[8]

In September, President Obama announced a new campaign to boost federal trafficking prosecutions by providing additional training for prosecutors, law enforcement officials and immigration judges. And federal contractors and subcontractors will be required to guarantee that their supply lines do not involve products manufactured with forced labor. He also backed efforts to give victims access to treatment, legal and employment services and a simplified visa process for those brought into the United States against their will.

Experts say trafficking in America will only be eliminated when ordinary citizens become aware of the problem and hold accountable those businesses that enable the trade — from hoteliers who rent rooms to traffickers to factory owners who employ trafficked laborers and website owners who advertise sex slaves.

As *New York Times* columnist Nicholas Kristof, who has campaigned relentlessly against human trafficking, wrote, "Sex trafficking is just as unacceptable in America as it is in Thailand or Nepal."[9]

— *Robert Kiener*

Katarlina, who at age 13 became a victim of domestic sex trafficking in Miami, Fla., is now an anti-trafficking advocate and teaches a course in trafficking at Trinity International University in Davie, Fla.

Getty Images/Sun Sentinal/Carey Wagner

[1] "Trafficking in Persons Report 2012," U.S. Department of State, 2012, p. 359, www.state.gov/documents/organization/192598.pdf.

[2] *Ibid.*, p. 360.

[3] "Hidden Slaves: Forced Labor in the United States," Free the Slaves and Human Rights Center, September 2004, p. 10, www.freetheslaves .net//Document.Doc?id=17. Also see "About Slavery FAQ," Free the Slaves, www.freetheslaves.net/SSLPage.aspx?pid=304.

[4] "Trafficking in Persons Report 2012," *op. cit.*

[5] *Ibid.* Also see Stephanie Hanes, "Human Trafficking: A misunderstood global scourge," *The Christian Science Monitor*, Sept. 9, 2012, www .csmonitor.com/World/Global-Issues/2012/0909/Human-trafficking-a-misunderstood-global-scourge.

[6] Nicholas D. Kristof, "Not quite a teen but sold for sex," *The New York Times*, April 19, 2012, www.nytimes.com/2012/04/19/opinion/ kristof-not-quite-a-teen-yet-sold-for-sex.html?_r=0.

[7] "FBI saves 79 kids held as sex slaves in U.S.," Fox News, June 25, 2012, www.foxnews.com/us/2012/06/25/fbi-rescues-7-kids-held-as-sex-slaves-in-us/.

[8] Siddharth Kara, *Sex Trafficking: Inside the Business of Modern Slavery* (2009), p. 196.

[9] Kristof, *op. cit.*

Instead, traffickers confiscated her passport and forced her into prostitution. She became pregnant, miscarried and contracted HIV. "I just wanted to get some money," she explained. "I never imagined this would happen."[14]

• Pakistani father Muhammad Ahsan "gave" his son, Sajjad, to his employer to pay off a $1,176 debt. The 10-year-old now works as a domestic in the employer's Lahore home, washing dishes and cleaning floors. "I am ashamed because I have in fact 'sold' my son," said the father, "and ended his schooling to do so."[15]

Human trafficking is booming, with an estimated $32 billion a year in profits, according to the ILO.[16] "It's been growing dramatically since the mid-1980s, thanks to factors like the ending of the Cold War, disappearing borders, globalization, deteriorating economies and the growth of international crime syndicates," explains Shelley.

Profits are high because expenses are so low. The potential supply of slave labor is massive — and cheap. The average annual cost of capturing, transporting and supporting a slave in the American South in 1850 was about $40,000 in today's money; today, a slave costs an average of $90 a

More Than Half the Victims Are Female

Of the 20.9 million people trafficked each year, more than 15 million are adults, or nearly three times the number of children. More than half — 11.4 million — are female.

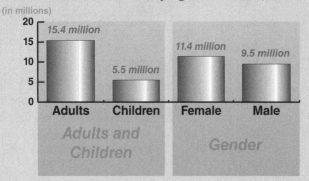

Trafficked Persons, by Age and Gender, 2012

(in millions)

- Adults: 15.4 million
- Children: 5.5 million
- Female: 11.4 million
- Male: 9.5 million

Adults and Children

Gender

Source: "ILO 2012 Global Estimate of Forced Labour," International Labour Organization, June 2012, www.ilo.org/wcmsp5/groups/public/@ed_norm/@declaration/documents/publication/wcms_181921.pdf

year.[17] Because of the abundant supply, traffickers do not spend a lot of money on their maintenance. If a slave gets sick or injured, outlives his usefulness or becomes troublesome, he may be "dumped or killed," according to the Washington, D.C.-based group, Free the Slaves.

As the problem has grown, the world has responded by adopting several treaties against slavery and human trafficking. The United Nations adopted an international treaty banning trafficking in 2000, and the United States' Trafficking Victims Protection Act (TVPA), also passed in 2000, mandates the cutoff of nonhumanitarian aid for nations that do not adequately address trafficking. Other countries have adopted similar anti-trafficking laws, using the U.N. treaty as a framework.[18]

But, as many observers have noted, the number of successful prosecutions has been disappointing. "This is the only category of serious crime treated with such leniency by the courts worldwide," said Shelley.[19] Others, such as TVPA co-author Rep. Chris Smith, R-N.J., say existing laws are sufficient but are not being enforced properly.

As experts debate how to stem a growing illicit trade that touches every corner of the globe, here are some of the questions being asked:

Are anti-trafficking laws tough enough?

While experts may differ on the effectiveness of today's anti-trafficking legislation, they all agree there are more laws on the books now than ever before.

Various forms of anti-trafficking legislation were passed in the late 20th century, including the 2000 Trafficking in Persons Protocol. Commonly known as the "Palermo Protocol," it was the first international legal instrument to define and criminalize trafficking. Unlike many other U.N. treaties, the protocol was created as a law enforcement treaty; parties that signed it were required to create domestic penalties for human trafficking. So far 117 countries have signed the treaty, but only 64 have outlawed all forms of human trafficking.[20] (*See map, p. 380, and graph, p. 384.*)

When the U.S. Congress passed the Trafficking Victims Protection Act in 2000, it targeted both domestic and international trafficking and established the State Department's Office to Monitor and Combat Trafficking in Persons. During his speech at the Clinton Global Initiative, Obama announced a new initiative to boost federal prosecutions and convictions of traffickers.[21]

Besides the 64 countries that have passed anti-trafficking laws, 49 U.S. states and the District of Columbia have followed suit.[22] And in 2008 the Council of Europe's Convention on Action Against Trafficking in Human Beings went into effect. "This domestic and international legislation is a testament to the growing awareness of human trafficking," says the Polaris Project's Ellison.

But with trafficking on the rise, many are asking whether the laws are tough enough. "The short answer is no," says George Mason University's Shelley. "Penalties need to be harsher and existing laws need to be better enforced. Given the size of the problem, there are almost no cases. And traffickers are often given minimal sentences because of corruption. There is a lack of political will to get tougher."

Activists in Europe complain that traffickers have "working relationships" with the police.[23] "We have had cases of police officers being complicit in the trafficking themselves," said Petya Nesporva, an expert on human trafficking at the Council of Europe in Strasbourg, France.[24]

"Other than the meager chance of being caught, there is almost no real risk to being a sex trafficker, because of the anemic penalties prescribed in the law," said Siddharth Kara, a fellow on human trafficking at Harvard University's Kennedy School of Government. For example, as Kara noted, in India there is no financial penalty for sex slavery; Italy and Thailand also have no financial penalties for sex trafficking.[25]

Some experts suggest that laws should target traffickers' bank accounts. "Too often trafficking is seen as a high-profit, low-risk crime. One way to change that is allow traffickers' assets to be confiscated and turned over to their victims," says Anti-Slavery International's Donohoe.

Kara calls for drastically increasing trafficking penalties. For instance, he said, the financial penalty for drug trafficking in India is "one hundred times more severe than the current fine for sex trafficking." To abolish trafficking, he wrote, the global community must be pressured to increase the financial penalties of human slavery "to a level at least equal to that of drug trafficking."[26]

As part of its ongoing worldwide investigation of anti-trafficking efforts required under the TVPA, the U.S. State Department issues annual (so-called "naming and shaming") reports on nations with weak, anti-trafficking legislation. In its most recent report, for instance, the State Department criticized India — where traffickers snatch tens of thousands of children a year — for its low conviction rate.[27]

"Nearly 450,000 cases of children trafficked for labor were reported in the past three years, but prosecutions were launched in just 25,000 of those cases, and 3,394 employers were convicted," according to *The Washington Post*.[28] The report urged India to pass a comprehensive anti-trafficking law and boost convictions, which it said

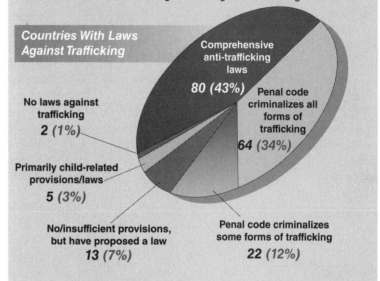

Only 80 Countries Have Laws Combating Trafficking

Fewer than half of the world's 192 countries have comprehensive anti-trafficking laws, and only about one-third criminalize all types of human trafficking, according to The Protection Project, a human rights research institute at The Johns Hopkins University School of Advanced International Studies in Washington, D.C. Many developing countries have weak or no regulations against trafficking.

Countries With Laws Against Trafficking

Comprehensive anti-trafficking laws
80 (43%)

Penal code criminalizes all forms of trafficking
64 (34%)

No laws against trafficking
2 (1%)

Primarily child-related provisions/laws
5 (3%)

No/insufficient provisions, but have proposed a law
13 (7%)

Penal code criminalizes some forms of trafficking
22 (12%)

Source: "The Protection Project Review of the Trafficking in Persons Report," The Protection Project, The Johns Hopkins University, July 2012, p. 53

are often blocked by alleged "official complicity."[29] Other critics point out that India's Immoral Trafficking of People Act fails even to define trafficking and that both citizens and legislators lack the will to halt the practice.[30]

Other countries need to strengthen their anti-trafficking laws as well. Libya, Sudan, Algeria, Syria, Cuba and North Korea are among the 17 countries the State Department has blacklisted as "Tier Three" nations — those doing little or nothing to combat trafficking. Under the TVPA, the United States may withhold or withdraw nonhumanitarian, non-trade-related foreign aid.

Critics say the TVPA, now awaiting congressional reauthorization, needs beefing up. For example, the United States critiques itself in the TVPA's annual report. "It's simply not ethical to rate yourself," says Norma Ramos, executive director of the New York-based Coalition Against Trafficking in Women (CATW). "You need an impartial third party."

Some believe the TVPA annual report treats allies too kindly. "It upgraded India [a tier on the TIP report], and that makes no sense at all," says Ramos. "India still has a huge sex trafficking industry, including open-air slave markets!"

Shelley agrees. "All countries are not treated equally in the report," she says. "It is still soft on some countries, such as the Gulf States."

TVPA sponsor Smith recently attacked the Obama administration as "unconscionable" for declining to invoke sanctions against several countries, such as Algeria, Kuwait and Yemen that were doing little to control human trafficking as mandated by the TVPA. "It's time to get serious with countries that enable or are complicit with human trafficking," he said.[31]

The Polaris Project's Ellison acknowledges that while there may be shortcomings in the State Department's annual rankings, the report "has shone a light on the problem of human trafficking." In addition, she says, nongovernmental organizations often understand there may be gaps in TVPA reporting for political reasons, but they can then use what has been reported as a basis for further investigation.

Others say the law and its naming and shaming reports force countries to address trafficking. Luis CdeBaca, ambassador-at-large for the State Department's Office to Monitor and Combat Trafficking in Persons, said the threat of sanctions and loss of foreign aid is "a major motivation" to get countries to comply with at least "the minimum standards for the elimination of trafficking."[32] The possibility of losing substantial U.S. funding is a powerful tool for countries to improve their anti-trafficking efforts.

To increase convictions, the U.N. Office on Drugs and Crime (UNODC) helps countries develop and strengthen anti-trafficking legislation. Thanks in part to such international assistance, Vietnam now has one of the highest trafficking conviction rates in the world.[33]

"Prosecutions and convictions are increasing. That is good news," explains UNICEF's Thatun. "But one person trafficked is one person too many."

Would legalizing prostitution reduce sex trafficking?

Nearly everyone involved in combating human trafficking and slavery finds prostitution a difficult subject.

"I've never seen so politically explosive a topic," says Andreas Kotsadam, a postdoctoral fellow at Norway's Oslo University and co-author of a study on prostitution and sex trafficking. "Both sides are ideologically motivated and are quick to ignore any data that doesn't support their arguments."[34]

The question of how to treat prostitution is loaded with issues of ethics, morality and politics. "Many use the topic as a political football," says Anti-Slavery International's Donohoe. "This can undermine the seriousness of the anti-trafficking debate."

U.N. agencies prefer to let member states decide for themselves whether to legalize prostitution. "It is a very emotional issue, and UNICEF doesn't take a position on prostitution," says Thatun, the UNICEF child-protection specialist.

Abolitionists say banning prostitution would put traffickers out of business. "Prostitution should be outlawed. Period," says CATW's Ramos. "It is oppression, it is violence against women and we envision a world free of it."

Legalizing prostitution, on the other hand, "is like hanging up a 'Welcome' sign to traffickers," she says. "Countries that have done so have seen an increase in demand for prostitution and the amount of sex trafficking it fuels." (*See "At Issue," p. 395.*) Amsterdam saw an increase in the number of trafficked women after it legalized prostitution, she says. She also cites a 2004 U.S. State Department report, which said, "Where prostitution is legalized or tolerated, there is a greater demand for human trafficking victims and nearly always an increase in the number of women and children trafficked into commercial sex slavery."[35]

But sex workers and more liberal proponents say legalizing or decriminalizing prostitution would make it easier to prosecute traffickers. Sarah Walker, a sex worker and member of the Prostitutes Collective in London, says, "Continuing to outlaw prostitution merely drives it underground, treats women as victims and does nothing to stem trafficking."

She and other legalization advocates cite New Zealand, which decriminalized prostitution in 2003 but saw no large, verifiable increase in sex trafficking. And sex trafficking fell in Sweden and Norway, in 1999 and 2009, respectively, after they outlawed procuring sex — but not selling it (charging clients but not the prostitutes).

"Trafficking of persons for commercial sexual exploitation is least prevalent in countries where prostitution is illegal, most prevalent in countries where prostitution is legalized and in between in those countries where prostitution is legal but procuring illegal," said one study.[36]

Abolitionists are quick to point out that sex trafficking rose in the Netherlands and Germany after those countries legalized prostitution, but abolition opponents claim the higher numbers reflect more efficient prosecutions rather than an increase in trafficking.

"The likely explanation for the increase is the intensification of investigations by the police and the public prosecution service, as well as the growing attention to human trafficking," a government report in the Netherlands noted. "It is also possible that there is greater awareness . . . of the need to report victims of human trafficking."[37]

"The problem here lies in the clandestine nature of both the prostitution and trafficking markets, making it difficult, perhaps impossible, to find hard evidence establishing [a] relationship" between legalizing prostitution and increased trafficking, economists Seo-Young Cho, Axel Dreher and Eric Neumayer write in a recent study.[38]

In Sweden outlawing the procurement of sex reportedly has cut down on trafficking. "The prohibition against the purchase of a sexual service has had a direct effect on trafficking in human beings," reported Kajsa Wahlberg, the country's National Rapporteur on Trafficking in Human Beings. "Victims of human trafficking for sexual purposes have told the police that traffickers and procurers talk about Sweden as a bad market for prostitution activities."[39]

But looking deeper, Sweden's success looks less certain. "The picture that advocates of the Swedish model are painting outside of Sweden is clearly very different [from] the reality inside Sweden," points out Wendy Lyon, a blogger and human rights activist in Ireland. "Furthermore, the Swedes don't seem unaware that they still have significant issues with prostitution and sex trafficking — they just don't want the rest of the world to know about it."[40] For instance, she noted, a Swedish county police commissioner recently claimed that sex trafficking in Sweden was "a business with huge income and little risk."[41]

Should all forms of child labor be outlawed?

As he crouches down to scrub a dirty motorbike, 6-year-old Nabeel Mukhtar begins to cry. The young Pakistani is forced to work nine hours a day, six days a week instead of attending school. "I want to study and become a doctor," he says, "but we don't have any money."[42]

Nearby, his mother Shazia explains, "From the bottom of my heart I want to send my son to school, but we have so many expenses. . . . We struggle to put food on the table."[43]

Despite international and national laws prohibiting most child labor, 215 million children, ages 5-17, are working illegally around the world.* Illegal child labor is defined as work a child is forced to do that prevents them from being educated or endangers them. And more than half of the world's child laborers are engaged in hazardous work, such as mining, waste-picking or other jobs that expose children to dangerous solvents or explosives.[44]

Experts say child labor abuses are directly linked to trafficking and slavery. Because children are not able to resist, most child labor is considered coerced, according to child welfare specialists. "Children rarely have a say when it comes to working, and their conditions can be slave-like," says UNICEF's Thatun.

Children are regularly sold by their parents or are kidnapped by traffickers to work as virtual slaves for little or no pay. In addition, thousands of child soldiers have been forced to fight in civil wars.[45]

While most people agree that forced or bonded labor should be illegal for children, some people question whether children shouldn't be allowed to work in certain circumstances. In impoverished countries where children must contribute to their family's income, child labor is a "necessary evil," say parents and government officials in developing countries.

"Working children are essential for survival in many families, as they were in our own heritage until the late 19th century," explains economist Thomas DeGregori of the libertarian Cato Institute in Washington. "So, while the struggle to end child labor is necessary, getting there often requires taking different routes."[46]

For instance, Indian lawmakers have long argued that young children must be allowed to help support their families. Indeed, although India ratified the Rights of the Child Convention in 1992, it declared that the provision would be "progressively implemented" because "it is not practical immediately to prescribe minimum ages for admission to each and every area of employment in India."[47] Thus, after years of falling below international guidelines on child labor, India is just now addressing the problem. Parliament is considering a law banning the employment of all children under 14 and 14- to 18-year olds in hazardous occupations.[48]

---

* Child labor is forbidden by the 1973 International Labour Organization's Convention No. 138 on the Minimum Age for Admission to Employment and the 1990 Convention of the Rights of the Child.

CHRONOLOGY

Ancient Times *Slavery is legal and flourishing as a way of life.*

2000 BC The first recorded mention of slavery is found in the Sumerian Code of Ur-Nammu.

7th Century BC Slaves are part of everyday life in ancient Greece; as many as 100,000 are in fifth-century Athens alone.

73 BC After the Third Servile War, led by Spartacus, more than 6,000 slaves are crucified along Rome's Appian Way.

1500s-1700s *Colonial expansion leads to increased slavery around the world, especially in the Atlantic Ocean, where a triangular trade involving slaves develops between Europe, West Africa and the New World.*

1500s Portuguese, Spanish, Dutch and English establish colonies and enslave indigenous people. . . . In mid-1500s Portugal establishes Atlantic slave trade. One in six slaves die during the journey from Africa to the Americas.

1780 Massachusetts becomes first U.S. state to ban slavery.

1800s *Abolitionist movements end the slave trade.*

1807 Britain and the United States pass laws outlawing the slave trade, but not slavery itself.

1833 Britain bans slavery in its empire. . . . France follows suit in 1848.

1863 In the middle of the U.S. Civil War, President Abraham Lincoln issues Emancipation Proclamation freeing slaves in the confederate states.

1865 13th Amendment abolishes slavery in the United States.

1900s *International organizations and treaties outlaw slavery and trafficking.*

1926 League of Nations adopts the Slavery Convention, charging the governments that sign it to suppress all forms of slavery.

1948 U.N.'s Universal Declaration of Human Rights prohibits slavery and the slave trade, but bonded and forced labor continue worldwide.

1949 U.N. adopts a convention prohibiting human trafficking.

1990s-Present *Elimination of European border controls and the collapse of the Soviet Union spur increase in human trafficking, prompting a global response.*

1991 Soviet Union's collapse leads to a surge in trafficking in Eastern Europe.

2000 International Labour Organization's Convention 182 to eliminate the worst forms of child labor goes into force after being ratified by more than 100 countries. . . . United States passes Trafficking Victims Protection Act, which increases penalties for trafficking in the United States and aids trafficking victims. U.N. adopts Trafficking in Persons Protocol, the first binding international instrument to define and criminalize human trafficking.

2002 U.S. State Department's first "Trafficking in Persons" report grades nations on their effectiveness at combating human trafficking.

2008 Council of Europe's Convention on Action Against Trafficking in Human Beings goes into effect.

2011 Police in China break up 3,200 human trafficking gangs, rescuing more than 24,000 abducted women and children. . . . California requires companies to ensure their products are not made with trafficked or slave labor.

2012 In a landmark speech to the Clinton Global Initiative, President Obama calls human trafficking "modern slavery" and announces new steps to combat exploitation of more than 20 million workers and children in the United States and abroad. He said victims include workers who toil for little pay, are abused and barred from leaving their jobs, child soldiers and impoverished girls sold into the sex trade.

The Many Faces of Exploitation

Trafficking definitions have been broadened.

The definitions of human trafficking are inexact and have evolved over the years. In the past, victims could be considered "trafficked" only if they had been transported into an exploitative situation, either domestically or across borders.

"The term is broader now," says Mary Ellison, director of public policy for the Polaris Project, an anti-trafficking organization in Washington, D.C. "It includes many different forms of exploitation and is less concerned with the means of trafficking."

According to the U.S. government, the phrase "trafficking in persons" denotes all the criminal conduct involved in forced labor and trafficking. "Despite a term that seems to connote movement, at the heart of the phenomenon of trafficking in persons are the many forms of enslavement, not the activities involved in international transportation," says a U.S. State Department web page defining trafficking.[1]

Similarly, the U.N. defines trafficking as "the recruitment, transport, transfer, harboring or receipt of a person by such means as threat or use of force or other forms of coercion, of abduction, or fraud or deception for the purpose of exploitation."[2] The key elements of both definitions are the recruitment, transfer or harboring of victims, the use of force or coercion and the carrying out of activity for the purpose of exploitation.

Given the global nature of human trafficking, it's not surprising that it takes so many different forms. They include:

Sex Trafficking —The International Labour Organization (ILO) estimates that one-fifth of all trafficking involves sexual exploitation, which falls into two categories. The first includes adults who have been coerced, forced or deceived into prostitution. Even if an individual initially agreed to engage in prostitution but then was held in service through physical or psychological force, he or she is still considered a trafficking victim. The second category is child sex trafficking, which includes all children exploited sexually for commercial reasons.[3]

Forced Labor — Includes people forced into labor inside their own country as well as those trafficked across borders. For example, a domestic worker kept as a virtual slave in her employer's quarters would be considered a victim of forced labor. Some forced laborers may also be referred to as slaves. Forced labor differs from slavery, however, in that slavery usually implies a physical abduction followed by forced labor without pay, where the victim is under the perpetrator's complete control. According to the State Department, a child is considered a forced laborer when "the child appears to be in the custody of a non-family member who has the child perform work that financially benefits someone outside the child's family and does not offer the child the option of leaving."[4] The ILO estimates that 68 percent of all trafficking is done for labor exploitation.[5]

Bonded Labor — Also known as "debt bondage," this includes workers forced to "work off" or "pay back" a debt they may have agreed to as part of the terms of their employment. Some bonded laborers, many of whom are children, may have "inherited" the debt from a parent, relative or friend.

Child Soldiers — Children under 18 are considered to have been trafficked if they are recruited into armed forces by threats or other verbal coercion, physical force or fraud by government, paramilitary or rebel forces. Child soldiers might work as combatants, cooks, servants or spies or even be forced to have sex with adult combatants. According to Child Soldiers International, an advocacy group in London, 20 countries have used children in hostilities since 2010.[6]

— *Robert Kiener*

---

[1] "What Is Trafficking in Persons?" U.S. Department of State, www.state.gov/documents/organization/194942.pdf.

[2] "Protocol to Prevent, Suppress and Punish Trafficking in Persons, Especially Women and Children, Supplementing the United Nations Convention Against Transnational Organized Crime," United Nations, 2000, www.uncjin.org/Documents/Conventions/dcatoc/final_documents_2/convention_%20traff_eng.pdf.

[3] "Trafficking in Persons Report 2012," U.S. Department of State, June 2012, p. 45.

[4] "What Is Trafficking in Persons?" *op. cit.*

[5] "Trafficking in Persons Report 2012," *op. cit.*

[6] "Louder than words: States still using child soldiers," Child Soldiers International, Sept. 12, 2012, www.child-soldiers.org/news_reader.php?id=584. Also see John Felton, "Child Soldiers," *CQ Global Researcher*, July 1, 2008, pp. 183-211.

According to child rights activists, India's tougher legislation is long overdue. "Employers preferred children, as they could be paid less, made to work longer hours and beaten into submission," explained Enakshi Ganguly Thukral, co-director of the New Delhi-based HAQ: Centre for Child Rights. "The only way to address child labour and poverty was to ensure that child labour was banned."[49]

But Canadian professors Sylvain Dessy and Stephane Pallage say banning the "worst forms" of child labor — such as drug trafficking, working in rock quarries or deep sea fishing — would lead to an overall drop in children's wages because more children would be available for the non-hazardous jobs, thus increasing poverty in developing nations. "The market for the worst forms of child labor helps to keep wages for the 'good' forms of child labor sufficiently high to help poor families finance their children's education," they wrote.[50] In Bolivia a union of young workers successfully lobbied the government to drop a proposed ban on all forms of child labor — which members feared would cost them much-needed jobs and income — for a less restrictive ban on forced and exploitative labor.[51]

Banning all child work can have negative consequences. When the United States suggested banning textile imports produced in Bangladesh by child labor, 500,000 children lost their garment factory jobs, and, according to DeGregori, many were forced into "prostitution and other dangerous behavior."[52]

Stung by the international criticism, Bangladesh in 2006 banned children from working in the textile factories but did nothing to ban child labor or abuses in other industries.

As with child trafficking and slavery, lack of enforcement exacerbates the child labor problem. For instance, in the West African country of Guinea, a law banning employment for anyone under 16 has had little effect, according to a recent report. Children as young as 5 reportedly are working in dangerous farming, mining and fishing jobs. "Guinea is good at developing laws, but applying them still poses some problems," said Gregoire Tonguino, an official with Guinea's Ministry of Children and the Family. Few child protection experts even know about the nation's child labor laws, he said.[53]

Child labor also keeps children from being educated, handicapping future generations and depriving societies of economic growth and development. "Until more governments introduce stricter child labor laws and give children

back their lives, these children — and the children they will someday have — will be doomed," says Cambodian human rights activist Mam. "There is a direct link between child labor, slavery and trafficking."

BACKGROUND

Ancient Practice

Slavery is nearly as old as human civilization, historians say. Indeed, some even say it existed in prehistoric hunting societies.[54] Slavery certainly existed in ancient civilizations in Mesopotamia and ancient Greece, China, India, Africa and pre-Columbian America.[55] The first recorded mention of slavery is in a law found in the Sumerian Code of Ur-Nammu, a tablet from around 2000 B.C.[56]

The later Babylonian Code of Hammurabi (1760 B.C.) contained numerous edicts on owning slaves, such as:

- "If any one take a male or female slave of the court, or a male or female slave of a freed man, outside the city gates, he shall be put to death."
- "If any one find runaway male or female slaves in the open country and bring them to their masters, the master of the slaves shall pay him two shekels of silver."[57]

In ancient societies slaves most often were taken as war booty. Others were abducted by pirates. Criminals were sometimes sentenced to slavery, as were delinquent debtors. Slaves usually worked as farm laborers or domestic servants. And, while slavery was accepted through much of the ancient world, the Essenes and Therapeutae — two early Jewish sects — forbade it.[58]

Slaves were a part of everyday life in ancient Greece, as early as the seventh century B.C., working jobs such as domestic servants, mineworkers, shopkeepers and ship's crew members. Sparta and Athens owed much of their success to slave labor. Historian Ursula Cliff wrote: "Slave labour allowed the citizens of Athens and Sparta to focus on the aspects of life they thought important, whether that be developing a grand system of government and culture or creating a military society to rival that of anywhere in the ancient world."[59]

In the fifth century B.C., slaves made up more than a third of the population of Athens, and many households had several slaves.[60] Slaves in Athens were generally treated better than elsewhere in Greece, and some could even earn their freedom. In Sparta, slaves were owned by the state and outnumbered their masters by about 10 to one.[61]

In ancient Rome, slaves performed a wide range of skilled and unskilled duties. As the Roman Empire expanded, conquered peoples were often enslaved. Many were common laborers, but some became teachers or even physicians.

Treatment was often brutal. Many who tried to escape were branded "FGV," Latin for *fugitivus* or "fugitive." Many mineworkers were whipped to make them work harder, farm workers often worked in chain gangs; others were made to work as prostitutes and sex slaves. Most infamously, some were forced to become gladiators, fighting wild animals, or one another, to the death for the amusement of Roman audiences.

Slave revolts, such as the uprising led by the slave-gladiator Spartacus in the first century B.C., were punished brutally, often by crucifixion. Indeed, after the Third Servile War, led by Spartacus in 73 B.C., more than 6,000 slaves were crucified along Rome's Appian Way.[62]

Although treatment was generally harsh in Rome, slaves — unlike in Greece — could earn their freedom. After the collapse of the Roman Empire in the fifth century A.D., slaves were more commonly used as household servants, office workers and soldiers than as gang laborers. Many were tied to a local lord's land and became serfs, dependent on their owners for their livelihood and survival.

Arabs were active in the slave trade, transporting millions of Africans, Europeans and Asians across the Mediterranean and northern Africa. Religion was no barrier: Muslims, Christians and Jews widely accepted slavery. However, the Catholic Church did not oppose slavery until Christians were being enslaved by what the church termed "infidels."[63] In 1488 Pope Innocent VII accepted 100 slaves as a gift from King Ferdinand of Aragon and offered them to some of his cardinals.[64]

Slavery flourished during the Middle Ages. The Vikings raided Britain and abducted slaves that they sold as far afield as Istanbul. In the 10th century, as the Germanic tribes expanded eastward, they captured so many Slavs that their name gave rise to the term "slave."[65] Slavery also existed in the Americas; North American Indians, Aztecs, Mayans and Incas all used slave labor.

Slave Trade Expands

The age of international exploration, expansionism and colonialism that began in the 15th century led to a dramatic increase in slavery. As the Portuguese, Spanish, Dutch and English established new colonies, they enslaved indigenous people to work in the mines and harvest sugar, cotton, rubber and tobacco.

Slavery became so entrenched that governments issued laws and edicts regulating the practice. King Louis XIV's *Code Noir* spelled out slaves' duties and how they should be treated throughout the French Empire. It proclaimed, "We declare slaves as movable property" and dictated punishments such as whipping and branding for minor crimes.[66]

Disease and poor conditions decimated the ranks of indigenous slaves, however, forcing the colonial powers to turn to Africa. African slaves were prized over their European counterparts because they were heartier, used to working in a tropical climate and resistant to many tropical diseases. They also usually had agricultural experience and expertise in handling livestock.

The Portuguese inaugurated the Atlantic slave trade, one of the earliest examples of mass trafficking in humans, followed by the Spanish. Between the middle of the 16th century and the mid-19th century, more than 10 million Africans were enslaved and shipped across the Atlantic to what is now Brazil, Haiti, Cuba and the Americas.[67]

Although the Portuguese, Dutch and others took part in the Atlantic slave trade, by the 18th century the British dominated the "triangular trade" in slaves. To ensure maximum return on their investment, ships brought firearms, cotton goods, alcohol and other items from Britain to West Africa, where they were traded for Africans captured in the interior. This human cargo was then transported to the Americas under the most horrendous conditions for the six- to eight-week journey known as the "middle passage."[68]

According to a U.N. report: Slaves were "chained together, with scarcely room to turn, traveling for months, seasick, surrounded by the filth of vomit-filled tubs, into which children often fell, some suffocating. The shrieks of the women and the groans of the dying render the whole scene of horror almost inconceivable. Death and disease are all around."[69] About one in six slaves died during the trip.[70]

Completing the triangle, the ship owners would sell their surviving human cargo in the West and buy rum, sugar, molasses, tobacco and hemp for sale in Europe.

In the 18th century, abolitionists protesting slavery met with widespread opposition from proponents, many of whom — anxious to retain the economic advantage of free labor — argued that the slaves were better off than in their homelands. "We ought to consider whether the negroes in a well-regulated plantation, under the protection of a kind master, do not enjoy as great, nay, even greater advantages then when under their own despotic governments," Liverpool merchant Michael Renwick Sergent noted in 1778.[71]

During the European Enlightenment of the latter 18th century, intellectuals and politicians began debating the morality of slavery. In 1774 British Quakers moved to expel any church member involved in the slave trade. In the United States, Massachusetts became the first state to abolish slavery, in 1780. Other Northern states soon did the same.

But Southern slave owners argued that slavery was an economic necessity. In 1787, the Southern states pressured the Constitutional Convention to agree that no law against slavery would be passed for 20 years.

France first abolished slavery in 1789, during the French Revolution, but Emperor Napoleon Bonaparte restored it in the French colonies in 1804, including an unsuccessful attempt to reimpose slavery in its Caribbean colony, Sainte-Domingue, where slaves had begun a revolution in 1791. They later declared their independence from France, effectively ending slavery in the country they renamed Haiti.[72]

In 1807 the slave trade, but not slavery itself, was outlawed in Britain and its colonies and in the United States. However, there were so many slaves working on American plantations and giving birth to new slaves that the ban on new arrivals did little to reduce slavery.

Elsewhere, slavery was beginning to disappear. Spain's colonies in South America, which gained their independence in the early 1800s, banned slavery. Britain, spurred on by Quakers and abolitionists such as William Wilberforce and John Wesley, banned slavery in 1833. France definitively abolished it in 1848, freeing all the slaves in its colonies. But slavery continued in the American South throughout the 1800s, spurred by a boom in cotton production ushered in by Eli Whitney's invention of the cotton gin in 1793.

It would take the Civil War to break slavery's hold on the South. In 1863, as the war raged, President Abraham Lincoln issued the Emancipation Proclamation, freeing all slaves in states "in rebellion against the United States." In 1865, after the war ended, slavery was abolished in all of the United States with passage of the 13th Amendment to the Constitution.

Spain outlawed slavery in Puerto Rico in 1873 and in Cuba in 1886; Brazil followed suit in 1888.

International Efforts

During the 20th century, several international treaties banned slavery around the globe as well as human trafficking, a relatively recent phenomenon.

Unlike slavery, trafficking was universally illegal. In 1904 The International Agreement for the Suppression of White Slave Traffic was ratified by 12 nations, including the United States. It sought to prevent the abduction of women for prostitution rings — dubbed "the white slave trade" — primarily in Europe and Asia.[73]

The League of Nations held an international conference in Geneva in 1921 to deal with "white" slavery, which they renamed as the more internationally (and racially) inclusive "trafficking in women and children." Thirty-three countries signed the International Convention for the Suppression of the Traffic in Women and Children.[74]

The League also addressed slavery with its 1926 Slavery Convention, which required signatories to "prevent and suppress the slave trade."[75] Research reports, created as part of the treaty, alerted the world to the growing problem of international trafficking.[76]

In 1948, the U.N.'s Universal Declaration of Human Rights held that "no one shall be held in slavery or servitude; slavery and the slave trade shall be prohibited in all their forms." The next year the U.N.'s Convention for the Suppression of the Traffic in Persons and of the Exploitation of the Prostitution of Others became the first legally binding treaty on trafficking. It prescribed procedures for the extradition of alleged traffickers. So far 82 of the world's 192 nations have ratified the convention.[77]

Until the 1980s, trafficking often was seen as related to prostitution. But a dramatic rise in international trafficking forced the world to broaden its understanding of the more widespread nature of trafficking. Since the mid-1980s, "Trafficking has increased dramatically with globalization, the rise of illicit trade and the end of Cold War," writes Shelley, the transnational crime expert.

"Human trafficking has flourished in the last two decades, and there is no end in sight."[78]

Shelley and other experts cite various reasons for the increase in trafficking: the breakup of the U.S.S.R., which led to floundering Eastern European economies as well as a rise in corruption and an increase in transnational criminal gangs. And, as globalization led to greater demand for goods and improved mobility, international cargo shipments skyrocketed, making human trafficking easier. Likewise, the elimination of border checks in Europe after creation of the European Union in 1993 paved the way for increased trafficking.

Meanwhile, "Human trafficking has gained increased prominence around the world over the past few years as has been evidenced by numerous international conferences and initiatives," according to Alayksandr Sychov, Belarus' permanent representative to international organizations.[79] In 2000 the U.N. passed the Palermo Protocol against trafficking, which expanded on the 1949 convention by defining human trafficking and outlawing all forms, not just prostitution-related trafficking.[80]

The Palermo Protocol also is notable because, unlike other U.N. treaties, it was created as a law enforcement instrument. In addition to requiring signers to penalize trafficking, it also required them to pass domestic laws that protect victims and offer them temporary or permanent residence.

When it enacted the Trafficking Victims Protection Act in 2000, the United States announced that it intended to target both domestic and foreign trafficking. The act, which must be regularly reauthorized by Congress, was allowed to expire in September 2011 and is now awaiting reauthorization.

Pursuant to the law, each year the State Department's Office to Monitor and Combat Trafficking reports on what countries are doing to end the trade, stressing the importance of the "three P's":[81]

- Prosecution: criminalizing trafficking and prosecuting offenders,
- Protection: identifying and aiding victims and
- Prevention: raising awareness of the trade.

Because human trafficking is a transnational crime, regional laws play a key role in combating the problem. Besides the U.S. law, the Council of Europe's Convention on Action Against Trafficking in Human Beings for the first time aimed to protect trafficked victims in Europe,

something many earlier agreements lacked.[82] And in 2005 several Asian nations (China, Laos, Cambodia, Thailand, Myanmar and Vietnam) established an initiative, COMMIT, to create anti-trafficking measures to serve as guidelines for each state's local anti-trafficking laws.

International and regional anti-trafficking treaties are only effective if local laws are strong and enforced. Individual countries are responsible for investigating, prosecuting and convicting human traffickers, but the complex nature of the crime makes this difficult. "It is a crime that goes beyond borders and one that is very complex to investigate and prosecute," says Elaine Panter, director of programs and planning at Georgetown University's Protection Project. Putting together a successful case against a trafficker who operates in several countries and violates laws in each is complicated and costly. "In many countries that have limited resources, it can be difficult to enforce these laws."

Training is another roadblock. Border guards, police, and federal officers all must be aware of both international and national anti-trafficking laws. To help educate and train anti-trafficking personnel the U.N. in 2007 established the United Nations Global Initiative to Fight Human Trafficking (GIFT) to coordinate and promote the global fight against trafficking.

"We are still in the early days of legislating and fighting this inhuman traffic," explains Panter. "There are international treaties and local laws in place, but much more still needs to be done."

"Human trafficking is a crime of such magnitude and atrocity that it cannot be dealt with successfully by any government alone," says a description of GIFT's mission. "This global problem requires a global, multi-stakeholder strategy that builds on national efforts throughout the world."[83]

CURRENT SITUATION

Boosting Enforcement

Slavery still exists worldwide, President Obama said in his dramatic September speech to the Clinton Global Initiative, which made international headlines.

"Now, I do not use that word, 'slavery' lightly," he said. "It evokes obviously one of the most painful chapters in our nation's history. But around the world, there's no denying the awful reality. When a man, desperate for work, finds himself in a factory or on a fishing boat or in a field, working, toiling, for little or no pay, and beaten if he tries to escape — that is slavery. When a woman is locked in a sweatshop, or trapped in a home as a domestic servant, alone and abused and incapable of leaving — that's slavery. When a little boy is kidnapped, turned into a child soldier, forced to kill or be killed — that's slavery. When a little girl is sold by her impoverished family — girls my daughters' age — runs away from home or is lured by the false promises of a better life and then imprisoned in a brothel and tortured if she resists — that's slavery. It is barbaric, and it is evil, and it has no place in a civilized world."[84]

For human rights activists Obama's speech was confirmation that trafficking and slavery are finally receiving the attention they deserve. "The president is telling the world that trafficking and slavery are growing problems and that the United States will pursue them. His speech and policy announcements represent a turning point in the fight against human trafficking," says the Polaris Project's executive director Bradley Myles.

Obama also announced new methods to strengthen the legal fight against traffickers. Many human rights experts believe this will underscore the importance of prosecutions. "It's important to keep pressuring nations to investigate, prosecute and convict these traffickers," says Slavery International's Donohoe.

Some say recent arrests and convictions suggest the problem is being taken more seriously by governments around the world:

- **China** — In 2011 police broke up 3,200 human trafficking gangs and rescued more than 15,000 abducted women and 8,660 children.[85] This past June police arrested 802 people on suspicion of child trafficking and recovered 181 children.[86] China's trafficking problems stem from its strict one-child policy, which has created a large black market for stolen baby boys, the preferred gender in many Chinese families. Additionally, a critical shortage of baby girls has led to increased trafficking of women and girls to serve as laborers or wives for unwed sons.[87]
- **Romania** — More than 900 human trafficking cases were investigated by police in 2011, up from 717 in 2010, and 480 traffickers were indicted, with more than half convicted. Some were sentenced, for the first time, to more than 10 years in jail.[88]

- **Nigeria** — Police rescued 300 children, ages 10-15, being trafficked inside the country.[89] In September Nigeria announced plans to set up anti-trafficking police units in each of its 36 states.[90]

The global fight against human trafficking and slavery is relatively new and is, as UNICEF's Thatun says, "Just beginning to show results."

Policing Suppliers

Corporations, concerned that human trafficking, slavery or forced labor may be contaminating their supply chains, have joined the battle against trafficking.

In fact, Obama noted in his September speech that in addition to harming companies' reputations, trafficking "distorts markets" when some companies use unpaid or underpaid "slaves" to manufacture goods.

Companies are taking steps to eliminate the potential for trafficked labor in their operations and supply chains. Iconic companies such as Coca Cola, Exxon-Mobil, Microsoft and Delta Airlines recently formed the Global Business Coalition Against Human Trafficking (gBCAT).[91]

Nestlé has willingly opened its supply chain to outside inspectors and uncovered child labor abuses. The Fair Labor Association (FLA) recently examined Nestlé's cocoa supply chain in the Ivory Coast and uncovered child laborers harvesting and processing the product. Nestlé not only made the report public but pledged to prevent further abuses. "The use of child labour in our cocoa supply chain goes against everything we stand for. As the FLA report makes clear, no company sourcing cocoa from Cote d'Ivoire (Ivory Coast) can guarantee that it doesn't happen, but what we can say is that tackling child labour is a top priority for our company," said José Lopez, Nestlé's executive vice president for operations.[92]

Campbell's Soup recently gave suppliers detailed standards they must meet in order to sell produce or other products to the company and announced new measures to "expand training on slavery and human trafficking" for everyone in their supply chain.[93]

Gap has a code of vendor conduct that bars factories producing Gap products from using involuntary labor of any kind. Other firms, from Microsoft to Best Buy, have similar codes.

But while many companies claim to investigate their supply chains, some have been criticized for "handing off"

Would decriminalizing prostitution reduce sex trafficking?

YES Cari Mitchell
Spokeswoman, English Collective of Prostitutes, London, England

Written for *CQ Global Researcher*, October 2012

Decriminalizing prostitution increases sex workers' safety by dismantling a legal system that forces women to work in isolation at risk of violence. The most compelling evidence comes from New Zealand, which decriminalized it in 2003. Sex workers are safer, attacks are cleared up quicker and women find it easier to leave prostitution, since they no longer are barred from other jobs by a criminal record.

But it's difficult to talk about this because trafficking has been so misrepresented. Fabricated or "speculative" figures about the numbers of victims are seized on by politicians, the media and what *The Guardian* called an "unlikely union of evangelical Christians with feminist campaigners" to justify claims that "80 percent of women in prostitution are controlled by traffickers." Britain's 2009 Policing and Crime Act, which increased the criminalization of sex workers under the cover of measures to criminalize clients, was the culmination of this moralistic crusade.

Prostitution has been pushed further underground and sex workers left more vulnerable to abuse and violence, exploitative working conditions, police illegality, rape and trafficking.

Three quarters of sex workers in London have suffered rape and other violence. Has this prompted soul-searching by government, police and the authorities? No. Instead, raids, arrests, convictions and even imprisonment of sex workers have risen.

Victims of trafficking have fared no better. A parliamentary inquiry found they are frequently deprived of "protection, access to services and justice" and "treated as immigration offenders facing detention and removals." Child victims, forced to work as servants, recently got compensation because the police systematically refused to investigate the horrific abuse they suffered.

It's no wonder prostitution is increasing in the U.K., given that at least 70 percent of sex workers are mothers and poverty caused by rising unemployment and benefit cuts is forcing one in five mothers to skip meals to feed their kids. Public concern about violence against female prostitutes is also increasing. The anti-rape initiative SlutWalk, with its purposeful inclusion of sex workers, is countering those prominent feminists who conflate prostitution with trafficking and dismiss sex workers.

Decriminalizing sex work would make it easier for trafficking victims to come forward and for police to pursue rapists and traffickers rather than sex workers and clients.

NO Norma Ramos, Esq.
Executive Director, Coalition Against Trafficking in Women New York, N.Y.

Written for *CQ Global Researcher*, October 2012

At its core, prostitution is the world's oldest oppression: a social injustice that arises primarily out of gender inequality exacerbated by poverty, racial and ethnic marginalization and childhood sexual abuse. In short, prostitution stems from *lack* of choice, not choice.

Prostitution creates a class of human beings who are not allowed to say no to unwanted sex. Many survivors of commercial sexual exploitation refer to prostitution as prepaid rape. Societies that care about social justice and gender equality do not look for ways to make a place where this gender-based violence can take place under "safer" conditions. "Safer prostitution" is an oxymoron.

The way to address oppression is to end it — not to legalize it, regulate it or make it more tolerable. Legalizing prostitution is not only a betrayal of the promise of equality for women and girls, it creates the legal and social conditions that encourage human trafficking and inevitably leads to an exponential expansion of sex trafficking.

Countries that either decriminalize or legalize prostitution send an unmistakable signal to human traffickers that they are welcome to conduct business in their country. Those countries that have legalized prostitution, such as Germany, have released official reports admitting that legalization has failed to make prostitution workable and safer, even going so far as to state that prostitution should not be considered a way to make a living.

The most effective way to address this commercial sexual exploitation is to penalize the buyers and offer those caught up in sex trafficking a way out, as has been done in Sweden, Norway and Iceland. Known as the Nordic model, this approach has discouraged sex trafficking. It is premised on the idea that women and girls have the right not to be bought and sold for sexual exploitation.

Prostitution teaches men and boys that women and girls can be rendered into sexual commodities that can be bought or sold for sexual use and abuse. It creates a callousness among men that undermines the human rights of all women and girls. Those who care about human rights and women's rights increasingly see legalization as a failed social policy and are embracing the Nordic model, the world's first law based on both human and women's rights. It is premised on the notion that women and girls are human beings and cannot be bought or sold for sex.

that responsibility to their suppliers or outside auditors. "Companies have to resist outsourcing ethical responsibility," says Anti-Slavery International's Donohoe.

"The global business community must invest more resources to ensure they are not facilitating human trafficking," says George Mason University's Shelley.

Legislators, often influenced by anti-trafficking activists, have begun mandating supply chain inspection. California's recently passed Supply Chain Transparency Act requires companies doing business in the state to disclose how they are ensuring their supply chains are free of trafficked and slave labor. Proponents are pushing for a similar federal law, and in fact the Obama administration recently introduced similar standards for federal contractors. (*See sidebar, p. 382.*)

Cyber Trafficking

Since the invention of the Internet, a sex slave or a child laborer is now only a mouse click away. In the United States and much of the world, the Internet is now the primary platform for traffickers buying and selling women and children for sex.

"The Internet has opened a whole new front in the war with human trafficking — allowing demand to run free without practical obstacles," said TVPA co-author Smith.[94]

"Victims trafficked through pimp-controlled sex trafficking, escort services, in-call and out-call services, chat rooms, pornography and brothels disguised as massage parlors are commonly marketed" on websites, according to the Polaris Project.[95] "Individuals advertising online for commercial sex are often made to appear that they are working independently, when in fact they are victims of sex trafficking," Polaris' Ellison says.

Illicit online employment agencies, marriage bureaus and chat rooms have been used to recruit "traffickable" victims. "If you don't think that most of the online dating and foreign bride sites are fronts for prostitution and human trafficking, then you have your head in the sand. Just Google it," said anti-trafficking activist Kathryn Griffin Townsend, founder of We've Been There, Done That, an organization to rehabilitate women who have been rescued from prostitution.[96] She and others say simply Googling "buy foreign women" reveals numerous questionable sites.

Closing these sites has been difficult. After public pressure, some sites, such as Craigslist, have agreed to remove sex-related listings. Others, such as backpage.com, have refused. The Communications Decency Act protects the owners of websites by absolving them of responsibility for the content of postings by site users. Critics claim closing down these sites, in a "whack-a-mole" fashion, is wrong-headed, because the owners will merely move their sites to another country. They recommend investing in programs to help those most vulnerable to trafficking and cooperating with sites to investigate and remove advertising that promotes trafficking.

Human rights advocates also propose using the Internet and other high-tech tools to combat traffickers. In his speech on trafficking, Obama said the State Department is using technology, such as the website www.SlaveryFootprint.org, to identify goods made with slave labor. In many countries, such as Ghana, villagers have been given cell phones to help report trafficking incidents. Microsoft, Google and Facebook are cooperating with authorities to help identify potential traffickers. Databases that contain traffickers' methods of operation help law enforcement uncover them.

"Traffickers are always one step ahead of us," says Ellison. "We need to use whatever technology we can to go after them."

OUTLOOK

Shifting Perceptions

Although the high-tech battle against human trafficking and slavery is still in its infancy, activists are optimistic that the world is taking the subject seriously. For example, 20 years ago few Westerners knew that slavery existed within their own countries or had any idea of the global reach of the human trafficking industry. (*See sidebar, p. 382.*)

UNICEF's Thatun remembers giving a talk on human slavery in Australia in 2007. When she asked, "Is there any trafficking here?" she remembers "Everyone said no, trafficking only happens in less developed nations. Today they know better."

Hundreds of organizations are now on the Internet devoted to publicizing and fighting trafficking. "There were far fewer a decade ago," says Polaris Project director of communications Meagan Fowler.

"We have been working on anti-trafficking issues since the late 1980s, and it's reassuring to see the world growing more and more aware of the extent of this problem," says Thatun. "The more the public and private sectors are aware of trafficking and slavery, the faster the problem will be solved."

Perceptions also are changing. Optimists point to developments such as the State Department's Trafficking in Persons report and its ("naming and shaming") country rankings as proof that the world is taking positive steps to deal with the problem. "I've seen a huge shift in the perception of these problems over the last 30 years," says Ramos of the Coalition Against Trafficking in Women. "We have a long road ahead of us, but we are making progress."

As more businesses — often under public pressure — regulate their supply chains, slave labor should lessen, activists say. And late last year Google gave $11.5 million to nonprofit and academic organizations for the fight against trafficking. "Our support will free more than 12,000 people from modern-day slavery and prevent millions more from being victimized," Google said.[97] Microsoft recently awarded $185,000 in research grants to explore how technology facilitates trafficking.[98] Other companies and organizations have joined the campaign as well.

Although the number of trafficking and slavery cases seems to grow larger each year, many experts attribute the increase to more victims being willing to come forward. "What was once taboo is now more accepted," says Thatun. "It has taken over a decade for that mind shift." Better reporting and improved law enforcement also have contributed to the increase.

While some say the increased international focus is helping to reduce slavery and trafficking, others disagree. "This is a growth field. It will only get bigger over the next decades," says Shelley. The transnational crime expert at George Mason University explains that climate change, which is already displacing people living on islands and coastal lowlands, could displace millions of others, who will be desperate to feed themselves and their families. The growing economic disparity in the world will also fuel the growth in trafficking, she says.

"Sadly, there is a growing supply of people vulnerable to traffickers," she says. "I am not optimistic."

Others are encouraged that attention now is focusing on prevention and protection of victims rather than just on convicting traffickers. "In the past, we too often waited for victims to come to us," says Thatun. "Now we are more focused on helping before they become victims." And victims are receiving crisis intervention, emotional assistance, financial help, rehabilitation and more.

In the final analysis, however, more countries must have the political will to combat the problem, activists say. If they don't, "Trafficking will be the defining issue of the 21st century," wrote Shelley in her global investigation of trafficking. And "humanity will be diminished by its prevalence."[99]

NOTES

1. Henry Mhango, "Malawi children falling victim to human traffickers," *The Guardian*, July 16, 2012, www.guardian.co.uk/global-development/2012/jul/16/malawi-children-victim-human-traffickers.

2. "Trafficking in Persons Report," U.S. Department of State, July 2012, p. 323, www.state.gov/documents/organization/192596.pdf.

3. Madalitso Kateta, "Child and women trafficking high in Malawi," Mywage.org, www.mywage.com/main/women-and-work/children-and-work/child-and-woman-trafficking-high-in-malawi.

4. "Trafficking in Persons: U.S. policy and issues for Congress," Congressional Research Service, Dec. 23, 2010, p. 20, http://fpc.state.gov/documents/organization/139278.pdf. Also see "Trafficking in Persons Report 2012," *op. cit.*

5. "Fact Sheet: Obama administration announces efforts to combat human trafficking at home and abroad," The White House, Sept, 25, 2012, www.whitehouse.gov/the-press-office/2012/09/25/fact-sheet-obama-administration-announces-efforts-combat-human-trafficki.

6. "Protocol to Prevent, Suppress and Punish Trafficking in Persons Especially Women and Children, supplementing the United Nations Convention against Transnational Organized Crime," Office of the United Nations High Commissioner for Human Rights, www2.ohchr.org/english/law/protocoltraffic.htm.

7. "ILO hails campaign against modern slavery," International Labour Organization, Sept. 28, 2012, www.ilo.org/global/about-the-ilo/newsroom/news/WCMS_190434/lang--en/index.htm.

8. "ILO 2012 Global Estimate of Forced Labour," International Labour Organization, June 1, 2012, www.ilo.org/wcmsp5/groups/public/@ed_norm/@declaration/documents/publication/wcms_181921.pdf.

9. *Ibid.*

10. Alison Holt, "British men forced into 'modern slavery' abroad," BBC, Feb. 1, 2012, www.bbc.co.uk/news/uk-16836065.

11. "Forced Labour," International Labour Organization, www.ilo.org/global/standards/subjects-covered-by-international-labour-standards/forced-labour/lang--en/index.htm. Also see "Children and Human Rights: Child Soldiers," Amnesty International, www.amnesty.org/en/children. For background, see John Felton, "Child Soldiers," *CQ Global Researcher*, July 1, 2008, pp. 183-211.

12. "General Assembly president calls for redoubling of efforts to end human trafficking," United Nations Office on Drugs and Crime, April 3, 2012, www.unodc.org/unodc/en/frontpage/2012/April/un-general-assembly-president-calls-for-re-doubled-efforts-to-end-human-trafficking.html.

13. "Thailand: Children trafficked to sell flowers and beg," IRIN News, June 4, 2012, www.irinnews.org/Report/95566/THAILAND-Children-trafficked-to-sell-flowers-and-beg.

14. "Uganda: Women trafficked into sex work," IRIN News, March 5, 2012, www.irinnews.org/report/95013/UGANDA-Women-trafficked-into-sex-work.

15. "Pakistan: Selling children to pay off a debt," IRIN News, June 6, 2011, www.irinnews.org/Report/92904/PAKISTAN-Selling-children-to-pay-off-a-debt.

16. "ILO action against trafficking in human beings," International Labour Organization, 2008, www.ilo.org/wcmsp5/groups/public/@ed_norm/@declaration/documents/publication/wcms_090356.pdf.

17. "About Slavery: Modern Slavery," Free the Slaves, www.freetheslaves.net/SSLPage.aspx?pid=301.

18. See "International Anti-Trafficking Legislation," The Protection Project, www.protectionproject.org/resources/law-library/international-anti-trafficking/.

19. Louise Shelley, *Human Trafficking* (2010), p. 12.

20. "The Protection Project Review of the Trafficking in Persons Report 2012," The Protection Project, www.protectionproject.org/wp-content/uploads/2012/07/TIP-Review-2012-Final.pdf.

21. Mark Memmott, "Obama focuses on 'outrage of human trafficking,'" NPR, Sept. 25, 2012, www.npr.org/blogs/thetwo-way/2012/09/25/161748574/obama-focuses-on-outrage-of-human-trafficking.

22. "International trafficking in persons laws," U.N. Inter-agency Project on Human Trafficking, www.no-trafficking.org/resources_int_tip_laws.html.

23. Nikolaj Nielsen, "Human traffickers evade conviction," *EU Observer*, June 25, 2012, http://euobserver.com/justice/116750.

24. *Ibid.*

25. Siddharth Kara, *Sex Trafficking: Inside the business of modern slavery* (2010), p. 40.

26. *Ibid.*, p. 209.

27. Simon Denver, "India slowly confronts epidemic of missing children," The Associated Press, Sept. 22, 2012, www.washingtonpost.com/world/asia_pacific/india-slowly-confronts-epidemic-of-missing-children/2012/09/22/395d51b0-fd95-11e1-b153-218509a954e1_story.html.

28. *Ibid.*

29. "Trafficking in Persons Report 2012," *op. cit.*

30. Namita Bhandare, "A blot on our conscience," *Hindustan Times*, Feb. 17, 2012, www.hindustantimes.com/News-Feed/ColumnsOthers/A-blot-on-our-conscience/Article1-813048.aspx.

31. Chuck Neubauer, "Libya's record won't stop US aid," *The Washington Times*, Sept. 17, 2012, www.washingtontimes.com/news/2012/sep/17/libyas-record-wont-stop-us-aid-among-nations-fault/.

32. Chuck Neubauer, "Top human traffickers need not fear Obama," *The Washington Times*, July 29, 2012, www.washingtontimes.com/news/2012/jul/29/the-failure-of-the-white-house-to-enforce-threaten/?page=all.

33. "Prosecuting human traffickers," United Nations Office on Drugs and Crime, www.unodc.org/unodc/en/human-trafficking/prosecution.html.

34. Niklas Jakobsson and Andreas Kotsadam, "The Law and Economics of International Sex Slavery: Prostitution laws and trafficking for sexual exploitation," University of Gothenburg, June 2010, https://gupea.ub.gu.se/bitstream/2077/22825/1/gupea_2077_22825_1.pdf.

35. "The Link Between Prostitution and Sex Trafficking," U.S. Dept. of State, 2004, http://2001-2009 .state.gov/documents/organization/38901.pdf.

36. *Ibid.*, p. 16.

37. "Trafficking in Human Beings: Ten Years of Independent Monitoring," Bureau of the Dutch National Rapporteur, 2010, http://english.bnrm.nl/ reports/eighth/.

38. Seo-Young Cho, Saxel Dreher and Eric Neumayer, "Does legalized prostitution increase human trafficking?" *Economics of Security*, June 2012, p. 21, www2 .vwl.wiso.uni-goettingen.de/courant-papers/CRC-PEG_DP_96.pdf.

39. Speech by Kajsa Wahlberg, Dec. 6, 2010, www.kvin deraad.dk/files/Kajsa_Wahlberg.pdf.

40. Wendy Lyon, "'There was no lack of buyers' — Swedish sex trafficking trial concludes," *Feminist Ire*, May 20, 2012, http://feministire.wordpress .com/2012/05/20/there-was-no-lack-of-buyers-swedish-sex-trafficking-trial-concludes/#comments.

41. Peter Linnaeus, "Severe punishments of trafficking scandal," *Goteborg Post*, Feb. 2, 2012 (translated), www.gp.se/nyheter/goteborg/1.943437-stranga-straff-i-traffickingharvan.

42. Serena Chaudry, "Millions pushed into child labor in Pakistan," Reuters, Feb. 7, 2012, www .reuters.com/article/2012/02/07/us-pakistan-child labour-idUSTRE8160LA20120207.

43. *Ibid.*

44. "Accelerating action against child labor," International Labour Organization, 2010, www .ilo.org/ipecinfo/product/viewProduct.do?pro ductId=13853.

45. For background, see John Felton, "Child Soldiers," *CQ Global Researcher*, July 1, 2008, pp. 183-211.

46. Thomas DeGregori, "Child labor or child prostitution," Cato Institute, Oct. 8, 2002, www.cato.org/ publications/commentary/child-labor-or-child-prostitution.

47. "Convention on the Rights of the Child," United Nations Treaty Collection, Aug. 10, 2012, http:// treaties.un.org/pages/viewdetails.aspx?src=treaty&mtdsg_ no=iv-11&chapter=4&lang=en#EndDec.

48. Enakshi Ganguly Thukral, "Finally the will for the right ban," *The Hindu*, Aug. 31, 2012, www.thehindu .com/opinion/op-ed/article3840962.ece.

49. *Ibid.*

50. David Harrison, "It's official: Child labor is a good thing," *The Telegraph*, Jan. 30, 2005, www.telegraph. co.uk/news/worldnews/northamerica/canada/ 1482368/Its-official-child-labour-is-a-good-thing .html; http://blogsocial.viabloga.com/files/DP-EJ.pdf.

51. Jean Friedman-Rudovsky, "In Latin America, looking at the positive side of child labor," *Time*, Nov. 16, 2011, www.time.com/time/world/article/0,8599, 2099200,00.html.

52. DeGregori, *op. cit.*

53. "Guinea-Mauritania: Worst forms of child labour still widespread," IRIN News, Oct. 10, 2011, www .irinnews.org/Report/93921/GUINEA-MAURITANIA-Worst-forms-of-child-labour-still-widespread.

54. Kristina Kangaspunta, "A short history of trafficking in persons," *Freedom From Fear*, Sept. 15, 2012, www .freedomfromfearmagazine.org/index .php?option=com_content&view=article&id=99:a-short-history-of-trafficking-in-persons& catid=37:issue-1&Itemid=159. Also see "A brief history of slavery," *New Internationalist*, Aug. 1, 2001, www.newint.org/features/2001/08/05/history/.

55. Hugh Thomas, "World History: The Story of Mankind from Prehistory to the Present," 1996, pp. 54-55.

56. "Ur-Nammu," *Ancient Encyclopedia History*, www .ancient.eu.com/Ur-Nammu/.

57. L. W. King (translator), "The Code of Hammurabi," The Avalon Project, http://avalon.law.yale.edu/ ancient/hamframe.asp.

58. "Faith In Action: Judaism," Free the Slaves, www .freetheslaves.net/page.aspx?pid=486.

59. Ursula Cliff, "Slavery in Ancient Greece," *Clio*, 2009, http://cliojournal.wikispaces.com/Slavery+ in+Ancient+Greece.

60. Robert A. Guisepi, *A History of Ancient Greece* (1998), http://history-world.org/greece%20economy.htm.

61. *Ibid.*

62. Lewis Napthali and Meyer Reinhold, *Roman Civilization: The republic and the Augustan Age* (1990), p. 245.

63. "A Brief History Of Slavery," *New Internationalist*, Aug. 1, 2001, www.newint.org/features/2001/08/05/history/.

64. Rodney Stark, "The truth about the Catholic Church and slavery," *Christianity Today*, July 1, 2003, www.christianitytoday.com/ct/2003/july web-only/7-14-53.0.html.

65. "Slovak, Slavic, Slavonic, "University of Pittsburgh, www.pitt.edu/~votruba/qsonhist/slavicslovak.html.

66. "Breaking the silence: Lest we forget," United Nations, www.un.org/events/slaveryremembrance/background.shtml.

67. "Assessing the Slave Trade," *Voyages, The trans-Atlantic slave trade database*, www.slavevoyages.org/tast/assessment/index.faces.

68. "The Middle Passage," *Recovered Histories*, www.recoveredhistories.org/storiesmiddle.php.

69. "Breaking the silence: Lest we forget," *op. cit.*

70. *Ibid.*

71. "Pro Slavery Lobbies," *Recovered Histories*, www.recoveredhistories.org/storiesproslavery.php.

72. For background, see Marjorie Valbrun and Roland Flamini, "Rebuilding Haiti," *CQ Global Researcher*, Oct. 2, 2012, pp. 449-472.

73. "International Agreements," Fight Slavery Now, http://fightslaverynow.org/why-fight-there-are-27-million-reasons/the-law-and-trafficking/international-agreements/.

74. "International Convention for the Suppression of the Traffic in Women and Children," United Nations Treaty Collection, Sept. 30, 1921, http://treaties.un.org/pages/ViewDetails.aspx?src=TREATY&mtdsg_no=VII-3&chapter=7&lang=en.

75. "Slavery Convention," Office of the United Nations Hugh Commissioner for Human Rights, www2.ohchr.org/english/law/slavery.htm.

76. Kangaspunta, *op. cit.*

77. "A Convention for the Suppression of the Traffic in Persons and of the Exploitation of the Prostitution of Others," United Nations Treaty Collection, March 21, 1950, http://treaties.un.org/Pages/ViewDetails.aspx?src=TREATY&mtdsg_no=VII-11-a&chapter=7&lang=en.

78. Shelley, *op. cit.*, pp. 37-58.

79. Alayksandr Sychov, "Human trafficking: A call for global action," Globality Studies, Oct. 22, 2009, http://globality.cc.stonybrook.edu/?p=114.

80. United Nations Treaty Collection, http://treaties.un.org/Pages/ViewDetails.aspx?src=IND&mtdsg_no=XVIII-12-a&chapter=18&lang=en.

81. "Trafficking in Persons Report 2011," U.S. Department of State, June 2011, www.state.gov/j/tip/rls/tiprpt/2011/index.htm.

82. "Council of Europe Convention on Action Against Trafficking in Human Beings CETS No. 197," May 16, 2005, www.conventions.coe.int/Treaty/Commun/QueVoulezVous.asp?NT=197&CM=1&CL=ENG.

83. "About UN GIFT," U.N. GIFT, www.ungift.org/knowledgehub/en/about/index.html.

84. "Remarks by the President to the Clinton Global Initiative," White House, Sept. 25, 2012, www.whitehouse.gov/the-press-office/2012/09/25/remarks-president-clinton-global-initiative.

85. "Thousands of Chinese trafficking victims rescued by police," The Associated Press, March 11, 2012, www.guardian.co.uk/world/2012/mar/11/chinese-trafficking-victims-rescued.

86. "China: Police crack down on child trafficking rings," The Associated Press, July 6 2012, www.nytimes.com/2012/07/07/world/asia/china-police-crack-down-on-child-trafficking-rings.html.

87. For background, see Robert Kiener, "Gendercide Crisis," *CQ Global Researcher*, Oct. 4, 2011, pp. 473-498.

88. "Romania, Bulgaria make trafficking cases a priority," *Turkish Weekly*, Sept. 19, 2012, www.turkishweekly.net/news/142194/romania-bulgaria-make-trafficking-cases-a-priority.html.

89. "Human Trafficking: Army rescues over 300 under-aged in Kogi," *Leadership*, July 30, 2012, www.leadership.ng/nga/articles/31177/2012/07/30/human_trafficking_army_rescues_over_300_underaged_kogi.html.

90. "Nigeria police state commands to get anti-trafficking units," *Afriquejet*, Sept. 26, 2012, www.afriquejet.com/nigeria-police-state-commands-to-get-anti-trafficking-units-2012092645953.html.

91. "Global Business Coalition Announces Human Trafficking Initiative," *Travel Blackboard*, Sept. 26, 2012, www.etravelblackboardasia.com/article/86616/global-business-coalition-announces-human-trafficking-initiative.

92. Emma Thomasson, "Nestlé pledges action on Ivorian cocoa child labor," Reuters, June 29, 2012, www.reuters.com/article/2012/06/29/nestle-labour-ivory-coast-idUSL6E8HT2A320120629.

93. "Campbell Soup Company Disclosure Statement on Human Trafficking and Slavery in the Supply Chain," Campbell's Soup Co., December 2011, www.campbellsoupcompany.com/pdf/Human_Trafficking_and_Slavery_in_the_Supply_Chain_Final_12_15_11.pdf.

94. Peter J. Smith, "Congressman says Internet-fueled sex trafficking too big for government alone," Lifesitenews, Sept. 17, 2010, www.lifesitenews.com/news/archive//ldn/2010/sep/10091707.

95. "Internet based," Polaris Project, www.polarisproject.org/human-trafficking/sex-trafficking-in-the-us/internet-based.

96. "Letter from National Association of Human Trafficking Victim Advocates," U.S. House of Representatives, March 29, 2012, http://blackburn.house.gov/uploadedfiles/letter_from_anti-trafficking_organizations.pdf.

97. Chenda Ngak, "Human trafficking gets attention from Google," "TechTalk," CBS News, Dec. 14, 2001, www.cbsnews.com/8301-501465_162-57342980-501465/human-trafficking-gets-attention-from-google/.

98. Samantha Doer, "Microsoft Names Research Grant Recipients in Fight Against Child Sex Trafficking," Technet, June 13, 2012, http://blogs.technet.com/b/microsoft_on_the_issues/archive/2012/06/13/microsoft-names-research-grant-recipients-in-fight-against-child-sex-trafficking.aspx.

99. Shelley, *op. cit.*, p. 324.

BIBLIOGRAPHY

Selected Sources

Books

Bales, Kevin, and Ron Soodalter, *The Slave Next Door: Human Trafficking and Slavery in America Today*, University of California Press, 2010.
A co-founder of the anti-slavery group Free the Slaves and a professor of contemporary slavery at the Wilberforce Institute at the University of Hull in the U.K. (Bales) and an anti-slavery activist (Soodalter) explore various forms of slave labor.

Batstone, David, *Not For Sale: The Return of the Global Slave Trade and How We Can Fight It*, Harper Collins, 2010.
A journalist profiles the modern generation of abolitionists.

DeStefano, Anthony M., *The War on Human Trafficking: U.S. Policy Assessed*, Rutgers University Press, 2008.
A journalist explains how the U.S. government is combating trafficking.

Kara, Siddharth, *Sex Trafficking: Inside the Business of Modern Slavery*, Columbia University Press, 2010.
A fellow on human trafficking at Harvard University's Kennedy School of Government examines the size, growth and profitability of the sex trafficking industry.

Shelley, Louise, *Human Trafficking: A Global Perspective*, Cambridge University Press, 2010.
A leading expert on transnational crime examines the human trafficking business.

Articles

"Nobbling nasty networks," *The Economist*, Aug. 1, 2012.
The magazine surveys new high-tech approaches to combating human trafficking.

Cabitza, Mattia, "Peru takes its 'first step' in the eradication of child labour," *The Guardian*, July 16, 2012, www.guardian.co.uk/global-development/2012/jul/16/peru-eradicate-child-labour-education.
A pilot project in Peru seeks to reduce child labor.

Denyer, Simon, "India slowly confronts epidemic of missing children," *The Washington Post*, Sept. 22, 2012.
About 90,000 children are abducted by traffickers each year in India.

Sharma, Nandita, "The old anti-trafficking propaganda," *Counterpunch*, Sept. 5, 2012, www.counter punch.org/2012/09/05/the-old-anti-trafficking-propaganda/.
An investigation into human trafficking concludes that many women rescued from brothels entered the industry voluntarily.

Skinner, E. Benjamin, "The Fishing Industry's Cruelest Catch," *Business Week*, Feb. 23, 2012, www .businessweek.com/articles/2012-02-23/the-fishing-industrys-cruelest-catch.
A journalist reports on his six-week investigation into debt bondage on fishing ships in New Zealand waters.

Stuart, Elizabeth, "Stolen innocence: The battle against modern-day slavery in the U.S.," *Deseret News*, Dec. 10, 2011.
Profiles of several trafficked Americans offer a glimpse into the U.S. sex trafficking industry.

Reports and Studies

"Collateral Damage: The Impact of Anti-Trafficking Measures on Human Rights Around the World," Global Alliance Against Traffic in Women, 2007, www .gaatw.org/Collateral%20Damage_Final/singlefile_ CollateralDamagefinal.pdf.
A nonprofit group that works to prevent trafficking of women assesses the results of anti-trafficking measures in eight countries.

"Global Report on Trafficking in Persons," U.N. Office on Drugs and Crime, February 2009, www.unodc.org/ unodc/en/human-trafficking/global-report-on-trafficking-in-persons.html.
Based on data from 155 countries, a U.N. study provides the first global assessment of human trafficking.

"Trafficking in Persons: International Dimensions and Foreign Policy Issues for Congress," Congressional Research Service, April 20, 2012, www.fas.org/sgp/ crs/row/R42497.pdf.
Trafficking affects human rights, criminal justice, migration, gender, public health and labor issues.

"Trafficking in Persons Report," U.S. Department of State, June 2012, www.state.gov/j/tip/rls/tiprpt/2012/ index.htm.
The State Department's annual analysis of modern slavery ranks nations on their attempts to eradicate human trafficking.

Jakobsson, Niklas, and Andreas Kotsadam, "The Law and Economics of International Sex Slavery: Prostitution laws and trafficking for sexual exploitation," University of Gothenburg, June 2010, http://andreaskotsadam .files.wordpress.com/2010/06/trafficking.pdf.
Norwegian academies show how trafficking for sexual exploitation is affected by laws governing prostitution.

Lagon, Mark, and Diana Taylor, "Slavery and Supply Chains: What Businesses Can Do to Fight Human Trafficking," Council on Foreign Relations, May 14, 2008, www.cfr.org/human-rights/slavery-supply-chains-businesses-can-do-fight-human-trafficking-video/p16208.
Video explains how the U.S. government advises businesses to prevent trafficking in their supply chains.

For More Information

Anti-Slavery International, Thomas Clarkson House, The Stableyard, Broomgrove Rd., London SW9 9TL, United Kingdom; +44 20 7501 8920; www.antislavery.org. A 170-year-old organization that works to eliminate slavery worldwide.

Coalition Against Trafficking in Women (CATW), P.O. Box 7427, JAF Station, New York, NY 10116; www.catw .org. Works to end human trafficking and the commercial sexual exploitation of women and children worldwide.

Free the Slaves, 1320 19th St., N.W., Suite 600, Washington, DC 20036; 202-775-7480; www.freetheslaves.net. Promotes freedom for enslaved victims.

Global Initiative to Fight Trafficking (GIFT), P.O. Box 500, 1400 Vienna, Austria; +43-1 26060-5687; www.ungift .org. A U.N. organization that supports the global fight against human trafficking based on U.N. treaties.

International Labour Organization, 4 route des Morillons, CH-1211 Geneva 22, Switzerland; +41 22 799 6111; www

.ILO.org. Founded in 1919, a U.N. organization that collects data on forced labor around the world.

International Prostitutes Collective, P.O. Box 287, London NW6 5QU, United Kingdom; +44 20 7482 2496; www .prostitutescollective.net. An advocacy group that campaigns against prostitution laws that criminalize sex workers and advocates economic alternatives and higher benefits and wages.

Polaris Project, P.O. Box 53315, Washington, DC 20009; 202-745-1001; www.polarisproject.org. Grass-roots organization that fights human trafficking and modern slavery and promotes legislation to combat both.

United Nations Children's Fund (UNICEF), 3 United Nations Plaza, New York, NY 10017; 212-326-7000; www.unicef.org. Works to assure improved quality of life for children worldwide.

United Nations Office on Drugs and Crime (UNODC), Vienna International Centre, P.O. Box 500, A 1400 Vienna Austria; +43 1 26060; www.unodc.org. Assists member states in their struggle against illicit drugs, organized crime and terrorism.

Voices From Abroad:

SINA CHUMA-MKANDAWIRE

Director, International Labour Organization, Nigeria

A collective effort

"Victims of human trafficking require complex assistance in order to regain their confidence and reintegrate into the society. This involves medical help, psychological support, legal assistance, shelter and everyday care. It is impossible for one organisation or agency to meet all these needs, hence there are many actors working to support victims of human trafficking. In order to have an effective response to these needs, there is an obligation to set up channels of coordination, collaboration and effective and proper communication amongst organisations providing services to trafficking victims."

This Day (Nigeria), August 2012

EILIS WARD

Political Science Lecturer National University of Ireland, Ireland

Not all are trafficked

"It is important to remember here that not all women in prostitution are trafficked. Not all women in prostitution consider themselves victims in need of rescue. Nor do they all believe that selling sex means that an act of violence is committed upon them. Moreover, not everyone in prostitution is female, and not all clients are male."

Irish Times, October 2011

JOY NGOZI EZEILO

Special Rapporteur on Trafficking, U.N. Office of the High Commissioner for Human Rights, Switzerland

More effort needed

"The UAE must be commended for its strong commitment to combat trafficking in persons both at the domestic level and in the Gulf region. However, it needs to devote greater attention to identification of countless victims of all forms of trafficking and guarantee their right to effective remedy."

The New Times (Rwanda), April 2012

FOLEN MURAPA

Spokesperson, International Organisation for Migration, Zimbabwe

Against their will

"Victims of trafficking to South Africa, Mozambique and Angola are reportedly being forced to perform duties against their will for the benefit of the trafficker. These include sexual exploitation, forced labour, domestic servitude — under horrific, ruthless and hazardous working conditions."

Zimbabwe Standard,
March 2012

SERGEI BELYAEV

Head, Organization for Security and Cooperation in Europe, Turkmenistan

An appalling trend

"Trafficking in human beings is in all cases an extremely grave crime, but trafficking in persons with disabilities is especially appalling."

Trend News Agency (Azerbaijan), October 2011

NOK (ANONYMOUS)

Sex worker, Thailand

Rescue not wanted

"Before I was arrested I was working happily, had no debt and was free to move around the city. Now I'm in debt, I'm scared most of the time, and it's not safe to move around. How can they call this 'help'?"

The Nation (Thailand), March 2012

ELENA JEFFREYS

President, Scarlet Alliance, Australia

Not much evidence

"Australia's anti-trafficking laws have resulted in thousands of raids, resources devoted to surveillance and investigations, but have found very little evidence of trafficking."

New Zealand Herald, July 2012

MADELEINE REES

Attorney against sex
trafficking, England

Different manifestations

"Trafficking for the purpose of sexual exploitation still goes on in most western countries — including here. It

Seattle Post Intelligencer/David Horsey

manifests differently in a post-conflict country like Bosnia because it can be characterised by extreme violence, and it is very obvious."

Birmingham (England) Evening Mail, November 2011

16

Vanishing Biodiversity

Reed Karaim

Commuters use a boat bridge in Dhaka, the capital of Bangladesh, where the Buriganga River is clogged by invasive water hyacinths. The dense foliage of the rapidly growing plant covers the river's surface, blocking light, killing native species and destroying the fragile food web. Non-native species like the hyacinth are disrupting ecosystems and threatening plants and animals around the world.

From *The CQ Researcher*, November 6, 2012.

A s scientists study the web of life that makes up Earth's shrinking biodiversity, they continue to find unexpected connections. Consider the sea otter and climate change.

A small marine mammal that lives in the frigid northern Pacific coastal waters, the sea otter has the densest fur in the animal kingdom, with up to a million hairs per square inch.[1] Sea otter fur was so prized they were hunted to the brink of extinction in the early 1900s, when only about 2,000 remained.[2] Thanks to changing fashions and conservation efforts, the sea otter population has recovered to number in the tens of thousands, although it's still far below what it once was.

Once their fur was no longer cherished, sea otters were seen merely as cute, playful creatures — until recently.

A new study indicates that the sea otter plays a measurable role in fighting global warming. Researchers at the University of California, Santa Cruz, found that the otters helped to protect Pacific seaweed forests by eating kelp-loving sea urchins.[3] Kelp consumes carbon dioxide (CO_2), a principal contributor to global warming. By eating the sea urchins, the otters enable kelp forests to process up to an additional 9.6 million tons of carbon dioxide a year, the researchers found.[4]

"From the perspective of trying to mitigate climate change, all the focus has been on [CO_2-consuming] plants — managing forests, that sort of thing — but this indicates that animals might have a strong impact on the carbon cycle. There might be win-win conservation-climate change scenarios," says assistant professor of environmental studies Chris Wilmers, the study's lead author.

Most Threatened Species Are in Asia, Western Hemisphere

More than 900 species have gone extinct worldwide in the last 500 years, and more than 10,000 are in danger of extinction, according to the International Union for the Conservation of Nature. Ecuador, which is rapidly losing its biodiversity-rich rainforests to oil exploration, logging and road building, has the world's largest number of species threatened by extinction. Indonesia, India and Mexico have the most endangered mammals.

Countries with the Most Threatened Species

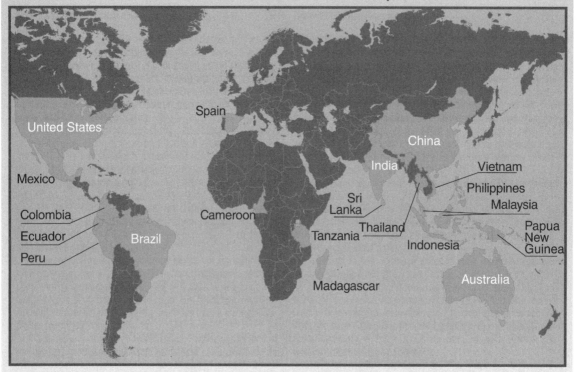

Source: "Threatened species in each country," "Red List," International Union for the Conservation of Nature, 2012, www.iucnredlist.org/documents/summarystatistics/2012_2_RL_Stats_Table_5.pdf. Map by Lewis Agrell

The sea otter study is one of several recent reports that are deepening scientific understanding of the importance of biodiversity and how humans affect it. For years, conservation biologists and other scientists have reported that the Earth is losing plant and animal species at an alarming rate. One new study, published in *Nature*, raises the possibility the planet is nearing a "state shift," or tipping point, in which the global ecosystem changes dramatically.[5]

Other recent research has taken a closer look at humanity's dependence on healthy ecosystems for everything from the food we eat to the water we drink and the clean air we breathe.[6]

"When we look at the bigger picture, we discover we depend on a whole lot of species," says Michel Loreau, director of the Centre for Biodiversity Theory and Modelling in Moulis, France.

Conservationists have made progress in some areas, including the Amazon, where forest clearing has slowed. "There's a lot more good news than people think," says Stuart Pimm, a conservation biologist with Duke University in Durham, N.C., and the University of

Pretoria in South Africa. "Globally, for example, we've reduced the rate of bird extinctions to about a quarter of what it would have been if we hadn't bothered."

Yet, overall, the Earth is still losing species. From large animals such as tigers and rhinoceroses to insects and plant varieties, populations are declining, and many species are believed to be going extinct. Estimates have ranged as high as 150 to 200 species a day, although some researchers believe the number could be significantly lower.[7] Part of the problem: No one knows how many species exist on Earth; estimates range from 2 million to 100 million.[8]

Scientists, however, can use the fossil record to compare the normal "background" rate of extinctions with the rate of recorded extinctions in more recent times. "We know the current extinction rates in the last four centuries are about 100 to 1,000 times higher than the background rates," says Loreau. Some projections, he says, show the Earth soon reaching extinction levels that are "10,000 times the background rates."

A few analysts are skeptical of such claims and even doubt a biodiversity crisis exists. Others believe the key to healthy ecosystems isn't the diversity of species but the health of key plants and animals. However, the level of biodiversity loss most experts see is alarming enough that many believe the planet is experiencing the "sixth great extinction" in Earth's history. But unlike previous mass extinctions, which were caused by natural disasters, this one largely is the work of humans, they say.

Researchers say there are five principal causes of biodiversity loss:

Tropical Species Are Declining

The populations of wild species in tropical climates have declined by more than 60 percent since 1970, while those in temperate climates have seen moderate growth (top graph). Freshwater and marine vertebrates in temperate climates have made gains, while those in tropical climates have declined 70 percent and 62 percent, respectively (bottom). The World Wildlife Fund's "Living Planet Index" has tracked population trends of more than 2,500 vertebrate species since 1970.

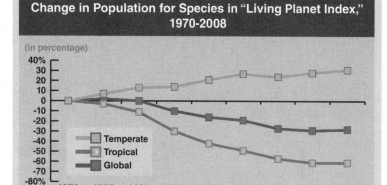

Change in Population for Species in "Living Planet Index," 1970-2008

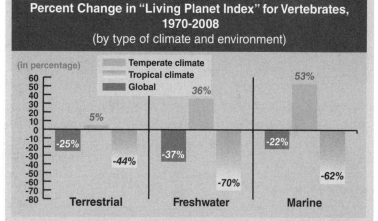

Percent Change in "Living Planet Index" for Vertebrates, 1970-2008 (by type of climate and environment)

Sources: "Living Planet Report 2012," World Wildlife Fund for Nature, 2012, p. 130, awsassets. panda.org/downloads/1_lpr_2012_online_full_size_single_pages_final_12051 6.pdf; "Living Planet Index Interactive Graph," World Wildlife Fund for Nature, 2012, wwf.panda.org/about_ our_earth/all_publications/living_planet_report/living_planet_report_graphics/l pi_interactive/

• Shrinking or fragmented natural habitat, largely caused by humanity's growing footprint;

Inside the 'Doomsday Vault,' Hope for Survival

But some conservationists ask: Is it enough?

High above the Arctic Circle, on the remote Norwegian island of Svalbard, a huge vault has been carved into the side of a mountain. If its isolated location, concrete walls and steel doors aren't security enough, the so-called "doomsday vault" is also surrounded by tall fences and motion detectors ready to sense any intruders.

The facility holds a treasure so common it can be found blowing in the wind on every continent, and yet it could hold the key to humanity's survival in the event of a global disaster.

The "doomsday vault" was built to hold seeds from wheat, corn, rice and other crop varieties from all around the world, a storehouse of genetic diversity intended to provide a final safeguard against the consequences of biodiversity loss. The collection is part of a system of some 1,400 other seed banks around the world.[1]

But some conservationists are asking whether even the doomsday vault and its sister vaults around the world are sufficient.

More than 740,000 seed samples are being kept in the chilled chambers of Svalbard, according to a recent estimate.[2] The project, a collaborative effort among the

The 24,200th seed sample — from a pink, wild banana native to China — is added to the 3.5 billion seeds stored in the sub-freezing vault at the Millennium Seed Bank in Sussex, England, on Oct. 15, 2009. Some 1,400 seed banks across the globe preserve thousands of plants to be used in the event of a global environmental disaster.

- Overuse, such as commercial fishing that has depleted bluefin tuna and other key marine species;
- Poisoning through pollution or agri-chemical runoff;
- Invasive species, often carried by humans into areas where they overwhelm native populations;
- Human-caused climate change.[9]

All the causes are tied to the rapid growth of population, expected to reach 9.5 billion by 2050. "Ultimately, it all comes back to how many people there are on Earth, and how much of the resources each of those people uses," says Anthony Barnosky, a professor of integrative biology at the University of California, Berkeley, who was lead author on the "state shift" study published in *Nature*.

The World Wildlife Fund (WWF), an international conservation group, has taken a leading role in tracking the state of biodiversity through its annual "Living Planet" report. The group's 2012 edition found that biodiversity has declined globally by around 30 percent between 1970 (the year the WWF began keeping track) and 2008.[10] The loss has been worst in the tropics, the richest storehouse of life on the planet, where it has fallen 60 percent.[11] (*For more details, see "Current Situation," p. 421.*)

Perhaps most alarmingly, the WWF estimates, every year humans use one-and-a-half years' worth of natural resources — in other words, 50 percent more resources than the Earth can replenish in a year. "In essence, the Earth has built up a bank account of natural resources, and what we're doing is eating into our principal," says Colby Loucks, WWF senior director for conservation science. By 2030, the fund projects, humans will need the equivalent of two planets worth of resources to meet their annual demands.

Norwegian government and several private organizations, reflects awareness of the precariousness of the genetic underpinnings of the world's food supply.

Selective breeding to boost crop productivity and other desirable features, such as early maturity, has led to a dramatic loss in plant diversity, about 75 percent, by most estimates.

Moreover, the genetic uniformity of major crops leaves them more vulnerable to diseases and environmental shifts like climate change. By including many different strains of various plants, the seed banks are meant to provide genetic ammunition to protect against such problems, or even to restore a species should it be wiped out by a calamity.

However, some experts say, the seed banks represent only a tiny portion of the genetic richness that once existed in the wild. Even more problematic, the seeds in storage represent nature frozen at a particular point in time, unable to evolve to meet changing conditions.

"Conservation is about keeping diversity in a dynamic state. . . . The Svalbard gene bank, and many others, focus only on collecting and preserving. . . . You can capture only so much, and in 100 years it will be useless because the planet will have changed," said Melaku Worede, an Ethiopian agronomist who has been in the forefront of efforts to keep different strains of important crops and their wild relatives alive in nature.[3]

Pat Mooney — executive director of ETC, an international organization based in Ottawa, Canada, that tracks the impact of biodiversity loss in the developing world — also questions the ability of the seed banks to respond to a major crisis, such as a new disease sweeping through one of the major food grains. "They have preserved quite a bit of diversity," Mooney says, "but their ability to crank up and produce enough seed is very low. They really can't do that quickly. The quality of the storage is also very variable. A lot of the collections are kind of poorly maintained, even in some of the major centers."

Mooney and Worede are among the experts who say it's important that the seed banks, while necessary as an emergency safeguard, not be seen as a sufficient substitute for maintaining genetic diversity on working farms around the world. "Farmers have been the custodians of biodiversity, and they need support," said Worede. "We lose everything if we lose diversity in the field."[4]

— *Reed Karaim*

[1]Charles Siebert, "Food Ark," *National Geographic*, July, 2011, http://ngm.nationalgeographic.com/2011/07/food-ark/siebert-text.

[2]Scott Stump, "'Doomsday Vault' holds seeds that could save the world," Today.com, March 2, 2012, http://today.msnbc.msn.com/id/46602078/ns/today.today_news/t/doomsday-vault-holds-seeds-could-save-world/#.UGx6rI4rzww.

[3]Melaku Worede, interview with *GRAIN*, April 22, 2009, www.grain.org/article/entries/709-melaku-worede-interview-in-english.

[4]*Ibid.*

Efforts are under way to reverse those trends. The Convention on Biodiversity, adopted by the United Nations in 1992 and eventually signed by 193 nations, commits participating countries to conserve biodiversity and promote sustainable development.[12] In 2002, the convention set a goal of achieving by 2010 "a significant reduction of the current rate of biodiversity loss at the global, regional and national level . . . to the benefit of all life" on Earth.[13]

But the convention's latest summary report bluntly concluded that this goal "has not been met."[14] In fact, none of the 110 nations that submitted individual reports had completely met their deadline, the report said. The study also found that nearly one-quarter of the planet's land surface has been degraded and lost biological productivity since 1980. Of 292 large river systems, two-thirds have become moderately or highly fragmented by dams and reservoirs, making it difficult for many species to survive. And more than 19,300 square miles of forests — crucial biodiverse habitats — are cleared every year by loggers, farmers, ranchers and developers. One bright spot: The species-rich Amazon rainforest is more protected now than in the past.

The news is grim for many wild animal populations. Various wild vertebrate species dwindled by an average of 31 percent between 1970 and 2006.[15] And many of those are teetering close to extinction. Even some domesticated creatures are at risk. One-fifth of all livestock breeds, such as cattle and sheep, could face extinction due to over-reliance on fewer and fewer breeds, leading to less genetic diversity and leaving them vulnerable to disease.[16]

"Our mathematical models and our observations and our experiments show that we're not necessarily doomed," said Paul Leadley, director of the Laboratoire d'Ecologie at the University of Paris at Orsay and one of the study's authors. "But they do show that if we don't do something now, we will be in big trouble."[17]

As conservationists and scientists assess the impact of biodiversity loss, here are some key questions being debated:

Is Earth at a global biodiversity-loss tipping point?

As they examine the degree to which human activity has changed the planet, some researchers believe the Earth could be nearing a "state shift," or a "tipping" point, in which the planet will see a dramatic change in its biodiversity. In an article in *Nature*, the researchers predicted it would likely include mass extinctions, drastic changes in species abundance, distribution and diversity and even new evolutionary trajectories for some forms of life.[18]

"Things will be different in a very noticeable way," says Barnosky, of UC-Berkley. "The last time one of these global state shifts happened — about 11,000 years ago, when the Earth moved from an ice age to the interglacial period (that we're still in) — we lost about 50 percent of the big-body animals and saw dramatic changes in what species lived where. That's the sort of changes we're talking about."

The last global state shift took about 1,600 years, but Barnosky says things could happen much more quickly this time because of the impact of the two principal drivers of change — climate change and an expanding human population. "What's happening now is much more intense than what happened then," he says.

It may seem hard to believe man's impact on the planet could be more significant than the retreat of the ice age, but at that time 30 percent of Earth's surface went from being covered by glaciers to being ice-free. Humans already have converted 43 percent of the globe's land for agricultural or urban use, with much of the remaining land cross-hatched with roads.[19]

The scientific consensus is that human activities also have increased the concentration of carbon dioxide and other gases that cause global warming. Higher CO_2 levels have increased ocean acidity, while polluted runoff from cities and chemically fertilized fields has damaged rivers and coastal areas.[20]

The cumulative impact of these changes is growing as the human population swells. By 2050, when the population is expected to reach 9.5 billion, "we'll have changed well over 50 percent of the planet's land surface," says Barnosky. "At that point, I'd say we would very likely see dramatic changes in the remaining places that aren't affected directly."

But some experts doubt a shift is at hand. "The concept of a tipping point drives me crazy," says Patrick Moore, a former Greenpeace member and co-founder who is now a frequent critic of current conservation claims.[21] "In a sense, every microsecond is a tipping point because everything is always changing.

"Change is the only constant. Stasis would mean the end of time," continues Moore, who now operates Greenspirit, a consulting firm in Vancouver, Canada, that advises and represents corporations on sustainable environmental policies. "It is inevitable there will be change, and the judgment as to whether or not that change is negative or positive is a value judgment."

Moore believes life on Earth is now more profuse than during most of the planet's history, part of an explosion of biodiversity that began many millions of years ago. He acknowledges that humans have been responsible for the extinction of many species but believes that trend, too, is overstated. "It's only been since 1930 that we cared whether a species went extinct or not, and since then I believe we have done a fairly good job," Moore says. "It's very likely that the rate of extinction has slowed."

However, Mikael Fortelius, a professor of evolutionary paleontology at the Institute of Biotechnology, University of Helsinki, Finland, and co-author of the *Nature* study, says the current rate of extinctions is cause for alarm. "If species were going extinct at the rate they've always done, we wouldn't have to worry, but they're going extinct at a thousand times that, so, yeah, we should be worried," he says. "It's not a difference in kind, but it's a huge difference in degree."

Fortelius' ongoing research supports the idea that state shifts can happen quickly. While cautioning that his results are preliminary, Fortelius says fossil records show that in the past, ecosystems, or "ecological packages," have remained stable for long periods — sometimes millions of years — before changing. "Then that state shift happens very quickly, comparatively, and the old system completely disappears and is replaced."

Looking at planetary changes occurring today, he agrees "we are getting into the range in several different areas where we are close to that 50 to 60 percent mark that is often associated with state shifts."

Many cases already exist of local ecosystems tipping into new states. J. Emmett Duffy, a professor at the Virginia Institute of Marine Science at the College of William and Mary, in Williamsburg, Va., points to the collapse of the cod fishery off the coast of Eastern Canada in the 1980s. "A moratorium was imposed. It was too late. The fish just wouldn't come back, and it wasn't clear why," he says.

Researchers finally realized cod had been predators of smaller fish that fed, among other things, on cod eggs. With the cod population decimated the number of these small fish boomed and by devouring the eggs of their former predators, they kept the cod population depleted. "The system had flipped past the tipping point," he says. "You ended up with a stable system that prevented cod from coming back."

One-Third of Species Are Threatened

Thirty-six percent of 47,677 plant and animal species being tracked by scientists were endangered, critically endangered or vulnerable to becoming endangered as of 2009,* according to the International Union for Conservation of Nature (IUCN), which reports on the status each year of select species of, among others, mammals, birds, amphibians, corals and conifers. Two percent of those species already had become extinct in 2009.

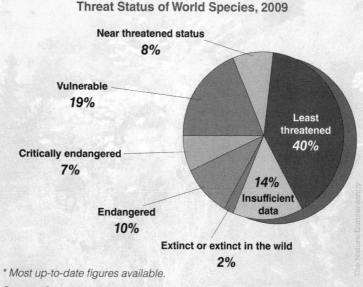

Threat Status of World Species, 2009

Near threatened status **8%**

Vulnerable **19%**

Critically endangered **7%**

Endangered **10%**

Least threatened **40%**

14% Insufficient data

Extinct or extinct in the wild **2%**

Most up-to-date figures available.

Source: Global Biodiversity Outlook 3, Convention on Biological Diversity, 2010, p. 27, www.cbd.int/doc/publications/gbo/gbo3-final-en.pdf. Information is drawn from the IUCN's

At that point, Duffy says, it takes another significant shift to move the system. In the North Atlantic, the cod appear to be returning after decades. Evidence indicates the small fish that had been devouring cod eggs eventually grew too numerous and cleaned out their own food supply, so their populations collapsed.[22]

But even some scientists who are worried about the degree of biodiversity loss doubt that the planet is on the verge of a global state shift. Charles Perrings, a professor of environmental economics at Arizona State University, Tempe, isn't sure there is a threshold at which biodiversity change takes place on a planetary scale. He believes shifts are likely to be confined to specific ecosystems.

"Are we at a global tipping point? I don't see that. I think, case by case, you can see these shifts, and in some instances, there may be a change of regime, or the system might just lose functionality," he says. "But I don't see the evidence for that globally."

Does monoculture agriculture threaten biodiversity?

Modern agriculture relies heavily on "monocrops" — or monoculture — in which large swaths of land are covered with one crop. It was a major component of the "Green Revolution" of the 1950s and '60s, which introduced higher-yielding crop varieties and modern farming methods to the developing world.

The worldwide spread of monoculture has been hailed for saving hundreds of millions of people from famine and with feeding a global human population that has more than doubled in less than 50 years.

AFP/Getty Images/Sonny Tumbelaka

Indonesian fishermen load tuna in Denpasar, Bali, on July 9, 2012. Many marine species and ecosystems, especially the bluefin tuna and coral reefs — have been decimated at an alarming rate in recent years by overfishing, coastal development, pollution and climate change.

The recent biotech revolution, which uses genetic engineering to create new plant varieties with very specific traits — such as tolerance of certain herbicides — also has pushed farmers toward monoculture. Genetically modified (GM) breeds are designed to be raised on fields planted in a single crop. The use of GM crops has exploded since they were introduced in the mid-1990s. Between 1996 and 2000, the number of acres planted worldwide in biotech crops jumped from 4.2 million acres to 109.2 million acres.[23]

Yet, the expansion of monoculture has significantly reduced the genetic variety of food plants around the world, according to the U.N. Food and Agriculture Organization (FAO), which estimates that 75 percent of crop diversity was lost between 1900 and 2000.[24]

A handful of breeds also now dominate among domesticated livestock, although the loss of livestock diversity has gotten less attention than dwindling plant diversity. Livestock loss has been "probably about 80 to 90 percent," says Pat Mooney, executive director of ETC, an international organization in Ottawa, Canada, that examines the impact of new technologies on traditional societies. "The loss there has been massive."

The genetic uniformity of crops and animals makes them susceptible to new diseases and pests, which can spread quickly through a monoculture field or herd without encountering much natural resistance. "In terms of biodiversity, there's not that much difference between paving something over for a city and clearing or replacing it with a monoculture of corn and soy. Those are equivalent, and to some extent if you add in all the pesticides that are going to go on that [crop], it may be even worse," says Kierán Suckling, executive director of the Center for Biological Diversity in Tucson, Ariz.

But Clive James, an agricultural scientist who worked with Norman Borlaug* at CIMMYT, a Mexican agricultural research center, believes bioengineered crops can take the Green Revolution one step further while helping to preserve biodiversity. Only genetic manipulation will enable the development of crops that can thrive on less water and nutrients and resist specific pests while yielding enough to feed the world's growing population, he says.

"We have 1.5 billion hectares [3.7 billion acres] of land in crops today, and if you want to protect the Amazon or other endangered habitats or areas that are biodiversity sanctuaries, the key is to increase productivity per hectare," James says. "What you have in biotechnology is a land-saving technology, allowing you to increase the production of food and fiber on existing land."

Twenty years ago, James founded the International Service for the Acquisition of Agri-biotech Applications (ISAAA), to share the benefits of crop biotechnology with farmers in developing countries. In the 15 years since bioengineered crops began to be used widely, farmers have boosted production by 276 million tons, he says. "Without those 276 million tons, you would have had to put another 91 million hectares [225 million acres] into production," he contends.

---

*Borlaug was a Nobel-Prize winning plant scientist hailed as the father of the Green Revolution.

CHRONOLOGY

1900-1940s *Concern about extinctions leads to first major efforts to protect endangered species.*

1901 President Theodore Roosevelt greatly expands wilderness preservation in the United States, eventually protecting 230 million acres.

1914 "Martha," the last passenger pigeon on Earth, dies at Cincinnati Zoo.

1934 Geneva Convention for the Regulation of Whaling is one of first international treaties to protect a species.

1936 The last Tasmanian tiger and the world's largest carnivorous marsupial go extinct.

1948 The world's first global environmental group, the International Union for the Protection of Nature (later the International Union for Conservation of Nature) is founded.

1960s-1980s *Modern environmental movement is born; biodiversity loss becomes global concern.*

1962 Government biologist Rachel Carson's best-selling book *Silent Spring* ties pesticides to declines of several wild species, helping to spur the environmental movement.

1970 World Wildlife Fund (WWF) launches Living Planet Index to track biodiversity.

1973 President Richard M. Nixon signs landmark Endangered Species Act to protect both species and their ecosystems. . . . Convention on International Trade in Endangered Species of Wild Fauna and Flora is first negotiated by a group of concerned nations and later signed by 176 countries.

1980 American biologist Thomas E. Lovejoy III coins the term "biological diversity."

1988 British ecologist Norman Myers, identifies 10 endangered global "hot spots" with exceptional biodiversity; list is later expanded to 34.

1990s *International community organizes to protect endangered species.*

1992 Convention on Biodiversity, intended to protect biodiversity and promote sustainable development, is signed by 150 nations at Earth Summit in Rio de Janiero, Brazil. President Bill Clinton signs it in 1993, but Senate fails to ratify it.

1995 International Coral Reef Initiative is launched to protect endangered reefs through collaborative, multinational efforts.

1997 More than 150 nations agree on Kyoto Protocol to reduce emissions causing global warming, considered a key cause of biodiversity loss; United States refuses to ratify it.

1998 U.N. declares 1998 the "Year of the Ocean" to promote awareness of threats to marine habitats.

2000-Present *Researchers forecast accelerating extinction rates as world population continues to rise.*

2002 Members of Convention on Biodiversity set targets for reducing biodiversity loss by 2010; heads of state later endorse the goals at World Summit on Sustainable Development.

2005 U.N.'s "Millennium Ecosystem Assessment" finds human activity has seriously degraded the services provided by 24 vital ecosystems.

2008 Norway becomes first country to support a Brazilian fund to preserve the rainforests, offering $1 billion for conservation efforts.

2010 Convention on Biodiversity acknowledges that the world has fallen short of 2010 targets for reducing biodiversity loss.

2012 Brazilian government says about 150 million acres of Amazon rainforest have been conserved, although deforestation continues, but at a slower pace. . . . WWF's "Living Planet Report" says biodiversity declined 30 percent from 1970 to 2008, mainly in bio-rich tropical regions. . . . Study in *Nature* says Earth may be reaching a "state shift," or tipping point, in which biodiversity loss significantly changes global ecosystems.

Mystery of the Disappearing Bees

New studies point to widely used pesticide for worldwide decline.

In the mid-2000s, beekeepers and others noticed that honeybee colonies — whose role as pollinators makes them critical to plant life and, thus, the entire food chain — were disappearing throughout the developed world at an alarming rate.

Since bees exist both in commercial hives and the wild, an exact tally of the losses are impossible, but millions of colonies and billions of bees have died. Everything from African viruses to global warming were suggested as possible causes for the disappearance. But now researchers believe they may have the solved the mystery. Three new studies, including two published in the respected journal *Science* earlier this year, blame a class of widely used pesticides known as "neonicotinoids."[1]

At least 142 million acres of corn, wheat and cotton-seeds in North America were treated in 2010 with the chemicals, which also are common in home gardening products.[2] Neonicotinoids, also known as "neonics," were developed in the 1980s and became common in the following decade. Bayer, the German chemical manufacturer, sold the first commercial version of neonics and still dominates the business.

A beekeeper tends a hive in southwestern France on June 1, 2012. Three new studies indicate that in the past decade widely used pesticides known as neonicotinoids may have caused the deaths of millions of colonies of bees — whose role as pollinators makes them critical to the entire food chain.

Trace elements of the insecticide are absorbed by plants and are present in the nectar on which bees feed and the pollen they gather. Studies confirm that the neonicotinoids — long

Some conservationists, however, such as Vandana Shiva, an international environmental activist who founded Navdanya, an Indian organization that promotes biodiversity conservation and organic farming, believe the benefits of bioengineering and monoculture have been vastly overstated. "Our work in Navdanya shows that biodiverse organic farming produces more food and nutrition per acre than chemical monocultures," she says. "Intensifying biodiversity is the solution to hunger."

Supporters of biotech crops include billionaire philanthropist Bill Gates, whose Bill and Melinda Gates Foundation has invested significantly in the development of genetically modified rice and cassava (a food staple for 250 million Africans) that provide enhanced nutrients. The foundation also has supported research into drought-resistant GM varieties of corn.

While acknowledging that widespread concerns persist about genetically modified crops, Gates believes the necessity of finding new ways to help developing nations feed themselves means seeking innovative approaches to boosting production. Speaking at the 2010 World Economic Forum in Davos, Switzerland, Gates said for some valuable crop characteristics, such as drought resistance, the GM approach "can probably do better than any other approach." He sees genetic engineering as "a tool, particularly for disease resistance" that could be "a real help" to developing world farmers.[25]

But Mooney notes that most bioengineered crops have been designed primarily to allow more chemical use. Prominent examples are Monsanto's Roundup Ready crops, which allow heavier applications of the company's Roundup herbicide.

suspected as a cause of the bee disappearance — can be deadly to bees in two ways. Research by scientists primarily affiliated with the University of Stirling in Scotland found that bee colonies that encountered the neonicotinoids had significantly reduced growth rates and an 85 percent reduction in the production of bee queens, critical for future survival.

"Given the scale of use of neonicotinoids, we suggest that they may be having a considerable negative effect on wild bumble bee populations across the developed world," the authors wrote.[3]

Another study by French researchers indicates that even nonlethal doses of the pesticide can impair bees' homing instincts that allow them to find their way back to their colonies. The scientists used tiny, radio transmitting chips to track bees exposed to neonicotinoids and found the damage was sufficient to lead to the collapse of colonies.[4] The study also provides an answer to another mystery that had puzzled researchers: Why they didn't find more dead bees when bee colonies died out.

A third study by Italian scientists found that dust containing the pesticide released during planting can also be lethal to bees.[5]

The three studies are likely to add to pressure on the U.S. Environmental Protection Agency to ban neonicotinoids. Several European nations have already instituted partial bans on the pesticides.[6]

Bee researchers and environmental activists say they still believe other environmental causes may also be playing a role in the disappearance of bees.[7] But the three studies indicate at least a large share of the mystery seems to have been solved.

— *Reed Karaim*

[1]Richard Schiffman, "Mystery of the disappearing bees: Solved!" Reuters, April 9, 2012, http://blogs.reuters.com/great-debate/2012/04/09/mystery-of-the-disappearing-bees-solved/.

[2]Tom Philpott, "3 New Studies Link Bee Decline to Bayer Pesticide," *Mother Jones*, March 29, 2012, www.motherjones.com/tom-philpott/2012/03/bayer-pesticide-bees-studies.

[3]Penelope P. Whithorn, *et al.*, "Neonicotinoid Pesticide Reduces Bumble Bee Colony Growth and Queen Production," *Science*, April 20, 2012, www.sciencemag.org/content/336/6079/351.abstract #aff-1.

[4]Mickaël Henry, *et al.*, "A Common Pesticide Decreases Foraging Success and Survival in Honey Bees," *Science*, April 20, 2012, www.sciencemag.org/content/336/6079/348.abstract.

[5]Andrea Tapparo, "Assessment of the environmental exposure of honeybees to particulate matter containing neonicotinoid insecticides coming from corn coated seeds," *Environmental Science and Technology*, March 6, 2012, www.ncbi.nlm.nih.gov/pubmed/22292570.

[6]"Colony Collapse Disorder: European Bans on Neonicotinoid Pesticides," Environmental Protection Agency, May 9, 2012, www.epa.gov/opp00001/about/intheworks/ccd-european-ban.html.

[7]Philpott, *op. cit.*

"Seventy-seven percent of the land area is in herbicide tolerant crops," he says. "It doesn't improve the yield. It's simply there to encourage the priority use of the herbicides the company sells." He notes that the increased use of herbicides and other pesticides can be devastating on other plants and creatures. "There's an indirect loss, which is quite substantial," Mooney says. "We've had a huge loss in pollinators — bees, which are absolutely essential. Two-thirds of our crops depend on wild pollinators." (*See sidebar, p. 416.*)

The wilder relatives of cultivated crops, known as "land races," which often grow along the edges of fields, also can be damaged by the chemicals used to protect monocrop agriculture. These land races mix genetically with their cultivated relatives, helping to provide natural, hardier hybrids, Shiva points out.

Genetically modified crops also reportedly have cross-pollinated with wild, non-GM species, breeding herbicide-resistant weeds. This creates a vicious cycle in which such "super weeds" require even more chemical use, increasing the damage to other "ecologically useful plant species," Shiva notes.

Nevertheless, even some scientists who are concerned about biodiversity loss in monocrop agriculture believe it's needed in order to balance environmental needs with those of a swelling human population.

"When you look at agriculture, you have two ways of growing: either extensively or intensively. Extensively means using more fields, more land. Intensively, you have more high-yielding plants, more fertilizer and so on," says Arizona State University's Perrings. "If you ask which is the biggest threat to biodiversity, it is the extensive growth of agriculture. Intensification is a much better solution to dealing with the challenge."

Does biodiversity loss threaten human civilization?

The extinctions of wild animals and plants sometimes are dismissed as having little practical impact on the well-being of the human race. Yet civilization is built on exploiting the planet's biological richness.

People rely on biological diversity for — among other things — food, medicines, shelter and clothing. More than 70,000 plant species are used in modern and traditional medicines alone, according to the International Union for the Conservation of Nature (IUCN), the world's oldest environmental organization.[26] Healthy, biodiverse ecosystems also provide goods and services, ranging from filtering fresh water to removing carbon dioxide from the air. The IUCN puts the value of those services, which humanity currently receives for free, at $16 trillion to $64 trillion.[27]

The possibility that the planet could be reaching an environmental tipping point because of the accelerated rate of extinctions raises the question of whether biodiversity loss threatens the human race. While scientists are not suggesting that humans themselves face extinction, some worry that biodiversity loss could have severe consequences for humankind. "Do I think there's a high likelihood of world catastrophe? I think it's a real possibility. No one knows the future, but if we don't change the way we're doing things today and just go blindly forward, we're setting ourselves up for disaster," says UC-Berkeley's Barnosky.

The point is approaching, he says, at which biodiversity loss could result in a fairly rapid reduction in the natural resources available. Agricultural production also could be significantly affected as growing patterns are changed by a shifting of global ecosystems. All of this would be occurring as human population growth puts added pressure on the planet's productive capacity.

"There will be more people, less clean water, less of all kinds of things," Barnosky says. "It's going to be harder to feed people. Where our agricultural lands are now — they're not going to be there, which leads to economic and political instability."

To avoid major disruptions, governments must address biodiversity loss in the next couple of decades, he says. "Here's the reality: By 2050, we've got 9 billion people we have to feed and provide for. We have to start now, because when we get to 2040, it's too late."

But some skeptics say the threat is seriously overstated. "It's part of the 'end is nigh' rhetoric, which has been with us since the beginning of humans," says Moore, of Greenspirit. "If they think the sky is falling, fine. I don't think it is. Certainly, there are places where species are endangered and some areas where we're seeing a loss of diversity, but I totally reject the idea that we're in a sixth mass extinction."

Moore believes the argument that extinction rates are 100 or 1,000 times the normal background rate is based on faulty science and mostly questionable estimates of how many species exist overall. He also thinks scientists who see the possibility of a catastrophe ahead are underestimating the ability of plants and animals to adapt to an environment altered by humans and of humans to extract the resources they need without seriously impacting biodiversity.

Environmentally responsible logging, for example, he says "is not responsible for much [biodiversity loss] at all." Biodiversity can flourish even where landscapes have been severely depleted through human interaction, he says. "With reclamation, it is often possible to return the land to a higher state of ecosystem biodiversity than was present initially, by contouring the land differently," he says. "We are actually capable of increasing biodiversity."

Other scientists believe losing biodiversity isn't critical if key species are preserved. "Just counting the number of species you've got is very misleading," says J. Philip Grime, a plant ecologist at the University of Sheffield in England. "The big questions are what kind of organisms are they, what do they do in the landscape and how are they going to respond to what we're doing to the planet. That's why [focusing on] biodiversity is not very helpful."

But Bradley J. Cardinale, principal author of the *Nature* paper assessing the cost of biodiversity loss, says it's critical to maintain complex ecosystems. "Losing biodiversity is going to reduce how productive and how sustainable most ecological processes are," he says, "and almost everything we care about, everything a biosystem gives to humanity, depends on those processes. It's the variety of life in nature that provides us with all the goods and services we count on."

Cardinale, a professor at the School of Natural Resources and Environment at the University of Michigan, Ann Arbor, says researchers continue to discover new connections that indicate how extinction or even a shrinking population of one species can have unexpected ramifications. One study, he says, found that the incidence of Lyme disease in humans is tied to the number of different species of mammals in forests. With more species, the ticks that carry the disease are spread thinner and the disease is diluted. "We have almost no idea how the well-being of our own species might be linked to the great variety of life that is the most striking feature of life on our planet," Cardinale says.

Without a better understanding of what's at stake, Cardinale believes, humans could be courting disaster. "We're maybe two centuries away from the situation being equivalent to a mass extinction where 75 percent of everything is gone. Can we survive that? That's the question everyone in the discipline is trying to answer," he says. "I don't think we have to act like it's doomsday. But I do think global loss of biodiversity ranks among the most important and dramatic problems in modern history."

BACKGROUND

Extinction Epochs

To the nonscientist, life can still seem so bountiful on Earth it's hard to imagine most of it disappearing. But five great extinction events have occurred during the planet's 4.5 billion-year history.[28] In each case, 75 percent or more of all species disappeared.[29]

Perhaps most well-known — and most recent — was the great extinction that occurred 65 million years ago, when many researchers believe the impact from a large asteroid kicked enough particulate matter into the air to change the climate and wipe out nearly all of the dinosaurs. Today's birds are generally thought to be the descendants of dinosaurs that managed to survive.[30]

But the most dramatic extinction, known as the Great Dying, occurred about 250 million years ago and resulted in the elimination of up to 96 percent of all species, including plants, insects and larger creatures. All of life on the planet today descended from the 4 percent of species that survived.[31]

Scientists aren't sure exactly what caused the Great Dying, but massive volcanic eruptions in Siberia, setting coalfields aflame and filling the air with both volcanic

Threats to Biodiversity

Construction of the world's third-largest hydroelectric project — the Belo Monte dam near Altamira, Brazil — will destroy up to 230 square miles of Amazon rainforest (top). Although nearly three-quarters of the 270,000 square miles of biodiverse forest habitats protected worldwide since 2003 have been in Brazil's biologically rich Amazon, deforestation continues in the region. The illegal trade in threatened species — such as these endangered sea turtles (bottom) that have been stuffed to sell to wildlife traffickers — is another threat to the planet's biodiversity. A worker from the Philippine Protected Areas and Wildlife Bureau in Manila displays one of the hundreds of turtles seized from Vietnamese fishermen last April off the southeast coast of the Philippines.

and coal ash, are thought to be a possible cause.[32] One or more asteroid strikes also may have played a role.

The other great extinctions occurred 440 million, 359 million and 200 million years ago. Causes vary, but a

Yemeni and foreign tourists admire a dragon blood tree, unique to the virtually untouched Yemeni island of Socotra, a site of global importance to biodiversity conservation. Located in the northwestern Indian Ocean, Socotra is sometimes referred to as "the Galapagos of the Indian Ocean" because of its unique and spectacular vegetation. The island's flora are among the world 10 most endangered island flora systems.

unifying element seems to be climate change caused by dust and dirt being hurled into the atmosphere after an asteroid collision, volcanic eruption or some other event.[33] "The evidence would support that each of the big five occurred at the same time that major shifts in the overall 'normal' for global climate occurred, and also to a large extent changes in ocean chemistry," says U.C. Berkeley's Barnosky. "This may be highly relevant to interpreting the present state of events, given that we are witnessing unusually fast changes in climate and ocean chemistry [acidification], this time of course caused by humans."

In more recent times, geologically speaking, large numbers of species disappeared during certain periods. About 73,000 years ago, some scientists believe the eruption of a mammoth volcano in Indonesia may have thrown so much ash into the air that it reduced the human population around the world to as few as 10,000 people.[34]

The advance and retreat of glaciers around the world during the last 100,000 years also caused periods of significant extinctions.[35] The current epoch — known as the Holocene — began about 11,700 years ago with the retreat of ice-age glaciers. The Holocene has been marked by the spread of what the University of Helsinki's Fortelius calls "the ultimate invasive species" — human beings.

Humans and Extinction

Giant mammals once roamed the Earth. The giant sloth, the woolly mammoth, the short-faced bear (which stood 13 feet tall on its hind legs and weighed nearly a ton), the giant condor and, in Australia, a giant kangaroo were just some examples of these "megafauna," as scientists call them.

These massive creatures had all disappeared by about 8000 B.C., probably due to human hunting, according to some scientists. Most megafauna in Australia disappeared relatively soon after the arrival of humans. "It was because these large, slow moving mammals had never had to run away from people with spears before," says Moore, of Greenspirit.

Humans also began selecting and breeding strains of plants for agriculture in pre-historic times. The earliest varieties of wheat were cultivated in the Middle East as long as 11,000 years ago.[36] Corn has similarly ancient origins. "We would never have maize (corn) today if farmers in Mexico hadn't selected from grasses, selected the best grain over a long period of time, thousands of years ago," says James, of the International Service for the Acquisition of Agri-biotech Applications.

By hunting some mammals to extinction and domesticating certain plants and animals, humans were altering the ecosystems in which they lived and impacting biodiversity long before recorded human civilization. "Part of the change we've witnessed in the last 10,000 years is directed change," notes Perrings, of Arizona State University. "It's the result of deliberate actions taken by people to promote certain species and get rid of others."

Humans continued to press species into — or to the edge of — extinction without much thought until relatively recently. The population of North American bison on the Great Plains was estimated at 60 million before being decimated by European-American hunters. By 1889 the population had fallen as low as 1,100, before conservation efforts began to rebuild numbers.[37]

Other creatures disappeared forever. "The dodo bird and the passenger pigeons were victims of overhunting for food; the Carolina parakeet, the only parrot that was native to North America, was eradicated by farmers because it ate their crops," wrote Moore in *Confessions of a Greenpeace Dropout: The Making of a Sensible Environmentalist.*[38]

Humans also have caused extinctions — either intentionally or accidentally — by introducing foreign species, particularly on islands or other contained ecosystems, that overwhelmed native creatures.[39] Finally, humans have pervasively changed their environment through the spread of agriculture. The grain fields that now cover thousands of square miles across the American Great Plains, for example, were once largely native grasslands, with a variety of species. Many animals that existed in this ecosystem were either forced to move to new territory or declined steeply in population.

In the last century, concern that commercial fishing was hunting whales to the brink of extinction led to one of the first international efforts to protect a species. The Geneva Convention for the Regulation of Whaling became effective in 1935, although it was ignored by some nations.[40] Other treaties and laws would follow as the conservation and environmental movements gained strength. The organized effort to protect some plants and animals marked a sea change in humanity's long relationship with its fellow inhabitants.

The 1973 U.S. Endangered Species Act, which extended federal protection to species identified as at risk, is considered a landmark step in the process.[41] The Center for Biological Diversity studied how many species have become extinct since the act became law. "We found that the vast majority of species that were listed (as endangered) in the act were saved from extinction," Suckling says. "The good news is we have a tool that works. Unfortunately, there are not that many Endangered Species Acts around the world."

Indeed, events around the world reveal very different situations regarding biodiversity loss and the range of government responses.

CURRENT SITUATION

Threats and Progress

Although the sheer profusion of life on Earth prevents researchers from developing an accurate estimate of how many species have gone extinct in recent years, reports by the World Wildlife Fund, the Convention on Biological Diversity and the International Union for the Conservation of Nature (IUCN) show a continuing and precipitous decline in many plant and animal species. The studies show that many of the species are headed for extinction if current trends are not reversed.

One of the most widely cited measures of plant and animal populations is the IUCN "Red List," which determines the likelihood a species may become extinct if current conditions persist. The list is based on information gathered by species scientists around the world. As of this year, 31 percent of the 63,837 species that had been evaluated were threatened with extinction.[42]

But while biodiversity loss continues, there have been advances on the political front. "Some 170 countries now have national biodiversity strategies and action plans. At the international level, financial resources have been mobilized and progress has been made in developing mechanisms for research, monitoring and scientific assessment of biodiversity," notes *Global Biodiversity Outlook 3*.[43]

Gains have been made in protecting some of the most critical and endangered habitats, including tropical forests and animal habitat. "Nations as a whole are now protecting 13 percent of their land surface in national parks, which is great news. The national parks aren't always in the places we'd like them to be, but nonetheless countries are coming together to protect more of the planet," says Pimm, of Duke University and the University of Pretoria.

Here is a look at important efforts in key parts of the globe:

Oceans — Oceans cover 70 percent of the planet's surface and hold some of the most critically endangered habitat and species.

Increased acidification and warmer water temperatures caused by climate change have made reef-forming corals among Earth's most endangered creatures. In less than 25 years, the number of ocean reefs with living coral on at least half of their surfaces has fallen from more than 60 percent to only 4 percent.[44]

"These are the rainforests of the sea. There's a huge diversity of species that live in coral reefs and nowhere else," says Duffy, of the Virginia Institute of Marine Science. Should the reefs die out, the *Global Biodiversity Outlook 3* concluded the repercussions on the ocean food chain could threaten the livelihoods and food security of hundreds of millions of people.[45]

Losing these ecosystems would also be tragic, Duffy adds, because "reefs are a major source of interesting chemical compounds that have led to new drugs and have been used in pharmaceuticals."

Is biodiversity loss reaching a critical stage?

YES

Colby Loucks
Senior Director, Conservation Science Program, World Wildlife Fund

Written for *CQ Global Researcher*, November 2012

Without a doubt, biodiversity loss is reaching a critical stage. The ever-growing human demand for natural resources continues to place tremendous pressures on Earth's biodiversity, threatening the very ecosystems and benefits that we rely on for security, health and well-being.

This trend is evident in the World Wildlife Fund's 2012 "Living Planet Report," a biennial assessment of the state of global biodiversity produced in collaboration with the Zoological Society of London and the Global Footprint Network. Overall, the report shows global biodiversity has declined nearly 30 percent since 1970, with tropical and freshwater species experiencing the most precipitous declines.

Meanwhile, humanity's ecological footprint — which compares our consumption against Earth's regenerative capacity — is rising. Currently, humans are consuming 50 percent more resources than the Earth can provide annually. We are living as if we have an extra planet at our disposal. In essence, we are overdrawing Earth's bank account — consuming the "principal" — which is clearly not sustainable.

By 2050, Earth must sustain a projected human population of 9-plus billion people while supporting healthy ecosystems and the invaluable free services they provide, such as purifying water, pollinating crops and absorbing the carbon dioxide emissions that contribute to global warming. While technology can replace some of nature's benefits — and buffer against their degradation — many are irreplaceable.

And therein lies the dilemma: How do we reduce the pressure on Earth's ability to regenerate itself while creating a prosperous future that provides food, water and energy for all?

The good news is we can reverse this decline in biodiversity and fragile ecosystems if we act now. The longer we wait, the more likely we'll reach a point of no return. Many ideas and actions can be taken now to head this off, including halting the loss of natural areas and preserving those that remain, increasing the efficiency of food supply chains and minimizing carbon emissions.

But that's just the start. We also must manage resources sustainably, scale up renewable energy production, consider environmental and social costs in national and corporate undertakings and foster equitable access to food, water and energy.

But first and foremost, humanity must recognize that we have a serious problem: We're running up a major ecological debt that is putting the health of our planet (and eventually us) in jeopardy. Let's deal with it now before the debt gets worse.

NO

Patrick Moore
Chairman and Chief Scientist, Greenspirit Enterprises, Vancouver, Canada; Author, Confessions of a Greenpeace Dropout: The Making of a Sensible Environmentalist

Written for *CQ Global Researcher*, November 2012

The idea that humans are driving a "sixth mass extinction" and that the planet's biodiversity is in peril is a myth. Biodiversity is higher in our era than it was 550 million years ago. This trend toward increased biodiversity has continued throughout the millennia despite five major extinction events — two of which severely reduced the number of species on Earth. During the Permian-Triassic extinction 250 million years ago, 90 percent of all species were exterminated, the nearest life ever came to being wiped off the planet. Then 65 million years ago the Cretaceous-Tertiary extinction caused the loss of dinosaurs and about 50 percent of all species. Both events likely were caused by large meteor impacts, which threw millions of tons of debris into the atmosphere and blocked the sun, reducing plant growth and causing mass starvation. After both events, however, biodiversity recovered and rose to a greater number of species than before.

Humans have caused species extinction ever since they migrated from Africa to new environments where indigenous species could not cope with human predation. When humans reached Australia 60,000 years ago, they hunted most of the large, slow-moving mammals — such as mammoths, mastodons and saber-toothed tigers — to extinction, as they did when they arrived in the New World about 15,000 years ago. When Micronesians discovered New Zealand around A.D. 1200 they hunted the giant flightless Moas to extinction. And most recently, when Europeans colonized Australia, New Zealand and the Pacific islands, many local species were exterminated by non-native species brought in by the settlers — such as rats, cats, foxes and snakes.

The scale of these human-caused extinctions is not remotely close to the mass extinctions caused by natural disasters. Until recently, human-caused extinction was considered a natural event. But serious efforts are now being made to prevent further extinctions, perhaps triggered by the human-induced extinction of the passenger pigeon in the 1920s. The imposition of large protected areas, control of non-indigenous species and establishment of captive breeding programs all have helped to reduce extinctions.

Species will always go extinct, and new species will continue to come into being. Chances are, in the long run, the historical trend toward ever increasing biodiversity will continue through the coming millennia.

Overfishing also threatens ocean fisheries, a critical source of the world's food. In Africa and South Asia alone, about 400 million people depend on fish for most of their animal protein.[46] The amount of fish taken out of the oceans has increased nearly five-fold since 1950.[47] Eighty percent of the fish populations assessed by researchers are either "exploited or fully exploited," according to *Biodiversity Outlook 3*.[48]

Some of the larger, slower-growing fish hunted by humans are the most vulnerable. "The poster child, in some ways, is the bluefin tuna. If this were a land vertebrate it would have been declared an endangered species long ago," says Duffy, "and yet it's [still] fished commercially."

The oceans remain largely wide open to exploitation. The nations attending the 2010 meeting of the Convention on Biodiversity in Nagoya, Japan, agreed to a plan that includes establishing marine protected areas covering 10 percent of the oceans by 2020. Currently, however, less than 1 percent of the oceans are in marine reserves.[49]

Amazon and Latin America — Species conservation efforts in recent years have been concentrated in Brazil's vast portion of the biologically rich Amazon rainforests. "The little-known secret is that the Amazon has gone from almost no protection to 57 percent protected, and while that's not enough it shows you can actually make a big difference," said Tom Lovejoy, head of the H. John Heinz III Center's biodiversity effort, based in Washington, D.C.[50]

In fact, of the 270,000 square miles worldwide that have been put in protected areas since 2003, nearly three-quarters have been in Brazil, largely through collaborative efforts between Brazil and a several other nations and international groups.[51] Norway, for example, is contributing $1 billion to a Brazilian fund to reduce deforestation.[52]

The conservationist group SavingSpecies, which Pimm chairs, has worked to connect and protect fragmented habitats in the coastal forests of northeastern Brazil, in an effort to save the endangered golden lion tamarin, a primate that went extinct in the wild before being reintroduced in its habitat, beginning in the mid-1980s.

Pimm says the project, which purchased 31 square miles of largely unproductive grazing land, illustrates how relatively small investments (in this case, about $300,000) can provide big returns. The group bought — and allowed

to return to their natural state — parcels of land that bridged the gaps between surviving areas of habitat, providing a much larger range for the animals to live in. "The simplest things you can do is buy small fragments of land and then reconnect them," Pimm says. "By reconnecting the land, we can have a disproportionate impact on biodiversity."

Despite these efforts, however, deforestation in the Amazon Basin continues, albeit more slowly, and has reached more than 17 percent of the original forest. Even if current conservation efforts are successful, it is expected to hit 20 percent by 2020.[53]

Other ecosystems in South and Central America also continue to suffer losses. Populations of tropical freshwater fish, both in Latin American and other equatorial regions, have declined by 74 percent since 1970, primarily due to habitat loss and fragmentation.[54] Amphibian species also are down in numbers worldwide but are at the greatest risk of extinction in Latin America and the Caribbean, according to *Global Biodiversity Outlook 3*.[55]

Asia and India — Tigers, Asian elephants, Indian rhinoceroses — some of the most well-known threatened species on the planet — live in Asia and India. Rapidly growing human populations have reduced the natural habitat for many large mammals, while illegal hunting remains a problem across much of the region.[56]

Tigers, for example, have lost 93 percent of their natural range. Their population has fallen to between 3,200 and 3,500 in the wild.[57] Despite conservation efforts, poachers continue to kill tigers for their bones, which are made into "tiger bone wine" used in traditional Chinese medicine. Rhinoceroses are killed for their horns, believed to have medicinal value.

"The increasing wealth of China and Vietnam is driving demand for more tiger bone," says WWF's Loucks. "Rhino horn, per kilo, is more expensive than gold and cocaine, so it's attracting organized crime into the field (in both Asia and Africa). The situation is pretty bad."

Krithi Karanth, a conservation biologist with the Centre for Wildlife Studies in Bangalore, India, has studied wild animal populations and their interactions with rural Indians. She says the fragmentation of habitat is causing difficulties for a variety of large mammals in the region. Although India has set aside about 5 percent of its land as nature parks, many are too small and isolated from other habitat, Karanth has found.

Endangered tigers are protected at a Buddhist temple in Kanchanaburi province in Thailand, one of 13 countries hosting fragile tiger populations. The animals are highly prized by international wildlife smugglers. Wild tiger populations have been decimated in recent decades, in part because their bones are sought by practitioners of traditional Chinese medicine. The world tiger population is estimated to have fallen to only 3,200 from about 100,000 a century ago.

Still, she sees attitudes on the subcontinent evolving. "For the first time in history there's a large Indian middle class," Karanth says, and with that more affluent population, has come increasing attention to conservation. "There's a lot of public support in India for animals like tigers and elephants. At least in the southern part of the country, you've seen a recovery of the tiger population."

She believes Indian culture provides hope. "Despite having a billion people, we still have a lot of wildlife left, and part of this is because in India there is a large amount of what we call cultural tolerance," she says. "I've talked to thousands of villagers and asked them why, if they have an agricultural loss (because of wild animals) they haven't reported it, and the answers are, 'It's their land, too,' or 'It's part of the natural process.'"

Iraq provides a surprising bright spot for habitat recovery in Asia. Under the regime of Saddam Hussein, 90 percent of the country's Mesopotamian marshes were drained. Since 2003, however, much of the drainage has been dismantled and by 2006 nearly 60 percent of the marshes had been flooded again, enabling the natural vegetation to recover.[58]

Africa — A coalition of conservation groups and scientists conducting the first continent-wide survey of habitat for the great African apes recently found that in the past two decades habitat has shrunk by more than 50 percent for the Cross River and eastern gorillas and 31 percent for western gorillas. Chimpanzee habitat also is disappearing across Africa.[59] Deforestation and overhunting threatens the apes. The meat of gorillas and chimpanzees, called bush meat, is a primary source of protein for many rural Africans and is considered a delicacy in some African cities.

"The situation is very dramatic. Many of the ape populations we still find today will disappear in the near future," said Hjalmar Kuehl, a primatologist with the Max Planck Institute for Evolutionary Anthropology in Leipzig, Germany, who helped organize the research.[60]

As in Asia, the African human population is growing rapidly, leading to extensive clearing of land for urban growth, agriculture and industry. Forests are losing their trees and biodiversity in waves emanating from major cities, according to the World Wildlife Fund. In Tanzania, for example, logging has advanced 75 miles from the city of Dar es Salaam in just 14 years, depleting all high-value timber within 124 miles.

"This first wave of degradation was followed by a second that removed medium-value timber, and a third that consumed the remaining woody biomass for charcoal production," according to the "Living Planet Report 2012."[61] Without alternatives for construction materials and fuel, this stripping of the forests is likely to continue around Africa's major cities.

North America and Europe — With established wildlife reserves, conservation laws and active environmental movements, the industrialized countries have not faced the same degree of biodiversity loss in recent years as those in the less developed world.

The WWF's "Living Planet Report 2012" found that the populations of some birds and land and marine mammals have increased in the temperate climate zones, which include North America and Europe, and that there has been an overall increase of biodiversity since 1970 in those regions.

But the industrialized countries cannot pat themselves too firmly on the back, says the WWF's Loucks, because they did their damage in earlier decades. "Prior to 1970, they were much more impacted," he says. Also, he adds, "There's naturally much more biodiversity in the tropics, so there's more to lose."

Despite overall positive trends, areas of concern still exist in the North. Since 1980, farmland bird populations have declined in Europe by an average of 50 percent, according to the Convention on Biological Diversity.[62] Wildflowers, including marigolds, cornflowers and poppies, also are disappearing from much of the English countryside, according to conservationists, who believe the increased use of agricultural herbicides may be responsible.[63]

The United States witnessed a conservation success story with the recent recovery of most of the nation's off-shore fisheries, which had been badly depleted, through a federal program that set quotas for total catch based on scientific assessments.[64] Regional councils then apportion that quota among commercial fishermen.

Despite the program's success and its support by commercial fisherman, however, it is controversial with recreational fishermen, who feel the program benefits large commercial fishermen at the expense of sports fishing. The U.S. House of Representatives voted last May to deny federal funds to expand the program. The two Republican lawmakers behind the bill, Florida's Rep. Steve Southerland and Rep. Michael Grimm of New York, declared the system was part of federal efforts "to destroy every aspect of American freedom under the guise of conservation."[65]

The bill has not advanced in the Senate.

OUTLOOK

Coming Changes

If the world is indeed nearing a global biodiversity state shift, as some scientists believe, then the natural environment could start to look very different in as little as 20 years or so. No one can predict the shape of that new world, except that many of the plants and animals we know now would not be around.

But even some scientists who believe a so-called tipping point is approaching say it could still be a century or more away. Conservation biologists and other researchers point out, however, that current rates of biodiversity loss will still result in significant changes in life on the planet, whether or not the ecosystem reaches a tipping point.

If the declines in population of tropical freshwater fish and many important ocean species are not reversed, much of the world's population could face a shortfall in one of its important food sources. If agricultural plant and livestock biodiversity continues to be lost, the prospect for a devastating disease sweeping through crops,

such as the strain of wheat rust now hurting farmers in Asia and Africa, grows more likely.

"Unfortunately, I'm not very optimistic regarding the long-term future, unless we take drastic measures," says Loreau, of the Centre for Biodiversity Theory and Modelling in France. "We live in a civilization that is based on the idea that humans are very different from everything else and should really dominate nature, and it leads us to completely downplay natural processes and the importance of ecosystems. To address the problem we have to recognize that humans are part of nature. We have to change our relationship with nature and how much we consume."

Karanth, of the Centre for Wildlife Studies in Bangalore, fears a confluence of environmental changes. "On the global level, it looks pretty grim," she says, "with climate change being the big factor. With huge areas becoming warmer, it's going to be hard to save much of what's here."

But others focus on the progress that has already been made. "Here in the U.S., where we have strong laws, lots of money for recovery and a democratic system that allows citizens to hold the government's feet to the fire, we can and do save species. So it is possible for us to turn this around," says Suckling, of the Center for Biological Diversity in Tucson.

"It's going to require a lot of effort and a lot of money and, in many countries, political reform," he says. "But we've done it in a lot of places."

Barnosky, of UC-Berkeley and the primary author of the state shift study, believes the future depends on bringing down the rate of world population growth. "It's all too easy to turn this into a 'gloom-and-doom, we're screwed' story. For me, the key point is, if we want to make a future for our kids as good as the one we live in now, there are things we have to recognize are happening and take steps to manage. We've got a window of time here.

"We're poised right on the cusp," he continues. "If we do the right thing, it's all going to turn out okay. If we don't, all hell can break loose."

NOTES

1. "Basic Facts about Sea Otters," Defenders of Wildlife, www.defenders.org/sea-otter/basic-facts.
2. *Ibid.*

3. Megan Gannon, "Sea Otters May Be Global Warming Warriors," *Live Science*, Sept. 7, 2012, www.livescience.com/23030-sea-otters-may-be-global-warming-warriors.html.

4. The figure is calculated by converting 8.7 teragrams to tons. The figure is taken from the abstract of the study by Chris Wilmers, *et al.*, "Do tropic cascades affect the storage and flux of atmospheric carbon? An analysis of sea otters and kelp forests," Ecological Society of America, www.esajournals.org/doi/abs/10.1890/110176.

5. Anthony D. Barnosky, *et al.*, "Approaching a state shift in Earth's biosphere," *Nature*, June 7, 2012, p. 52.

6. Bradley J. Cardinale, *et al.*, "Biodiversity loss and its impact on humanity," *Nature*, June 7, 2012, p. 59.

7. "Biodiversity Is Life," United Nations Educational, Scientific and Cultural Organization, 2010, p. 3, www.cbd.int/iyb/doc/partners/iyb-unesco-uk-school-pack-en.pdf. Also see Richard Knight, "Biodiversity loss: How accurate are the numbers?" BBC News, April 24, 2012, www.bbc.co.uk/news/magazine-17826898.

8. *Ibid.*

9. *Global Biodiversity Outlook 3*, Secretariat of the Convention on Biological Diversity, 2012, p. 9, www.cbd.int/gbo3/.

10. "Living Planet Report 2012: Biodiversity, biocapacity and better choices," World Wildlife Fund, 2012, p. 12, www.panda.org/about_our_earth/all_publications/living_planet_report/.

11. *Ibid.*

12. "List of parties," Convention on Biological Diversity, www.cbd.int/convention/parties/list/.

13. *Global Biodiversity Outlook 3, op. cit.*, p. 9.

14. *Ibid.*

15. *Ibid.*, p. 24.

16. *Ibid.*, p. 53.

17. *Global Biodiversity Outlook 3* video presentation, Secretariat of the Convention on Biological Diversity, 2012, www.cbd.int/gbo3/.

18. Barnosky, *et al., op. cit.*, p. 55.

19. *Ibid.*, p. 54.

20. *Ibid.*

21. Patrick Moore was an early member and leader of Greenpeace for several years, but the organization disputes his characterization of his level of involvement.

22. A fuller explanation can be found in Emmett Duffy's "Resurrection of a collapsed ecosystem: Cod rebound in the North Atlantic," SeaMonster blog, Aug. 15, 2011, http://theseamonster.net/2011/08/resurrection-of-a-collapsed-ecosystem-cod-rebound-in-north-atlantic/.

23. For background, see Jason McLure, "Genetically Modified Food," *CQ Researcher*, Aug. 31, 2012, pp. 717-740.

24. "Crop biodiversity: use it or lose it," FAO Media Center, Food and Agriculture Organization, www.fao.org/news/story/en/item/46803/icode/.

25. "Bill Gates backs genetically modified food research," 2010 World Economic Forum, www.dailymotion.com/video/xggd8o_bill-gates-backs-genetically-modified-food-research_news.

26. "Why we need biodiversity," International Union for the Conservation of Nature, www.iucn.org/what/tpas/biodiversity/about/biodiversity/.

27. *Ibid.*

28. For a list of the five extinctions with time of occurrence see "Big Five mass extinction events," BBC Nature, 2012, www.bbc.co.uk/nature/extinction_events.

29. Bryan Walsh, "The Next Great Extinction Could Be Coming Sooner Than You Think," *Time*, March 3, 2011, http://science.time.com/2011/03/03/the-next-great-extinction-could-be-coming-sooner-than-you-think/.

30. Richard Stone, "Dinosaurs Living Descendants," *Smithsonian*, December 2010, www.smithsonianmag.com/science-nature/Dinosaurs-Living-Descendants.html.

31. "Big Five mass extinction events," *op. cit.*

32. Jennifer Walsh, "New Suspect in 'Great Dying:' Massive Prehistoric Coal Explosion," *Live Science*,

Dec. 20, 2011, www.livescience.com/17577-great-dying-coal-eruption.html.

33. "Big Five mass extinction events," *op. cit.*

34. "Mass extinctions" timeline, Discovery.com, http://dsc.discovery.com/earth/wide-angle/mass-extinctions-timeline.html.

35. "Helping Unravel Causes of Ice Age Extinctions," *ScienceDaily*, Nov. 2, 2011, www.sciencedaily.com/releases/2011/11/111102161253.htm.

36. Sue College and James Connelly, eds., "The Origins and Spread of Domestic Plants in Southwest Asia and Europe," Left Coast Press, June 2007, p. 40, http://books.google.com/books?id=D2nym35k_EcC&pg=PA40#v=onepage&q&f=false.

37. "Bison," An Educator's Guide to the Natural Resources of South Dakota," Northern State University, www3.northern.edu/natsource/MAMMALS/Bison1.htm.

38. Patrick Moore, *Confessions of a Greenpeace Dropout: The Making of a Sensible Environmentalist* (2010), Location 6895, Kindle edition.

39. *Ibid.*

40. Kieran Mulvaney, *The Whaling Season: An Inside Account of The Struggle to Stop Commercial Whaling* (2003), p. 115. For background, see Marc Leepson, "Whaling: End of an Era," *Editorial Research Reports*, 1985, vol. II; available at *CQ Researcher Plus Archive*.

41. For background see, Mary H. Cooper, "Endangered Species Act," *CQ Researcher*, June 3, 2005 (Updated Sept. 22, 2010), pp. 493-516.

42. "Table 1: Numbers of threatened species by major groups of organisms (1996-2012)," IUCN "Red List," www.iucnredlist.org/documents/summary statistics/2012_1_RL_Stats_Table_1.pdf.

43. *Global Biodiversity Outlook 3, op. cit.*, p. 9.

44. *Ibid.*, p. 47. Also see "Living Planet Report 2012," *op. cit.*, p. 93.

45. *Global Biodiversity Outlook 3, op. cit.*, p. 11.

46. Gaia Vince, "How the world's oceans could be running out of fish," BBC.com, Sept. 21, 2012, www.bbc.com/future/story/20120920-are-we-running-out-of-fish.

47. "Living Planet Report 2012," *op. cit.*, p.13.

48. *Global Biodiversity Outlook 3, op. cit.*, p. 48.

49. Gaia Vince, "How the world's oceans could be running out of fish," BBC News, Sept. 21, 2012, www.bbc.com/future/story/20120920-are-we-running-out-of-fish/1.

50. *Global Biodiversity Outlook 3*, video, *op. cit.* Also see Doug Struck, "Disappearing Forests," *CQ Global Researcher*, Jan. 18, 2011, pp. 27-52.

51. David Braun, "Brazil beefs up protection of Atlantic rain forest," *National Geographic*, June 14, 2010, http://newswatch.nationalgeographic.com/2010/06/14/brazil_adds_parks_in_atlantic_forest/.

52. "Norway donates $1 billion to Brazilian rainforest fund," Norway.org, www.norway.org/ARCHIVE/policy/environment/regnskogen_i_brasil_en/.

53. *Global Biodiversity Outlook 3, op. cit.*, p. 33.

54. *Ibid.*, video.

55. *Global Biodiversity Outlook 3, op. cit.*, p. 26.

56. For background, see Robert Kiener, "Wildlife Smuggling," *CQ Global Researcher*, Oct. 1, 2010, pp. 235-262.

57. "Living Planet Report 2012," *op. cit.*, p. 27.

58. *Global Biodiversity Outlook 3, op. cit.*, p. 42.

59. Matt Walker, "Great ape habitat in Africa has dramatically declined," BBC Nature, Sept. 28, 2012, www.bbc.co.uk/nature/19731343.

60. *Ibid.*

61. "Living Planet Report," *op. cit.*, p. 78.

62. *Global Biodiversity Outlook 3, op. cit.*, p. 24.

63. Emily Beament, "Arable plant species disappearing," *The Independent*, Aug. 1, 2012, www.independent.co.uk/environment/nature/arable-plant-species-disappearing-7998249.html.

64. "Plenty more fish in the sea," *The Economist*, May 26, 2012, www.economist.com/node/21555960.

65. "The Grand Old Party and the Sea," *The New York Times*, May 16, 2012, www.nytimes.com/2012/05/17/opinion/the-grand-old-party-and-the-sea.html.

BIBLIOGRAPHY

Selected Sources

Books

Moore, Patrick, *Confessions of a Greenpeace Dropout: The Making of a Sensible Environmentalist*, Beatty Street Publishing, 2010.
A founder of Greenpeace, who broke with the organization when he felt its positions became too extreme, contends there is no real evidence that biodiversity is threatened by mass extinctions today.

Shiva, Vandana, *Monocultures of the Mind: Perspectives on Biodiversity and Biotechnology*, Zed Books, 1993.
In a seminal work on biodiversity loss, a leading critic of monoculture agriculture and biotechnology examines their impacts on biodiversity and indigenous farmers in the developing world.

Wilson, Edward O., *The Diversity of Life*, W.W. Norton, 1999.
A renowned Harvard biologist and outspoken proponent of maintaining biodiversity updates his landmark work on the topic, with a forward examining the status of Earth's biodiversity at the dawn of the 21st century.

Articles

Barnosky, Anthony D., *et al.*, "Approaching a state shift in Earth's biosphere," *Nature*, June 2012, www.nature.com/nature/journal/v486/n7401/full/nature11018.html.
A professor of integrative biology and his collaborators believe biodiversity loss could be leading to a tipping point in which Earth's ecosystems change rapidly and significantly.

Cardinal, Bradley J., *et al.*, "Biodiversity loss and its impact on humanity," *Nature*, June 2012, www.nature.com/nature/journal/v486/n7401/full/nature11148.html.
A University of Michigan professor and other scientists review the latest research on how biodiversity loss will alter ecosystems and their ability to provide for humans.

Chestney, Nina, "Chance of saving most coral reefs is dwindling — study," Reuters, Sept. 16, 2012, www.reuters.com/article/2012/09/16/coral-climate-idUSL5E8KE4HE20120916.
About 70 percent of the world's coral reefs will suffer serious harm by 2030 due to climate change, according to researchers in Canada and Australia.

Gaia, Vince, "How the world's oceans could be running out of fish," BBC Future, Sept. 21, 2012, www.bbc.com/future/story/20120920-are-we-running-out-of-fish.
Studies indicate that humans could be depleting the world's ocean fisheries to such an extent that future generations will not be able to catch fish from the oceans.

Knight, Richard, "Biodiversity loss: How accurate are the numbers?" BBC News, April 24, 2012, www.bbc.co.uk/news/magazine-17826898.
Some experts say researchers are significantly overestimating the numbers of species being lost around the world.

Lomborg, Bjorn, "Research Is The Way Ahead for Preserving Biodiversity," *Forbes India*, Sept. 25, 2012, http://forbesindia.com/article/environment-special/research-is-the-way-ahead-for-preserving-biodiversity/33120/1.
A Copenhagen Business School professor who is a frequent critic of modern environmentalism says scientists should focus on boosting agricultural productivity on existing lands to save biodiversity elsewhere.

Siebert, Charles, "Food Ark," *National Geographic*, July 2011, http://ngm.nationalgeographic.com/2011/07/food-ark/siebert-text.
Siebert discusses global efforts to protect biodiversity, including establishing a "doomsday vault" of seeds.

Studies and Reports

Global Biodiversity Outlook 3, Secretariat of the Convention on Biodiversity, 2010, www.cbd.int/gbo3/.
This comprehensive report on the state of global biodiversity is issued periodically by the U.N. agency charged with supporting the goals of the Convention on Biodiversity.

"The IUCN Red List of Threatened Species," International Union for the Conservation of Nature, 2012, www.iucnredlist.org.
An online, searchable database developed by an international conservation organization provides updated

information on endangered species of plants and animals around the world.

Grooten, Monique, *et al.*, "Living Planet Report 2012: Biodiversity, biocapacity and better choices," World Wildlife Fund International and the Global Footprint Network, 2012, wwf.panda.org/about_ our_earth/all_publications/living_planet_report/.
A leading wildlife conservation organization and an international think tank devoted to sustainability

assess declining global biodiversity and what can be done about it.

Suckling, Kieran, *et al.*, "Extinction and the Endangered Species Act," Center for Biological Diversity, May 1, 2004, www.biologicaldiversity.org/ swcbd/PROGRAMS/policy/ESA/eesa.pdf.
A U.S. conservation group finds that the Endangered Species Act has been largely successful.

For More Information

Center for Biological Diversity, P.O. Box 710, Tucson, AZ 85702; 520-623-5252; center@biologicaldiversity.org. A leading advocacy organization for protecting biodiversity in the United States.

Conservation International, 2011 Crystal Dr., Suite 500, Arlington, VA 22202; 703-341-2400; www.conservation.org. Promotes biological research and works with national governments and businesses to protect 34 biodiversity hot spots worldwide.

Defenders of Wildlife, 1130 17th St., N.W., Washington, DC 20036; 202-682-9400; www.defenders.org. An advocacy group dedicated to the preservation of all wild animals and native plants in their natural communities.

The International Union for Conservation of Nature, UCN Conservation Centre, Rue Mauverny 28, 1196 Gland, Switzerland; +41 22 999-0000; www.iucn.org. The world's oldest and largest global environmental organization; maintains the "Red List," which identifies species at risk of extinction.

The Nature Conservancy, 4245 North Fairfax Dr., Suite 100, Arlington, VA 22203-1606; 703-841-5300; www .nature.org. Supports land conservation to protect wildlife habitat in the U.S. and more than 30 nations.

Secretariat of the Convention on Biological Diversity, 413, Saint Jacques St., Suite 800, Montreal QC, H2Y 1N9, Canada; +1 514 288-2220; www.cbd.int. U.N. agency charged with supporting the goals of the Convention on Biological Diversity.

World Resources Institute, 10 G St., N.E., Suite 800, Washington, DC 20002; 202-729-7600; www.wri.org. Conducts research on ecosystem threats and works with indigenous communities to balance human and wildlife needs.

World Wildlife Fund International, Av. du Mont-Blanc 1196, Gland, Switzerland; +41 22 364 91 11; wwf.panda .org. Works to protect endangered species around the world and publishes the omnibus "Living Planet" reports.

Voices From Abroad:

ERACH BHARUCHA

Director, Bharati Vidyapeeth Institute of Environment
Education and Research, India

A multi-pronged strategy

"Planning a strategy for biodiversity conservation must also include breeding of endangered species. . . . Preserving corridors between protected areas to facilitate movement of animals is crucial to maintain wildlife population. Identifying ecologically sensitive areas around parks and sanctuaries to form buffers is necessary to protect animals inside the protected areas and reduce conflict with local people's needs."

Economic Times (India), April 2012

SALIHU DAHIRU

Head, United Nations Initiative on Reducing Emissions from
Deforestation and Forest Degradation, Nigeria

Sharing the costs

"The cost of such additional investments [in biodiversity] must be fairly shared between those countries that demand forest-related emission reductions and those that supply them."

Daily Trust (Nigeria), December 2011

DIANE KLAIMI

Program Officer U.N. Environment Programme,
Regional Office West Asia, Bahrain

Accelerated loss

"The Gulf region is under pressure from urban growth and development, and they are drivers of biodiversity loss. Biodiversity loss has reached 1,000 times more than it used to be 50 years ago; we are trying to bring these figures to policymakers and the business sector and see how they can implement biodiversity conservation."

Gulf Daily News (Bahrain), May 2011

IN A WORLD WITHOUT BEES, WE'LL HAVE TO DO OUR OWN POLLINATING

Seattle Post Intelligencer/David Horsey

NAOKI ADACHI

President, Response Ability (an environmental consulting firm), Japan

A wise business decision

"Until recently, most companies considered their businesses and biodiversity separate issues. But now they realize that without healthy biodiversity, they cannot maintain their businesses."

Japan Times, October 2010

TRACY REES

Deputy Director, Business in the Community,* Wales

Superficial reporting

"Biodiversity and ecosystem services are usually treated superficially in company reports and are rarely seen as financially material or relevant to annual financial reporting."

Western Mail (Wales), January 2012

ABSALOM SHIGWEDHA

Environmental journalist, Namibia

More than just wildlife

"Biodiversity is not just about wildlife or wild places. It includes the crops that we eat, the insects that pollinate them and the bacteria that create soil that sustains farming."

New Era (Namibia), December 2011

IAN SPELLERBERG

Professor of Nature Conservation, Lincoln University, New Zealand

More to do

"New Zealand is seen as a world leader in nature conservation — but let's not forget that nature conservation is not a luxury. It is the most fundamental of all the pillars of sustainability. We have achieved a lot in nature conservation, but it's more than just about saving iconic species. . . . A lot more has to be done to conserve and ensure sustainable, equitable use of nature's goods and services. Diversity in nature is the key, whether it is

diversity of biota in the soils, genetic diversity or diversity within ecosystems."

New Zealand Herald, November 2010

CATHERINE NAMUGALA

Minister of Tourism Environment and Natural Resources, Zambia

Tourism depends on it

"Without natural resources, it would be very difficult to attract tourists. We also need to balance the ecological, economical, ethical and scientific roles in the country. In short, we all depend on biological diversity."

Times of Zambia, October 2010

---

*A charity that promotes corporate social responsibility.